THE ROYAL INSCRIPTIONS OF ASHURBANIPAL (668–631 BC), AŠŠUR-ETEL-ILĀNI (630–627 BC), AND SÎN-ŠARRA-IŠKUN (626–612 BC), KINGS OF ASSYRIA, PART 3

THE ROYAL INSCRIPTIONS OF THE NEO-ASSYRIAN PERIOD

EDITORIAL BOARD

Grant Frame (Philadelphia)
Director and Editor-in-Chief

Barry L. Eichler (New York)

Karen Radner (Munich)

Steve Tinney (Philadelphia)

PROJECT CONSULTANTS

Robert K. Englund† (Los Angeles)

A. Kirk Grayson (Toronto)

Simo Parpola (Helsinki)

Volumes Published

1 The Royal Inscriptions of Tiglath-pileser III (744–727 BC) and Shalmaneser V (726–722 BC), Kings of Assyria
HAYIM TADMOR and SHIGEO YAMADA

2 The Royal Inscriptions of Sargon II, King of Assyria (721–705 BC)
GRANT FRAME

3/1 The Royal Inscriptions of Sennacherib, King of Assyria (704–681 BC), Part 1
A. KIRK GRAYSON and JAMIE NOVOTNY

3/2 The Royal Inscriptions of Sennacherib, King of Assyria (704–681 BC), Part 2
A. KIRK GRAYSON and JAMIE NOVOTNY

4 The Royal Inscriptions of Esarhaddon, King of Assyria (680–669 BC)
ERLE LEICHTY

5/1 The Royal Inscriptions of Ashurbanipal (668–631 BC), Aššur-etel-ilāni (630–627 BC), and Sîn-šarra-iškun (626–612 BC), Kings of Assyria, Part 1
JAMIE NOVOTNY and JOSHUA JEFFERS

5/2 The Royal Inscriptions of Ashurbanipal (668–631 BC), Aššur-etel-ilāni (630–627 BC), and Sîn-šarra-iškun (626–612 BC), Kings of Assyria, Part 2
JOSHUA JEFFERS and JAMIE NOVOTNY

THE ROYAL INSCRIPTIONS OF THE NEO-ASSYRIAN PERIOD

VOLUME 5/3

The Royal Inscriptions of Ashurbanipal (668–631 BC), Aššur-etel-ilāni (630–627 BC), and Sîn-šarra-iškun (626–612 BC), Kings of Assyria, Part 3

JAMIE NOVOTNY, JOSHUA JEFFERS,
and GRANT FRAME

EISENBRAUNS
University Park, Pennsylvania

Printed in the United States of America on acid-free paper.

ISBN 978-1-64602-262-5

The research and publication of this volume have been supported by the National Endowment for the Humanities, the Alexander von Humboldt Foundation, the University of Pennsylvania, Ludwig-Maximilians-Universität München, and the Gerda Henkel Stiftung.

Cover illustration: Ashurbanipal carrying a basket on his head as depicted on a pink marble stele (BM 90864) discovered at Babylon. Drawing by Sabrina Nortey.

The text editions in this work were produced using Oracc. See http://oracc.org for further information.

Library of Congress Cataloging-in-Publication Data

Names: Ashurbanipal, King of Assyria, active 668 B.C.–627 B.C., author. | Assur-etal-ilani, King of Assyria, active 630 B.C.–627 B.C., author. | Sin-sarra-iskun, King of Assyria, active 626 B.C.–612 B.C., author. | Novotny, Jamie R., editor. | Jeffers, Joshua, 1977– editor. | Frame, Grant, editor.
Title: The royal inscriptions of Ashurbanipal (668–631 BC), Assur-etal-ilani (630–627 BC), and Sin-sarra-iskun (626–612 BC), kings of Assyria / [edited by] Jamie Novotny, Joshua Jeffers and Grant Frame.
Other titles: Royal inscriptions of the neo-Assyrian period.
Description: University Park, Pennsylvania : Eisenbrauns, [2023]– | Series: The royal inscriptions of the neo-Assyrian period | Includes bibliographical references.
Summary: "A collection of updated editions and English translations of 106 historical inscriptions from Babylonia, the East Tigris Region, and outside the Assyrian Empire attributed to Ashurbanipal as well as his family and loyal officials"—Provided by publisher.
Identifiers: LCCN 2018036039 | ISBN 9781646022625 (cloth : alk. paper)
Subjects: LCSH: Ashurbanipal, King of Assyria, active 668 B.C.–627 B.C. | Assur-etal-ilani, King of Assyria, active 630 B.C.–627 B.C. | Sin-sarra-iskun, King of Assyria, active 626 B.C.–612 B.C. | Cuneiform inscriptions, Akkadian. | Assyria—History—Sources. | Akkadian language—Texts. | Assyria—Kings and rulers.
Classification: LCC PJ3837.A6 N68 2023 | DDC 492/.1—dc23
LC record available at https://lccn.loc.gov/2018036039

Eisenbrauns is an imprint of The Pennsylvania State University Press.
The Pennsylvania State University Press is a member of the Association of University Presses.
The paper used in this publication meets the minimum requirements of the American National Standard for Information Sciences—Permanence of Paper for Printed Library Materials, ANSI Z39.48-1984.

To A. Kirk Grayson

Contents

Detailed Table of Contents xi
List of Figures xvi
Contents of Scores xvii
Foreword xix
Preface xxi
Editorial Notes xxiii
Bibliographical Abbreviations xxv
Other Abbreviations xxxv
Object Signatures xxxvii

Introduction 1

I. Ashurbanipal
Babylonia
Babylon
Clay Cylinders — Nos. 241–245 47
Stone Steles — No. 246 58
Bricks — Nos. 247–251 62
Agade
Clay Cylinder — No. 252 69
Borsippa
Clay Cylinders — No. 253 70
Stone Stele — No. 254 72
Clay Tablet — No. 255 75
Dūr-Kurigalzu
Bricks — No. 256 76
Mê-Turān
Bricks — No. 257 77
Nippur
Clay Cylinders — No. 258 78
Bricks — Nos. 259–261 81
Sippar
Clay Cylinders — No. 262 86
Uruk
Clay Cylinders — No. 263 88
Clay Tablet — No. 264 91
East Tigris Region
Dēr
Clay Cylinder — No. 265 93

Iran
Persepolis
Eyestones and Beads — Nos. 266–268 95
Stone Vessel — No. 269 97
Uncertain Provenance
Silver Vessel — No. 270 98
II. Ashurbanipal — Uncertain Texts
Clay Tablets — Nos. 1001–1029 100
Rock Face— No. 1030 127
III. Ashurbanipal — High Officials and Royal Women
Nos. 2001–2002 Introduction 133
Libbāli-šarrat
Aššur
Stone Stele — No. 2001 133
Queen of Ashurbanipal (name not preserved)
Nineveh
Clay Tablet — No. 2002 134
Sîn-balāssu-iqbi
Ur
Nos. 2003–2018 Introduction 136
Stone Door Socket — No. 2003 136
Clay Nails — Nos. 2004–2005 138
Clay Disks — No. 2006 140
Clay (Drum-shaped) Object — No. 2007 142
Bricks — Nos. 2008–2018 144
IV. Aššur-etel-ilāni
Introduction 157
Assyria
Kalḫu
Bricks — No. 1 157
Babylonia
Babylon
Clay Tablets — Nos. 2–3 159
Dilbat
Brick — No. 4 163
Nippur
Brick — No. 5 164
Uncertain Provenance
Clay Cylinders and Tablets — No. 6 165
V. Sîn-šuma-līšir
Introduction 168
VI. Sîn-šarra-iškun
Introduction 169
Assyria
Nineveh
Clay Cylinders — Nos. 1–5 169
Clay Tablet — No. 6 178

Aššur
Clay Prisms — Nos. 7–9 180
Clay Cylinders — No. 10 189
Clay Cones — No. 11 193
Stone Block — No. 12 196
Bricks — Nos. 13–14 197
Clay Tablets — No. 15–18 200
Kalḫu
Clay Cylinders — No. 19 205
Clay Bulla — No. 20 209
Uncertain Provenance
Stone Vessel — No. 21 210
VII. Sîn-šarra-iškun — High Officials and Royal Women
Ana-Tašmētu-taklāk
Nineveh
Stone Bowl — No. 2001 212
VIII. Aššur-uballiṭ II
Introduction 213

Minor Variants and Comments 215
Index of Museum Numbers 219
Index of Excavation Numbers 225
Index of Names 227
Concordances of Selected Publications 231
Scores of Inscriptions (on Oracc) 1–56
(the pdf of the scores is available at http://oracc.museum.upenn.edu/rinap/scores/)

Detailed Table of Contents

Introduction 1

I. Ashurbanipal

Babylonia

Babylon

Clay Cylinders

No. 241 — Cylinder L[ondon][6] / Cylinder P[runkinschrift][2] / Frame, RIMB 2 B.6.32.1 47

No. 242 — Cylinder P[runkinschrift][1] / Frame, RIMB 2 B.6.32.6 51

No. 243 — BE 28510 / Frame, RIMB 2 B.6.32.3 52

No. 244 — Cylinder L[ondon][1] / Frame, RIMB 2 B.6.32.4 54

No. 245 — Emaḫ Cylinder / Frame, RIMB 2 B.6.32.5 56

Stone Steles

No. 246 — S[tele][3] / Frame, RIMB 2 B.6.32.2 58

Bricks

No. 247 — Marzahn, FuB 27 (1989) no. VIII (nos. 14–16) / Frame, RIMB 2 B.6.32.7 62

No. 248 — Walker, CBI no. 78 / Marzahn, FuB 27 (1989) no. IX (nos. 17–19) / Frame, RIMB 2 B.6.32.8 64

No. 249 — Marzahn, FuB 27 (1989) no. VI (no. 10) / Frame, RIMB 2 B.6.32.11 66

No. 250 — BE 41186 / Frame, RIMB 2 B.6.32.10 66

No. 251 — Walker, CBI no. 79 / Marzahn, FuB 27 (1989) no. VII (nos. 11–13) / Frame, RIMB 2 B.6.32.9 67

Agade

Clay Cylinder

No. 252 — Frame, Mesopotamia 28 (1993) pp. 45–48 / Frame, RIMB 2 B.6.32.20 69

Borsippa

Clay Cylinders

No. 253 — Frame, RIMB 2 pp. 215–216 B.6.32.13 / Frame, CTMMA 4 no. 163 70

Stone Stele

No. 254 — S[tele][2] / Frame, RIMB 2 B.6.32.14 72

Clay Tablet

No. 255 — Clay, BE 8/1 no. 142 / Lambert, AfO 18 (1957–58) pp. 385–386 and pl. XXV / Frame, RIMB 2 B.6.32.23 75

Dūr-Kurigalzu

Bricks

No. 256 — Al-Jumaily, Sumer 27 (1971) pl. 14 fig. 30 / Frame, RIMB 2 B.6.32.21 76

Mê-Turān

Bricks

No. 257 — Rashid, Sumer 37 (1981) pp. 72–80 / Frame, RIMB 2 B.6.32.22 77

Nippur

Clay Cylinders

No. 258 — Gerardi, Studies Sjöberg pp. 207–215 / Frame, RIMB 2 B.6.32.15 78

Bricks
No. 259 — Hilprecht, BE 1/1 no. 82 / Walker, CBI no. 80 / Frame, RIMB 2 B.6.32.16 81
No. 260 — Legrain, PBS 15 no. 74 / Frame, RIMB 2 B.6.32.17 84
No. 261 — Gerardi, ARRIM 4 (1986) p. 37 / Frame, RIMB 2 B.6.32.18 85
Sippar
Clay Cylinders
No. 262 — Cylinder L[ondon][2] / Frame, RIMB 2 B.6.32.12 86
Uruk
Clay Cylinders
No. 263 — Clay, YOS 1 no. 42 / Keiser, BIN 2 no. 35 / Frame, RIMB 2 B.6.32.19 88
Clay Tablet
No. 264 — von Weiher, SuTU 2 no. 31 91
East Tigris Region
Dēr
Clay Cylinder
No. 265 — Frahm, Studies Parpola pp. 59–64 93
Iran
Persepolis
Eyestones and Beads
No. 266 — PT4 455 / Schmidt, Persepolis 2 p. 58 and pl. 25 no. 3 95
No. 267 — PT4 1180 / Schmidt, Persepolis 2 p. 59 96
No. 268 — PT4 1173 / Schmidt, Persepolis 2 pp. 57–58 96
Stone Vessel
No. 269 — PT4 368 + PT5 156 + PT5 244 / Schmidt, Persepolis 2 pp. 83–84 and pl. 49 no. 1 97
Miscellaneous
Silver Vessel
No. 270 — Miho Museum, SF 4.061 98
II. Ashurbanipal — Uncertain Texts
Clay Tablets
No. 1001 — Sm 1937 100
No. 1002 — K 9155 101
No. 1003 — K 6371 102
No. 1004 — 82-3-23,125 103
No. 1005 — K 14127 104
No. 1006 — 81-2-4,286 104
No. 1007 — K 4496 105
No. 1008 — K 16776 106
No. 1009 — K 19448 107
No. 1010 — K 6868 + K 9248 108
No. 1011 — K 18219 109
No. 1012 — K 19386 110
No. 1013 — Rm 283 110
No. 1014 — K 3150 112
No. 1015 — K 6370 113
No. 1016 — K 10621 114
No. 1017 — K 17809 114
No. 1018 — K 17999 115

No. 1019 — K 22138 116
No. 1020 — Rm 2,467 117
No. 1021 — K 13749 117
No. 1022 — 81-7-27,280 118
No. 1023 — K 16899 + Sm 1048 119
No. 1024 — Rm 337 + Rm 451 120
No. 1025 — K 4498 122
No. 1026 — K 8361 123
No. 1027 — K 6681 124
No. 1028 — K 6806 125
No. 1029 — Bu 91-5-9,204 126
Rock Face
No. 1030 — Shakaft-i Gulgul Rock Relief Inscription / Grayson and Levine, Iranica Antiqua 11 (1975) pp. 29–38. 127
III. Ashurbanipal — High Officials and Royal Women
Nos. 2001–2002 Introduction 133
Libbāli-šarrat
Aššur
Stone Stele
No. 2001 — VA 8847 / Andrae, Stelenreihen pp. 6–8 and pl. 10 no. 1 133
Queen of Ashurbanipal (name not preserved)
Nineveh
Clay Tablet
No. 2002 — 83-1-18,332 / Johns, ADD 1 p. 498 no. 644 134
Sîn-balāssu-iqbi
Ur
Nos. 2003–2018 Introduction 136
Stone Door Socket
No. 2003 — Gadd, UET 1 no. 169 / Frame, RIMB 2 B.6.32.2001 136
Clay Nails
No. 2004 — Gadd, UET 1 no. 183 / Frame, RIMB 2 B.6.32.2002 138
No. 2005 — Gadd, UET 1 no. 171 / Frame, RIMB 2 B.6.32.2014 139
Clay Disks
No. 2006 — Sollberger, UET 8 no. 102 / Frame, RIMB 2 B.6.32.2015 140
Clay (Drum-shaped) Object
No. 2007 — Gadd, UET 1 no. 172 / Frame, RIMB 2 B.6.32.2016 142
Bricks
No. 2008 — Gadd, UET 1 no. 170 / Walker, CBI no. 82 / Frame, RIMB 2 B.6.32.2003 144
No. 2009 — Gadd, UET 1 no. 168 / Walker, CBI no. 81 / Frame, RIMB 2 B.6.32.2004 145
No. 2010 — Gadd, UET 1 nos. 173–174 / Frame, RIMB 2 B.6.32.2005 146
No. 2011 — Gadd, UET 1 no. 175 / Frame, RIMB 2 B.6.32.2006 148
No. 2012 — Gadd, UET 1 no. 176 / Frame, RIMB 2 B.6.32.2007 148
No. 2013 — Gadd, UET 1 no. 180 / Frame, RIMB 2 B.6.32.2008 149
No. 2014 — Gadd, UET 1 no. 181 / Frame, RIMB 2 B.6.32.2009 150
No. 2015 — Gadd, UET 1 no. 182 / Walker, CBI no. 86 / Frame, RIMB 2 B.6.32.2010 151
No. 2016 — Gadd, UET 1 no. 177 / Walker, CBI no. 83 / Frame, RIMB 2 B.6.32.2011 152
No. 2017 — Gadd, UET 1 no. 178 / Walker, CBI no. 84 / Frame, RIMB 2 B.6.32.2012 154

No. 2018 — Gadd, UET 1 no. 173 / Walker, CBI no. 85 / Frame, RIMB 2 B.6.32.2013 155

IV. Aššur-etel-ilāni

Introduction 157

Assyria

Kalḫu

Bricks

No. 1 — 1 R pl. 8 no. 3 / Walker CBI no. 190 157

Babylonia

Babylon

Clay Tablets

No. 2 — PTS 2253 / Leichty, JAOS 103 (1983) pp. 217–220 / Frame, RIMB 2 B.6.35.1 159

No. 3 — BE 42262 / Marzahn and Frame, JCS 48 (1996) pp. 95–96 161

Dilbat

Brick

No. 4 — Langdon, OECT 1 pl. 29 / Walker, CBI no. 87 / Frame, RIMB 2 B.6.35.3 163

Nippur

Brick

No. 5 — Edzard, AfO 19 (1959–60) p. 143 / Frame, RIMB 2 B.6.35.4 164

Uncertain Provenance

Clay Cylinders and Tablets

No. 6 — Clay, YOS 1 no. 43 / Stephens, YOS 9 no. 81 / Frame, RIMB 2 B.6.35.5 165

V. Sîn-šuma-līšir

Introduction 168

VI. Sîn-šarra-iškun

Introduction 169

Assyria

Nineveh

Clay Cylinders

No. 1 — Cylinder C 169

No. 2 — Cylinder D 173

No. 3 — BM 122613 / Millard, Iraq 30 pl. XXVII 175

No. 4 — 80-7-19,13 / King, CT 34 pl. 3 176

No. 5 — K 8540 + 82-5-22,28 / King, CT 34 pl. 4 177

Clay Tablet

No. 6 — Cylinder C 178

Aššur

Clay Prisms

No. 7 — Cylinder A 180

No. 8 — VAT 9524 (+) A 494 / Frahm, KAL 3 pp. 89–91 and 230 186

No. 9 — VA 7506 (+) VA 7518 / Schroeder, KAH 2 nos. 130 and 132 187

Clay Cylinders

No. 10 — Cylinder A 189

Clay Cones

No. 11 — Schroeder, KAH 2 nos. 129 and 133 / Donbaz and Grayson, RICCA pp. 55–60 and pls. 32–64 nos. 236–248 193

Stone Block

No. 12 — Kessler, ISIMU 14–15 (2011–12) pp. 39–43 196

Bricks
No. 13 — Schroeder, KAH 2 no. 134 / Walker, CBI no. 189 / Jakob-Rost and Marzahn, VAS 23 nos. 143–145, 148, and 151 197
No. 14 — Messerschmidt, KAH 1 no. 56 200
Clay Tablets
No. 15 — VAT 9948 / Falkner, AfO 16 (1952–53) pp. 305–307 and pl. XV 200
No. 16 — VAT 9948 / Falkner, AfO 16 (1952–53) pp. 305–307 and pl. XV 201
No. 17 — VAT 9975 / Schroeder, KAV no. 171 203
No. 18 — VAT 9975 / Schroeder, KAV no. 171 204
Kalḫu
Clay Cylinders
No. 19 — Cylinder B 205
Clay Bulla
No. 20 — ND 6228 / Dalley and Postgate, Fort Shalmaneser p. 139 and pl. 45 no. 83 209
Uncertain Provenance
Stone Vessel
No. 21 — 81-2-4,25A / Searight, Assyrian Stone Vessels pp. 58–59 and fig. 30 no. 418 210
VII. Sîn-šarra-iškun — High Officials and Royal Women
Ana-Tašmētu-taklāk
Nineveh
Stone Bowl
No. 2001 — 55-12-5,252 / Searight, Assyrian Stone Vessels p. 74 and fig. 49 no. 511 212
VIII. Aššur-uballiṭ II
Introduction 213

List of Figures

Figure 1. Map showing cities in Babylonia and the East Tigris region where clay cylinders of Ashurbanipal have been discovered . . . 4

Figure 2. Annotated plan of the ruins of the eastern half of the inner city of Babylon . . . 19

Figure 3. Map showing the principal Assyrian cities where Aššur-etel-ilāni and Sîn-šarra-iškun undertook building activities . . . 31

Figure 4. Plan of the Nabû temple at Aššur and the earlier ruins of the Ištar temple . . . 34

Figure 5. Obverse and reverse of the "Fall of Nineveh Chronicle" (BM 21901) . . . 35

Figure 6. VA Bab 601 (Asb. 241 ex. 10), a clay cylinder found at Babylon that is inscribed with a text recording the restoration of Nēmetti-Enlil and its gates . . . 49

Figure 7. BM 90864 (Asb. 246), a marble stele depicting Ashurbanipal carrying a basket on his head and recording that king's restoration of Ekarzagina, the temple of the god Ea at Babylon . . . 60

Figure 8. Annotated plan of the ruins of the Eridu district of Babylon and the Esagil temple complex . 64

Figure 9. UM L-29-632+633+636 (Asb. 258 ex. 1), a damaged clay cylinder recording Ashurbanipal's restoration of the god Enlil's ziggurat at Nippur . . . 79

Figure 10. CBS 8654 (Asb. 259 ex. 9), a brick from Nippur with a Sumerian inscription recording that Ashurbanipal (re)built Ekur, the temple of the god Enlil . . . 82

Figure 11. VA 8847 (Ass 15756 + Ass 15758; Asb. 2001), fragments of the upper portion of a stele of Ashurbanipal's wife Libbāli-šarrat that were discovered in the "row of steles" at Aššur . . . 133

Figure 12. BM 119014 (Asb. 2007), a clay drum-shaped object with a Sumerian inscription of the Ur III king Amar-Suen and an Akkadian text of Sîn-balāssu-iqbi, a governor of Ur during the reign of Ashurbanipal . . . 143

Figure 13. PTS 2253 (Aei 2), a crudely-fashioned, single-column clay tablet inscribed with a text recording the dedication of an offering table to the god Marduk . . . 160

Figure 14. The Nabû temple at Aššur showing the general find spots of inscribed objects of Sîn-šarra-iškun . . . 181

Figure 15. VA 8419 + VA 5059 (Ass 13266 + Ass 13594; Ssi 7 ex. 3), a fragment of a clay prism with an inscription recording Sîn-šarra-iškun building the Nabû temple at Aššur. . . . 183

Figure 16. VA Ass 2316 (Ass 13158 [+] Ass 13158a; Ssi 10 ex. 2), a fragmentarily-preserved clay cylinder inscribed with a text recording the construction of the temple of the god Nabû at Aššur. . . . 191

Figure 17. VA 8416 (Ass 12727; Ssi 11 ex. 1), a clay cone discovered at Aššur recording Sîn-šarra-iškun's construction of Nabû's temple . . . 195

Figure 18. BM 115697 (Ass 13467; Ssi 13 ex. 23), a brick with an Akkadian inscription recording the construction of the temple of the god Nabû . . . 198

Contents of Scores

(the pdf is available at http://oracc.museum.upenn.edu/rinap/scores/)

I. Ashurbanipal

Babylonia

Babylon

Clay Cylinders

No. 241 — Cylinder L[ondon][6] / Cylinder P[runkinschrift][2] / Frame, RIMB 2 B.6.32.1 1

No. 244 — Cylinder L[ondon][1] / Frame, RIMB 2 B.6.32.4 11

No. 245 — Emaḫ Cylinder / Frame, RIMB 2 B.6.32.5 13

Borsippa

Clay Cylinders

No. 253 — Frame, RIMB 2 pp. 215–216 B.6.32.13 / Frame, CTMMA 4 no. 163 15

Mê-Turān

Bricks

No. 257 — Rashid, Sumer 37 (1981) pp. 72–80 / Frame, RIMB 2 B.6.32.22 18

Nippur

Clay Cylinders

No. 258 — Gerardi, Studies Sjöberg pp. 207–215 / Frame, RIMB 2 B.6.32.15 19

Sippar

Clay Cylinders

No. 262 — Cylinder L[ondon][2] / Frame, RIMB 2 B.6.32.12 21

Uruk

Clay Cylinders

No. 263 — Clay, YOS 1 no. 42 / Keiser, BIN 2 no. 35 / Frame, RIMB 2 B.6.32.19 24

III. Ashurbanipal — High Officials and Royal Women

Sîn-balāssu-iqbi

Ur

Clay Nails

No. 2005 — Gadd, UET 1 no. 171 / Frame, RIMB 2 B.6.32.2014 27

Clay Disks

No. 2006 — Sollberger, UET 8 no. 102 / Frame, RIMB 2 B.6.32.2015 30

IV. Aššur-etel-ilāni

Babylonia

Uncertain Provenance

Clay Cylinders and Tablets

No. 6 — Clay, YOS 1 no. 43 / Stephens, YOS 9 no. 81 / Frame, RIMB 2 B.6.35.5 33

VI. Sîn-šarra-iškun

Assyria

Nineveh

Clay Cylinders

No. 1 — Cylinder C 35

Aššur

Clay Prisms

No. 7 — Cylinder A 38

Clay Cylinders
No. 10 — Cylinder A 46
Clay Cones
No. 11 — Schroeder, KAH 2 nos. 129 and 133 / Donbaz and Grayson, RICCA pp. 55–60 and pls. 32–64 nos. 236–248 50
Kalḫu
Clay Cylinders
No. 19 — Cylinder B 52

Foreword

The present series of publications, Royal Inscriptions of the Neo-Assyrian Period (RINAP), is intended to present up-to-date editions of the royal inscriptions of a number of Neo-Assyrian rulers. It is modeled on the publications of the now-defunct Royal Inscriptions of Mesopotamia (RIM) series and carries on where the RIMA (Royal Inscriptions of Mesopotamia, Assyrian Periods) publications ended. The RIM Project was initiated by A. Kirk Grayson at the University of Toronto in 1979 and over the years received extensive support from the Social Sciences and Humanities Research Council of Canada, the University of Toronto, and private individuals, in particular Laurence Shiff. In all, it produced ten volumes in its various sub-series. Grayson retired from the University of Toronto in 2000 and a few years later found it necessary to cease scholarly pursuits due to personal and family illnesses. At that time, he handed over responsibility for the work of the project to me, formerly the assistant director and at times acting director of the RIM Project. When I took up a position at the University of Pennsylvania in 2006 and the last RIM volume (RIME 1 by Douglas R. Frayne) appeared in early 2008, the RIM Project officially ceased to exist. Work on several further volumes of inscriptions of Assyrian and Babylonian rulers had already begun during the time of the RIM Project and Grayson passed on responsibility for the materials and manuscripts to me. In 2007, I initiated the current project in order to continue the task of making the official inscriptions of the several important Neo-Assyrian rulers available in modern, scholarly editions. While the volumes in the new series resemble the format of the RIM volumes in most matters, the RINAP volumes include indices of proper names, and editions of the texts are also available online, in connection with the Cuneiform Digital Library Initiative (CDLI) and the Open Richly Annotated Cuneiform Corpus Initiative (Oracc).

Seven volumes have already appeared in this series: RINAP 1, comprising the inscriptions of Tiglath-pileser III and Shalmaneser V (begun by Hayim Tadmor and completed by Shigeo Yamada); RINAP 2, comprising the inscriptions of Sargon II (by Grant Frame, with the collaboration of Andreas Fuchs for two texts); RINAP 3/1–2, comprising the inscriptions of Sennacherib (begun by A. Kirk Grayson and completed by his collaborator Jamie Novotny); RINAP 4, comprising the inscriptions of Esarhaddon (by Erle Leichty, with a contribution by Grant Frame); RINAP 5/1, comprising some of the inscriptions of Ashurbanipal (by Jamie Novotny and Joshua Jeffers); and RINAP 5/2, which included Ashurbanipal's inscriptions written on clay tablets discovered at Nineveh (by Joshua Jeffers and Jamie Novotny). This volume (RINAP 5/3, by Jamie Novotny, Joshua Jeffers, and Grant Frame), the eighth book to appear, is the penultimate installment. The final volume (RINAP 6, by Jamie Novotny) will include some corrections and additions, as well as complete indexes of museum and excavation numbers and names for the entire RINAP series.

The National Endowment for the Humanities awarded the RINAP Project research grants in 2008, 2010, 2012, 2015, and 2017 to help carry out its work and my thanks must be expressed to it. My appreciation must also be extended to the University of Pennsylvania and to the University of Pennsylvania Museum of Archaeology and Anthropology, where the project is based, for their support. Additional funding for the preparation of RINAP 5/2 was provided by the Alexander von Humboldt Foundation (through the establishment of the Alexander von Humboldt Professorship for Ancient History of the Near and Middle East), Ludwig-Maximilians-Universität München (Historisches Seminar - Abteilung Alte Geschichte), and the Gerda Henkel Stiftung (grant no. AZ 09/V/21). I am grateful to Karen Radner for providing additional financial support for the project.

Philadelphia
January 2023

Grant Frame
Editor-in-Chief

Preface

The history of the Ashurbanipal project up to the publication of the RINAP 5/1 and RINAP 5/2 volumes has been outlined in the prefaces to those books. The authors are once again extremely grateful to the individuals and institutions named in those prefaces for their past contributions and continuing support which has gone into the preparation of RINAP 5/3.

The present volume contains: (1) Ashurbanipal's inscriptions from Babylonia (Babylon, Agade?, Borsippa, Dūr-Kurigalzu, Mê-Turān, Nippur, Sippar, and Uruk), the East Tigris Region (Dēr), and Iran (Persepolis); (2) texts (chiefly written on clay tablets found at Nineveh) attributed to Ashurbanipal, but whose assignments to him are not firmly established; (3) inscriptions written by some members of the royal family (especially his queen Libbāli-šarrat) and officials (namely Sîn-balāssu-iqbi, governor of Ur); and (4) the official inscriptions of his sons and successors Aššur-etel-ilāni and Sîn-šarra-iškun. Note, however, that the official texts of Ashurbanipal's older brother Šamaš-šuma-ukīn, the king of Babylon, are not edited in RINAP 5/3; for editions of those inscriptions, see Frame, RIMB 2 pp. 248–259 B.6.33.1–2001.

With regard to the Babylonian inscriptions of Ashurbanipal and Aššur-etel-ilāni included in the present volume, they were published by Frame in 1995, in RIMB 2 (pp. 194–247 B.6.32.1–2016 and pp. 261–268 B.6.35.1–5). This material was converted and (moderately) adapted by Novotny in 2014–15 into the Oracc format and lemmatized (linguistically tagged) by Alexa Bartelmus in 2015–16, in connection with the "Babylon 6" sub-project of open-access Royal Inscriptions of Babylonia online (RIBo) Project, which is part of the LMU-Munich-based Munich Open-access Cuneiform Corpus Initiative (MOCCI). In 2022, Frame updated and modified the introductions, catalogues, commentaries, bibliographies, and editions of the RIMB 2 texts, while Novotny also made additional changes to the text introductions, catalogues, and commentaries.

As for the other inscriptions included in RINAP 5/3, Novotny carried out the initial work on the 1000- and 2000-number texts, as well as on the inscriptions of Ashurbanipal from Persepolis, between 1997 and 2003. From 2009 to 2018, Novotny prepared the introductions, catalogues, bibliographies, and editions of the brick inscription of Aššur-etel-ilāni from Kalḫu and Sîn-šarra-iškun's inscriptions; this material was lemmatized by him in 2018, after the completion of RINAP 5/1. Starting in 2018, in connection with the preparation of RINAP 5/2, Jeffers began updating Novotny's work, including collating some texts that had not been examined from originals in the British Museum (London) and Vorderasiatisches Museum (Berlin) or from (Aššur excavation) photographs. In 2022, Jeffers completed the work on the 1000-number texts inscribed on clay tablets and produced their text introductions (incorporating earlier comments of Novotny for a number of texts), wrote the commentary of Aššur-etel-ilāni's one Assyrian inscription and six of the eight commentaries of Sîn-šarra-iškun's inscriptions (Ssi 3 and 21 were written by Novotny), updated and expanded the bibliographies, and prepared the minor variants and comments of those texts; he also lemmatized the 1000-number texts, standardized Novotny's translations, and completed the score transliterations. In 2021–22, Novotny prepared most of the front and back material, wrote the book's introduction, organized the arrangement of the texts, prepared the editions of the Ashurbanipal clay cylinder from Dēr and the rock relief from Shakaft-i Gulgul, created/edited/annotated the figures, and provided additional input on the texts edited by Frame and Jeffers. Lastly, he undertook the time-consuming task of generating and formatting the text catalogues.

Work on the present corpus of texts necessitated extensive travel for collation of previously published inscriptions and for examination of unpublished material. The authors wish to thank the various museums and museum authorities that have cooperated in the preparation of this book. They would like to thank the directors, keepers, curators, and assistants of the British Museum (London), the Louvre (Paris), Oriental Institute of the University of Chicago (Chicago), the University of Pennsylvania Museum of Archaeology and

Anthropology, and the Vorderasiatisches Museum (Berlin). Specifically, the authors express their gratitude to Katherine Blanchard, John Brinkman, John Curtis, Irving Finkel, Joachim Marzahn, Jonathan Taylor, Ariane Thomas, and Christopher Walker. These colleagues, and their staff, have been extremely helpful and have extended every courtesy and assistance.

As usual with a volume in this series, numerous individuals aided in the production of the volume in some way. Since the preparation of this book has spanned more than two decades, it is impossible to name everyone who has contributed to RINAP 5/3 and thus any omissions are unintentional. While the authors have collated most of the texts themselves, other scholars have kindly collated some texts, provided information on pieces, or aided in some way. These include Veysel Donbaz, Zsombor Földi, Pamela Gerardi, A. Kirk Grayson, Enrique Jiménez, Tonio Mitto, Olof Pedersén, Karen Radner, Julian Reade, Michael Roaf, Daniel Schwemer, Laurence Shiff, Aaron Schmitt, Ira Spar, Ronald Sweet, Jonathan Taylor, Greta Van Buylaere, Klaus Wagensonner, Christopher Walker, and Cornelia Wunsch. Updated information about and transliterations of some of Ashurbanipal's inscriptions from Babylon now in Istanbul was kindly made accessible through the publication project led by Andreas Schachner (Deutsches Archäologisches Institut, Istanbul), in particular from Greta Van Buylaere, who is presently preparing new editions of this material within the framework of the Deutsche Forschungsgemeinschaft-funded project *The Cuneiform Documents in the Babylon Collection of the Istanbul Archaeological Museums (Eski Şark Eserleri Müzesi)* (project number 438042051), directed by Nils Heeßel (Marburg University) and Daniel Schwemer (Würzburg University). The authors would like to express their thanks for being permitted to incorporate this new information from Babylon (B) collection in this volume. In Toronto, during the RIM years, and later in Philadelphia and Munich, several individuals contributed to the technical preparation of the volume and they deserve credit for performing tedious and time-consuming tasks. For the Toronto stage of production (1997–2004), the authors offer their gratitude to Hope Grau and Jill Ruby for performing various tasks in connection with the Ashurbanipal manuscripts. For the Munich and Philadelphia stages of production (2014–22), the authors would like to thank Michael Chapin, Niclas Dannehl, Louisa Grill, and Jona Volohonsky, student assistants who checked the bibliographies, museum numbers, excavation numbers, and index of names in order to help ensure their accuracy. Special thanks must be given to Steve Tinney for undertaking the arduous task of helping generate the final camera-ready copy and converting and preparing the texts for the online version.

The penultimate manuscript of the 5/3 volume was read by Andreas Fuchs, Nicholas Postgate, and Martin Worthington. These reviewers made numerous astute comments, welcome criticisms, and suggestions for improvement, particularly on the transliterations and translations, for which the authors are grateful. Members of the RINAP editorial board (especially Karen Radner) and the project consultants offered helpful suggestions at various times near the completion of the volume. Their time, care, and generosity are greatly appreciated.

The authors' appreciation goes out to the Alexander von Humboldt Foundation, the Gerda Henkel Stiftung, Ludwig-Maximilians-Universität München (Historisches Seminar - Alte Geschichte), the National Endowment for the Humanities, the Social Sciences and Humanities Research Council of Canada, the University of Pennsylvania, the University of Toronto, and several private individuals, in particular Laurence Shiff and Malcolm Horsnell, whose financial support allowed for travel to the numerous museums cited above and provided the funding necessary for them to conduct research on Ashurbanipal's inscriptions and to publish this volume.

Last, but by no means least, the authors wish to record their gratitude for the ongoing support and encouragement of their families: Denise Bolton, Robert and Diana Novotny, and Jennifer Novotny; and Jordan Wesolowski, Dave and Kathy Jeffers, and Heather Zeigler.

Munich
Philadelphia
Philadelphia
January 2023

Jamie Novotny
Joshua Jeffers
Grant Frame

Editorial Notes

The volumes in the RINAP series are modeled upon the publications of the now-defunct Royal Inscriptions of Mesopotamia (RIM) Project, with a few modifications, in particular the addition of indices of proper names. Like the RIM volumes, the volumes in this series are not intended to provide analytical or synthetic studies, but rather to provide basic text editions that can serve as the foundations for such studies. Thus, extensive discussions of the contents of the texts are not presented, and the core of each volume is the edition of the relevant texts.

In this volume, the order of the texts is based for the most part upon the following two criteria:

(1) The city at which the structure dealt with in the building or dedicatory portion of the text was located. If that information is not preserved on the text, the provenance of the inscribed object is the determining factor.

(2) The type of object upon which the inscription is written (prism, cylinder, tablet, etc.).

In the volumes of the RINAP series, the term "exemplar" is employed to designate a single inscription found on one object. The term "text" is employed to refer to an inscription that existed in antiquity and that may be represented by a number of more or less duplicate exemplars. In these editions, exemplars of one text are edited together as a "master text," with a single transliteration and translation. Variants to the "master text" are provided either on page (major variants) or at the back of the volume (minor variants).

Each text edition is normally supplied with a brief introduction containing general information. This is followed by a catalogue containing basic information about all exemplars. This includes museum and excavation numbers (the symbol + is added between fragments that belong to the same object), provenance, lines preserved, and indication of whether or not the inscription has been collated (c = collated with the original, (c) = partially collated with the original, p = collated by means of a photograph, (p) = partially collated from a photograph; and n = not collated). The next section is normally a commentary containing further technical information and notes. The bibliography then follows. Items are arranged chronologically, earliest to latest, with notes in parentheses after each bibliographic entry. These notes indicate the exemplars with which the item is concerned and the nature of the publication, using the following key words: photo, copy, edition, translation, study, provenance, and collations. Certain standard reference works (e.g., the various volumes of "Keilschriftbibliographie" and "Register Assyriologie" published in Orientalia and Archiv für Orientforschung respectively; Borger, HKL 1–3; AHw; CAD; and Seux, ERAS) are not normally cited, although they were essential in the collecting and editing of these texts. While the bibliographies should contain all major relevant items, they are not necessarily exhaustive; a vast amount of scattered literature exists on many of the inscriptions edited in this volume and much of this literature is of only limited scholarly interest.

As noted earlier, a distinction is made between major and minor variants to a "master text"; the major variants are placed at the bottom of the page and the minor variants at the back of the book. In brief, major variants are essentially non-orthographic in nature, while minor variants are orthographic variations. Orthographic variants of proper names may at times be significant and thus on occasion these will also appear on the page as major variants. Complete transliterations of all exemplars in the style of musical scores are found in the pdf on Oracc at http://oracc.museum.upenn.edu/rinap/scores/ and thus any reader who finds the notes on variants insufficient for his/her needs may check the full reading of any exemplar (the pdfs of the scores for previous RINAP volumes are also now available on Oracc).

Several photographs are included in this volume. These are intended to show a few of the object types upon which Ashurbanipal's inscriptions were written and to aid the reader in understanding the current state of preservation of some of the inscriptions.

As is the normal practice for transliterating cuneiform inscriptions, lowercase Roman is used for Sumerian and lowercase italics for Akkadian; logograms in Akkadian texts appear in capitals. The system of sign values in Borger, Mesopotamisches Zeichenlexikon, is generally followed. Italics in the English translation indicate either an uncertain translation or a word in the original language. In general, the rendering of geographical names follows the Répertoire Géographique des Textes Cunéiformes (Rép. Géogr.), personal names follows The Prosopography of the Neo-Assyrian Empire (PNA), and the translation of temple names follows George, House Most High; note, however, the names of Babylonian rulers follow the spelling used in RIMB 2.

There are several differences between the RIM and RINAP styles. Among these, the most notable is that all partially preserved or damaged signs, regardless of how they are broken, now appear between half brackets (⸢ and ⸣). Thus, no partially preserved sign has square brackets ([and]) inserted in its transliteration; for example, [DINGI]R and LUGA[L KU]R appear in the transliteration as ⸢DINGIR⸣ and ⸢LUGAL KUR⸣ respectively. This change was made to ensure compatibility of the online RINAP editions with the standards of the Open Richly Annotated Cuneiform Corpus (Oracc), the parent site and project where RINAP Online is housed. This change was implemented in the print version in order to present identical editions in RINAP 5 and RINAP Online. Note, however, that the translations may give more indication of damage than their corresponding transliterations, as the translations were prepared according to standard Assyriological practices; for example, ⸢DINGIR⸣ (= [DINGI]R) and ⸢LUGAL KUR⸣ (= LUGA[L KU]R) are translated as "[the go]d" and "king [of the lan]d," and not "the god" and "king of the land."

In addition to the indices of museum and excavation numbers and selected publications found in the RIM volumes, the RINAP volumes also contain indices of proper names (personal names, topographical names, and divine names). Searchable online versions of the manuscripts are maintained on Oracc by MOCCI (Munich Open-access Cuneiform Corpus Initiative). Web versions of the editions are also hosted on CDLI (Cuneiform Digital Library Initiative).

Philadelphia
January 2023

Grant Frame
Editor-in-Chief

Bibliographical Abbreviations

Abel and Winckler, Keilschrifttexte	L. Abel and H. Winckler, Keilschrifttexte zum Gebrauch bei Vorlesungen. Berlin, 1890
Achämenidenhof	B. Jacobs and R. Rollinger (eds.), Der Achämenidenhof. The Achaemenid Court: Akten des 2. Internationalen Kolloquiums zum Thema »Vorderasien im Spannungsfeld klassischer und altorientalischer Überlieferungen« Landgut Castelen bei Basel, 23.–25. Mai 2007 (=Classica et Orientalia 2). Wiesbaden, 2010
AfK	Archiv für Keilschriftforschung, vols. 1–2. Berlin, 1923–25
AfO	Archiv für Orientforschung, vol. 3– (vols. 1–2 = AfK). Berlin, Graz, and Horn, 1926–
AJ	The Antiquaries Journal, Being the Journal of the Society of Antiquaries of London. London, 1921–
Altertum	Das Altertum. Berlin, 1955–
AMI NF	Archaeologische Mitteilungen aus Iran. Neue Folge. Berlin, 1968–
Andrae, JIT	W. Andrae, Die jüngeren Ischtar-Tempel in Assur (=WVDOG 58). Leipzig, 1935
Andrae, Stelenreihen	W. Andrae, Die Stelenreihen in Assur (=WVDOG 24). Leipzig, 1913
Andrae, WEA	W. Andrae, Das wiedererstandene Assur, 1. Auflage. Leipzig, 1938; 2. Auflage. Munich, 1977
André-Salvini, Babylone	Catalogue de l'exposition "Babylone," Paris, musée du Louvre, 14 mars–2 juin 2008. Paris, 2008
ANEP^2	J.B. Pritchard (ed.), The Ancient Near East in Pictures Relating to the Old Testament, 2nd edition. Princeton, 1969
ANET^3	J.B. Pritchard (ed.), Ancient Near Eastern Texts Relating to the Old Testament, 3rd edition. Princeton, 1969
AO	Der Alte Orient, 43 vols. Leipzig, 1899–1945
AOAT	Alter Orient und Altes Testament. Neukirchen-Vluyn, Kevelaer, and Münster, 1968–
AoF	Altorientalische Forschungen. Berlin, 1974–
ARRIM	Annual Review of the Royal Inscriptions of Mesopotamia Project. Toronto, 1983–91
Aynard, Prisme	J.M. Aynard, Le prisme du Louvre AO 19.939. Paris, 1957
Babelon, Manual	E. Babelon, Manual of Oriental Antiquities Including the Architecture, Sculpture, and Industrial Arts of Chaldæa, Assyria, Persia, Syria, Judæa, Phoenicia, and Carthage, new edition. London, 1906
Babylon: Myth and Reality	I.L. Finkel and M.J. Seymour (eds.), Babylon: Myth and Reality. London, 2008
Babylon: Wahrheit	J. Marzahn and G. Schauerte (eds.), Babylon: Wahrheit. Munich, 2008
Bär, Ischtar-Tempel	J, Bär, Die älteren Ischtar-Tempel in Assur: Stratigraphie, Architektur und Funde eines altorientalischen Heiligtums von der zweiten Hälfte des 3. Jahrtausends bis zur Mitte des 2. Jahrtausends v. Chr (=WVDOG 105). Saarbrücken, 2003
Bagg, Rép. Géogr. 7	A.M. Bagg, Die Orts- und Gewässernamen der neuassyrischen Zeit, 5 parts (=Répertoire Géographique des Textes Cunéiformes 7). Wiesbaden, 2007–2020
Bagh. Mitt.	Baghdader Mitteilungen. Berlin, 1960–
Barnett, Sculptures from the North Palace	R.D. Barnett, Sculptures from the North Palace of Ashurbanipal at Nineveh (668–627 B.C.). London, 1976
Barnett and Lorenzini, Assyrian Sculpture	R.D. Barnett and A. Lorenzini, Assyrian Sculpture in the British Museum. Toronto, 1975
Barnett et al., Sculptures from the Southwest Palace	R.D. Barnett, E. Bleibtreu, and G. Turner, Sculptures from the Southwest Palace of Sennacherib at Nineveh, 2 vols. London, 1998
Bauer, Asb.	T. Bauer, Das Inschriftenwerk Assurbanipals (=Assyriologische Bibliothek, Neue Folge 1–2). Leipzig, 1933
BE	Babylonian Expedition of the University of Pennsylvania, Series A: Cuneiform Texts, 14 vols. Philadelphia, 1893–1914
Beaulieu, History of Babylon	P.-A. Beaulieu, A History of Babylon, 2200 BC–AD 75. Hoboken, 2018

Beaulieu, Nabonidus	P.-A. Beaulieu, The Reign of Nabonidus, King of Babylon 556–539 BC (=Yale Near Eastern Researches 10). New Haven and London, 1989
Beaulieu, Pantheon of Uruk	P.-A. Beaulieu, The Pantheon of Uruk During the Neo-Babylonian Period (=Cuneiform Monographs 23). Leiden and Boston, 2003
Beek, Atlas	M.A. Beek, Atlas of Mesopotamia. A Survey of the History and Civilisation of Mesopotamia from the Stone Age to the Fall of Babylon. Trans. by D.R. Welsh; H.H. Rowley (ed.). London and Edinburgh, 1962
Befund und Historierung	S. Heinsch, W. Kuntner, and R. Rollinger (eds.), Befund und Historierung: Dokumentation und ihre Interpretationsspielräume (=Araxes 1). Turnhout, 2021
Berytus	Berytus, Archaeological Studies. Beirut, 1934–
Bezold, Cat.	C. Bezold, Catalogue of the Cuneiform Tablets in the Kouyunjik Collection of the British Museum, 5 vols. London, 1889–99
Bezold, Literatur	C. Bezold, Kurzgefasster Überblick über die babylonisch-assyrische Literatur, nebst einem chronologischen Excurs, zwei Registern und einem Index zu 1700 Thontafeln des British-Museum's. Leipzig, 1886
Bezold, Ninive und Babylon^{4}	C. Bezold, Ninive und Babylon, 4th edition (=Monographien zur Weltgeschichte 18). Bielefeld and Leipzig, 1926
BIN	Babylonian Inscriptions in the Collection of J.B. Nies. New Haven, 1917–
BiOr	Bibliotheca Orientalis. Leiden, 1943–
Bittel et al., Yazılıkaya	K. Bittel, R. Naumann, and H. Otto, Yazılıkaya: Architektur, Felsbilder, Inschriften und Kleinfunde (=WVDOG 61). Leipzig, 1941
Bleibtreu, Vergoldeter Silberbecher	E. Bleibtreu, Ein vergoldeter Silberbecher der Zeit Assurbanipals im Miho Museum: Historische Darstellungen des 7. Jahrhunderts v. Chr. (=AfO Beiheft 28). Vienna and Horn, 1999
BM Guide	British Museum. A Guide to the Babylonian and Assyrian Antiquities, 3rd edition. London, 1922
Bock, Kinderheit	U. Bock, "Von seiner Kinderheit bis zum Erwachsenenalter": Die Darstellung der Kinderheit des Herrschers in mesopotamischen und kleinasiatischen Herrscherinschriften und literarischen Texten (=AOAT 383). Münster, 2012
Böhl, Chrestomathy 1	F.M.T. Böhl, Akkadian Chrestomathy, Volume 1: Selected Cuneiform Texts. Leiden, 1947
Böhl, MLVS	F.M.T. Böhl, Mededeelingen uit de Leidsche verzameling van spijkerschrift-inscripties, 3 parts. Amsterdam, 1933–36
Börker-Klähn, Bildstelen	J. Börker-Klähn, Altvorderasiatische Bildstelen und vergleichbare Felsreliefs, 2 vols (=Baghdader Forschungen 4). Mainz am Rhein, 1982
Borger, Asarh.	R. Borger, Die Inschriften Asarhaddons, Königs von Assyrien (=AfO Beiheft 9). Graz, 1956
Borger, BIWA	R. Borger, Beiträge zum Inschriftenwerk Assurbanipals: Die Prismenklassen A, B, C = K, D, E, F, G, H, J und T sowie andere Inschriften. Wiesbaden, 1996
Borger, EAK 1	R. Borger, Einleitung in die assyrischen Königsinschriften, Erster Teil: Das zweite Jahrtausend v. Chr. (=Handbuch der Orientalistik Ergänzungsband V/1/1). Leiden, 1961
Borger, HKL	R. Borger, Handbuch der Keilschriftliteratur, 3 vols. Berlin, 1967–75
Borger, MZ	R. Borger, Mesopotamisches Zeichenlexikon (=AOAT 305). Münster, 2004
Brereton, I am Ashurbanipal	G. Brereton (ed.), I am Ashurbanipal, King of the World, King of Assyria. London, 2018
Brinkman, PKB	J.A. Brinkman, A Political History of Post-Kassite Babylonia, 1158–722 B.C. (=AnOr 43). Rome, 1963
BSA	Bulletin on Sumerian Agriculture. Cambridge, 1984–
BSMS	Bulletin of the (Canadian) Society for Mesopotamian Studies. Toronto, 1981–2006
CAD	The Assyrian Dictionary of the Oriental Institute of the University of Chicago, 21 vols. Chicago, 1956–2010
CAH^{2} 3/2	J. Boardman et al. (eds.), The Cambridge Ancient History, 2nd edition, vol. 3, part 2: The Assyrian and Babylonian Empires and Other States of the Near East, from the Eighth to the Sixth Centuries B.C. Cambridge, 1991
Carter and Stolper, Elam	E. Carter and M.W. Stolper, Elam: Surveys of Political History and Archaeology (=University of California Publications: Near Eastern Studies 25). Berkeley, 1984
Champdor, Babylon	A. Champdor, Babylon. Translated from the French by Elsa Coult. London and New York, 1958
Clay, BE 8/1	A.T. Clay, Legal and Commercial Transactions Dated in the Assyrian, Neo-Babylonian and Persian Periods Chiefly from Nippur. Philadelphia, 1908
Clay, YOS 1	A.T. Clay, Miscellaneous Inscriptions in the Yale Babylonian Collection (=YOS 1). New Haven, 1915

de Clercq, Collection	H.F.X. de Clercq and J. Ménant, Collection de Clercq, catalogue méthodique et raisonné, antiquités assyriennes, cylindres orientaux, cachets, briques, bronzes, bas-reliefs, etc., 2 vols. Paris, 1888/1903
Cole, SAAS 4	S.W. Cole, Nippur in Neo-Assyrian Times c. 755–612 BC (=SAAS 4). Helsinki, 1996
Cole and Machinist, SAA 13	S.W. Cole and P. Machinist, Letters from Assyrian and Babylonian Priests to the Kings Esarhaddon and Assurbanipal (=SAA 13). Helsinki, 1998
Contenau, Manuel d'archéologie orientale	G. Contenau, Manuel d'archéologie orientale depuis les origines jusqu'à l'époque d'Alexandre, 4 vols. Paris, 1927–47
Continuity of Empire	G.B. Lanfranchi, M. Roaf, and R. Rollinger (eds.), Continuity of Empire (?). Assyria, Media, Persia (=History of the Ancient Near East, Monographs 5). Padua, 2003
CRRA 47	S. Parpola and R.M. Whiting (eds.), Sex and Gender in the Ancient Near East: Proceedings of the 47th Rencontre Assyriologique Internationale, Helsinki, July 2–6, 2001. Helsinki, 2002
CRRA 56	L. Feliu, J. Llop, et al. (eds.), Time and History in the Ancient Near East. Proceedings of the 56th Rencontre Assyriologique Internationale at Barcelona, 26–30 July 2010. Winona Lake, 2013
CT	Cuneiform Texts from Babylonian Tablets in the British Museum. London, 1896–
CTMMA	Cuneiform Texts in the Metropolitan Museum of Art. New York, Winona Lake, and University Park, 1988–
CTMMA 2	I. Spar and W.G. Lambert, Literary and Scholastic Texts of the First Millennium B.C. (=CTMMA 2). New York, 2005
Current Research in Cuneiform Palaeography	E. Devecchi, G.G.W. Müller, and J. Mynářová (eds.), Current Research in Cuneiform Palaeography: Proceedings of the Workshop Organized at the 60th Rencontre Assyriologique Internationale, Warsaw 2014. Gladbeck, 2015
Curtis and Reade, Art and Empire	J.E. Curtis and J.E. Reade, Art and Empire: Treasures from Assyria in the British Museum. New York, 1995
CUSAS 17	A.R. George (ed.), Cuneiform Royal Inscriptions and Related Texts in the Schøyen Collection (=Cornell University Studies in Assyriology and Sumerology 17). Bethesda, MD, 2011
Dalley, City of Babylon	S. Dalley, The City of Babylon: A History c. 2000 BC–AD 116. Cambridge, 2021
Dalley, Hanging Garden	S. Dalley, The Mystery of the Hanging Garden of Babylon: An Elusive World Wonder Traced. Oxford, 2013
Dalley and Postgate, Fort Shalmaneser	S. Dalley and J.N. Postgate, The Tablets from Fort Shalmaneser (=Cuneiform Texts from Nimrud 3). London, 1984
Da Riva, GMTR 4	R. Da Riva, The Neo-Babylonian Royal Inscriptions (=Guides to the Mesopotamian Textual Records 4). Münster, 2008
Da Riva, SANER 3	R. Da Riva, The Inscriptions of Nabopolassar, Amel-Marduk and Neriglissar (=Studies in Ancient Near Eastern Records 3). Boston and Berlin, 2013
Dictionnaire de la Bible 6	H. Cazelles (ed.), Dictionnaire de la bible: Supplément 6: Mystères – Passion. Paris, 1960
Donbaz and Grayson, RICCA	V. Donbaz and A.K. Grayson, Royal Inscriptions on Clay Cones from Ashur Now in Istanbul (=RIMS 1). Toronto, 1984
Ellis, Foundation Deposits	R.S. Ellis, Foundation Deposits in Ancient Mesopotamia (=Yale Near Eastern Researches 2). New Haven and London, 1968
Fales, ARIN	F.M. Fales (ed.), Assyrian Royal Inscriptions: New Horizons in Literary, Ideological, and Historical Analysis. Papers of a Symposium Held in Cetona (Siena) June 26–28, 1980. Rome, 1981
Frahm, Companion to Assyria	E. Frahm, A Companion to Assyria. Hoboken, 2017
Frahm, KAL 3	E. Frahm, Historische und historisch-literarische Texte (=Keilschrifttexte aus Assur literarischen Inhalts 3 and WVDOG 121). Wiesbaden, 2009
Frahm, Sanherib	E. Frahm, Einleitung in die Sanherib-Inschriften (=AfO Beiheft 26). Vienna and Horn, 1997
Frame, Babylonia	G. Frame, Babylonia 689–627 B.C.: A Political History. Leiden, 1992
Frame, RIMB 2	G. Frame, Rulers of Babylonia from the Second Dynasty of Isin to the End of Assyrian Domination (1157–612 BC) (=RIMB 2). Toronto, 1995
Frame, RINAP 2	G. Frame, The Royal Inscriptions of Sargon II, King of Assyria (721–705 BC) (=RINAP 2). University Park, 2021
Frayne, RIME 3/2	D. Frayne, Ur III Period (2112–2004 BC) (=RIME 3/2). Toronto, 1997
Frazer, Akkadian Royal Letters	M. Frazer, Akkadian Royal Letters. Berlin, 2023
FuB	Forschungen und Berichte. Berlin, 1957–91
Gadd, UET 1	C.J. Gadd, L. Legrain, and S. Smith, Royal Inscriptions (=UET 1). London, 1928
Galter, Ea/Enki	H.D. Galter, Der Gott Ea/Enki in der akkadischen Überlieferung: Eine

	Bestandsaufnahme des vorhandenen Materials (=Dissertationen der Karl-Franzens-Universität Graz 58). Graz, 1983
Geers, Heft	F.W. Geers, Heft: Unpublished volumes of copies of texts and fragments from the British Museum Kouyunjik collection. 1924–39
George, BTT	A.R. George, Babylonian Topographical Texts (=Orientalia Lovaniensia Analecta 40). Leuven, 1992
George, House Most High	A.R. George, House Most High: The Temples of Ancient Mesopotamia (=Mesopotamian Civilizations 5). Winona Lake, IN, 1993
Glassner, Chronicles	J.-J. Glassner, Mesopotamian Chronicles (=Writings from the Ancient World 19). Atlanta, 2004
Gnoli and Vernant, La mort	G. Gnoli and J.-P. Vernant (eds.), La mort, les morts dans les sociétés anciennes. Cambridge and Paris, 1982
Grayson, ARI	A.K. Grayson, Assyrian Royal Inscriptions, 2 vols. Wiesbaden, 1972–1976
Grayson, Chronicles	A.K. Grayson, Assyrian and Babylonian Chronicles (=Texts from Cuneiform Sources 5). Locust Valley, NY, 1975
Grayson and Novotny, RINAP 3/1	A.K. Grayson and J. Novotny, The Royal Inscriptions of Sennacherib, King of Assyria (704–681 BC), Part 1 (=RINAP 3/1). Winona Lake, IN, 2012
Grayson and Novotny, RINAP 3/2	A.K. Grayson and J. Novotny, The Royal Inscriptions of Sennacherib, King of Assyria (704–681 BC), Part 2 (=RINAP 3/2). Winona Lake, IN, 2014
Hätinen, dubsar 20	A. Hätinen, The Moon God Sîn in Neo-Assyrian and Neo-Babylonian Times (=Dubsar 20). Münster, 2021
Harper, Literature	R.F. Harper, Assyrian and Babylonian Literature: Selected Translations. New York, 1904
Hebraica	Hebraica, vols. 1–11. Chicago, 1884–95
Herrschaftslegitimation	C. Levin and R. Müller (eds.), Herrschaftslegitimation in vorderorientalischen Reichen der Eisenzeit. Tübingen, 2017
Hilprecht, BE 1	H.V. Hilprecht, Old Babylonian Inscriptions Chiefly from Nippur (=BE 1), 2 vols. Philadelphia, 1893 and 1896
Hilprecht, Excavations	H.V. Hilprecht, The Excavations in Assyria and Babylonia (=BE Res 1). Philadelphia, 1904
Hilprecht, Explorations	H.V. Hilprecht, Explorations in Bible Lands during the 19th Century. Philadelphia, 1903
Hunger, Kolophone	H. Hunger, Babylonische und assyrische Kolophone (=AOAT 2). Kevelaer and Neukirchen-Vluyn, 1968
Imperien und Reiche	M. Gehler and R. Rollinger (eds.), Imperien und Reiche in der Weltgeschichte. Epochenübergreifende und globalhistorische Vergleiche. Wiesbaden, 2014
IOS Annual 22	Y. Cohen, A. Gilan, N. Wasserman, L. Cerqueglini, and B. Sheyhatovitch (eds.), The IOS Annual Volume 22: "Telling of Olden Kings," Leiden, 2022
Iran	Iran. Journal of the British Institute of Persian Studies. London, 1963–
IrAnt	Iranica Antiqua. Leiden, 1961–
Iraq	Iraq. London, 1934–
ISIMU	ISIMU: Revista sobre Oriente Próximo y Egipto en la antigüedad. Madrid, 1998–
Jakob-Rost and Marzahn, VAS 23	L. Jakob-Rost and J. Marzahn, Assyrische Königsinschriften auf Ziegeln aus Assur (=VAS 23 and VAS Neue Folge 7). Berlin, 1985
JAOS	Journal of the American Oriental Society. New Haven, 1893–
Jastrow, Religion	M. Jastrow, Die Religion Babyloniens und Assyriens, 2 vols. Giessen, 1905–12
JCS	Journal of Cuneiform Studies. New Haven and Cambridge, 1947–
JCSMS	Journal of the Canadian Society for Mesopotamian Studies. 2006–
Jeffers and Novotny, RINAP 5/2	J. Jeffers and J. Novotny, The Royal Inscriptions of Ashurbanipal (668–631 BC), Aššur-etel-ilāni (630–627 BC), and Sîn-šarra-iškun (626–612 BC), Kings of Assyria, Part 2 (=RINAP 5/2). University Park, PA, 2023
Jeremias, HAOG^2	A. Jeremias, Handbuch der altorientalischen Geisteskultur, 2nd edition. Leipzig, 1929
JNES	Journal of Near Eastern Studies. Chicago, 1942–
Johns, ADD	C.H.W. Johns, Assyrian Deeds and Documents, Recording the Transfer of Property, Including the So-called Private Contracts, Legal Decisions and Proclamations Preserved in the Kouyunjik Collections of the British Museum, Chiefly of the 7th Century B.C., 4 vols. Cambridge, 1898–1923
JRAS	Journal of the Royal Asiatic Society. London, 1834–
Jursa, Die Babylonier	M. Jursa, M., Die Babylonier. Geschichte, Gesellschaft, Kultur. Munich, 2004
Kämmerer and Metzler, Weltschöpfungsepos	T.R. Kämmerer and K.A. Metzler (eds.), Das babylonische Weltschöpfungsepos Enūma elîš (=AOAT 375). Münster, 2012
Kaskal	Kaskal. Rivista di storia, ambiente e culture del Vicino Oriente Antico. Padua, 2004–

Kataja and Whiting, SAA 12	L. Kataja and R. Whiting, Grants, Decrees and Gifts of the Neo-Assyrian Period (=SAA 12). Helsinki, 1995
Keiser, BIN 2	C. Keiser and J.B. Nies, Historical Religious and Economic Texts and Antiquities. New Haven, 1920
King, Cat.	L.W. King, Catalogue of the Cuneiform Tablets in the Kouyunjik Collection of the British Museum, Supplement. London, 1914
King, History	L.W. King, A History of Babylon from the Foundation of the Monarchy to the Persian Conquest. London, 1915
Kitchen, Third Intermediate Period^4	K.A. Kitchen, The Third Intermediate Period in Egypt, 1100-650 BC, 4th edition. Oxford, 2009
Klengel-Brandt, Reise	E. Klengel-Brandt, Reise in das alte Babylon. Leipzig, 1970
Koldewey, Tempel	R. Koldewey, Die Tempel von Babylon und Borsippa (=WVDOG 15). Leipzig, 1911
Koldewey, WEB^4	R. Koldewey, Das wieder erstehende Babylon: Die bisherigen Ergebnisse der deutschen Ausgrabungen, 4th edition. Leipzig, 1925
Koldewey, WEB^5	R. Koldewey, Das wieder erstehende Babylon: Die bisherigen Ergebnisse der deutschen Ausgrabungen, 5th edition. Leipzig, 1990
Kuhrt, Persian Empire	A. Kuhrt, The Persian Empire: A Corpus of Sources from the Achaemenid Period. London and New York, 2007
Kulturelle Schnittstelle	L. Müller-Funk, S. Procházka, G. Selz and A. Telič (eds), Kulturelle Schnittstelle. Mesopotamien, Anatolien, Kurdistan. Geschichte. Sprachen. Vienna, 2014
Lambert, Babylonian Creation Myths	W.G. Lambert, Babylonian Creation Myths (=Mesopotamian Civilizations 16). Winona Lake, IN, 2013
Lambert, Cat.	W.G. Lambert, Catalogue of the Cuneiform Tablets in the Kouyunjik Collection of the British Museum, 3rd Supplement. London, 1992
Lambert and Millard, Cat.	W.G. Lambert and A.R. Millard, Catalogue of the Cuneiform Tablets in the Kouyunjik Collection of the British Museum, 2nd Supplement. London, 1968
Langdon, Kish 1	S. Langdon and L. Watelin, Excavations at Kish, the Hebert Weld and Field Museum of Natural History Expedition to Mesopotamia, 4 vols. Paris, 1924–34
Langdon, OECT 1	S. Langdon, The H. Weld-Blundell Collection in the Ashmolean Museum, vol. 1: Sumerian and Semitic Religious and Historical Texts. Oxford, 1923
Lawson, Concept of Fate	J.N. Lawson, The Concept of Fate in Ancient Mesopotamia of the First Millennium: Towards an Understanding of šīmtu. Wiesbaden, 1994
Legrain, PBS 15	L. Legrain, Royal Inscriptions and Fragments from Nippur and Babylon. Philadelphia, 1926
Lehmann-Haupt, Šamaššumukîn	C.F. Lehmann[-Haupt], Šamaššumukîn, König von Babylonien 668–648 v. Chr. (=Assyriologische Bibliothek 8). Leipzig, 1892
Leichty, RINAP 4	E. Leichty, The Royal Inscriptions of Esarhaddon, King of Assyria (680–669 BC) (=RINAP 4). Winona Lake, IN, 2011
Leichty, Sippar	E. Leichty, J.J. Finkelstein, and C.B.F. Walker, Tablets from Sippar, 3 vols. (=Catalogue of the Babylonian Tablets in the British Museum 6–8). London, 1986–88
Lenfant, Ctésias de Cnide	D. Lenfant, Ctésias de Cnide: la Perse; l'Inde; autres fragments. Paris, 2004
Lippolis, Sennacherib Wall Reliefs	C. Lippolis (ed.), The Sennacherib Wall Reliefs at Nineveh (=Monografie di Mesopotamia 15). Firenze, 2011
Livingstone, SAA 3	A. Livingstone, Court Poetry and Literary Miscellanea (=SAA 3). Helsinki, 1989
Luckenbill, ARAB	D.D. Luckenbill, Ancient Records of Assyria and Babylonia, 2 vols. Chicago, 1926–27
Lyon, Manual	D.G. Lyon, An Assyrian Manual for the Use of Beginners in the Study of the Assyrian Language. Chicago, 1886
LZB	Literarisches Zentralblatt für Deutschland. Leipzig, 1924–43
Macgregor, SAAS 21	S.L. Macgregor, Beyond Hearth and Home: Women in the Public Sphere in Neo-Assyrian Society (=SAAS 21). Helsinki, 2012
Magdalene, Wunsch, and Wells, Fault, Responsibility and Administrative Law	F.R. Magdalene, C. Wunsch, and B. Wells, Fault, Responsibility and Administrative Law in Late Babylonian Legal Texts (=Mesopotamian Civilizations 23). University Park, 2019
MAOG	Mitteilungen der Altorientalischen Gesellschaft. Leipzig, 1925–43
Margueron, Mesopotamia	J.-C. Margueron, Mesopotamia (=Archaeologia Mundi). Cleveland, 1965
Marzahn and Jakob-Rost, Ziegeln 1	J. Marzahn and L. Jakob-Rost, Die Inschriften der assyrischen Könige auf Ziegeln aus Assur, Teil 1. Berlin, 1984
MDOG	Mitteilungen der Deutschen Orient-Gesellschaft zu Berlin. Berlin, 1898–
Meinhold, Ištar	W. Meinhold, Ištar in Aššur: Untersuchung eines Lokalkultes von ca. 2500 bis 614 v. Chr. (=AOAT 367). Münster, 2009
Meissner, BuA	B. Meissner, Babylonien und Assyrien, 2 vols. Heidelberg, 1920 and 1925

Meissner, Grundzüge	B. Meissner, Grundzüge der babylonisch-assyrischen Plastik (=Der Alte Orient 15). Leipzig, 1915
Melville, SAAS 9	S.C. Melville, The Role of Naqia/Zakutu in Sargonid Politics (=SAAS 9). Helsinki, 1999
Mesopotamia	Mesopotamia: Rivista di archeologia, epigrafia e storia orientale antica. Turin, 1966–
Messerschmidt, KAH 1	L. Messerschmidt, Keilschrifttexte aus Assur historischen Inhalts, erstes Heft (=WVDOG 16). Leipzig, 1911
Millard, SAAS 2	A.R. Millard, The Eponyms of the Assyrian Empire 910–612 BC (=SAAS 2). Helsinki, 1994
MJ	Museum Journal of the University Museum, University of Pennsylvania, vols. 1–24. Philadelphia, 1910–35
Moortgat, Kunst	A. Moortgat, Die Kunst des alten Mesopotamien. Die klassische Kunst Vorderasiens. Cologne, 1967
Morgenbladet	Morgenbladet, Oslo, 1819–
Münchner Jahrbuch der bildenden Kunst	Münchner Jahrbuch der bildenden Kunst. Munich, 1906–
MVAG	Mitteilungen der Vorderasiatisch-Aegyptischen Gesellschaft. Leipzig and Berlin, 1896–1944
NABU	Nouvelles assyriologiques brèves et utilitaires. Paris, 1987–
Novotny, Eḫulḫul	J.R. Novotny, Eḫulḫul, Egipar, Emelamana, and Sîn's *Akītu*-House: A Study of Assyrian Building Activities at Ḫarrān. PhD dissertation, University of Toronto, 2003
Novotny and Jeffers, RINAP 5/1	J. Novotny and J. Jeffers, The Royal Inscriptions of Ashurbanipal (668–631 BC), Aššur-etel-ilāni (630–627 BC), and Sîn-šarra-iškun (626–612 BC), Kings of Assyria, Part 1 (=RINAP 5/1). University Park, PA, 2018
Nunn, Knaufplatten	A. Nunn, Knaufplatten und Knäufe aus Assur (=WVDOG 112). Saarwellingen, 2006
D. Oates and J. Oates, Nimrud	J. Oates and D. Oates, Nimrud: An Assyrian Imperial City Revealed. London, 2001
J. Oates, Babylon	J. Oates, Babylon (=Ancient Peoples and Places 94). London, 1979
OECT	Oxford Editions of Cuneiform Texts. Oxford, London, and Paris, 1923–
OLZ	Orientalistische Literaturzeitung. Berlin and Leipzig, 1898–
OMROL	Oudheidkundige Mededelingen uit het Rijksmuseum van Oudheden te Leiden. Leiden, 1907–
Onasch, ÄAT 27	H.-U. Onasch, Die assyrischen Eroberungen Ägyptens, 2 vols. (=Ägypten und Altes Testament 27). Wiesbaden, 1994
OrAnt	Oriens Antiquus. Rome, 1962–90
Orientalia NS	Orientalia. Nova Series. Rome, 1932–
Parker and Dubberstein, Babylonian Chronology	R. Parker and W. Dubberstein, Babylonian Chronology 626 B.C.–A.D. 75 (=Brown University Studies 19). Providence, 1956
Parpola, LAS	S. Parpola, Letters from Assyrian Scholars to the Kings Esarhaddon and Assurbanipal, 2 vols. (=AOAT 5/1–2). Kevelaer and Neukirchen, 1970 and 1983
Parpola, SAA 9	S. Parpola, Assyrian Prophecies (=SAA 9). Helsinki, 1997
Parpola, SAA 10	S. Parpola, Letters from Assyrian and Babylonian Scholars (=SAA 10). Helsinki, 1993
Parpola and Watanabe, SAA 2	S. Parpola and K. Watanabe, Neo-Assyrian Treaties and Loyalty Oaths (=State Archives of Assyria 2). Helsinki, 1988
Parpola and Whiting, Assyria 1995	S. Parpola and R.M. Whiting (eds.), Assyria 1995: Proceedings of the 10th Anniversary Symposium of the Neo-Assyrian Text Corpus Project, Helsinki, September 7–11, 1995. Helsinki, 1997
Parrot, Assyria	A. Parrot, The Arts of Assyria. New York, 1961
Payam-e Bastan Shenas	Payam-e Bastan Shenas. Tehran, 2004–
Pazhohesh-ha-ye Bastanshenasi Iran	Pazhohesh-ha-ye Bastanshenasi Iran. Tehran, 2012–
PBS	Publications of the Babylonian Section, University Museum, University of Pennsylvania, 15 vols. Philadelphia, 1911–26
Pedersén, Archives	O. Pedersén, Archives and Libraries in the City of Assur: A Survey of the Material from the German Excavations, 2 vols. (=Studia Semitica Upsaliensia 6 and 8). Uppsala, 1985–86
Pedersén, Babylon	O. Pedersén, Babylon: The Great City. Münster, 2021
Pedersén, Katalog	O. Pedersén, Katalog der beschrifteten Objekte aus Assur: Die Schriftträger mit Ausnahme der Tontafeln und ähnlicher Archivtexte (=Abhandlungen der Deutschen Orient-Gesellschaft 23). Saarbrücken, 1997
PIHANS	Publications de l'Institut historique-archéologique néerlandais de Stamboul. Leiden, 1956–
PNA	H.D. Baker and K. Radner (eds.), The Prosopography of the Neo-Assyrian Empire. Helsinki, 1998–

Pognon, Bavian	H. Pognon, L'inscription de Bavian, texte, traduction et commentaire philologique. Paris, 1879–80
Porter, Trees, Kings, and Politics	B.N. Porter, Trees, Kings, and Politics: Studies in Assyrian Iconography (=Orbis Biblicus et Orientalis 197). Freiburg and Göttingen, 2003
Postgate, Governor's Palace	J.N. Postgate, The Governor's Palace Archive (=Cuneiform Texts from Nimrud 2). London, 1973
Postgate, Royal Grants	J.N. Postgate, Neo-Assyrian Royal Grants and Decrees (=Studia Pohl, Series Maior 1). Rome, 1969
PSBA	Proceedings of the Society of Biblical Archaeology, 40 vols. London, 1878–1918
1 R	H.C. Rawlinson and E. Norris, The Cuneiform Inscriptions of Western Asia, vol. 1: A Selection from the Historical Inscriptions of Chaldaea, Assyria, and Babylonia. London, 1861
3 R	H.C. Rawlinson and G. Smith, The Cuneiform Inscriptions of Western Asia, vol. 3: A Selection from the Miscellaneous Inscriptions of Assyria. London, 1870
5 R	H.C. Rawlinson and T.G. Pinches, The Cuneiform Inscriptions of Western Asia, vol. 5: A Selection from the Miscellaneous Inscriptions of Assyria and Babylonia. London, 1880–84
RA	Revue d'assyriologie et d'archéologie orientale. Paris, 1886–
Radner, A Short History of Babylon	K. Radner, A Short History of Babylon. London, 2020
Radner, Tall Šēḫ Ḥamad	K. Radner, Die neuassyrischen Texte aus Tall Šēḫ Hamad. Mit Beiträgen von Wolfgang Röllig zu den Aramäischen Beischriften (=Berichte Der Ausgrabung Tall Šēḫ Hamad / Dūr-Katlimmu 6). Berlin, 2002
RB	Revue biblique. Paris, 1892–
Reade, Assyrian Sculpture	J. Reade, Assyrian Sculpture. Cambridge, MA 1983
Rép. Géogr.	W. Röllig (ed.), Beihefte zum Tübinger Atlas des vorderen Orients, Reihe B, Nr. 7: Répertoire géographique des textes cuneiformes. Wiesbaden, 1974–
Reuther, Merkes	O. Reuther, Die Innenstadt von Babylon (Merkes) (=WVDOG 47). Leipzig, 1926
Reynolds, SAA 18	F. Reynolds, The Babylonian Correspondence of Esarhaddon (=SAA 18). Helsinki, 2003
RIMB	The Royal Inscriptions of Mesopotamia, Babylonian Periods, 1 vol. Toronto, 1995
RIME	The Royal Inscriptions of Mesopotamia, Early Periods, 5 vols. Toronto, 1990–2008
RIMS	The Royal Inscriptions of Mesopotamia, Supplements, 1 vol. Toronto, 1984
RINAP	The Royal Inscriptions of the Neo-Assyrian Period. Winona Lake and University Park, IN, 2011–
RINBE	The Royal Inscriptions of the Neo-Babylonian Empire. University Park, IN, 2020–
RLA	Reallexikon der Assyriologie und Vorderasiatischen Archäologie, 15 vols. Berlin, 1932–2018
RLV	Reallexikon der Vorgeschichte, 15 vols. Berlin, 1924–32
Rost and Marzahn, Babylon	L. Jakob-Rost and J. Marzahn, Babylon (=Vorderasiatisches Museum, Kleine Schriften 4). Berlin, 1983
J.M. Russell, Final Sack	J.M. Russell, The Final Sack of Nineveh: The Discovery, Documentation, and Destruction of King Sennacherib's Throne Room at Nineveh, Iraq. New Haven and London, 1998
J.M. Russell, Senn.'s Palace	J.M. Russell, Sennacherib's Palace Without Rival at Nineveh. Chicago and London, 1991
SAA	State Archives of Assyria. Helsinki, 1987–
SAAB	State Archives of Assyria Bulletin. Padua, 1987–
SAAS	State Archives of Assyria Studies. Helsinki, 1992–
SAAS 29	G.B. Lanfranchi, R. Mattila, and R. Rollinger (eds.), Writing Neo-Assyrian history: sources, problems, and approaches (=SAAS 29). Helsinki, 2019
Salonen, Ziegeleien	A. Salonen, Die Ziegeleien im alten Mesopotamien (=Annales Academiae Scientiarum Fennicae, Series B 171). Helsinki, 1972
Schaudig, Inschriften Nabonids	H. Schaudig, Die Inschriften Nabonids von Babylon und Kyros' des Grossen samt den in ihrem Umfeld enstandenen Tendenzschriften: Textausgabe und Grammatik (=AOAT 256). Münster, 1997
Scheil, Prisme	V. Scheil, Le prisme d'Asarhaddon, roi d'Assyrie 681–668 (=Bibliothèque de l'École des Haute Études 208). Paris, 1914
Schmidt, Persepolis 2	E.F. Schmidt, Persepolis II: Contents of the Treasury and Other Discoveries (=OIP 69). Chicago, 1957
Schmitt, Ischtar-Tempel	A.W. Schmitt, Die jüngeren Ischtar-Tempel und der Nabû-Tempel in Assur (=WVDOG 137). Wiesbaden, 2012
Schrader, KB	E. Schrader, Keilinschriftliche Bibliothek, Sammlung von assyrischen und babylonischen Texten in Umschrift und Übersetzung, 6 vols. Berlin, 1889–1915

Schrader, KB 2	E. Schrader, Sammlung von assyrischen und babylonischen Texten in Umschrift und Übersetzung (=Keilinschriftliche Bibliothek 2). Berlin, 1890
Schroeder, KAH 2	O. Schroeder, Keilschrifttexte aus Assur historischen Inhalts, Zweites Heft (=WVDOG 37). Leipzig, 1922
Schroeder, KAV	O. Schroeder, Keilschrifttexte aus Assur verschiedenen Inhalts (=WVDOG 35). Leipzig, 1920
Searight, Assyrian Stone Vessels	A. Searight, J. Reade, and I. Finkel, Assyrian Stone Vessels and Related Material in the British Museum. Oxford, 2008
Seipel, 7000 Jahre	W. Seipel (ed.), 7000 Jahre persische Kunst: Meisterwerke aus dem Iranischen Nationalmuseum in Tehran (=Kunsthistorisches Museum 22). Milan and Vienna, 2000
Śilwa, Cracow and Jena	J. Śilwa and E. Kluwe, From the Archaeological Collections of Cracow and Jena. Warsaw and Cracow, 1988
Sjöberg, Temple Hymns	A.W. Sjöberg and E. Bergmann, The Collection of the Sumerian Temple Hymns (=Texts from Cuneiform Sources 3). Locust Valley, 1969
G. Smith, Assyrian Discoveries	G. Smith, Assyrian Discoveries; An Account of Explorations and Discoveries on the Site of Nineveh, During 1873 and 1874. New York, 1875
G. Smith, Notebook 17	G. Smith, Notebook 17. The British Library, London, Department of Manuscripts, Add. MS. 30413
Sollberger, UET 8	E. Sollberger, Royal Inscriptions Part 2. London, 1965
Sollberger and Kupper, IRSA	E. Sollberger and J.R. Kupper, Inscriptions royales sumériennes et akkadiennes. Paris, 1971
Source	Source: Notes in the History of Art. Chicago, 1981–
Spar and Jursa, CTMMA 4	I. Spar and M. Jursa, Cuneiform Texts in the Metropolitan Museum of Art 4: Temple Archive and Other Texts From the First and Second Millennium B.C. New York, 2014
Starr, SAA 4	I. Starr, Queries to the Sungod: Divination and Politics in Sargonid Assyria (=SAA 4). Helsinki, 1990
Steible, NSBW	H. Steible, Die neusumerischen Bau- und Weihinschriften, 2 vols. (=Freiburger Altorientalische Studien 9:1–2) Stuttgart, 1991
Stephens, YOS 9	F.J. Stephens, Votive and Historical Texts from Babylonia and Assyria (=YOS 9). New Haven, 1937
Strassmaier, AV	J.N. Strassmaier, Alphabetisches Verzeichniss der assyrischen und akkadischen Wörter der Cuneiform Inscriptions of Western Asia, vol. II, sowie anderer meist unveröffentlichter Inschriften. Mit zahlreichen Ergänzungen und Verbesserungen und einem Wörterverzeichniss zu den in den Verhandlungen des VI. Orientalisten-Congresses zu Leiden veröffentlichten babylonischen Inschriften (=Assyriologische Bibliothek 4). Leipzig, 1886
Streck, Asb.	M. Streck, Assurbanipal und die letzten assyrischen Könige bis zum Untergange Niniveh's, 3 vols. (=Vorderasiatische Bibliothek 7). Leipzig, 1916
Strommenger and Hirmer, Mesopotamien	E. Strommenger and M. Hirmer, Fünf Jahrtausende Mesopotamien: Die Kunst von den Anfängen um 5000 v. Chr. bis zu Alexander dem Grossen. Munich, 1962
Studia Chaburensia 8	S. Hasegawa and K. Radner (eds.), The Reach of the Assyrian and Babylonian Empires: Case Studies in Eastern and Western Peripheries (=Studia Chaburensia 8). Wiesbaden, 2020
Studies Böhl	M.A. Beek, A.a. Kampman, C. Nijland, and J. Ryckmans (eds.) Symbolae Biblicae et Mesopotamicae Francisco Mario Theodoro De Liagre Böhl. Leiden 1973
Studies Borger	S.M. Maul (ed.), Festschrift für Rykle Borger zu seinem 65. Geburtstag am 24. Mai 1994: *tikip santakki mala bašmu* ... Groningen, 1998
Studies Deimel	Miscellanea Orientalia Dedicata A. Deimel Annos LXX Complenti (=AnOr 12). Rome, 1935
Studies Edhem	Halil Edhem Hâtira Kitabi: Cilt 1 (In Memoriam Halil Edhem Vol. 1) (=Türk Tarih Kurumu yayınları 7/5). Ankara, 1947
Studies Ellis	M.J. Boda and J. Novotny (eds.), From the Foundations to the Crenellations: Essays on Temple Building in the Ancient Near East and Hebrew Bible (=AOAT 366). Münster, 2010
Studies Grayson	G. Frame (ed.), From the Upper Sea to the Lower Sea: Studies on the History of Assyria and Babylonia in Honour of A.K. Grayson (=PIHANS 101). Leiden, 2004
Studies Immerwahr	A.P. Chapin (ed.), Charis: Essays in Honor of Sara A. Immerwahr (=Hesperia, Supplement 33). Princeton, 2004
Studies Oded	G. Galil, M. Geller, and A.R. Millard (eds.), Homeland and Exile: Biblical and Ancient Near Eastern Studies in Honour of Bustenay Oded (=Vetus Testamentum Supplements 130). Leiden and Boston, 2009
Studies Oelsner	J. Marzahn and H. Neumann (eds.), Babylonien und seine Nachbarn in neu- und

	spätbabylonischer Zeit: Wissenschaftliches Kolloquium aus Anlass des 75. Geburtstags von Joachim Oelsner Jena, 2. und 3. März 2007 (=AOAT 369). Münster, 2014.
Studies Oppenheim	R.D. Biggs and J.A. Brinkman (eds.), Studies Presented to A. Leo Oppenheim, June 7, 1964. Chicago, 1964
Studies Parpola	M. Luukko, S. Svärd, and R. Mattila (eds.), Of God(s), Trees, Kings, and Scholars: Neo-Assyrian and Related Studies in Honour of Simo Parpola (=StOr 106). Helsinki, 2009
Studies Puech	Mélanges d'histoire des religions offerts à Henri-Charles Puech, sous le patronage et avec le concours du Collège de France et de la Section des sciences religieuses de l'École pratique des hautes Études, Paris, 1974
Studies Renger	B. Böck, E. Cancik-Kirschbaum, and T. Richter (eds.), Munuscula Mesopotamica: Festschrift für Johannes Renger (=AOAT 267). Münster, 1999
Studies Rochberg	C.J. Crisostomo, E.A. Escobar, T. Tanaka, and N. Veldhuis (eds.), The Scaffolding of Our Thoughts: Essays on Assyriology and the History of Science in Honor of Francesca Rochberg. Leiden and Boston, 2018
Studies Römer	M. Dietrich and O. Loretz (eds.), dubsar anta-men: Studien zur Altorientalistik. Feschrift für Willem H.Ph. Römer zur Vollendung seines 70. Lebensjahres mit Beiträgen von Freunden, Schülern und Kollegen (=AOAT 253). Münster, 1998
Studies Sjöberg	H. Behrens, et al. (eds.), Dumu-e_2-dub-ba-a: Studies in Honor of Ake W. Sjöberg (=Occasional Publications of the Samuel Noah Kramer Fund 11). Philadelphia, 1989
Studies Stolper	M. Kozuh, W.F.M. Henkelman, C.E. Jones, and C. Woods (eds.), Extraction and Control: Studies in Honor of Matthew W. Stolper (=Studies in Ancient Oriental Civilization 68), Chicago, 2014
Studies Strommenger	B. Hrouda (ed.), Von Uruk nach Tuttul: Eine Festschrift für Eva Strommenger. Munich, 1992
Studies H. and M. Tadmor	I. Ephʿal, A. Ben-Tor, and P. Machinist (eds.), Hayim and Miriam Tadmor Volume (=Eretz-Israel 27). Jerusalem, 2003
Studies Winnett	J.W. Wevers and D.B. Redford (eds.), Studies on the Ancient Palestinian World Presented to Professor F. V. Winnett on the occasion of his retirement 1 July 1971. Toronto, 1972
Sumer	Sumer: A Journal of Archaeology in Iraq. Baghdad, 1945–
Susa and Elam	K. De Graef and J. Tavernier (eds.), Susa and Elam. Archaeological, Philological, Historical and Geographical Perspectives. Proceedings of the International Congress Held at Ghent University, December 14–17, 2009 (=Mémoires de la Délégation en Perse 58). Leiden and Boston, 2013
Svärd, Power and Women	S. Svärd, Power and Women in the Neo-Assyrian Palaces. PhD dissertation, University of Helsinki, 2012
Svärd, SAAS 23	S. Svärd, Power and Women in the Neo-Assyrian Palaces (=SAAS 23). Helsinki, 2015
Tadmor and Yamada, RINAP 1	H. Tadmor and S. Yamada, The Royal Inscriptions of Tiglath-pileser III (744–727 BC) and Shalmaneser V (726–722 BC), Kings of Assyria (=RINAP 1). Winona Lake, IN, 2011
Tallqvist, Götterepitheta	K. Tallqvist, Akkadische Götterepitheta, mit einem Götterverzeichnis und einer Liste der prädikativen Elemente der sumerischen Götternamen (=Studia Orientalia 7). Helsinki, 1938
Texts and Contexts	P. Delnero and J. Lauinger (eds.), Texts and contexts: The Circulation and Transmission of Cuneiform Texts in Social Space (=SANER 9). Berlin, 2015
TUAT	O. Kaiser (ed.), Texte aus der Umwelt des Alten Testaments. Gütersloh, 1982–2001
TUAT^2	B. Janowski and G. Wilhelm (eds.), Texte aus der Umwelt des Alten Testaments, Neue Folge. Munich, 2004–
UCP	University of California Publications in Semitic Philology, vols. 1–24. Berkeley, 1907–63
UE	Ur Excavations. Oxford, London, and Philadelphia, 1926–
UET	Ur Excavations, Texts. London, 1928–
Unger, Babylon	E. Unger, Babylon: die heilige Stadt nach der Beschreibung der Babylonier. Berlin and Leipzig, 1931
Ungnad, ARU	A. Ungnad and J. Kohler, Assyrische Rechtsurkunden. Leipzig, 1913
UVB	Vorläufiger Bericht über die von (dem Deutschen Archäologischen Institut und der Deutschen Orient-Gesellschaft aus Mitteln) der Deutschen Forschungsgemeinschaft unternommenen Ausgrabungen in Uruk-Warka. Berlin, 1930–
UVB 1	J. Jordan and A. Schott, Erster vorläufiger Bericht über die von der Notgemeinschaft der Deutschen Wissenschaft in Uruk-Warka unternommenen Ausgrabungen. Berlin, 1930
Van Buren, Found.	E.D. Van Buren, Foundation Figurines and Offerings. Berlin, 1931

VAS	Vorderasiatische Schriftdenkmäler der Königlichen Museen zu Berlin. Leipzig and Berlin, 1907–
Vera Chamaza, Omnipotenz	G.W. Vera Chamaza, Die Omnipotenz Aššurs: Entwicklungen in der Aššur-Theologie unter den Sargoniden Sargon II., Sanherib und Asarhaddon (=AOAT 295). Münster, 2002
Vorderasiatisches Museum	L. Jakob-Rost (ed.), Das Vorderasiatische Museum, Berlin. Mainz am Rhein, 1992
Walker, CBI	C.B.F. Walker, Cuneiform Brick Inscriptions in the British Museum, the Ashmolean Museum, Oxford, the City of Birmingham Museums and Art Gallery, the City of Bristol Museum and Art Gallery. London, 1981
Weiershäuser and Novotny, RINBE 1/1	Frauke Weiershäuser and Jamie Novotny, The Royal Inscriptions of Nabopolassar (625–605 BC) and Nebuchadnezzar II (604–562 BC), Kings of Babylon, Part 1 (=RINBE 1/1). University Park, PA, forthcoming
Weiershäuser and Novotny, RINBE 2	F. Weiershäuser and J. Novotny, The Royal Inscriptions of Amēl-Marduk (561–560 BC), Neriglissar (559–556 BC), and Nabonidus (555–539 BC), Kings of Babylon (=RINBE 2). University Park, PA, 2020
von Weiher, SpTU 2	E. von Weiher, Spätbabylonische Texte aus Uruk, Teil II (=Ausgrabungen der Deutschen Forschungsgemeinschaft in Uruk-Warka 10). Berlin, 1983
Weissbach, Miscellen	F.H. Weissbach, Babylonische Miscellen (=WVDOG 4). Leipzig, 1903
Wetzel, Stadtmauern	F. Wetzel, Die Stadmauern von Babylon (=WVDOG 48). Leipzig, 1930
Wetzel and Weissbach, Hauptheiligtum	F. Wetzel and F.H. Weissbach, Das Hauptheiligtum des Marduk in Babylon, Esagila und Etemenanki (=WVDOG 59). Leipzig, 1938
Winckler, AOF	H. Winckler, Altorientalische Forschungen, 3 vols. Leipzig, 1893–1905
Wiseman, Chronicles	D.J. Wiseman, Chronicles of Chaldean kings (626–556 B.C.) in the British Museum. London, 1956
WO	Die Welt des Orients. Wuppertal, Stuttgart, and Göttingen, 1947–
Woolley, UE 5	C.L. Woolley, The Ziggurat and Its Surroundings (=UE 5). London and Philadelphia, 1939
Woolley, UE 8	C.L. Woolley, The Kassite Period and the Period of the Assyrian Kings (=UE 8). London, 1965
Woolley, UE 9	C.L. Woolley, The Neo-Babylonian and Persian Periods (=UE 9). London, 1962
Woolley and Moorey, Ur	C.L. Woolley, Ur "of the Chaldees," rev. and updated by P.R.S. Moorey. London, 1982
Worthington, Textual Criticism	M. Worthington, Principles of Akkadian Textual Criticism (=Studies in Ancient Near Eastern Records 1). Berlin and Boston, 2012
WVDOG	Wissenschaftliche Veröffentlichungen der Deutschen Orient-Gesellschaft. Leipzig, Berlin, and Wiesbaden, 1900–
WZJ	Wissenschaftliche Zeitschrift der Friedrich Schiller Universität Jena. Jena, 1951–
Yamada, SAAS 28	S. Yamada (ed.), Neo-Assyrian Sources in Context: Thematic Studies of Texts, History, and Culture (=SAAS 28). Helsinki, 2018
YOS	Yale Oriental Studies, Babylonian Texts. New Haven, 1915–
ZA	Zeitschrift für Assyriologie und Vorderasiatische Archäologie. Berlin, 1886–
Zadok, Rép. Géogr. 8	R. Zadok, Geographical Names According to New- and Late-Babylonian texts (=Répertoire géographique des textes cunéiformes 8). Wiesbaden, 1985
Zawadzki, Fall of Assyria	S. Zawadzki, The Fall of Assyria and Median-Babylonian Relations in Light of the Nabopolassar Chronicle. Delft, The Netherlands, 1988
Zettler, Inanna Temple	R.L. Zettler, The Ur III Temple of Inanna at Nippur: The Operation and Organization of Urban Religious Institutions in Mesopotamia in the Late Third Millennium B.C. (=Berliner Beiträge zum Vorderen Orient 11). Berlin, 1992
ZK	Zeitschrift für Keilschriftforschung und verwandte Gebiete, 2 vols. Leipzig, 1884–85

Other Abbreviations

8°-Heft	microfiche 1–6 in Borger, BIWA
Aei	Aššur-etel-ilāni
Asb.	Ashurbanipal
Asn.	Ashurnasirpal II
Ass	Aššur
c	collated
ca.	circa
cf.	*confer* (lit. "compare")
cm	centimeter(s)
col(s).	column(s)
coll.	collection
comm.	commentary
dia.	diameter
DN	divine name
E	east
ed(s).	editor(s)
Esar.	Esarhaddon
esp.	especially
et al.	*et alii* (lit. "and others")
ex(s).	exemplar(s)
fig(s).	figure(s)
frgm(s).	fragment(s)
g	gram(s)
gen.	gentilic
kg	kilogram(s)
lbs	pounds
LoBl	lose Blätter, microfiche 12–13 in Borger, BIWA
m	meter(s)
max.	maximum
MS	manuscript
n	not collated
N	north
NA	Neo-Assyrian
n(n).	note(s)
no(s).	number(s)
NS	Nova Series/New Series
obv.	obverse
p	collated from photo
p(p).	page(s)
ph(s)	photo(s)
pl(s).	plate(s)
rev.	reverse
RN	royal name
S	south
SEB	South-East Building (Kalḫu)
Ssi	Sîn-šarra-iškun
vol(s).	volume(s)
W	west

+	Between object numbers indicates physical join
(+)	Indicates fragments from same object but no physical join

Object Signatures

A	Aššur collection of the Arkeoloji Müzeleri, Istanbul
A Babylon	Collection of the Nebuchadnezzar Museum, Babylon
AH	Abu Habba collection of the British Museum, London
AO	Collection of Antiquités Orientales of the Musée du Louvre, Paris
Ash	Ashmolean Museum, Oxford
Ass	Prefix for excavation numbers from the German excavations at Aššur
B	Signature of tablets in the Babylon collection of the Arkeoloji Müzeleri, Istanbul
BE	Prefix for excavation numbers from the German excavations at Babylon
BM	British Museum, London
Bu	E.A.W. Budge collection of the British Museum, London
CBS	Babylonian Section of the University Museum, Philadelphia
D	Signature of tablets in the Arkeoloji Müzeleri, Istanbul
DT	Daily Telegraph collection of the British Museum, London
EŞ	Eşki Şark Eserleri Müzesi of the Arkeoloji Müzeleri, Istanbul
H	Signature of objects in the collections of the City of Bristol Museum and Art Gallery
HMA	Signature of objects in Hearst Museum of Anthropology of the University of California at Berkeley
HS	Hilprecht collection of Babylonian Antiquities of Fr. Schiller Universität, Jena
IM	Iraq Museum, Baghdad
K	Kuyunjik collection of the British Museum, London
Ki	L.W. King collection of the British Museum, London
LB	A.F.M.Th. de Liagre Böhl Collection, Leiden
ML	Signature of cuneiform materials in the McLennan Library belonging to the McGill University Ethnological collections, Montreal
MMA	Metropolitan Museum of Art, New York
N	1) Nippur collection of the University Museum, Philadelphia 2) Siglum (infix) for excavation numbers from the American excavations at Nippur
NBC	James B. Nies collection of the Yale Babylonian Collection, New Haven
ND	Prefix for excavation numbers from the British excavations at Nimrud
NT	Excavation numbers of inscribed objects from the American excavations at Nippur
PMA	Philadelphia Museum of Art
PT	Prefix for excavation numbers for objects found on the Persepolis terrace by the Oriental Institute expedition
PTS	Princeton Theological Seminary
Rm	H. Rassam collection of the British Museum, London
SE	Signature of objects in the collections of the Couvent Saint-Étienne, Jerusalem
SF	Signature of objects in the Miho Museum, Koka
Sm	G. Smith collection of the British Museum, London
U	Prefix of excavation numbers from the British-American excavations at Ur (Tell al Muqayyar)
UM	University of Pennsylvania Museum of Archaeology and Anthropology, Philadelphia
VA	Vorderasiatisches Museum, Berlin
VA Ass	Aššur collection of the Vorderasiatisches Museum, Berlin
VA Bab	Babylon collection of the Vorderasiatisches Museum, Berlin
VAG	Casts (Güsse) in the collection of the Vorderasiatisches Museum, Berlin
VAT	Tablets in the collection of the Vorderasiatisches Museum, Berlin
W	Prefix for excavation numbers from the German excavations at Uruk/Warka
W-B	Signature of objects in the Weld-Blundell collection of the Ashmolean Museum, Oxford
WML	Signature of objects in collections of the the World Museum Liverpool, Liverpool
YBC	Babylonian collection of the Yale University Library, New Haven

Introduction

In the mid-650s, a few years before Egypt declared itself independent under Psammetichus I with the help of Carian and Ionian mercenaries and before Šamaš-šuma-ukīn rebelled, the Assyrian Empire had reached the apex of its territorial expansion.[1] Ashurbanipal's vast holdings stretched from the Zagros Mountains in the east to the Mediterranean Sea and Cilicia in the west. Ruling from the capital Nineveh, he managed his extensive kingdom with the aid of his trusted officials, including at least seventy-one provincial governors.[2] Moreover, the Empire had close ties with no less than thirty-nine client states,[3] including many important Phoenician port cities in the Levant, who regularly supplied building materials for building projects in the Assyrian heartland, the so-called "Aššur-Nineveh-Arbela" triangle. Although Ashurbanipal declared victory over his older brother in late 648 (after 30-V), when Šamaš-šuma-ukīn committed suicide or was killed and when the citizens of Babylon voluntarily opened the city's eight gates after a protracted siege,[4] the strength of the Assyrian Empire was waning and its reputation was in tatters. The loss of Egypt as a client a few years earlier (ca. 653) did not help. The punitive military expeditions that Ashurbanipal launched in 647–644, especially against Elam in western Iran and the Qedarite tribal leaders on the Arabian peninsula, only made matters worse, especially after the Assyrian army had destroyed the Elamite religious center Susa.[5] The well-oiled machine that was the Assyrian Empire was visibly starting to rust and, if its collapse had not yet been written on the wall, it was at least imaginable, something that would have been unfathomable only a few years earlier, before Ashurbanipal and Šamaš-šuma-ukīn went to war. Assyria's fortunes continued to decline during Ashurbanipal's final years on the throne, as well as during the reigns of his successors, Aššur-etel-ilāni, Sîn-šuma-līšir, and Sîn-šarra-iškun. Ashurbanipal's inability or failure to closely manage the transition of power, as his father Esarhaddon and grandmother Naqī'a (Zakūtu) had carefully done, further weakened Assyria, both at home and with its contemporaries (especially in Babylonia),[6] as members of the royal family and influential officials vied for power. In 612, less than twenty years after Ashurbanipal's death, the once-grand and once-all-important Assyrian metropolis Nineveh was captured and destroyed by a Babylonian-Median alliance led by Nabopolassar and Cyaxares (Umakištar) and its final Aššur-appointed king, Sîn-šarra-iškun, was dead. Three years later, in 609, the Assyrian Empire ceased to exist when its last ruler, Aššur-uballiṭ II, fled the city of Ḫarrān before an advancing Babylonian army and was never heard from again. The Assyrian Empire was gone, but not forgotten.

Some aspects of Ashurbanipal's reign and his inscriptions have already been discussed in the introduction to Parts 1 and 2 and that information will not be repeated here. Therefore, interested readers should consult the introductions of RINAP 5/1 and RINAP 5/2 for surveys of Ashurbanipal's inscribed objects from Assyrian cities, an overview of previous editions, studies of his military campaigns and building activities in Assyria, information about the chronology of his long reign, and translations of relevant passages in king lists and

[1] According to a Babylonian chronicle, the Šamaš-šuma-ukīn rebellion began on 19-X-652. For an overview of the so-called "Brothers' War," see Novotny and Jeffers, RINAP 5/1 pp. 22–23; and, for a chronological outline of the revolt, see Frame, Babylonia pp. 188–190.

[2] For details about the Assyrian provinces, see Radner, RLA 11/1–2 (2006) pp. 42–68.

[3] Lauinger, Texts and Contexts pp. 289–290; and Radner, SAAS 29 pp. 313–314 (with n. 25).

[4] Babylon fell sometime after 30-V-648; BM 40577 is the last economic document from Babylon dated by Šamaš-šuma-ukīn's regnal years. Ashurbanipal's own inscriptions state that the gods threw the king of Babylon into a raging conflagration. It is uncertain from this cryptic remark whether Šamaš-šuma-ukīn took his own life or was murdered by his once-loyal supporters. For some details, see Novotny and Jeffers, RINAP 5/1 p. 23 n. 146.

[5] For overviews of these campaigns, see Novotny and Jeffers, RINAP 5/1 pp. 23–26.

[6] Nabopolassar, a "son of a nobody," seized the throne of Babylon while Sîn-šuma-līšir and Sîn-šarra-iškun fought for control of Assyria after the death of Aššur-etel-ilāni. For further information, see the section *Aššur-etel-ilāni and His Chief Eunuch Sîn-šuma-līšir* below.

Babylonian chronicles. The introduction to the present volume includes information about the texts included in Part 3 and the texts excluded from RINAP 5; a survey of the inscribed objects included in Part 3; Ashurbanipal's building Activities in Babylonia and the East Tigris Region; the end of Ashurbanipal's reign; and Assyria under the Empire's last rulers Aššur-etel-ilāni, Sîn-šuma-līšir, Sîn-šarra-iškun, and Aššur-uballiṭ II. The introduction also includes English translations of three Babylonian Chronicles, including the so-called "Fall of Nineveh Chronicle," which documents the final years of Assyria as a political entity.

Texts Included in Part 3

RINAP 5 was originally conceived as being split into three parts. Part 1 was to include all of the historical inscriptions on clay prisms, clay cylinders, and wall slabs and other stone objects from Nineveh, Aššur, and Kalḫu; Part 2 was to edit together the texts of Ashurbanipal preserved on clay tablets; and Part 3 was to contain all of Ashurbanipal's Babylonian inscriptions, the royal inscriptions of Aššur-etel-ilāni and Sîn-šarra-iškun, as well as the texts whose attribution is uncertain (the 1000-numbered texts) and inscriptions written in the names of other members of the royal family (the queens) and officials (including loyal supporters in Babylonia). In 2018, however, the authors had felt that RINAP 5 should be published in two parts, rather than in three parts; this is stated several times in Part 1, especially in the book's introduction. During the course of the preparation of Part 2, it became increasingly clear that the original plan to split the corpus of inscriptions of Ashurbanipal, Aššur-etel-ilāni, and Sîn-šarra-iškun into three parts was the most viable option for publishing this large group of texts. Thus, RINAP 5 once again became a three-part volume.

Part 3 contains all of the certainly-identifiable and positively-attributable inscriptions of Ashurbanipal discovered in Babylonia (mostly from Babylon), in the East Tigris Region (Dēr), and outside of the Assyrian Empire, mostly at the Persian capital Persepolis, together with some texts that have been tentatively attributed to Ashurbanipal (the 1000-number texts, as defined in the Editorial Notes), inscriptions of some members of Ashurbanipal's family — his wife Libbāli-šarrat, as well as his sons and successors Aššur-etel-ilāni and Sîn-šarra-iškun[7] — and loyal officials (namely Sîn-balāssu-iqbi, governor of Ur). In total, 106 inscriptions are edited in the present volume. The contents of these texts fall into three broad categories: (1) building and display inscriptions, (2) dedicatory inscriptions, and (3) proprietary labels. Other subgenres of royal compositions (for example, historical-literary texts, colophons, and land grants in the form of dedications) are excluded entirely from RINAP 5; see below for details.

Most of the inscriptions included in Part 3 are composed in the Standard Babylonian dialect of Akkadian (with Assyrianisms). A handful of inscriptions, mostly written or stamped on bricks, were composed in Sumerian. The texts from Assyria are written in Neo-Assyrian script, while those from Babylonia are usually, but not always, in contemporary or archaizing Neo-Babylonian script.

Texts Excluded from RINAP 5/3

Numerous textual sources relating to Ashurbanipal fall outside the scope of this volume. In particular, the numerous Ashurbanipal colophons,[8] which one could classify as a type of royal inscription, and the texts assigned to the reign of Ashurbanipal and his successors that are edited in the SAA series are excluded from RINAP 5, as already mentioned in the introduction of Part 2.[9] There are numerous texts that were catalogued, copied, edited, referred to, or transliterated in Bauer, Asb. and Borger, BIWA that the authors decided not to include in Part 3, thereby excluding them entirely from RINAP 5. In the case of some of the texts, the decision was fairly easy and straightforward, whereas in the case of others, it was not since it was difficult to determine whether the text should be regarded as a royal inscription (in the strictest sense; for example, an annalistic text or a summary inscription in the style of the inscriptions written on clay prisms or a dedicatory inscription) or as a historical-literary composition (for example, the Ashurbanipal Epic or the Epical Narrative Relating to Ashurbanipal's Elamite Wars).[10] Texts that were regarded as royal inscriptions, but whose

---

[7] The inscriptions of Ashurbanipal's older brother Šamaš-šuma-ukīn are not edited in RINAP 5. For editions of the inscriptions of that king of Babylon, see Frame, RIMB 2 pp. 248–259 B.6.33.1–2001.

[8] This rich source material, however, will be soon be edited as part of the Reading the Library of Ashurbanipal Project, a collaborative, online project between the British Museum and Ludwig-Maximilians-Universität München directed by Enrique Jiménez and Jonathan Taylor.

[9] See Jeffers and Novotny, RINAP 5/2 p. 3 for further details.

[10] See, for example, Livingstone, SAA 3 pp. 48–52 nos. 19–22.

attribution to Ashurbanipal is (highly) uncertain, are sometimes edited as 1000-numbers in this volume and sometimes excluded from RINAP 5 altogether, depending on those texts' current states of preservation. Texts that the authors considered to be historical-literary compositions are also not included in RINAP 5; the majority of these were edited or catalogued in Bauer, Asb. pp. 71–82.[11] As it is not yet possible to categorize the genre and assign a royal 'author' of each and every one of these fragments with a high degree of confidence, it is inevitable that not every previously published Ashurbanipal royal inscription has made it into RINAP 5. Therefore, it is very likely that the authors of the present volume excluded some texts that should have been included in Part 3, even as a 1000-number. Given the poor state of preservation of some of the texts, this was unavoidable. Through new joins and new pieces, hopefully some of the issues the present authors faced in the preparation of this volume will be eventually resolved.

YBC 2171 (Stephens, YOS 9 no. 80), an Assyrian inscription written on a clay cylinder that A.K. Grayson attributed to Sîn-šarra-iškun, is not included with the inscriptions of that Assyrian ruler since the present authors see no conclusive proof that that text was composed while Sîn-šarra-iškun was king of Assyria.[12] As already proposed by R. Borger and J.A. Brinkman, that inscription likely dates to the time of the much earlier Assyrian king Ninurta-tukultī-Aššur and, thus, is not edited in RINAP 5/3.[13]

Moreover, there are numerous still-to-be-published and still-to-be-attributed Neo-Assyrian royal inscriptions whose royal 'authors' are yet to be positively identified. The bulk of these badly-damaged texts are in the DT, K, Rm, and Sm collections of the British Museum (London). Although many of these texts have been transliterated since the 1980s by G. Frame, A.K. Grayson, E. Leichty, and other scholars associated directly or indirectly with the RIM and RINAP projects, this large group of Assyrian 'historical' texts are not edited in RINAP 5/3, despite it being the last volume of inscriptions to appear in the RIMA and RINAP series. Instead, these poorly-preserved sources will first be disseminated online, in an open-access format and, thus, the work of these scholars will be made accessible via CDLI, eBL, and Oracc, principally through RIAo and RINAPo.[14]

Survey of the Inscribed Objects Included in Part 3

The corpus of firmly identifiable inscriptions of Ashurbanipal and his successors Aššur-etel-ilāni and Sîn-šarra-iškun currently comprises 295 texts; a further 30 late Neo-Assyrian inscriptions which might be attributed to Ashurbanipal, although some very arbitrarily, are also edited here (Asb. 1001–1030). In addition, two texts are ascribed to his wife/wives, including a round-topped stele of Libbāli-šarrat (Asb. 2001), and sixteen are written in the name of a loyal official of his in Babylonia, Sîn-balāssu-iqbi, the governor of Ur. Inscriptions of Assyria's last rulers, including those edited in Parts 1 and 2, are presently found on a wide variety of clay, stone, and metal objects, specifically:

Object Type	*Text No.*
Clay prisms	Asb. 1–8, 9 (exs. 1–6, 8–28, 30–31, 33–34, 37–56, 58–95, 97–145, 148–153, 155–159, 162–163, 165–171, 173–203, 205–41*), 10–20; Ssi 7–9
Clay vertical cylinders	Asb. 9 (exs. 7, 29, 32, 35–36, 57, 96, 146–147, 154, 160–161, 164, 172, 204)
Clay tablets	Asb. 72–240, 255, 264, 1001–1029, 2002; Aei 2–3, 6 (ex. 2); Ssi 6, 15–18
Clay cylinders	Asb. 21, 241–245, 252–253, 258, 262–263, 265; Aei 6 (exs. 1, 3); Ssi 1–5, 10, 19
Clay cones/nails	Asb. 2004–2005; Ssi 11
Clay bulla	Ssi 20
Clay disks	Asb. 2006
Clay drum-shaped object	Asb. 2007
Bricks (including glazed bricks)	Asb. 71, 247–251, 256–257, 259–261, 2008–2018; Aei 1, 4–5; Ssi 13–14

[11] Most of these texts will eventually be included in the fragmentarium of Enrique Jiménez' Electronic Babylonian Literature (eBL) Project (https://www.ebl.lmu.de/ [last accessed January 25, 2023]).
[12] Grayson, Studies Winnett p. 168; and Grayson, ARI 1 p. 143 §933. The object is often referred to as a "prism" in earlier literature.
[13] Borger, EAK 1 pp. 100–102; and Brinkman, PKB p. 102 n. 557.
[14] Respectively https://cdli.ucla.edu, https://www.ebl.lmu.de/, http://oracc.org/riao/, and http://oracc.org/rinap/.

Object Type	*Text No.*
Stone anthropomorphic statues	Asb. 63
Stone tablets	Asb. 61–62
Stone human-headed bull colossi	Asb. 64 (ex. 1)
Wall slabs (including slabs with reliefs)	Asb. 22–58, 64 (ex. 2)
Stone blocks and paving stones	Asb. 59–60; Ssi 12
Stone door sockets	Asb. 2003
Stone vessels (various types)	Asb. 68–70, 269; Ssi 21–2001
Small stone objects (including beads)	Asb. 266–268
Stamp seals (including impressions)	Asb. 65–67
Steles	Asb. 246, 254, 2001
Rock faces	Asb. 1030
Gold beaker	Asb. 270

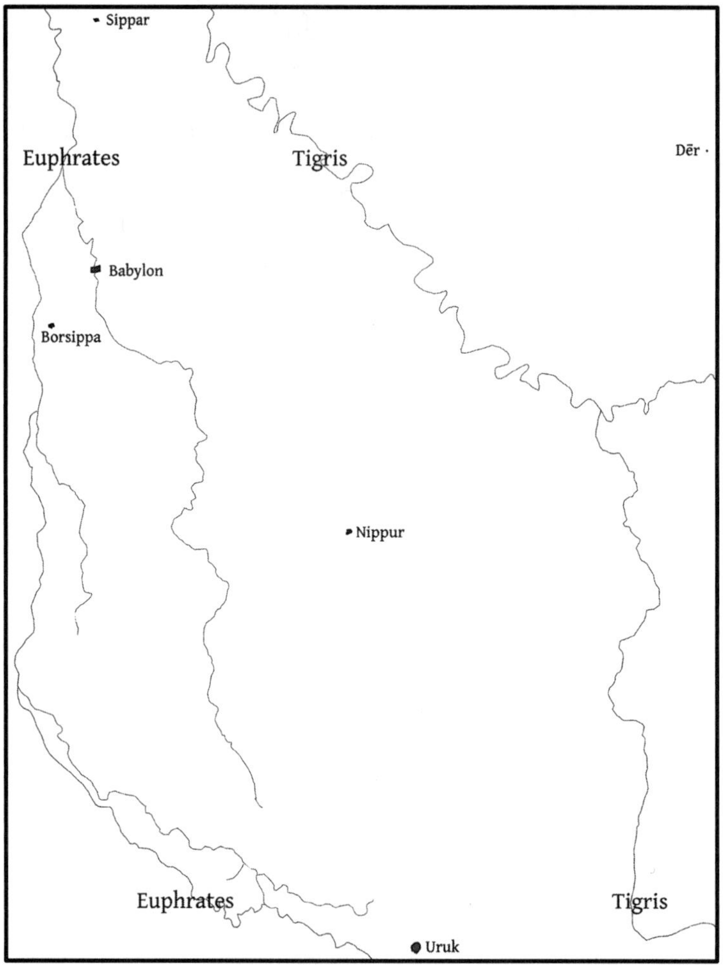

Figure 1. Map showing cities in Babylonia and the East Tigris region where clay cylinders of Ashurbanipal have been discovered.

Clay Cylinders

Numerous building and display inscriptions of Ashurbanipal from Babylonia and the East Tigris region were written on clay cylinders.[15] These originate from Agade (modern identification unknown), Babylon, Borsippa (modern Birs Nimrud), Dēr (modern Tell Aqar), Nippur (modern Nuffar), Sippar (modern Tell Abu Habbah), and

[15] Asb. 241–245, 252–253, 258, 262–263, and 265.

Uruk (modern Warka). All of these texts are written in Akkadian (Standard Babylonian, with Assyrianisms), but the script in which they are written varies. The texts are generally inscribed in contemporary or archaizing Neo-Babylonian script, but a few texts are either written (on different exemplars) in both contemporary and archaizing Neo-Babylonian script and in Neo-Assyrian script.[16] The inscriptions, when completely preserved, vary in length from twenty-four to thirty-three lines of text and are always written in a single column. These building inscriptions and display inscriptions follow four basic patterns. The first, which is a dedicatory inscription, contains: (1) a dedication to the deity whose temple, shrine, sanctuary, or ziggurat was being renovated/rebuilt; (2) the king's name, titles, and epithets; (3) a statement about what Ashurbanipal accomplished in Babylon during his reign; (4) a short building account; and (5) a concluding formula, with advice to future rulers and blessings and curses for those who obey and disregard Ashurbanipal's instructions on how to treat his inscribed objects.[17] The second, which is also classified as a dedicatory inscription, comprises the following five sections: (1) a dedication to a god or goddess; (2) the king's name, titles, and epithets; (3) a brief statement on why Ashurbanipal undertook the work; (4) a short building account; and (5) a statement about what the deity for whom the construction work was undertaken should do in response to Ashurbanipal's pious deeds.[18] The third group of dedicatory inscriptions combines elements from both of the Ashurbanipal dedicatory inscription types described above and it includes: (1) an opening dedication; (2) the king's name, titles, and epithets; (3) a statement about what Ashurbanipal accomplished in Babylon during his reign; (4) a short building account; (5) a statement about what the deity for whom the construction work was undertaken should do in response to Ashurbanipal's pious deeds; and (6) concluding formula, with advice to future rulers with blessings and curses.[19] The fourth type is a building, or display, inscription, which contains: (1) the king's name, titles, and epithets; (2) a statement about what Ashurbanipal accomplished in Babylon during his reign; (3) a short building account; (4) a passage describing what the deity for whom the repair work was carried out should do on account of Ashurbanipal's pious deeds; and (5) Ashurbanipal's advice against destroying his inscribed objects, with accompanying curses for anyone who harms his foundation documents.[20] Regarding the contents of the building accounts included in these inscriptions, they record some of the numerous building projects completed by Ashurbanipal at Babylon, including the renovation of its walls Imgur-Enlil ("The God Enlil Has Shown Favor") and Nēmetti-Enlil ("Bulwark of the God Enlil"); the restoration of Ṭābi-supūršu ("Its Fold Is Pleasant"), the city wall of Borsippa; the reconstruction of Egigunû, the ziggurat temple of the god Enlil at Nippur; the rebuilding of Ebabbar ("Shining House"), the temple of the sun-god Šamaš at Sippar; the restoration of Eanna ("House of Heaven"), the temple of the goddess Ištar at Uruk; and the rebuilding of Edimgalkalama ("House, Great Bond of the Land"), the temple of the god Anu rabû ("Great Anu" = Ištarān) at Dēr.[21] Most of the inscriptions were written before the outbreak of hostilities with his older brother Šamaš-šuma-ukīn in 652 since those texts mention him in a favorable manner.[22] None of Ashurbanipal's cylinders are dated, as one expects from Babylonian cylinder inscriptions.

A twenty-line Akkadian inscription of Aššur-etel-ilāni is preserved on two clay cylinders.[23] The text records that that Assyrian king returned the body of the Chaldean sheikh Šamaš-ibni to its proper burial place; the bones of that ruler had been in Assyria since the time of his grandfather Esarhaddon. Since all of the copies of

---

[16] Asb. 248, 252, 253 (ex. 3), 258, 263, and 265 are written in contemporary Neo-Babylonian script. Asb. 242 and 247 are written in an archaizing script. Copies of Asb. 241 and 262 are written in both contemporary and archaizing Neo-Babylonian scripts. Asb. 243–245 and 253 (exs. 1–2 and 4) are written in Neo-Assyrian script.

[17] Asb. 241 and 253. Section 1 begins with *ana* DN "to DN"; section 2 starts with *anāku Aššur-bāni-apli* "I, Ashurbanipal"; section 3 opens with *ina palêya* "during my reign"; section 4 commences with *ina ūmēšūma* "at that time"; and section 5 begins with *rubû arkû* "O future ruler." In Asb. 253, the opening two words of section 3 are completely restored and the first words of sections 4–5 are partially preserved.

[18] Asb. 258. Section 1 begins with *ana* DN "to DN"; section 2 starts with *Aššur-bāni-apli* "Ashurbanipal"; section 3 opens with *ana balāṭīšu* "in order to ensure his good health"; section 4 commences with the name of the building being renovated; and section 5 begins with *ana šatti* "on account of this."

[19] Asb. 263. Section 1 begins *ana* DN "to DN"; section 2 starts with *Aššur-bāni-apli* "Ashurbanipal"; section 3 opens with *ina palêya* "during my reign"; section 4 commences with *ina ūmēšūma* "at that time"; section 5 begins with *ana šatti* "on account of this"; and section 6 starts with *ayyumma rubû arkû* "any future ruler."

[20] Asb. 242–245 and 262. There are two subtypes. As for the first subtype (Asb. 243–245), section 1 begins with *Aššur-bāni-apli* "Ashurbanipal"; section 2 starts with *šipir Esagil ša abu bānû'a lā uqattû* "the work on Esagil that the father who engendered me had not finished"; section 3 commences with *ina ūmēšūma* "at that time"; section 4 begins with the name of the deity for whom the work was undertaken or *ana šatti* "on account of this"; and section 5 starts with *ša šumī šaṭru* "(but as for) the one who ... my inscribed name." As for the second subtype (Asb. 242 and 262), section 1 begins with *Aššur-bāni-apli* "Ashurbanipal"; section 2 opens with *ina palêya* "during my reign"; section 3 starts with *ina ūmēšūma* "at that time"; section 4 begins with *ana šatti* "on account of this"; section 5 begins with *matīma ina aḫrât ūmē* "at any time in the future"; and section 6 commences with *ša šumī šaṭru* "(but as for) the one who ... my inscribed name."

[21] See the section *Ashurbanipal's Building Activities in Babylonia and the East Tigris Region* below for further information.

[22] For details, see the section *Dates of Ashurbanipal's Babylonian Inscriptions* below.

[23] Aei 6 exs. 1 and 3.

this inscription were purchased, including one written on a clay tablet (see below), the original find spots of this text are not known.

Seven extant inscriptions of Sîn-šarra-iškun are written on clay cylinders.[24] These were discovered at Aššur (modern Qalʿat Širqāt), Kalḫu (modern Nimrud), and Nineveh (modern Kuyunjik). These building (or display) inscriptions are always written in (Standard Babylonian) Akkadian, in Neo-Assyrian script, and in a single column of text. Some of the cylinders have ruling lines between each line of text, or every second line of text, while others have no ruling lines at all, apart from before and after the line containing the date when the cylinder was inscribed.[25] These inscriptions record some of Sîn-šarra-iškun's building activities, especially his rebuilding of the Nabû temples Egidrukalamasumu ("House Which Bestows the Scepter of the Land") and Ezida ("True House"), as well as repairs that he had made to his great-grandfather Sennacherib's palace (Egalzagdinutukua, The "Palace Without a Rival"; = the South-West Palace).[26] The inscriptions, as far as they are preserved, can all be classified as building (or display) inscriptions. These begin with Sîn-šarra-iškun's name, a (detailed) statement about how the gods actively support him — which ultimately resulted in him becoming the king of Assyria — and his genealogy (which he traces back four generations to his great-great-grandfather Sargon II).[27] This is followed by a passage about his piety and devotion towards supporting Assyria's temples and cults[28] and the main topic of the text: the building account.[29] The inscriptions conclude with advice to future rulers, together with applicable blessings and curses.[30] The cylinders, at least the ones that are presently-known, are always dated. The preserved dates record that Sîn-šarra-iškun's cylinders were inscribed in the eponymies of Bēl-aḫu-uṣur (palace overseer; Ssi 10), Dādî (chief treasurer; Ssi 19), Nabû-tappûtī-alik (chief eunuch; Ssi 1), and Sîn-šarru-uṣur, (governor of Ḫindānu; Ssi 3).[31]

Clay Prisms

Seven fragmentarily-preserved, multi-faceted clay prisms of Sîn-šarra-iškun survive today.[32] They all come from Aššur and are inscribed with texts recording Sîn-šarra-iškun's construction of the Nabû temple at Aššur. One text (Ssi 7) duplicates verbatim an inscription that is also written on clay cylinders (Ssi 10; see the previous section) and one text (Ssi 9) is an earlier version of that inscription (Ssi 7 and 10).[33] Interestingly, Sîn-šarra-iškun's scribes first wrote out building inscriptions for Nabû's temple at Aššur on clay prisms before changing the medium of those texts to clay cylinders. This is the opposite of what Esarhaddon did for inscriptions of his recording his rebuilding of Ešarra ("House of the Universe"), the Aššur temple at Aššur.[34]

Clay Tablets

Numerous clay tablets and tablet fragments with inscriptions of late Neo-Assyrian rulers are known, especially from the reigns of Sennacherib, Esarhaddon, and Ashurbanipal. These objects principally come from Nineveh, but also from other important cities in the Assyrian heartland, namely Aššur, Dūr-Šarrukīn (modern Khorsabad), Kalḫu, and Uruk.[35] In addition to the 140 inscriptions of Ashurbanipal written on tablets edited in

[24] Ssi 1–5, 10, and 19. YBC 2171 (Stephens, YOS 9 no. 80), as mentioned above, is not included here. See the section *Texts Excluded from RINAP 5/3* above.

[25] Ssi 1–5 and 19 have horizontal rulings between each line of text. Ssi 10 exs. 1 and 3 have rulings after every second line of text. Ssi 10 ex. 2 is not ruled, except for before and after its date line.

[26] See the section *Sîn-šarra-iškun, Aššur-uballiṭ II, and the End of the Assyrian Empire* below for details on this king's building activities.

[27] These inscriptions always start with *anāku Sîn-šarra-iškun* "I, Sîn-šarra-iškun" and end with the name of his great-great-grandfather Sargon II. Sîn-šarra-iškun is unusual in that he traces his genealogy back four generations. For example, Esarhaddon and Ashurbanipal give only the names of their fathers and grandfathers.

[28] This section begins with *ina rēš šarrūtīya*, "at the beginning of my reign," or *ultu Aššur ... qātū'a umallû*, "after the god Aššur placed ... into my hands."

[29] The building report usually commences with *ina ūmēšū(ma)* "at that time," but it can also start with *ina rēš šarrūtīya*, "at the beginning of my reign."

[30] This section begins with *rubû arkû* "(May) a future ruler." Ssi 1 includes only blessings, while Ssi 10 and 19 have both blessings and curses.

[31] The names of the eponym-officials are presented in alphabetical order. For a discussion of their chronological sequence, see the section *Eponym Dates* below.

[32] Ssi 7–9. All of Ashurbanipal's inscriptions written on clay prisms are discussed and edited in Novotny and Jeffers, RINAP 5/1 pp. 2–4 and 37–290 Asb. 1–20.

[33] Ssi 8 is not sufficiently preserved to be able to determine whether it is earlier or later than Ssi 7, 9, and 10. VA 7506 (+) VA 7518 (Ssi 9) was inscribed in the eponymy of Aššur-mātu-taqqin, governor of (U)pummu, and VA 5060 (+) LB 1323 (Ssi 10 ex. 1) was inscribed in the eponymate of the palace overseer Bēl-aḫu-uṣur. On the sequence of these two *limmu*-officials, see the *Eponym Dates* section below (p. 41).

[34] Esarhaddon 59 (Aššur B) was written before Esarhaddon 57 (Aššur A) and, presumably, Esarhaddon 58 (Aššur B). For editions of these texts, see Leichty, RINAP 4 pp. 119–134.

[35] For discussions of these, see Tadmor and Yamada, RINAP 1 pp. 9–10; Frame, RINAP 2 p. 7; Grayson and Novotny, RINAP 3/2 pp. 5–8; Leichty, RINAP 4 pp. 3–4; and Jeffers and Novotny, RINAP 5/2 pp. 3–9.

Part 2, 3 additional Akkadian texts known only from tablets date with certainty to Ashurbanipal's reign.[36] The first is an archival copy of an inscription of a wife of Ashurbanipal (possibly Libbāli-šarrat) that she had written on the reddish gold plating of an object that she had had made and dedicated to the goddess Tašmētu, the wife of the god Nabû.[37] The second is an archival copy of an inscription that had been written on the metal plating of a ceremonial cart (*attaru*) dedicated to a deity at Uruk, possibly that city's tutelary goddess Ištar.[38] The third might record the dedication of a lamp to the god Marduk at Babylon or the god Nabû at Borsippa, but, since virtually nothing of that inscription survives, that interpretation is far from certain.[39]

Six tablets bearing three Akkadian inscriptions of Aššur-etel-ilāni and five Akkadian inscriptions of Sîn-šarra-iškun are known.[40] These texts of the former ruler come from Babylonia and, thus, are generally written in contemporary Neo-Babylonian script,[41] while those of the latter king originate from Aššur and Nineveh and are written in Neo-Assyrian script. Six of the eight texts are archival copies or drafts of short dedicatory inscriptions that had been written on the metal plating of an object dedicated to one of the king's patron deities. Aššur-etel-ilāni's dedicatory texts record the creation of a *musukkannu*-wood offering table (*paššuru*) and a gold scepter (*haṭṭu*) for Marduk at Babylon and Sippar-Aruru (Dūr-Šarrukku).[42] The dedicatory inscriptions of Sîn-šarra-iškun from Aššur record the fashioning of a *kallu*-bowl and a *šulpu*-bowl for the god Nabû, a silver spoon (*itqūru*) for the goddess Tašmētu, and *musukkannu*-wood offering tables (*paššuru*) for the goddesses Antu and Šala.[43] As for the other two inscriptions on tablets, one records that Aššur-etel-ilāni returned the body of the Chaldean sheikh Šamaš-ibni to its proper burial place, while the other gives an account of Sîn-šarra-iškun's work on the city wall of Nineveh.[44] The latter tablet is an archival copy of an inscription that was written on clay cylinders deposited in the mud-brick structure of Nineveh's wall Badnigalbilukurašušu ("Wall Whose Brilliance Overwhelms Enemies").[45] Unusually, the tablet is dated. It was inscribed in the month Ulūlu (VI), in the eponymy of the palace overseer Bēl-aḫu-uṣur.[46]

A number of fragmentarily-preserved clay tablets bearing Akkadian inscriptions are arbitrarily edited in this volume.[47] Given their heavily-damaged state of preservation, their attribution to Ashurbanipal or to another late Neo-Assyrian king (for example, Sennacherib or Esarhaddon) is uncertain. These fragments merit no further comment, especially since it is not possible to determine these texts' subgenre (for example, dedicatory inscription or annalistic text).

Clay Cones

It has been remarked that clay cones "are certainly the most unusual of the variety of objects upon which Assyrian royal inscriptions were inscribed. Unlike bricks, statues, reliefs, steles, and even clay tablets, the form and function of which are immediately recognizable, the clay cones do not fit any pattern familiar to our modern minds."[48] Moreover, "cone" — or "knob," "boss," "peg," or "nail" as used in other scholarly literature — is not really an adequate translation of the Akkadian word *sikkatu*, the term for these objects that appears regularly in the corpus of Assyrian royal inscriptions. Although there is quite a diversity in the shape of these *sikkatu*, the cones all have a tapered shaft that comes almost to a point and a large, hollow, semi-spherical head; the shaft was sometimes inserted into the center of a decorated clay plate and the combined cone and

---

36 Asb. 255, 264, and 2002.
37 Libbāli-šarrat is the only known-by-name wife of Ashurbanipal and, therefore, it is possible that this inscription was also written in her name.
38 The text is not sufficiently preserved to be certain to whom the ceremonial cart had been dedicated. The attribution of the inscription to Ashurbanipal is based solely on the fact that the tablet (W 22669/3) was discovered at Uruk.
39 CBS 733 + CBS 1757 contains a second, longer inscription, very likely written in the name of Ashurbanipal's older brother, Šamaš-šuma-ukīn, the king of Babylon. See Frame, RIMB 2 pp. 256–257 B.6.33.5 for an edition of and further information about that text.
40 Aei 2–3 and 6 (ex. 2); and Ssi 6 and 15–18.
41 Aei 3 (VAT 13142), which was found at Babylon, is written in Neo-Assyrian script.
42 Aei 2–3. PTS 2253 (Aei 2) includes a private two-line note at the end which mentions food offerings of a certain Nādin, son of Bēl-aḫḫē-iqīša, that were delivered in the 3rd year of the reign of the Achaemenid king Cambyses II (527). Thus, PTS 2253 is a much later copy of that Akkadian inscription of Aššur-etel-ilāni. The tablet might originate from Uruk, rather than Babylon, since Nādin, son of Bēl-aḫḫē-iqīša (line 22), is probably to be identified with a scribe by that name who is known at Uruk from the reign of Neriglissar into the reign of Cambyses. See the commentary of Aei 2 for further details.
43 Ssi 15–18.
44 Aei 6 (ex. 2) and Ssi 6.
45 The Sumerian ceremonial name of Nineveh's wall (*dūru*) is known from Sennacherib's inscriptions. See Grayson and Novotny, RINAP 3/1 pp. 17–19. No clay cylinders bearing this inscription have yet been positively identified.
46 On the date, see the section *Eponym Dates* below.
47 Asb. 1001–1029.
48 Donbaz and Grayson, RICCA p. 1.

plate were placed in the interior room of a building with the plate flat against the wall and the head of the cone protruding.[49] The cones themselves, like their companion plates, could be enameled with a variety of colors (black, white, yellow, brown, red, green, and blue).

At present, the only known Akkadian inscription written on clay cones from the 668–612 period dates to the reign of Sîn-šarra-iškun.[50] That Akkadian text, which is known from at least fifteen cones inscribed in the eponymy of the chief cook Sa'īlu (see the section *Eponym Dates* below), records in a very cursory fashion Sîn-šarra-iškun's construction of the god Nabû's temple at Aššur.[51]

In addition, at least two Sumerian inscriptions of Sîn-balāssu-iqbi, one of the governors of Ur while Ashurbanipal was king, were written on clay cones (which are more in the shape of a nail), all of which originate from Ur (modern Tell Muqayyar).[52] The first text, which is known from a single exemplar, states that that governor restored Etemennigurru ("House, Foundation Clad in Awe-Inspiring Radiance"), the ziggurat terrace of Ekišnugal, the temple complex of the moon-god at Ur.[53] The second inscription, which is attested from thirteen different exemplars, states that Sîn-balāssu-iqbi rebuilt Gipāru(ku) and constructed a statue for the goddess Ningal, the consort of Sîn (Nanna).[54]

Miscellaneous Clay Objects

Less than a handful of inscriptions are written on other types of clay objects. These are: (1) a bulla with a clay sealing discovered in the Review Palace at Kalḫu bearing a two-word proprietary label of Sîn-šarra-iškun; (2) eight clay disks from Ur inscribed with a sixteen-line Akkadian inscription of Sîn-balāssu-iqbi, the governor of Ur, recording that that official rebuilt a well named Puḫilituma ("Well That Brings Luxuriance") in the Sîn temple at Ur "in order to ensure the good health of Ashurbanipal, king of Assyria"; and (3) a clay drum-shaped object with a copy of a Sumerian inscription of the Ur III king Amar-Suena (2046–2038) and a colophon of Sîn-balāssu-iqbi stating that he had found an inscribed brick of that king while looking for the ground plan of Ekišnugal.[55] The texts on the drum-shaped object, which might have been a model for an altar or dais, were prepared on behalf of Sîn-balāssu-iqbi by Nabû-šuma-iddin, a lamentation-priest of the god Sîn.[56]

Bricks

Given the numerous building activities that Ashurbanipal, Aššur-etel-ilāni, and Sîn-šarra-iškun, as well as Sîn-balāssu-iqbi of Ur (on behalf of Ashurbanipal), sponsored in the Assyrian heartland and in Babylonia, it is no surprise that over 150 inscribed/stamped bricks of these men are now found in museum collections all over the world, especially in the British Museum (London) and the Vorderasiatisches Museum (Berlin), or were copied or photographed by archaeologists shortly after their discovery in the nineteenth and early twentieth centuries.[57] At present, twenty-three different brick inscriptions are known from Aššur and Kalḫu in Assyria, and Babylon, Dilbat (modern Deilam), Dūr-Kurigalzu (modern Aqar Quf), Mê-Turān (modern Tell Ḥaddād), Nippur, and Ur in Babylonia. The bricks vary in size and shape (usually square or rectangular, but occasionally well-head, that is, bricks used in the construction of round wells and conduits). The text is sometimes stamped and sometimes inscribed by hand on the face and/or the edge of the brick.[58] The inscriptions from Assyria (reigns of Aššur-etel-ilāni and Sîn-šarra-iškun)[59] are always in Akkadian, using Neo-Assyrian script. The texts from Babylonia (reigns of Ashurbanipal and Aššur-etel-ilāni), however, are sometimes in Akkadian and sometimes in Sumerian,[60] and the script is either contemporary Neo-Babylonian, archaizing Neo-Babylonian (which is modelled on Old Babylonian monumental script), or a mixture of contemporary and archaizing Neo-

---

[49] For further details on cones and plates (with references to earlier studies, photographs, and drawings), see Donbaz and Grayson, RICCA pp. 1–4; and Nunn, Knaufplatten *passim*. The majority of the known Assyrian clay cones come from Aššur.
[50] Ssi 11.
[51] George, House Most High p. 94 no. 397.
[52] Asb. 2004–2005.
[53] George, House Most High p. 114 no. 653 and p. 149 no. 1090.
[54] George, House Most High p. 93 no. 385.
[55] Respectively, Ssi 20, Asb. 2006, and Asb. 2007. For an edition of the Amar-Suena inscription, see Frayne, RIME 3/2 pp. 256–257 E3/2.1.3.11.
[56] On the poor quality of the copy of the Sumerian text, see the commentary of Asb. 2007.
[57] Asb. 247–251, 256–257, 259–261, and 2008–2018; Aei 1, 4–5; and Ssi 13–14. The exact number of extant bricks is unknown since the actual number of bricks bearing Asb. 257 has never been published/recorded in scholarly publications.
[58] At times, the text might be inscribed within an area that has been impressed, thus, providing a border for the text. In some scholarly literature these inscriptions are usually described as stamped, rather than, more accurately, as inscribed.
[59] No inscribed bricks of Ashurbanipal from Assyria are presently known. All of that king's brick inscriptions come from Babylonia.
[60] Asb. 247–250 and 256–257 (Babylon, Dūr-Kurigalzu, and Mê-Turān) and Aei 4 (Dilbat) are in Akkadian. Asb. 251, 259–261, and 2008–2018 (Babylon, Nippur, and Ur) and Aei 5 (Nippur) are in Sumerian.

Babylonian sign forms.[61] The inscriptions vary in length, from three to sixteen lines of text. All of the Babylonian brick inscriptions are dedicatory in nature, that is, they are addressed to the deity whose temple, shrine, sanctuary, or ziggurat was being restored.[62] For example, Asb. 248 reads:

> For the god Marduk, his lord: Ashurbanipal, king of the world (and) king of Assyria, son of Esarhaddon, king of the world, king of Assyria, (and) king of Babylon, had baked bricks made anew for Etemenanki.

The brick inscriptions from Assyria, on the other hand, are commemorative labels.[63] The short texts denote ownership, but also add a brief statement about the building in whose structure the bricks are incorporated. For example, Ssi 13 reads:

> I, Sîn-šarra-iškun, great king, strong king, king of the world, king of Assyria; son of Ashurbanipal, great king, strong king, king of the world, king of Assyria, king of the land of Sumer and Akkad, king of the four quarters (of the world); son of Esarhaddon, great king, strong king, king of the world, king of Assyria, (5) governor of Babylon, king of the land of Sumer and Akkad; son of Sennacherib, great king, strong king, king of the world, king of Assyria, ruler who has no rival; descendant of Sargon (II), great king, strong king, king of the world, king of Assyria, governor of Babylon, king of the land of Sumer and Akkad; (10) the one who renovates the chapels of the temple of the god Nabû, my lord, that is inside Baltil (Aššur): I repaired its (lit. "that") enclosed courtyard with baked bricks, the craft of the god Nunurra.

Steles

Only four round-topped steles are currently known from the reign of Ashurbanipal, but more of these monuments certainly existed in antiquity.[64] Three of the monuments come from Babylonia (Babylon and Borsippa) and these are inscribed with building inscriptions of Ashurbanipal, specifically recording the restoration of Ekarzagina ("House, Quay of Lapis Lazuli" or "House, Pure Quay"), the temple of the god Ea in the Esagil complex at Babylon,[65] and the rebuilding of the enclosure wall of Ezida ("True House"), the temple of Nabû at Borsippa.[66] The fronts of the steles, which are made from pink marble, have frontal depictions of Ashurbanipal holding a work-basket on his head, indicating his (symbolic) role in the restorations. The inscriptions are generally written in contemporary Neo-Babylonian script[67] and were commissioned by Ashurbanipal before 652 since they all mention Šamaš-šuma-ukīn in a favorable manner. The other monument comes from Aššur, from the so-called "row of steles," and it is inscribed with a five-line (proprietary) Akkadian inscription of Ashurbanipal's wife Libbāli-šarrat.[68] The Assyrian queen, shown with a mural crown representing a city wall and its towers, is depicted on the face of the monument and her inscription is engraved on the back.

Stone Blocks

A stone block discovered at Aššur with a sixteen-line Akkadian inscription of Sîn-šarra-iškun written on it is the only presently-attested inscribed stone block from the last sixty years of the Assyrian Empire.[69] The text records that Sîn-šarra-iškun constructed the Nabû temple at Aššur anew on an empty plot of land. Interestingly, this account contradicts the one presented in inscriptions written on clay cylinders and prisms, which state that the temple had been rebuilt on its earlier Middle and Neo-Assyrian plans.[70] The findspot of the

---

[61] Asb. 247–250, 256–257, and 2008–2018 (Babylon, Dūr-Kurigalzu, Mê-Turān, and Ur) and Aei 4 (Dilbat) are in contemporary Babylonian script. Asb. 259–261 (Nippur) are in archaizing Babylonian script. Asb. 251 (Babylon) and Aei 5 (Nippur) have mixed sign forms.

[62] Grayson, Orientalia NS 49 (1980) pp. 156–157.

[63] Grayson, Orientalia NS 49 (1980) pp. 155–156.

[64] Asb. 246, 254, and 2001. It is certain from the concluding formula of K 2694 + K 3050 (Asb. 220 [L^{4}] iv 1′–5′); Jeffers and Novotny, RINAP 5/2 pp. 319–328) that the text written on that multi-column clay tablet was a draft of an inscription that was to be engraved on a stele erected in Babylon, presumably in Marduk's temple Esagil. That monument is not presently known.

[65] Asb. 246 ex. 1 (lines 65b–67a). The building report of Asb. 246 ex. 2 is not preserved and, thus, it is quite possible that that stele did not describe the restoration of Ea's shrine Ekarzagina.

[66] Asb. 254 (lines 33–36). A similar stele of Šamaš-šuma-ukīn (BM 90866) was found at Borsippa in 1880, in the room southwest of Room C2 of Ezida, together with this stele of Ashurbanipal (BM 90865). For an edition of that text, see Frame, RIMB 2 pp. 252–253 B.6.33.3.

[67] Asb. 254 has some Neo-Assyrian sign forms.

[68] Asb. 2001.

[69] Ssi 12. Inscriptions on this material support are well attested from the reigns of Sennacherib and Esarhaddon. See Grayson and Novotny, RINAP 3/2 pp. 13–14 and pp. 249–270 Sennacherib 169–189 and pp. 317–327 Sennacherib 224–229; and Leichty, RINAP 4 pp. 137–144 Esarhaddon 61–67, pp. 164–165 Esarhaddon 81–82, and p. 314 Esarhaddon 2002.

[70] For details on that building project, see the section *Sîn-šarra-iškun's Building Activities* below.

stone block at Aššur is not known so it is unclear whether or not it was actually incorporated into the physical structure of that holy building.[71]

Stone Door Sockets

The only inscribed door socket attested from the reigns of the last kings of Assyria comes from Ur. The object, which was recycled from the upper part of an older *kudurru* (boundary stone) and which is in the shape of a coiled snake, was found in situ in Edublalmaḫ ("House, Exalted Door Socket"), an especially holy part the moon-god temple Ekišnugal at Ur.[72] The bottom is inscribed with a thirty-eight-line Sumerian inscription of Sîn-balāssu-iqbi of Ur. This dedicatory inscription, which is written in two equal-length columns, records that the governor of Ur, a son of the previous governor Ningal-iddin, commissioned a new door for Etemennigurru, which he had placed on its former position and over a foundation deposit; the door was made from boxwood (Sumerian *taškarin*) and outfitted with silver and copper fixtures. The text concludes with a curse against anyone who erases Sîn-balāssu-iqbi's inscription or alters the door socket's location.

Stone and Metal Vessels

Numerous stone vessels are inscribed with a one-line proprietary inscription stating that the objects belonged to Ashurbanipal.[73] Most come from Nineveh, one was discovered at Aššur, and one was found at Persepolis. Some of the stone vessels bearing an Ashurbanipal proprietary label have images of a table and a lion incised to the left of the inscription. In the repertoire of Assyrian 'hieroglyphs,' the lion represents the king and, thus, these vessels were probably used to serve Ashurbanipal's meals, that is, these are the objects that were used specifically for "the king's table" (TABLE + LION).[74] In addition, several stone vessels have a single-line proprietary inscription of Sîn-šarra-iškun written on them, as well as that of a late Neo-Assyrian queen Ana-Tašmētu-taklāk.[75]

An ornately-decorated and gold-leafed silver goblet with a proprietary inscription of Ashurbanipal is also known.[76] Although the text appears to be a genuine inscription, the authenticity of the object itself cannot be verified since its provenance is uncertain and since such a highly-decorated metal vessel is presently not otherwise attested for the late Neo-Assyrian period.[77]

Small Stone Objects, Including Stone Beads

Three beads inscribed with short texts of Ashurbanipal were found in the Treasury of the Persian capital Persepolis.[78] Two of these small inscribed stones — a polished banded white, grey, and pink chalcedony cylinder and a grey scorched onyx eyestone — bear dedication inscriptions to the goddess Sutītu.

Rock Reliefs

Very few monuments (round-topped steles and rock reliefs) of Ashurbanipal are known to have been set up outside of the Assyrian heartland and Babylonia. A poorly-preserved Assyrian relief, with a thirty-six-line Akkadian inscription, carved into a rock face at Shakaft-i Gulgul — which is located in the Zagros Mountains, on the southwestern slopes of the Kabir Kuh, a mountainous ridge that separates western and eastern Luristan — might be the only-presently-attested rock relief of Assyria's last great king, although the attribution to him is not entirely certain.[79] The prologue of the weathered monument, which could have also been carved during the reign of his father Esarhaddon,[80] states that (1) the god Aššur determined the king's royal destiny while he

---

71 K. Kessler (ISIMU 14–15 [2011–12] pp. 39-43) notes only that the stone block was in the Aššur Site Museum until at least 1987.

72 Asb. 2003. See George, House Most High p. 79 no. 203 for further details on Edublalmaḫ.

73 Novotny and Jeffers, RINAP 5/1 pp. 362–366 Asb. 68–70; and, in this volume, Asb. 269. PT4 368 + PT5 156 + PT5 244 (Asb. 269), which was found in Hall 41 and Corridor 31 of the Treasury at Persepolis, is an impressive sculptured bowl with four lion handles.

74 For further details and bibliography on Assyrian hieroglyphs, see Leichty, RINAP 4 pp. 238–243 Esarhaddon 115; Nadali, Iraq 70 (2008) pp. 87–104; and Niederreiter, Iraq 70 (2008) pp. 51–86.

75 Ssi 21–2001. For other possible vessels of this king (or his brother Aššur-etel-ilāni), see Novotny and Jeffers, RINAP 5/1 pp. 362–365 Asb. 68 (exs. 1*–19*) and Asb. 69 (exs. 1*–3*). On the identity of Ana-Tašmētu-taklāk, see the commentary of Ssi 2001.

76 Asb. 270.

77 The only other metal vessel known from the late Neo-Assyrian period is a silver bucket that is inscribed with a two-line dedicatory inscription of Esarhaddon (Leichty, RINAP 4 pp. 281–282 Esarhaddon 140). That object was discovered in 1992 by the Iranian Department of Antiquities in a hoard of silver vessels found in a cave in the Luristan region.

78 Asb. 266–268.

79 Asb. 1030. For an earlier edition and study of this monument, see Grayson and Levine, IrAnt 11 (1975) pp. 29–38.

80 The king's name and the name of his father in Asb. 1030 lines 4–5 are completely missing. For further information about the royal

was still in his mother's womb, (2) the god Enlil called the king by name to rule over the land and people, (3) the gods Sîn and Šamaš gave auspicious signs about the establishment of the author's reign, (4) the gods Nabû and Marduk bestowed the king with intelligence and wisdom, and (5) the great gods placed the king safely on the throne of his father. The passage recording the principal reason(s) the monument was commissioned, which might have given us further clues about identity of the Assyrian king in whose name the inscription was written, is almost completely destroyed; only a few signs remain.[81] The text concludes with a short building report recording the creation of the monument, advice to a future ruler to respect the carved image and accompanying texts, and curses against anyone who alters or destroys the king's record of his (pious) deeds, which was created "for the admiration of the kings, [my] descendants."[82]

Military Campaigns

Numerous inscriptions edited in RINAP 5 include accounts of Ashurbanipal's victories on the battlefield. Since all of these campaigns were briefly discussed in Part 1 (pp. 14–26), there is no reason to include that information here. However, the authors feel that it is necessary to provide a few tables for easy reference. Only texts preserving military narration are included. Details on the military campaigns narrated in the texts edited in RINAP 5/1 and RINAP 5/2 are presented in Tables 1–2 below.

Table 1: "Incidents" Arranged by Campaign Report[83]

Incident(s)	Source(s)
Egypt 1	**2** iii 6–iv 1′; **3** i 48–i 90; **4** i 38–75; **6** ii 4′–2′′; **7** ii 1′–18′′; **8** ii 1′–12′; **11** i 52–117; **72** ii 1′–21′; **73** i 1–8; **117** 1–12; **118** 1′–3′; **119** 1′–3′; **196** 10–21; **197** 1′–4′′; **207** 6′–36′
Egypt 2	**2** iv 2′–v 12; **3** i 91–ii 37; **4** i 76–ii 11′; **6** ii 3′′–iii 57′; **7** ii 19′′–iii 15′; **8** ii 13′–33′; **9** i 34–54; **11** i 118–ii 48; **12** ii 7′–14′a; **73** rev. i′ 1′–4′; **93** 1′–3′; **118** 4′–14′; **119** 4′–5′; **121** 5′–6′; **122** 1′–9′; **197** 5′′–6′′, 10′′–24′′; **207** 37′–rev. 11; **233** 1′–2′
Tyre, Arwad 1–2, Ḫilakku, Tabal, Lydia 1–2	**1** vi 11–31′; **2** vi 14–vii 3′; **3** ii 38–iii 4; **4** ii 12′–72′; **6** iii 58′–iv 7′; **7** iii 16′–30′′; **8** iii 1′–45′; **9** i 55–ii 20; **11** ii 49–125; **12** ii 14′b–24′; **13** iii 1′–13′; **74** ii 1′–11′; **91** i 1′–16′; **92** ii 1′–8′; **93** 4′–12′; **124** 1′–7′; **125** Side A 1′–7′; **207** rev. 19–37
Qirbit	**1** vi 1–10; **2** v 1′–vi 13; **3** iii 5–15; **4** ii 73′–iii 8; **6** iv 8′–19′; **7** iii 31′′–35′′; **207** rev. 12–18; **238** 1′–rev. 11
Mannea, Media, Urarṭu 1	**3** iii 16–iv 14; **4** iii 9–iv 8; **6** iv 1′′–v 23; **7** iv 1′–74′′; **8** iv 1′–22′′; **9** ii 21–52; **11** ii 126–iii 26; **12** iii 1′′–9′′; **13** iii 1′′–9′′; **74** iii 1′–iv 16; **75** 1′–9′; **76** ii′ 1′–9′; **77** i′ 1′–7′; **78** 1′–rev. 3; **91** ii 1′–11′; **92** iii 1′; **171** 1′–11′; **195** rev. 10–14
Elam 1–2	**3** iv 15–79; **4** iv 9–49′; **6** v 24–107; **7** iv 75′′–v 47; **12** iii 10′′–iv 12′; **79** i 1–16, ii 1–18; **80** i′ 1′–22′; **81** 1′–7′; **82** 1′–13′; **119** rev. 4–14; **120** 1′–12′; **121** 1′–4′; **135** 3′–5′; **186** 15–23; **197** 7′′–9′′; **240** 1′–8′
Elam 3	**3** iv 80–vi 9; **4** iv 50′–vi 12; **6** v 1′–vii 10; **7** v 48–vi 22′; **8** v 1′–vii 10′; **9** ii 53–71; **11** iii 27–49; **12** v 1–5; **79** ii 19–iv 13′; **83** i′ 1–13; **84** i′ 1′–10′; **85** i 1′–10′; **86** i 1′–9′; **92** iii 2′–15′; **126** rev. 1–4; **128** 1′–9′; **135** rev. 1; **155** 6′–8′; **161** i 1–ii 14, iii 9′–27′; **162** 3′–l.e. 3; **163** 1′–rev. 5; **164** 1′–12′; **165** 1–13, rev. 7′–8′; **166** 1′–7′; **168** 1′–8′; **169** 1′–10′; **170** 1′–11′; **171** rev.? 1′–10′; **195** rev. 1–9; **200** 7–rev. 14; **201** 1′–12′; **202** 1′–20′; **228** 13′–14′; **233** 6′–11′; **234** i′ 1′–4′
Gambulu	**3** vi 10–85; **4** vi 13–95; **6** vii 11–47′; **7** vi 23′–vii 35; **8** vii 11′–17′′; **9** ii 72–iii 5; **11** iii 50–69; **12** v 6–13; **79** iv 14′; **86** i 10′–ii 15′; **89** i 1–ii 12′; **92** iii 16′–26′; **125** Side A 8′–9′; **127** 1–9; **161** ii 15–iii 8′, 28′–iv 16; **162** 1′–2′; **163** rev. 6–8; **165** rev. 1′–6′, 9′–15′; **167** 1′–13′; **169** 11′–17′; **170** 12′–15′; **195** 10–28
Elam 4, Šamaš-šuma-ukīn rebellion	**3** vi 86–vii 76; **4** vi 96–vii 79; **6** vii 48′–ix 52′′; **7** vii 36–ix 9; **8** viii 1′–ix 37′; **9** iii 6–32; **11** iii 70–iv 109; **85** rev. i′ 1–6; **86** iii 1′; **87** ii 1–6; **88** ii′ 1′–21′; **89** ii 13′–vi 14; **92** iii 27′–iv 4; **94** i 1′–12′; **95** i 1–11; **105** rev.? i 1′–12′a; **106** 1′–10′; **107** ii′ 1′–13′; **112** ii 1–18; **126** rev. 5–11; **127** rev. 1′–15′; **130** 5′–rev. 9, l.e. 1–4; **131** 1′–7′; **132** 1′–12′; **133** rev. 1–5; **134** 1′–21′; **135** rev. 2–3; **137** 1′–9′a; **147** 1′–9′; **150** 1′–16′; **151** 6′–14′; **155** 9′–rev. 6; **172** 1–22; **173** i 1′–ii 11′, iv 1′–9′; **174** 1′–4′, rev. 2′–9′; **175** i 1′–14′, ii 1′–iii 14′; **176** 1–17; **177** 2′–10′; **178** 1′–rev. 22; **179** 1′–14′; **180** 2′–7′, rev.? 7–15; **181** 1′–5′, rev.? 2′–9′; **182** 1′–rev.? 8′; **183** 3′–7′; **184** 8′–9′; **188** 1–6; **197** 1′′′–rev. 12; **203** 13–rev. 8; **204** 1′–rev. 6; **205** 1′–11′; **228** 15′–25′, rev. 23–26; **229** ii 1′–16′
Elam 5	**7** ix 10–63′′; **8** ix 29′′–x 16′; **9** iii 33–iv 16; **11** iv 110–v 62; **91** iv 1–8′; **112** iii 1′–8′; **133** rev. 6–16; **136** rev. 1–18; **137** 9′b–16′; **197** rev. 13–23; **228** 26′–29′; **229** iii 1′–4′; **234** ii′ 1′–17′
Elam 6–7	**9** iv 17–vi 21; **10** iv 12–v 32; **11** v 63–vii 81; **91** v 1–vi 17; **92** v 1–4; **94** ii 1′–iii 23′; **95** rev. i′ 1′–6′; **96** rev. i′

'author' of the Shakaft-i Gulgul inscription, see the commentary of Asb. 1030.

[81] Asb. 1030 lines 17b–25a.

[82] Asb. 1030 lines 24b–25a.

[83] Tables 1–2 combine information provided in Parts 1 and 2. All of the text numbers mentioned in these two tables refer to inscriptions of Ashurbanipal, despite the absence of the "Asb." prefix. The abbreviations for the "incidents" follow the designation of Grayson, ZA 70 (1980) pp. 240–244 (with minor changes); Gambulu is treated separately from Elam 3 here. See Novotny and Jeffers, RINAP 5/1 pp. 14–26 for more details about Ashurbanipal's campaigns and Grayson's classifications of them. There are a few incidents that are not included in Tables 1–2. These are Jeffers and Novotny, RINAP 5/2 p. 101 Asb. 110 lines 10′–13′ (mentions Bīt-Ḫumbê); p. 256 Asb. 197 lines 25′′–27′′ and p. 365 Asb. 233 lines 3′–5′ (tribute from kings in the Levant); and p. 337 Asb. 224 line 25 (Sandak-šatru incident), which is subsumed under the Tugdammî incident.

	1′–13′; **97** rev. i′ 1′–4′; **100** ii′ 1′–10′; **101** rev. ii′ 1′–7′; **102** i′ 1′–rev. 12; **103** ii′ 1′–8′; **108** rev.[?] i′ 1′–19′; **112** iii 9′–16′; **133** rev. 17–20; **134** 22′–30′; **135** rev. 4–8; **138** 1′–9′; **139** 1′–11′; **140** 1′–rev. 4; **141** 1′–14′; **142** rev. 1′–7′; **143** 1′–3′; **152** 1′–6′; **154** 1′–10′; **155** rev. 7–14; **188** 7–rev. 2; **194** v 24–vi 23; **197** rev. 24–41; **198** rev. 1′–11′; **199** rev. 1′–7′; **215** iii 2′–iv 35; **217** 1′–rev. 19′; **224** 18–19; **227** rev. 1–17; **228** rev. 1–22; **229** iii 1′–v 12; **234** rev. i 1′–9′; **235** 1′–7′
Arabs 1	**3** vii 77–viii 55; **4** vii 80–viii 57; **6** x 1′–18″; **7** ix 64″–x 52′; **8** ix 38′–28″; **11** vii 82–viii 64; **86** iii 2′–iv 18′; **90** i 1′–13′, ii 1′–9′; **129** 1′–rev. 7; **172** rev. 1′–9′; **180** 8′–rev.[?] 5; **194** i 1–iii 11
Arabs 2	**11** viii 65–x 5; **109** i′ 1′–10′; **156** 20–rev. 12; **194** iii 12–v 2; **215** v 1–13
Elam 8	**11** x 6–39; **110** 1′–5′; **143** 4′–11′; **144** 1′–9′; **145** rev. 1′–9′a; **157** 6–14; **158** 4′–5′; **194** vi 27–43
Urarṭu 2	**11** x 40–50; **110** 6′–9′
Cyrus	**12** vi 7′–13′
Ḫudimiri	**12** vi 14′–25′
Tugdammî	**13** viii 6–11′; **224** 20–25

Table 2: Proposed Chronology of "Incidents"[84]

Date	Incident(s)	Source(s)
668	Qirbit	**1** vi 1–10; **2** v 1′–vi 13; **3** iii 5–15; **4** ii 73′–iii 8; **6** iv 8′–19′; **7** iii 31″–35″; **207** rev. 12–18; **238** 1′–rev. 11
667	Arwad 1	**3** ii 63–72; **4** ii 34′–46′; **6** iii 89′–103′; **7** iii 44′–4″; **8** iii 15′–29′; **9** i 69–74; **11** ii 63–67; **13** iii 9′–13′; **91** i 9′–16′; **207** rev. 33–37
667	Egypt 1	**2** iii 6–iv 1′; **3** i 48–i 90; **4** i 38–75; **6** ii 4′–2″; **7** ii 1′–18″; **8** ii 1′–12′; **11** i 52–117; **72** ii 1′–21′; **73** i 1–8; **117** 1–12; **118** 1′–3′; **119** 1′–3′; **196** 10–21; **197** 1′–4″; **207** 6′–36′
ca. 666–665	Lydia 1	**1** vi 11–31′; **2** vi 14–vii 3′; **3** ii 86b–iii 4; **4** ii 61′–72′; **6** iv 1′–7′; **7** iii 17″–30″; **9** ii 10–20; **11** ii 95–110; **74** ii 1′–11′; **92** ii 2′–8′; **125** Side A 1′–7′; **207** rev. 19–27
ca. 666–664	Egypt 2	**2** iv 2′–v 12; **3** i 91–ii 37; **4** i 76–ii 11′; **6** ii 3″–iii 57′; **7** ii 19″–iii 15′; **8** ii 13′–33′; **9** i 34–54; **11** i 118–ii 48; **12** ii 7′–14′a; **73** rev. i′ 1′–4′; **93** 1′–3′; **118** 4′–14′; **119** 4′–5′; **121** 5′–6′; **122** 1′–9′; **197** 5″–6″, 10″–24″; **207** 37′–rev. 11; **233** 1′–2′
ca. 664	Elam 1	**3** iv 15–48; **4** iv 9–17′; **6** v 24–72; **7** iv 75″–v 16; **12** iii 10″–iv 10′; **79** i 1–16; **80** i′ 1′–22′; **119** rev. 4–8; **186** 15–16; **197** 7″
664	Elam 2	**3** iv 49–79; **4** iv 18′–49′; **6** v 73–107; **7** v 17–47; **12** iv 11′–12′; **79** ii 1–18; **81** 1′–7′; **82** 1′–13′; **119** rev. 9–14; **120** 1′–12′; **121** 1′–4′; **135** 3′–5′; **186** 17–23; **197** 8″–9″; **240** 1′–8′
ca. 662	Tyre	**3** ii 38–62; **4** ii 12′–33′; **6** iii 58′–88′; **7** iii 16′–43′; **8** iii 1′–14′; **9** i 55–68; **11** ii 49–62; **12** ii 14′b–24′; **13** iii 1′–8′; **91** i 1′–8′; **93** 4′–12′; **124** 1′–7′
ca. 662	Ḫilakku, Tabal	**3** ii 63–74; **4** ii 34′–48′; **6** iii 89′–105′; **7** iii 44′–6″; **8** iii 15′–31′; **9** i 69–76; **11** ii 68–80; **207** rev. 28–32
ca. 662	Arwad 2	**3** ii 75–86a; **4** ii 49′–60′; **6** iii 106′–iv 1; **7** iii 7″–16″; **8** iii 32′–45′; **9** i 77–ii 9; **11** ii 81–94; **92** ii 1′
ca. 660	Mannea	**3** iii 16–92a; **4** iii 9–15′; **6** iv 1″–v 5; **7** iv 1′–58″; **8** iv 1′–21″; **9** ii 21–52; **11** ii 126–iii 26; **12** iii 1″–9″; **13** iii 1″–9″; **74** iii 1′–iv 11; **75** 1′–9′; **76** ii′ 1′–9′; **77** i′ 1′–7′; **78** 1′–3′; **91** ii 1′–11′; **92** iii 1′; **171** 1′–11′; **195** rev. 10–14
ca. 658	Media	**3** iii 92b–iv 5; **4** iii 16′–22′; **6** v 6–12; **7** iv 59″–65″; **8** iv 22″; **74** iv 12–16; **78** 4′–6′
ca. 657	Urarṭu 1	**3** iv 6–14; **4** iv 1–8; **6** v 13–23; **7** iv 66″–74″; **78** rev. 1–3
653	Elam 3	**3** iv 80–vi 9; **4** iv 50′–vi 12; **6** v 1′–vii 10; **7** v 48–vi 22′; **8** v 1′–vii 10′; **9** ii 53–71; **11** iii 27–49; **12** v 1–5; **79** ii 19–iv 13′; **83** i′ 1–13; **84** i′ 1′–10′; **85** i 1′–10′; **86** i 1′–9′; **92** iii 2′–15′; **126** rev. 1–4; **128** 1′–9′; **135** rev. 1; **155** 6′–8′; **161** i 1–ii 14, iii 9′–27′; **162** 3′–l.e. 3; **163** 1′–rev. 5; **164** 1′–12′; **165** 1–13, rev. 7′–8′; **166** 1′–7′; **168** 1′–8′; **169** 1′–10′; **170** 1′–11′; **171** rev.[?] 1′–10′; **195** rev. 1–9; **200** 7–rev. 14; **201** 1′–12′; **202** 1′–20′; **228** 13′–14′; **233** 6′–11′; **234** i′ 1′–4′
653	Gambulu	**3** vi 10–85; **4** vi 13–95; **6** vii 11–47′; **7** vi 23′–vii 35; **8** vii 11′–17″; **9** ii 72–iii 5; **11** iii 50–69; **12** v 6–13; **79** iv 14′; **86** i 10′–ii 15′; **89** i 1–ii 12′; **92** iii 16′–26′; **125** Side A 8′–9′; **127** 1–9; **161** ii 15–iii 8′, 28′–iv 16; **162** 1′–2′; **163** rev. 6–8; **165** rev. 1′–6′, 9′–15′; **167** 1′–13′; **169** 11′–17′; **170** 12′–15′; **195** 10–28
before 652 and ca. 650	Arabs 1	**3** vii 77–viii 55; **4** vii 80–viii 57; **6** x 1′–18″; **7** ix 64″–x 52′; **8** ix 38′–28″; **11** vii 82–viii 64; **86** iii 2′–iv 18′; **90** i 1′–13′, ii 1′–9′; **129** 1′–rev. 7; **172** rev. 1′–9′; **180** 8′–rev.[?] 5; **194** i 1–iii 11
652–648	Šamaš-šuma-ukīn rebellion	**6** viii 9‴b–ix 10″; **7** viii 1′–79′; **8** viii 1‴–36⁗; **11** iii 70–135, iv 41b–109; **89** iv 2′b–v 18″; **94** i 1′–12′; **105** rev.[?] i 1′–12′a; **130** 5′–rev. 9, l.e. 1–4; **134** 1′–21′; **172** 9–22; **173** ii 9′–11′; **174** 1′–4′; **175** i 1′–7′, ii 1′–25′; **176** 1–8; **180** 2′–7′; **181** rev.[?] 2′–9′; **183** 3′–7′; **228** rev. 23–26
ca. 651–650	Elam 4	**3** vi 86–vii 76; **4** vi 96–vii 79; **6** vii 48′–viii 9‴a and ix 11″–52″; **7** vii 36–viii 12 and viii 80′–ix 9; **8** viii 1′–34″ and viii 37⁗–ix 37′; **9** iii 6–32; **11** iii 136–iv 41a; **85** rev. i′ 1–6; **86** iii 1′; **87** ii 1–6; **88** ii′ 1′–21′; **89** ii 13′–iv 2′a, v 19″–vi 14; **92** iii 27′–iv 4; **95** i 1–11; **106** 1′–10′; **107** ii′ 1′–13′; **112** ii 1–18; **126** rev. 5–11; **127** rev. 1′–15′; **131** 1′–7′; **132** 1′–12′; **133** rev. 1–5; **135** rev. 2–3; **137** 1′–9′a; **147** 1′–9′; **150** 1′–16′; **151** 1′–14′; **155** 9′–rev. 6; **172** 1–8; **173** i 1′–ii 8′, iv 1′–9′; **174** rev. 2′–9′; **175** i 8′–14′, ii 26–iii 14′; **176** 9–17; **177** 2′–10′; **178** 1′–rev. 22; **179** 1′–14′; **180** rev.[?] 7–15; **181** 1′–5′; **182** 1′–rev.[?] 8′; **184** 8′–9′; **188** 1–6; **197** 1‴–rev. 12; **203** 13–rev. 8; **204** 1′–rev. 6; **205** 1′–11′; **228** 15′–25′; **229** ii 1′–16′
647	Elam 5	**7** ix 10–63″; **8** ix 29″–x 16′; **9** iii 33–iv 16; **11** iv 110–v 62; **91** iv 1–8′; **112** iii 1′–8′; **133** rev. 6–16; **136** rev. 1–18; **137** 9′b–16′; **197** rev. 13–23; **228** 26′–29′; **229** iii 1′–4′; **234** ii′ 1′–17′

[84] Information on the dates can be found in Novotny and Jeffers, RINAP 5/1 pp. 16–26.

Date	Incident(s)	Source(s)
646	Elam 6	**9** iv 17–vi 21; **10** iv 12–v 32; **11** v 63–vii 8; **91** v 1–vi 17; **92** v 1–4; **94** ii 1′–iii 23′; **95** rev. i′ 1′–6′; **96** rev. i′ 1′–13′; **97** rev. i′ 1′–4′; **100** ii′ 1′–10′; **101** rev. ii′ 1′–7′; **102** i′ 1′–rev. 12; **103** ii′ 1′–8′; **108** rev.? i′ 1′–19′; **112** iii 9′–16′; **133** rev. 17–20; **134** 22′–30′; **135** rev. 4–6; **138** 1′–9′; **139** 1′–11′; **140** 1′–rev. 4; **141** 1′–14′; **152** 1′–6′; **154** 1′–10′; **155** rev. 7–14; **188** 7–rev. 2; **197** rev. 24–41; **198** rev. 1′–11′; **199** rev. 1′–7′; **215** iii 2′–iv 35; **217** 1′–rev. 19′; **224** 18–19; **227** rev. 1–17; **228** rev. 1–22; **229** iii 1′–iv 13; **234** rev. i 1′–9′; **235** 1′–7′
ca. 645	Elam 7	**11** vii 9–81; **135** rev. 7–8; **142** rev. 1′–7′; **143** 1′–3′; **194** v 24–vi 23; **229** v 1–12
ca. 645–643	Arabs 2	**11** viii 65–x 5; **109** i′ 1′–10′; **156** 20–rev. 12; **194** iii 12–v 2; **215** v 1–13
ca. 645–643	Elam 8	**11** x 6–39; **110** 1′–5′; **143** 4′–11′; **144** 1′–9′; **145** rev. 1′–9′a; **157** 6–14; **158** 4′–5′; **194** vi 27–43
ca. 645–643	Lydia 2	**11** ii 111–125
ca. 645–643	Urarṭu 2	**11** x 40–50; **110** 6′–9′
ca. 642–640	Cyrus	**12** vi 7′–13′
ca. 642–640	Ḫudimiri	**12** vi 14′–25′
ca. 640–639	Tugdammî	**13** viii 6–11′; **224** 20–25

Ashurbanipal's Building Activities in Babylonia and the East Tigris Region

Numerous texts describe Ashurbanipal's many building activities in Babylonia. In the prologues of some of his annalistic texts and building inscriptions written on multi-faceted clay prisms, the king provides a vague overview of his (temple) building activities, stating:

> (As for) the sanctua[ries of A]ssyria (and) the land Akkad whose foundation(s) Esarh[addon], king of Assyria, the father who had engendered me, had laid, but whose construction he had not finished, I myself now completed their work by the command of the great gods, my lords.[85]

> I built (and) completed the sanctuaries of Assyria (and) the land Akkad in their en[ti]rety. I made every type of temple appurtenance there is from silver (and) gold, (and) I a[d]ded (them) to those of the kings, my ancestors. I made the great gods who support me reside in their exalted inner sanctums. I offered sumptuous offerings before them (and) presented (them) with my gif[ts]. I made regular offerings (and) contributions more plenti[ful] than those of distant [day]s.[86]

From the textual and archaeological records, it is known that Ashurbanipal had sponsored building programs in at least ten Babylonian cities: Agade, Babylon, Borsippa, Cutha, Dūr-Kurigalzu, Mê-Turān, Nippur, Sippar, Ur, and Uruk. He also carried out construction in the East Tigris region, at Dēr. Full details about Ashurbanipal's building activities in Assyria are given in the introduction of Jeffers and Novotny, RINAP 5/2 (pp. 11–25). For general studies, see in particular Frame, RIMB 2 pp. 194–195 and 261; and Grayson, CAH^2 3/2 pp. 155–158. Ashurbanipal's Babylonian and East-Tigridian building projects will be discussed alphabetically by city.

Agade

According to the Neo-Babylonian king Nabonidus (555–539), Babylon's last native king, Ashurbanipal was one of two Assyrian kings who had rebuilt Eulmaš, the temple of the goddess Ištar at Agade, the capital of the third-millennium ruler Sargon whose location is still unknown.[87] Nabonidus stated that both Ashurbanipal and his father Esarhaddon had failed to properly rebuild Eulmaš since neither of them had been able to find the temple's original, divinely-sanctioned foundations, which had been laid by Sargon of Agade.[88] That king claimed:

> Esarhaddon, king of Assyria, and Ashurbanipal, his son, to whom the god Sîn, king of the gods, granted the totality of (all) lands, sought out the (original) foundation(s) of Eulmaš, but did not reach (them). They put down in writing, saying: "I sought out the (original) foundation(s) of that Eulmaš, but I did

[85] Novotny and Jeffers, RINAP 5/1 p. 111 Asb. 6 (Prism C) i 5′–10′.
[86] Novotny and Jeffers, RINAP 5/1 p. 218 Asb. 10 (Prism T) iii 35b–49a.
[87] Weiershäuser and Novotny, RINBE 2 p. 87 Nabonidus 10 ii 1′–4′ and p. 137 Nabonidus 27 ii 37–45a. Asb. 252 is probably an inscription recording work on Eulmaš at Agade, but its building account is completely missing. For the attribution of the text written on clay cylinder fragment 81-2-4,174 to Ashurbanipal, see the commentary of Asb. 252. For information on Eulmaš, see Frame, Mesopotamia 28 (1993) pp. 21–50; George, House Most High p. 155 no. 1168; Bartelmus and Taylor, JCS 66 (2014) pp. 113–128; and Weiershäuser and Novotny, RINBE 2 p. 8.
[88] Nabonidus makes the same claim for one of the Kassite kings named Kurigalzu (probably the first king of this name) and for Nebuchadnezzar II. For a discussion of Nabonidus criticizing Nebuchadnezzar, see Schaudig, Studies Ellis pp. 155–161.

> not reach (them). I cut down poplar(s) and *maštû*-tree(s) and (then) built a replacement Eulmaš and gave (it) to the goddess Ištar of Agade, great lady, my lady."[89]

Since such admissions would not have been included in Assyrian royal inscriptions, it can be confidently assumed that Nabonidus' scribes drafted Ashurbanipal's "confession" of not constructing Eulmaš precisely on its ancient, Sargonic-period foundations and with durable, high-quality materials. Presumably, Esarhaddon and Ashurbanipal gave the temple of Ištar at Agade the care it deserved when rebuilding that sacred structure. Unfortunately, no contemporary witness presently survives to give those Assyrian kings' testimonies about their work on Eulmaš.[90]

Babylon

In 689, Sennacherib captured, looted, and destroyed Babylon,[91] as he described in his so-called "Bavian Inscription":

> I destroyed, devastated, (and) burned with fire the city, and (its) buildings, from its foundations to its crenellations. I removed the brick(s) and earth, as much as there was, from the (inner) wall and outer wall, the temples, (and) the ziggurat, (and) I threw (it) into the Araḫtu river. I dug canals into the center of that city and (thus) leveled their site with water. I destroyed the outline of its foundations and (thereby) made its destruction surpass that of the Deluge. So that in the future, the site of that city and (its) temples will be unrecognizable, I dissolved it (Babylon) in water and annihilated (it), (making it) like a meadow.[92]

Although the actual destruction was probably not as bad as described in royal inscriptions, Babylon, with the god Marduk's temple Esagil ("House Whose Head Is High") at its heart, ceased to be the bond that linked heaven and earth. That connection was severed when Esagil, the most sacred building in the city's Eridu district, had been destroyed and when Marduk's statue and its paraphernalia (including an ornately-decorated bed) had been carried off to Assyria and placed in Ešarra ("House of the Universe"), the temple of the Assyrian national god Aššur, located in the Baltil quarter of Aššur.[93]

Soon after becoming king in late 681, in the wake of Sennacherib's murder,[94] probably during his 2nd regnal year (679), Esarhaddon, Ashurbanipal's and Šamaš-šuma-ukīn's father, initiated construction in Babylon so that that important Babylonian city would once again be a bond between heaven and earth.[95] From that time

---

[89] Weiershäuser and Novotny, RINBE p. 137 Nabonidus 27 ii 37–45a.

[90] According to two Babylonian chronicles (Leichty, RINAP 4 pp. 7–8), the statue of the goddess Ištar of Agade, together with the statues of other gods of that city, that had been in Elam (presumably in its religious capital Susa) were returned to Agade on 10-XII-674, at the very end of Esarhaddon's seventh regnal year, presumably as part of a treaty agreement between Assyria and Elam. The return of that cult image was very likely the principal reason that Esarhaddon undertook work on Eulmaš. Given that this project began late in Esarhaddon's reign, this work was probably unfinished in late 669 and, therefore, the task of completing it fell to his successors. Based on Nabonidus' inscriptions, it was Ashurbanipal, not Šamaš-šuma-ukīn, who took responsibility for ensuring the completion of this temple of Ištar of Agade.

[91] Four books on this important Mesopotamian city have recently been published. These are Beaulieu, History of Babylon; Radner, A Short History of Babylon; Pedersén, Babylon; and Dalley, City of Babylon.

[92] Grayson and Novotny, RINAP 3/2 pp. 316–317 Sennacherib 223 lines 50b–54a. The event and the period following the second conquest of Babylon are also recorded in the Chronicle Concerning the Period from Nabû-nāṣir to Šamaš-šuma-ukīn, the Esarhaddon Chronicle, the Akītu Chronicle, Babylonian Kinglist A, the Ptolemaic Canon, and the Synchronistic King List. For translations, see Grayson and Novotny, RINAP 3/1 pp. 23–27. Inscriptions of Esarhaddon record the destruction of the city, but those accounts remove all human agency from the events. See, for example, Leichty, RINAP 4 p. 196 Esarhaddon 104 i 34–ii 1a: "The Enlil of the gods, the god Marduk, became angry and plotted evilly to level the land (and) to destroy its people. The river Araḫtu, (normally) a river of abundance, turned into an angry wave, a raging tide, a huge flood like the deluge. It swept (its) waters destructively across the city (and) its dwellings and turned (them) into ruins. The gods dwelling in it flew up to the heavens like birds; the people living in it were hidden in another place and took refuge in an [unknown] land."

[93] Babylon, according the 1,092-line Babylonian Epic of Creation *Enūma eliš* ("When on high"), had been created to not only be the center of the universe but also the eternal link between humans and gods. For recent editions and studies of *Enūma eliš*, see Kämmerer and Metzler, Das babylonische Weltschöpfungsepos; and Lambert, Babylonian Creation Myths pp. 3–277 and 439–492. Babylon and Esagil are regularly described as being the bond of heaven and earth in cuneiform sources. See, for example, George BTT pp. 38–39 no. 1 (Tintir = Babylon) Tablet I line 6 and pp. 80–81 no. 5 (Esagil commentary) lines 25–26. For a recent study of Marduk's Babylon linking heaven and earth, see Radner, A Short History of Babylon pp. 75–87.

[94] For a brief study of the murder of Sennacherib, see Grayson and Novotny, RINAP 3/2 pp. 28–29 (with references to earlier studies). For the opinion that Esarhaddon, rather than Urdu-Mullissu, was the son who murdered his father, see also Knapp, JAOS 140 (2020) pp. 165–181. For the most recent discussion on the matter, see Dalley and Siddall, Iraq 83 (2021) pp. 45–56.

[95] Esarhaddon's work on Babylon might have started during his 2nd year (679), after the 28th/29th of Simānu (III). On the date, see Novotny, JCS 67 (2015) pp. 151–152. With regard to work on Esagil, it is possible that that project had not progressed very far by 672 or 671. For this opinion, see Frame, Babylonia pp. 77–78; and George, Iraq 57 (1995) p. 178 n. 38.

onwards, until his death on 10-VIII-669, Esarhaddon made a concerted effort to restore Babylon, its city walls Imgur-Enlil ("The God Enlil Has Shown Favor") and Nēmetti-Enlil ("Bulwark of the God Enlil"), and its temples, especially its most sacred buildings Esagil and Etemenanki ("House, Foundation Platform of Heaven and Netherworld").[96] This Assyrian king described the rebuilding of Babylon's most important structures as follows:

> [In] a favorable month, on a propitious day, I laid its foundation platform over its previous foundations (and) in (exact) accordance with its earlier plan I did not diminish (it) by one cubit nor increase (it) by half a cubit. I built (and) completed Esagil, the palace of the gods, an image of the *apsû*, a replica of Ešarra, a likeness of the abode of the god Ea, (and) a replica of (the square of) Pegasus (*ikû*); I had (Esagil) ingeni[ously] built (and) I laid out (its) square. For its roof, I stretched out magnificent cedar beams, grown on Mount Amanus, the pure mountain, (and) fastened bands of gold (and) silver on doors of cypress, whose fragrance is sweet, and installed (them) in its gates.[97]
>
> I built anew Etemenanki, the ziggurat, on the site where it previously stood — its length is one *ašlu* (and) one *ṣuppān*, (and) its width is one *ašlu* (and) one *ṣuppān*.[98]
>
> With the large *aslu*-cubit, I measured the dimensions of Imgur-Enlil, its great wall — each length (and) width was thirty *ašlus*. I had (it) built as it was before and raised (its top) up like a mountain. I built (and) [completed] Nēmetti-Enlil, its outer wall, (and) filled (it) with [splend]or (making it) [an object of wonder] for [all of] the people.[99]

---

[96] For Esarhaddon's "Babylon Inscriptions," see Leichty, RINAP 4 pp. 193–258 Esarhaddon 104–126; and Novotny, JCS 67 (2015) pp. 145–168. See also the "Aššur-Babylon Inscriptions": Leichty, RINAP 4 pp. 103–115 Esarhaddon 48–49 and 51–53 and pp. 134–137 Esarhaddon 60. For Esagil and Etemenanki, see George, House Most High pp. 139–140 no. 967 and p. 149 no. 1088. For Imgur-Enlil and Nēmetti-Enlil, with their eight gates, see George, BTT pp. 336–351 (commentary to Tintir V lines 49–58, which are edited on pp. 66–67).

[97] Leichty, RINAP 4 p. 198 Esarhaddon 104 iii 41b–iv 8. The square-shaped (or diamond-shaped) "Sublime Court" (also known as the "Court of Bel") of Esagil was the earthly replica of the "Field" (*ikû*), its heavenly counterpart. The Field, which we now refer to as the "Square of Pegasus," was a large diamond shape that was formed by four near-equally-bright stars: Markab ("saddle"; α Pegasi), Scheat ("shoulder"; β Pegasi), Algenib ("the flank"; γ Pegasi) and Alpheratz ("the mare"; α Andromedae); see Radner, A Short History of Babylon pp. 79–81. After 689, Sennacherib built a new square courtyard onto Ešarra, the so-called "Ostanbau" (see Grayson and Novotny, RINAP 3/2 pp. 20–21 [with references to previous studies]); that part of Aššur's temple at Aššur was modelled on Esagil's Sublime Court/Court of Bēl. The statement in Esarhaddon's inscriptions that Marduk's temple was "a replica of Ešarra" refers to the *ikû*-shaped eastern annex building constructed by Sennacherib. This addition was to make Aššur's temple the new bond between heaven and earth; Leichty, RINAP 4 p. 109 Esarhaddon 48 (Aššur-Babylon A) lines 98b-99a refer to that sacred building as the "bond of heaven and earth" (*markas šamê u erṣetim*).

[98] Leichty, RINAP 4 p. 207 Esarhaddon 105 vi 27b–32. The base of Etemenanki measured 91.5 × 91.5 m (8400 m^2). The core of unbaked mud bricks was surrounded with a 15.75-meter-thick baked-brick outer mantle. Information about Etemenanki prior to the Assyrian domination of Babylonia (728–626) is very sparse and comes entirely from narrative poems (*Enūma Eliš* and the Poem of Erra) and scholarly compilations (Tintir = Babylon) and, thus, it is not entirely certain when Marduk's ziggurat at Babylon was founded. It has often been suggested that Nebuchadnezzar I (1125–1104), the fourth ruler of the Second Dynasty of Isin, was its founder; this would coincide with the period during which *Enūma eliš* is generally thought to have been composed. Given the lack of textual and archaeological evidence, this assumption cannot be confirmed with any degree of certainty and one cannot rule out the possibility that the Etemenanki was founded much earlier, perhaps even in Old Babylonian times. Esarhaddon is the first known builder of Marduk's ziggurat. In the reign of the Neo-Babylonian king Nebuchadnezzar II (604–562), Etemenanki is sometimes thought to have had seven stages, six lower tiers with a blue-glazed-brick temple construction on top; for a discussion and digital reconstructions, see Pedersén, Babylon pp. 153–165. This view has gained support over the last decade because Babylon's ziggurat is depicted on the now-famous "Tower of Babel" Stele (George, CUSAS 17 pp. 153–169 no. 76), however, this understanding is now less certain as that monument might be a modern fake (Dalley, BiOr 72 [2016] col. 754; Lunde, Morgenbladet 2022/29 pp. 26–33; and Dalley, BiOr 79 [2022] forthcoming). Given the current textual and archaeological evidence, it is uncertain how many stages Marduk's ziggurat had during Esarhaddon's reign. For further details about the textual sources and the archaeological remains, see Wetzel and Weissbach, Hauptheiligtum; George, BTT pp. 298–300 (the commentary to Tintir IV line 2, which is edited on pp. 58–58) and 430–433 (commentary to the E-sagil Tablet lines 41–42, which are edited on pp. 116–117); and Pedersén, Babylon pp. 142–165.

[99] Leichty, RINAP 4 p. 207 Esarhaddon 105 vi 33–vii 4. According to Esarhaddon's inscriptions, Babylon's city walls formed a perfect square; however, the northern and southern stretches of the wall are 2,700 m in length, while the eastern and western sides are significantly shorter, being each 1,700 m in length. According to an inscription of the Neo-Babylonian king Nabonidus (Weiershäuer and Novotny, RINBE 2 p. 54 Nabonidus 1 [Imgur-Enlil Cylinder] i 22), Imgur-Enlil measured "20 UŠ." An UŠ is a unit for measuring length, but its precise interpretation is uncertain since the sections of the lexical series Ea (Tablet VI) and Aa dealing with UŠ are missing. According to M. Powell (RLA 7/5–6 [1989] pp. 459 and 465–467 §I.2k), 1 UŠ equals 6 ropes, 12 *ṣuppu*, 60 *nindan*-rods, 120 reeds, and 720 cubits, that is, approximately 360 m; for UŠ = *šuššān*, see Ossendrijver, NABU 2022/2 pp. 156–157 no. 68. According to the aforementioned inscription of Nabonidus, Imgur-Enlil measured 20 UŠ (UŠ.20.TA.A), which would be approximately 7,200 m (= 360 m × 20). A.R. George (BTT pp. 135–136) has demonstrated that the actual length of Imgur-Enlil in the Neo-Babylonian period was 8,015 m, while O. Pedersén (Babylon p. 42 and 280) gives the length of the walls as 7,200 m, with the assumption that the stretches of walls within the area of palace are disregarded. In the time of Nabopolassar and his son Nebuchadnezzar II, Imgur-Enlil and Nēmetti-Enlil were respectively 6.5 m and 3.7 m thick, with reconstructed heights of 15 m and 8 m. These impressive structures would have been made from an estimated 96,800,000 (Imgur-Enlil) and 28,500,000 (Nēmeti-Enlil) unbaked bricks. For a recent study of Imgur-Enlil and Nēmetti-Enlil from the textual sources and the archaeological remains, see Pedersén, Babylon pp. 39–88.

From sometime after 28/29-III-679 until 10-VIII-669, Esarhaddon rebuilt Imgur-Enlil, Nēmetti-Enlil, Esagil, Etemenanki, the processional way, and Eniggidrukalamasuma ("House Which Bestows the Scepter of the Land"), the temple of the god Nabû of the *ḫarû*.[100] To promote urban renewal, the Assyrian king, as the *de facto* ruler of Babylon, strongly encouraged Babylon's citizens to resettle the city, build houses, plant orchards, and dig canals.[101] At home, in an appropriate workshop in the religious capital Aššur, in the Aššur temple Ešarra, Esarhaddon had skilled craftsmen restore the divine statues of Marduk and his entourage (Bēltīya [Zarpanītu], Bēlet-Bābili [Ištar], Ea, and Mandānu) and had several cult objects fashioned.[102] Despite Esarhaddon's best efforts, and contrary to what his inscriptions record, work on Esagil (and Etemenanki) remained unfinished and the refurbished statue of Marduk remained in Assyria when he died in late 669.[103] The completion of that work fell to Ashurbanipal and Šamaš-šuma-ukīn, whom Esarhaddon had officially designated to replace him in II-672.[104]

Shortly after his official coronation as king of Assyria in I-668, in the month Ayyāru (II), Ashurbanipal traveled south to Babylon with his older brother Šamaš-šuma-ukīn, the statues of Marduk and his entourage, and numerous priests and temple personnel.[105] The Assyrian king describes the trip from Baltil (Aššur) to Šuanna (Babylon) as follows:

---

[100] For Eniggidrukalamasuma, see George, House Most High pp. 132–133; and Pedersén, Babylon pp. 167–174. Moreover, Esarhaddon (and Ashurbanipal) built a baked-brick pedestal or altar in front of the larger, eastern gate to the ziggurat area, ca. 190 m from the precinct wall. For the baked-brick pillar, see Reuther, Merkes pp. 70–71; and Pedersén, Babylon pp. 154–155 and p. 213 fig. 5.14. Furthermore, it has been suggested that Esarhaddon was the king responsible for the "lion of Babylon"; for this proposal, see Dalley, City of Babylon pp. 201 and p. 202 fig. 7.9; and Dalley, BiOr 79 (2022) forthcoming.

Because Esarhaddon states that he refurbished the statues of Bēlet-Bābili (Ištar), Ea, and Mandānu, together with those of Marduk and Bēltīya (Zarpanītu), he presumably also undertook work on the temples of those three deities: respectively Eturkalama ("House, Cattle-Pen of the Land"), Ekarzagina ("House, Quay of Lapis Lazuli" or "House, Pure Quay"), and Erabriri ("House of the Shackle Which Holds in Check"). This proposal is supported by the fact that Ashurbanipal is known to have sponsored construction on Eturkalama and Ekarzagina; see below. All three temples were located inside the Esagil complex.

[101] Esarhaddon never took the hand of Marduk during an *akītu*-festival (New Year's festival) and, therefore, he was never officially regarded as Marduk's divinely-appointed earthly representative. This was because Marduk's statue was damaged and in Baltil (Aššur), probably in the Aššur temple. For these reasons, all of his "Babylon Inscriptions" written on clay prisms are dated to his "accession year" (*rēš šarrūti*). For details, see Novotny, JCS 67 (2015) pp. 149–151.

[102] Leichty, RINAP 4 pp. 107–108 Esarhaddon 48 (Aššur-Babylon A) lines 61b–93; compare p. 198 Esarhaddon 104 (Babylon A) iv 9–20. The statues of the deities Amurru, Abšušu, and Abtagigi were also renovated/repaired at that time. A seat (*šubtu*) and footstool (*gišzappu*) for the goddess Tašmētu were chief among the items that Esarhaddon had made or restored for Babylon.

[103] Several inscriptions of Esarhaddon prematurely record Marduk's triumphant return to Esagil and the installation of Šamaš-šuma-ukīn as king of Babylon. See Leichty, RINAP 4 p. 113 Esarhaddon 52 (Aššur-Babylon H) and pp. 114–115 Esarhaddon 53 (Aššur-Babylon G). Esarhaddon likely planned to return Marduk and his entourage in time for the fall *akītu*-festival at Babylon, the one held in the month Tašrītu (VII), in 670 (his 11th regnal year as the king of Assyria). Those plans, however, were derailed when the king ordered an intercalary Ulūlu (VI2) to be added, thus postponing the New Year's festival in Babylon by one entire month; this is recorded in K 930, a letter attributed to the chief exorcist Marduk-šākin-šumi addressed to the king (Parpola, SAA 10 p. 200 no. 253). S. Parpola (LAS 2 pp. 185–188 no. 190) dates this piece of correspondence to 1-VI-670 (= August 7th 670), an interpretation that was perhaps (at least partially) influenced by the contents of 81-1-18,54 (Cole and Machinst, SAA 13 pp. 54–55 no. 60), a letter attributed to Urdu-Nabû, a priest of the Nabû temple at Kalḫu, who pressed the king about whether or not the *akītu*-festival would take place since nobles from Babylon and Borsippa had come to him asking about the matter. The decision to intercalate Ulūlu (VI2), rather than Addaru (XII2), seems to have taken place at the outset of Ulūlu, despite the fact that Esarhaddon's advisors were aware that 670 would be a "leap year" from the beginning of the year, although it was unclear at that time whether the intercalation would take after Ulūlu or Addaru; see K 185 (Parpola, SAA 10 pp. 32–33 no. 42), a letter written by the astrologer Balasî, probably in Nisannu (I) of that year. The slight shift in the calendar meant that the Tašrītu (VII) 670 *akītu*-festival did not take place and, thus, Esarhaddon did not escort Marduk and his entourage to Babylon, take the hand of Babylon's tutelary deity during the New Year's festival, and officially become the king of Babylon as he had intended. The inscriptions written on tablet fragments Sm 1079 (Aššur-Babylon H) and K 5382b (Aššur-Babylon G) were likely written shortly before Esarhaddon ordered an intercalary Ulūlu, resulting in him not returning Marduk to Esagil and not placing Šamaš-šuma-ukīn on the throne of Babylon as those texts recorded.

Of course, other factors might have also contributed to Esarhaddon not returning Marduk to Esagil. One postponement might have been due to an inauspicious event that occurred in the fortified city Labbanat, which prompted Esarhaddon to order that the statues be returned to Assyria rather than continuing the journey to Babylon; for some details on K 527 (Parpola SAA 10 p. 19 no. 24) — a letter written by Ištar-šumu-ēreš, Adad-šumu-uṣur, and Marduk-šākin-šumi, possibly on 18-II-669 — see Frame, Babylonia pp. 77–78. Moreover, the restoration of Esagil might not have been sufficiently completed to have warranted the return of the cult statues. This might have been due in part to the fact that Esarhaddon's architects had not sufficiently raised the temple above the water table and that Esagil's inadequately waterproofed floor needed to be fixed. This problem with the temple's flooring is suggested by the fact that Ashurbanipal raised the level of the pavement in Esagil's main courtyard by nearly a half meter; see the comments in George, Iraq 57 (1995) p. 178 n. 48. Moreover, Esarhaddon's decision to campaign against Egypt for a third time in 669 might have also delayed the return of Marduk's statue.

[104] For a brief overview, see Novotny and Jeffers, RINAP 5/1 pp. 13–14.

[105] Late in Nisannu (I) 668, Ashurbanipal instructed his diviners to determine whether Šamaš-šuma-ukīn should take the hand of Marduk during that year and take that god's statue back to Babylon; see Starr, SAA 4 pp. 236–237 no. 262. On 28-I-668, the king's haruspices returned with a 'firm yes' from the gods Šamaš and Marduk and the journey to Babylon set out shortly thereafter. According to three Babylonian Chronicles, Šamaš-šuma-ukīn and Marduk entered Babylon in the month Ayyāru (II). The Chronicle Concerning the Period from Nabû-nāṣir to Šamaš-šuma-ukīn (iv 34–36) records that the entry into Babylon took place on either the 14th or 24th day of the month,

> [... m]e, [Ashurbanipal, ..., he blessed ...]. Šamaš-šuma-ukīn, (my) favorite brother whom I presen[ted to the god Marduk], took the hands of his great divinity and was marching be[fore him]. *Āšipu*-priest(s) ... [...], lamentation priests with *manz*[*û*-drums (and) *ḫalḫallatu*-drums ...], (and) singers with lyre(s) [*were singing*] the praise of [his] lordshi[p. Maumuša ...]. From the quay of Baltil (Aššur) to the quay of Babylon, wherever they stopped for the n[ight], sheep were butchered, bulls were slaughtered, (and) *armannu*-aromatics were scattered *o*[*n*] the ...s. They brought befo[re him] everything there was for morning (and) evening meals. Piles of brushwood were lit (and) torches ignited (so that) [th]ere was lig[ht] for one league. All of my troops were arranged in a circle (around him) like a rainbow (and) there were joyous celebrations day and night. The deities the Lady of Akkad, Nanāya, Uṣur-amāssa, Ḫanibiya, (and) Ada... had taken up residence on the banks of the river, waiting for the king of the gods, the lord of lords. The god Nergal, mightiest of the gods, came out of Emeslam, his princely residence, (and) approached the quay of Babylon amidst a joyous celebration, arriving safely. The god Nabû, the triumphant heir, took the direct ro[ad] from Borsippa. The god Šamaš rushed from Sippar, emitting radiance onto Babylon. The gods of the land of Sumer and Akkad (in their hurry) *looked exhausted* like tired foals. With the craft of the sage — "the wa[shing] of the mouth," ["the opening of the mouth," bathing, (and) purification] — he (Marduk) entered the fruit orchards of the luxuriant gardens of Karzagina ("Pure Quay" or "Quay of Lapis Lazuli"), a pur[e] place, before the stars of heaven — the deities Ea, Šamaš, Asalluḫi, Bēlet-ilī, Kusu, (and) Nin[girima] — an[d ... inside] it (Esagil) he took up residence on (his) [eternal] d[ais].[106]

Marduk, Bēltīya (Zarpanītu), Bēlet-Bābili (Ištar), Ea, and Mandānu were returned to their temples and Šamaš-šuma-ukīn was placed on the throne, just as Esarhaddon had intended to do while he was still alive.[107]

As work in Babylon was still incomplete in II-668, Ashurbanipal — despite the fact that Šamaš-šuma-ukīn was the king of Babylon, although not yet officially since he still had to take the hand of Marduk during an *akītu*-festival — took it upon himself to finish what his father had started.[108] First and foremost was the completion of Babylon's two most important structures: Marduk's temple and ziggurat Esagil and Etemenanki, together with their shrines, platforms, and daises.[109] As for Esagil, Ashurbanipal finished its structure;[110] adorned its interior, especially Eumuša ("House of Command"),[111] Marduk's cella, which he "made glisten like the stars (lit. 'writing') of the firmament"; roofed it with beams of cedar (*erēnu*) and cypress (*šurmēnu*) imported from Mount Amanus and Mount Lebanon in the Levant;[112] hung doors of boxwood (*taskarinnu*), *musukkannu*-

---

while the Esarhaddon Chronicle (lines 35′–37′) states that that event occurred on the 24th or 25th of Ayyāru, and the Akītu Chronicle (lines 5–8) mentions that Šamaš-šuma-ukīn and Marduk came into Babylon on the 24th. See Novotny and Jeffers, RINAP 5/1 pp. 34–35 for translations of these passages.

[106] Jeffers and Novotny, RINAP 5/2 p. 326 Asb. 220 (L[4]) iii 1′–22′ (with restorations from iv 8′–20′ on p. 328). Note that iii 1′–6′ are presented here as they would have appeared on the now-lost stele that Ashurbanipal had set up in Esagil after Marduk's return to his temple in II-668, rather than as how these lines of texts were inscribed in the draft version preserved on clay tablet K 2694+. For details, see Jeffers and Novotny, RINAP 5/2 pp. 5–6, 320–321, 326, and 328.

[107] Perhaps already in VII-670; see n. 103 above. As pointed out by G. Frame (Babylonia p. 78), the promotion of Šamaš-šuma-ukīn to heir designate of Babylon in II-672 might have prompted the return of Marduk's statue.

[108] This work is recorded in Novotny and Jeffers, RINAP 5/1 pp. 103–104 Asb. 5 (Prism I) i 8′–ii 5; pp. 111 and 114 Asb. 6 (Prism C) i 18′–43′; p. 139 Asb. 7 (Prism Kh) i 1′–13′; pp. 212 and 216 Asb. 10 (Prism T) i 21–54; pp. 266–267 Asb. 12 (Prism H) i 1′–3′; pp. 275 and 278 Asb. 13 (Prism J) ii 1′–14′ and viii 12′–17′; p. 282 Asb. 15 ii 10–21; p. 285 Asb. 17 i′ 6′–9′; p. 293 Asb. 22 i 1′–4′; pp. 302–303 Asb. 23 (IIT) lines 41–53; and p. 355 Asb. 61 lines 13–33; Jeffers and Novotny, RINAP 5/2 p. 84 Asb. 98 i 1′–6′; p. 85 Asb. 99 i 1′–11′; p. 111 Asb. 116 i 2′–9′a; p. 238 Asb. 191 rev.[?] 1–15; pp. 307–308 Asb. 215 (Edition L) i 1′–25′; p. 318 Asb. 219 obv. 1′–12′; p. 331 Asb. 222 lines 7–14a; pp. 333–334 Asb. 223 iii 36′–40′ and iv 11′–19′; pp. 337–338 Asb. 224 lines 26–32; p. 342 Asb. 225 rev. 24′; p. 343 Asb. 226 rev. 3–7; and 354 Asb. 229 i 1′–9′; and, in the present volume, Asb. 241 lines 3–22; Asb. 242 lines 7b–20a; Asb. 243 lines 7b–11; Asb. 244 lines 8–14a; Asb. 245 lines 8–14a; Asb. 246 lines 36b–67a; Asb. 247–251; Asb. 253 lines 7–18; Asb. 254 lines 1–32; Asb. 262 lines 1–15; and Asb. 263 lines 7–22a. For the archaeological evidence, see Pedersén, Babylon *passim*. A.R. George (Iraq 57 [1995] p. 178 n. 38) has proposed the following about the state of Esagil's completion at the very beginning of Ashurbanipal's reign: "[M]ost, if not all, of the basic work must have been completed by the time that the cult-statues eventually returned to Babylon, at the accession of Šamaš-šuma-ukīn in 668 B.C., although some furnishings, notably Marduk's bed and chariot, were not installed until much later (654 and 653 B.C. respectively). Though six months elapsed between the death of Esarhaddon and Šamaš-šuma-ukīn's arrival in Babylon with the cult-statue of Marduk, it remains unlikely that the walls of the central courtyard and other structural parts of the main building had yet to be built at the time of Aššurbanipal's accession. What is probable, however, is that some, if not all, of the secondary brickwork known to have been the work of Aššurbanipal, rather than his father — the raising and repaving of the floors, and maybe the addition of the *kisû* on the exterior walls — dated to this time."

[109] Esagil and Etemenanki were located in the Eridu quarter of Babylon, not in Šuanna as Ashurbanipal's inscriptions record.

[110] This work is attested from numerous bricks with a nine-line Akkadian inscription (Asb. 247) stamped into them. They come from Floor k (3rd pavement) and Floor l (4th pavement); see Pedersén, Babylon p. 143; and the catalogue of Asb. 247 in the present volume.

[111] George, House Most High p. 156 no. 1176.

[112] The wood was probably supplied by one or more of Assyria's vassals in the Levant. It is possible that Ba'alu of Tyre, Milki-ašapa of Byblos, Iakīn-Lû (Ikkilû) of Arwad, and Abī-Ba'al of Samsimurruna aided in the transport of the timber.

wood,[113] juniper (*burāšu*), and cedar in its (principal) gateways; and donated metal, wooden, and stone vessels for the cult. With regard to Etemenanki, he had its massive brick structure completed. In addition, Ashurbanipal claims to have built anew Ekarzagina ("House, Quay of Lapis Lazuli" or "House, Pure Quay"), the temple of the god Ea); Eturkalama ("House, Cattle-Pen of the Land"), the temple of Ištar of Babylon (Bēlet-Bābili), and Emaḫ ("Exalted House"), the temple of the goddess Ninmaḫ.[114] The arduous task of finishing the construction of Imgur-Enlil and Nēmetti-Enlil, the (inner) wall (*dūru*) and outer wall (*šalḫû*), was also accomplished;[115] this included hanging new doors in the (eight) city gates.[116]

At various times between 668 and 652, Ashurbanipal made significant donations to Marduk in Esagil. After the Egyptian metropolis Thebes was captured and plundered (ca. 664), the Assyrian army brought an abundance of gold, silver, and *zaḫalû*-metal back to the Assyrian capital Nineveh.[117] Two obelisks that were reported to have been "cast with shiny *zaḫalû*-metal" and to have weighed 2,500 talents (*biltu*) each, provided Ashurbanipal with a massive amount of metal for making the temples of his patron deities shine like daylight.[118] Esagil was one of the beneficiaries of Assyria's successes in Egypt. Ashurbanipal created an entirely new throne-dais (*paramāḫu*) for Marduk, one more resplendent than Aššur's Dais of Destinies in Ešarra at Aššur.[119] This new seat, which might have gone by the name "Tiʾāmat,"[120] was constructed from bricks cast from 50 talents (1,500 kg/3307 lbs) of *zaḫalû*-metal.[121] Around the same time, or in conjunction with the creation of the cast-brick throne-dais, Ashurbanipal had his craftsmen build a canopy (*ermi Anu*) from *musukkannu*-wood

---

113 On the identification of *musukkannu*-wood as *Dalbergia sissoo*, see, for example, Postgate, BSA 6 (1992) p. 183.

114 George, House Most High p. 108 no. 569, p. 119 no. 715 and p. 151 no. 1117. For Emaḫ, see also Pedersén, Babylon pp. 181–189. Ekarzagina and Eturkalama were located in the Esagil temple complex, whereas Emaḫ was in the Ka-dingirra district, which was north of the Eridu district. Although Ashurbanipal states that he built Ekarzagina and Eturkalama anew (Asb. 244 and 246), it is possible that Esarhaddon had already taken some steps to renovate those two temples. This is suggested by the fact that Ashurbanipal's father states that he refurbished the statues of Bēlet-Bābili (Ištar) and Ea, together with those of Marduk, Bēltīya (Zarpanītu), and Mandānu. Because Ashurbanipal reports that these two religious structures were "built anew" (*eššiš ušēpiš*), it is quite possible that little had been accomplished on Ekarzagina's and Eturkalama's rebuilding during Esarhaddon's reign and, therefore, Ashurbanipal felt that he could take full credit for these two temple's reconstructions; note also that he does not refer to his father's work on Babylon's city walls. Because the passage recording Marduk's return in the so-called "School Days Inscription" refers to the area of Ea's temple as Karzagina ("Quay of Lapis Lazuli"), instead of Ekarzagina ("House, Quay of Lapis Lazuli"), like his father Esarhaddon does, one could tentatively suggest that the brick structure of Ekarzagina had not been built by II-668 and, therefore, Ashurbanipal's statement about him constructing Ea's temple anew was not unfounded; compare Jeffers and Novotny, RINAP 5/2 p. 327 Asb. 220 [L^4] iii 19′ to Leichty, RINAP 4 Esarhaddon 60 (Aššur-Babylon E) line 46′. In addition, it is likely that Ashurbanipal also worked on Erabriri ("House of the Shackle Which Holds in Check"), the temple of the god Mandānu, which was inside the Esagil temple complex, since that deity's statue was returned to Babylon in II-668; see George, House Most High p. 137 no. 936.

115 Asb. 241 (lines 16b–22) does not refer at all to his father's work on Imgur-Enlil and Nēmetti-Enlil. That text records that Ashurbanipal rebuilt (that section of) Babylon's inner and outer walls because they had become old and had buckled or collapsed. This might imply that Esarhaddon had not yet started work on that stretch of Imgur-Enlil and Nēmetti-Enlil or that the work was still in the early stages of construction. Cyrus II, in his so-called "Cyrus Cylinder Inscription" (Schaudig, Inschriften Nabonids pp. 550–556), mentions that he discovered foundation documents of Ashurbanipal in the mudbrick structure of Babylon's walls when he was rebuilding them.

116 None of Babylon's eight city gates are mentioned by name in Ashurbanipal's inscriptions. These gates, starting with the southwesternmost gate of east Babylon, and moving counterclockwise, are the Uraš Gate (Ikkibšu-nakarī), the Zababa Gate (Izēr-âršu), the Marduk Gate (Šuʾâšu-rēʾi), the Ištar Gate (Ištar-sākipat-tēbîšu), the Enlil Gate (Enlil-munabbiršu), the King's Gate (Libūr-nādûšu), the Adad Gate (Adad-napišti-ummāni-uṣur), and the Šamaš Gate (Šamaš-išid-ummāni-kīn).

117 In Asb. 3 (Prism B) ii 26–34a (Novotny and Jeffers, RINAP 5/1 p. 61), for example, Ashurbanipal states: "[Si]lver, gold, precious stones, as much property of his palace as there was, garment(s) with multi-colored trim, linen garments, large horses, people — male and female — two tall obelisks cast with shiny *zaḫalû*-metal, whose *weight* was 2,500 talents (and which) stood at a temple gate, I ripped (them) from where they were erected and took (them) to Assyria. I carried off substantial booty, (which was) without number, from inside the city Thebes."

118 The two obelisks were removed from a temple at Thebes (possibly the Amun temple at Karnak). Some scholars have suggested that the (seven-meter-tall) obelisks were solid metal and date to the reign of Tuthmosis III (1504–1450). For this opinion, see, for example, Desroches-Noblecourt, Revue d'Égyptologie 8 (1951) pp. 47–61; Aynard, Prisme pp. 23–25; Kitchen, Third Intermediate Period[4] p. 394 (with n. 891); and Onasch, ÄAT 27/1 p. 158. Note that A.L. Oppenheim (ANET[3] p. 295 n. 13) has proposed that the obelisks were only metal plated.

According to M.A. Powell (RLA 7/7–8 [1990] p. 510 §V.6), one talent was approximately thirty kilograms (= sixty minas). Thus, each obelisk might have weighed about 75,000 kg (165,346 lbs) and, therefore, the pair might have yielded around 150,000 kg (330,693 lbs) of *zaḫalû*-metal. At least seventy talents (2,100 kg/4630 lbs) of that silver alloy was used to decorate the cella of the moon-god Sîn's temple Eḫulḫul; see Novotny, Studia Chaburensia 8 pp. 78–80; and Jeffers and Novotny, RINAP 5/2 p. 25 (with n. 109).

119 As for the Dais of Destinies (*parak šīmāte*), Esarhaddon (Leichty, RINAP 4 p. 136 Esarhaddon 60 lines 26′–29′a) records that he had it entirely rebuilt from *ešmarû*-metal and had images of both him and his son Ashurbanipal (then heir designate) depicted on its outer facing. For further details, see Grayson and Novotny, RINAP 3/2 pp. 21–22 (esp. n. 56).

120 George, BTT pp. 44–45 no. 1 (Tintir) Tablet II line 1. According to A.R. George (ibid. pp. 268–269), "Tiʾāmat" was the seat of Marduk (Bēl) in Eumuša, the cella of Marduk in Esagil. According to Asb. 15 ii 19–21 (Novotny and Jeffers, RINAP 5/1 p. 282), the throne-dais was "[placed over the massive body of the ro]iling [sea (Tiāmat)]."

121 For the opinion that the *zaḫalû*-metal came from the obelisks plundered from Thebes, see Onasch, ÄAT 27/1 p. 80 n. 386 and pp. 156–158 and 161; and Novotny, Orientalia NS 72 (2003) pp. 211–215.

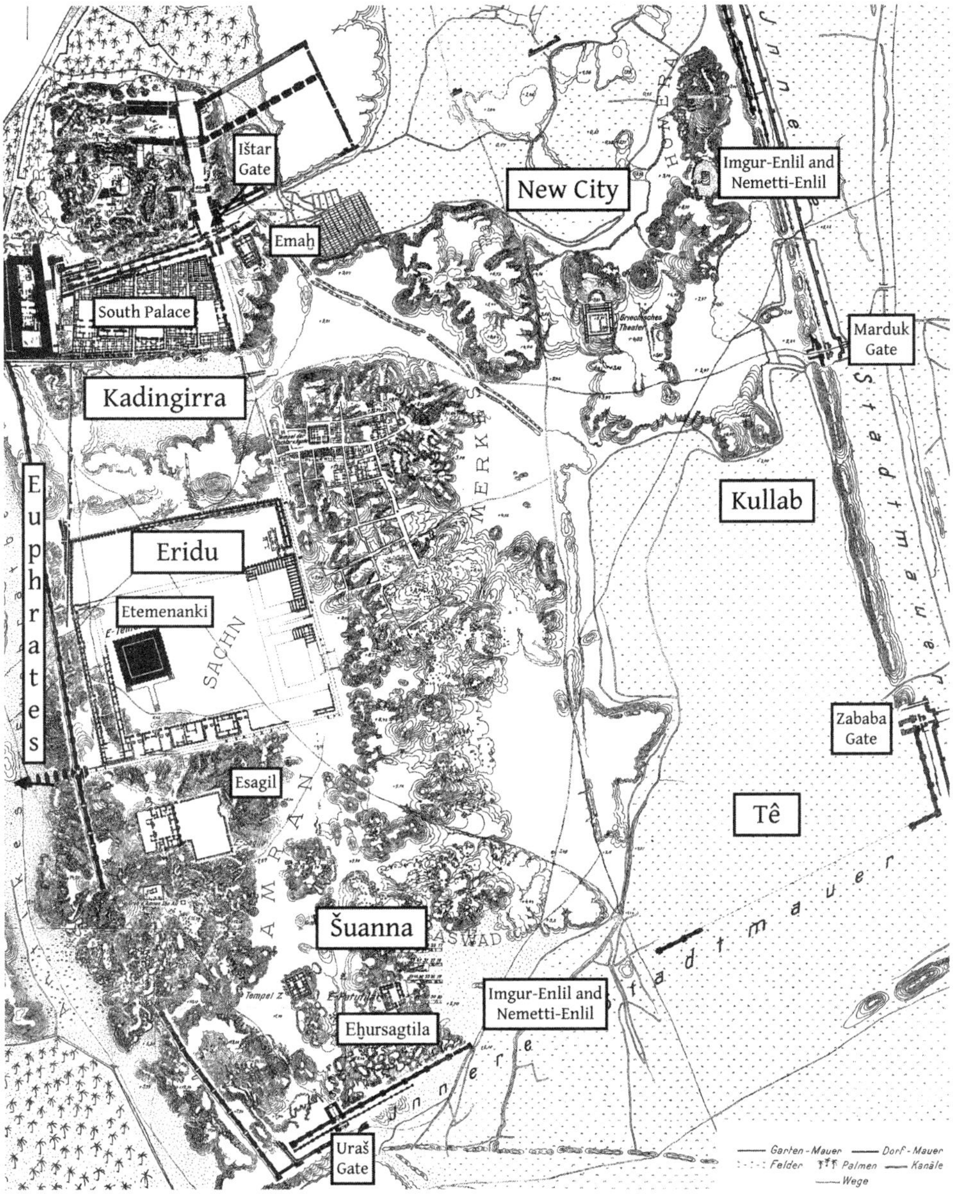

Figure 2. Annotated plan of the ruins of the eastern half of the inner city of Babylon. Adapted from Koldewey, WEB[5] fig. 256.

and clad with thirty-four talents and twenty minas (1020.8 kg/2250 lbs) of reddish gold. That covering was stretched out over Marduk's statue, which sat atop the throne-dais.

In 656, or at the very beginning of 655 at the latest, Ashurbanipal was made aware of the fact that several objects of Marduk and his wife Zarpanītu that had been taken to Assyria by his grandfather Sennacherib in 689 in the wake of the destruction and plundering of Babylon and Esagil were still in the Aššur temple at Aššur. Sennacherib had given Babylon's tutelary deity's bed (*eršu*) and throne (*kussû*) to the Assyrian national god as part of his religious reforms that made the Aššur cult more like that of Marduk's at Babylon.[122] Before

[122] During his final years on the throne (late 689–681), Sennacherib instituted numerous religious reforms, the foremost being the remodeling of the temple, cult, and New Year's festival of the god Aššur at Aššur on those of Babylon, and having Assyrian scribes (re)write *Enūma eliš* so that the Assyrian Empire's national god, rather the Babylon's tutelary deity Marduk, was the chief protagonist and the city of Aššur, instead of Babylon, was the bond that held the universe together. For Sennacherib's religious reforms, see in particular Machinist, Wissenschaftskollegs zu Berlin Jahrbuch (1984–85) pp. 353–364; Frahm, Sanherib pp. 20 and 282–288; and Vera Chamaza, Omnipotenz pp. 111–167.

dedicating those objects to Aššur, Sennacherib had his scribes place inscriptions written in his name on them.[123] When Ashurbanipal learned of this appropriation of cultic objects, he reclaimed the bed and throne for Marduk. First, he had his scribes make copies of his grandfather's inscription(s) and record detailed descriptions of the objects.[124] Next, he had the metal-plating with Sennacherib's inscriptions removed, had the bed and throne refurbished, and had those objects clad anew with metal platings bearing Ashurbanipal's own dedicatory inscription.[125] At the same time, Ashurbanipal had a new chariot (*narkabtu*) made for Babylon's patron god. That exquisite gift was adorned with trappings of gold, silver, and precious stones; the metal plating probably bore (an) Akkadian inscription(s). The bed, throne, and chariot entered Esagil on 27-III-655.[126] The bed was placed in Kaḫilisu ("Gate Sprinkled with Luxuriance"), the bed chamber (*maštaku*) of Zarpanītu.[127] The dedication of these items by Ashurbanipal might have caused a bit of friction with Šamaš-šuma-ukīn, who was losing patience with his brother's constant interference in internal religious and political affairs of Babylonia. These actions might have widened the rift between the two brothers.

Ashurbanipal also had an ornately-decorated writing board (*lē'u*) dedicated to Marduk. Unfortunately, the clay tablet upon which this copy of the text is written is not sufficiently preserved to be able to determine when the text was composed or when the writing board, which bore an image of the Assyrian king, was placed in Esagil.[128]

---

[123] These texts were dedicatory inscriptions, with Aššur as the divine recipient. For the inscription(s) written on the appropriated bed and throne of Marduk, see Grayson and Novotny, RINAP 3/2 p. 227 Sennacherib 161 lines 1–20 and pp. 229–231 Sennacherib 162 ii 1–iii 16′. According to the subscript of Sennacherib 161 (Grayson and Novotny, RINAP 3/2 p. 228 rev. 9′–11′), the same inscription was written on the throne. That scribal note also states that the text written on a chest (*pitnu*) was not copied. The two tablets bearing these texts were inscribed by Ashurbanipal's scribes in 656 or in early 655, sometime before 27-III-655. For details, see Grayson and Novotny, RINAP 3/2 p. 8 and 225–229; and Jeffers and Novotny, RINAP 5/2 pp. 8–9.

[124] For the texts, see the note immediately above. For the description of the bed, see Grayson and Novotny, RINAP 3/2 p. 228 Sennacherib 161 rev. 1′–2′ and p. 231 Sennacherib 162 iii 17′–29′. For that of Marduk's throne, see ibid p. 228 Sennacherib 161 rev. 3′–8′ and p. 231 Sennacherib 162 iii 30′–35′.

[125] For a copy of that text, see Jeffers and Novotny, RINAP 5/2 pp. 333–334 Asb. 223 iv 1′–29′. K 2411, the tablet inscribed with that text, was composed shortly after 27-III-655.

[126] For the date, see Jeffers and Novotny, RINAP 5/2 p. 333 Asb. 223 iii 36′–40′: "Wording (of the inscription) that was erased from the bed (and) the throne of the god Bēl (Marduk), which were deposited in the temple of (the god) Aššur, (and that of the inscription) written upon (them) in the name of Ashurbanipal. Simānu (III), the twenty-seventh day, eponymy of Awiānu (655), th[ey were returned t]o Ba[byl]on [(...)]." Marduk's throne is not specifically mentioned or referred to in Ashurbanipal's own inscriptions. This is in contrast to the bed and the chariot, which are regularly mentioned in the prologues of that king's inscriptions. See, for example, Novotny and Jeffers, RINAP 5/1 p. 216 Asb. 10 (Prism T) i 39–54.

The Šamaš-šuma-ukīn Chronicle (Novotny and Jeffers, RINAP 5/1 pp. 34–35) line 4 records that the "former bed of the god Bēl" returned to Babylon in the 14th year. The text, at least according for the entry for the 4th year (lines 2–3), should be dated by the regnal years of Šamaš-šuma-ukīn, and, therefore, the return of Marduk's bed occurred in 654 (Šamaš-šuma-ukīn 14th year = Ashurbanipal's 15th year), which is a year later than is recorded by contemporary inscriptions (Novotny and Jeffers, RINAP 5/1 pp. 354–256 Asb. 61; and Jeffers and Novotny, RINAP 5/2 p. 333 Asb. 223 iii 36′–40′), which state that the bed (and throne) of Marduk were returned early in the eponymy of Awiānu, governor of Que. That official, at least according to the so-called "Eponym Lists" (Millard, SAAS 2 p. 53 sub 655 A3 v 5′), was *limmu* in Ashurbanipal's 14th regnal year (655). It is not impossible that the author/compiler of the Šamaš-šuma-ukīn Chronicle confused Šamaš-šuma-ukīn's and Ashurbanipal's regnal years, and wrote down 14th year (which would be correct for the Assyrian king, but not for the king of Babylon) rather than 13th year (which would be correct for the king of Babylon, but not for the king of Assyria). The same confusion seems to have taken place for the 15th year in line 5 (of the Šamaš-šuma-ukīn Chronicle). The scribe dates the entry of the "new chariot of the god Bēl" to the 15th year, which surely must be to Ashurbanipal's 15th year as king (654 = Year 14 of the king of Babylon), rather than Šamaš-šuma-ukīn's 15th regnal year (653).

The date for the entry of Marduk's new chariot into Babylon seems to conflict with two inscriptions of Ashurbanipal, which imply that the chariot was already given to Marduk in 655, probably before 27-III of that year. The inscriptions in question are Novotny and Jeffers, RINAP 5/1 pp. 354–256 Asb. 61; and Jeffers and Novotny, RINAP 5/2 pp. 331–334 Asb. 223, which were written in VII-655 and shortly after 27-III-655 respectively. Assuming that Ashurbanipal dedicated the chariot at the same time as Marduk's bed, as that king's inscriptions suggest, then the compiler of the Šamaš-šuma-ukīn Chronicle, for reasons unknown, recorded the receipt of the Assyrian king's donations to Marduk in two separate and sequential years, rather than in one and the same year. This (arbitrary) splitting of events over two years also happens for entries in the Babylonian Chronicle for Esarhaddon's 4th and 5th regnal years (677 and 676). In the Chronicle Concerning the Period from Nabû-nāṣir to Šamaš-šuma-ukīn and the Esarhaddon Chronicle (Leichty, RINAP 4 pp. 7–8), the decapitations of Abdi-Milkūti of Sidon and Sanda-uarri of Kundu and Sissû are erroneously recorded as taking place at the end of the 5th year (676), rather than at the end of the 4th year (677), after the capture of the Phoenician city Sidon. It is clear from Esarhaddon's own inscriptions, in particular, "Nineveh B" (Leichty, RINAP 4 pp. 27–35 Esarhaddon 2), that Abdi-Milkūti and Sanda-uarri were beheaded in late 677. It is certain since the earliest known copy of that text (ex. 1 [IM 59046]) is dated to 22-II-676, which is over four months before VII-676 and XII-676, when those rulers lost their heads according to the chronicles. That error in dating in the Babylonian Chronicle has been long known; see, for example, Tadmor, Studies Grayson p. 272. The entries for the return of Marduk's bed and entry of his new chariot into Babylon might contain a similarly erroneous account of events.

[127] George, House Most High p. 107 no. 555. Kaḫilisu is a byname of Eḫalanki ("House of the Secrets of Heaven and Netherworld") and named in Ashurbanipal's inscriptions instead of Edara'ana ("House of the Ibex of Heaven"), the actual name of the cella of Zarpanītu in Esagil. The destinations of the throne and chariot are not recorded in Ashurbanipal's inscriptions.

[128] Clay tablet 81-7-27,70 = Jeffers and Novotny, RINAP 5/2 pp. 342–343 Asb. 226.

After the suppression of the Šamaš-šuma-ukīn rebellion (sometime after V-648) and while Kandalānu (647–627) was king of Babylon, Ashurbanipal continued to undertake building projects in Babylon. Probably in 647, he made repairs to Duku ("Pure Mound"), the seat of Marduk as Lugaldimmeranki in Ubšukkina ("Court of Assembly") in Esagil.[129] This part of Babylon's most sacred building might have sustained damage during the Brothers' War. Much later in his reign, around his 30th regnal year (639), Ashurbanipal is known to have sponsored construction at Babylon. Sometime before II-639, he dedicated an (inscribed) and reddish-gold-plated ebony bed to Marduk, renovated a sanctuary of Marduk, and began rebuilding Esabad ("House of the Open Ear"), the temple of the goddess Gula in the Tuba quarter in west Babylon.[130] In 638 (or slightly later, perhaps in 637), construction on Esabad was completed.[131] After finishing Gula's temple, or shortly before completing its construction, Ashurbanipal renovated Marduk's *akītu*-house, which was located outside of the city, north of the Ištar Gate.[132] In and after 639 and 638, the Assyrian king had utensils of metal and stone, including two gold baskets (*masabbu*), made for Esagil.[133]

It is possible that Ashurbanipal worked on other temples around this same time, perhaps the Ninurta temple Eḫursagtila ("House Which Exterminates the Mountains"),[134] a sacred building located in Šuanna quarter of east Babylon. Ashurbanipal, or possibly Esarhaddon, might be the unnamed former king who the founder of the Neo-Babylonian Empire, Nabopolassar (625–605), claims had started building the temple but had not completed its construction.[135] If Ashurbanipal was in fact a previous builder of Eḫursagtila, then it is probable that work began on the temple (shortly) before his death in 631, which might explain why it was never finished.[136]

Borsippa

Sometime between 668 and 652, Ashurbanipal set up four silver-plated (and inscribed) statues of wild bulls (*rīmu*) in two prominent gateways of Ezida ("True House"), the temple of the god Nabû at Borsippa: in the Gate of the Rising Sun and the Gate of Lamma-RA.BI.[137] Later in his reign, sometime after V-648 and before 6-II-639, although Kandalānu was the king of Babylon, Ashurbanipal stationed an additional pair of wild bulls in the Luguduene Gate, as well as outfitting the god of scribes' temple with lavish appurtenances and architectural features, including (re)casting Kizalaga ("Bright Place"), the seat of the god Nūru, from a large amount of

---

[129] George, House Most High p. 77 no. 180 and p. 154 no. 1160. The full names of Duku and Ubšukkina are Dukukinamtartarrede ("Pure Mound Where Destinies are Determined") and Ubšukkinamezuhalhala ("Court of the Assembly Which Allots the Known *Mes*"). The byname of Duku is *parak šīmāti* ("Dais of Destinies").

[130] The ebony bed and the sanctuary (*ayyakku*) are both mentioned in Asb. 22 (i 1′–4′; Novotny and Jeffers, RINAP 5/1 pp. 293), an inscription whose approximate date of composition is ca. 642–640. Work on Gula's temple was presumably underway when Asb. 12 (Prism H; ibid. pp. 265–271) was composed. The principal copy of that text (EŞ 7832), whose now-lost building account would have recorded the rebuilding of Esabad, was inscribed on 6-II-639.

[131] Esabad was completed before Asb. 13 (Prism J: Novotny and Jeffers, RINAP 5/1 pp. 271–278) and Asb. 23 (IIT; ibid. pp. 296–311) were composed. Those two texts were written no earlier than Ashurbanipal's 31st regnal year (638). The date of Prism J is not preserved on any of the known exemplars of that text and the limestone slab engraved with the IIT text is not dated.

[132] The Sumerian ceremonial name of the *akītu*-house at Babylon is Esiskur ("House of the Sacrifice"); see George, House Most High p. 142 no. 993. Work on the temple was in progress when Asb. 13 (Prism J; Novotny and Jeffers, RINAP 5/1 pp. 271–278) was composed and, thus, it might have been completed in 638 (or in 637), perhaps before the fall New Year's festival in the month Tašrītu (VII).

[133] One of the baskets was inscribed with a fifty-line inscription, while the other had a fifty-five-line text written on it. These Akkadian inscriptions are Asb. 224 and 225 respectively, which were composed sometime after 638 since they mention the Cimmerian ruler Tugdammî's successor Sandak-šatru; see Jeffers and Novotny, RINAP 5/2 pp. 334–342.

[134] George, House Most High p. 102 no. 489; and Pedersén. Babylon pp. 190–193.

[135] Weisershäuser and Novotny, RINBE 1/1 Nabopolassar 7 (Eḫursagtila Cylinder) lines 22–24; see also Da Riva, SANER 3 pp. 54 §2.2.2 (É-PA-GÌN-ti-la Inscription [C12]).

[136] No remains of this stage of the temple's history ("Level 0") have been excavated. The earliest phase of construction ("Level 1") dates to the time of Nabopolassar. See Pedersén. Babylon pp. 190–193 for details. Note that a single brick inscribed with a Sumerian inscription of Esarhaddon (BE 15316; Leichty, RINAP 4 pp. 256–258 Esarhaddon 126 ex. 1) was discovered in the Ninurta temple, in the South gate, courtyard door, which might point to Esarhaddon having worked on Eḫursagtila. Despite Aššur-etel-ilāni's short reign (see below), one cannot entirely exclude the possibility that he, rather than his father or grandfather, undertook construction on Ninurta's temple at Babylon. Given the current textual record, it seems more likely that the unnamed previous building of that sacred structure was Ashurbanipal.

[137] Novotny and Jeffers, RINAP 5/1 p. 104 Asb. 5 (Prism I) ii 6–8; p. 114 Asb. 6 (Prism C) i 44′–47′; p. 139 Asb. 7 (Prism Kh) i 14′–17′; p. 216 Asb. 10 (Prism T) ii 1–6; and Jeffers and Novotny, RINAP 5/2 p. 308 Asb. 215 (Edition L) i 26′–29′: and p. 354 Asb. 229 i 10′–13′. Ashurbanipal's father Esarhaddon and the Neo-Babylonian king Nabonidus also set up statues of wild bulls in gateways of Ezida. See Leichty, RINAP 4 p. 117 Esarhaddon 54 (Smlt.) rev. 10b–16a; and Weiershäuser and Novotny, RINBE 2 p. 76 Nabonidus 4 Frgm. 7 ii′ 1′–11′. Tablet fragment K 6806 (Asb. 1028) preserves parts of the last two lines of an inscription that was written on the metal plating of wild bulls erected in Ezida at Borsippa, which is evident from the subscript (rev. 3′), which reads "That which (is written) upon the wild bulls of Borsippa [(...)]." It is uncertain if this inscription was composed in the name of Esarhaddon or Ashurbanipal. For information on this Ezida temple, see George, House Most High pp. 159–160 no. 1236.

zaḫalû-metal (a silver alloy); setting up silver(-plated) *pirkus* (meaning uncertain) in the gates Kamaḫ and Kanamtila; and fashioning a reddish gold threshold (*askuppu*).[138]

In addition, prior to the outbreak of the Brothers' War in 652, Ashurbanipal restored Borsippa's city wall, Ṭābi-supūršu ("Its Fold Is Pleasant").[139]

Cutha

During his third decade as king, while Kandalānu sat on the throne of Babylon, Ashurbanipal had Emeslam ("House, Warrior of the Netherworld"), the temple of the god Nergal at Cutha, built anew "from its foundations to its crenellations."[140] That sacred building, according to preserved inscriptions, was in a woeful state of repair. Not only was its brick superstructure old, its foundations were out of alignment. In an auspicious month and on a propitious day, Ashurbanipal's workmen relaid Emeslam's foundations on their correct (divinely-sanctioned) positions, together with the appropriate accompanying foundation deposits. The new temple was built in accordance with the craft of the brick-god Kulla and with crushed pieces of aromatics ceremoniously mixed into (some of) the bricks.[141] The structure was adorned with a variety of woods (*musukkannu*-wood, KA-wood, ebony, boxwood, *ḫilēpu*-wood, and UMBIN-wood); its roof was made from long beams of cedar that had been imported from Mount Sirāra and Mount Lebanon in the Levant; and its doors were made from white cedar (*liāru*). In a gateway near Nergal's cella, Ashurbanipal stationed (metal-plated and inscribed) statues of lion-headed eagles (*anzû*).[142] As for when this work was carried out, it appears to have begun after Susa was looted and destroyed in 646, when the Assyrians brought back from the Elamite religious capital a statue of the goddess Nanāya, along with numerous other royal and divine objects looted from Babylonia (including Cutha) or sent there as bribes by former kings of Babylon, including his own brother Šamaš-šuma-ukīn. The project was probably completed sometime between 642 and 640.[143]

Dēr

After the Šamaš-šuma-ukīn rebellion was suppressed in 648, Ashurbanipal renovated, rebuilt, or repaired Edimgalkalama ("House, Great Bond of the Land"), the temple of the god Anu rabû, perhaps since it had sustained damage during that bloody, four-year war.[144] After the construction of its brick superstructure, which was said to have been "raised as high as a mountain," was completed, sometime before Abu (V) 645,[145] Ashurbanipal had its interior decorated and adorned with metal-plated objects and had its divine occupants (Anu rabû, Šarrat-Dēr, and Mār-bīti) placed once again on their daises.[146]

---

[138] Novotny and Jeffers, RINAP 5/1 p. 267 Asb. 12 (Prism H) i 4′–13′a; pp. 275–276 Asb. 13 (Prism J) ii 15′–30′; pp. 293–294 Asb. 22 i 5′–12′; and p. 303 Asb. 23 (IIT) lines 54–59.

[139] Asb. 253.

[140] Novotny and Jeffers, RINAP 5/1 p. 267 Asb. 12 (Prism H) i 13′b–25′; p. 291 Asb. 21 line 10′b–12′a; p. 294 Asb. 22 i 14′b–21′; and p. 303 Asb. 23 (IIT) lines 61b–63; and Jeffers and Novotny, RINAP 5/2 pp. 347–348 Asb. 227 (Nergal-Laṣ Inscription) rev. 18–29; p. 352 Asb. 228 (Nergal-Laṣ Inscription) rev. 27–28; p. 356 Asb. 229 v 1′′–3′′; and p. 357 Asb. 230 rev. i′ 2′–6′. For a brief study of Emeslam, see George, House Most High pp. 126–127 no. 802.

[141] Ashurbanipal claims that the bricks were fashioned in molds made from ebony and *musukkannu*-wood.

[142] There were statues of lion-headed eagles stationed in a gateway of Emeslam's cella (*papāḫu*) since the reign of the Ur III king Šulgi (2094–2047). See Frayne, RIME 3/2 p. 135 E3/2.1.2.26 rev. i 13′–14′.

[143] Susa was destroyed during Ashurbanipal's second war with Ummanaldašu (Ḫumban-ḫaltaš III), sometime before 1-IX-646 since the Assyrian king claims to have made the statue of Nanāya that he had found in that city enter its "rightful" place in Uruk on the first of Kislīmu (IX); see the section *Uruk* below for more details, as well as Novotny and Jeffers, RINAP 5/1 pp. 23–25 (for the Assyrian campaigns against the Elamite king Ummanaldašu). When items from Emeslam were returned to Cutha from Susa, probably on Ashurbanipal's return march home in 646 from Susa via Uruk, the Assyrian king might have seen the condition that Nergal's temple was in and decided to have it rebuilt and refurbished.

The date of completion is based on the proposed date of composition for Asb. 22, which is likely the earliest presently-attested inscription of Ashurbanipal recording work on Nergal's temple at Cutha; for details, see Novotny and Jeffers, RINAP 5/1 p. 293.

[144] Novotny and Jeffers, RINAP 5/1 p. 217 Asb. 10 (Prism T) iii 15–17; and p. 304 Asb. 23 (IIT) lines 73–75; and in the present volume Asb. 265 lines 1′–3′a. Work on the temple is also recorded in the historical-literary text written on K 2632 (Bauer, Asb. p. 76 and pls. 23–24 iii 17–20). For information about Edimgalkalama, see George, House Most High p. 76 no. 166; and Frahm, Studies Parpola pp. 51–64.

[145] The inclusion of the completion of Edimgalkalama in the prologue of Asb. 10 (Prism T: Novotny and Jeffers, RINAP 5/1 pp. 209–221, specifically p. 217 iii 15–17) seems to indicate that construction on that sacred building had come to an end. K 1729 (ex. 2) is the earliest dated copy of that inscription and it was inscribed on 6-V-645 (eponymy of Nabû-šar-aḫḫēšu). On the date of that post-canonical eponym, see Novotny and Jeffers, RINAP 5/1 p. 32.

[146] Asb. 23 (IIT) lines 74–75 (Novotny and Jeffers, RINAP 5/1 p. 304) record that Ashurbanipal had Great Anu's (Ištarān's) *musukkannu*-wood seat (*šubtu*) clad with silver (*kaspu*) and that he had had another item made from silver and reddish gold (*ḫurāṣu ruššû*). The inscription is not sufficiently preserved to be able to determine what that item might have been.

Dūr-Kurigalzu

Ashurbanipal repaired Enlil's ziggurat at Dūr-Kurigalzu.[147] This work is attested from a single inscribed brick built into the southwest façade of the temple-tower.[148]

Mê-Turān

A large number of bricks discovered at Tell Ḥaddād attest to Ashurbanipal's building activities at Mê-Turān.[149] The Akkadian inscription written on those square bricks, which were found in situ, state that the Assyrian king enlarged the courtyard of Ešaḫula ("House of the Happy Heart"), the temple of the god Nergal in that city[150] and made its processional way "shine like daylight." The inscribed bricks, which are said to have been baked in a "(ritually) pure kiln" (*utūnu elletu*), were used to pave the temple's courtyard and processional way.

Nippur

Just like his father Esarhaddon, Ashurbanipal rebuilt Ekur ("House, Mountain"), the temple of the god Enlil at Nippur.[151] Moreover, he restored the Egigunû, the temple on top of Enlil's ziggurat, together with some part of its cella Eḫursaggalama ("House, Skillfully-Built Mountain" or "House Stepped Mountain).[152] Numerous stamped and inscribed bricks attest to the renovations. Work on the ziggurat temple was carried out since its enclosure wall (*igāru*) had become old and eroded, perhaps due to water damage.[153] Since Ashurbanipal refers to himself as "the king of the land of Sumer and Akkad" in an Akkadian inscription written on a clay cylinder recording the renovation of that sacred building, the work at Nippur was probably carried out at a time when there was no separate king of Babylon, or at least not one acknowledged by the text's composer(s).[154] Thus, Ashurbanipal probably sponsored the work sometime after the suppression of the Šamaš-šuma-ukīn rebellion (652–648). The pro-Assyrian governor (*šandabakku*) of Nippur, Enlil-bāni, assuming he was still in office at the time, might have overseen the work on Ashurbanipal's behalf.[155]

It is possible that Ashurbanipal might have also worked on Nippur's city wall, but that project is not attested in the extant textual record.[156]

Sippar

While Šamaš-šuma-ukīn was king of Babylon and certainly before his older brother incited a rebellion against him in 652, Ashurbanipal sponsored work on the most important Babylonian temple of the sun-god: Ebabbar ("Shining House"), the temple of Šamaš at Sippar.[157] Few details about the project itself are recorded in contemporary sources, but the construction, as is usually the case, was undertaken because the temple's

---

[147] Asb. 256. According to the Kuyunjik Ziggurat List (George, House Most High p. 46 no. 4: 7), the Sumerian ceremonial name of the ziggurat was Egirin ("Pure House"). On the reading of KUR.TI.KI as Dūr-Kurigalzu (or its older name Parsâ), see George, House Most High p. 45, commentary to no. 3 line 42′.

[148] The brick is reported to have been reused, that is, it was not found in its original position.

[149] Asb. 257.

[150] George, House Most High p. 144 no. 1020. Ešaḫula was located in Sirara, the temple district of Mê-Turān.

[151] Asb. 258–261. For Esarhaddon's Nippur inscriptions, see Leichty, RINAP 4 pp. 260–270 Esarhaddon 128–132. For Ekur's building history, see George, House Most High p. 116 no. 677.

[152] George, House Most High p. 92 no. 373 and pp. 100-101 no. 480; and Sjöberg, Temple Hymns p. 50. For a study of Ashurbanipal's work on the ziggurat, see Clayden and Schneider, Kaskal 12 (2015) pp. 349–382. Asb. 258 (lines 15–19) gives the impression that Egigunû was the ziggurat, but it is more likely only the temple on top of it, as A.R. George (House Most High p. 92 no. 373) has already suggested. Moreover, Egigunû might be a noun (with É as a preceding determinative for a building), rather than a ceremonial name; see, for example, CAD G pp. 67–70 sub *gigunû*. Thus, one might read Asb. 258 line 15 as É.*gi-gu-nu-ú ziq-qur-rat* NIBRU.KI, "the sacred building of the ziggurat of Nippur," instead of *é-gi-gu-nu-ú ziq-qur-rat* NIBRU.KI, "Egigunû, the ziggurat of Nippur." It is unclear what part of Eḫursaggalama Ashurbanipal had repaired since the reading of the relevant passage in Asb. 261 (line 10) is uncertain and differs in the known copies of the text.

[153] The known exemplars of Asb. 261 are both well-head bricks, which means that they were intended to be used in a round well or conduit. This might support the notion that the ziggurat and its sacred temple had sustained damage from water. On the conduit built by Ashurbanipal on the northeast façade of the ziggurat, see Clayden and Schneider, Kaskal 12 (2015) pp. 364–365 and 367.

[154] Asb. 258 (line 10). On the date, see the commentary to that text, as well as Clayden and Schneider, Kaskal 12 (2015) p. 354. As noted by G. Frame (RIMB 2 p. 220), the work could have been carried out during the rebellion, but that would be highly unusual since Babylonia was in turmoil.

[155] For details on this important man, see Frame, Babylonia p. 121; Cole, SAAS 4 pp. 54–55; Weszeli, PNA 2/1 p. 519 sub Illil-bāni no. 2; and Reynolds, SAA 18 p. XXXII.

[156] This wall was built on top of the Ur III city wall. Only one or two courses of this five-meter-thick wall have survived. For details, including its attribution to Ashurbanipal, see Gibson, Zettler, and Armstrong, Sumer 39 (1983) pp. 177 and 184–189.

[157] Jeffers and Novotny, RINAP 5/2 pp. 358–359 Asb. 231; and in the present volume Asb. 262. For details about Ebabbar, see, for example, George, House Most High p. 70 no. 97 and Weiershäuser and Novotny, RINBE 2 pp. 9–10.

brickwork was old and needed to be replaced. We do know, however, that Ashurbanipal roofed Šamaš' earthly abode with cedar beams transported all the way from Mount Sirāra and Mount Lebanon in the Levant and had doors of cedar installed in its (principal) gateways.

Since one inscription states that Sippar was in an abysmal state before the work on Ebabbar had started, it is likely that Ashurbanipal, either on his own or in collaboration with Šamaš-šuma-ukīn, undertook other construction projects in that city.[158] For example, Ashurbanipal might have assisted his older brother when the latter had Sippar's city wall Badullisâ ("Wall Named in Ancient Times") rebuilt.[159]

Ur

At Ur, the most important cult center of the moon-god in Babylonia,[160] Sîn-balāssu-iqbi, the governor of that city, undertook construction on Sîn's temple Ekišnugal on behalf of the Assyrian king (Ashurbanipal), rather than on that of the king of Babylon (Šamaš-šuma-ukīn).[161] That important official, as far as his inscriptions are preserved, rebuilt and restored Eadgigi ("House of the Counsellor"), the abode of the god Nusku; Eankikuga ("House of Pure Heaven and Netherworld"), the station of the god Kusu; Eanšar, a "royal abode" (of Sîn?); É.AŠ.AN.AMAR (exact reading uncertain), the abode of the god Enlil; Eešbanda ("House Little Chamber"), the abode of the goddess Šuzianna; É.DUB.galekura (exact reading uncertain), the abode of the god Ninimma; Elugalgalgasisa ("House of the King who Lets Counsel Flourish"), the ziggurat; Ešaduga ("House Which Pleases the Heart"), the "abode of Enlilship" (of Sîn?); Etemennigurru ("House, Foundation Clad in Awe-Inspiring Radiance"), the ziggurat terrace; Eušumgalana ("House of the Dragon of Heaven"), the station of the goddess Ninkasi; É...gukuga (name not fully preserved), an abode or seat of the god Ennugi; Gipāru(ku), a sanctuary of the goddess Ningal; and Puḫilituma ("Well That Brings Luxuriance"), a well located in the temple complex. While carrying out the work, Sîn-balāssu-iqbi's workmen found an inscribed brick of the Ur III king Amar-Suena (2046–2038). Sîn-balāssu-iqbi had Nabû-šuma-iddin, a lamentation-priest of Sîn, make a copy of that text and had the new inscribed object, a clay drum-shaped object, deposited inside the structure of the moon-god's temple.[162] In addition, Sîn-balāssu-iqbi constructed a statue for Ningal and had it placed inside Gipāru. He also commissioned a new door for Etemennigurru, which he had placed on its former position and over a foundation deposit; the door was made from boxwood (Sumerian *taškarin*) and outfitted with silver and copper fixtures.

Uruk

While Šamaš-šuma-ukīn was king of Babylon and after Baʾalu of Tyre had reaffirmed his loyalty to Assyria (ca. 662)[163] and Ḫundāru of Dilmun became a tribute-paying client (or reconfirmed his status as such),[164]

---

[158] Jeffers and Novotny, RINAP 5/2 p. 358 Asb. 231 lines 3′b–5′a: "The city of privileged-status, which is depicted as the 'Crab' in the heavens and ... [...] its foundations were tottering. The abode of his city was torn out and one could not examine [its] structu[re ...] its [*plain*]s were full of lions instead of oxen and sheep."

[159] Frame, RIMB 2 pp. 249–251 B.6.33.1. The name of Sippar's city wall is called Baduldua ("Wall Built in Ancient Times") in the Kuyunjik Ziggurat List (George House Most High p. 47 no. 4 line 33).

[160] Ḫarrān, with its principal temple Eḫulḫul, located in the northwestern part of the Empire, near the Baliḫ River, was the most important cult center of Sîn in Assyria. See Novotny, Eḫulḫul; Groß, Kulturelle Schnittstelle pp. 139–154; Novotny, Studia Chaburensia 8 pp. 73–94; Weiershäuser and Novotny, RINBE 2 pp. 10–11; Hätinen, dubsar 20 *passim*, but particularly pp. 384-416; and Jeffers and Novotny, RINAP 5/2 pp. 23–25.

[161] Asb. 2003–2018; note that only Asb. 2006 and 2008–2009 specifically state that the work was carried out on Ashurbanipal's behalf. These inscriptions, nearly all of which were composed in Sumerian (rather than Akkadian), were written on a wide variety of objects: clay cones, clay disks, and clay drum-shaped objects, bricks, and a stone door socket (made from a reused boundary stone). For details on the Ekišnugal temple complex and its various temples, shrines, and sanctuaries, see George House Most High p. 65 no. 42 (Eadgigi), p. 67 no. 71 (Eankikuga), p. 68 no. 81 (Eanšar), p. 69 no. 91 (E.AŠ.AN.AMAR), p. 79 no. 202 (É.DUB.galekura) and no. 203 (Edublalmaḫ), p. 83 no. 265 (Eešbanda), p. 93 no. 385 (Egipgar), p. 114 no. 653 (Ekišnugal), p. 119 no. 706 (Elugalgalgasisa), p. 149 no. 1090 (Etemennigurru),p. 158 no. 1214 (Eušumgalana), and p. 161 no. 1255 (É-...gukuga); and Zettler and Hafford RLA 14/5–6 (2015) pp. 370–375 §3.1. For information about Sîn-balāssu-iqbi, a son of Ningal-iddin, see Brinkman, Orientalia NS 34 (1965) pp. 248–253; Frame, Babylonia pp. 98–101 and 278; Baker, PNA 3/1 pp. 1129–1130 sub Sîn-balāssu-iqbi no. 3; Brinkman, RLA 12/7–8 (2011) p. 514; and the general introduction to Asb. 2003–2018 in the present volume (p. 135).

[162] Asb. 2007. For the Amar-Suena inscription, see Frayne, RIME 3/2 pp. 256–257 E3/2.1.3.11.

[163] See Novotny and Jeffers, RINAP 5/1 pp. 17–18 for details and textual references.

[164] Dilmun is mentioned twice as a vassal of Assyria in extant inscriptions: once in Asb. 23 (Novotny and Jeffers, RINAP 5/1 p. 308 IIT lines 131b–132, as well as line 137) and once in Asb. 263 (line 9). It is clear from Asb. 263 that its ruler (Ḫundāru) was already sending regular payments to Assyria prior to the outbreak of the Šamaš-šuma-ukīn rebellion in 652 since the king of Babylon is mentioned favorably in that text. This is interesting since the only other inscription mentioning that king of Dilmun dates to ca. 638. For details about this ruler of Dilmun, who is also mentioned in royal correspondence, see Brinkman, PNA 2/1 p. 479 sub Ḫundāru 2.

Ashurbanipal repaired the enclosure wall of Eanna ("House of Heaven"), the temple of the goddess Ištar, at Uruk.[165]

During the second war with the Elamite king Ummanaldašu (Ḫumban-ḫaltaš III) in 646, the Assyrian army thoroughly looted and destroyed the important religious center Susa, together with its principal temples and ziggurat.[166] At least two inscriptions record the countless wonders that Ashurbanipal had discovered in that city's palaces and sacred buildings, which included royal and divine objects that had been looted from Babylonia by Elamite kings (on seven different occasions) or that had been sent there as bribes by former kings of Babylon, including his own brother Šamaš-šuma-ukīn.[167] Of the numerous items kept in Susa's treasuries, the most important, at least according to the textual record, was a statue of the goddess Nanāya, which Ashurbanipal believed had been carried off to Elam "1635 years" earlier (during the Old Babylonian Period).[168] That statue, together with those of the goddesses Uṣur-amassa and Urkayītu, which were apparently also discovered at Susa, was ceremoniously returned on 1-XI-646 to its "rightful" place in Eḫiliana ("House of the Luxuriance of Heaven"), which was located in the Eanna temple complex.[169] After this time, Ashurbanipal appears to have sponsored some work on Eḫiliana, but since none of the texts of this king (thought to be) written for objects deposited or displayed are sufficiently preserved, it is unclear what he did for Nanāya's cella

---

165 Asb. 263 (lines 22b–24a). For a brief history of Eanna, see George, House Most High pp. 67–68 no. 75.

166 For information about the Assyrian campaigns against the Elamite king Ummanaldašu, see Novotny and Jeffers, RINAP 5/1 pp. 23–25.

167 Novotny and Jeffers, RINAP 5/1 p. 202 Asb. 9 (Prism F) v 3–18 and p. 249 Asb. 11 (Prism A) vi 7–26.

168 Most inscriptions record the number of years that Nanāya was in Elam as 1,635, but a few texts state that she was in Susa either 1630, 1535, or 1530 years. For details, see Novotny and Jeffers, RINAP 5/1 p. 204 on-page note to Asb. 9 (Prism F) v 72. Asb. 227 obv. 12–15 (Jeffers and Novotny, RINAP 5/2 p. 346) states that Kudur-Nanḫundu, a king of Elam, abducted Nanāya. Scholars have identified that Elamite ruler with either (1) Kutir-Naḫḫunte I, a contemporary of the Old Babylonian kings Samsu-iluna (1749–1712) and Abī-ešuḫ (1711–1684), or (2) Kutir-Naḫḫunte III, an Elamite ruler who held authority in Babylonia after the fall of the Kassite Dynasty in the mid-12th century. For the proposal that it was the former Elamite ruler who had taken Nanāya's statue to Susa, see, for example, Scheil, RA 29 (1932) pp. 67–76, especially p. 76; König, RLA 2/5 (1938) p. 330; Hinz, RLA 6/5–6 (1983) pp. 383–384; van Koppen, Susa and Elam pp. 380–384 (with references to previous studies); and Janssen, NABU 2021/3 pp. 186–188 no. 81. For the suggestion that it was the later Kutir-Naḫḫunte III who had carried off the goddess Nanāya, see, for example, Stolper in Carter and Stolper, Elam pp. 88–89 n. 323; and Vallat, NABU 1993/1 pp. 25–26 no. 31 (with references to earlier studies). As pointed out by F. van Koppen (Susa and Elam p. 381), the Kutir-Naḫḫunte in question can only be the earlier Elamite ruler as it would be very difficult to reconcile the 1635-year span of time (*Distanzangabe*) with the later ruler; the abduction of the statue of Nanāya might have taken place while Abī-ešuḫ, Ḫammu-rāpi's grandson, was on the throne. He also suggested that Ashurbanipal's scholars arrived at the number 1635 using (a) source(s) comparable to the Babylonian King List A (Grayson, RLA 6/1–2 [1980] pp. 90–96 §3.3): "We are not familiar with the sources for Babylonian history used by Ashurbanipal's scholars, but may assume that their figures resembled those of the *Babylonian King List A*, with 368 years for the First Sealand Dynasty and 576 years and 9 months for the Kassite Dynasty" (van Koppen, Susa and Elam p. 381 n. 35). It is unclear, as stated already by van Koppen, precisely which Old Babylonian king's reign was the starting point used by Ashurbanipal's scholars to calculate the length of Nanāya's residence in the Elamite capital Susa. Recently, however, T. Janssen (NABU 2021/3 pp. 186–188) has suggested that the variant 1535-year span began with Abī-ešuḫ's immediate successor Ammī-ditāna (1683–1647) — thus excluding the reigns of Ḫammu-rāpi (1792–1750), Samsu-iluna, and Abī-ešuḫ — and ended with the battle of Tīl-Tūba in 653, rather than with the sack of Susa in 646, the year when Nanāya's statue was actually recovered and returned to its "rightful" place in Eḫiliana: 89 (Babylon I Dynasty after Abī-ešuḫ) + 368 (entire Sealand I Dynasty) + 576 (entire Kassite Dynasty) + 502 (post-Kassite period until 653) = 1535. If Janssen's proposal proves correct, in that the 1535 years begin after the reign of Abī-ešuḫ, then the more-commonly-used span of 1635 years would have placed that Urukian goddess' abduction during the first half of Ḫammu-rāpi's tenure as king. For the evidence that Kutir-Naḫḫunte I might have taken the statue of Nanāya while Abī-ešuḫ, Ḫammu-rāpi's grandson, was on the throne, see van Koppen, Susa and Elam pp. 380–384. As for the 1630-year span, could that number refer to the time from Ḫammu-rāpi's first regnal year to Ashurbanipal's first year as king? One arrives at that number as follows: 43 (Ḫammu-rāpi's reign) + 38 (Samsu-iluna's reign) + 28 (Abī-ešuḫ's reign) + 89 (Babylon I Dynasty after Abī-ešuḫ) + 368 (entire Sealand I Dynasty) + 577 (= 576 years and 9 months; entire Kassite Dynasty) + 487 (post-Kassite period until 668) = 1630. Given the variants 1635, 1535, and 1530, it is less certain that Ashurbanipal's scribes regarded the start of his reign as the end date of Nanāya's stay in Susa, which would have been far too early and, thus, the 1630-year period ended closer to that goddess' return to Uruk, perhaps even in 653, as Janssen has suggested. That proposal might find some contemporary textual support from Asb. 126 rev. 5–7 (Jeffers and Novotny, RINAP 5/2 p. 123), a damaged passage that seems to record that Ummanigaš (Ḫumban-nikaš II) — the son of Urtaku whom Ashurbanipal placed on the Elamite throne shortly after Teumman was beheaded during the battle at Tīl-Tūba in 653 — failed to send Nanāya's statue back to Uruk. The number 1630 in reports about the fifth Elamite campaign was changed to 1635, a figure that became the most-commonly-used *Distanzangabe*; for details, see Jeffers, ZA 108 (2018) pp. 215–216 §2.5. It is unlikely that the addition of five years was random and, therefore, there must be some logical explanation for the change. Perhaps this alteration (using exclusive counting) reflects the time between the death of Teumman in 653 — assuming that that year was the original endpoint of the 1630 (and 1530) years — and Ummanaldašu (Ḫumban-ḫaltaš III) assuming power in 648. Apart from the five-year period between the start of the Šamaš-šuma-ukīn rebellion in 651 and the sack of Susa in 646 (also using exclusive counting), the present authors are not aware of any major events in (Babylonia and) Elam that would have necessitated the five-year change. Assuming that Ashurbanipal's scribes' calculations were based on source(s) comparable to the Babylonian King List A, as van Koppen has suggested, then the 1530 and 1535 time spans would have placed Nanāya's departure at the beginning of Ammī-ditāna's reign (around his fifth year as king); and the 1630 and 1635 time spans would have regarded that event as having taken place during the reign of the more-famous Ḫammu-rāpi, who was a contemporary of Šamšī-Adad I (1813–1781), a ruler of Assyria well-known to Ashurbanipal's scribes. Given the lack of firm information from extant sources, these issues must remain a matter of speculation.

169 The date that Nanāya entered Eḫiliana is recorded in Novotny and Jeffers, RINAP 5/1 p. 251 Asb. 11 (Prism A) vi 122: *ina* ITI.GAN UD.1.KÁM "in the month Kislīmu (IX), on the first day." For details on Eḫiliana, see George, House Most High pp. 98–99 no. 459.

at Uruk after XI-646.[170] Because a statue of Nanāya was already in Eḫiliana at the time, as is clear from at least two inscriptions of his father Esarhaddon,[171] it is not known if Ashurbanipal replaced the then-residing Nanāya statue with the one he had taken from Susa or if that long-absent image was placed elsewhere in the Eanna complex. How this dilemma was resolved is not recorded in presently-available sources. It is certain, however, that Nabopolassar (625–605), returned the Nanāya statue that Ashurbanipal brought into Eḫiliana in 646 BC to Susa in his accession year (626) BC.[172]

A clay tablet containing an archival copy of an inscription of Ashurbanipal discovered at Uruk records that the Assyrian king had a metal-plated (and inscribed) ceremonial cart (*attaru*) dedicated to one of that city's gods or goddesses.[173] Given the poor state of preservation of that text, it is uncertain to whom the cart was given — Ištar, Nanāya, or some other deity (Uṣur-amassa or Urkayītu) — and when the inscription was composed, either before the outbreak of the Šamaš-šuma-ukīn rebellion in 652 or after the conclusion of the second war with Ummanaldašu in 646. Since Ištar was the goddess of war, it is likely that the cart had been dedicated to her, probably in connection with Ashurbanipal's restoration of Eanna's enclosure wall, sometime before 652, although this cannot be proven with certainty.

Ashurbanipal's Death

Classical sources give an account of the final days of the Assyrian Empire, an event also documented in one cuneiform source: the so-called "Fall of Nineveh Chronicle" (see the section *Chronicles* below for a translation). According to the "History of Persia" written by Ctesias of Cnidus,[174] a Greek physician living at the Persian court in the late 5th century, the "last" king of Assyria, Sardanapalus — a man identified with Ashurbanipal rather than his son Sîn-šarra-iškun, the last Assyrian king to have ruled from Nineveh — committed suicide when he thought that Nineveh was about to fall to the Babylonian and Median forces laying siege to his capital. This fictional account narrates the Assyrian king's tragic death as follows:

> Then the king [Sardanapalus] ... gave up hope of being saved. To avoid falling into the hands of the foes, he prepared a massive pyre in the palace and piled on it gold and silver, as well as all the royal garments; then he shut the concubines and eunuchs into a room which had been got ready in the midst of the pyre, and consigned himself together with them and the palace to the flames.[175]

This account, which inspired Lord Byron's tragedy *Sardanapalus* and Eugene Delacroix's *La mort de Sardanapale*,[176] appears to have conflated Ashurbanipal's death with that of his brother Šamaš-šuma-ukīn, who, according to Ashurbanipal's inscriptions, was burned alive in his palace in late 648,[177] or that of his son Sîn-šarra-iškun, who died when the Babylonians and Medes sacked Nineveh in 612.[178]

---

[170] Jeffers and Novotny, RINAP 5/2 pp. 359–368 Asb. 232–236. The subscript of Asb. 236 (ibid. p. 368 rev. ii′ 1′–2′) implies that the text written on the tablet to which fragment K 13360 belongs was inscribed on an object, possibly a foundation document (likely a clay prism), displayed or deposited in a (sacred) building at Uruk. The prominent mention of Nanāya indicates that the inscription was composed after that goddess' return to Eḫiliana in late 646. Work on Eḫiliana might have also been recorded in Novotny and Jeffers, RINAP 5/1 p. 291 Asb. 21 (line 12′), but that text is badly damaged, so it is unclear if it records Nanāya's return to Uruk or her return to Eḫiliana and Ashurbanipal's subsequent work on that sacred structure.

[171] Leichty, RINAP 4 p. 276 Esarhaddon 135 (Uruk C) lines 11–15 and p. 278 Esarhaddon 136 (Uruk D) lines 11–17. Esarhaddon's renovation of Eḫiliana was prompted by him returning the statue of Nanāya that his father Sennacherib had taken to Assyria in 693, after Assyrian troops had captured and looted Uruk and Eanna. For a letter recording some of the details of the repair of the statues of Uruk's deities, see Parpola SAA 10 pp. 284–285 no. 349. Esarhaddon claims that the Kassite king Nazi-Maruttaš (re)built or renovated that holy part of Eanna. If this reflects historical reality, then Nanāya's cult at Uruk, despite the abduction of its cult statue several hundreds of years earlier (see n. 168 above), had been restored in or before this time. Clearly, a new cult statue had been created and was worshipped in Eḫiliana from the Middle Babylonian Period onwards. Esarhaddon also names Erība-Marduk, a member of the Bīt-Yakīn tribe in the Sealand who became the king of Babylon, as a previous builder of Nanāya's cella. Erība-Marduk's work on Eanna was not favorably remembered in the Neo-Babylonian Period. For details, see Beaulieu, Pantheon of Uruk pp. 136–138; and Da Riva and Novotny, IOS Annual 22 pp. 21–22.

[172] This is recorded in the Chronicle Concerning the Early Years of Nabopolassar lines 15b–17 (see p. 43).

[173] Asb. 264. The opening dedication and building report are not preserved. The association of the inscription with Uruk is based solely on the provenance of the tablet (W 22669/3).

[174] For example, see Lenfant, Ctésias de Cnide; and Rollinger in Frahm, Companion to Assyria pp. 571–572.

[175] Kuhrt, Persian Empire p. 41 no. 16 §27.

[176] For images of Ashurbanipal in later tradition, see Frahm, Studies H. and M. Tadmor pp. 37*–48*. Because nothing about Ashurbanipal's death is recorded in cuneiform sources, it has been sometimes suggested that Ashurbanipal died by fire; see Frame, Babylonia p. 155.

[177] Novotny and Jeffers, RINAP 5/1 p. 158 Asb. 7 (Prism Kh) viii 55′–61′ and p. 243 Asb. 11 (Prism A) iv 46–52. W. von Soden, (ZA 62 [1972] pp. 84–85) has suggested that an official by the name of Nabû-qātē-ṣabat threw Šamaš-šuma-ukīn into the fire; for evidence against that proposal, see Frame, Babylonia p. 154 n. 101. Ctesias' account of the death of Ashurbanipal might have mistaken the death of the Assyrian king at Nineveh with that of the king of Babylon. If that Classical description of Ashurbanipal's death was based on the death of Šamaš-šuma-ukīn, then the king of Babylon might have committed suicide. For this opinion, see Frahm, Studies H. and M. Tadmor p. 39*; and

After Ashurbanipal died, he was succeeded by his son Aššur-etel-ilāni. When and how Ashurbanipal's death occurred has been a subject of debate since few sources shed light on the matter,[179] and, thus, scholars generally believe that he ruled over Assyria until 631, 630, or 627.[180] Based on contemporary (Babylonian) evidence, Ashurbanipal was king (of Assyria) until at least Simānu (III) of his 38th year (631),[181] but, according to an inscription of Nabonidus' mother Adad-guppī (Hadad-ḫappī), he reigned until his 42nd year (627).[182] At present, the "Adad-guppi Stele Inscription" is the only Akkadian source that gives a length of reign for Ashurbanipal. The relevant passages of that "pseudo-autobiographical" text, which is engraved on two round-topped monuments discovered in and near Ḫarrān, reads:

> From the twentieth year of Ashurbanipal, king of Assyria, (during) which I (Adad-guppī) was born, until the forty-second year of Ashurbanipal, the third year of Aššur-etel-ilāni, his son, the twenty-first year of Nabopolassar, the forty-third year of Nebuchadnezzar (II), the second year of Amēl-Marduk, (and) the fourth year of Neriglissar, after (these) ninety-five years, ... From the time of Ashurbanipal, king of Assyria, until the ninth year of Nabonidus, king of Babylon, (my) son, my own offspring, he (Sîn) kept me alive for 104 good years on account of the reverence that the god Sîn, king of the gods, had placed in my heart.[183]

It is clear from this inscription — which was written by Nabonidus (555–539) on his mother's behalf a few years after her death in 547, perhaps during his 14th (542) or 15th (541) year as king[184] — that there is an obvious discrepancy between the age given for Adad-guppī in the text (104) and the actual number of years between Ashurbanipal's 20th year and Nabonidus' 9th year (102).[185] Much ink has been spilt on the matter, especially about the lengths of Ashurbanipal's and Aššur-etel-ilāni's reigns. Can the information presented in Adad-guppī's biographical account of her long life be reconciled with other Babylonian documents? Possibly, yes.

It is clear from other extant chronographic sources that the composer(s) of the Adad-guppi Stele Inscription had a firm grasp on the length of reigns for the Neo-Babylonian kings, starting with Nabopolassar, the first ruler of the "Neo-Babylonian Dynasty." The chronographer correctly assigns twenty-one years to Nabopolassar (625–605), forty-three years of Nebuchadnezar II (604–562), two years to Amēl-Marduk (561–560), and four years to Neriglissar (559–556).[186] Because the short reign of Lâbâši-Marduk (556), which lasted only two

---

MacGinnis, Sumer 45 (1987–88) pp. 40–43. Note that Šamaš-šuma-ukīn's death is also recorded in the Amherst Papyrus 63.

178 According to Berossos, a Hellenistic-era priest of the god Bēl (Marduk) who wrote a Greek history of Babylonia (*Babyloniaca*), Sarakos (Sîn-šarra-iškun) was afraid of being captured and thus committed suicide by burning down his palace around him; see Burstein, SANE 1/5 p. 26. It is possible that Berossos, who was writing long after the events of 612, confused Sîn-šarra-iškun's death with that of Ashurbanipal or more likely that of his brother Šamaš-šuma-ukīn, a king of Babylon who is known with certainty to have died in a conflagration.

179 Assyrian chronographic sources are of no use since: (1) the Assyrian King list, the so-called "SDAS List," ends with the reign of Shalmaneser V (Gelb, JNES 13 [1954] pp. 209–230; and Grayson, RLA 6/1-2 [1980] pp. 101–115 §3.9); and (2) the latest preserved entries in the Assyrian Eponym Chronicle and Eponym Canon are respectively for the years 699 and 649 (Millard, SAAS 2 pp. 49 and 54). Babylonian chronographic texts are also of no help since Ashurbanipal is not included in Babylonian King List A (Novotny and Jeffers, RINAP 5/1 p. 29) or the Ptolemaic Canon (ibid. p. 30). The Uruk King List (ibid. p. 29) probably mentions Ashurbanipal, but states that he ruled over Babylonia jointly with his brother Šamaš-šuma-ukīn for twenty-one years (669–648), before Kandalānu was king for twenty-one years (647–627). Although Synchronistic King Lists (ibid. pp. 29–30) mention Ashurbanipal, those texts do not record the lengths of the kings' reigns. Moreover, the Babylonian Chronicles (ibid. pp. 34–36; and the present volume pp. 42–46) are not preserved for the years 647 (Ashurbanipal's 22nd year) to 628 (Kandalānu's 20th regnal year = Aššur-etel-ilāni's 3rd year as king); part of the entry for 627 is extant and his son Sîn-šarra-iškun is mentioned in the report for that year.

180 See, for example, Na'aman, ZA 81 (1991) pp. 243–267, especially pp. 243–255; Zawadzki, ZA 85 (1995) pp. 67–73; Beaulieu, Bagh. Mitt. 28 (1997) pp. 367–394; Gerber, ZA 88 (1998) pp. 72–93; Reade, Orientalia NS 67 (1998) pp. 255–265; Oelsner, Studies Renger pp. 643–666, especially pp. 644–645; Liebig, ZA 90 (2000) pp. 281–284; and Fuchs, Studies Oelsner pp. 25–28 and 35.

181 Brinkman and Kennedy, JCS 35 (1983) p. 24 no. J.38. N 4016 comes from Nippur. This document is dated to 20-III-631. It is possible that Ashurbanipal could have died prior to this and news of his death had not yet reached Nippur from the Assyrian capital.

182 Weiershäuser and Novotny, RINBE 2 p. 225 Nabonidus 2001 (Adad-guppi Stele) i 30.

183 Weiershäuser and Novotny, RINBE 2 pp. 225–226 Nabonidus 2001 (Adad-guppi Stele) i 29–33a and ii 26–29a.

184 According to the Nabonidus Chronicle (Weiershäuser and Novotny, RINBE 2 p. 26) ii 13–15a, Adad-guppī died on 5-I-547 (= April 6th 547) in the city Dūr-karašu, which was on the Euphrates River, upstream of Sippar. On the date of composition of the Adad-guppi Stele, see Beaulieu, Nabonidus p. 68 n. 1; and Schaudig, Inschriften Nabonids p. 501.

185 The composer(s) of the text used inclusive, rather than exclusive, dating for Adad-guppī's age, that is, Nabonidus Year 9 is included in the counting of years, even though the king's mother only lived five days into her son's 9th regnal year.

186 These dates are more or less confirmed by the Uruk King List and the Ptolemaic Canon (Weiershäuser and Novotny, RINBE 2 p. 24). Note that the Uruk King List records that Neriglissar ruled for three years and eight months and that his young son Lâbâši-Marduk was king for only three months. Berossus assigns nine months to the reign Lâbâši-Marduk. Based on economic documents, a reign of two or three months is likely for Neriglissar's young son, but not the nine stated by Berossus, since his reign is attested only for the months Nisannu (I), Ayyāru (II), and Simānu (III) of his accession year; see Beaulieu, Nabonidus pp. 86–87. Based on date formulae of business documents, the Uruk King List appears to give too long a reign to Neriglissar, who appears to have died a few days into his 4th regnal year; the latest presently-attested document dated by his reign was written at Uruk on 6-*I* (YBC 3433; Parker and Dubberstein, Babylonian Chronology

or three months, took place during the same year as the 4th and final year of his father Neriglissar, that short-reigned ruler is omitted from the list of rulers during whose reigns Adad-guppī lived. The reigns of the four aforementioned Babylonian rulers account for seventy of the ninety-five years of Adad-guppī's life before her son officially became king, which took place on 1-I-555 (during the Nisannu New Year's festival). The queen mother lived until 5-I-547, the 5th of Nisannu (I) of Nabonidus' 9th year.

The composer(s) of the Adad-guppi Stele Inscription, however, had less of a grasp on Assyrian history, in particular, the length of the reigns of Ashurbanipal, in whose country and during whose reign Adad-guppī was born, and his first successor Aššur-etel-ilāni.[187] Information about Assyria's last three kings — Sîn-šuma-līšir, Sîn-šarra-iškun, and Aššur-uballiṭ II — was not essential because Sîn-šuma-līšir's and Sîn-šarra-iškun's reigns began (and ended in the case of the former) in a year in which Aššur-etel-ilāni was still king[188] and the tenures of Sîn-šarra-iškun and Aššur-uballiṭ overlapped with Nabopolassar's reign. Because the requisite years were subsumed under Aššur-etel-ilāni or Nabopolassar there was no need to mention Sîn-šuma-līšir, Sîn-šarra-iškun, or Aššur-uballiṭ II in the list of rulers during whose reigns Adad-guppī lived.[189] Moreover, the same was true of Kandalānu, the king of Babylon who was placed on the throne by Ashurbanipal and ruled over Babylonia for twenty-one years,[190] since his tenure took place while Ashurbanipal and Aššur-etel-ilāni ruled Assyria.[191] The text's chronographer(s) appear not to have had concrete information about the reigns of Assyria's last kings, very likely as that information was not readily available.[192] They were, however, certain about two things: (1) there were twenty-two years between the end of the Šamaš-šuma-ukīn rebellion in 648 — as that piece of information was recorded in several Babylonian Chronicles — and the first year of Nabopolassar in 625;[193] and

---

p. 12). Despite the fact that Neriglissar was king for only a short time after the start of his 4th regnal year, he is credited with a four-year reign by the composer(s) of the Adad-guppi Stele Inscription. That year (556) was regarded as Neriglissar Year 4, Lâbâši-Marduk Year 0, and Nabonidus Year 0. For a recent study on the date of Nabonidus' accession to the throne, see Frame, Studies Rochberg pp. 287–295.

[187] Adad-guppī was very likely born in (or at least near) Ḫarrān. W. Mayer (Studies Römer pp. 250–256) has suggested that Adad-guppī might have been a daughter of the Assyrian prince Aššur-etel-šamê-erṣeti-muballissu (Pempe, PNA 1/1 pp. 184–185; Novotny and Singletary, Studies Parpola pp. 170–171) and, therefore, a granddaughter of Esarhaddon, but there is no extant textual evidence to support this proposal.

In scholarly literature, Nabonidus' mother is sometimes referred to as a priestess of the god Sîn of Ḫarrān on account of the devotion she claims to have given to the moon-god in the stele inscription written in her name. However, this need not be the case, since it is equally as plausible that Adad-guppī was simply a pious, upper class lay-woman. The piety expressed in her pseudo-autobiographical account of her life does not necessarily have to be interpreted as cultic obligations of a priestess. See the discussions in Dhorme, RB 5 (1908) p. 131; Garelli, Dictionnaire de la Bible 6 (1960) p. 274; Funck, Altertum 34 (1988) p. 53; W. Mayer, Studies Römer (1998) pp. 253–256; and Jursa, Die Babylonier p. 37. Note that many years ago B. Landsberger (Studies Edhem p. 149) already argued against the idea of Adad-guppi being an *ēntu*-priestess of the moon-god at Ḫarrān and that P. Michalowski (Studies Stolper p. 207) believed that this proposal is "an unsubstantiated modern rumor."

[188] Sîn-šuma-līšir's months-long reign (= his accession year) took place during the final year of Aššur-etel-ilāni's reign and at the same time as the accession year of Sîn-šarra-iškun. It also took place during the final year that Kandalānu, the king of Babylon, was alive (his 21st regnal year).

[189] With the exception of Sîn-šarra-iškun's accession year, which was the year before Nabopolassar became king, the entire reign of Assyria's penultimate king overlaps with the tenure of the founder of the Neo-Babylonian Empire. The entire duration of Aššur-uballiṭ II's reign also took place while Nabopolassar was king of Babylon. Moreover, Sîn-šarra-iškun Year 1 took place during the posthumous Kandalānu Year 22 (see the note immediately below).

[190] The Uruk King List (Novotny and Jeffers, RINAP 5/1 p. 29) credits Kandalānu with a twenty-one-year reign, but the Ptolemaic Canon (ibid. p. 30) states that he was king for twenty-two years. The length of Kandalānu's reign is broken away in Babylonian King List A (ibid. p. 29), but it might have been twenty-one years since that text also appears to list Sîn-šuma-līšir (reading uncertain) as a king of Babylon. The attribution of twenty-two years to Kandalānu comes from economic documents that are posthumously dated to his 22nd regnal year; see Brinkman and Kennedy, JCS 35 (1983) p. 49 no. L 163, which comes from Babylon and is dated to 2-VIII-626, which was twenty-four days before Nabopolassar became king (26-VIII-626). Kandalānu died early in his 21st regnal year, perhaps in late Ayyāru (II) or early Simānu (III). The latest economic document not posthumously dated to his reign was written on 8-III-627 (ibid. p. 49 no. L.159) and the earliest text posthumously dated to his tenure is 1-VIII-627 (ibid. p. 49 no. L.160). Because no one (Sîn-šarra-iškun or Nabopolassar) was in a position to take the hand of Marduk during the *akītu*-festival at Babylon on 1-I-626, the New Year's festival did not take place, as the Akītu Chronicle records (see the section *Chronicles* below) and nobody was officially crowned as the king of Babylon; thus, some economic documents continued to be dated by Kandalānu's reign. Rather than recording a one-year kingless period, the Ptolemaic Canon gives an extra year of reign to Kandalānu. Note that this text also assigns an extra year to Esarhaddon, attributing to him a thirteen-year-long reign. The additional year covers Šamaš-šuma-ukīn's accession year (668).

[191] Adad-guppī was probably living in Assyria until Nabopolassar captured and destroyed Ḫarrān in 610 and, thus, from her perspective (as composed by Nabonidus' scribes after her death), Ashurbanipal and Aššur-etel-ilāni were kings before Nabopolassar came to power. Therefore, one would not expect the queen mother to regard Kandalānu, or even Šamaš-šuma-ukīn, as a king during whose reign she had lived since they were Babylonian kings who were contemporaries of Ashurbanipal and his son Aššur-etel-ilāni.

[192] See n. 179 above.

[193] Based on extant chronographic sources, the end of the Šamaš-šuma-ukīn rebellion would very likely have been recorded for that king of Babylon's 20th regnal year (648) in the Esarhaddon Chronicle and the Šamaš-šuma-ukīn Chronicle; see Novotny and Jeffers, RINAP 5/1 pp. 34–35. The Akītu Chronicle (lines 23–27) records that the New Year's Festival did not take place during the 20th year (of Šamaš-šuma-ukīn), the last year of the Brothers' War, as well as in Nabopolassar's accession year (626 = posthumous Kandalānu Year 22). The twenty-

(2) Aššur-etel-ilāni succeeded his father as king of Assyria for a short time and that his tenure did not overlap with that of Nabopolassar, unlike his successors Sîn-šarra-iškun and Aššur-uballiṭ II. The composer(s) of the Adad-guppi Stele Inscription, who very likely did not have precise information at hand, assigned a forty-two-year reign to Ashurbanipal and a three-year reign to Aššur-etel-ilāni.[194] This timeframe — Ashurbanipal's 21st to 42nd regnal years[195] and Aššur-etel-ilāni 1st to 3rd regnal years — covered the remaining twenty-five years of the ninety-five years that Adad-guppī had lived before Nabonidus officially became the king of Babylon. In total, Nabonidus' mother is said to have lived 104 years, which is impossible as there were only 102 years from 649 (Ashurbanipal's 20th year) to 547 (Nabonidus' 9th year). Because Nabonidus' literary craftsmen were aware of the number of years that had transpired between Adad-guppī's (purported) birth and her (recorded) death, they must have known that they had assigned too many years to the life of the centenarian queen mother.

Presumably in order not to give the impression that Ashurbanipal's reign was not immediately followed by Nabopolassar's, the chronographer(s)/composer(s) included Aššur-etel-ilāni in the list of kings, even though it was abundantly clear that adding that ruler's regnal years was superfluous and that the total for Adad-guppī's lifespan would be more than she actually lived.[196] If the three double-counted years for Aššur-etel-ilāni's reign are excluded from the year count, the total is reduced to 101, which is one year shy of the needed 102 years between 649 and 547. If Nabonidus' scholars actually knew how many years had passed since Ashurbanipal's 20th regnal year, they would have been aware that there were twenty-three years between 649 and 626, not twenty-two as they record.[197] Thus, they should have assigned Ashurbanipal a forty-three-year reign, but they did not. The missing year would then bring the count back up to the required 102 years. The subtraction of three years and the miscalculation of the date of Ashurbanipal's 20th year (which is off by one year) seems a rather unlikely scenario, especially as it is needlessly complex. The double counting can easily be accounted for, but the missing year for Ashurbanipal that is then accurately accounted for cannot. There must have been a simpler, more rational explanation for how Nabonidus' chronographer(s) calculated the age of his very old mother.

Based on the extant sources currently at our disposal, Babylonian Chronicles in particular, it appears that Nabonidus' scholars wrongly identified Ashurbanipal's 20th year (649): they seem to have confused it with Šamaš-šuma-ukīn's 20th and final year (648), the milestone year that his rebellion ended, as well as a year in which the New Year's festival at Babylon did not take place.[198] There are precisely twenty-two years between the end of Šamaš-šuma-ukīn's tenure as king and the 1st year of Nabopolassar's reign, as well as between interruptions in the *akītu*-festival at Babylon in 648 and 626. Moreover, these years match the number of years attributed to Kandalānu by the Ptolemaic Canon and economic documents.[199] Given that the 20th year loomed large in Babylonian (and Assyrian) historical memory, since it was the year the protracted war between

---

two-year period in question corresponds to the reign of Kandalānu according to the Ptolemaic Canon and economic documents dated to that king's tenure (627–626) or to the twenty-one-year period for Kandalānu's reign (647–627) and the joint one-year reign for Sîn-šuma-līšir and Sîn-šarra-iškun (626), which overlapped with Nabopolassar's accession year, according to the Uruk King List and probably also Babylonian King List A (ibid. p. 29). Posthumous Kandalānu Year 22 is recorded as "for one (entire) year, there was no king in the land (Akkad)" in lines 14–15a of the Chronicle Concerning the Early Years of Nabopolassar (see the section *Chronicles* below). From surviving Babylonian Chronicles and King Lists, Nabonidus' scribes were clearly aware of the number of years between the end of Ashurbanipal's war with Šamaš-šuma-ukīn and the accession of Nabopolassar. Presumably, the missing entries in the Babylonian Chronicle would have been dated by Kandalānu's regnal years.

194 Information about Aššur-etel-ilāni's 4th year as king appears to have gone unnoticed by the composer(s) of the Adad-guppi Stele Inscription. This is not surprising as Babylonian business documents dated to his reign come only from Nippur and only one is known for his 4th and final year as king (Brinkman and Kennedy, JCS 35 [1983] p. 53 no. M12). Four texts, however, are dated by his 3rd year; see ibid. p. 53 nos. M8–M11. Because there are so few presently-attested dated documents for the fourth year of Aššur-etel-ilāni's reign and since 627 was a chaotic year, with four kings by which to date business transactions (Kandalānu, Aššur-etel-ilāni, Sîn-šuma-līšir, and Sîn-šarra-iškun), it is not surprising that this Assyrian king is credited by Nabonidus' scribes as having ruled for only three years.

195 Based on the information provided about Ashurbanipal's length of reign in the Adad-guppi Stele Inscription, some scholars (especially S. Zawadzki [Fall of Assyria pp. 57–63]) have suggested that Ashurbanipal and Kandalānu were one and the same person, but this seems unlikely, as already pointed out by J.A. Brinkman (for example, CAH^2 3/2 pp. 60–62) and G. Frame (Babylonia pp. 191–213, especially 193–195, and 296–306).

196 This is evident from the fact that Nabonidus' scholars were aware that there were only twenty-two years between the end of the Šamaš-šuma-ukīn rebellion and the 1st regnal year of Nabopolassar. Thus, any regnal years assigned to Aššur-etel-ilāni would have been regarded as a double count since those years were already included in the regnal count for Ashurbanipal.

197 The composer(s) added twenty-two years to the 20th regnal year of Ashurbanipal to arrive at a total of forty-two years. The math, however, is off by one year when one counts from Ashurbanipal's actual 20th year as king. It is unclear, however, whether that year would have been 648 or 626.

198 The Akītu Chronicle line 23 (Novotny and Jeffers, RINAP 5/1 p. 36) records the following for the 20th year (of Šamaš-šuma-ukīn's): "The twentieth year (648): The god Nabû did not go (and) the god Bēl did not come out." Presumably other chronicles would have noted the same information and given additional details about the end of the rebellion.

199 See n. 190 above.

Ashurbanipal and Šamaš-šuma-ukīn concluded, it should not come as a surprise that more than one hundred years later Nabonidus' chronographer(s) regarded the 20th year in texts accessible to them as Ashurbanipal's, not Šamaš-šuma-ukīn's, 20th regnal year. They would not have been the only men to have confused or mixed up the dates of past events, as it is clear that there are a number of errors in extant Babylonian Chronicles. For example, the Šamaš-šuma-ukīn Chronicle wrongly states that a bed of Marduk entered Babylon in the "14th year (of Šamaš-šuma-ukīn [654])," when it should have been the "13th year (of Šamaš-šuma-ukīn [655])," since that text dates events by the regnal years of the king of Babylon. The 14th year would be correct if the year refers to Ashurbanipal's 14th regnal year (655).[200] Thus, it is not implausible for Nabonidus' scribes to have regarded Šamaš-šuma-ukīn's 20th year as Ashurbanipal's 20th year. If this was the case, does the math add up? Yes. There are 101 years between 648 ("Ashurbanipal's" 20th year; 648 = Šamaš-šuma-ukīn Year 20) and 547 (Nabonidus' 9th year) and 104 years when the double-counted three-year reign of Aššur-etel-ilāni are taken into account.[201] Moreover, the twenty-two years of Ashurbanipal during which Adad-guppī claims to lived corresponds exactly to the requisite number of years between the end of Šamaš-šuma-ukīn rebellion and the first year of Nabopolassar's reign. Thus, it seems highly probable that Nabonidus' mother was born in 648, and not in 649, as previously thought.[202]

Chart 1: Side by side comparisons of the regnal years of Ashurbanipal, Aššur-etel-ilāni, Nabopolassar, and their contemporaries (Šamaš-šuma-ukīn, Kandalānu, Sîn-šuma-līšir, and Sîn-šarra-iškun) from 649 to 625.

Year	Ashurbanipal (actual)	Ashurbanipal (Adad-guppi Stele)	Aššur-etel-ilāni	Nabopolassar	Other Kings
649	**20**	[[19]]	—	—	Šamaš-šuma-ukīn 19
648	21	**20**	—	—	**Šamaš-šuma-ukīn 20** Kandalānu 0
647	22	21	—	—	Kandalānu 1
646	23	22	—	—	Kandalānu 2
645	24	23	—	—	Kandalānu 3
644	25	24	—	—	Kandalānu 4
643	26	25	—	—	Kandalānu 5
642	27	26	—	—	Kandalānu 6
641	28	27	—	—	Kandalānu 7
640	29	28	—	—	Kandalānu 8
639	30	29	—	—	Kandalānu 9
638	31	30	—	—	Kandalānu 10
637	32	31	—	—	Kandalānu 11
636	33	32	—	—	Kandalānu 12
635	34	33	—	—	Kandalānu 13
634	35	34	—	—	Kandalānu 14
633	36	35	—	—	Kandalānu 15
632	37	36	—	—	Kandalānu 16
631	38	37	0	—	Kandalānu 17
630	[[39]]	38	1	—	Kandalānu 18
629	[[40]]	39	2	—	Kandalānu 19
628	[[41]]	40	3	—	Kandalānu 20
627	[[42]]	41	4	—	Kandalānu 21 Sîn-šuma-līšir 0 Sîn-šarra-iškun 0
626	—	42	—	**0**	**Kandalānu 22** Ssi 1
625	—	—	—	1	Ssi 2

year counted in Adad-guppi Stele   year double counted in Adad-guppi Stele   [[42]] year not attested in source(s)

20 year confused by Nabonidus' chronographer(s)   **0** same year, confirmed from Babylonian Chronicles

[200] On this confusion and at least one other error in the Babylonian Chronicle, see the discussion in n. 126 above.

[201] If one counts the number of months from 648 to 547, then Adad-guppī' would have lived to 104 years of age since there were thirty-six (or possibly thirty-seven) intercalary months during Nabonidus' mother's long life, which is the equivalent of three years. There was an Intercalary Ulūlu (VI2) in the years 643, 640, 629, 621, 616, 611, 607, 603, 600, 598, 596, 584, 574, 564; and an Intercalary Addaru (XII2) in the years 646, 638, 635, 624, 619, 614, 606, 594, 591, 588, 582, 579, 577, 572, 569, 563, 560, 557, 555, 553, and 550. In addition, intercalary months were expected in 632 and between 629 and 624 (possibly in 625). The count would be one month more if Adad-guppī' were to have been born in 649, rather than in 648, since that year had an Intercalary Addaru (XII2).

[202] This would mean that Adad-guppī' was 101, not 102, years old.

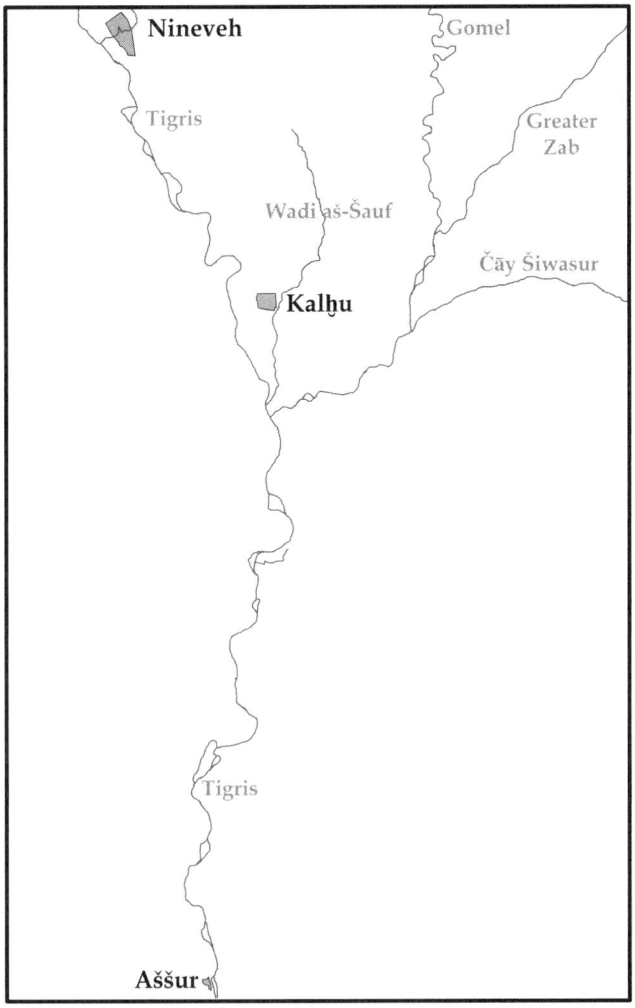

Figure 3. Map showing the principal Assyrian cities where Aššur-etel-ilāni and Sîn-šarra-iškun undertook building activities.

Based on the available evidence, it appears that Ashurbanipal reigned until early 631, as evidenced from the latest Babylonian economic documents dated to his reign. Thus, his son and first successor Aššur-etel-ilāni was probably king 630–627 and his son and second successor Sîn-šarra-iškun likely ruled over Assyria 626–612.

Aššur-etel-ilāni and His Chief Eunuch Sîn-šuma-līšir

When Ashurbanipal died, a certain Nabû-rēḫtu-uṣur incited a rebellion. The chief eunuch Sîn-šuma-līšir and men from his estate, including his cohort commander Ṭāb-šār-papāḫi, brought order back to the Assyrian heartland and installed Ashurbanipal's young and inexperienced son Aššur-etel-ilāni (630–627) on the throne.[203] Aššur-etel-ilāni, whose short reign is not well documented in contemporary or later sources, was king for four years, at least according to one economic text from Nippur.[204]

[203] Two grants of land with tax exemptions (Kataja and Whiting, SAA 12 pp. 36–41 nos. 35–36) record that Sîn-šuma-līšir aided Aššur-etel-ilāni, who was still a minor when Ashurbanipal died. Kataja and Whiting, SAA 12 pp. 38–39 no. 36 obv. 4–9 read: "After my father and begetter had dep[arted], no father brought me up or taught me to spread my [wings], no mother cared for me or saw to my [education], Sîn-šuma-līšir, the chief eunuch, [one who had deserved well] of my father and be[getter, who had led me constantly like a father, installed me] safely on the throne of my father and begetter [and made the people of Assyria, great and small, keep] watch over [my kingship during] my minority, and respected [my royalty]." For further information about Sîn-šuma-līšir, see, for example, J. Oates, CAH^2 3/2 pp. 162–163, 168–170, and 172–176; Na'aman, ZA 81 (1991) pp. 243–257; Frame, RIMB 2 p. 269 B.6.36; Mattila, PNA 3/1 p. 1148 sub Sîn-šumu-lēšir; Fuchs, Studies Oelsner pp. 54–58 §3.1; and Schaudig, RLA 12/7–8 (2011) pp. 524–525.

[204] For biographical sketches of Ashurbanipal's first successor, see, for example, J. Oates, CAH^2 3/2 pp. 162–176, 184, and 186; Frame, RIMB 2 p. 261 B.6.35; Brinkman, PNA 1/1 pp. 183–184 sub Aššūr-etel-ilāni no. 2; and Fuchs, Studies Oelsner pp. 54–58 §3.1. Because his reign was

In Assyria, he sponsored construction on Ezida ("True House"), the temple of the god Nabû at Kalḫu.[205] Since his brother and successor Sîn-šarra-iškun (see below) also undertook work on that sacred building, construction on that temple appears to have been unfinished when Aššur-etel-ilāni's tenure as king came to an end.

Despite Kandalānu being the king of Babylon, Aššur-etel-ilāni held authority over parts of Babylonia,[206] and, like his father before him, he sponsored building projects in several Babylonian cities. This is evident from a few of his inscriptions.[207] These record that he dedicated a *musukkannu*-wood offering table to the god Marduk (presumably at Babylon); made a gold scepter for Marduk and had it placed in Eešerke, that god's place of worship in the city Sippar-Aruru;[208] renovated E-ibbi-Anum ("House the God Anu Named"), the temple of the god Uraš and the goddess Ninegal at Dilbat; and rebuilt Ekur ("House, Mountain"), the temple of the god Enlil at Nippur. In addition, the young Assyrian king returned the body of Šamaš-ibni, a Chaldean sheikh who had been taken to Assyria and executed by Esarhaddon in 678, to Dūru-ša-Ladīni, a fortified settlement in the area of the Bīt-Dakkūri tribe.[209]

Although Aššur-etel-ilāni was king, it was Sîn-šuma-līšir, his chief eunuch, who held real power over Assyria.[210] This might have led to friction between the king's top officials and members of the royal family. In 627 (or possibly already in 628), civil war broke out. The ambitious Sîn-šuma-līšir, who was not a member of the royal family,[211] declared himself king and took control of (parts of) Assyria, as well as parts of Babylonia, which he was able to do since Kandalānu, the king of Babylon, had recently died.[212] Aššur-etel-ilāni, Sîn-šuma-līšir, Sîn-šarra-iškun (another son of Ashurbanipal), and perhaps a few other members of the royal family vied for power in the Assyrian heartland and in Babylonia.[213] Sîn-šarra-iškun, Aššur-etel-ilāni's brother, eventually won

---

contemporaneous with that of Kandalānu, Aššur-etel-ilāni is not included in the various lists of rulers of Babylonia, which state that Sîn-šuma-līšir (and Sîn-šarra-iškun) or Nabopolassar was king of Babylon after Kandalānu; see Novotny and Jeffers, RINAP 5/1 pp. 29–30.

According to CBS 2152, an economic document from Nippur (Brinkman and Kennedy, JCS 35 [1983] p. 53 no. M.12), Aššūr-etel-ilāni was king until at least 1-VIII-627. Note, however, that the pseudo-autobiographical text of Adad-guppi, the mother of the Babylonian king Nabonidus (555–539), from Ḫarrān (Weiershäuser and Novotny, RINBE 2 p. 225 Nabonidus 2001 [Adad-guppi stele] i 30) states that Aššur-etel-ilāni was king for only three years; see above for details.

205 Aei 1. Twenty-six exemplars of this seven-line Akkadian inscription are presently known. For an overview of the building history of the Ezida temple at Kalḫu, see George, House Most High p. 160 no. 1239; and Novotny and Van Buylaere, Studies Oded pp. 215 and 218. For a discussion of the archaeological remains of that temple, see, for example, D. Oates, Iraq 19 (1957) pp. 26–39; and D. Oates and J. Oates, Nimrud pp. 111–123. For information on Kalḫu, see in particular D. Oates and J. Oates, Nimrud; and the open-access, Oracc-based Nimrud: Materialities of Assyrian Knowledge Production website (http://oracc.org/nimrud [last accessed January 25, 2023).

206 Although none of Aššur-etel-ilāni's inscriptions ever specifically call him "king of Babylon," "governor of Babylon," or "king of Sumer and Akkad," his authority over (the northern) parts of Babylonia is evident from that fact that twelve economic documents from Nippur are dated by his regnal years, rather than those of Kandalānu. For a catalogue of these texts, which refer to him as either "the king of Assyria" or "the king of the lands," see Brinkman and Kennedy, JCS 35 (1983) pp. 52–53 nos. M.1–M.12.

207 Aei 2–5.

208 This temple, whose Sumerian ceremonial name means "House, Shrine of Weeping," is not otherwise attested and it might be a corrupted writing of Ešeriga ("House Which Gleans Barley"), the temple of the deity Šidada at Dūr-Šarrukku (= Sippar-Aruru); see George, House Most High p. 83 no. 269.

209 Aei 6. For further information about Šamaš-ibni, See Frame, Babylonia pp. 79–80; and p. 165 of the present volume.

210 See n. 203 above.

211 As pointed out by E. Frahm (Companion to Assyria p. 198 n. 22), Sîn-šuma-līšir's "family background remains unknown and ... it cannot be entirely excluded that he too was a member of the royal family."

212 This is evident from the fact that Babylonian King List A and the Uruk King List name him as Kandalānu's successor (see Novotny and Jeffers, RINAP 5/1 p. 29) and that seven economic documents from Babylon and Nippur (Brinkman and Kennedy, JCS 35 [1983] pp. 53–54 nos. N.1–N.7) are dated by his accession year. The latest firmly dated text from Kandalānu was written on 8-III-627 (ibid. p. 48 no. L.159), although it is possible that that document could have been drafted shortly after that king of Babylon's death since the earliest dated Babylonian economic document for Sîn-šuma-līšir is 12-III-627.

213 Since one document from Nippur is dated to 1-VIII of Aššur-etel-ilāni's 4th regnal year (Brinkman and Kennedy, JCS 35 [1983] p. 53 no. M.12) — which is later than the earliest-known economic documents dated by the accession years of Sîn-šuma-līšir and Sîn-šarra-iškun, which are dated to the 12th of Simānu (III) and the 8th of Tašrītu (VII) respectively (ibid. pp. 53–54 nos. N.1 and O.1) — it is certain that Aššur-etel-ilāni was still alive when the civil war broke out. It is unclear, however, who set the civil war in motion: Sîn-šuma-līšir, Sîn-šarra-iškun, or someone else.

It is possible that Sîn-šarra-iškun, with the backing of several influential officials, made the first move. This ambitious prince might have taken the opportunity when Aššur-etel-ilāni sent his protector Sîn-šuma-līšir to Babylon upon the death of Kandalānu. One conjectural scenario is as follows. With Sîn-šuma-līšir far away in Babylonia, presumably to be the next king of Babylon, Sîn-šarra-iškun and his supporters tried to depose Aššur-etel-ilāni. With the Assyrian heartland in chaos, Sîn-šuma-līšir saw his chance to grab power for himself, marched back to Assyria with his men, declared himself king, and fought his rivals, principally Sîn-šarra-iškun, for control of Assyria. His efforts, however, were in vain. Sîn-šarra-iškun gained the upper hand and forced Sîn-šuma-līšir to retreat south to Babylonia, where he assumed he would be safe. This would not be the case, since Nabopolassar, an influential man from Uruk with ambitions of his own, captured and executed him. This, of course, is conjectural, but one possible scenario for how events played out in Assyria in 627, especially since it is equally likely that Sîn-šuma-līšir rebelled against Aššur-etel-ilāni and that Sîn-šarra-iškun countered the chief

the day, ascended the Assyrian throne, and restored order to his kingdom.[214] Sîn-šuma-līšir, who is probably to be identified with the "all-powerful chief eunuch" (*rab ša rēši dandannu*) of the "Nabopolassar Epic," appears to have gone to Babylonia, where he was captured and publicly executed on the orders of Nabopolassar, a "son of a nobody" who would soon become the next king of Babylon.[215]

Sîn-šarra-iškun, Aššur-uballiṭ II, and the End of the Assyrian Empire

Despite restoring power to the hands of the royal family, which could trace its origins back over a thousand years to its founder Bēl-bāni (the son of Adāsi),[216] and bringing civil order to Assyria, Sîn-šarra-iškun (626–612) was unable to prevent the collapse and disappearance of the Assyrian Empire.[217] Nevertheless, he was able to keep it alive for another fifteen years. During that time, at least until his 11th regnal year (616), he was able to keep his principal rival, the Babylonian king Nabopolassar, at bay (that is, out of the Assyrian heartland) and, thus, he could sponsor several largescale building activities in the Aššur–Nineveh–Arbela triangle.

Sîn-šarra-iškun's Building Activities

Extant inscriptions record that Sîn-šarra-iškun undertook construction in the three most important cities of the heartland: Aššur, Kalḫu, and Nineveh.[218] Most of the work was very likely carried out before 615, at which point Assyria was fighting for its very existence.[219]

In the religious capital Aššur, he built a new temple for the god Nabû, since that god's place of worship was then inside Eme-Inanna ("House of the *Mes* of Inanna"), the temple of the Assyrian Ištar.[220] Sîn-šarra-iškun had Egidrukalamasumu ("House Which Bestows the Scepter of the Land") constructed on a vacant plot of land, which concealed the ruins of earlier, long-abandoned Ištar temples.[221] Nabû's new earthly abode took several

---

eunuch's bid for the Assyrian crown only after that ambitious man had tried to remove his brother from the throne. Until new textual evidence comes to light, this matter will remain a subject of scholarly debate.

[214] A few of his inscriptions seem to imply that he was young when he came to the throne; see, for example, Ssi 10 lines 16b–19. However, he could not have been that young when he came to power since Aššur-uballiṭ II, assuming that he was indeed a son of his, must have been old enough to take over the duties of king when his father died in 612 and, therefore, Aššur-uballiṭ must have been born prior to Sîn-šarra-iškun becoming king in late 627. It is not impossible that Sîn-šarra-iškun was an older brother of Aššur-etel-ilāni.

[215] Da Riva, JNES 76 (2017) p. 82 ii 10′–16′. See Gerber, ZA 88 (1998) p. 83; and Tadmor, Studies Borger pp. 353–357. Sîn-šarra-iškun might have put an end to his rivalry with Sîn-šuma-līšir by forming an alliance, albeit a very short-lived one, with Nabopolassar, who, seeking power for himself, agreed to the (terms of a bilateral) treaty since it was in his own interest to have Sîn-šuma-līšir out of the way. Nabopolassar, a self-described "son of a nobody," appears to have come from a family that had strong Assyrian ties, with several of its members having served as high officials on behalf of Assyrian kings in Uruk. It is possible that he might have served as the governor of that Babylonian city. For details, see Jursa, RA 101 (2007) pp. 125–136. For brief biographical sketches of this Neo-Babylonian ruler, see, for example, Brinkman, RLA 9/1–2 (1998) pp. 12–16; and Da Riva, GMTR 4 pp. 2–7 §1.2.1.

[216] Seven inscriptions of Esarhaddon and one text of Ashurbanipal trace the royal family's origins back to the Old Assyrian king Bēl-bāni, son of Adāsi (Brinkman, PNA 1/2 p. 288 sub Bēl-bāni no. 1). See, for example, Leichty, RINAP 4 p. 262 Esarhaddon 128 (Nippur A) line 14; and Novotny and Jeffers, RINAP 5/1 p. 220 Asb. 10 (Prism T) v 40–41.

[217] For his reign, see, for example, J. Oates, CAH^2 3/2 pp. 175–182; Frame, RIMB 2 p. 270 B.6.37; Novotny, PNA 3/1 pp. 1143–1145 sub Sîn-šarru-iškun; Schaudig, RLA 12/7–8 (2011) pp. 522–524; and Frahm, Companion to Assyria pp. 191–192. Because his reign was contemporaneous with that of Kandalānu and Nabopolassar, this Assyrian king is usually not included in the various lists of rulers of Babylonia; see Novotny and Jeffers, RINAP 5/1 pp. 29–30. He is mentioned, however, in the Uruk King List (ibid. p. 29) as ruling over southern Mesopotamia for one year together with Sîn-šuma-līšir. His name might have also appeared in King List A, but the relevant section of that text is now missing. Sîn-šarra-iškun (and Sîn-šuma-līšir) are probably included in the Uruk King List because the length of Kandalānu's reign is given as twenty-one, instead of twenty-two, years.

[218] See also Novotny and Van Buylaere, Studies Oded pp. 215–219. It is unlikely that Sîn-šarra-iškun rebuilt Ešaḫula, the temple of the god Nergal in Sirara, the temple district of Mê-Turān, since the text recording that work (Stephens, YOS 9 no. 80) was probably written in the name of Ninurta-tukultī-Aššur, and not that of Sîn-šarra-iškun; see the section *Texts Excluded from RINAP 5/3* above.

[219] See the section *Eponym Dates* below for discussions of the dates of Sîn-šarra-iškun's inscriptions (and associated building projects).

[220] Ssi 7–14. For Egidrukalamasumu, see, for example, George, House Most High p. 94 no. 397; Novotny and Van Buylaere, Studies Oded pp. 216–218; Schmitt, Ischtar-Tempel pp. 82–100; Novotny, Kaskal 11 (2014) pp. 159–169; and Novotny in Yamada, SAAS 28 pp. 262–263. For Eme-Inanna, see, for example, George, House Most High pp. 122–123 no. 756; and Schmitt, Ischtar-Tempel pp. 26–81.

[221] The western part of the temple was constructed directly above Ištar Temples H, G, GF, E, and D, and the Ištar temple that had been built by Tukultī-Ninurta I. Its northern wall abutted the southern wall of the still-in-use Ištar temple that had been originally constructed by Aššur-rēšī-iši I. See Novotny, Kaskal 11 (2014) p. 163 fig. 1. Sîn-šarra-iškun's scribes, at least according to the building account of the so-called "Cylinder A Inscription" (for example, Ssi 10 lines 22b–27a), regarded the ruins to be the remains of earlier Nabû temples constructed by the Middle Assyrian kings Shalmaneser I (1273–1244) and Aššur-rēšī-iši I (1132–1115) and the Neo-Assyrian ruler Adad-nārārī III (810–783). That same inscription (line 29) claims that the temple was erected "according to its original plan, on its former site," which was not the case, because the new Nabû temple was constructed over the ruins of previous Ištar temples. Ssi 12 (lines 8–14a), a text engraved on a stone block, however, correctly states that the temple was built on an empty lot. For a brief study on the discrepancy between the textual and archaeological records, see Novotny, Kaskal 11 (2014) pp. 162–165. Note that the general ground plan of the Nabû temple at Aššur is very similar to that of the Ezida temple at Kalḫu. Compare fig. 4 with D. Oates and J. Oates, Nimrud p. 112 fig. 67.

years to complete[222] and, once it was finished, the statues of the god of scribes and his wife Tašmētu were ushered into the temple during a grand ceremony; at that time, prize bulls and fat-tailed sheep were presented as offerings. Although Sîn-šarra-iškun claims to have made the new temple "shine like daylight," no details about its sumptuous decoration are recorded in extant texts. We do know, however, that he presented (inscribed) reddish gold *kallu*-and *šulpu*-bowls to Nabû, a silver spoon (*itqūru*) to Tašmētu, and *musukkannu*-wood offering tables (*paššuru*) to the goddesses Antu and Šala.[223]

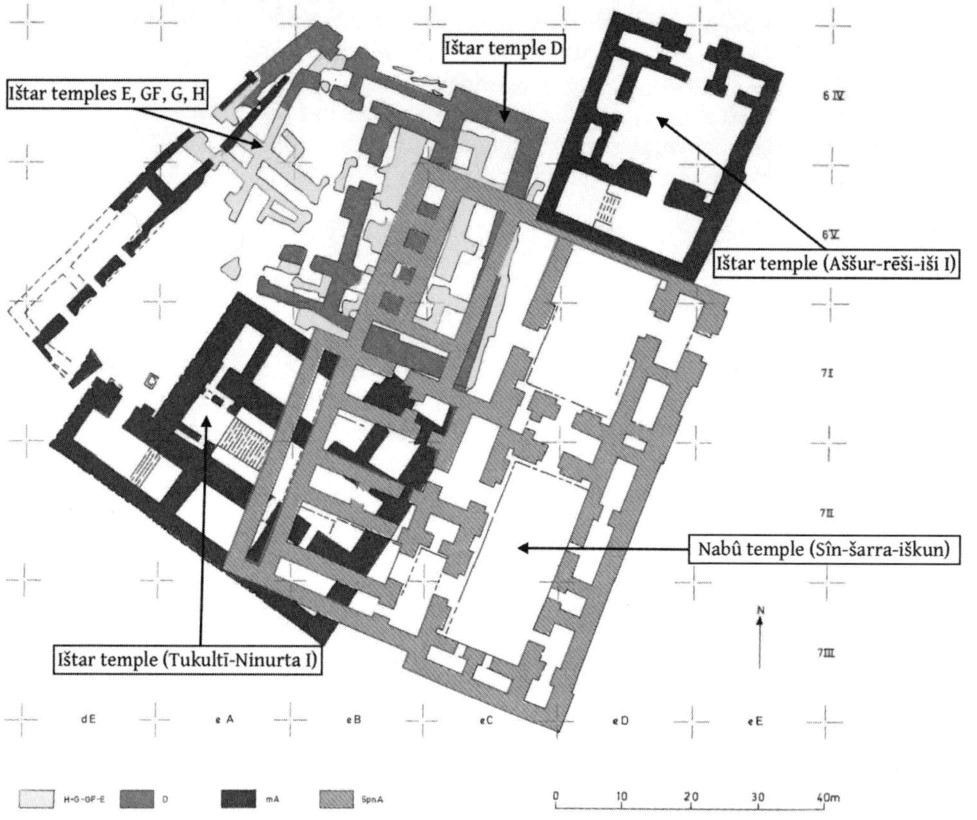

Figure 4. Plan of the Nabû temple at Aššur and the earlier ruins of the Ištar temple. Adapted from Bär, Ischtar-Tempel p. 391 fig. 5.

At Kalḫu, Sîn-šarra-iškun completed his brother Aššur-etel-ilāni's work on Ezida ("True House"), Nabû's temple in that city, since construction on that sacred building remained unfinished when Sîn-šarra-iškun became king.[224]

At his capital, Nineveh, he made repairs to the mud-brick structure of the city wall Badnigalbilukurašušu ("Wall Whose Brilliance Overwhelms Enemies"), renovated the western part of the South-West Palace (Egalzagdinutukua ["Palace Without a Rival"] = Sennacherib's palace), and, probably, sponsored a few other projects in that metropolis.[225] As for work on the "Alabaster House" (=the South-West Palace), which served as

[222] According to the dates of Sîn-šarra-iškun's inscription, construction on this sacred building took at least three years to complete. See the section *Eponym Dates* below for further information.
[223] Ssi 15–18.
[224] Ssi 19 (lines 30–37). For bibliographical references to Ezida, see n. 205 above.
[225] Ssi 1–6. The building report of Ssi 1 (lines 12′–15′) records work on the Alabaster House and that of Ssi 6, at least according to its subscript (rev. 13′), would have described construction on Nineveh's city wall. The building accounts of other inscriptions of his from Nineveh (Ssi 2–5) are either completely missing or not sufficiently preserved to be able to determine what accomplishment of Sîn-šarra-iškun they commemorated. For information on Sennacherib's palace, see, for example, Reade, RLA 9/5–6 (2000) pp. 411–416 §§14.2–3; Grayson and Novotny, RINAP 3/1 p. 17; and Jeffers and Novotny, RINAP 5/2 p. 15. For a detailed and comprehensive study of the "Palace Without a Rival" (=the South-West Palace), see J.M. Russell, Senn.'s Palace. For information on the palace reliefs, see Barnett et al., Sculptures from the Southwest Palace; Lippolis, Sennacherib Wall Reliefs; and J.M. Russell, Final Sack. For studies on Nineveh's wall, see Reade, RLA 9/5–6 (2000) pp. 397–403 §§11.1–4; Grayson and Novotny, RINAP 3/1 pp. 17–19; and Reade, SAAB 22 (2016) pp. 39–93.

an administrative center,[226] Sîn-šarra-iškun's renovations might have included (1) partially redecorating Room XXII with scenes of the landscape around Nineveh and a triumphal procession of men wearing foliage on their heads; (2) recarving the walls of Court XIX and Room XXVIII with scenes of warfare; and (3) removing the former images of the wall panels in Room XLII and Court XLIX so that they could be resculpted with new images.[227] Presumably in 613 (if not earlier), he strengthened the vulnerable spots in Nineveh's defenses, principally by reinforcing its eighteen gates and narrowing their central corridors with large blocks of stone;[228] Sîn-šarra-iškun was able to do this since his rival Nabopolassar was preoccupied with a rebellion in Sūḫu, a kingdom situated in the Middle Euphrates region.[229]

Figure 5. Obverse and reverse of the "Fall of Nineveh Chronicle" (BM 21901). © Trustees of the British Museum.

Sîn-šarra-iškun's Wars with Nabopolassar

Two Babylonian Chronicles — the so-called "Chronicle Concerning the Early Years of Nabopolassar" and "Fall of Nineveh Chronicle" (see below for translations) — provide the backbone for the long war between Sîn-šarra-iškun and Nabopolassar.[230] These two chronographic documents, together with the dates of Babylonian

[226] For details, see Reade, RLA 9/5–6 (2000) p. 415 §14.3.
[227] Some of these changes might have taken place already during the reign of his father Ashurbanipal, as stated already in Jeffers and Novotny, RINAP 5/2 (p. 15).
[228] For the evidence from the Adad, Halzi, and Šamaš Gates, see Stronach in Parpola and Whiting, Assyria 1995 pp. 307–324; and Pickworth, Iraq 67 (2005) pp. 295–316. Sîn-šarra-iškun might have also strengthened the western part of the South-West Palace since it could be accessed from the Step Gate of the Palace and the Step Gate of the Gardens.
[229] Fall of Nineveh Chronicle lines 31–37; see the *Chronicles* section below for a translation of that passage.
[230] The former chronographic text, as far as it is preserved, records events from 627 (Sîn-šarra-iškun's accession year) to 623 (Sîn-šarra-iškun Year 4 = Nabopolassar Year 3), but it would have included descriptions of the clashes between Assyria and Babylonia up to the year 617 (Sîn-šarra-iškun Year 10 = Nabopolassar Year 9). Based on information presented in the latter chronicle, which records the events of 616 (Sîn-šarra-iškun Year 11 = Nabopolassar Year 10) to 609 (Aššur-uballiṭ Year 3 = Nabopolassar Year 17), the accounts for the years 622–617 would likely have narrated how Nabopolassar and his army expelled the Assyrians from Babylonia, which they were able to do in 620 (Sîn-šarra-iškun Year 7 = Nabopolassar Year 6), at least based on the date formulae of business documents.

economic documents,[231] chart the two rulers' fight for control over Babylonia between 626 and 620[232] and then the Babylonian and Median invasion of the Assyrian heartland and annihilation of its cities and cult centers between 616 and 612.

Up until 615, his 12th year as king, Sîn-šarra-iškun, with the assistance of allied troops from Egypt, was able to keep Nabopolassar at bay, mostly because the battles fought between the two rulers took place in northern Babylonia or in the Middle Euphrates region, and not on Assyrian soil. Everything, however, changed in 615, when Cyaxares (Umakištar), "the king of the Umman-manda" (Medes), joined the fight. In that turn-of-events year, Nabopolassar invaded the Assyrian heartland and attacked Aššur. He failed to capture that important religious center and was forced to retreat south, as far as the city Takritain (modern Tikrit). In the following year, 614, Cyaxares marched straight into the heart of Assyria and roamed effortlessly through it, first capturing Tarbiṣu, a city in very close proximity to Nineveh, and then Aššur, which the Babylonians had failed to take in 615.[233] Upon hearing this news, Nabopolassar quickly marched north and forged an alliance with the Median king. The unexpected union not only gave fresh impetus to Nabopolassar's years-long war with Sîn-šarra-iškun, but also removed any hopes that the Assyrian king might have had about the survival of his kingdom. Sîn-šarra-iškun could clearly see the writing on the wall and he took what measures he could to fortify Nineveh.[234] In 613 (if not earlier, in 614 or 615), that city's gates were reinforced by narrowing them with massive blocks of stone. The death blow for Sîn-šarra-iškun and his capital came during the following year, in 612. Nineveh's fortifications, even with the improvements made to its defenses, were not sufficient to prevent a joint Babylonian-Median assault from breaching the city's walls.After a three-month siege — from the month Simānu (III) to the month Abu (V) — Nineveh fell and was looted and destroyed.[235] Before the city succumbed to the enemy,[236] Sîn-šarra-iškun died. Unfortunately, the true nature of his death — whether he committed

---

[231] For a catalogue of the economic texts dated by his reign, see Brinkman and Kennedy, JCS 35 (1983) pp. 54–59. Those business documents, the earliest of which date to his accession year and the latest to his 7th year as king, come from Babylon (Accession Year), Kār-Aššur (Year 7), Maši... (year damaged), Nippur (Years 2–6), Sippar (Accession Year, Years 2–3), and Uruk (Years 5–7).

[232] The two men vied for control over Babylon, Nippur, Sippar, and Uruk. It is clear that Uruk changed hands on more than one occasion; see Beaulieu, Bagh. Mitt. 28 (1997) pp. 367–394. The latest economic document dated to Sîn-šarra-iškun's reign from Babylonia comes from Uruk and is dated to 12-X-620 (Brinkman and Kennedy, JCS 35 [1983] p. 58 no. O.45). This may well mark the end of Assyria's presence in Babylonia.

[233] On the last days of the city Aššur, see Miglus, ISIMU 3 (2000) pp. 85–99; and Miglus, Befund und Historierung pp. 9–11. There is evidence of burning throughout the city. The Assyrian kings' tombs, which were located in the Old Palace, were looted, their sarcophagi smashed, and their bones scattered and (probably) destroyed; see Ass ph 6785 (MacGinnis in Brereton, I am Ashurbanipal p. 284 fig. 292), which shows the smashed remains of an Assyrian royal tomb. It has been suggested that this destruction might have been the work of Elamite troops, who were paying Assyria back for Ashurbanipal's desecration of Elamite royal tombs in Susa in 646, which is described as follows: "I destroyed (and) demolished the tombs of their earlier and later kings, (men) who had not revered (the god) Aššur and the goddess Ištar, my lords, (and) who had disturbed the kings, my ancestors; I exposed (them) to the sun. I took their bones to Assyria. I prevented their ghosts from sleeping (and) deprived them of funerary libations" (Novotny and Jeffers, RINAP 5/1 p. 250 Asb. 11 [Prism A] vi 70–76).

Kalḫu was also destroyed in 614 and again in 612. See D. Oates and J. Oates, Nimrud *passim*; and Miglus, Befund und Historierung pp. 8–9. A well in Ashurnasirpal II's palace (Northwest Palace) filled with the remains of over one hundred people attests to the city's violent end (D. Oates and J. Oates, Nimrud pp. 100–104). Some of the remains might have been removed from (royal) tombs desecrated during Kalḫu's sack, while other bodies were thrown down there alive, as suggested from the fact that the excavators found skeletons with shackles still on their hands and feet. While Nabû's temple Ezida was being looted and destroyed, the copies of Esarhaddon's Succession Treaty (Parpola and Watanabe, SAA 2 pp. XXIX–XXXI and 28–58 no. 6) that had been stored (and displayed) in that holy building were smashed to pieces on the floor. For evidence of the selective mutilation of bas reliefs in the Northwest Palace, see Porter, Studies Parpola pp. 201–220, esp. pp. 210–218. For an overview of the widespread destruction of Assyria's cities, see MacGinnis in Brereton, I am Ashurbanipal pp. 280–283.

[234] As J. MacGinnis (in Brereton, I am Ashurbanipal p. 280) has pointed out, "the very size of the city [Nineveh] proved to be its fatal weakness. The length of its wall — a circuit of almost 12 kilometres — made it impossible to defend effectively at all places." The fact that Nineveh had eighteen gates, plus the Tigris River nearby, did not help.

[235] For evidence of Nineveh's destruction, which included the deliberate mutilation of individuals depicted on sculpted slabs adorning the walls of Sennacherib's South-West Palace and Ashurbanipal's North Palace, see, for example, Reade, AMI NF 9 (1976) p. 105; Reade, Assyrian Sculpture p. 51 fig. 73; Curtis and Reade, Art and Empire pp. 72–77 (with figs. 20–22), 86–87 (with figs. 28–29), and 122–123; Stronach in Parpola and Whiting, Assyria 1995 pp. 307–324 (with references to earlier studies); Reade, RLA 9/5–6 (2000) pp. 415–416 §14.3 and pp. 427–428 §18; Porter, Studies Parpola pp. 203–207; Reade, in Brereton, I am Ashurbanipal pp. 32–33 (with fig. 28); and Macginnis in Brereton, I am Ashurbanipal p. 281. One of the more striking examples of the selected mutilation by Assyria's enemies is the wide gash across Sennacherib's face in the so-called "Lachish Reliefs" (BM 124911) in Room XXXVI of the South-West Palace (Reade, Assyrian Sculpture p. 51 fig. 73). There is evidence of heavy burning in the palaces. The intensity of Nineveh's last stand is evidenced by excavation of the Halzi Gate, where excavators discovered the remains of people (including a baby) who had been cut down by a barrage of arrows as they tried to flee Nineveh while parts of the city were on fire. See Stronach in Parpola and Whiting, Assyria 1995 p. 319 pls. IIIa–b.

[236] Some (fictional) correspondence between Sîn-šarra-iškun and Nabopolassar from the final days of the Assyrian Empire exists in the form of the so-called "Declaring War" and "Letter of Sîn-šarra-iškun" texts. The former (BM 55467; Gerardi, AfO 33 [1986] pp. 30–38), which is known from a tablet dating to the Achaemenid or Seleucid Period, was allegedly written by Nabopolassar to an unnamed Assyrian king (certainly Sîn-šarra-iškun) accusing him of various atrocities and declaring war on the Assyrian, stating: "[*On account*] of the crimes against the land Akkad that you have committed, the god Marduk, the great lord, [*and the great gods*] shall call [*you*] to account [...] I shall destroy

suicide, was murdered by one or more of his officials, or was executed by the troops of Nabopolassar or Cyaxares — is not recorded in cuneiform sources, including the Fall of Nineveh Chronicle (see below).[237]

Aššur-uballiṭ II and the End of the Assyrian Empire

Although Nineveh was in ruins and Sîn-šarra-iškun was dead, the Assyrian Empire still had a little bit of fight in her. Aššur-uballiṭ II (611–609), a man who was very likely the son and designated heir of Sîn-šarra-iškun, declared himself king of Assyria in Ḫarrān, an important provincial capital located in the northwestern part of Assyria, near the Baliḫ River (close to modern Urfa).[238] Assyria's last ruler — who could not officially be crowned king of Assyria since the Aššur temple at Aššur was in ruins and, thus, the ancient coronation ceremony that would confirm him as Aššur's earthly representative could not be performed[239] — relied upon Assyria's last remaining ally: Egypt. While Nabopolassar's armies consolidated Babylonia's hold over the Assyrian heartland in 611, Aššur-uballiṭ was able to prepare for battle in his makeshift capital. In 610, Nabopolassar, together with Cyaxares, marched west, crossed the Euphrates River, and headed directly for Ḫarrān, Assyria's last bastion. As the Babylonian and Median forces approached the city, Aššur-uballiṭ and his supporters fled since any fight would have been futile. By saving his own skin, this Assyrian ruler put off the final death blow of his kingdom by one year. When the armies of Nabopolassar and Cyaxares arrived at Ḫarrān, they thoroughly looted and destroyed it and its principal temple Eḫulḫul, which was dedicated to the moon-god Sîn. During the following year, 609, Aššur-uballiṭ returned with a large Egyptian army and attacked the Babylonian garrisons that Nabopolassar had stationed near Ḫarrān. Despite this minor victory, he failed to retake the city. By the time, the king of Babylon arrived on the scene, Aššur-uballiṭ and his Egyptian allies were no longer in the vicinity of Ḫarrān and, therefore, he marched to the land Izalla and attacked it instead. Aššur-uballiṭ was never to be heard from again. The once-great Assyrian Empire was gone, but not forgotten.[240]

Some key events of the Neo-Assyrian Period were recorded in the Bible, the writings of Greek and Roman historians (for example, Berossus, Ctesias of Cnidus, Herodotus, and Josephus), and Aramaic and Demotic tales (for example, the tale of Ahiqar, the Inaros Cycle, and the Brothers' War [Amherst Papyrus 63]) and these sources, with their portrayals of Assyria and some of its more memorable kings and their deeds (or misdeeds), kept the memory of the Assyrian Empire alive until Assyria's rediscovery in the mid-19th century, when its capital cities began to be unearthed and native, contemporary cuneiform sources written in the Akkadian language came to light.[241]

Dating and Chronology

Unless it is stated otherwise, the dates given in this volume (excluding those in bibliographical citations) are all BC. Each ancient Mesopotamian year has been given a single Julian year equivalent even though the ancient year actually encompassed parts of two Julian years, with the ancient year beginning around the time of the vernal equinox. Thus, for example, the 1st regnal year of Ashurbanipal (the eponymy of Mār-larīm) is indicated

you [...]" (rev. 10–14). The (fictional) response is a fragmentary letter (MMA 86.11.370a + MMA 86.11.370c +MMA 86.11.383c–e; Lambert, CTMMA 2 pp. 203–210 no. 44), known from a Seleucid Period copy, purported to have been written by Sîn-šarra-iškun to Nabopolassar while the Assyrian capital Nineveh was under siege, pleading to the Babylonian king, whom the besieged Assyrian humbly refers to as "my lord," to be allowed to remain in power. For further details about these texts, see, for example, Lambert, CTMMA 2 pp. 203–210 no. 44; Frahm, NABU 2005/2 pp. 43–46 no. 43; Da Riva, JNES 76 (2017) pp. 80–81; and Frazer, Akkadian Royal Letters.

[237] See the section *Ashurbanipal's Death* above, esp. n. 178, for more information.

[238] On Aššur-uballiṭ II, see, for example, J. Oates, CAH² 3/2 p. 182; Brinkman, PNA 1/1 p. 228 sub Aššūr-uballiṭ no. 2; Radner, Tall Šēḫ Ḥamad pp. 17–19; Frahm, Companion to Assyria p. 192; Radner in Yamada, SAAS 28 pp. 135–142; and MacGinnis in Brereton, I am Ashurbanipal pp. 283–284.

[239] On Aššur-uballiṭ remaining as the heir designate, rather than the king, of Assyria, see Radner in Yamada, SAAS 28 pp. 135–142.

[240] For Assyria after 612, its "afterlife," and legacy (with references to previous literature), see, for example, Curtis, Continuity of Empire pp. 157–167; Frahm, Companion to Assyria pp. 193–196; and Hauser in Frahm, Companion to Assyria pp. 229–246. For Nabopolassar (625–605) and Nebuchadnezzar II (604–562) modelling the organization of their central palace bureaucracy and imperial administration on Assyria's, see Jursa, Achämenidenhof pp. 67–106; and Jursa, Imperien und Reiche pp. 121–148. Urban life continued to some extent in Assyria's once-grand metropolises and the cult of the god Aššur survived in Aššur. See, for example, Miglus, Studies Strommenger pp. 135–142; Dalley, AoF 20 (1993) pp. 134–147; Dalley, Hanging Garden pp. 179–202; Frahm, Companion to Assyria pp. 193–194; and Radner, Herrschaftslegitimation pp. 77–96. A handful of "post-Assyrian" legal contracts have been discovered at Dur-Katlimmu (modern Tell Sheikh Hamad), a site on the eastern bank of the Khabur River. These texts come from the early reign of the Neo-Babylonian king Nebuchadnezzar II, between 603 and 600; see Postgate, SAAB 7 (1993) pp. 109–124; and Radner, Tall Šēḫ Ḥamad pp. 61–69 nos. 37–40.

[241] For Assyria in the Hebrew Bible and in Classical Sources, see respectively Frahm, Companion to Assyria pp. 556–569; and Rollinger in Frahm, Companion to Assyria pp. 570–582.

to be 668, although it actually ended in early 667 and, thus, events which took place late in the ancient year "668" actually took place early in the Julian year 667.

Texts edited in this volume occasionally mention contemporary dates and the charts in this section are intended to aid the reader in understanding those dates.

The traditional order of the Mesopotamian month names and their modern equivalents are:

I	Nisannu	March–April	VII	Tašrītu	September–October
II	Ayyāru	April–May	VIII	Araḫsamna	October–November
III	Simānu	May–June	IX	Kislīmu	November–December
IV	Du'ūzu	June–July	X	Ṭebētu, Kanūnu	December–January
V	Abu	July–August	XI	Šabāṭu	January–February
VI	Ulūlu	August–September	XII	Addaru	February–March
VI_2	Intercalary Ulūlu		XII_2	Intercalary Addaru	

Based on evidence from Babylonia, Intercalary Addaru (XII_2) was (sometimes) placed before the "normal" twelfth month, just as it is still done today in the Jewish calendar.[242] This might have also been the case for Intercalary Ulūlu (VI_2). In Assyria, it is unknown if one or both of these inserted months were added prior to, instead of after, Ulūlu (VI) and Addaru (XII). A letter from Mār-Ištar, Esarhaddon's agent in Babylonia,[243] concerning the interruption of a festival in Ulūlu might provide seventh-century evidence for Intercalary Ulūlu (VI_2) coming before the "normal" Ulūlu. The relevant portion of that piece of correspondence reads as follows:

> As to what the king, my lord, wrote to me: "The month Ulūlu (VI) is intercalary; do not perform the ceremonies this month" — Ammu-salām entered Babylon on the evening of the 6th day; the god Nabû had come before him, on the 3rd. The gate was kept open before the gods Bēl and Nabû on the 4th, the 5th and the 6th, and sacrifices were performed. When I saw the king my lord's sealed order, I issued the order: the rest of the ceremonies of Ulūlu (VI) will be performed in the coming month, as the king, my lord, wrote to me.[244]

Although it is not explicitly stated by Mār-Ištar, one could tentatively assume that an Intercalary Ulūlu was added (last minute) before the "normal" Ulūlu, thereby causing the in-progress festival to be postponed one month so that it could be performed during the "normal" Ulūlu, rather than in the then Intercalary Ulūlu.[245] Because the festival was to take place during a regularly scheduled month, the king and his advisors were keenly aware of the importance of maintaining the (various) cultic calendar(s), especially during a year in which an intercalary month was added. Therefore, it is not unreasonable to assumed that "normal" Ulūlu and Addaru took place immediately before Nisannu (I) and Tašrītu (VII) respectively, rather than being separated from them by an intercalary month. This would seemingly ensure that there were no major disruptions between ceremonies and festivals that were celebrated just before the *akītu*-festival (New Year's festival). Should this actually have been the case during the (late) Neo-Assyrian Period, then the revised order of the Mesopotamian month names and their modern equivalents should be:

I	Nisannu	March–April	VII	Tašrītu	September–October
II	Ayyāru	April–May	VIII	Araḫsamna	October–November
III	Simānu	May–June	IX	Kislīmu	November–December
IV	Du'ūzu	June–July	X	Ṭebētu, Kanūnu	December–January
V	Abu	July–August	XI	Šabāṭu	January–February
VI_2	Intercalary Ulūlu		XII_2	Intercalary Addaru	
VI	Ulūlu	August–September	XII	Addaru	February–March

[242] For details on the presently-available evidence (from the reign of Nabonidus), see Magdalene, Wunsch, and Wells, Fault, Responsibility and Administrative Law pp. 464–465.

[243] For a brief overview of his correspondence, see Baker, PNA 2/2 pp. 739–740 sub Mār-Issār no. 18.

[244] Parpola, SAA 10 p. 295 no. 357. The translation is S. Parpola's, but with a few minor modifications to match RINAP's editorial style.

[245] S. Parpola (LAS 2 pp. 284–285, commentary to no. 287) states the following: "While the intercalation of a second Ulūlu did not alter the name of the month in which the festival took place, it was necessary to postpone part of the ceremonies till the following month since the festival of Ulūlu was originally connected with the New Year's festival of Tašrītu, and it would have been unthinkable to break the sequence of cultic events leading from one festival to the other by a hiatus of a month or more."

For a table attempting to precisely convert Assyrian dates to Julian ones for the first twenty-one years of Ashurbanipal's reign and translations of relevant passages in six king lists (including Babylonian King List A, the Uruk King List, and the Ptolemaic Canon), see Novotny and Jeffers, RINAP 5/1 pp. 28–30.

Eponym Dates

In Assyria, each eponym-year, called a *limmu* or *līmu* in Akkadian, was named after a high state official. Lists of these officials (eponyms) were compiled by Assyrian scribes. The eponym list for Ashurbanipal's reign breaks off after his 20th regnal year and, thus, the exact sequence from 648 to the end of the Assyrian empire (609) is unknown, so every scholar who has attempted to order the eponyms after 648 has his/her own sequence, most notably M. Falkner (AfO 17 [1954–56] pp. 100–120), S. Parpola (PNA 1/1 pp. XVIII–XX), and J.E. Reade (Orientalia NS 67 [1998] pp. 255–265). P. Miglus (Befund und Historierung pp. 11–14) has carefully assessed the proposed sequences of eponyms against the dated texts in twenty-three Neo-Assyrian archives at Aššur and has concluded Parpola's proposed reconstruction for Sîn-šarra-iškun's eponyms for the years 614-612 cannot be reconciled with the archaeological findings from Aššur, whereas Reade's suggested arrangement for this same three-year period does.[246] Charts comparing Falkner's, Parpola's, and Reade's suggested arrangement of the post-canonical eponyms have been recently published in Baker, PNA 4/1 pp. 265–266 and Novotny and Jeffers, RINAP 5/1 pp. 31–32, and, therefore, not reprinted here. The chart below provides the proposed eponyms for the second half of Ashurbanipal's reign (648–631), as well as for the complete reigns of Aššur-etel-ilāni, Sîn-šarra-iškun, and Aššur-uballiṭ II.

Year	*Regnal Year*	*Falkner*	*Parpola*	*Reade*
Ashurbanipal				
648	21	Bēlšunu, governor of Ḫindānu	Bēlšunu, governor of Ḫindānu	Bēlšunu, governor of Ḫindānu
647	22	Nabû-da''inanni, governor of Que	Nabû-nādin-aḫi, governor of Kār-Shalmaneser	Nabû-nādin-aḫi, governor of Kār-Shalmaneser
646	23	Nabû-šar-aḫḫēšu, governor of Samaria	Nabû-šar-aḫḫēšu, governor of Samaria	Nabû-šar-aḫḫēšu, governor of Samaria
645	24	Nabû-šarru-uṣur, chief eunuch	Šamaš-da''inanni, governor of Babylon	Nabû-da''inanni, governor of Que
644	25	Marduk-rēmanni, governor of Kilīzu	Nabû-šarru-uṣur, chief eunuch	Šamaš-da''inanni, governor of Babylon
643	26	Aššur-šarru-uṣur, governor of Maraš	Aššur-šarru-uṣur, governor of Maraš	Nabû-šarru-uṣur, chief eunuch
642	27	Mušallim-Aššur, governor of Aliḫi	Nabû-da''inanni, governor of Que	Šarru-mētu-uballiṭ, governor of Māzamua
641	28	Aššur-gimillu-tēre, chief fuller	Aššur-gārū'a-nēre, chief cupbearer	Aššur-šarru-uṣur, governor of Maraš
640	29	Zababa-erība (unknown rank)	Šarru-mētu-uballiṭ, governor of Māzamua	Aššur-gārū'a-nēre, chief cupbearer
639	30	Sîn-šarru-uṣur, governor of Ḫindānu / Sîn-šarru-uṣur, governor of Nineveh	Mušallim-Aššur, governor of Aliḫi	Bulluṭu, chief singer Upāqa-ana-Arbail (unknown rank)
638	31	Bēlu-lū-dāri (unknown rank)	Aššur-gimillu-tēre, chief fuller	Upāqa-ana-Arbail (unknown rank)
637	32	Šarru-mētu-uballiṭ, governor of Māzamua	Zababa-erība (unknown rank)	Mušallim-Aššur, governor of Aliḫi

[246] P. Miglus (Befund und Historierung pp. 13–14) makes the following statement about the post-canonical eponym sequence for the years 614–612: "Zusammenfassend ist festzustellen, dass die von Simo Parpola vorgenommene Rekonstruktion der Eponymen-Abfolge für die Jahre 614-12 v. Chr. mit den archäologischen Befunden in Assur nicht in Einklang zu bringen ist. Sie setzt eine Kontinuität der Privatarchive voraus, von denen mindestens neun die Eroberung der Stadt unbeschadet überdauert haben müssten. Dies würde bedeuten, dass ihre Besitzer in einer völlig neuen politischen und wirtschaftlichen Lage unverändert ihren bisherigen Geschäften hätten nachgehen können. Julian Reade listet als Eponymen für 614 v. Chr. Sîn-šarru-uṣur, den Statthalter von Ninive, auf, für 613 v. Chr. Marduk-rēmanni, den Statthalter von Kalizi, und für 612 v. Chr. Nabû-mār-šarri-uṣur (Tab. 1.2). In Assur findet man lediglich den ersten auf dem Schuldschein 1.23 im Archiv 52a. Das Dokument datiert vom 22. Elūlu (VI.) und dürfte somit unmittelbar vor der Stadteroberung verfasst worden sein. Die beiden anderen Namen sind hingegen in Assur nicht belegt, was die von Reade vorgenommene Rekonstruktion der postkanonischen Eponymenreihe für diesen Zeitabschnitt zu bestätigen scheint."

Year	*Regnal Year*	*Falkner*	*Parpola*	*Reade*
636	33	Šamaš-da''inanni, governor of Babylon / Šarru-mētu-uballiṭ, governor of Māzamua	Sîn-šarru-uṣur, governor of Ḫindānu	Aššur-gimillu-tēre, chief fuller
635	34	Aššur-gārū'a-nēre, chief cupbearer	Bēlu-lū-dāri (unknown rank)	Zababa-erība (unknown rank)
634	35	Nabû-nādin-aḫi, governor of Kār-Shalmaneser	Bulluṭu, chief singer	Sîn-šarru-uṣur, governor of Ḫindānu
633	36	Ashurbanipal, king	Upāqa-ana-Arbail (unknown rank)	Bēlu-lū-dāri (unknown rank)
632	37	Bulluṭu, chief singer	Ṭāb-ṣil-Sîn (unknown rank)	Adad-rēmanni (unknown rank)
631	38	Upāqa-ana-Arbail (unknown rank)	Adad-rēmanni (unknown rank)	Marduk-šarru-uṣur, governor of Que
Aššur-etel-ilāni				
630	1	Adad-rēmanni (unknown rank)	Ṣalam-šarri-iqbi, field marshal of Kummuḫu	Bēl-šaddû'a (unknown rank)
629	2	Bēl-šarru-na'id (unknown rank)	Nabû-šarru-uṣur "the later," palace scribe	Nabû-sagībi, governor of Laḫīru
628	3	Nabû-sagībi, governor of Laḫīru	after Nabû-šarru-uṣur, palace scribe	Sîn-šarru-uṣur, palace scribe; Sîn-šarru-uṣur, "the later" (unknown rank); Nūr-ṣalam-ṣarpi (unknown rank)
627	4[247]	Mannu-kī-aḫḫē, governor of Ṣimirra (hapax Nineveh)	Marduk-šarru-uṣur, governor of Que	Kanūnāyu, governor of Dūr-Šarrukīn
Sîn-šarra-iškun				
626	1	Nabû-šarru-uṣur "the later," palace scribe	Marduk-rēmanni, governor of Kilīzu; Iqbi-ilāni (unknown rank)	Aššur-mātu-taqqin, governor of (U)pummu
625	2	after Nabû-šarru-uṣur, palace scribe	Sîn-šumu-ibni (unknown rank; hapax Nineveh); Sîn-šarru-uṣur, palace scribe	Aššur-rēmanni, chief eunuch of the crown prince
624	3	Aššur-mātu-taqqin, governor of (U)pummu	Kanūnāyu, governor of Dūr-Šarrukīn	Nabû-šarru-uṣur "the later," palace scribe
623	4	Ṣalam-šarri-iqbi, field marshal of Kummuḫu	Aššur-mātu-taqqin, governor of (U)pummu	Ṣalam-šarri-iqbi, field marshal of Kummuḫu
622	5	Sîn-šarru-uṣur, palace scribe	Dādî, (chief) treasurer	Dādî, (chief) treasurer
621	6	Aššur-rēmanni, chief eunuch of the crown prince	Bēl-iqbi, governor of Tušḫan	Bēl-aḫu-uṣur, palace overseer
620	7	Dādî, (chief) treasurer	Sa'īlu, chief cook	Sa'īlu, chief cook
619	8	Bēl-aḫu-uṣur, palace overseer	Mannu-kī-aḫḫē, governor of Ṣimirra (hapax Nineveh)	Bēl-iqbi, governor of Tušḫan
618	9	Sa'īlu, chief cook	Nabû-sagībi, governor of Laḫīru	Iqbi-ilāni (unknown rank)
617	10	Nabû-tappûtī-alik, chief eunuch	Aššur-rēmanni, chief eunuch of the crown prince	Sîn-ālik-pāni, chamberlain
616	11	Bēl-iqbi, governor of Tušḫan	Bēl-aḫu-uṣur, palace overseer	Nabû-tappûtī-alik, chief eunuch (= Pašî)
615	12	Iqbi-ilāni (unknown rank); Sîn-ālik-pāni, chamberlain	Sîn-ālik-pāni, chamberlain	Šamaš-šarru-ibni, field marshal
614	13	Sîn-kēnu-īdi	Pašî (unknown rank)	Sîn-šarru-uṣur, governor of Nineveh
613	14	Šamaš-šarru-ibni, field marshal	Nabû-tappûtī-alik, chief eunuch	Marduk-rēmanni, governor of Kilīzu
612	15[248]	Nabû-mār-šarri-uṣur, field marshal	Šamaš-šarru-ibni, field marshal	Nabû-mār-šarri-uṣur, field marshal

247 627, Aššur-etel-ilāni's 4th regnal year, is also the accession years of Sîn-šuma-līšir and Sîn-šarra-iškun.

248 612, Sîn-šarra-iškun's 15th regnal year, is also the accession year of Aššur-uballiṭ II, starting in late Abu (V) or early Ulūlu (VI) of that year, based on the extant account of the year 612 in the Fall of Nineveh Chronicle (lines 38–52); see p. 45 below.

Year	*Regnal Year*	*Falkner*	*Parpola*	*Reade*
Aššur-uballiṭ II				
611	1	—	Nabû-mār-šarri-uṣur, field marshal	—
610	2	—	Nabû-šarru-uṣur, chief judge	—
609	3	—	Gargamisāyu (unknown rank)	—

Seven inscriptions of Sîn-šarra-iškun bear dates. These are as follows:

Eponym	*Falkner*	*Parpola*	*Reade*	*Dated Sîn-šarra-iškun Texts*
Aššur-mātu-taqqin, governor of (U)pummu	624	623	626	9 (Aššur)
Bēl-aḫu-uṣur, palace overseer	619	616	621	6 (Nineveh), 10 (Aššur)
Dādî, (chief) treasurer	620	622	622	19 (Kalḫu)
Nabû-tappûtī-alik, chief eunuch[249]	617	613	616	1 (Nineveh)
Sa'īlu, chief cook	618	620	620	11 (Aššur)
Sîn-šarru-uṣur, governor of Ḫindānu	639	636	634	3 (Nineveh)

Given that Sîn-šarra-iškun's inscriptions from Kalḫu and Nineveh record different building projects,[250] it is not possible to establish a chronological sequence for Bēl-aḫu-uṣur, Dādî, Nabû-tappûtī-alik, and Sîn-šarru-uṣur (governor of Ḫindānu) based solely on those texts. However, since all of the dated inscriptions of Sîn-šarra-iškun from Aššur record the construction of the Nabû temple at Aššur, it might be possible to suggest an order for the eponymies of Aššur-mātu-taqqin, Bēl-aḫu-uṣur, and Sa'īlu. As proposed already by Falkner and Reade,[251] the chronological order of these three eponym-officials is likely Aššur-mātu-taqqin, Bēl-aḫu-uṣur, and Sa'īlu. There is probably no gap or an interlude of not more than a year (or two) between Aššur-mātu-taqqin and Bēl-aḫu-uṣur.[252] The provisional order is based on (1) the fact that Ssi 9 (Ass 3518+) is a shorter version of Ssi 10 (Cylinder A) and (2) the assumption that Ssi 11, an inscription written on clay cones adorning the interior walls (once they had been built), would have been written after Ssi 10, a text copied onto clay cylinders (and prisms) deposited inside the structure of the temple (as its walls were being built). Given the size of this building, it is tentatively proposed here that Aššur-mātu-taqqin, Bēl-aḫu-uṣur, and Sa'īlu held the post of eponym one after the other, with no gaps, or with no more than one year between their tenures. If this proves correct, then the end date for this three- to five-year period might have been 620 (Sîn-šarra-iškun's 7th year as king) — or 619, 618, 617, or even 616 (his 8th–11th regnal years) at the absolute latest — since Nabopolassar besieged Aššur in Ayyāru (II) and Simānu (III) of 615 and the Medes under Cyaxares (Umakištar) captured and destroyed Assyria's traditional religious capital sometime after Abu (V) 614.[253] Given what little we know about Sîn-šarra-iškun's reign, most of which comes from the Fall of Nineveh Chronicle (see below), Aššur-mātu-taqqin, Bēl-aḫu-uṣur, and Sa'īlu were most likely eponyms earlier in Sîn-šarra-iškun's tenure as king, perhaps starting in 626, 625, 624, or 623. An early date for Aššur-mātu-taqqin's stint as eponym is fairly certain since, as already pointed out by J.E. Reade,[254] a Babylonian-style legal text from Nippur is dated by his eponymy and, therefore, that governor of (U)pummu must have been eponym before 620, at the absolute latest, because the last documents from Babylonia dated by Sîn-šarra-iškun's regnal years are from that year.[255] Given that transactions from Nippur are dated by his 2nd to 6th regnal years, it is likely that the legal transaction in question (Ni 2534) dates to near the beginning of Sîn-šarra-iškun's reign, possibly either to his 1st (626), as proposed by Reade, or 2nd (625) year as king.[256] The year 625 is tentatively preferred here for the eponymy of Aššur-mātu-taqqin (1) since the year 627 was extremely turbulent;[257] (2) because Sîn-šarra-iškun, at least

[249] J.E. Reade (Orientalia NS 67 [1998] p. 259) proposes that Pašî was an alternate name used for Nabû-tappûtī-alik at Aššur.

[250] Ssi 1 (lines 12′–15′) records work on the "Alabaster House" at Nineveh (=the South-West Palace), Ssi 6 would have described the construction on Nineveh's city wall, and Ssi 19 (lines 30–37) gives an account of the rebuilding of the Nabû temple (Ezida) at Kalḫu. The building account of Ssi 3 is not sufficiently preserved to be able to identify which building at Nineveh that text commemorated.

[251] For this opinion, see also Novotny, Kaskal 11 (2014) p. 164 n. 11.

[252] This would mean that it took Sîn-šarra-iškun five or six years to build the superstructure of Nabû's temple at Aššur. Based on S. Parpola's arrangement of these eponyms, it would have taken him eight years to build the temple.

[253] Fall of Nineveh Chronicle lines 16–30 (see p. 44).

[254] Reade, Orientalia NS 67 (1998) p. 258.

[255] See n. 231 above.

[256] Brinkman and Kennedy, JCS 35 (1983) p. 62 no. Sn.2.

[257] One could suggest, for example, that Sîn-šarru-uṣur the palace scribe (attested in date formulae for months I–X), Sîn-šarru-uṣur "the

according to his own inscriptions, spent a great deal of time and effort preparing the building site that he could construct Nabû's temple at Aššur; and (3) since Aššur-mātu-taqqin's tenure as eponym was shortly after that of Kanūnāyu, governor of Dūr-Šarrukīn, and there do not appear to have been any irregularities during the period that Kanūnāyu was eponym.[258]

With regard to Parpola's suggestion that Nabû-tappûtī-alik was eponym in 613, this seems highly unlikely,[259] unless, however, the work on the western part of the South-West Palace was a last-minute effort to strengthen it from potential breaches via the Step Gate of the Palace and the Step Gate of the Gardens. If that was not the case, then one should expect that Nabû-tappûtī-alik held that prestigious post before Babylonian and Median forces started campaigning in the Assyrian heartland, that is, before 615, as Falkner and Reade suggest.

Dates of Ashurbanipal's Babylonian Inscriptions

A number of Ashurbanipal's inscriptions from Babylonia mention his older brother Šamaš-šuma-ukīn in a positive light and, thus, were certainly composed before the start of the Brothers' War in 652. The inscriptions of Ashurbanipal that do not refer to Šamaš-šuma-ukīn and that were written on clay cylinders are presumed to have been written after Babylon opened its gates to Ashurbanipal in late 648, while Kandalānu, Ashurbanipal's hand-selected replacement as the king of Babylon, sat on the throne.

The inscriptions of Sîn-balāssu-iqbi (Asb. 2003–2018), the governor of Ur, also predate the Šamaš-šuma-ukīn rebellion. That governor of Ur — who undertook construction of the moon-god temple Ekišnugal on Ashurbanipal's behalf, rather than Šamaš-šuma-ukīn's — is attested as the governor of Ur only for the years 658 and 657, although he undoubtedly held that position for a much longer period of time. A pre-652 date for these texts is confirmed by the fact that his (younger?) brother Sîn-šarru-uṣur had replaced him as governor of Ur (shortly) before the outbreak of the Šamaš-šuma-ukīn rebellion.[260]

Chronicles

Three Mesopotamian chronicles provide useful information both on events of the reigns of Assyria's last two rulers Sîn-šarra-iškun and Aššur-uballiṭ II and on the order of those events.[261] The standard edition of Mesopotamian chronicles is the edition of A.K. Grayson (Grayson, Chronicles), but note also the more-recent edition by J.-J. Glassner (Glassner, Chronicles) and the ongoing work by I. Finkel and R.J. van der Spek (see https://www.livius.org/sources/about/mesopotamian-chronicles/ [last accessed January 25, 2023]). For the convenience of the user of this volume, it has been thought useful to present translations of the relevant passages here; these translations are adapted from the aforementioned works.

1. *Chronicle Concerning the Early Years of Nabopolassar*
   (Grayson, Chronicles pp. 87–90 no. 2; Glassner, Chronicles pp. 214–219 no. 21)[262]

1–4a) [...] when he[263] had sent [*troops*] to Babylon, [*they entered the city*] during the night. *Then*, they did battle inside the city for an entire day. [*They inflicted a defeat* (*on them and*)[264] the garriso]n of Sîn-šarra-iškun[265] fled to Assyria. The city (Babylon) was entrusted to [...].[266]

4b–9) On the twelfth day of the month Ulūlu (VI), the troops of Assyria [*went down to Akkad*], entered the

later" (IX–XI), and Nūr-ṣalam-ṣarpi (XII) were all eponym in 627, while Sîn-šuma-līšir and Sîn-šarra-iškun vied for power.

258 For the evidence that Aššur-mātu-taqqin (immediately) followed Kanūnāyu as eponym, see Dalley and Postgate, Fort Shalmaneser pp. 55–56 and pl. 2 no. 6.

259 P. Miglus (Befund und Historierung pp. 13–14) has also come to this conclusion; see n. 246 above.

260 Note that another of Sîn-balāssu-iqbi's brothers, Sîn-tabni-uṣur, was governor of Ur in 650–649. See, for example, Frame, Babylonia pp. 278–279.

261 For translations of the four Mesopotamian chronicles that provide information on events of the reigns of Ashurbanipal and Šamaš-šuma-ukīn, see Novotny and Jeffers, RINAP 5/1 pp. 33–36.

262 For a recent study of lines 1–17, see Fuchs, Studies Oelsner pp. 64–65.

263 Lines 1–9 likely record events that took place during 627. J.J. Glassner (Chronicles pp. 216–217) reads the beginning of line 1 as [*ina* ITI.*x* mdAG-IBILA-ÙRU ERIM.MEŠ] *ana* TIN.TIR.KI *ki-i iš-pu-ru*, which he translates as "[in the month of ..., Nabopolassar] having sent [troops] to Babylon." As the events recorded here took place before Ulūlu (VI), presumably in 627, it is unclear whether or not Nabopolassar was involved at Babylon at that time. It is not impossible that this passage refers to infighting between Sîn-šuma-līšir and Sîn-šarra-iškun.

264 J.J. Glassner (Chronicles p. 217) translates this passage as "they inflicted a defeat on Assyria," but restores only [BAD$_5$.BAD$_5$ GAR.MEŠ].

265 It is possible that Sîn-šarra-iškun could be an error for Sîn-šuma-līšir.

266 A.K. Grayson (Chronicles p. 88) translates the first part of line 4 as "he appointed [*officials* with]in the city."

city Šasnaku,[267] (and) set fire to (its) temple (and) [*had (its) property brought out*]. Then, in the month Tašrītu (VII), the gods of Kish went to Babylon. [*On the ...th day*, the troops o]f Assyria marched to Nippur and Nabopolassar retreated before them. [The troops of As]syria and the citizens of Nippur went after him as fa[r] as Uruk. At Uruk, they did battle against Nabopolassar, but (then) retreated before Nabopolassar.

10–13) In the month Ayyāru (II),[268] the troops of Assyria went down to Akkad. On the twelfth day of the month Tašrītu (VII), when the troops of Assyria had marched against Babylon (and) when the Babylonians had come out of Babylon, on that (very) day, they (the Babylonians) did battle against the troops of Assyria. They inflicted a major defeat upon the troops of Assyria and took them as prisoners.

14–15a) For one (entire) year, there was no king in the land (Akkad). On the twenty-sixth day of the month Araḫsamna (VIII), Nabopolassar ascended the throne in Babylon.

15b–17) The accession year of Nabopolassar (626): In the month Addaru (XIII), Nabopolassar returned the gods of Susa to Susa, whom (the king of) Assyria had carried off and made reside in Uruk.[269]

18–19) The first year of Nabopolassar (625): On the seventeenth day of the month Nisannu (I), terror fell upon the city (Šapazzu). The god Šamaš and the gods of the city Šapazzu (Bāṣ) went to Babylon.[270]

20) On the twenty-first day of the month Ayyāru (II), the troops of Assyria [en]tered the city Sal[lāte][271] (and) had (its) property brought out.

21–24) On the twentieth day <of the month Simānu (III)/Duʾūzu (IV)>, the gods of Sippar we[nt] to Babylon [and], on the ninth day of the month Abu (V), Nabopolassar and his troops [marched] to the city Sall[āte] and did battle against the city Sallāte, but he did not take the city. The troops of Assyria arriv[e]d and he (Nabopolassar) retreated before them and withdrew.

25–28) [The second year] of Nabopolassar (624): At the beginning of the month Ulūlu (VI), the troops of Assyria went down [to Akkad] and set up camp by the Banītu canal. They did [battle against Nab]opolassar, but *achieved nothing.* [...] ...[272] and (then) they withdrew.

29–34) [The third year (623)]: On the eighth [day of the month ...], Dēr rebelled against Assyria. On the fifteenth day of the month Tašrītu (VII), [...[273] (In)] that (same) [year], the king of Assyria and his troops went down to Akkad and [*took Uruk.*[274] *He had (its) property brought out*] and made (it) enter Nippur. Afterwards, Itti-ili [*rebelled. When the king of Assyria hea*]*rd (this),*[275] he posted a garrison in Nippur [*(and) went back to his land. Itti-ili set out from*] (the area) Across the River (Ebēr nāri), came up, and [...] against [*(the city)* ...]. He ravaged [the city ...]nu. Then, he set out towards Nineveh.

35–40) [...],[276] who had come to do battle against him, [... *whe*]*n* they saw him, they bowed down before him. [...]. The rebel king [...] one hundred days [...] ... when [... the] rebel [*king* ...].

2. *Fall of Nineveh Chronicle*
(Grayson, Chronicles pp. 90–96 no. 3; Glassner, Chronicles pp. 218–225 no. 22)

1–2) The tenth year of Nabopolassar (616): In the month Ayyāru (II), he mustered the troops of Akkad and

[267] Šasnaku is probably not far from Sippar. On its location, see Zadok, Rép. Géogr. 8 pp. 289–290.
[268] Lines 10–17 probably record the events that occurred in 626.
[269] The Assyrian in question is Ashurbanipal, who sacked and plundered Susa in 646; see the section *Uruk* above for some details.
[270] Šapazzu, which is also known as Bāṣ, is a city in the vicinity of Sippar. See Bagg, Rép. Géogr. 7/3 p. 102. Its principal god is Bēl-ṣarbi.
[271] Sallāte is a city in northern Babylonia, on the east bank of the Euphrates, in the vicinity of Sippar; see M.P. Streck, RLA 11/7–8 (2008) p. 578; Zadok, Rép. Géogr. 8 p. 285; and Bagg, Rép. Géogr. 7/3 p. 499. This city is not to be confused with the Assyrian city Raqamātu, which is located in the Habur triangle, west of Naṣibina and north of Guzana; see Bagg, Rép. Géogr. 7/2 pp. 505–506.
[272] J.J. Glassner (Mesopotamian Chronicles p. 216) reads the beginning of line 28 as [ERIM.MEŠ KUR *aš-šur* ...]-*suḫ-ma* "[the troops of Assyria *broke up ca*]*mp*."
[273] J.J. Glassner (Mesopotamian Chronicles p. 216) restores here ^{m}*i-ti*-DINGIR *ṣal-tú ana* NIBRU.KI DÙ ("Itti-ili did battle against Nippur"), but without justification.
[274] The interpretation of lines 31–34 follows Fuchs, Studies Oelsner p. 34 (with nn. 29 and 31). J.J. Glassner (Chronicles p. 216) tentatively restores BÀD.AN.KI ("Dēr") in line 31.
[275] J.J. Glassner (Chronicles p. 216) restores after EGIR ^{m}*i-ti*-DINGIR ("after Itti-ili") GIN UNUG.KI *iḫ-te*]-*pe-e-ma*, thus understanding the end of line 31 and the beginning of line 32 as "[He pursued] Itti-ili, ravaged [*Uruk*]." Note that A. Fuchs (Studies Oelsner p. 34 n. 29) proposes Uruk's conquest was mentioned at the beginning of line 31, and not in line 32, as Glassner suggests.
[276] J.J. Glassner (Chronicles p. 218) reads the beginning of line 35 as [ERIM.MEŠ *šá* ^{md}30-LUGAL-GAR-*un* LUGAL KUR *aš*]-*šur* ["the troops of Sîn-šarra-iškun, the king of Ass]yria."

marched along the bank of the Euphrates River. Moreover, the Sūḫeans (and) Ḫindāneans did not do battle against him, (but) placed their possessions before him.

3–6a) In the month Abu (V), the troops of Assyria assembled in the city Gablīni[277] and Nabopolassar went up against them. Then, on the twelfth day of the month Abu (V), he did battle against the troops of Assyria and the troops of Assyria retreated before him. He then inflicted a major defeat upon Assyria (and) took many of them as prisoners. He captured the Manneans, who had come to their aid, and the officials of Assyria. On that (very) day, he (also) took the city Gablīni.

6b–8a) Also in the month Abu (V), the king of Akkad (and) his troops w[en]t up to the cities Manê, Saḫiri, and Balīḫu [a]nd took them as the spoils of war. They carried off much of their booty (and) abducted their gods.

8b–9) In the month Ulūlu (VI), the king of Akkad and his troops returned and, on his way, he took (the people of) the city Ḫindānu and its gods to Babylon.

10–11a) In the month Tašrītu (VII), the troops of Egypt and the troops of Assyria pursued the king of Akkad as far as the city [G]ablīni, but they did not overtake the king of Akkad (and so) they withdrew.

11b–15) In the month Addaru (XII), the troops of Assyria and the troops of Akkad did battle against one another at the city Madānu, which (is in the territory of) the city Arrapḫa, and the troops of Assyria retreated before the troops of Akkad. They (the troops of Akkad) inflicted a major defeat upon them (the Assyrian troops) (and) they drove them to the (Lower) Zab. They captured [t]heir char[iots] and their horses (and) took many of them as prisoners. They made many of their (text: its) [...] cross the Tigris River with them and ushered (them) into Babylon.

16–18) [The eleventh year (615): The king of] Akkad mustered his troops and marched along the bank of the Tigris River. Then, in the month Ayyāru (II), he encamped against Baltil (Aššur). [On the ...th day] of the month Simānu (III), he did battle against the city, but he did not take the city. The king of Assyria mustered his troops, pushed the king of Akkad back from Baltil (Aššur), and pursued him as far as the city Tagrita'in, [a city] on the (west) bank of the Tigris River.[278]

19–22) The king of Akkad posted his troops as a garrison in the fortress of the city Tagrita'in. The king of Assyria and his troops encamped against the troops of the king of Akkad who had been posted in the city Tagrita'in. Then, for ten days, they did battle against them, but he (the king of Assyria) did not take the city. The troops of the king of Akkad, who had been posted in the fortress, inflicted a major defeat upon Assyria. [*They pushed*] the king of Assyria and his troops [*back*] and he (the king of Assyria) returned to his land.

23) In the month Araḫsamna (VIII), the Medes went down to the city Arrapḫa and [...] ... [...].

24–27) The twelfth year (614): In the month Abu (V), when the Medes [*had set out*] against Nineveh, [*the king of Assyria and his troops*] speedily came [*to its aid*], but (nevertheless) they took Tarbiṣu, a city in the province of Nineveh. [...] they (the Medes) went along [the Ti]gris [River] and encamped against Baltil (Aššur). They did battle against the city and [...] destroyed [...]. They inflicted a terrible defeat upon a great people. He took it (Baltil) as the spoils of war (and) [carried off its] bo[oty].

28–30) [The king of A]kkad and his troops, who had gone to help the Medes, did not arrive (in time for) the battle. [When] the cit[y was taken, the king of Akka]d [and] C[yax]ares (Umakištar) met one another by the city (and) they brought about friendly relations and a peace agreement with each other. [*Afterwards*, Cyaxa]res and his troops returned to his land. The king of Akkad and his troops (also) returned to his (own) land.

31–37) [The thirteenth year (613): In the month Ayyā]ru (II), the Sūḫeans rebelled against the king of Akkad and began a war. [The king of Akkad] mustered his [tr]oops and marched to the land Sūḫu. On the fourth day of the month Simānu (III), he did [battle against the c]ity Raḫi-ilu, a city which is (on an island) in the middle of the Euphrates River, and, at that time, he took the city. He built his [...]. The men who (live) on the bank(s) of the Euphrates River came down to him (and) [...]. He encamped [against] the city Anat. [*He had*] (siege) tower[s *cross over*] *fr*[*om*] the western side, [...], brought th(os)e (siege) towers close to (Anat's) city wall. He did battle against the [city], but [*he did not take*] the c[ity.[279]

[277] Gablīni is located near where the Ḫabur joins the Euphrates; see Zadok, Rép. Géogr. 8 p. 135.

[278] Tagrita'in (Tagariteyāni) is modern Takrīt; see Zadok, Rép. Géogr. 8 p. 301; and Bagg, Rép. Géogr. 7/2 p. 582.

[279] A.K. Grayson (Chronicles p. 94) tentatively translates this passage as "and *captured it*."

... the king of] Assyria and his troops came down and [*they pushed back*] the king of Akkad and his troops.[280]

38–41) [The fourteenth year (612)]: The king of Akkad muster[ed] his troops [and march]ed [to *Assyria*]. The king of the Ummān-manda [*marched*] towards the king of Akkad. [*Then, the king of Akkad and Cyaxares*] met one another [*by the city* ...]*û*. [The k]ing of Akkad [*and his troops crossed the Tigris River and* Cy]axares had (his troops) cross [the *Rad*]*ānu* [*River*] and (then) they marched along the bank of the Tigris River. [*On the ...th day of Simānu (III)*, they encamp]ed against Nineve[h].

42–46) From the month Simānu (III) until the month Abu (V), for three [months, they ...] (and) did intensive battle against the city.[281] [On the ...th day] of the month Abu (V), they inflicted a major [defeat upon a g]reat [people]. At that time, Sîn-šarra-iškun, the king of Ass[yria, *died*. ...]. They carried off substantial booty from the city and (its) temple(s). [They turned the c]ity into a mound of ru[ins (lit. "a mound and ruins"). The ...] of Assyria escaped from the enemy and, in order to (save his own) life, he *g*[*rasped*] the feet of the king of Akkad.

47–49a) On the twentieth day of the month Ulūlu (VI), Cyaxares and his troops returned to his land. Afterwards, the king of Akka[d *and his troops*] marched as far as the city Naṣībīna. [They ...] prisoners and deportees. Moreover, they brought the (people of) the land Raṣappa (Ruṣapa) to Nineveh, before the king of Akkad.

49b–52) On [the ...th day of the] month [..., *Aššur-uballiṭ (II)*] ascended the throne in Ḫarrān to exercise the kingship of Assyria. Until [*the ...th day of*] the month [..., ...] in Nineveh. [F]rom the twentieth day of the month [...], the king of [*Akkad*] *took away* [...] and [...] in the city [...].

53–55) The fifteenth year (611): In the month Du'[ūzu (IV) the ki]ng of Akkad [mustered his troops and] marched to Assyria [and marched about] triumphantly [in Assyria]. He captured [the ...] of the lands [...] and Šu[...]a, took them as the spoils of war, (and) [carried off] their sub[stantial] booty.

56–57) In the mon[th Araḫsamn]a (VIII), the king of Akkad t[ook] the lead of his troops [and marched] against the city *Ru*[*g*]*gu*[*lītu*]. He did battle against the city and, on the twenty-eighth day of the month Araḫsamna (VIII), he took the city. [...] did not [spare] a single person (among them). He returned [to his land].

58–60) The sixteenth year (610): In the month Ayyāru (II), the king of Akkad mustered his troops [a]nd marched to Assyria. Fr[om the month ...] until the month Araḫsamna (VIII), he marched about triumphantly in Assyria. In the month Araḫsamna (VIII), the Ummān-manda came [*to the ai*]*d of* the king of Akkad. Then, they *consolidated* their troops together and marched to Ḫarrān, [agains]t [Aššur-uball]iṭ (II), who had ascended the throne in Assyria.

61–64a) Then, fear of the enemy fell over Aššur-uballiṭ (II) and the troops of Eg[ypt, who] had come [to his aid]; they aban[doned] the city [and] crossed [*the Euphrates River*]. The king of Akkad reached Ḫarrān, [did battle against *the city*, and] took the city. He carried off substantial booty from the city and (its) temple(s).

64b–65) In the month Addaru (XII), the king of Akkad left [*his troops and*] their [*camp*] and he (himself) returned to his land. Moreover, the Ummān-manda, who had co[me] to the aid [of] the king of Akkad, [with]drew.

66–68) <The seventeenth year (609)>: In the month Du'ūzu (IV), Aššur-uballiṭ (II), the king of Assyria, [(...)] the numerous troops of Egypt, [(...)], crossed the (Euphrates) River, and marched against Ḫarrān in order to conquer (the troops that the king of Akkad had posted there). [They (... *and*) *to*]*ok* [...]. They massacred the garrison that the king of Akkad had posted inside. [Wh]en they [had kill]ed (the enemy), they encamp[ed] against Ḫarrān.

(69–71) Until the month Ulūlu (VI), they did battle against the city, but ach[ieved nothing and] did not [with]draw. The king of Akkad went to the aid of his troops, but [*did not do battle*]. He went up [to the land I]zalla and he burned with fire the [...] of numerous cities in the mountains.

72–75) At that time, the troops of [... ma]rched as far as the province of Urarṭu (Urašṭu). In the *land* [...],

---

[280] A.K. Grayson (Chronicles p. 94) tentatively translates this passage as "and ... the king of Akkad and his army. *He (the king of Akkad) went home*."

[281] A.K. Grayson (Chronicles p. 94) translates this passage as "they subjected the city to a heavy siege."

they (the troops of the king of Akkad) took them as the spoils of war. They [*took awa*]y the garrison that the king of [... had posted inside it] and went up to the city [...]. The king of Akkad returned to his land.

76–77) In the [eighteenth] ye[ar (608): In the month Ulū]lu (VI), the king of Akkad mustered his troops and (...).

78) Let [the one who] lo[ve]s the gods [Na]bû and Marduk protect (this tablet and) not let (it) fall into (enemy) hands.

3. *Akītu Chronicle*

(Grayson, Chronicles pp. 131–132 no. 16; Glassner, Chronicles pp. 212–215 no. 20)

24–27) After Kandalānu,[282] in the accession year of Nabopolassar (626): There were insurrections in Assyria and Akkad. Hostilities (and) warfare were constant. The god Nabû did not go (and) the god Bēl did not come out.

----

[282] The phrase *arki Kandalānu*, "after Kandalānu," is also attested as a date formula for two Babylonian economic documents written after the death of that king of Babylon. There is one presently-attested tablet that is posthumously dated to Kandalānu's 22nd year (626); BM 40039 (Wiseman, Chronicles pp. 89–90 and pls. XVIII–XIX) was written on "Araḫsamna (VIII), 2nd day, year twenty-two, after Kandalānu, king of Babylon." This tablet was inscribed twenty-four days before Nabopolassar ascended the throne in Babylon (26-VIII-626).

241

Ashurbanipal's restoration of Nēmetti-Enlil ("Bulwark of the God Enlil"), Babylon's outer city wall, and its gates is recorded on numerous clay cylinders discovered at Babylon. The mention of Šamaš-šuma-ukīn, Ashurbanipal's older brother and the king of Babylon, in a positive manner indicates that the text was composed prior to the commencement of Šamaš-šuma-ukīn's rebellion in 652. This Akkadian inscription is sometimes referred to as "Cylinder L[ondon][6]" and "Cylinder P[runkinschrift][2]" in previous editions.

CATALOGUE

Ex.	Museum Number	Excavation/ Registration No.	Photograph Number	Provenance	Dimensions (cm)	Lines Preserved	cpn
1	BM 86918	1900-3-10,2	—	Purchased from J.E. Gejou; probably from Babylon	Length: 18.5; Dia. of ends: 5.9	1–30	c
2	Bibliothèque Nationale Inv. 65 no. 5929	—	—	Probably Babylon	15.8×7.4	1–29	c
3	B 9 (former D 240)	BE 8763	Bab ph 554	Babylon, Kasr 24n, South Palace, main court, in debris	—	1–2, 19–29	c
4	B 15 (former D 251)	BE 12131	Bab ph 559	Babylon, Kasr 23o, South Palace, in debris above the north wall of the main court	—	3–12	c
5	VA 4902	BE 29275	Bab ph 680–684	Babylon, eastern side of the inner city wall, 40 cm under the surface in the vicinity of the western face of the mud brick outer wall, in debris by tower 4 of the main wall	Length: 17.5; R dia.: 5.5; L dia.: 5.8	1–30	c
6	VA Bab 634	BE 29362	Bab ph 691	Babylon, Kasr, 22u, South Palace	Length: 15	1–30	c
7	VA Bab 602	BE 30112	Bab ph 688–689	Babylon, eastern side of the inner city wall, in the vicinity of the western face of the outer wall, in debris by tower 10 of the main wall	Length: 17.3; R dia.: 5.1; L dia.: 5.2	1–30	c
8	VA Bab 604	BE 30130	Bab ph 690	Babylon, in the vicinity of tower 8 of the main wall	Length: 15.8; R dia.: 5.5; L dia.: 5.2	1–30	c
9	VA Bab 603	BE 30160	Bab ph 706	As ex. 8	Length: 16.3; R dia.: 5.1; L dia.: 4.8	1–30	c
10	VA Bab 601	BE 30161	Bab ph 704	As ex. 8	Length: 16.5; Dia.: 7.3	1–30	c
11	VA Bab 632	BE 30164	Bab ph 705	As ex. 8	Length: 17.7; R dia.: 5.6; L dia.: 5.6	1–30	c
12	BM 47655	81-11-3,360	—	Acquired from H. Rassam's work in Babylonia; probably from Babylon	4.2×3.6	1–4, 27–28, 30	c
13	BM 47656	81-11-3,361	—	As ex. 12	4.2×3.6	1, 23, 25–29	c
14	BM 50662	82-3-23,1653	—	As ex. 12	9.1×6	1–10	c

15	BM 68613	82-9-18,8612	—	As ex. 12	11×5.8	1–6, 8–11, 28–30	c
16	BM 77223	83-6-30,3	—	Purchased from J.M. Shemtob; probably from Babylon	7.5×7	1–3, 25–30	c
17	A Babylon 55	—	—	Babylon, in a clay box, inside the inner wall, about 9 m from the point where it meets the Ištar Gate, near the fifth tower from the southeast corner	16.6×6.45	1–30	p
18	A Babylon 9	—	—	Babylon, in filling of vaulted building	—	—	n
19	IM 124171	81-B-3	—	Babylon, in debris of the inner wall 150 m east of the Ištar Gate	11.5×6	1–8, 27–30	p
20	B 42 (former D 277)	BE 33896	Bab ph 1301	Babylon, Merkes 26pI	—	5–10	c

COMMENTARY

Ex. 1 was purchased by the British Museum from J.E. Gejou (Paris) and ex. 16 from J.M. Shemtob (London). Exs. 3–11 come from the excavations of the Deutsche Orient-Gesellschaft at Babylon, exs. 12–15 from H. Rassam's work in Babylonia (see Reade in Leichty, Sippar 1 pp. xxxii–xxxiii), and exs. 17–19 from work by the Iraqi State Organization for Antiquities and Heritage at Babylon between 1979 and 1981. Exs. 12 and 13 might come from the same cylinder, but they do not physically join. See Wetzel, Stadtmauern pls. 32–33 for the exact findspots of exs. 5, 7, and 8. Information about exs. 3, 4, and 20 was kindly provided by G. Van Buylaere, who is presently preparing new editions of this material within the framework of the DFG-funded project *The Cuneiform Documents in the Babylon Collection of the Istanbul Archaeological Museums (Eski Şark Eserleri Müzesi)* (project number 438042051), directed by Nils Heeßel (Marburg University) and Daniel Schwemer (Würzburg University). Photos of exs. 5–11 were kindly provided to Frame by J. Marzahn. Parts of lines 1–8 of ex. 6 which are no longer preserved in Berlin with the main section of the exemplar are visible on Babylon photo 691; the score uses the photo for those portions of these lines. Parts of lines 23–25 of ex. 8 are no longer preserved but appear on Babylon photo 690; the score also includes those portions visible only on the photo. Ex. 10 was kindly collated by Marzahn; VAN 11306 is a photo of this exemplar. Exs. 4 are 20 were collated by D. Schwemer; transliterations of the pieces in the score are based on his examination of the fragments. A score of the text is presented on Oracc and the minor (orthographic) variants are listed at the back of the book.

Ex. 1 is written in archaizing Babylonian script and exs. 2–17 and 19–20 are in contemporary Babylonian script; the script of ex. 18 is not known. The number and arrangement of lines varies a great deal between the exemplars. When complete, the inscription is found upon 26 lines (ex. 17), 27 lines (exs. 2, 6, 7, and 10), 28 lines (exs. 5, 8, and 9), 29 lines (ex. 11) or 30 lines (ex. 1). The line arrangement follows ex. 1, as does the master line (with help from ex. 17 for lines 4, 12–19, 22–23, and 28 and from ex. 7 for line 21), with the exception of *ap-qid* and *li-ḫal-liq* in lines 14 and 30 respectively.

E. Unger (in Wetzel, Stadtmauern p. 80) states that BE 30113 is an exemplar of this inscription, but it actually has an inscription of Nabonidus; that clay cylinder, as far as it is preserved, appears to bear a copy of that king's "Eḫulḫul Cylinder" inscription (Weiershäuser and Novotny, RINBE 2 pp. 140–151 Nabonidus 28, ex. 51). The fragment BM 83001, which was cited as a duplicate of this inscription in Lambert, Cat. p. 75, probably comes from the same cylinder as the fragment BM 83000 and is presented with that fragment as ex. 2 of Asb. 253. A poorly preserved cylinder fragment in the Babylon collection of the Eşki Şark Eserleri Müzesi (Istanbul) with the number B 46 (formerly D 281) has a mostly illegible eight-line inscription. The phrase [... *áš*]-⸢*šú dan-nu a-na*⸣ S[IG$^{?}$ *la ḫa-ba-li* ...], which is otherwise only attested in inscriptions of Ashurbanipal (Asb. 241 line 13, Asb. 242 line 13, Asb. 243 lines 10–11 [mostly restored], Asb. 244 line 11, Asb. 245 line 11, Asb. 246 lines 50–51, Asb. 253 line 16 [restored], Asb. 254 line 30, Asb. 262 line 11, and Asb. 263 line 18), may appear in line 5'; however, it is very difficult to identify any of the traces in the preceding and following lines with other parts of Ashurbanipal's inscriptions. Moreover, the traces would seem to fit *e*[*n-ši* better than S[IG, while no presently-known inscription of Ashurbanipal uses a syllabic writing for this word in the phrase. Photos and information on B 46 were kindly supplied by G. Van Buylaere.

Because lines 13–14 and 27 mention the king of Babylon, Šamaš-šuma-ukīn, in a favorable manner, the inscription must have been composed before 652, the start of Ashurbanipal's older brother's rebellion.

BIBLIOGRAPHY

1880 Pognon, Bavian p. 122 and n. 1 (ex. 2, study)
1886 Strassmaier, AV passim (ex. 2, study)
1892 Lehmann-Haupt, Šamaššumukîn 1 p. 27, and 2 p. 62 and pls. XXX–XXXI no. 11 (P^{2}) (ex. 2, copy, study)
1900 King, CT 9 pls. 6–7 (ex. 1, copy)
1901 Koldewey, MDOG 8 p. 4 (ex. 3, study)
1905 Koldewey, MDOG 26 pp. 17–18 (exs. 5, 7–8, provenance)
1905–6 Fossey, ZA 19 pp. 371–377 (ex. 1, edition)
1916 Streck, Asb. pp. XLIII, XCI, 234–239 no. 4 (L^{6} [P^{2}]), 412, and 835–836 (exs. 1–2, edition; exs. 3–11, study)
1922 BM Guide p. 230 no. 37 (ex. 1, study)
1924–25 Unger, AfK 2 p. 23 no. 17 (exs. 3–11, study)
1925 Koldewey, WEB^{4} p. 149–51 and fig. 96 (exs. 3–11, provenance, translation [by Delitzsch]; ex. 11, photo)
1927 Luckenbill, ARAB 2 pp. 372–373 §§963–964 (exs. 1–2, translation)
1930 Unger in Wetzel, Stadtmauern p. 80 (exs. 3–11, study)
1933 Bauer, Asb. 2 p. 50 (exs. 1–11, study)
1970 Klengel-Brandt, Reise p. 26 fig. 11 (ex. 10, photo)
1985 Al-Rawi, Sumer 41 p. 25 (exs. 17–18, study)
1991 Al-Rawi, ARRIM 9 pp. 1–3 nos. 1–2 (ex. 17, copy, transliteration; ex. 19, photo)
1992 George, BTT pp. 345–346 (ex. 1, partial edition)
1994 Lawson, Concept of Fate p. 77 n. 31 (line 16a, study)
1995 Frame, RIMB 2 pp. 196–198 B.6.32.1 (exs. 1–19, edition)
1996 Borger, BIWA p. 387 to Streck pp. 234–239 no. 4 P^{2} and LoBl 105, 107, 110, and 112 (exs. 12–16, transliteration)
1998 Borger, BiOr 55 col. 847 (study)
2008 Frame, JCSMS 3 p. 29 (lines 10–14a, translation)
2012 Worthington, Textual Criticism p. 180 (line 16a, edition)
2020 Radner, A Short History of Babylon pp. 106–108 (ex. 17, photo; translation)
2021 Dalley, City of Babylon p. 211 (lines 10–13a, 14b–15, translation)
2021 Pedersén, Babylon pp. 42 and 48 (study; ex. 17, provenance)

Figure 6. VA Bab 601 (Asb. 241 ex. 10), a clay cylinder found at Babylon that is inscribed with a text recording the restoration of Nēmetti-Enlil and its gates. Photo: Olaf M. Teßmer.

TEXT

1) *a-na* ^{d}AMAR.UTU LUGAL ŠÁR ^{d}*í-gì-gì u* ^{d}*a-nun-na-ki ba-ni* AN-*e u* KI-*tim mu-kin giš-ḫur-ru*

2) *a-ši-ib é-sag-íl* EN KÁ.DINGIR.RA.KI EN GAL-*i be-li-ia*

3) *a-na-ku* ^{m}AN.ŠÁR-DÙ-A LUGAL GAL LUGAL *dan-nu* LUGAL ŠÁR LUGAL KUR *aš-šur* LUGAL *kib-rat* LÍMMU-*ti*

4) DUMU ^{m}AN.ŠÁR-ŠEŠ-SUM.NA LUGAL GAL LUGAL *dan-nu* LUGAL ŠÁR LUGAL KUR *aš-šur* GÌR.NÍTA

1–2) For the god Marduk, king of all the Igīgū gods and Anunnakū gods, creator of heaven and netherworld, who establishes archetypes (and) dwells in Esagil, lord of Babylon, great lord, my lord:

3–9) I, Ashurbanipal, great king, strong king, king of the world, king of Assyria, king of the four quarters (of the world); son of Esarhaddon, great king, strong king, king of the world, king of Assyria, governor of Babylon, king of the land of Sumer and Akkad, who (re)settled

TIN.TIR.KI
5) LUGAL KUR EME.GI$_7$ *u* URI.KI *mu-še-šib* KÁ.DINGIR.RA.KI *e-piš é-sag-íl*
6) *mu-ud-diš eš-re-e-ti kul-lat ma-ḫa-zi šá i-na qer-bi-ši-na*
7) *iš-tak-ka-nu si-ma-a-ti ù sat-tuk-ki-ši-na baṭ-lu-tu ú-ki-nu*
8) *par-ṣe ki-du-de-e ki-ma la-bi-ri-im-ma ú-te-ru áš-ru-uš-šu-un*
9) DUMU DUMU ^{md}30-ŠEŠ.MEŠ-SU LUGAL GAL LUGAL *dan-nu* LUGAL ŠÁR LUGAL KUR *aš-šur a-na-ku-ma*
10) *ina* BALA-*e-a* EN GAL ^{d}AMAR.UTU *ina ri-šá-a-ti a-na* TIN.TIR.KI *i-ru-um-ma*
11) *ina é-sag-íl šá da-ra-a-ti šu-bat-su ir-me sat-tuk-ki é-sag-íl*
12) *ù* DINGIR.MEŠ TIN.TIR.KI *ú-ki-in ki-din-nu-ú-tu* TIN.TIR.KI *ak-ṣur*
13) *áš-šú dan-nu a-na* SIG *la ḫa-ba-li* ^{md}GIŠ.NU$_{11}$-MU-GI.NA ŠEŠ *ta-li-mì*
14) *a-na* LUGAL-*ú-tu* KÁ.DINGIR.RA.KI *ap-qid ù i-na* KÙ.BABBAR KÙ.GI
15) *ni-siq-ti* NA$_4$.MEŠ *é-sag-íl az-nu-un-ma*
16) *ki-ma ši-ṭir bu-ru-mu ú-nam-mir é-umuš-a ina u$_4$-me-šú-ma*
17) *im-gur-*^{d}EN.LÍL BÀD KÁ.DINGIR.RA.KI *né-met-*^{d}EN.LÍL *šal-ḫu-ú-šú*
18) *ša la-ba-riš il-lik-ú-ma i-qu-pu in-na-ab-tu*
19) *áš-šú ma-aṣ-ṣar-ti é-sag-íl ù eš-re-e-ti* KÁ.DINGIR.RA.KI
20) *du-un-nu-nu ina e-muq um-ma-na-a-ti-ia sur-riš né-met-*^{d}EN.LÍL
21) *šal-ḫu-ú-šú ina ši-pir* ^{d}*kulla eš-šiš ú-še-piš-ma* KÁ.GAL.MEŠ-*šú ú-rak-kis*
22) GIŠ.IG.MEŠ *ú-še-piš-ma ú-rat-ta-a ina* KÁ.MEŠ-*šú*
23) NUN *ar-ku-ú šá ina* BALA-*e-šú ši-pir šu-a-ti in-na-ḫu um-ma-ni en-qu-tu*
24) *ši-ta-ʾa-al im-gur-*^{d}EN.LÍL BÀD *né-met-*^{d}EN.LÍL *šal-ḫu-ú*
25) *ki-ma si-ma-ti-šú-nu la-bi-ra-a-ti e-pu-uš* MU.SAR-*u-a a-mur-ma*
26) Ì.GIŠ *pu-šu-uš* UDU.SISKUR BAL-*qí it-ti* MU.SAR-*e-ka šu-kun*
27) *ik-ri-bi-ka* ^{d}AMAR.UTU *i-šem-me šá šu-mì šaṭ-ru u* MU *ta-lim-ia*
28) *ina ši-pir ni-kil-ti i-ab-bat* MU.SAR-*u-a it-ti* MU.SAR-*e-šú la i-šak-ka-nu*
29) ^{d}AMAR.UTU LUGAL *gi-im-ri ag-giš lik-kil-me-šú-ma*
30) MU-*šú* NUMUN-*šú i-na* KUR.KUR *li-ḫal-liq*

Babylon, (re)built Esagil, renovated the sanctuaries of all the cult centers, constantly established appropriate procedures in them, and (re)confirmed their interrupted regular offerings, (who) restored the rites (and) rituals according to the old pattern; grandson of Sennacherib, great king, strong king, king of the world, king of Assyria, I —

10–16a) During my reign, the great lord, the god Marduk, entered Babylon amidst rejoicing and took up his residence in Esagil for evermore. I (re)confirmed the regular offerings for Esagil and the gods of Babylon. I (re-)established the privileged status of Babylon (and) appointed Šamaš-šuma-ukīn, my favorite brother, to the kingship of Babylon in order that the strong might not harm the weak. Moreover, I *decorated* Esagil with silver, gold, (and) precious stones and made Eumuša glisten like the stars (lit. "writing") of the firmament.

16b–22) At that time, (with regard to) Imgur-Enlil, the (city) wall of Babylon, (and) Nēmetti-Enlil, its outer wall, which had become old and buckled (and) collapsed, in order to increase the security of Esagil and the (other) sanctuaries of Babylon, with the strength of my labor forces I had Nēmetti-Enlil, its outer wall, built quickly anew with the craft of the god Kulla and I refitted its gates. I had (new) doors made and fixed (them) in its gateways.

23–27a) O (you) future ruler, during whose reign this work falls into disrepair, question skilled craftsmen! (Re)build Imgur-Enlil, the (city) wall, (and) Nēmetti-Enlil, the outer wall, according to their ancient specifications! Look at my inscribed object, anoint (it) with oil, offer a sacrifice, (and) place (it) with your (own) inscribed object! The god Marduk will (then) listen to your prayers.

27b–30) (But) as for the one who destroys my inscribed name or the name of my favorite (brother) by some crafty device, (or) does not place my inscribed object with his (own) inscribed object, may the god Marduk, king of everything, glare at him angrily and make his name (and) his descendant(s) disappear from the lands!

---

13 *áš-šú dan-nu a-na* SIG *la ḫa-ba-li* "in order that the strong might not harm the weak": Cf. the prologue of the Code of Ḫammu-rāpi i 37–39: *dan-nu-um / en-ša-am / a-na la ḫa-ba-li-im.* ŠEŠ *ta-li-mì* "my favorite brother": For a discussion of the meaning of the term *talīmu* "favorite," see Bartelmus, SAAB 16 (2007) pp. 287–302. She concludes that the term "was the official designation of the highest possible rank among the king's relatives, but obviously of lower position than that of the king himself" (ibid., p. 299).

16 For the reading of the name of Marduk's cella in Esagil as *é-umuš-a* and for information on this holy room, see George, BTT pp. 273 and 389–391.

242

This Akkadian inscription, which is written on a clay cylinder (presumably from Babylon), records Ashurbanipal's work on the platforms and daises of Esagil, the temple of the god Marduk in the Eridu district of Babylon. Like the other known clay cylinder inscriptions of this Assyrian king, the text was composed sometime between 668 and 652, during the first half of Ashurbanipal's reign. In scholarly literature, this text is occasionally called the "Cylinder P[runkinschrift][1] [Inscription]."

CATALOGUE

Museum Number	Provenance	Dimensions (cm)	cpn
collection de Clercq	Probably Babylon	15.6×7.5×5.9	n

COMMENTARY

Neither this inscription's original provenance nor present location are known, although the piece was once in the collection de Clercq. The inscription is written in archaizing script and has been edited from the published heliographic reproductions of the cylinder (de Clercq, Collection 2 figs. A.I–III following p. 116, and pls. XXIV–XXV).

As implied from Šamaš-šuma-ukīn's favorable mention in lines 13–15 and 24–25, the inscription was composed before the king of Babylon revolted against Ashurbanipal, his younger brother, in 652.

BIBLIOGRAPHY

1870 3 R pl. 16 no. 5 (copy in type)
1886 Bezold, Literatur p. 113 §64.3.a (study)
1890 Jensen in Schrader, KB 2 pp. 258–261 (edition)
1903 de Clercq, Collection 2 pp. 148–154, figs. A.I–III following p. 116, and pls. XXIV–XXV (photo [heliograph], copy in type, edition, study)
1892 Lehmann-Haupt, Šamaššumukîn 1 pp. 26–27 and 2 p. 62 and pls. XXVIII–XXIX no. 10 (P^{1}) (copy, study)
1916 Streck, Asb. pp. XLII–XLIII and 232–235 no. 3 (P^{1}) (edition)
1916 Weissbach, LZB 430 (study)
1927 Luckenbill, ARAB 2 p. 372 §§960–962 (translation)
1938 Wetzel and Weissbach, Hauptheiligtum pp. 77–78 (study)
1995 Frame, RIMB 2 pp. 206–208 B.6.32.6 (edition)
1996 Borger, BIWA p. 387 to Streck pp. 232-235 no. 3 P^{2} and LoBl 134 (transliteration, study)
1998 Borger, BiOr 55 col. 848 (study)
2021 Pedersén, Babylon pp. 150–151 (study)

TEXT

1) ^{m}AN.ŠÁR-DÙ-A LUGAL GAL LUGAL *dan-nu* LUGAL ŠÁR
2) LUGAL KUR *aš-šur* LUGAL *kib-rat* LÍMMU-*ti* LUGAL LUGAL.MEŠ
3) NUN *la šá-na-an* DUMU ^{m}AN.ŠÁR-ŠEŠ-SUM.NA
4) LUGAL GAL LUGAL *dan-nu* LUGAL ŠÁR LUGAL KUR *aš-šur*
5) GÌR.NÍTA TIN.TIR.KI LUGAL KUR EME.GI_{7} *u* URI.KI
6) DUMU DUMU ^{md}30-ŠEŠ.MEŠ-SU LUGAL GAL

1–7a) Ashurbanipal, great king, strong king, king of the world, king of Assyria, king of the four quarters (of the world), king of kings, ruler who has no rival; son of Esarhaddon, great king, strong king, king of the world, king of Assyria, (5) governor of Babylon, king of the land of Sumer and Akkad; grandson of Sennacherib, great king, strong king, king of the world, king of Assyria, I —

LUGAL *dan-nu*
7) LUGAL ŠÁR LUGAL KUR *aš-šur a-na-ku-ma* EN GAL ^{d}AMAR.UTU
8) *šá ina* BALA-*e* LUGAL *maḫ-ri ina ma-ḫar* AD *ba-ni-i-šú*
9) *ú-ši-bu ina qé-reb bal-til*.KI *ina* u$_{4}$-*me* BALA-*ia*
10) *ina ri-šá-a-ti a-na* TIN.TIR.KI *i-ru-um-ma*
11) *sat-tuk-ki é-sag-íl u* DINGIR.MEŠ TIN.TIR.KI *ú-kin*
12) *ki-din-nu-ú-tu* TIN.TIR.KI *ak-*⸢*ṣur*⸣
13) ⸢*áš*⸣-*šú dan-nu a-na* SIG *la ḫa-ba-li*
14) ^{md}GIŠ.NU$_{11}$-MU-GI.NA ŠEŠ *ta-li-mì*
15) *a-na* LUGAL-*ú-tu* TIN.TIR.KI *ap-qí-di*
16) *ù ši-pir é-sag-*⸢*íl šá*⸣ *za-ru-ú-a*
17) *la* ⸢*ú*⸣-*qa-at-tu-ú a-na-ku ú-*⸢*šak*⸣-*lil*

7b–17) During my reign, the great lord, the god Marduk, who during the reign of a previous king had resided in Baltil (Aššur) in the presence of the father who had created him, (10) entered Babylon amidst rejoicing. I (re)confirmed the regular offerings for Esagil and the gods of Babylon. I (re-)established the privileged status of Babylon (and) appointed Šamaš-šuma-ukīn, my favorite brother, (15) to the kingship of Babylon in order that the strong might not harm the weak. I completed the work on Esagil which my father had not finished.

18) *ina* u$_{4}$-*me-šú-*⸢*ma*⸣ *di-ʾa-a-ni u* ⸢BÁRA.MEŠ *šá*⸣ *si-*⸢*ḫir*⸣-*ti*
19) *é-sag-*⸢*íl*⸣ *ki-i* ⸢*si*⸣-*ma-a-ti-šú-nu la-bi-ra-a-ti*
20) *ina áš-ri-šú-nu lu-u ad-di a-na šat-*⸢*ti*⸣ ^{d}AMAR.UTU EN GAL
21) *ep-še-ti-ia dam-qa-a-*⸢*ti*⸣ *ḫa-di-iš* IGI.BAR-*ma*
22) TI u$_{4}$-*me* SÙ.MEŠ *še-bé-e lit-tu-tu ṭu-ub* UZU
23) *ù ḫu-ud lìb-bi li-šim ši-ma-ti*
24) *ù šá* ^{md}GIŠ.NU$_{11}$-MU-GI.NA LUGAL TIN.TIR.KI
25) ŠEŠ *ta-lim-ia* u$_{4}$-*me-šú li-ri-ku liš-bi bu-ʾa-a-ri*

18–20a) At that time, I (re-)erected the platforms and daises of all of Esagil in their (original) positions according to their ancient specifications.

20b–25) On account of this, may the god Marduk, the great lord, look upon my good deeds with pleasure and determine as my fate a long life, fullness of old age, good health, and happiness! Moreover, with regard to Šamaš-šuma-ukīn, king of Babylon, my favorite brother, may his days be long and may he be fully satisfied with (his) good fortune!

26) *ma-ti-ma ina aḫ-rat* u$_{4}$-*me* NUN *ar-ku-u šá ina* u$_{4}$-*me* BALA-*šú*
27) *ši-pir šu-a-ti in-na-ḫu an-ḫu-us-su lu-ud-diš*
28) *šu-mì it-ti* MU-*šú liš-ṭur* MU.SAR-*u-a li-mur-ma*
29) Ì.GIŠ *lip-šu-uš* UDU.SÍSKUR BAL-*qí ina áš-ri-šú liš-kun*

26–30a) If at any time in the future, during the days of the reign of some future ruler, this work falls into disrepair, may (that ruler) repair its dilapidated state! May he write my name with his (own) name! May he find my inscribed object, anoint (it) with oil, offer a sacrifice, (and) set (my inscribed object back) in its place! The god Marduk will (then) hearken to his prayers.

30) *ik-ri-bi-i-šú* ^{d}AMAR.UTU *i-šem-me* [*šá*] *šu-mì šaṭ-ru*
31) *i-pa-áš-ši-ṭu* MU.SAR-*ú-a i-ab-ba-tu*
32) *lu-u a-šar-šú ú-nak-ka-ru* EN GAL ^{d}AMAR.UTU *ag-gi-iš*
33) *lik-kil-me-šú-ma* MU-*šú* NUMUN-*šú i-na* KUR.KUR ⸢*li*⸣-*ḫal-liq*

30b–33) [(But) as for the one who] erases my inscribed name, (or) destroys my inscribed object, or changes its position, may the great lord, the god Marduk, glare at him angrily and make his name (and) his descendant(s) disappear from the lands!

243

A fragment of a clay cylinder discovered at Babylon preserves part of an Akkadian inscription of Ashurbanipal. The text appears to record some deed that the king of Assyria undertook on behalf of the god Ea, possibly the renovation of that deity's temple Ekarzagina ("House, Quay of Lapis Lazuli" or "House, Pure Quay"). The favorable mention of Ashurbanipal's older brother, Šamaš-šuma-ukīn, suggests that the inscription was composed at some point between 668 and 652.

CATALOGUE

Museum Number	Excavation Number	Photograph Number	Provenance	Dimensions (cm)	cpn
EŞ 7893	BE 28510	Bab ph 558	Babylon, Kasr, 21s, South Palace	7.3×7	c

COMMENTARY

This cylinder fragment was found at Babylon in December 1903 and is shown on Babylon photo 558. Approximately one-half of the original circumference of the left end is preserved. The inscription is written in Neo-Assyrian script. The restorations are based upon Asb. 245 lines 1–12 and 21–24; however, there does not appear to be sufficient space at the end of line 5 to restore all the titles usually accorded to Esarhaddon in other inscriptions. Two cylinder fragments, VA Bab 614 and B 65, which are presented under text Asb. 244 (exs. 1* and 2*), could conceivably be duplicates of this inscription.

Ashurbanipal renovated Ekarzagina, the temple of the god Ea located inside the Esagil complex, and had his action recorded on at least one stele (Asb. 246). Since this cylinder inscription probably deals with a structure associated with Ea and since it comes from Babylon, it is quite likely that it also commemorated work on Ekarzagina. The inscription is similar to other inscriptions of Ashurbanipal, in particular those describing his work on the temples of the goddesses Ištar and Ninmaḫ in the Eridu and Ka-dingirra districts of Babylon (Asb. 244–245).

Because the inscription preserves part of a passage describing Ashurbanipal's appointment of his older brother Šamaš-šuma-ukīn as king of Babylon (line 11), the text must have been composed before the latter's rebellion, which commenced in 652.

BIBLIOGRAPHY

1904 Koldewey, MDOG 21 p. 7 (provenance; partial translation, study [by Delitzsch])

1916 Streck, Asb. pp. XC–XCI (partial translation, study [by Delitzsch])

1927 Nassouhi, MAOG 3/1–2 p. 35 no. 16 (photo)

1931 Unger, Babylon p. 225 no. 16 (study)

1938 Wetzel and Weissbach, Hauptheiligtum p. 77 n. 1 (study)

1995 Frame, RIMB 2 pp. 202–203 B.6.32.3 (edition)

2021 Pedersén, Babylon pp. 150–151 (study)

TEXT

1) ^{m}AN.ŠÁR-*ba-a-ni*-IBILA LUGAL ⸢GAL⸣ [LUGAL *dan-nu* LUGAL ŠÁR]

2) LUGAL KUR *aš-šur* LUGAL *kib-ra-a*-⸢*ti*⸣ [LÍMMU-*ti* LUGAL LUGAL.MEŠ]

3) NUN *la šá-na-an šá ul*-⸢*tu*⸣ [*tam-tim e-liti a-di tam-tim*]

4) *šap-liti i-be-lu-ma gi*-[*mir ma-li-ki ú-šak-niš še-pu-uš-šú*]

5) DUMU ^{m}AN.ŠÁR-ŠEŠ-SUM.NA LUGAL ⸢GAL⸣ [(LUGAL *dan-nu*) (LUGAL ŠÁR) (LUGAL KUR *aš-šur*)]

6) LUGAL KUR EME.GI$_{7}$ *u* URI.KI DUMU [DUMU ^{md}30-PAP.MEŠ-SU LUGAL *dan-nu*]

1–7a) Ashurbanipal, [great] king, [mighty king, king of the world], king of Assyria, king of the [four] quarters (of the world), [king of kings], ruler who has no rival, who rules from [the Upper Sea to the] Lower [Sea] and [who made] all [rulers bow down at his feet]; (5) son of Esarhaddon, [great] king, [(mighty king), (king of the world), (king of Assyria), (governor of Babylon)], king of the land of Sumer and Akkad; [grand]son of [Sennacherib, (great king), mighty king], king of the world, king of Assyria, I —

7) LUGAL ŠÁR LUGAL KUR *aš-šur a-na-ku*-[*ma ši-pir é-sag-íl*]

8) *šá* AD *ba-nu-ú-a la ú*-[*qa-at-tu-u a-na-ku ú-šak-lil*]

9) *sat-tuk-ki é-sag-íl* [*u* DINGIR.MEŠ TIN.TIR.KI *ú-kin*]

7b–11) [I completed the work on Esagil] which (my) father who had engendered me had not [finished. I (re)confirmed] the regular offerings for Esagil [and the gods of Babylon. I (re-)established] the privileged status of B[abylon (and) appointed Šamas-šuma-ukīn, my favorite brother, to the kingship of Babylon in

10) *ki-din-nu-ut* ⸢KÁ⸣.[DINGIR.RA.KI *ak-ṣur áš-šú dan-nu*]
11) [*a*]-⸢*na*⸣ SIG [*la ḫa-ba-li* ^{md}GIŠ.NU$_{11}$-MU-GI.NA]
Lacuna
1′) MU.⸢SAR⸣-[*u-a i-ab-ba-tu lu-u a-šar-šú ú-nak-ka-ru*]
2′) ^{d}*é-a* LUGAL ⸢ABZU$^{?}$⸣ [*ina ma-ḫar* ^{d}EN ^{d}GAŠAN-*ía* MUNUS.ḪUL-*šú lit-tas-qar*]
3′) MU-*šú* NUMUN-*šú i-na* [KUR.KUR *li-ḫal-liq*]

order that the strong might not harm] the weak.

Lacuna
1′–3′) [(But) as for the one who ... destroys my] inscri[bed object, or changes its position], may the god Ea, king of the Wat[ery Abyss (*apsû*), speak evil of him before the god Bēl (Marduk) (and) the goddess Bēltīya (Zarpanītu) and make] his name (and) his descendant(s) [disappear] from [the lands]!

244

Ashurbanipal's renovation of Eturkalama ("House, Cattle-Pen of the Land"), the temple of the goddess Ištar in the Esagil temple complex, is known from at least two clay cylinders. The Akkadian inscription was composed during the first half of the reign of Ashurbanipal (668–652). This text is sometimes called "Cylinder L[ondon][1]."

CATALOGUE

Ex.	Museum Number	Excavation/ Registration No.	Photograph Number	Provenance	Dimensions (cm)	Lines Preserved	cpn
1	BM 90935 (=BM 12064)	81-2-1,103	—	Acquired by H. Rassam from Babylon	Length: 17.6; Dia. of ends: 5.3	1–24	c
2	BM 40074	81-2-1,38	—	Purchased by Spartali & Co.; probably from Babylon	7.1×6.8	7–21	c

CATALOGUE OF UNCERTAIN EXEMPLARS

Ex.	Museum Number	Excavation/ Registration No.	Photograph Number	Provenance	Dimensions (cm)	Lines Preserved	cpn
1*	VA Bab 614	BE 29482	Bab ph 707	Babylon, Kasr 24q, South Palace, gate building, in debris	9.1×7.5	1–4, 19–24	c
2*	B 65 (former D 300)	BE 38119	Bab ph 2198, 2691	Babylon, "outside" (the Merkes)	—	1–5, 22–24	c

COMMENTARY

Ex. 1 was brought from Babylon by H. Rassam, according to S.A. Strong (JRAS 1891 p. 472). There is not enough of the building accounts of exs. 1* and 2* preserved to be certain they are duplicates of this inscription and not of either Asb. 243 or Asb. 245. Because of the major variant in line 23 of exs. 1*–2*, those exemplars might well represent a new and hither-to previously unidentified inscription. All ex-

243 line 2′ ⸢ABZU$^{?}$⸣ "Wat[ery Abyss (*apsû*)]": Or ⸢*ap*⸣-[*si-i*].

emplars are written in Neo-Assyrian script. The master line follows ex. 1, with help from ex. 1* in line 21. Restorations in lines 18–21 follow Asb. 245 lines 18–21. A score of the text is presented on Oracc and the minor (orthographic) variants are listed at the back of the book.

The Babylon excavation register indicates that ex. 2* (B 65) was found "außerhalb"; since the immediately preceding and following items in the register are said to have been found in "Merkes," the register might simply mean that the piece was not found in the Merkes city quarter. This information is courtesy of J. Marzahn. B 65 was kindly collated by G. Van Buylaere.

Because lines 11–12 and 19–21 mention Šamaš-šuma-ukīn, the older brother of Ashurbanipal, in a positive way, the inscription was certainly composed before he rebelled against Assyria in 652.

BIBLIOGRAPHY

1885	Lehmann-[Haupt], ZK 2 pp. 360–361 (ex. 1, study)
1886	Bezold, Literatur p. 113 §64.3.b (ex. 1, study)
1891	Strong, JRAS pp. 471–475 (ex. 1, copy in type, edition)
1892	Lehmann-Haupt, Šamaššumukîn 1 p. 25 and 2 p. 61 and pls. XXIII–XXIV no. 8 (L^{1}) (exs. 1–2, copy, study)
1916	Streck, Asb. pp. XLI and 226–229 no. 1 (L^{1}) (exs. 1–2, edition)
1922	BM Guide p. 230 no. 35 (ex. 1, study)
1927	Luckenbill, ARAB 2 pp. 369–370 §§953–955 (exs. 1–2, translation)
1930	Unger in Wetzel, Stadtmauern p. 80 (ex. 1*, study)
1995	Frame, RIMB 2 pp. 203–204 B.6.32.4 (exs. 1–2*, edition)

TEXT

1) ^{m}AN.ŠÁR-DÙ-IBILA LUGAL GAL LUGAL *dan-nu* LUGAL ŠÁR LUGAL KUR *aš-šur* 2) LUGAL *kib-rat* LÍMMU-*ti* LUGAL LUGAL.MEŠ NUN *la šá-na-an* 3) *ša ul-tu tam-tim e-liti a-di tam-tim šap-liti i-be-lu-ma* 4) *gi-mir ma-li-ki ú-šak-niš še-pu-uš-šú* 5) DUMU ^{m}AN.ŠÁR-ŠEŠ-SUM.NA LUGAL GAL LUGAL *dan-nu* LUGAL ŠÁR LUGAL KUR *aš-šur* 6) GÌR.NÍTA KÁ.DINGIR.RA.KI LUGAL KUR EME.GI$_7$ *ù* URI.KI 7) DUMU DUMU ^{md}30-PAP.MEŠ-SU LUGAL *dan-nu* LUGAL ŠÁR LUGAL KUR *aš-šur a-na-ku-ma*	1–7) Ashurbanipal, great king, strong king, king of the world, king of Assyria, king of the four quarters (of the world), king of kings, ruler who has no rival, who rules from the Upper Sea to the Lower Sea and who made all rulers bow down at his feet; (5) son of Esarhaddon, great king, strong king, king of the world, king of Assyria, governor of Babylon, king of the land of Sumer and Akkad; grandson of Sennacherib, strong king, king of the world, king of Assyria, I —
8) *ši-pir é-sag-íl šá* AD *ba-nu-u-a la ú-qa-at-tu-u* 9) *a-na-ku ú-šak-lil sat-tuk-ki é-sag-íl u* DINGIR.MEŠ TIN.TIR.KI 10) *ú-ki-in ki-din-nu-tu* KÁ.DINGIR.RA.KI *ak-ṣur* 11) *áš-šú dan-nu a-na* SIG *la ḫa-ba-li* ^{md}GIŠ.NU$_{11}$-<MU>-GI.NA 12) ŠEŠ *ta-li-mì a-na* LUGAL-*u-ti* KÁ.DINGIR.RA.KI *ap-qid*	8–12) I completed the work on Esagil which (my) father who had engendered me had not finished. I (re)confirmed the regular offerings for Esagil and the gods of Babylon. (10) I (re-)established the privileged status of Babylon (and) appointed Šamaš-<šuma>-ukīn, my favorite brother, to the kingship of Babylon in order that the strong might not harm the weak.
13) *ina u$_4$-me-šú-ma é-tùr-kalam-ma* É ^{d}INANNA TIN.TIR.KI 14) *eš-šiš ú-še-piš* ^{d}INANNA TIN.TIR.KI ^{d}GAŠAN *ṣir-tu* 15) *ep-še-te-ia* MUNUS.SIG$_5$.MEŠ *ḫa-diš lip-pal-lis-ma* 16) *u$_4$-me-šam-ma ma-ḫar* ^{d}EN ^{d}GAŠAN-*ía lit-tas-qar da-mì-iq-ti* 17) TI *u$_4$-me* SÙ.MEŠ *li-šim ši-ma-ti* 18) [*it*]-*ti* AN-*e ù* KI-*tim lu-ki-in* BALA-*ú-a* 19) [*ù šá* ^{md}]⸢GIŠ.NU$_{11}$⸣-<MU>-GI.NA LUGAL	13–14a) At that time, I had Eturkalama, the temple of the goddess Ištar of Babylon, (re)built anew. 14b–20) May the goddess Ištar of Babylon, the exalted lady, look upon my good deeds with pleasure and may she say good things about me daily before the god Bēl (Marduk) and the goddess Bēltīya (Zarpanītu)! May she determine as my fate a long life (and) make my reign [as] firm as heaven and netherworld! [Moreover, with regard to] Šamaš-<šuma>-ukīn, king of Babylon, [my

4 *ú-šak-niš*: One expects the verb to be in the subjunctive (*ušaknišu*); see also Asb. 245 line 4, Asb. 246 line 12, Asb. 254 line 7, Asb. 262 line 3, Asb. 263 line 8, and Asb. 243 line 4 (restored).

KÁ.DINGIR.RA.KI
20) [ŠEŠ *ta-lim-ia* u_4*-me-šu*] *li-ri-ku liš-bi lit-tu-tu*
21) [*ša šu-mì šaṭ-ru u* MU *ta*]*-lim-ia ina ši-pir ni-kil-ti i-pa-áš-ši-ṭu*
22) MU.⸢SAR⸣*-u-a i-ab-ba-tu lu-u a-šar-šú ú-nak-ka-ru*
23) ^{d}INANNA TIN.TIR.KI *ina ma-*⸢*ḫar*⸣ ^{d}EN ^{d}GAŠAN-*ía* MUNUS.ḪUL-*šú*
24) *lit-tas-qar* MU-*šú* NUMUN-*šú ina* KUR.KUR *li-ḫal-liq*

favorite brother], may [his days] be long and may he experience the fullness of old age!
21–24) [(But) as for the one who] erases [my inscribed name or the name of] my [fav]orite (brother) by some crafty device, (or) destroys my inscribed object, or changes its position, may the goddess Ištar of Babylon speak evil of him before the god Bēl (and) the goddess Bēltīya (and) make his name (and) his descendant(s) disappear from the lands!

245

Two clay cylinders discovered at Babylon are inscribed with an Akkadian text that commemorates Ashurbanipal's restoration of Emaḫ ("Exalted House"), a temple in the Ka-dingirra district of Babylon. According to Tintir IV 18 (George, BTT pp. 58–59 and 313), Emaḫ was the temple of the mother goddess Bēlet-ilī and R. Borger takes ^{d}NIN.MAḪ in lines 13, 14, and 23 of this inscription to be a logogram for Bēlet-ilī (BiOr 55 [1998] col. 847; and see also Borger, MZ p. 451). It is uncertain, however, if ^{d}NIN.MAḪ would have been pronounced in Akkadian as Bēlet-ilī or read, more learnedly, as Sumerian Ninmaḫ in this inscription. Following previous editions of this text, we tentatively assume that the name of the goddess was pronounced Ninmaḫ here. (See also Beaulieu, Iraq 59 [1997] pp. 93–96 in connection with a cylinder inscription from the reign of Nebuchadnezzar II.) The inscription, which is similar to Asb. 243–244, was also composed before the outbreak of the Šamaš-šuma-ukīn rebellion in 652. M. Streck referred to this text as the "Emaḫ Cylinder [Inscription]."

CATALOGUE

Ex.	Museum Number	Excavation/ Registration No.	Photograph Number	Provenance	Dimensions (cm)	Lines Preserved	cpn
1	VA 8409	BE 5457	Bab ph 494, 495, 530	Babylon, Emaḫ, southwestern cella (E), 10 m below the surface	Length: 14.8; Dia. of ends: 6.2	1–24	c
2	BM 33338	Rm 3,11	—	Acquired by H. Rassam; probably from Babylon	Length: 9.4; L. dia.: 5.1	1–24	c

COMMENTARY

For the precise find spot of ex. 1, see Koldewey, Tempel pl. III (noted as "CYL" in the room designated A.2). Ex. 2 was part of a shipment sent by H. Rassam to the British Museum in 1879 which included items from Babylon, Borsippa, and Telloh, as well as a brick from the Assyrian religious capital Aššur; see Reade in Leichty, Sippar 1 p. xxix. In view of the contents of the inscription, BM 33338 probably also originates from Babylon, like ex. 1. Both exemplars are written in Neo-Assyrian script. VA Bab 614 and B 65 might

244 line 23 Exs. 1*–2* have [... ^{d}]⸢AMAR⸣.UTU ^{d}EN-*ía* MUNUS.ḪUL-*šú* and [...] ⸢AMAR.UTU EN⸣-*ía* MUNUS.ḪUL-⸢*šú*⸣ respectively, "[...] evil of him [before (...) the god] Marduk, my lord," instead of "evil of him before the god Bēl (and) the goddess Bēltīya."

be two further exemplars of this inscription; see Asb. 244 exs. 1*–2* and the commentary to that text. The master line follows ex. 1. A score of the text is presented on Oracc and the minor (orthographic) variants are listed at the back of the book.

As can be implied from the positive reference to the appointment of Šamaš-šuma-ukīn, Ashurbanipal's "favorite brother" (*aḫu talīmu*), to the kingship of Babylon in lines 11–12, this text was composed prior to the commencement of Šamaš-šuma-ukīn's revolt in 652.

BIBLIOGRAPHY

1900 Koldewey, MDOG 4 pp. 6–7 (ex. 1, provenance, translation [by Meissner])
1903 Weissbach, Miscellen no. 8 (ex. 1, copy, edition)
1905 Jastrow, Religion 1 pp. 418–419 (ex. 1, partial translation)
1911 Koldewey, Tempel pp. 4, 13, 14 fig. 17, and 67 (ex. 1, provenance, photo, edition [by Delitzsch])
1916 Streck, Asb. pp. XLIII–XLIV and 238–241 no. 5 (E-maḫ) (ex. 1, edition)
1924–25 Unger, AfK 2 p. 23 no. 16 (ex. 1, study)
1925 Koldewey, WEB^{4} pp. 59–60 and fig. 41 (ex. 1, copy)
1927 Luckenbill, ARAB 2 p. 373 §§965–967 (ex. 1, partial translation)
1983 Rost and Marzahn, Babylon pp. 15 and 17 (ex. 1, translation)
1995 Frame, RIMB 2 pp. 205–206 B.6.32.5 (exs. 1–2, edition)
1996 Borger, BIWA LoBl 123 (ex. 2, transliteration)
1998 Borger, BiOr 55 col. 847 (study)
2021 Pedersén, Babylon p. 183 (study)

TEXT

1) ^{m}AN.ŠÁR-DÙ-A LUGAL GAL LUGAL *dan-nu* LUGAL ŠÁR LUGAL KUR *aš-šur*
2) LUGAL *kib-rat* LÍMMU-*ti* LUGAL LUGAL.MEŠ NUN *la šá-na-an*
3) *ša ul-tu tam-tim e-liti a-di tam-tim šap-liti i-be-lu-ma*
4) *gi-mir ma-li-ki ú-šak-niš še-pu-uš-šú*
5) DUMU ^{m}AN.ŠÁR-ŠEŠ-SUM.NA LUGAL GAL LUGAL *dan-nu* LUGAL ŠÁR LUGAL KUR *aš-šur*
6) GÌR.NÍTA KÁ.DINGIR.RA.KI LUGAL KUR EME.GI$_{7}$ *ù* URI.KI
7) DUMU DUMU ^{md}30-PAP.MEŠ-SU LUGAL *dan-nu* LUGAL ŠÁR LUGAL KUR *aš-šur a-na-ku-ma*

1–7) Ashurbanipal, great king, strong king, king of the world, king of Assyria, king of the four quarters (of the world), king of kings, ruler who has no rival, who rules from the Upper Sea to the Lower Sea and who made all rulers bow down at his feet; (5) son of Esarhaddon, great king, strong king, king of the world, king of Assyria, governor of Babylon, king of the land of Sumer and Akkad; grandson of Sennacherib, strong king, king of the world, king of Assyria, I —

8) *ši-pir é-sag-íl šá* AD *ba-nu-u-a la ú-qa-at-tu-u*
9) *a-na-ku ú-šak-lil sat-tuk-ki é-sag-íl u* DINGIR.MEŠ TIN.TIR.KI
10) *ú-kin ki-di-nu-tu* KÁ.DINGIR.RA.KI *ak-ṣur*
11) *áš-šú dan-nu a-na* SIG *la ḫa-ba-li* ^{md}GIŠ.NU$_{11}$-MU-GI.NA
12) ŠEŠ *ta-li-mì a-na* LUGAL-*u-tu* KÁ.DINGIR.RA.KI *ap-qid*

8–12) I completed the work on Esagil which (my) father who had engendered me had not finished. I (re)confirmed the regular offerings for Esagil and the gods of Babylon. (10) I (re-)established the privileged status of Babylon (and) appointed Šamaš-šuma-ukīn, my favorite brother, to the kingship of Babylon in order that the strong might not harm the weak.

13) *ina u$_{4}$-me-šú-ma é-maḫ* É ^{d}NIN.MAḪ *šá qé-reb* KÁ.DINGIR.RA.KI

13–14a) At that time, I had Emaḫ, the temple of the goddess Ninmaḫ (or Bēlet-ilī) that is inside Babylon, (re)built anew.

14) *eš-šiš ú-še-piš a-na šat-ti* ^{d}NIN.MAḪ GAŠAN *ṣir-tu*
15) *ep-še-te-ia* MUNUS.SIG$_{5}$.MEŠ *ḫa-diš lip-pal-lis-ma*
16) *u$_{4}$-me-šam-ma ma-ḫar* ^{d}EN ^{d}GAŠAN-*ía lit-tas-qar da-mì-iq-ti*
17) TI *u$_{4}$-me* SÙ.MEŠ *li-šim ši-ma-ti*
18) *it-ti* AN-*e u* KI-*tim lu-ki-in* BALA-*ú-a*
19) *ù šá* ^{md}GIŠ.NU$_{11}$-MU-GI.NA LUGAL KÁ.DINGIR.RA.KI

14b–20) On account of this, may the goddess Ninmaḫ, the exalted lady, look upon my good deeds with pleasure and say good things about me daily before the god Bēl (Marduk) and the goddess Bēltīya (Zarpanītu)! May she determine as my fate a long life (and) make my reign as firm as heaven and netherworld! Moreover, with regard to Šamaš-šuma-ukīn, king of Babylon, my favorite brother, may his days be long and may he experience the fullness of old age!

20) ŠEŠ *ta-lim-ía* *u_4-me-šú li-ri-ku liš-bi lit-tu-tu*
21) *ša šu-mì šaṭ-ru ù* MU *ta-lim-ia ina ši-pir ni-kil-ti i-pa-áš-ši-ṭu*
22) MU.SAR-*u-a i-ab-ba-tu lu-u a-šar-šú ú-nak-ka-ru*
23) ^{d}NIN.MAḪ *ina ma-ḫar* ^{d}EN ^{d}GAŠAN-*ía* MUNUS.ḪUL-*šú lit-tas-qar*
24) MU-*šú* NUMUN-*šú ina* KUR.KUR *li-ḫal-liq*

21–24) (But) as for the one who erases my inscribed name or the name of my favorite (brother) by some crafty device, (or) destroys my inscribed object, or changes its position, may the goddess Ninmaḫ speak evil of him before the god Bēl (and) the goddess Bēltīya and make his name (and) his descendant(s) disappear from the lands!

246

One or two stone steles are engraved with an Akkadian inscription of Ashurbanipal that records his restoration of Ekarzagina ("House, Quay of Lapis Lazuli" or "House, Pure Quay"), the temple of the god Ea in the Esagil temple complex, in the Eridu district of Babylon. Because the text mentions Šamaš-šuma-ukīn, the king of Babylon and Ashurbanipal's older brother, in a positive manner, it is certain that the inscription dates to the first part of Ashurbanipal's reign (668–652). This inscription is sometimes referred to as "S[tele]^{3}" in previous editions.

CATALOGUE

Ex.	Museum Number	Registration Number	Provenance	Dimensions (cm)	Lines Preserved	cpn
1	BM 90864 (=BM 12110)	81-3-24,367	Babylon, area of Esagil	35.9×22.2×6.4	1–100	c
2	BM 22533	94-1-15,335	Purchased in 1894; reportedly from Babylon	4×7.5	18–22	p

COMMENTARY

A relief of Ashurbanipal carrying a basket on his head (that is, personally aiding in the restoration of Ea's temple) is found on the front of ex. 1, a stele of pink marble discovered in an area of Esagil, the god Marduk's temple at Babylon. Similar reliefs have been found on steles in Ezida ("True House"), the temple of the god Nabû at Borsippa (Asb. 254 and Frame, RIMB 2 pp. 252–253 B.6.33.3 [written in the name of Šamaš-šuma-ukīn]). B.N. Porter presents a study on the representation of Ashurbanipal as a "basket-bearing king" in Babylonia in her book Trees, Kings, and Politics, pp. 47–58.

Ex. 2 is a small fragment of pink marble with a relief showing part of a garment similar to the one worn by Ashurbanipal on ex. 1. The object was purchased in 1894 and is said to have come from Babylon (see Reade and Walker, AfO 28 [1981–82] p. 119). Very little of ex. 2 is preserved and none of the building section remains. Thus, it is quite likely that this exemplar did not describe the restoration of Ekarzagina, but instead recorded Ashurbanipal's work on another temple at Babylon. K. Hecker (TUAT^{2} 6 p. 34 n. 42) tentatively suggested that this piece might be a fragment from a stele of Šamaš-šuma-ukīn.

Rather than present a score for this inscription on Oracc, the edition below follows ex. 1 (with lines 30–41 and 68–88 restored following Asb. 254 lines 21–26a and 38b–70 respectively). Ex. 2 has the following:

Lacuna
1′) [...]-⸢*dul*⸣-*lum šá ep*-[...]
2′) [... U]GU *ṣal-mat* S[AG$^{?}$ ...]
3′) [... A]N.ŠÁR-Š[EŠ$^{?}$-...]
4′) [... *da*]*n*$^{?}$-*n*[*u*$^{?}$ ...]
Lacuna

Thus, ex. 2 has the following variants to ex. 1:

[*an*]-⸢*dul*⸣-*lum* for *an-dul-lu* in line 18 and [U]GU for *e-li* in line 19. With regard to ex. 1, lines 1–28, 29–55, 56–84, and 85–100 are on the front, right side, back, and left side of the stele respectively. The inscription is written in contemporary Babylonian script.

Šamaš-šuma-ukīn's positive mention in lines 5–55 and 74–76 indicates that the inscription was composed before the onset of his rebellion against his brother Ashurbanipal in 652.

BIBLIOGRAPHY

1886 Bezold, Literatur pp. 113–114 §64.3.d (ex. 1, study)
1889–91 Evetts, PSBA 13 p. 158 (ex. 1, study)
1891 Strong, JRAS pp. 469–471 (ex. 1, partial copy in type, partial edition)
1892 Lehmann-Haupt, Šamaššumukîn 1 frontpiece and p. 25, and 2 pp. 14–19, 59–61 and pls. XVII–XXII no. 7 (S^{3}) (ex. 1, photo, copy, edition)
1895 Quentin, RB 4 pp. 553–562 (ex. 1, copy in type, edition)
1906 Babelon, Manual p. 89 fig. 64 (ex. 1, photo)
1913 Curtius, Münchner Jahrbuch der bildenden Kunst 8 pp. 11–12 and fig. 6 (ex. 1, photo, study [of relief])
1915 King, History pl. following p. 272 (ex. 1, photo)
1915 Meissner, AO 15 p. 74 fig. 131 (ex. 1, photo)
1916 Streck, Asb. pp. XLV and 244–249 no. 7 (S^{3}) (ex. 1, edition)
1920 Meissner, BuA 1 pl. 38 fig. 40 (ex. 1, photo)
1922 BM Guide p. 74 no. 300 and pl. XXVIII (ex. 1, photo, study)
1924–25 Unger, AfK 2 p. 23 no. 10 (ex. 1, study)
1926 Bezold, Ninive und Babylon^{4} fig. 126 (ex. 1, photo)
1926 Unger, RLV 4 /2 pl. 267c (ex. 1, photo)
1927 Luckenbill, ARAB 2 p. 376 §§978–980 (ex. 1, partial translation)
1929 Jeremias, HAOG^{2} p. 18 fig. 8 (ex. 1, photo)
1931 Contenau, Manuel d'archéologie orientale 3 p. 1299 and fig. 822 (ex. 1, photo, study)
1931 Unger, Babylon p. 225 no. 12 (ex. 1, study)
1958 Champdor, Babylon p. 137 fig. 89 (ex. 1, photo)
1961 Parrot, Assyria p. 35 fig. 40A (ex. 1, photo)
1961 Potratz, Orientalia NS 30 pp. 14–15 and pl. I fig. 3 (ex. 1, photo, study [of relief])
1962 Beek, Atlas p. 28 fig. 39 (ex. 1, photo)
1962 Strommenger and Hirmer, Mesopotamien pl. 262 (ex. 1, photo)
1966 Ellis, Berytus 16 pp. 47–48 and pl. VIII fig. 3 (ex. 1, photo, study)
1967 Margueron, Mesopotamia fig. 58 (ex. 1, photo)
1967 Moortgat, Kunst p. 157 and pl. 282 (ex. 1, photo, study)
1968 Ellis, Foundation Deposits pp. 24–25 (ex. 1, study)
1969 Pritchard, ANEP^{2} no. 450 (ex. 1, photo)
1972 Salonen, Ziegeleien pl. XIII (ex. 1, photo)
1975 Barnett and Lorenzini, Assyrian Sculpture p. 35 (ex. 1, photo)
1976 Barnett, Assyrian Sculptures from the North Palace pl. 1 (ex. 1, photo)
1979 J. Oates, Babylon p. 122 (ex. 1, photo)
1981–82 Reade and Walker, AfO 28 p. 119 (ex. 2, photo, transliteration)
1982 Börker-Klähn, Bildstelen no. 224 (ex. 1, photo, study)
1983 Galter, Ea/Enki pp. 199–200 (ex. 1, study)
1988 Parpola and Watanabe, SAA 2 p. 60 fig. 19 (ex. 1, photo)
1992 Frame, Babylonia cover (ex. 1, photo)
1994 Lawson, Concept of Fate p. 77 n. 31 (line 14b, edition, study)
1995 Frame, RIMB 2 pp. 199–202 B.6.32.2 (exs. 1–2, edition)
2003 Porter, Trees, Kings, and Politics pl. 11 (ex. 1, photo)
2004 Porter, Studies Immerwahr pp. 268–270 (ex. 1, photo; exs. 1–2, study)
2008 André-Salvini, Babylone p. 139 no. 95 (ex. 1, photo, lines 36b–57, translation; study)
2008 Marzahn, Babylon: Wahrheit pp. 162–164 no. 80 with fig. 96 (ex. 1, photo; lines 36b–57 [André-Salvini], translation; study)
2008 Reade, Babylon: Myth and Reality p. 79 with fig. 59 (ex. 1, photo, study)
2010 Novotny, Studies Ellis p. 120 n. 69 and p. 130 (lines 61–63, study)
2011 Hecker, TUAT^{2} 6 pp. 33–35 (ex. 1, translation, photo, study)
2018 Novotny in Brereton, I am Ashurbanipal pp. 202–203 Fig. 224 (ex. 1, photo)
2021 Pedersén, Babylon pp. 150–151 (study)

TEXT

1) *a-na-ku*
2) ^{m}AN.ŠÁR-DÙ-A
3) MAN GAL MAN *dan-nu*
4) MAN ŠÚ MAN KUR *aš-šur*
5) MAN *kib-rat* LÍMMU-*ti*
6) LUGAL LUGAL.ME NUN *la šá-na-an*
7) *šá ina a-mat* AN.ŠÁR ^{d}UTU
8) *u* ^{d}AMAR.UTU
9) *ul-tú tam-tim*
10) *e-liti a-di tam-tim*
11) *šap-liti i-be-lu-ma*
12) *gi-mir ma-liki ú-šak-niš*
13) *še-pu-uš-šú za-nin é-sag-íl*

1–36a) I, Ashurbanipal, great king, strong king, king of the world, king of Assyria, king of the four quarters (of the world), king of kings, ruler who has no rival, who by the command of the gods Aššur, Šamaš, and Marduk rules from the Upper Sea (10) to the Lower Sea and who made all rulers bow down at his feet, who provides for Esagil, the palace of the gods — whose doorbolt I made glisten like the stars (lit. "writing") of the firmament —, who repaired the damaged parts of all their sanctuaries, (who) established (my) protection over all cult centers, whose deeds are pleasing to all the gods (and) (20) whose shepherdship is sweet to the black-headed people; son of Esarhaddon,

Figure 7. BM 90864 (Asb. 246), a marble stele depicting Ashurbanipal carrying a basket on his head and recording that king's restoration of Ekarzagina, the temple of the god Ea at Babylon. © Trustees of the British Museum.

14) É.GAL DINGIR.MEŠ *šá ki-ma ši-ṭir bu-ru-mu*
15) *ú-nam-mir* SI.GAR-*šú*
16) *u šá eš-re-e-te ka-li-ši-na*
17) *ḫi-bil-ta-ši-na ú-šal-lim*
18) *e-li kul-lat ma-ḫa-zi ú-kin an-dul-lu*
19) *šá ep-še-tu-šú* UGU *kal* DINGIR.MEŠ DÙG.GA *e-li*
20) *ṣal-mat* SAG.DU *du-uš-šu-pat* SIPA-*us-su*
21) DUMU ^{m}AN.ŠÁR-ŠEŠ-SUM.NA MAN GAL
22) MAN *dan-nu* MAN ŠÚ MAN KUR *aš-šur* GÌR.NÍTA KÁ.DIŠ
23) MAN KUR *šu-me-ri u* URI.KI* *mu-še-šib* TIN.TIR.KI
24) *e-piš é-sag-íl mu-ud-diš*
25) *eš-re-e-te kul-lat ma-ḫa-zu*
26) *šá ina qé-reb-ši-na iš-tak-*⸢*kan*⸣

great king, strong king, king of the world, king of Assyria, governor of Babylon, king of the land of Sumer and Akkad, who (re)settled Babylon, (re)built Esagil, renovated the sanctuaries of all the cult centers, constantly established appropriate procedures in them, and (re)confirmed their interrupted offerings, (who) restored the rites and rituals according (30) to the old pattern; grandson of Senna[cherib], great king, strong king, king of the world, king of Ass[yria], I —

23 KI*: The text has KU$^{?}$ for KI.

27) si-ma-a-ti
28) u sat-tuk-ki-ši-na baṭ-lu-tú ú-ki-nu
29) par-ṣe ⌜ki-du-de-e⌝
30) ki-ma la-bi-⌜rim⌝-[ma]
31) ú-⌜ter-ru⌝
32) a-na áš-⌜ri?⌝-[šu-un]
33) A A ^{md}30-⌜ŠEŠ?⌝.[MEŠ-SU]
34) MAN GAL MAN ⌜dan-nu⌝
35) MAN ŠÚ MAN KUR aš-[šur]
36) a-na-ku-ma EN [GAL]
37) ^{d}AMAR.UTU šá ina ⌜BALA⌝-[e]
38) LUGAL maḫ-[ri]
39) ina ma-ḫar AD ba-ni-[i-šú]
40) ú-ši-bu ina qé-[reb]
41) bal-til.KI ina u_4-[me]
42) BALA-ía ina ri-šá-⌜ti⌝
43) a-na TIN.TIR.KI
44) i-ru-um-ma
45) sat-⌜tuk-ki⌝
46) é-⌜sag⌝-íl
47) u DINGIR.⌜MEŠ⌝ KÁ.DINGIR
48) ú-⌜kin ki⌝-din-nu-ut
49) TIN.⌜TIR.KI⌝ ak-⌜ṣur⌝
50) áš-šú ⌜dan⌝-nu a-na
51) SIG ⌜la ḫa⌝-ba-lu
52) ^{md}GIŠ.⌜NU$_{11}$⌝-MU-GI.NA
53) ŠEŠ ⌜ta⌝-li-me
54) ⌜a-na LUGAL-ú-ut⌝
55) TIN.⌜TIR⌝.[KI] ⌜ap⌝-qid
56) u ši-pir é-⌜sag⌝-íl
57) ⌜šá⌝ za-ru-u-a la ú-qa-at-tu-u
58) a-na-ku ú-šak-lil GIŠ.ÙR.MEŠ
59) GIŠ.ere-nu u GIŠ.ŠUR.MÌN ṣi-ru-tú tar-bi-ti
60) KUR.ḫa-ma-nu u KUR.lab-na-nu e-li-⌜šú⌝
61) ⌜ú⌝-šat-ri-ṣi GIŠ.IG.MEŠ GIŠ.TÚG GIŠ.MES.⌜MÁ.KAN.NA⌝
62) ⌜GIŠ⌝.LI GIŠ.ere-nu ú-še-piš-ma ú-rat-⌜ta⌝-[a]
63) [ina] KÁ.MEŠ-šú ú-na-a-te KÙ.GI KÙ.BABBAR ⌜ZABAR⌝
64) ⌜AN⌝.BAR GIŠ.⌜MEŠ⌝ u NA$_4$.MEŠ DÙ-ma ú-kin
65) [ina] ⌜qé⌝-reb-šú ⌜ina u_4⌝-me-šú-ma é-kar-za-gìn-na
66) ⌜É⌝ ^{d}⌜é⌝-[a] šá qé-reb é-sag-íl eš-šiš
67) ⌜ú⌝-še-⌜piš ^{d}⌝é-a LUGAL ZU.AB ši-⌜pir⌝
68) ⌜šu⌝-a-⌜ti⌝ [ḫa]-⌜diš⌝ IGI.BAR-ma ia-a-ti ^{m}⌜AN⌝.[ŠÁR]-⌜DÙ⌝-A
69) MAN KUR aš-⌜šur⌝ [NUN] pa-liḫ-šú a-mat MUNUS.SIG$_5$-ía liš-⌜šá-kin⌝
70) šap-tuš-⌜šú⌝ TIN u_4-me SÙ.MEŠ še-bé-e ⌜lit-tu-tú⌝
71) ṭu-ub ⌜UZU⌝ u ⌜ḫu-ud⌝ lìb-bi li-šim ši-ma-ti
72) ⌜SUḪUŠ GIŠ.GU.ZA⌝ [LUGAL-u]-⌜ti⌝-ía ki-ma KUR-i
73) ⌜li⌝-[šar-šid] ⌜it⌝-ti AN-e u ⌜KI-tim⌝
74) ⌜lu⌝-kin ⌜BALA-u⌝-a u šá ^{md}GIŠ.NU$_{11}$-MU-[GI].⌜NA⌝

36b–65a) During my reign, the [great] lord, the god Marduk, who during the reign of a previous king (40) had resided in Baltil (Aššur) in the presence of the father who created [him], entered Babylon amidst rejoicing. I (re)confirmed the regular offerings for Esagil and the gods of Babylon. I (re-)established the privileged status of Babylon (and) (50) in order that the strong might not harm the weak, I appointed Šamaš-šuma-ukīn, my favorite brother, to the kingship of Babylon. I completed the work on Esagil which my father had not finished. I roofed it with long beams of cedar and cypress, the produce of (60) Mount Amanus and Mount Lebanon. I had doors made of boxwood, *musukkannu*-wood, juniper, and cedar and I fixed (them) [in] its gates. I had vessels made of gold, silver, bronze, iron, wood, and (precious) stones and I placed (them) inside it.

65b–67a) At that [time], I had Ekarzagina, the temple of the god E[a] that is inside (the) Esagil (temple complex), (re)built anew.

67b–76a) May the god Ea, king of the Watery Abyss (*apsû*), look upon this work with [pleasure] and may a good word for me — [Ashurba]nipal, king of Ass[yria, ruler] who reveres him — be set (70) upon his lips! May he determine as my fate a long life, fullness of ol[d a]ge, good health, and happiness! May he [make] the foundation of my [royal th]ro[ne as secure] as a mountain! May he make my reign as firm as heaven and netherworld! Moreover, with regard to Šamaš-šuma-[uk]īn, king of Babylon, my favorite brother,

61 Following I. Gershevitch, J.N. Postgate has supported the identification of *musukkannu*-wood (a valuable hardwood) with *Dalbergia sissoo*; see Postgate, BSA 6 (1992) p. 183.

75) LUGAL TIN.⸢TIR⸣.KI ŠEŠ *ta-lim-ia* u_4*-me-šú*

76) *li-ri-ku liš-bi bu-ʾa-a-*⸢*ri*⸣ *ma-*⸢*ti*⸣*-ma*

77) *ina aḫ-rat* u_4*-me* ⸢NUN⸣ *ar-ku-u* ⸢*šá ina*⸣ [u_4]-⸢*me* BALA-*šú*⸣

78) ⸢*ši*⸣*-pir* ⸢*šu*⸣*-a-ti in-na-ḫu an-ḫu-us-*⸢*su*⸣

79) ⸢*lu-ud*⸣*-diš ṣa-lam* ⸢LUGAL⸣*-u-ti-ía li-*⸢*mur*⸣*-ma*

80) [Ì.GIŠ *lip*]*-šu-*⸢*uš*⸣ UDU.SISKUR BAL-*qí it-ti*

81) ⸢*ṣa-lam-i*⸣*-šú* ⸢*liš*⸣*-kun ik-ri-bi-*⸢*šú*⸣

82) ⸢^{d}⸣*é-a* ⸢*i-šem-me*⸣ *šá šu-*⸢*mì*⸣ *šaṭ-*⸢*ru*⸣

83) *i-*⸢*pa*⸣-[*áš*]-⸢*ši-ṭu ṣa-lam* LUGAL⸣*-u-ti-*⸢*ía*⸣

84) [*i-ab-ba*]-⸢*tu*⸣

85) ⸢*lu*⸣*-u* ⸢*a*⸣*-šar-šú*

86) [*ú*]-⸢*na-kar*⸣-[(*u*)]-⸢*ma*⸣

87) [*it*]-⸢*ti*⸣ *ṣa-*[*lam-šú*]

88) *la i-šak-*[*kan*]

89) ^{d}*é-a* EN

90) *ṣi-i-ru*

91) *ag-gi-iš*

92) *lik-kil-me-šú-ma*

93) GIŠ.GU.ZA LUGAL-*ti-šú*

94) *li-šá-bal-kit-ma*

95) *li-ṭi-ir*

96) *be-lut-su* MU-*šú*

97) NUMUN-*šú ina* KUR.KUR

98) *li-ḫal-liq-ma*

99) *a-a ir-ši-šú*

100) *re-e-mu*

may his days be long and may he be fully satisfied with (his) good fortune!

76b–82a) If at any time in the future, [during the days] of the reign of some future ruler, this work falls into disrepair, [may (that ruler) re]pair its dilapidated state! May he look at my royal image, (80) [an]oint (it) [with oil], offer a sacrifice, (and) place (my image) with his (own) image! The god Ea will (then) listen to his prayers.

82b–100) (But) as for the one who e[ras]es my inscribed name, (or) [destroys] my royal statue, or [*ch*]*an*[*ges*] its position [and] does not pla[ce] (it) with [his] (own) im[age], may the god Ea, (90) exalted lord, glare at him angrily, overthrow his royal rule, and take away his sovereignty. May he (Ea) make his name (and) his descendant(s) disappear from the lands and have no pity on him!

247

A short Akkadian inscription of Ashurbanipal is stamped upon numerous bricks found at Babylon. The nine-line text states that the Assyrian king had had bricks made for Esagil ("House Whose Top Is High") and Etemenanki ("House, Foundation of Heaven and Netherworld"), the temple and ziggurat of Babylon's patron god Marduk, both located in the Eridu district of that city.

CATALOGUE

Ex.	Museum Number	Excavation Number	Photograph Number	Provenance	Dimensions (cm)	Lines Preserved	FuB 27	cpn
1	VA Bab 4052	BE 8086	Bab ph 872	Babylon, Esagil, Room 6, 4th pavement (Floor l)	37×37	1–9	—	p
2	VA Bab 4052i	BE 8083	—	Babylon, Esagil, court, 4th pavement (Floor l)	37×37×10	1–9	14	n
3	VA Bab 4052k	—	—	Probably Babylon	37×37×7.5	1–9	15	n
4	VA Bab 4073a	—	—	As ex. 3	37×37×7.5	1–9	16	n
5	VA Bab —?	BE 8072	—	As ex. 1	37×37	1–9	—	n
6	VA Bab —?	BE 8010	—	Babylon, Esagil, court, 3rd pavement (Floor k)	—	—	—	n

7	VA Bab —?	BE 8044	—	As ex. 6	30×30	—	—	n
8	VA Bab —	BE 8045	—	As ex. 6	30×30	—	—	n
9	VA Bab —?	BE 8046	—	As ex. 6	30×30	—	—	n
10	VA Bab —?	BE 8047	—	As ex. 6	30×30	—	—	n
11	VA Bab —?	BE 8048	—	As ex. 6	30×30	—	—	n
12	VA Bab —?	BE 8049	—	As ex. 6	30×30	—	—	n
13	VA Bab —?	BE 8051	—	As ex. 6	—	—	—	n
14	VA Bab —?	BE 8052	—	As ex. 6	—	—	—	n
15	VA Bab —?	BE 8053	—	As ex. 6	—	—	—	n
16	VA Bab —?	BE 8054	—	As ex. 6	—	—	—	n
17	VA Bab —?	BE 8073	—	As ex. 2	37×37	—	—	n
18	VA Bab —?	BE 8074	—	As ex. 2	37×37	—	—	n
19	VA Bab —?	BE 8075	—	As ex. 2	37×37	—	—	n
20	VA Bab —?	BE 8076	—	As ex. 2	37×37	—	—	n
21	VA Bab —?	BE 8077	—	As ex. 2	37×37	—	—	n
22	VA Bab —?	BE 8078	—	As ex. 2	37×37	—	—	n
23	VA Bab —?	BE 8079	Bab ph 870	As ex. 2	37×37	1–9	—	p
24	VA Bab 4073	BE 8080	—	As ex. 2	37×37	—	—	n
25	VA Bab 4052	BE 8081	—	As ex. 2	37×37	—	—	n
26	VA Bab —?	BE 8082	—	As ex. 2	37×37	—	—	n
27	EŞ —	—	—	Probably Babylon	—	1–9	—	p

COMMENTARY

The excavations of the Deutsche Orient-Gesellschaft at Babylon in November 1900 either certainly or probably produced all of the exemplars. See Marzahn, FuB 27 (1989) pp. 58 and 64 n. 12 (against Wetzel and Weissbach, Hauptheiligtum p. 86) with regard to the provenance of ex. 2 (assuming that VA Bab 4052i and BE 8083 are identical). Exs. 3–4 and 27 might also be listed under Babylon excavation numbers. Where known, the inscription is stamped on the brick's face. The stamp used on ex. 2 measures 16.5×7.7 cm and 16.8×6.8 cm on exs. 3–4. The inscription is in a somewhat archaizing Babylonian script. The only variant reported for the inscription is MEŠ for ME in line 4 (exs. 2–4; see Marzahn, FuB 27 [1989] p. 58). Following RINAP editorial practices, no score for this brick inscription is presented on Oracc.

BIBLIOGRAPHY

1900–1 Koldewey, MDOG 7 pp. 22–23 (ex. 5, provenance, translation)

1911 Koldewey, Tempel pp. 44 and 72 no. 10 (ex. 5, provenance, edition)

1916 Streck, Asb. pp. LXIII and 350–351 no. 3.a.β (ex. 5, edition)

1924–25 Unger, AfK 2 p. 23 no. 12 (exs. 1, 5, study)

1925 Koldewey, WEB^{4} pp. 202 and 203 fig. 125 (ex. 1, photo, study)

1927 Luckenbill, ARAB 2 p. 405 §§1119–1120 (ex. 5, translation)

1931 Unger, Babylon p. 280 no. 22 (exs. 1, 5, translation)

1938 Wetzel and Weissbach, Hauptheiligtum p. 39 no. A.II.a and pp. 86–87 (exs. 1–2, 5–26, provenance, edition)

1989 Marzahn, FuB 27 p. 58 no. VIII, nos. 14–16 and fig. 7 (transliteration; ex. 2, copy; exs. 2–4, study)

1995 Frame, RIMB 2 pp. 208–209 B.6.32.7 (exs. 1–27, edition)

2010 Novotny, Studies Ellis p. 110 and p. 127 n. 121 (lines 4–9; ex. 2, study)

2021 Pedersén, Babylon pp. 150–151 and 157 (study)

TEXT

1) *ana* ^{d}AMAR.UTU UMUN-*šú*
2) ^{m}AN.ŠÁR-DÙ-A
3) MAN ŠÚ MAN KUR *aš-šur*
4) *ana* TIN ZI.ME-*šú*
5) *a-gur-ri*
6) *é-sag-gíl*
7) *u é-temen-an-ki*
8) *eš-šiš*
9) *ú-šal-bi-in*

1–9) For the god Marduk, his lord: Ashurbanipal, king of the world (and) king of Assyria, in order to ensure his good health (5) had baked bricks made anew for Esagil and Etemenanki.

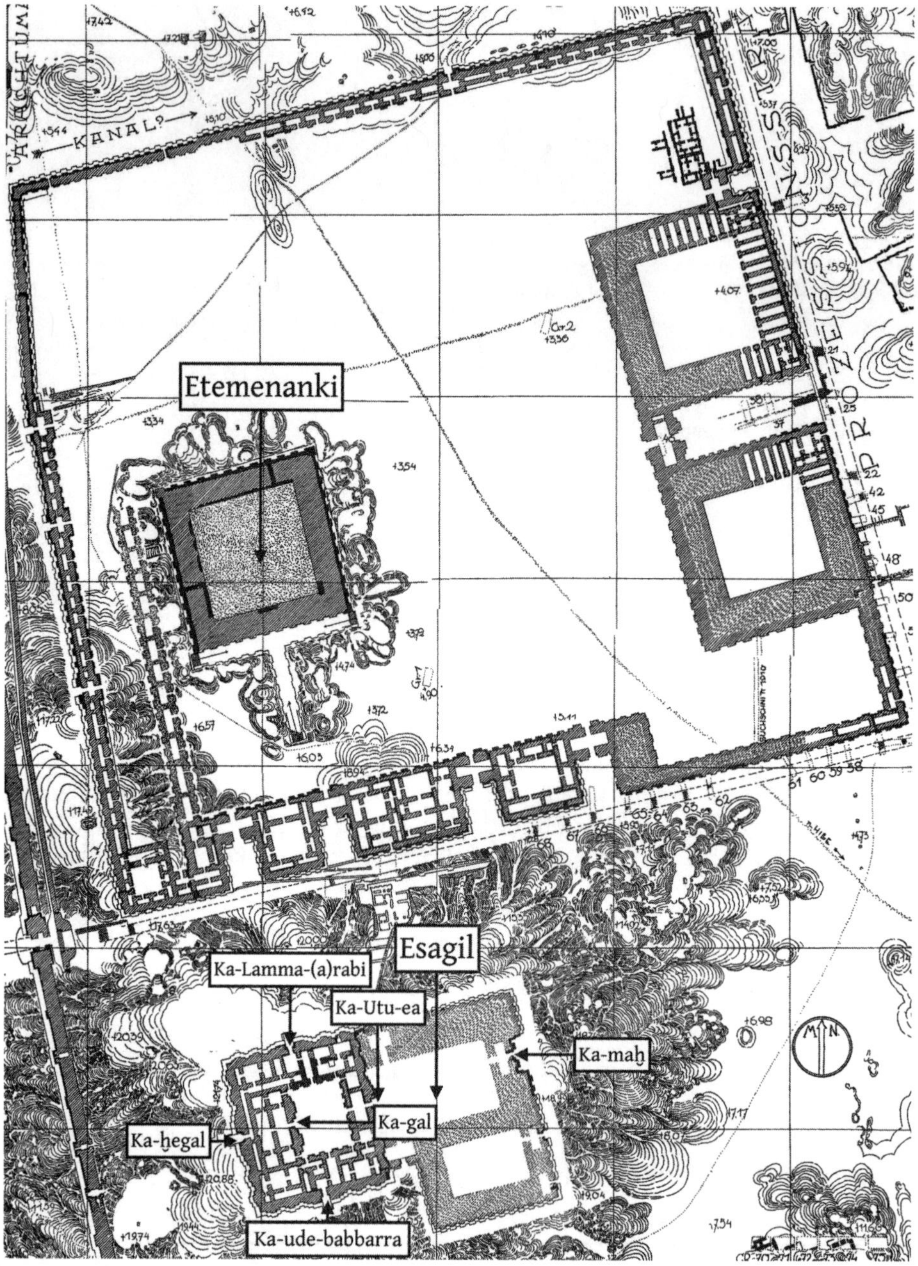

Figure 8. Annotated plan of the ruins of the Eridu district of Babylon and the Esagil temple complex. Adapted from Koldewey, WEB[5] fig. 256.

248

Five bricks from Babylon have an Akkadian inscription stamped upon them. This ten-line text mentions that Ashurbanipal had had bricks made for the ziggurat Etemenanki, which was located in east Babylon, in the sacred Eridu district.

CATALOGUE

Ex.	Museum Number	Excavation/ Registration No.	Photograph Number	Provenance	Dimensions (cm)	Lines Preserved	FuB 27	cpn
1	BM 90285	DT 381	—	Babylon	31.5×25×6.5	1–10	—	p
2	VA Bab 4073b	BE 40145	Bab ph 1892	Babylon, Merkes 22qII	32×32×8.5	1–10	17	p
3	EŞ 9027	BE 40855	Bab ph 1965	Babylon, Sachn 37ak, south wall	31×31	1–10	—	p
4	VA Bab 4073c	BE 41032	—	Babylon, Sachn 37af, south	16.5×23×7.5	6–10	18	n
5	VA Bab 4073d	BE 41232	—	Babylon, Sachn 36ab, south	24×31×9	1–10	19	n

COMMENTARY

G. Smith states that ex. 1 was found at Bablyon (Assyrian Discoveries p. 380), although it was obtained by the expedition to Nineveh led by him on behalf of the Daily Telegraph newspaper in 1873. The Deutsche Orient-Gesellachaft discovered exs. 2–5 during excavations at Babylon. The exact findspot of ex. 3 is noted on pl. 12 of Wetzel and Weissbach, Hauptheiligtum (cited erroneously as "[BE] 40856"); ex. 4 was found in January 1910. For the provenance of ex. 5, see Marzahn, FuB 27 (1989) p. 59 and p. 64 n. 14 (contra Wetzel and Weissbach, Hauptheiligtum p. 86). Each brick is stamped on the face. The area stamped on ex. 1 measures 13.3×7.1 cm, on ex. 2 10.3×8.0 cm, on ex. 4 4.5×7.9 cm, and on ex. 5 11.2×7.8 cm. The inscription is in contemporary Babylonian script. The line arrangement follows ex. 1; exs. 2–5 have lines 9 and 10 of ex. 1 on a single line. Smith refers to having found a nine-line exemplar, but this must refer to ex. 1 since it is registered as having come from his expedition to Iraq. According to C.B.F. Walker (CBI p. 67), a copy of the inscription on BM 90285 is found in G. Smith, Notebook 17 (=Add. MS 30413) fol. 19, no. 36. Exs. 2–3 and 5 have *aš-šur* not AN.ŠÁR in line 2. No score for this brick inscription is presented on Oracc, following RINAP editorial practices.

BIBLIOGRAPHY

1875 G. Smith, Assyrian Discoveries p. 380 (ex. 1, translation)
1886 Bezold, Literatur p. 116 §65.4.m (ex. 1, study)
1916 Streck, Asb. pp. LXIII and 350–351 no. 3.a.α (ex. 1, edition)
1922 BM Guide p. 74 no. 302 (ex. 1, study)
1924–25 Unger, AfK 2 p. 23 nos. 13–14 (ex. 1, study)
1927 Luckenbill, ARAB 2 p. 405 §1118 (ex. 1, translation)
1938 Wetzel and Weissbach, Hauptheiligtum p. 40 no. A.II.d and pp. 86–87 (exs. 2–5, provenance, edition)
1981 Walker, CBI pp. 66–67 no. 78 (ex. 1, transliteration)
1989 Marzahn, FuB 27 p. 59 no. IX, nos. 17–19 and fig. 8 (transliteration; ex. 5, copy; exs. 2, 4, 5, study)
1995 Frame, RIMB 2 pp. 209–210 B.6.32.8 (exs. 1–5, edition)
2021 Pedersén, Babylon p. 157 (study)

TEXT

1) *ana* dAMAR.UTU UMUN-*šú*
2) mAN.ŠÁR-DÙ-A
3) MAN ŠÚ MAN KUR AŠ
4) A m*aš-šur*-PAP-AŠ
5) MAN ŠÚ MAN KUR AŠ
6) MAN KÁ.DIŠ.KI
7) *a-gur-ri*
8) *é-temen-an-ki*
9) *eš-šiš*
10) *ú-še-piš*

1–10) For the god Marduk, his lord: Ashurbanipal, king of the world (and) king of Assyria, son of Esarhaddon, (5) king of the world, king of Assyria, (and) king of Babylon, had baked bricks made anew for Etemenanki.

249

A third Akkadian inscription stamped on a single brick from Babylon records that Ashurbanipal had bricks made for Marduk's ziggurat, Etemenanki.

CATALOGUE

Museum Number	Excavation Number	Photograph Number	Provenance	Dimensions (cm)	cpn
VA Bab 4052h	BE 41143	Bab ph 2030	Babylon, Sachn 38ao, south	31.5×31.5×8.5	p

COMMENTARY

The brick was found in Babylon on March 3, 1910. The inscription is stamped on its face and is in contemporary Babylonian script. The text has been edited from the published photograph, supplemented by the published collations by J. Marzahn.

BIBLIOGRAPHY

1910 Wetzel, MDOG 43 p. 23 (provenance)
1916 Streck, Asb. pp. LXIII and 837 no. 8 (edition)
1924–25 Unger, AfK 2 p. 23 no. 15 (study)
1925 Koldewey, WEB^{4} p. 183 fig. 117 (photo)
1938 Wetzel and Weissbach, Hauptheiligtum p. 40 no. A.II.c and pp. 86–87 (provenance, edition)
1989 Marzahn, FuB 27 p. 57 no. VI, no. 10 and fig. 5 (copy, transliteration, study)
1995 Frame, RIMB 2 p. 212 B.6.32.11 (edition)
2021 Pedersén, Babylon p. 157 (study)

TEXT

1) *ana* ⸢^{d}⸣AMAR.UTU UMUN-*šú* ^{m}AN.ŠÁR-DÙ-A MAN ŠÚ
2) MAN ⸢KUR⸣ *aš-šur a-gur-ri é-temen-an-ki*
3) *a-*⸢*na*⸣ TIN-⸢*šú eš*⸣-*šiš* ⸢*ú*⸣-*šal-bi-in*

1–3) For the god Marduk, his lord: Ashurbanipal, king of the world (and) king of Assyria, for the sake of his life had baked bricks made anew for Etemenanki.

250

A brick fragment discovered at Babylon preserves part of a four-line Akkadian inscription of Ashurbanipal. The text, which is stamped on the brick, records the making of baked bricks for the ziggurat Etemenanki.

CATALOGUE

Museum Number	Excavation Number	Provenance	Dimensions (cm)	cpn
—	BE 41186	Babylon, Sachn 34ai, south	—	n

COMMENTARY

German excavators found this brick fragment (BE 41186) at Babylon on March 16, 1910. According to O. Pedersén (personal communication), the brick's present location is in the Vorderasiatisches Museum (Berlin). The edition of the inscription is based upon that of F.H. Weissbach because no photograph of the fragment appears to have been made. Weissbach states that there does not appear to have been room to restore more than the name of Ashurbanipal at the end of line 1 and suggests that the lack of any title for Ashurbanipal might indicate that the text dates to the period before Ashurbanipal became king (that is, during the reign of Esarhaddon, but after Ashurbanipal had been named heir to the throne). There is, however, no evidence to suggest that Ashurbanipal held any authority in Babylonia during the reign of Esarhaddon or was active there with regard to building projects at that time. Since it was not possible to verify the spacing on the original piece, such a suggested date must remain improbable.

BIBLIOGRAPHY

1938 Wetzel and Weissbach, Hauptheiligtum p. 40 no. A.II.b and p. 86 (provenance, edition)

1995 Frame, RIMB 2 pp. 211–212 B.6.32.10 (edition)

2021 Pedersén, Babylon p. 157 (study)

TEXT

1) [*ana*] ^{d}AMAR.UTU UMUN-*šu* ^{m}AN.ŠÁR-[DÙ-A]
2) A ^{m}AN.ŠÁR-PAP-AŠ MAN ŠÚ [MAN KUR AŠ]
3) *a-gur-ri é-temen-*⸢*an*⸣-[*ki*]
4) *eš-šiš ú*-[*še-piš*]

1–4) [For] the god Marduk, his lord: Ashur[banipal], son of Esarhaddon, king of the world (and) [king of Assyria had] baked bricks [made] anew for Etemena[nki].

251

Eight bricks discovered at Babylon are stamped with a Sumerian inscription of Ashurbanipal. This short, four-line text states that the Assyrian king had Etemenanki ("House, Foundation of Heaven and Netherworld"), Marduk's ziggurat, rebuilt anew.

250 line 4 *ú*-[*še-piš*]: Or possibly *ú*-[*šal-bi-in*]; compare for example Asb. 249 line 3.

CATALOGUE

Ex.	Museum Number	Excavation/ Registration No.	Photograph Number	Provenance	Dimensions (cm)	Lines Preserved	FuB 27	cpn
1	BM 130712	1942-1-28,1	—	Aquired by B.A Varty; probably Babylon	23×9.5×3.5	1–4	—	c
2	EŞ 9028	BE 39849	Bab ph 1192	Babylon, city area	—	1–4	—	p
3	VA Bab 4054c	BE 41252	—	Babylon, Sachn 36ab, southwest	30.5×30.5×8.5	1–4	13	n
4	VA Bab 4054a	BE 36072	Bab ph 1914, 1916	Babylon, Merkes 27nII, +8.50	25×18×8.5	1–4	11	p
5	VA Bab 4054b	BE 39436	Bab ph 1916	Babylon, Merkes 24qII, +8.00	21×19×8.5	1–4	12	p
6	VA —	BE 39807	Bab ph 1916	Babylon, Sachn 37am, south	—	1–4	—	p
7	VA —$^{?}$	BE 41171	—	Babylon, Sachn 26z, west	—	—	—	n
8	—	BE 46433	Bab ph 3283	Babylon, Merkes 37s, baked brick pillar	—	2–4	—	p

COMMENTARY

B.A. Varty presented ex. 1 to the British Museum and exs. 2–8 come from the excavations at Babylon by the Deutsche Orient-Gesellschaft in 1908–12. All of the exemplars are stamped on the brick's face. The area stamped on ex. 1 measures 5.3×20.7 cm, on ex. 3 5.5×20.7 cm, and on exs. 4–5 5.5×9.5 cm. The script is a mixture of (contemporary and archaic) sign forms. For example, lugal is written five times with the Old Babylonian form and the sixth time with the Neo-Babylonian form. Ex. 1 was kindly collated by C.B.F. Walker. No variants are attested and, thus, no score of this text is presented on Oracc.

Although the inscription appears to have been written in Sumerian, the writing *eš-šiš* ("anew") in line 4 and ma-da *aš-šur*.KI ("Assyria") in lines 2 and 3 would suggest that at least part of the inscription was read in Akkadian.

BIBLIOGRAPHY

1938 Wetzel and Weissbach, Hauptheiligtum p. 40 no. A.II.e and pp. 86–87 (exs. 2–8, provenance, edition)
1981 Walker, CBI p. 67 no. 79 (ex. 1, transliteration)
1989 Marzahn, FuB 27 pp. 57–58 no. VII, nos. 11–13 and fig. 6 (transliteration; ex. 3, copy; exs. 3–5, study)
1995 Frame, RIMB 2 pp. 210–211 B.6.32.9 (exs. 1–8, edition)
2013 May, CRRA 56 pp. 206–207 (study)
2021 Pedersén, Babylon p. 157 (study)

TEXT

1) ^{d}asar-ri umun gal lugal-a-ni-ir ^{m}AN.ŠÁR-DÙ-A
2) lugal imin lugal ma-da *aš-šur*.KI dumu ^{m}AN.ŠÁR-PAP-AŠ
3) lugal imin lugal ma-da *aš-šur*.KI lugal TIN.TIR.KI
4) nam-ti-la-bi-šè é-temen-an-ki *eš-šiš* mu-na-dím

1–4) For the god Asari, great lord, his lord: Ashurbanipal, king of the world (and) king of Assyria, son of Esarhaddon, king of the world, king of Assyria, (and) king of Babylon, for the sake of his life had constructed Etemenanki anew.

3 inim, the number seven, is used here for the Akkadian word *kiššatu*, "world, totality"; see AHw p. 492 and CAD K p. 457.

252

A fragment of a clay cylinder now in the British Museum preserves a small portion of Akkadian inscription referring to a temple of the goddess Ištar, as well as to the goddess Ištar of Agade (Akkad). Although the name of the king in whose name the text was written is no longer preserved, the inscription should probably be attributed to Ashurbanipal because the wording of the text is similar to that found in other (Babylonian) inscriptions of his.

CATALOGUE

Museum Number	Registration Number	Provenance	Dimensions (cm)	cpn
—	81-2-4,174	Babylon or Agade	8.2×7.5	c

COMMENTARY

The fragment is part of the British Museum's Kuyunjik collection and, thus, it might come from that site, although some pieces from other places (for example, Borsippa) have been mistakenly placed in that collection. The piece is shown on British Museum photograph 230549. The inscription is in contemporary Babylonian script and has been edited from the original.

The wording of the inscription is similar to that found on several other clay cylinder inscriptions of Ashurbanipal from Babylonia, in particular his text recording work on the city wall of Babylon (Asb. 241 lines 23–28; see also Asb. 253 lines 23–27 and Asb. 262 lines 23–28), although the placement of some phrases is different in this inscription; the proposed restorations are based on Asb. 241 and 253. M. Streck (Asb. pp. XLI–XLII) included this fragment among his exemplars for the inscription of Ashurbanipal describing the restoration of the Ebabbar temple at Sippar (Asb. 262), but it is clear that he had not actually seen the piece and that he placed it there because of a comment by H. Winckler (OLZ 1 [1898] col. 76).

Since the name of the deity whose temple was built or restored is normally the deity mentioned in the curse formula, it is likely that it was a temple of the goddess Ištar of Agade (often called Bēlet-Agade) which was of concern in the text. Nabonidus records that Ashurbanipal had carried out work on Eulmaš, the temple of Ištar of Agade at Agade (Weiershäuser and Novotny, RINBE 2 p. 137 Nabonidus 27 ii 37–45), thus this fragment might very well describe the restoration of that (still-undiscovered) temple. With regard to the history of the Eulmaš temple at Agade, see, for example, Frame, Mesopotamia 28 (1993) pp. 21–50. However, there was also a temple of Ištar of Agade in the Ka-dingirra district of Babylon, Emašdari ("House of Animal Offerings"), and in view of Ashurbanipal's other work at that city, it is likely that this inscription refers to that temple, rather than the one at Agade.

BIBLIOGRAPHY

1896 Bezold, Cat. 4 p. 1768 (study)
1993 Frame, Mesopotamia 28 pp. 45–48 (copy, edition, study)
1995 Frame, RIMB 2 pp. 227–228 B.6.32.20 (edition)

TEXT

Lacuna

1′) [ši]-⌜pir? šu-a⌝-ti ⌜in-na⌝-[ḫu ...]

2′) en-qu-ú-tu ši-ta-⌜al⌝ [...]

3′) ⌜É ^{d}15⌝ ki-i si-⌜ma⌝-[ti-šu? la-bi-ra-a-ti e-pu-uš (...) ik-ri-bi-ka ^{d}INANNA (a-ga-dè.KI)]

4′) i-⌜šem⌝-me MU.SAR-⌜ú?⌝-[a a-mur-ma Ì.GIŠ pu-šu-uš UDU.SISKUR BAL-qí]

5′) it-ti MU.⌜SAR⌝-e-ka ⌜šu⌝-[kun šá šu-mì šaṭ-ru ina ši-pir ni-kil-ti i-pa-áš-ši-ṭu šu-mì]

6′) it-ti MU-šú la i-šaṭ-ṭa-⌜ru⌝ [MU.SAR-ú-a i-ab-ba-tu-ma it-ti MU.SAR-e-šú]

7′) ⌜la i-šak-ka-nu qí?-bit?⌝ x [...]

8′) ^{d}INANNA a-ga-⌜dè⌝.[KI ...]

Lacuna

1′–5′a) this [*work*] falls into dis[repair ...], question skilled [craftsmen! ... Rebuild (...)], the temple of the goddess Ištar according to [*its* ancient] specifi[cations! (...) *The goddess Ištar* (*of Agade*)] will (then) listen to [your prayers. Look at my] inscribed object, [anoint (it) with oil, offer a sacrifice, (and)] s[et] (my inscribed object) with your (own) inscribed object!

5′b–8′) [(But) as for the one who erases my inscribed name by some crafty device], (or) does not write [my name] with his name, (or) [destroys my inscribed object], (or) does not set [my inscribed object with his (own) inscribed object] ... [...] the goddess Ištar of Agade [will ...].

253

Several clay cylinders are inscribed with an Akkadian inscription of Ashurbanipal that records his restoration of Borsippa's city wall, Ṭābi-supūršu ("Its Fold Is Pleasant"), and its gates. Because the king's older brother Šamaš-šuma-ukīn is mentioned favorably, the text was composed prior to the outbreak of his rebellion against Assyria in 652.

CATALOGUE

Ex.	Museum Number	Registration Number	Provenance	Dimensions (cm)	Lines Preserved	cpn
1	VA 3587	—	Purchased; possibly from Borsippa	12×5.7	1–28	c
2	BM 83000 (+) BM 83001	83-1-21,163 (+) 83-1-21,164	Acquired by H. Rassam; probably from Borsippa	5.6×6; 5×4.5	18–27; 2–22, 24–28	c
3	AO 7752	—	Probably from Borsippa	12×6.8×4,4	1–12, 26–28	c
4	MMA 86.11.51	—	As ex. 1	6.4×10.8	15–23	c

COMMENTARY

Ex. 1 was purchased by the Vorderasiatisches Museum, ex. 3 by the Louvre Museum, and ex. 4 by the Metropolitan Museum of Art; ex. 2 is thought to come from H. Rassam's work (see Leichty, Sippar 3 pp. xiii and 327; Lambert, Cat. p. 75 indicates that BM 83001 comes from Nineveh [modern Kuyunjik]). Exemplars 1–2 and 4 are written in Neo-Assyrian script and ex. 3 is in contemporary Babylonian script, although D. Arnaud states that some of its signs diverge from the forms expected in Neo-Babylonian writing (Studies Puech p. 27). The line arrangement follows ex. 1. The master line is a conflation of the various exemplars, although only ex. 1 preserves parts of lines 13–14. The restoration of lines 7–23 and 25–28 is based upon Asb. 241 lines 3–23 and 25b–29. Note, however, that line 6 is partially restored from an inscription of Šamaš-šuma-ukīn; see Frame, RIMB 2 p. 254 B.6.33.4 line 10. A score of the text is presented on Oracc and the minor (orthographic) variants are listed at the back of the book.

The favorable mention of Ashurbanipal's appointment of his older brother Šamaš-šuma-ukīn as the king of Babylon in lines 16–17 (partially restored) indicates that the text must have been composed sometime between 668 and 652.

BIBLIOGRAPHY

1939–41 Weidner, AfO 13 pp. 217–118 and pl. XVI (ex. 1, copy, edition)
1974 Arnaud, Studies Puech pp. 27–32 (ex. 3, edition)
1974 Arnaud, RA 68 p. 191 (ex. 3, study)
1991–93 Frame, JCS 43–45 pp. 119–120 (ex. 2, copy, edition)
1995 Frame, RIMB 2 pp. 215–216 B.6.32.13 (exs. 1–2, edition)
1996 Borger, BIWA pp. 383 and 385 (study)
1998 Borger, BiOr 55 col. 848 (study)
2014 Frame in Spar and Jursa, CTMMA 4 pp. 275–277 and pl. 129 no. 163 (ex. 4 copy [Spar], transliteration; exs. 1–4, translation)

TEXT

1) *a-na* ^{d}AG IBILA *gaš-⸢ri⸣ x (x)* [...] *⸢ur$^{?}$⸣-šá-ni* DINGIR.MEŠ *ti-iz-qar šá-qu-u muš-tar-ḫu*
2) DUB.⸢SAR⸣ *é-sag-⸢íl⸣ ma-⸢ru$^{?}$⸣ a-[šá-re-du ...] ⸢na⸣-šu-u ṭup-pi* NAM.MEŠ DINGIR.MEŠ *šá gu-um-mur/muru te-re-e-ti*
3) *e-tel-⸢li⸣* DINGIR.MEŠ ⸢GAL⸣.[MEŠ ... ^{d}]*⸢a-nun-na⸣-ki šá-kin ši-tul-tú a-na* DINGIR.MEŠ *šu-ut* AN KI
4) *kap-ka-pu x x x x (x)-a-ti x x* [...] *⸢šá⸣ la iš-šá-an-na-nu* GIŠ.TUKUL.MEŠ-*šú*
5) *bu-kúr* ^{d}*asar-ri ⸢reš-tu⸣-ú i-⸢lit⸣-ti* ⸢^{d}⸣[*e$_{4}$-ru$_{6}$-u$_{8}$* ...] *šá šur-ba-a-ti e-nu-us-su*
6) *a-šib é-zi-⸢da⸣* É [*ki*]-*⸢i⸣-ni* EN *bár-⸢sipa⸣*.[KI *ma-ḫa-zu*] *⸢ra-áš⸣-bu* EN GAL EN-*ia*

1–6) To the god Nabû, the powerful heir [... *h*]*ero* of the gods, eminent, exalted, splendid, scribe of Esagil, f[oremost] son, [...], who bears the tablet of the fates of the gods, who controls the omens, prince of the g[reat] gods, [(...) *the one who directs the Igīgū and*] Anunnakū gods, who gives advice to the gods of heaven (and) netherworld, powerful ... [...] whose weapons cannot be equaled, (5) firstborn son of the god Asari (Marduk), offspring of the goddess [Erua (Zarpanītu), ...] whose lordship is supreme, who dwells in Ezida — the proper temple — lord of Borsi[ppa — the] awesome [cult center] — great lord, my lord:

7) *a-na-ku* ^{m}AN.ŠÁR-DÙ-A ⸢MAN GAL⸣ MAN *dan-nu* MAN ŠÚ MAN KUR [*aš*]-⸢*šur*⸣ LUGAL *kib-rat* LÍMMU-*ti*
8) DUMU ^{m}AN.ŠÁR-ŠEŠ-SUM.NA MAN GAL MAN *dan-nu* MAN ŠÚ MAN KUR *aš*-[*šur* GÌR.NÍTA TIN].⸢TIR⸣.KI LUGAL KUR EME.GI$_{7}$ *u* URI.⸢KI⸣
9) *mu-še-šib* KÁ.DINGIR.⸢RA.KI⸣ [*e-piš é-sag-íl mu-ud-diš eš-re-e*]-*⸢ti⸣ kul-lat ma-ḫa-zi*
10) *ša ina qer-bi-ši-⸢na⸣ iš-tak-⸢ka⸣-*[*nu si-ma-a-ti ù sat-tuk-ki-ši-na*] *⸢baṭ⸣-lu-tú ú-ki-⸢nu⸣*
11) *par-ṣe ki-du-⸢de⸣-*[*e ki-ma la-bi-ri-im-ma ú-ter-ru áš*]-*⸢ru⸣-uš-šu-un*
12) [DUMU DUMU] $^{m⸢d}$30-ŠEŠ⸣.[MEŠ-SU MAN GAL MAN *dan-nu* MAN ŠÁR MAN KUR *aš*]-⸢*šur*⸣ *a-na-ku-⸢ma⸣*

7–12) I, Ashurbanipal, [gr]eat k[ing], mighty king, king of the world, king of [Ass]yria, king of the four quarters (of the world); son of Esarhaddon, great king, mighty king, king of the world, king of As[syria, governor of Babyl]on, king of the land of Sumer and Akkad, who (re)settled Babylon, [(re)built Esagil, (and) renovated the sanctuaries] of all cult centers; (10) who constantly establ[ished appropriate procedures] in them, (re)confirmed [their int]errupted [regular offerings, (and) restor]ed the rites (and) ritua[ls according to the old pattern; grandson of] Sennac[herib, great king, mighty king, king of the world, king of Assy]ria, I —

13) [*ina* BALA-*e-a* EN GAL ^{d}AMAR.UTU *ina ri-šá-a-ti a-na* TIN.TIR.KI] *⸢i⸣-ru-um-⸢ma⸣*
14) [*ina é-sag-íl šá da-ra-a-ti šu-bat-su ir-me*

13–18) [During my reign, the great lord, the god Marduk], entered [Babylon amidst rejoicing] and [took up his residence in the eternal Esagil. I (re)confirmed

2 The translation "who controls the omens" assumes that *gu-um-mur*(*u*) is a D stem stative subjunctive (see also Frame, RIMB 2 p. 254 B.6.33.4 [Šamaš-šuma-ukīn] line 3, *gu-um-mu-ru*) rather than a D stem infinitive ("... tablet of the fates of the gods for the control of the omens").

3 Nabû is at times called "the light (*nūru*) of the Igīgū and Anunnakū gods" and "the one who directs (*āširu*) the Igīgū and Anunnakū gods." See Tallqvist, Götterepitheta pp. 382–383 and Leichty, RINAP 4 p. 104 Esarhaddon 48 (Aššur-Babylon A) line 9.

7 The reading of lines 7 and 8 comes partly from ex. 1, which uses LUGAL for *šarru* ("king"), and partly from ex. 3, which uses MAN. In the later restorations in line 12, MAN is used arbitrarily.

8 LUGAL is preserved only on ex. 1 and it is likely that ex. 3 would have had MAN here. Since ex. 1 does not preserve any of the MANs in the royal titles in lines 7, 8 or 12, it may well have originally had LUGAL instead of MAN in those places as well.

sat-tuk]-⸢*ki*⸣ *é-sag-*⸢*íl*?⸣

15) ⸢*ù* DINGIR.MEŠ⸣.DINGIR.⸢MEŠ⸣ [TIN.TIR.KI *ú-kin ki-din-nu-(ú)-tu* TIN].⸢TIR?⸣.KI *ak-*⸢*ṣur*⸣

16) *áš-šú dan-nu a-na* SIG *la ḫa-*⸢*ba*⸣*-*[*li* ^{md}GIŠ.NU_{11}-MU-GI.NA] ⸢ŠEŠ⸣ *ta-li-mì*

17) *a-na* LUGAL-*ú-ut* KÁ.DINGIR.RA.KI ⸢*ap-qid*⸣ [*ù i-na* KÙ.BABBAR KÙ.GI] *ni-siq-ti* NA_4.MEŠ

18) ⸢*é-sag-íl az*⸣*-nun-ma ki-ma ši-ṭir* ⸢*bu*⸣*-*[*ru-mu ú*]-⸢*nam*⸣*-mir é-umuš-a*

19) *ina* [u_4-*me*]-⸢*šú-ma* DÙG.GA⸣-*su-pur-šú* BÀD *bár-sipa*.KI ⸢*ša*⸣ [*la-ba*]-⸢*riš*⸣ *il-lik-ú-ma*

20) ⸢*i*⸣*-*[*qu-pu*] ⸢*in-nab-tu*⸣ *áš-šú* EN.⸢NUN⸣ *é-zi-da* ⸢*ù*⸣ *eš-re-e-te bár sipa*.KI *dun-nu-nu*

21) [*ina e-muq um*]-⸢*ma*⸣*-na-ti-ia* [*sur-riš* DÙG].GA-*su-pur-šú* BÀD *bár-sipa*.KI *ina ši-pir* ^{d}*kulla eš-šiš ú-še-piš-ma*

22) [KÁ.GAL.MEŠ-*šú*] ⸢*ú*⸣*-rak-ki-si* GIŠ.IG.MEŠ *ab-ni-ma ú-rat-ta-a ina* KÁ.MEŠ-*šú*

23) [NUN *ar*]-⸢*ku*⸣*-ú ša ina* BALA-*e-šú ši-pir šu-a-ti in-na-ḫu* LÚ.*um-ma-a-ni en-qu-tu*

24) ⸢*ši*⸣*-ta-ʾa-al* [DÙG.GA]-⸢*su*⸣*-pur-šú* BÀD *bár-sipa*.KI *ki-ma si-ma-ti-šú la-bi-ra-a-te e-pu-uš*

25) [MU.SAR-*u-a*] ⸢*a*⸣*-mur-ma* Ì.GIŠ *pu-šu-uš* UDU.SISKUR BAL-*qí it-ti* MU.SAR-*e-ka šu-kun*

26) [*ik-ri-bi*]-⸢*ka*⸣ ^{d}*na-bi-*⸢*um*⸣ [*i*]-⸢*šem*⸣*-me ša šu-mì šaṭ-ru ù* MU *ta-lim-ia*

27) [*ina ši-pir ni-kil-ti*] *i-ab-*[*bat* MU].⸢SAR⸣*-u-a it-ti* MU.SAR-*e-šú la i-šak-ka-nu*

28) [^{d}*na-bi-um* (...) *ag-giš lik*]-*kil-me-šú-ma* MU-*šú* NUMUN-*šú ina* KUR.KUR *li-ḫal-liq*

the regular offer]ings for Esagil (15) and the gods [of Babylon]. I (re-)established [the privileged status of Babyl]on (and) appointed [Šamaš-šuma-ukīn], (my) favorite brother, to the kingship of Babylon in order that the strong might not har[m] the weak. I decorated Esagil [with silver, gold], (and) precious stones and [made] Eumuša glisten like the stars (lit. "writing") of the fi[rmament].

19–22) At [th]at [time], (with regard to) Ṭābi-supūršu, the (city) wall of Borsippa, wh[ich] had become [ol]d, (20) [buckled (and) c]ollapsed, in order to increase the security of Ezida and the (other) sanctuaries of Borsippa, [with the strength of] my [labor] forces I had [Ṭā]bi-supūršu, the (city) wall of Borsippa, built [quickly] anew with the work of the god Kulla and refitted [its gates]. I built (new) doors and installed (them) in its gates.

23–26a) [O (you) futu]re [ruler], during whose reign this work falls into disrepair, question skilled craftsmen. (Re)build [Ṭābi-s]upūršu, the (city) wall of Borsippa, according to its ancient specifications. (25) Look at [my inscribed object], anoint (it) with oil, offer a sacrifice, (and) place (my inscribed object) with your (own) inscribed object. The god Nabû will (then) [lis]ten [to you]r [prayers].

26b–28) (But) as for the one who des[troys] my inscribed name or the name of my favorite (brother) [by some crafty device], (or) does not place my inscribed object with his (own) inscribed object, [may the god Nabû, (...)], glare at him [angrily] and make his name (and) his descendant(s) disappear from the lands.

254

A stone stele discovered at Borsippa is engraved with an Akkadian inscription of Ashurbanipal recording the restoration of Ezida ("True House"), the temple of the god Nabû in that city. A relief of the king carrying a basket on his head is carved on the front of the stele (see also Asb. 246); this image depicts the king personally aiding in the restoration work. Like many of Ashurbanipal's inscriptions, this eighty-one-line text was composed at some point between 668 and 652, that is, during the first half of the reign of Ashurbanipal. This inscription is sometimes referred to as "S[tele][2]" in previous editions.

CATALOGUE

Museum Number	Registration Number	Provenance	Dimensions (cm)	cpn
BM 90865	80-6-17,2	Borsippa, Ezida, in the room southwest of room C2	39×15.5×13	c

COMMENTARY

BM 90865 (80-6-17,2) was found during excavations at Borsippa in 1880 under the general direction of H. Rassam. The object was found in the same room of Ezida (the chamber southwest of room C2) as a stele with a similar inscription of his older brother Šamaš-šuma-ukīn (Frame, RIMB 2 pp. 252–253 B.6.33.3), which has a relief depicting that king of Babylon with a basket on his head. It was not found at Babylon as has sometimes been thought (for example, Unger, AfK 2 [1924–25] p. 23 no. 11). The inscription is for the most part in contemporary Babylonian script, although some Neo-Assyrian sign forms do appear. Lines 1–49 are on the back of the stele and lines 50–81 on the monument's side.

The friendly mention of Šamaš-šuma-ukīn in lines 3–32 and 46–48 indicates that the inscription must date before 652. Note that "Prism T", which was composed in the eponymy of Nabû-šar-ahhēšu, the governor of Samaria (645), records that Ashurbanipal had four silver(-plated) statues of wild bulls (*rīmu*) stationed in two prominent gateways of the Ezida temple at Borsippa (Novotny and Jeffers, RINAP 5/1 p. 216 Asb. 10 [Prism T] ii 1–6). For further details about Ashurbanipal's activities at Borsippa, see the introduction of the present volume (pp. 21–22).

BIBLIOGRAPHY

1886 Bezold, Literatur pp. 113–114 §64.3.d and 347 (study)
1889–91 Evetts, PSBA 13 p. 158 (study)
1891 Strong, JRAS pp. 457–468 (copy in type, edition)
1892 Lehmann-Haupt, Šamaššumukîn 1 p. 25 and 2 pp. 59–61 and pls. XIII–XVI no. 6 (S^{2}) (copy, study)
1904 Smith in Harper, Literature pp. 127–129 (translation)
1910 Delitzsch, AO 11/1 p. 36 fig. 17 (photo [inscription not visible])
1916 Streck, Asb. pp. XLIV–XLV and 240–245 no. 6 (S^{2}) (edition)
1922 BM Guide p. 74 no. 301 (study)
1924–25 Unger, AfK 2 p. 23 no. 11 (study)
1926 Unger, RLV 4/2 pl. 267d (photo [inscription not visible])
1927 Luckenbill, ARAB 2 pp. 375–376 §§974–977 (translation)
1931 Unger, Babylon p. 225 no. 13 and pl. 37 fig. 57 (photo [inscription not visible], study)
1962 Potratz, Orientalia NS 31 p. 46 and pl. I fig. 2 (photo [inscription not visible])
1968 Ellis, Foundation Deposits pp. 24–25 and 179 no. 24 (partial edition, study)
1976 Barnett, Assyrian Sculptures from the North Palace pl. 1 (photo)
1981 Reade in Fales, ARIN pl. II fig. 3 (photo [inscription not visible])
1982 Börker-Klähn, Bildstelen no. 225 (photo [inscription not visible], study)
1986 Reade, Iraq 48 p. 109 and pl. XIII (provenance)
1992 Frame, Babylonia p. 352 fig. 2 (photo [inscription not visible])
1994 Lawson, Concept of Fate p. 77 n. 31 (line 9a, study)
1995 Frame, RIMB 2 pp. 217–219 B.6.32.14 (edition)
2003 Porter, Trees, Kings, and Politics pl. 13 (photo)
2004 Porter, Studies Immerwahr pp. 271–272 (photo, study)
2010 Novotny, Studies Ellis p. 120 n. 69 (study)
2018 Beaulieu, History of Babylon p. 212 fig. 8.3 (photo [inscription not visible], study)
2018 Brereton, I am Ashurbanipal pp. 18–19 Fig. 11 (photo)

TEXT

1) *a-na-ku* ⸢AN⸣.ŠÁR-DÙ-A
2) ⸢MAN⸣ GAL MAN *dan-nu* MAN ŠÚ MAN KUR *aš-šur*
3) ⸢MAN⸣ *kib-rat* LÍMMU-*ti* LUGAL LUGAL.MEŠ
4) ⸢NUN⸣ *la šá-na-an šá ina a-mat* AN.ŠÁR ^{d}⸢UTU⸣
5) ⸢*ù*⸣ ^{d}AMAR.UTU *ul-tu tam-tim e*-⸢*liti*⸣
6) ⸢*a*⸣-*di* [(*x*)] *tam-tim šap-liti i-be*-⸢*lu-ma*⸣
7) ⸢*gi*⸣-*mir ma-liki ú-šak-niš še-pu-uš*-⸢*šú*⸣
8) [*za*]-⸢*nin*⸣ *é-sag-íl* É.GAL DINGIR.MEŠ

1–23a) I, Ashurbanipal, great [kin]g, strong king, king of the world, king of Assyria, king of the four quarters (of the world), king of kings, ruler who has no rival, who by the command of the gods Aššur, Šamaš, (5) and Marduk rules from the Upper Sea to the Lower Sea and who made all rulers bow down at his feet, [who provi]des for Esagil, the palace of the gods — [who]se [doorbo]lt I made glisten like the stars (lit. "writing") of the firmament —

9) [*šá ki*]-*ma ši-ṭir bu-ru-mu ú-nam-mir*
10) ⸢SI.GAR⸣-*šú ù šá eš-re-e-ti ka-li-ši-na*
11) *ḫi-bil-ta-ši-na ú-šal-lim e-li kul-lat*
12) *ma-ḫa-zi ú-kin an-dul-lum šá ep-še-e-tú*-[*šú*]
13) UGU *kal* DINGIR.MEŠ DÙG.GA UGU *ṣal-mat* SAG.DU
14) *du-šu-pat* SIPA-*us-su* DUMU ^{m}AN.ŠÁR-ŠEŠ-MU
15) MAN ŠÚ MAN KUR *aš-šur* GÌR.NÍTA KÁ.DINGIR.RA.KI
16) MAN KUR EME.GI$_{7}$ *ù* URI.KI *mu-še-šib* TIN.TIR.KI
17) *e-piš é-sag-íl mu-ud-diš eš-re-e-ti*
18) *kul-lat ma-ḫa-zi šá ina qer-bi-ši-na*
19) *iš tak-kan si-ma-te sat-tuk-ki*-⸢*ši-na*⸣
20) ⸢*baṭ*⸣-*lu-tú ú-ki-nu par-ṣe ki-du*-⸢*de*⸣-[*e*]
21) ⸢*ki*⸣-*ma la-bi-rim-ma ú-ter-ru a*-⸢*na*⸣
22) *áš-ri-šu-un* DUMU DUMU ^{md}30-ŠEŠ.⸢MEŠ-SU⸣
23) MAN ŠÚ MAN KUR *aš-šur a-na-ku-ma* EN GAL ^{d}AMAR.⸢UTU⸣
24) *šá ina* BALA-*e* LUGAL *maḫ-ri ina ma-ḫar*
25) AD *ba-ni-i-šú ú-ši-bu ina qé-reb*
26) ⸢*bal*⸣-*til*.KI *ina u$_{4}$-me* BALA-*e-a ina ri-šá-a*-[*ti*]
27) ⸢*a*⸣-*na* TIN.TIR.KI *i-ru-um-ma sat-tuk*-⸢*ki*⸣
28) *é-sag-íl u* DINGIR.MEŠ TIN.TIR.KI *ú-kin*
29) *ki-din-nu-ti* KÁ.DINGIR.RA.KI *ak-ṣur*
30) *áš-šú dan-nu a-na* SIG *la ḫa-ba-li*
31) ^{md}GIŠ.NU$_{11}$-MU-GI.NA ŠEŠ *ta-lim/limi*
32) *a-na* LUGAL-*ú-ti* TIN.TIR.KI *ap-qid*
33) *ina u$_{4}$-me-šú-ma* É.GAR$_{8}$ *é-zi-da*
34) *šá la-ba-riš il-lik-u-ma i-ni*-⸢*šú*⸣
35) *tem-me-en-šú ina* BALA-*e-a an-ḫu-us*-⸢*su*⸣
36) *lu-diš-ma ú-za-aq-qí-ir ḫur-sa*-⸢*niš*⸣
37) *a-na šat-ti* ^{d}*na-bi-um* EN *ṣi-ru*
38) *ep-še-te-ia* MUNUS.SIG$_{5}$.MEŠ *ḫa-diš* IGI.BAR-⸢*ma*⸣
39) *ia-a-ti* ^{m}AN.ŠÁR-DÙ-A NUN *pa-liḫ-šú*
40) *a-mat da-mi-iq-ti-ía liš-šá-kin šap-tuš-šú*
41) TIN *u$_{4}$-me* SÙ.MEŠ *še-bé-e lit-tu-tu*
42) *ṭu-ub* UZU *ḫu-ud lìb-bi li-šim*
43) *ši-ma-ti* SUḪUŠ GIŠ.GU.ZA LUGAL-*u-ti-ia*
44) *ki-ma* KUR-*i li-šar-šid it-ti*
45) ⸢AN⸣-*e u* KI-*tim lu-kin* BALA-*u-a*
46) ⸢*ù*⸣ *šá* ^{md}GIŠ.NU$_{11}$-MU-GI.NA
47) [LUGAL] TIN.TIR.KI ŠEŠ *ta-lim-ía u$_{4}$-me-šú*
48) [*li*]-*ri-ku liš-bi bu-ʾa-a-ri*
49) [*ma*]-⸢*ti-ma*⸣ *ina aḫ-rat u$_{4}$-me* NUN ⸢EGIR-*u*⸣
50) *šá ina u$_{4}$-me* BALA-*šú*
51) ⸢*ši*⸣-*pir šu-a-ti*
52) ⸢*in*⸣-*na-ḫu*
53) *an-ḫu-us-su*
54) ⸢*lu*⸣-*ud-diš ṣa-lam*
55) LUGAL-*ti-ia*
56) *li-mur-ma* Ì.GIŠ
57) ⸢*lip-šu-uš*⸣ UDU.SISKUR
58) ⸢BAL-*qí it*⸣-*ti*
59) *ṣa*-⸢*lam-i*⸣-*šú*

who repaired the damaged parts (10) of all their sanctuaries, (who) established (my) protection over all cult centers, the one who[se] deeds are pleasing to all the gods (and) whose shepherdship is sweet to the black-headed people; son of Esarhaddon, (15) king of the world, king of Assyria, governor of Babylon, king of the land of Sumer and Akkad, who (re)settled Babylon, (re)built Esagil, renovated the sanctuaries of all the cult centers, constantly established appropriate procedures in them, (and) (20) (re)confirmed [thei]r [inter]rupted regular offerings, (who) restored the rites and rituals according to the old pattern; grandson of Sennache[rib], king of the world, king of Assyria, I —

23b–32) During my reign, the great lord, the god Mard[uk], who during the reign of a previous king (25) had resided in Baltil (Aššur) in the presence of the father who created him, entered Babylon amidst rejoicing. I (re)confirmed the regular offerings for Esagil and the gods of Babylon. I (re-)established the privileged status of Babylon (and) (30) in order that the strong might not harm the weak I appointed Šamaš-šuma-ukīn, my favorite brother, to the kingship of Babylon.

33–36) At that time, (with regard to) the (enclosure) wall of Ezida ("True House") which had become old and whose foundation had become weak, during my reign I indeed renovated its dilapidated sections and made (it) as high as a mountain.

37–48) On account of this, may the god Nabû, the exalted lord, look upon my good deeds with pleasure and (40) may a good word for me — Ashurbanipal, ruler who reveres him — be set upon his lips! May he determine as my fate a long life, fullness of old age, good health, and happiness! May he make the foundation of my royal throne as secure as a mountain! (45) May he make my reign as firm as heaven and netherworld! Moreover, with regard to Šamaš-šuma-ukīn, [king] of Babylon, my favorite brother, may his days be long and may he be fully satisfied with (his) good fortune!

49–62) [If at] any time in the future, during the days of the reign of some future ruler, this work falls into disrepair, may (that ruler) repair its dilapidated state! May he look at (55) my royal image, anoint (it) with oil, offer a sacrifice, (and) place (my image) with his (own) image! The god Nabû will (then) listen to his prayers.

60) *li-⸢iš⸣-kun**
61) *ik-ri-⸢bi⸣-i-šú*
62) ^{d}⸢AG⸣ *i-šem-me*
63) *šá šu-⸢mì⸣ šaṭ-ru*
64) *i-⸢pa⸣-áš-ši-ṭu*
65) *ṣa-lam* ⸢LUGAL⸣-*ti-ia*
66) *i-ab-⸢ba⸣-tu*
67) ⸢*lu*⸣-*u a-⸢šar⸣-šú*
68) *ú-⸢nak⸣-ka-ru-ma*
69) *it-⸢ti⸣ ṣa-lam-šú*
70) *la i-⸢šak⸣-kan*
71) ^{d}*na-⸢bi⸣-um*
72) EN ⸢*šur*⸣-*bu-ú*
73) *ag-gi-iš*
74) *lik-kil-⸢me⸣-šú-ma*
75) GIŠ.GU.ZA ⸢LUGAL⸣-*ti-šú*
76) *li-⸢šá⸣-bal-kit-ma*
77) *li-ṭir be-lut-su*
78) ⸢MU⸣-*šú* NUMUN-*šú ina* KUR.KUR
79) ⸢*li*⸣-*ḫal-liq-ma*
80) ⸢*a*⸣-*a ir-ši-šú*
81) *re-e-mu*

63–81) (But) as for the one who erases my inscribed name, (or) destroys my royal statue, or changes its position and (70) does not place (it) with his (own) image, may the god Nabû, supreme lord, glare at him angrily, overthrow (75) his royal rule, and take away his sovereignty! May he (Nabû) make his name (and) his descendant(s) disappear from the lands and have no pity on him!

255

A poorly preserved clay tablet now in the Penn Museum (Philadelphia) bears copies of two dedicatory texts, both of which are written in Akkadian. The first and much shorter inscription only mentions Ashurbanipal, while the second and longer one mentions both Šamaš-šuma-ukīn and Ashurbanipal. The former is thought to have been written in the name of Ashurbanipal, while the latter is generally believed to have been composed in the name of his older brother, Šamaš-šuma-ukīn (Frame, RIMB 2 pp. 256–257 B.6.33.5); however, it is not inconceivable that both inscriptions should be attributed to Ashurbanipal. The badly damaged inscription might concern an object dedicated to the god Nabû at Borsippa (see the commentary).

CATALOGUE

Museum Number	Provenance	Dimensions (cm)	cpn
CBS 733 + CBS 1757	Possibly Borsippa	9.3×5.7×2.7	c

COMMENTARY

The two fragments, CBS 733 + CBS 1757, were joined by W.G. Lambert. The inscription is written in contemporary Babylonian script and is separated from an inscription of Ashurbanipal's brother Šamaš-šuma-ukīn (Frame, RIMB 2 pp. 256–257 B.6.33.5) by a horizontal ruling.

Due to the poor state of preservation of the tablet, it is uncertain with what object or structure the inscription was concerned. The name of Marduk's temple at Babylon, Esagil, is found in line 2 and the second inscription on the tablet, which is written in the name of Šamaš-šuma-ukīn, likely deals with a piece of equipment for the sacred boat of the god Nabû at Borsippa. As Lambert has already pointed out, in view of these facts and the appearance of the phrase "that light" in line 3, it is possible that the text "commemorates the giving of a lamp or lampstand to Marduk or Nabû" (AfO 18 [1957–58] p. 386).

BIBLIOGRAPHY

1908 Clay, BE 8/1 no. 142 (copy [only CBS 733])
1909 Ungnad, ZA 22 pp. 13–16 (edition [only CBS 733])
1957–58 Lambert, AfO 18 pp. 385–386 and pl. XXV (copy, edition)
1995 Frame, RIMB 2 p. 230 B.6.32.23 (edition)

TEXT

1) [*x* (*x*)] *x x x x* [...]
2) [(*x*)] *x qé-reb é-sag-*⸢*íl*⸣ [...]
3) ⸢*e*⸣*-nu-ma nu-ú-ru šu-a-*⸢*ti*⸣ [...]
4) ⸢MUNUS⸣.SIG$_5$-*tim* AN.ŠÁR-DÙ-A LUGAL KUR.[KUR? ...]
5) *u*$_4$*-mi-šam lit-*⸢*tas*⸣*-x x x* [(...)]

1–5) ... [...] in Esagi[l ...]. When that light [...] the good of Ashurbanipal, king of the land[s ...]. Let him daily ... [(...)].

256

A four-line dedicatory inscription of Ashurbanipal is inscribed on a brick that was found in the structure of the ziggurat at Dūr-Kurigalzu (modern Aqar Quf). It is possible that this Akkadian text is addressed to the god Enlil.

CATALOGUE

Source	Provenance	Dimensions (cm)	cpn
Al-Jumaily, Sumer 27 pl. 14 fig. 30	Dūr-Kurigalzu, built into the ziggurat's southwest façade	—	p

255 line 5 *lit-*⸢*tas*⸣*-x*: We might expect *lit-tas-qar* "may he/she say" (compare for example Asb. 244 line 16 and 245 line 16), but the traces do not fit a reading QAR of QA-AR.

COMMENTARY

The brick was built into the southwest façade of the ziggurat at Aqar Quf, which is reported not to have been its original position. Iraqi archaeologists excavated that part of the temple-tower in 1968–69. No excavation or museum number for the object is known. The text is inscribed, not stamped, in contemporary Babylonian script and it is edited from the published photograph. The suggested reading of the divine name in line 1 is uncertain, but is supported by the fact that most royal inscriptions from Dūr-Kurigalzu were dedicated to the god Enlil.

BIBLIOGRAPHY

1971 Al-Jumaily, Sumer 27 pp. 84 and 89, and pl. 14 fig. 30 following p. 98 [Arabic section] (provenance, photo)

1992 Frame, Babylonia p. 113 n. 60 (partial transliteration, study)

1995 Frame, RIMB 2 p. 228 B.6.32.21 (edition)

TEXT

1) ⸢*a*$^{?}$-*na*$^{?}$ ^{d}EN$^{?}$.LÍL$^{?}$⸣ [(...) EN-*šú*$^{?}$]
2) ^{m}AN.⸢ŠÁR$^{?}$⸣-DÙ-A MAN ŠÚ MAN ⸢KUR⸣ [*aš-šur*.KI (...)]
3) MAN *kib*-⸢*rat*⸣ LÍMMU-⸢*tim*$^{?}$⸣ [(...)]
4) *a-na* TI-*šú ú-še*-⸢*piš*$^{?}$⸣ [(...)]

1–4) *For the god Enlil,* [(...) *his lord*] Ashurbanipal, king of the world, king of [Assyria, (...)] king of the four quarters (of the world), had (this) [(...)] built for the sake of his life.

257

An Akkadian inscription of Ashurbanipal that describes how the king enlarged the courtyard of the temple Ešaḫula ("House of the Happy Heart") with bricks baked in a ritually-pure kiln and made its processional way "shine like daylight" is found on numerous bricks discovered in a temple dedicated to the god Nergal, "the lord of Sirara," at Mê-Turān/Mê-Turnat (modern Tell Ḥaddād).

CATALOGUE

Ex.	Source	Provenance	Dimensions (cm)	cpn
1	Rashid, Sumer 37 pp. 72–80	Mê-Turān, in the pavement of the Nergal temple	40×40×8	n
2	Rashid, Sumer 37 pp. 72–80	As ex. 1	40×40×8	n

COMMENTARY

The bricks were found in situ in 1980. The texts are inscribed (not stamped) and the script is contemporary Babylonian. No excavation or museum numbers are known for any of the bricks. According to F. Rashid, the numerous copies of the text differ from one another with regard to the particular cuneiform signs used and with regard to the length of the titles given to the god Nergal, the divine owner of Ešaḫula. Rashid published hand-drawn facsimiles and editions of two of the bricks. These two objects have not been seen, neither in the original nor in photograph, and are thus edited from the published copies.

The edition presented below follows ex. 1. Since the first two lines of ex. 2 diverge substantially from ex. 1, they are presented separately here:

1) *a-na* ^{d}U.GUR *dan-dan-nu** DINGIR.[ME]Š *šur-*⸢*bu*⸣-*ú* ⸢*kaš*⸣-[*kaš* (DINGIR.MEŠ)]

2) *a-šib é-šà-ḫúl*-la* EN *si-ra-ra*.KI ...

1–2) For the god Nergal, mightiest of the gods, the supreme, most over[powering (of the gods)], the one who dwells in (the temple) Ešaḫula, the lord of Sirara,

Both exemplars are presented in full in the score on Oracc, but without a master line.

BIBLIOGRAPHY

1981 F. Rashid, Sumer 37 pp. 72–80 [Arabic section] (exs. 1–2, copy, edition, study)

1982 Hannoun, BSMS 2 p. 6 (study)

1995 Frame, RIMB 2 p. 229 B.6.32.22 (edition)

TEXT

1) *a-na* ^{d}U.GUR *dan-dan-nu** DINGIR.MEŠ *kaš-kaš* DINGIR.MEŠ *šur-bu-ú gít-ma-la*

2) *mut-tal-la e-tel-lu* ŠEŠ-*šú a-šib é-šà-ḫúl*-la* EN *si-ra-ra*.KI

3) EN-*šú* ^{m}AN.ŠÁR-DÙ-IBILA MAN GAL MAN *dan-nu** MAN ŠÚ MAN KUR *aš-šur*.KI

4) DUMU ^{m}AN.ŠÁR-ŠEŠ-SUM.NA MAN GAL MAN *dan-nu** MAN ŠÚ MAN KUR *aš-šur*.KI

5) MAN TIN.TIR.KI MAN KUR *šu-me-ri ù* URI.KI

6) DUMU DUMU ^{md}30-ŠEŠ.MEŠ-SU MAN GAL MAN *dan-nu** MAN ŠÚ

7) MAN KUR *aš-šur*.KI-*ma ana* TIN ZI.MEŠ-*šú*

8) *i-na a-gur-ru* UDUN KÙ*-*tim ki-sal-li*

9) *é-šà-ḫúl*-la ú-ra-bi-i-ma*

10) *tal-lak-ta-šú ki-ma u*$_{4}$*-me ú-nam-mir*

1–3a) For the god Nergal, mightiest of the gods, most overpowering of the gods, the supreme, perfect, (and) noble sovereign of his brother(s), the one who dwells in (the temple) Ešaḫula, the lord of Sirara, his lord: 3b–7a) Ashurbanipal, great king, strong king, king of the world, king of Assyria; son of Esarhaddon, great king, strong king, king of the world, king of Assyria, (5) king of Babylon, king of the land of Sumer and Akkad; grandson of Sennacherib, great king, strong king, king of the world, (who was) also king of Assyria —

7b–10) In order to ensure his good health, he enlarged the courtyard of (the temple) Ešaḫula with baked bricks from a (ritually) pure kiln and made its processional way shine like daylight.

258

Two damaged clay cylinders found at Nippur preserve part of an Akkadian inscription of Ashurbanipal. That text describes the restoration of the ziggurat (or possibly only just the temple on top of it) for the god Enlil, the patron of Nippur. The renovation of that same structure is recorded on a brick inscription (Asb. 260).

CATALOGUE

Ex.	Museum Number	Excavation Number	Provenance	Dimensions (cm)	Lines Preserved	cpn
1	UM L-29-632+633+636 = PMA F29-6-387a+b+e	—	Nippur, in debris covering pavement of Ashurbanipal, near east corner of court of the ziggurat	Length: 8.5; Dia. of left end: 5.2	1–6, 8–25	c
2	UM 55-21-384	3 NT 840	Nippur, sounding K 2, near virgin soil	7.5×4.7	4–15	c

COMMENTARY

Ex. 1 has "an unusual conical shape, rather like a cone with the tip cut off" and ex. 2 would originally have been of similar size and shape (Gerardi, Studies Sjöberg p. 207). Ex. 1 was found by the University of Pennsylvania expedition to Nippur at the end of the nineteenth century and is on loan to the Penn Museum (Philadelphia) from the Philadelphia Museum of Art. Ex. 2 was found by the Oriental Institute and the Penn Museum expedition to Nippur in 1951–52. Both copies of the text are written in contemporary Babylonian script. The line arrangement and master line follow ex. 1, but with help from ex. 2 for lines 6–8 and 15. The restoration at the end of line 2 follows an inscription dating to the reign of the Babylonian king Nabû-nāṣir (747–734); see Frame, RIMB 2 p. 128 B.6.15.2001 line 3. A score of the text is presented on Oracc and the minor (orthographic) variants are listed at the back of the book.

Because Šamaš-šuma-ukīn is not mentioned in the inscription and because Nippur was kept under direct Assyrian control after the 652–648 rebellion (that is, it was not placed under the authority of the new king of Babylon Kandalānu [647–627]), it is more likely that this inscription comes from the time after the beginning of the rebellion than before it. Only a few fragmentary Assyrian inscriptions give Ashurbanipal the title "king of the land of Sumer and Akkad," and this is the only one from Babylonia to do so (see Frame, Babylonia pp. 304–306). The attribution of this title to Ashurbanipal could suggest that the inscription dates to a time when there was no separate king of Babylon, or at least none acknowledged by the scribes at Nippur. This could point to the time of the rebellion itself as the date of composition for the text, but one might not expect restoration work to have been carried out while the land was in turmoil.

Figure 9. UM L-29-632+633+636 (Asb. 258 ex. 1), a damaged clay cylinder recording Ashurbanipal's restoration of the god Enlil's ziggurat at Nippur. © Penn Museum of the University of Pennsylvania.

BIBLIOGRAPHY

1903 Hilprecht, Explorations pp. 460–462 (ex. 1, provenance, photo, partial translation)
1904 Hilprecht, Excavations pp. 460–462 (ex. 1, provenance, photo, partial translation)
1916 Streck, Asb. pp. LXIV and 352–353 no. 4 (ex. 1, partial translation)
1927 Luckenbill, ARAB 2 p. 390 §1019 (ex. 1, partial translation)
1989 Gerardi, Studies Sjöberg pp. 207–215 (exs. 1–2, copy, edition, study)
1995 Frame, RIMB 2 pp. 219–221 B.6.32.15 (exs. 1–2, edition)
1998 Borger, BiOr 55 col. 848 (study)
2010 Novotny, Studies Ellis p. 127 n. 118 (lines 17–19 study)
2015 Clayden and Schneider, Kaskal 12 pp. 349 and 360 (lines 15–19, translation; ex. 1, provenance)

TEXT

1) *a-na* ^{d}EN.LÍL LUGAL DINGIR.DINGIR ⸢EN⸣ AN-*e ù* KI-*tim* NUN *x* [...]
2) *pa-ri-is pu-ru-us-su-ú šá la in-nin-nu-*⸢*ú*⸣ [*qí-bit-su*$^{?}$]
3) *a-šá-red* ^{d}*í-gì-gì ma-am-lu*$_{4}$ ^{d}*a-nun-na-ki mu-ma-*[*ʾe-er* ...]
4) *ta-mi-iḫ ṣer-ret gi-im-ri sa-ni-*[*iq mit-ḫur-ti*$^{?}$]
5) EN KUR.KUR IGI.GÁL DINGIR.MEŠ *a-šib é-kur šá qé-*⸢*reb*⸣ [NIBRU.KI (EN GAL-*i*) EN-*šú*]

1–5) For the god Enlil, king of the gods, lord of heaven and netherworld, prince [...], one who renders decisions, who[se *order*] cannot be changed, foremost of the Igīgū gods, hero of the Anunnakū gods, who ru[les ...], one who holds the lead-rope of every(one), one who makes [*opposing forces*] agr[ee], lord of the lands, wisest of the gods, one who dwells in Ekur which is inside [Nippur, (the great lord), his lord]:

6) AN.⸢ŠÁR-DÙ-IBILA⸣ [LUGAL GAL] ⸢LUGAL⸣ *dan-nu* LUGAL ⸢*kiš*⸣-[*šat* LUGAL KUR *aš-šur*.KI]
7) [... LUGAL *šá ina kul-lat*] KUR.KUR *ma-ḫi-*⸢*ru*⸣ [*la i-šu-u*]
8) [DUMU ^{m}AN.ŠÁR-ŠEŠ-SUM.NA LUGAL GAL LUGAL] ⸢*dan*⸣*-nu* LUGAL *kiš-šat* LUGAL ⸢KUR⸣ [*aš-šur*.KI]
9) [A A] ⸢^{d}30-ŠEŠ.MEŠ-SU⸣ LUGAL GAL LUGAL *dan-nu* LUGAL *kiš-šat* LUGAL KUR *aš-šur*.KI-⸢*ma*⸣
10) ⸢LUGAL⸣ KUR EME.<<UR>>.GI$_{7}$ *u* URI.KI GÌR.NÍTA AN.ŠÁR ^{d}EN.LÍL *u* ^{d}*nin-urta*
11) *za-nin ma-ḫa-zi* E MA TAR DU DÙ *sì-ma-ak-ku*

6–11) Ash[ur]b[ani]p[al, great king], strong [kin]g, king of the wor[ld, king of Assyria, ... king who has no] equal [in all] the lands; [son of Esarhaddon, great king], strong [king], king of the world, king [of Assyria; grandson of Sennacherib], great king, strong king, king of the world, (who was) also king of Assyria; (10) king of the land of Sumer and Akkad, vice-regent for the gods Aššur, Enlil and Ninurta, one who provides for the cult centers, ... sanctuaries —

12) *a-na ba-laṭ* ZI-*šu ur-ruk u*$_{4}$*-me-šú šu-un-mur* SU-*šú šu-ul-lum* NUMUN-*šú*
13) *e-*⸢*li*⸣ *a-a-bi-šu ú-zu-uz-zu* BALA.MEŠ-*šú la-ba-ri* GIŠ.GIDRU-*šú šu-te-šu-ri*
14) EN-*us-*⸢*su*⸣ [UGU] ⸢KUR⸣-*šú šu-ṭúb-bi* UN.MEŠ-*šú ina ṭuḫ-di u nu-uḫ-šú i-tar-ri-i*

12–14) In order to ensure his good health, to prolong his days, to make his appearance (lit. "body") radiant, to ensure the well-being of his offspring, so that he stand (victoriously) over his enemies, that his reign endure, that he lead (his people) aright *with* his staff, that his rule please his [land], (and) that he guide his people in abundant prosperity,

15) *é-gi-gu-nu-ú ziq-qur-rat* NIBRU.KI *šá ina i-rat* ZU.AB *šur-šu-du tem-me-en-šú*
16) *šá i-ga-ri-šú la-ba-*⸢*riš il-li*⸣*-ku-ma ib-ba-šu-ú se-ri-iḫ-šú*

15–19) (With regard to) Egigunû, the ziggurat of Nippur, whose foundation is made secure on the breast of the Watery Abyss (*apsû*), whose enclosure wall had become old and *eroded*, I repaired its dilapidated

9 There does not seem to be room to restore DUMU DUMU at the beginning of the line, so the restoration follows Asb. 246 line 33.
11 E MA TAR DU DÙ: R. Borger (BiOr NS 55 [1988] col. 848) suggested reading *e-ma qud-du-u*$^{??}$ *x*, but without providing a translation. DÙ could stand for *bāni*, "builder" (of the sanctuaries), or *kal* "all" (of the sanctuaries) (Gerardi, Studies Sjöberg p. 210 n. 9).
13 GIŠ.GIDRU-*šú šu-te-šu-ri*, "that he lead (his people) aright *with* his staff": R. Borger (BiOr NS 55 [1988] col. 848) suggested taking "staff" as the subject of the infinitive and translated the passage as "damit sein Zepter regiert."
15 Instead of taking *é-gi-gi-nu-ú* as a name, "Egiginû" here and in line 21 (note also Asb. 260 line 10 é-gi-gun-⸢na⸣), one might translate "high temple." It is possible that the *é* should not be pronounced and instead be taken as a determinative (see George, House Most High p. 92 no. 373).
16 *se-ri-iḫ-šú*: The meaning of this word in the phrase *ibbašû seriḫšu*, tentatively translated "*eroded*" (literally "its *serḫu* has occurred"), is not clear. The word appears in only one other text; and CAD S p. 313 (sub *sirḫu*) and AHw p. 1037 (sub *serḫu*) take it to mean "earth wall(?)" and "Erosionsschutt" respectively.

17) *ina* SIG$_4$.AL.ÙR.RA UDUN KÙ-*tim ma-qit-*⸢*ta*⸣*-šú* ⸢*ak-šìr-ma*⸣ *ú-šak-lil bu-na-a-šú*
18) *ina ši-pir* ^{d}*kulla eš-šiš ú-še-piš-ma ú-nam-mir-šú ki-ma u*$_4$*-mu*
19) *re-ši-šu ki-ma šá-di-i ul-li-ma ú-šá-an-bi-iṭ zi-*⸢*mi*⸣*-*[*šú*]
20) *a-na šat-ti* ^{d}EN.LÍL LUGAL DINGIR.MEŠ ^{d}EN.LÍL DINGIR.MEŠ EN [GAL$^{?}$ (EN-*šú*)]
21) *é-gi-gu-nu-ú ṣa-ad-di ma-a-tim ḫa-diš ina nap-*⸢*lu*⸣*-*[*si-šú*]
22) *šá* AN.ŠÁR-DÙ-IBILA LUGAL KUR *aš-šur*.KI SIPA *ki-i-nu pa-liḫ* DINGIR-*u-ti-*⸢*šú*⸣ [GAL-*ti*$^{?}$]
23) LUGAL-*us-su lik-tar-rab* BALA.MEŠ-*šú li-iṣ-ṣur ana* UD.⸢MEŠ⸣ [SÙ.MEŠ]
24) GIŠ.GIDRU SIPA-*tú sa-ni-qat mit-ḫur-ti li-šat-*⸢*mi*⸣*-*[*iḫ-šú*$^{?}$]
25) UGU KUR-*šú liš-ṭib re-é-ut-su* UGU *na-ki-*⸢*ri*⸣*-*[*šú li-iš-zi-iz*$^{?}$]

section(s) with baked bricks from a (ritually) pure kiln, and completed its structure. I had it built anew with the craft of the god Kulla and made it shine like daylight. I raised its top (as high) as a mountain and made [its] appearance resplendent.

20–25) On account of this, when the god Enlil, king of the gods, chief god (lit. "Enlil") of the gods, [*great*] lord, [(*his lord*)], loo[ks] upon Egigunû, the sign of the lands, with pleasure, may he (Enlil) constantly bless the kingship of Ashurbanipal — king of Assyria, true shepherd who reveres his [*great*] divinity — (and) keep his reign safe until [far-off] days! May he *cause* [*him to*] *gr*[*asp*] a staff of shepherdship which makes opposing forces agree! May he make his shepherdship pleasant to his land! [*May he make* (*him*) *stand* (*victoriously*)] over [his] enemy!

259

This is the first of three Sumerian brick inscriptions of Ashurbanipal from Nippur. It states that Ashurbanipal had Ekur ("House, Mountain"), the temple of the god Enlil in Nippur, (re)built. The text is found stamped sometimes on the face of the brick and sometimes on its side.

CATALOGUE

Ex.	Museum Number	Excavation/ Registration No.	Provenance	Dimensions (cm)	Lines Preserved	cpn
1	BM 90807	51-10-9,78R	Purchased from H.C. Rawlinson; probably Nippur	14×12×6	4–11	c
2	BM 114299	1919-10-11,4743	Nippur	28.5×19×7.5	1–11	c
3	Ash 1922.181	W-B 181	Purchased; probably Nippur	23×12.5×6.5	1–11	c
4	Ash 1924.627	—	Acquired by S. Langdon; probably Tal Laḫam	32×32×7	1–11	c
5	Bristol H 5097	—	Gift from Sir. L. Woolley; probably Nippur	16×11×7	1–6	n
6	CBS 1632a	—	As ex. 2	23×14.5×4.5	1–11	c
7	CBS 8632	—	Nippur III, ziggurat, inner wall	30×29×7	1–11	c
8	CBS 8633	—	As ex. 2	18×12×5	1–11	c
9	CBS 8654	—	As ex. 2	30×30×8	1–11	c
10	UM 84-26-8	—	As ex. 2	32.5×28×8	1–11	c
11	UM 84-26-9	—	As ex. 2	30×28×7.5	1–11	c
12	UM 84-26-10	—	As ex. 2	29×29×8	1–11	c

258 line 17 ⸢*ak-šìr-ma*⸣: Collation suggests that AK (thus "I repaired") is more likely than IK (thus "he repaired") even though this results in an awkward shift of person. The other verbs in lines 15–19 referring to Ashurbanipal can be either in the first person singular or the third person singular, while in the remainder of the inscription he is referred to in the third person.
258 line 20 ^{d}EN.LÍL DINGIR.MEŠ EN [GAL$^{?}$ (EN-*šú*)], "chief god of the gods, [*great*] lord [(*his lord*)]": R. Borger (BiOr 55 [1988] col. 848) suggested restoring the end of the line as EN.[LÍL.KI] and translated the passage as "'Enlil' der Götter von Nippur."
258 line 24 *sa-ni-qat mit-ḫur-ti* "which makes opposing forces agree": The translation follows CAD M/2 pp. 137–138. See also line 4 of this text (partially restored), Aei 6 line 18, and Grayson and Novotny, RINAP 3/1 p. 234 Senn. 36 obv. 11 for the phrase *sāniq mitḫurti*.

13	UM 84-26-11, face	—	As ex. 2	28×14×7	1–11	c
14	—	—	As ex. 2	28×14×7	1–11	c
15	EŞ —	—	Probably Nippur	29×29.5×6.5	1–11	p
16	EŞ —	—	As ex. 15	15.5×30.5×7	1–11	p
17	EŞ —	—	As ex. 15	15.5×30.5×7	1–11	p
18	EŞ —	—	As ex. 15	29×29.5×7	1–11	p
19	EŞ —	—	As ex. 15	29×30×7.5	1–11	p
20	EŞ —	—	As ex. 15	29×30×7.5	1–11	p
21	YBC 2372	—	As ex. 15	19.1×11×3	1–11	c
22	R.F. Harper coll.	—	As ex. 2	—	1–11	n
23	—	5 NT 703	Nippur, entrance gate of Inanna temple, level I	—	—	n
24	HS 2981	—	As ex. 2	17.5×9×2.5	1–11	n
25	McGill Ethnological Collections ML 1.18	—	As ex. 15	17.8×10.4	1–11	p
26	Rijksmuseum van Oudheden, Leiden 1968/12.1	—	As ex. 15	27×28.5×8.5	1–11	p
27	MMA 59.41.85	—	As ex. 15	41.3×41.3×7	1–11	c
28	WML unnumbered 1	—	As ex. 15	—	1–11	p

Figure 10. CBS 8654 (Asb. 259 ex. 9), a brick from Nippur with a Sumerian inscription recording that Ashurbanipal (re)built Ekur, the temple of the god Enlil. © Penn Museum of the University of Pennsylvania.

COMMENTARY

The British Museum purchased ex. 1 from H.C. Rawlinson. Collations for it and ex. 2 were kindly supplied by C.B.F. Walker. Ex. 3 is from the H. Weld Blundell collection. In 1923–24, S. Langdon acquired a brick with this inscription (ex. 4) and was told that it came from "Tal Laḫam," which some located "a short distance north-east of Afaj, and some south-east of Duraihim." He suggested that the name had been distorted and stood for "Tal Dulaihim, eleven miles south-east of Afaj" (Kish 1 p. 108). Ex. 5 was presented to the Bristol museum by Sir L. Woolley. H.V. Hilprecht states that other bricks with this inscription were found in the same structure as ex. 7 (BE 1/1 p. 52). He also notes that Ashurbanipal's inscribed bricks were "sometimes green (originally blue) enamelled on the edges" (Hilprecht, Explorations p. 376). Some of the bricks found by him are likely to be identified with exs. 6 and 8–20. Photographs and measurements of exs. 15–20 were kindly supplied by H. Galter. A cast of ex. 23 in the Oriental Institute, Chicago, was examined. With regard to bricks from Nippur attributed to Ashurbanipal, see Clayden and Schneider, Kaskal 12 (2015) pp. 349–382.

The inscription is sometimes stamped on the face of the brick (e.g., exs. 1–5, 7, 9–10, and 16–17) and sometimes on the edge (e.g., exs. 11–12); one brick has the inscriptions in both places (exs. 13–14). In some cases, it is uncertain where the inscription appears (e.g., if the piece is known only from a photograph or if the brick has been cut down in size in modern times). The stamped area measures 14.5–15×6.5–7.1 cm. The script is archaizing Babylonian, perhaps intended to look Sumerian. The last sign of line 10 (-ta) is placed at the very end of the line and as a result the final vertical wedge of the sign often appears either to be omitted because of a lack of space or to have been obscured by the edge of the stamp. No variants are attested and no score for this brick inscription is presented online.

The inscription was not assigned to Ashurbanipal by the first editors of the text because of the unusual writing of the ruler's name (line 4). This inscription was likely modelled upon one of the Kassite ruler Adad-šuma-uṣur (BE 1/1 no. 81, and duplicates), as noted by M. Streck (Asb. p. LXIV). An inscription of Aššur-etel-ilāni (Aei 5 in the present volume) appears to have been modelled upon the same inscription of Adad-šuma-uṣur.

BIBLIOGRAPHY

1889–90 Pinches, Hebraica 6 pp. 55–58 (ex. 22, copy, edition)
1893 Hilprecht, BE 1/1 no. 82 and pp. 35–36 (ex. 7, copy, edition)
1893 Hilprecht, ZA 8 pp. 389–391 (study)
1903 Hilprecht, Explorations pp. 312, 371, 375, and 376 (provenance, translation)
1904 Hilprecht, Excavations pp. 312, 371, 375, and 376 (provenance, translation)
1916 Streck, Asb. pp. LXIII–LXIV and 352–353 no. 3.b (ex. 7, 22, edition)
1924 Langdon, Kish 1 pp. 108–109 (ex. 4, study)
1927 Luckenbill, ARAB 2 p. 405 §1121 (ex. 7, 22, translation)
1981 Walker, CBI pp. 67–68 no. 80 (exs. 1–5, transliteration)
1982 van Soldt, OMROL 63 pp. 50 and 59 no. 12 (ex. 26, photo, edition)
1985 Behrens, JCS 37 p. 239 no. 53 (exs. 6–14, study)
1988 Beckman, ARRIM 6 p. 2 (ex. 21, study)
1988 Oeslner in Śilwa, Cracow and Jena p. 19 (ex. 24 study)
1989 Frame, ARRIM 7 pp. 42 and 45 no. 40 (ex. 25, photo, study)
1992 Zettler, Inanna Temple p. 50 n. 42 (ex. 23, study)
1995 Frame, RIMB 2 pp. 221–222 B.6.32.16 (exs. 1–25, edition)
2013 May, CRRA 56 pp. 206–207 (study)
2014 Frame in Spar and Jursa, CTMMA 4 pp. 277–278 and pl. 130 no. 164 (ex. 27, copy [by Spar], edition, study)
2015 Clayden and Schneider, Kaskal 12 pp. 355–356 (edition, study) and p. 369 Figs. 4, 4.1 and 4.2 (copy [by Meyer]; exs. 3–4, photo)

TEXT

1) ^{d}en-líl-lá
2) lugal kur-kur-ra
3) lugal-a-ni-ir
4) AN.ŠÁR-*ba-an-ap-lu*
5) sipa še-ga-bi
6) lugal kala-ga
7) lugal ub-da límmu-ba
8) é-kur

1–11) For the god Enlil, lord of the lands, his lord: Ashurbanipal, (5) his obedient shepherd, mighty king, king of the four quarters (of the world), (re)built Ekur, his beloved temple, with baked bricks.

9) é ki ág-gá-a-ni
10) sig$_4$ al-ùr-ra-ta
11) mu-un-na-dù

260

A brick discovered at Nippur has a twelve-line Sumerian text inscribed on its edge. That inscription states that Ashurbanipal had the high temple (Egigunû) of the god Enlil's ziggurat rebuilt; the restoration of the same structure is recorded in text Asb. 258.

CATALOGUE

Museum Number	Excavation Number	Provenance	Dimensions (cm)	cpn
CBS 8644	—	Nippur	30×7.5×7.5	c

BIBLIOGRAPHY

1926 Legrain, PBS 15 no. 74 (copy, edition)
1928 Poebel, OLZ 31 col. 698 (study)
1985 Behrens, JCS 37 p. 240 no. 54 (study)
1993 George, House Most High p. 92 sub no. 373 (study to line 10)
1995 Frame, RIMB 2 p. 223 B.6.32.17 (edition)
2013 May, CRRA 56 pp. 206–207 (study)
2015 Clayden and Schneider, Kaskal 12 pp. 356–357 (edition)

TEXT

1) ^{d}en-líl-lá
2) lugal ⸢digir-re⸣-e-ne-ke$_4$
3) nir-gál an ki-a
4) nun nam tar-tar-ra
5) lugal-a-ni-ir
6) AN.ŠÁR-*ba-an*-IBILA
7) sipa še-ga-bi
8) lugal kala-ga
9) lugal ki-šár$^{?}$-ra$^{?}$ x
10) é-gi-gùn-⸢na⸣
11) sig$_4$ al-ùr-ra
12) mu-un-na-dù

1–12) For the god Enlil, king of the gods, sovereign of heaven (and) netherworld, prince (who decides) the fates, (5) his lord: Ashurbanipal, his obedient shepherd, mighty king, king *of the world*, (re)built Egigunû with baked bricks.

259 line 9 ág-gá-a-ni: C.B.F. Walker read ág-gá-ni on several bricks with this inscription in England (CBI p. 67), but this is a typographical error; see Frame in Spar and Jursa, CTMMA 4 pp. 277–278 note to line 9.
260 line 9 ki-šár$^{?}$-ra$^{?}$ x, "*of the world*": The reading is based on Asb. 261 line 9 since, except for the sections dealing with the structures being rebuilt and the writing of the royal name, the two texts are duplicates. The signs, however, seem to be closer to ki-ub-da$^{?}$, thus possibly "king *of the four quarters* (of the world)."
260 line 10 See the on-page note to Asb. 258 line 15.

261

Two bricks intended to be used in a well bear a Sumerian text that records that Ashurbanipal had some structure built within Eḫursaggalama ("House, Skillfully-Built Mountain"), the cella of the god Enlil at Nippur.

CATALOGUE

Ex.	Museum Number	Excavation Number	Provenance	Dimensions (cm)	Lines Preserved	cpn
1	UM 84-26-12	—	Probably Nippur	36/20×23.5×7.5	1–16	c
2	—	18 N —	Nippur, WC-2, Building C, in the lining of the mouth of the well in the courtyard	36/20×23.5×7.5	—	n

COMMENTARY

Ex. 1 is a "well-head" brick housed among the Penn Museum's collection of bricks from Nippur and Ur. In view of its inscription, it probably comes from the former site. The inscription is found on the outer edge of the brick and is written in archaizing Babylonian script. Information about ex. 2 comes from J.A. Armstrong and R.D. Biggs; for provenance of this brick, see Armstrong's unpublished doctoral dissertation, The Archaeology of Nippur from the Decline of the Kassite Kingdom until the Rise of the Neo-Babylonian Empire (University of Chicago, 1989) p. 42, where it is described as an "Ashurbanipal Ekur brick." The edition presented in the present volume is based on ex. 1.

Eḫursaggalama ("House, Skillfully-Built Mountain" or "House, Stepped/Storied Mountain") was the cella of the god Enlil, which was located on the highest tier of the ziggurat; see George, House Most High pp. 100–101 no. 480; and Sjöberg, Temple Hymns p. 50 and the references cited there.

BIBLIOGRAPHY

1985 Behrens, JCS 37 p. 240 no. 55 (ex. 1, study)
1986 Gerardi, ARRIM 4 p. 37 (ex. 1, copy, edition)
1993 George, House Most High p. 100 (study)
1995 Frame, RIMB 2 pp. 223–224 B.6.32.18 (exs. 1–2, edition)
2015 Clayden and Schneider, Kaskal 12 p. 357 (edition)

TEXT

1) ^{d}en-líl-lá
2) lugal digir-re-e-ne-ke$_4$
3) nir-gál an ki-a
4) nun nam tar-tar-ra
5) lugal-a-ni-ir
6) AN.ŠÁR-DÙ-IBILA
7) sipa še-ga-bi
8) lugal kala-ga
9) lugal ki-šár-ra
10) A-x
11) šà é-ḫur-sag-galam-ma-ke$_4$

1–16) For the god Enlil, king of the gods, sovereign of heaven (and) netherworld, prince (who decides) the fates, (5) his lord: Ashurbanipal, his obedient shepherd, mighty king, king of the world, skillfully (re)built (10) with baked bricks ... within Eḫursaggalama, his ancient royal cella.

10 Line 10 should record the name of the structure being restored, but the identification of the final sign(s) is not certain. Ex. 1 has: A-x (see minor variants [p. 216]) and ex. 2 appears to have A-NE.UD. A. George read the line as A.GÀR-DIŠ and suggested that it might refer to a baked-brick fitting of some sort (House Most High p. 100 no. 480).

12) pa-pa-ḫi nam-lugal-a-ni
13) libir-ra-bi-ta*
14) galam-bi
15) sig$_4$ al-ùr-ra
16) mu-un-na-dù

262

Several clay cylinders, all presumably from Sippar, preserve an inscription that records Ashurbanipal's restoration of Ebabbar ("Shining House"), the temple of the sun-god Šamaš. The favorable mention of the king of Babylon, Ashurbanipal's older brother Šamaš-šuma-ukīn, indicates that the text was composed before 652, therefore, at some point between Ashurbanipal's first regnal year (668) and the start of the Šamaš-šuma-ukīn Revolt (652). This text is sometimes called "Cylinder L[ondon]^{2}."

CATALOGUE

Ex.	Museum Number	Registration Number	Provenance	Dimensions (cm)	Lines Preserved	cpn
1	BM 91115	82-7-14,1043	Sippar	Length: 14.5; R dia.: 4.5; L dia.: 4.6	1–29	c
2	BM 56639	82-7-14,1044	As ex. 1	10.9×6.8×4.3	9–17	c
3	DT 272	—	Acquired by G. Smith; probably from Sippar	7.1×5.1	24–26, 28–29	c
4	BM 56634	82-7-14,1032	As ex. 1	10.7×8.7×6.5	1–27	c
5	BM 78264	Bu 88-5-12,120	Purchased by E.A.W. Budge; probably from Sippar	Length: 2.75″; segmental arc: 2.25″; chord: 2″	2–11	n
6	MMA —	—	Acquired by the Wolfe expedition	—	11–12	n
7	BM 28384 + BM 50843	98-10-11,20 + 82-3-23,1837	Acquired from H. Rassam and purchased from K. Minassian; probably Sippar	Length: 7.5; L dia.: 4.3	1–29	c

COMMENTARY

H. Rassam found exs. 1–2 and 4 at Sippar; ex. 3 comes from G. Smith's expedition to Kuyunjik, but was probably not found at that site. Ex. 5 was purchased by E.A.W. Budge and ex. 6 comes from the Wolfe expedition of 1885. Part of ex. 7 (BM 28384) was acquired by the British Museum from K. Minassian and part (BM 50843) comes from a shipment sent by Rassam, some of whose pieces came from Sippar.

Exs. 1–3, 5 and 7 are written in contemporary Babylonian script, while ex. 4 is in archaizing Babylonian script. Exs. 5–6 could not be located for collation when Frame was working on RIMB 2; however, R. Borger later saw ex. 5 and the edition for this exemplar in the score follows his transliteration in BIWA. Ex. 6 is said to have (parts of) lines 11–12; since similar, though not exactly duplicate, lines appear in other inscriptions of Ashurbanipal (for example, Asb. 242 lines 12b–16a), it is not impossible that MMA — (ex. 6) does not bear a copy of this inscription. Following a comment by H. Winckler (OLZ

261 line 13 *ta**: The final vertical wedge is omitted on ex. 1. Ex. 2 appears to have ⸢*gin*$_7$⸣, which would allow the translation "(re)built with baked bricks his ancient royal cella within Eḫursaggalama as (it had been) of old."

1 [1898] col. 76), M. Streck included the fragment 81-2-4,174 among the exemplars of this text (Streck, Asb. p. XLII). For that small piece, see Asb. 252. The line arrangement and master line follow ex. 1, with help from ex. 4 for the end of line 18, from ex. 7 for the ends of lines 21–26, and from Asb. 263 lines 25–26 for the ends of lines 19–20. A score of the text is presented on Oracc and the minor (orthographic) variants are listed at the back of the book.

This inscription must have been composed prior to 652, when Šamaš-šuma-ukīn, the king of Babylon and Ashurbanipal's brother, began a rebellion against Assyrian control over Babylonia, since lines 11–12, 21–22, and 26 refer to him in a positive manner.

BIBLIOGRAPHY

1884	5 R pl. 62 no. 1 (ex. 1, copy in type)
1885–86	Craig and Harper, Hebraica 2 pp. 87–89 (ex. 1, edition)
1886	Bezold, Literatur pp. 113 §64.3.c and 349 (ex. 1, study)
1886	Lyon, Manual pp. 23–24 and 74–75 (ex. 1, transliteration, study)
1890	Abel and Winckler, Keilschrifttexte p. 31 (ex. 1, copy)
1892	Lehmann-Haupt, Šamaššumukîn 1 pp. 25–26, and 2 pp. 18–21 and 61 and pls. XXV–XXVII no. 9 (L^2 (exs. 1–4, copy, edition; exs. 1–4, 6, study)
1898	Winckler, OLZ 1 cols. 75 and 77 (exs. 3, 5, study)
1904	Smith in Harper, Literature pp. 129–130 (ex. 1, translation)
1905	Jastrow, Religion 1 p. 418 (ex. 1, partial translation)
1916	Streck, Asb. pp. XLI–XLII and 228–233 no. 2 (L^2) (exs. 1–6, edition)
1922	BM Guide p. 230 no. 36 (ex. 1, study)
1927	Luckenbill, ARAB 2 pp. 370–372 §§956–959 (ex. 1, translation)
1994	Lawson, Concept of Fate p. 77 n. 31 (line 14a, study)
1995	Frame, RIMB 2 pp. 212–214 B.6.32.12 (exs. 1–7, edition)
1996	Borger, BIWA p. 387 to Streck pp. 228–233 no. 2 L^2 and LoBl pp. 108 and 112 (exs. 5 and 7, transliteration)
2010	Novotny, Studies Ellis pp. 111, 120, and 127 (lines 16–18, study)

TEXT

1) ^{m}AN.ŠÁR-DÙ-A LUGAL GAL LUGAL *dan-nu* LUGAL ŠÁR LUGAL KUR *aš-šur* LUGAL *kib-rat* LÍMMU-*ti*

2) LUGAL LUGAL.MEŠ NUN *la šá-na-an šá ina a-mat* DINGIR.MEŠ *ti-ik-li-šú ul-tu tam-tim e-liti*

3) *a-di tam-tim šap-liti i-be-lu-ma gi-mir ma-liki ú-šak-niš še-pu-uš-šú*

4) DUMU ^{m}AN.ŠÁR-ŠEŠ-SUM.NA LUGAL GAL LUGAL *dan-nu* LUGAL ŠÁR LUGAL KUR *aš-šur* GÌR.NÍTA TIN.TIR.KI

5) LUGAL KUR EME.GI$_7$ *u* URI.KI *mu-še-šib* TIN.TIR.KI *e-piš é-sag-íl*

6) *mu-ud-diš eš-re-e-ti kul-lat ma-ḫa-zi šá ina qé-reb-ši-na iš-tak-kan si-ma-ti*

7) *ù sat-tuk-ki-ši-na baṭ-lu-tu ú-ki-nu* DUMU DUMU ^{md}30-ŠEŠ.MEŠ-SU LUGAL GAL

8) LUGAL *dan-nu* LUGAL ŠÁR LUGAL KUR *aš-šur a-na-ku-ma ina* BALA-*e-a* EN GAL ^{d}AMAR.UTU *ina ri-šá-a-*⸢*ti*⸣

9) *a-na* TIN.⸢TIR⸣.KI *i-ru-um-ma ina é-sag-íl šá da-ra-ti šu-bat-su ir-me*

10) *sat-*⸢*tuk*⸣*-ki é-sag-íl u* DINGIR.MEŠ TIN.TIR.KI *ú-kin ki-din-nu-tu* TIN.TIR.KI

11) *ak-ṣur áš-šú dan-nu a-na* SIG *la ḫa-ba-li* ^{md}GIŠ.NU$_{11}$-MU-GI.NA ŠEŠ *ta-li-mì*

12) *a-na* LUGAL-*ú-ut* TIN.TIR.KI *ap-qid ù ši-pir é-sag-íl la qa-ta-a*

13) *ú-šak-lil ina* KÙ.BABBAR KÙ.GI *ni-siq-ti* NA$_4$.MEŠ *é-sag-íl az-nun-ma*

1–8a) Ashurbanipal, great king, strong king, king of the world, king of Assyria, king of the four quarters (of the world), king of kings, ruler who has no rival, who by the command of the gods, his helpers, rules from the Upper Sea to the Lower Sea and who made all rulers bow down at his feet; son of Esarhaddon, great king, strong king, king of the world, king of Assyria, governor of Babylon, (5) king of the land of Sumer and Akkad, who (re)settled Babylon, (re)built Esagil, renovated the sanctuaries of all the cult centers, constantly established appropriate procedures in them, and (re)confirmed their interrupted regular offerings; grandson of Sennacherib, great king, strong king, king of the world, king of Assyria, I —

8b–15) During my reign, the great lord, the god Marduk, entered Babylon amidst rejoicing and took up his residence in the eternal Esagil. (10) I (re)confirmed the regular offerings for Esagil and the gods of Babylon. I (re-)established the privileged status of Babylon (and) appointed Šamaš-šuma-ukīn, my favorite brother, to the kingship of Babylon in order that the strong might not harm the weak. I completed the unfinished work on Esagil. I *decorated* Esagil with silver, gold, (and) precious stones and made Eumuša glisten like the stars (lit. "writing") of the firmament. I restored the damage done to all the sanctuaries. I extended (my) protection over all the cult centers.

---

5 Ex. 7 has ⸢*mu*⸣-[...] instead of *e-piš é-sag-íl*, "(re)built Esagil."

14) *ki-ma ši-ṭir bu-ru-mu ú-nam-mir é-umuš-a ù šá eš-re-e-ti ka-li-ši-na*

15) *ḫi-bil-ta-ši-na ú-šal-lim e-li kul-lat ma-ḫa-zi ú-šat-ri-ṣi an-dul-lum*

16) *ina* u_4*-me-šú-ma é-babbar-ra šá qé-reb* ZIMBIR.KI É ^{d}UTU EN GAL EN-*ía šá la-ba-riš*

17) *il-lik-u-ma i-qu-pu in-nab-tu áš-ra-ti-šú áš-te-'e ina ši-pir* ^{d}*kulla*

18) *eš-šiš ú-še-piš-ma ki-ma* KUR-*i re-e-ši-i-šú ul-li a-na šat-ti* ^{d}UTU

19) DI.KUD.GAL DINGIR.MEŠ EN GAL EN-*ía ep-še-ti-ia dam-qa-a-ti ḫa-diš lip-*⸢*pa*⸣-[*lis*]-*ma*

20) *a-na ia-a-ši* ^{m}AN.ŠÁR-DÙ-A LUGAL KUR *aš-šur* NUN *pa-liḫ-šú* TIN u_4*-me* SÙ.MEŠ *še-bé-e* ⸢*lit*⸣-[*tu-tu*]

21) *ṭu-ub* UZU *u ḫu-ud lìb-bi li-šim ši-ma-ti u šá* ^{md}GIŠ.NU_{11}-MU-GI.NA

22) LUGAL TIN.TIR.KI ŠEŠ *ta-lim-ia* u_4*-me-šú li-ri-ku liš-bi bu-'a-a-ri ma-ti-ma*

23) *ina aḫ-rat* u_4*-me* NUN *ar-ku-ú šá ina* u_4*-me* BALA-*šú ši-pir šu-a-ti in-na-ḫu*

24) *an-ḫu-us-su lu-ud-diš šu-mì it-ti* MU-*šú liš-ṭur* MU.SAR-*u-a li-mur-ma*

25) Ì.GIŠ *lip-šu-uš* UDU.SISKUR BAL-*qí it-ti* MU.SAR-*e-šú liš-kun ik-ri-bi-šú*

26) ^{d}UTU *i-šem-me šá šu-mì šaṭ-ru ù* MU *ta-lim-ia ina ši-pir ni-kil-ti*

27) *i-pa-áš-ši-ṭu šu-mì it-ti* MU-*šú la i-šaṭ-ṭa-ru* MU.SAR-*ú-a*

28) *i-ab-ba-tu-ma it-ti* MU.SAR-*e-šú la i-šak-ka-nu* ^{d}UTU EN *e-la-ti u šap-la-ti*

29) *ag-gi-iš lik-kil-me-šú-ma* MU-*šú* NUMUN-*šú ina* KUR.KUR *li-ḫal-liq*

16–18a) At that time, I sought the (original) emplacement of Ebabbar, which is inside Sippar, the temple of the god Šamaš, the great lord, my lord, which had become old, buckled, and collapsed. I had (it) built anew with the craft of the god Kulla and raised its top (as high) as a mountain.

18b–22a) On account of this, may the god Šamaš, great judge of the gods, great lord, my lord, look upon my good deeds with pleasure! May he determine (20) for me — Ashurbanipal, king of Assyria, the ruler who reveres him — as my fate, a long life, fullness of [old age], good health, and happiness! Moreover, with regard to Šamaš-šuma-ukīn, the king of Babylon, my favorite (brother), may his days be long and may he be fully satisfied with (his) good fortune!

22b–26a) If at any time in the future, during the days of the reign of some future ruler, this work falls into disrepair, may (that ruler) renovate its dilapidated sections! May he write my name with his (own) name! May he find my inscribed object, (25) anoint (it) with oil, offer a sacrifice, (and) place (my inscribed object) with his (own) inscribed object! The god Šamaš will (then) listen to his prayers.

26b–29) (But) as for the one who erases my inscribed name or the name of my favorite (brother) by some crafty device, (or) does not write my name with his (own) name, (or) destroys my inscribed object, (or) does not place (my inscribed object) with his (own) inscribed object, may the god Šamaš, lord of the upper world and the netherworld, glare at him angrily and make his name (and) his descendant(s) disappear from the lands!

263

Four clay cylinders bear an Akkadian inscription that records that Ashurbanipal restored Eanna ("House of Heaven"), the temple of the goddess Ištar at Uruk. The text dates to the first half of Ashurbanipal's reign (668–652).

CATALOGUE

Ex.	Museum Number	Excavation Number	Photograph Number	Provenance	Dimensions (cm)	Lines Preserved	cpn
1	YBC 2180	—	—	Probably Uruk	20.4×9.4	1–32	c
2	HMA 9-1793 (formerly UCBC 1206)	—	—	Purchased by H.F. Lutz; probably Uruk	20.2×9.5; dia. of end: 5.5	1–32	c
3	NBC 2507 +? W 4444	W 4444	Warka ph 828 (W 4444)	Warka, NE of building J in Qc XVI 5 (W 4444)	6.5×7 (NBC 2507)	24–32	c; p
4	(Heidelberg)	W 20942	Warka ph 10191–10192	Warka, surface in the area of the archive ("im Archivgelände")	—	1–3, 2–32	p

COMMENTARY

K. Wagensonner kindly provided additional collations to ex. 1. H.F. Lutz purchased ex. 2 for the University of California at Berkeley in 1930. Regrettably, the copy of the piece published by Lutz is inaccurate in a number of places. In addition to numerous errors by the modern copyist (for example, *ša* for *kin*, *su* for *šu*, and *ta* for *ṭa* in line 10 [lines 10–11 of the exemplar]; omission of *-šú* after ŠÈG.MEŠ in line 11; omission of *si* in line 22 [line 23]; *gu* for *kám* in line 23 [line 24]; and addition of an *u* after UZU in line 26 [27]), the copy has *iš-tu* for ⸢*e-li*⸣ in line 9; for the start of line 28 (line 29 of the exemplar) the copy has *ina aḫ-rat* u_4*-me um-ma*, while the piece simply has ⸢*a-a*⸣*-um-ma*. As is the normal procedure in the RINAP volumes, a transliteration of the piece is found in the score but such errors of the modern copyist are not specifically noted. Some additional collations for this exemplar were kindly provided by D.A. Foxvog. With regard to ex. 3, it is uncertain if W 4444 joins NBC 2507 or not, but the two are tentatively kept together here. NBC 2507 has been collated from the original and W 4444 from a photo (on which line 24 is not legible owing to the curvature of the piece). Ex. 4 was found during the 21st season of excavations at Uruk (1962–63).

The script of all four exemplars is contemporary Babylonian. The line arrangement follows ex. 1; ex. 2 has the inscription on 33 lines. The master line follows ex. 1, with help from ex. 2 for lines 1–5. A score of the text is presented on Oracc and the minor (orthographic) variants are listed at the back of the book.

According to R. Koldewey (WEB[4] p. 164), a piece of a cylinder describing Ashurbanipal's work on Eanna was found at Babylon. Its inscription may be this one, but this cannot be determined since neither the excavation number nor the present location of the fragment mentioned by Koldewey is known. With regard to this object, see also Unger, AfK 2 (1924–25) p. 24; and Unger, Babylon p. 225 no. 15.

Since the text mentions Ashurbanipal's appointment of his brother Šamaš-šuma-ukīn to the kingship of Babylon in a positive manner (lines 18–19) and includes his brother in the invocation to the goddess (line 27), the inscription must date before the commencement of the latter's rebellion in 652.

BIBLIOGRAPHY

1915 Clay, YOS 1 no. 42 (ex. 1, copy)
1917–18 Ungnad, ZA 31 pp. 33–37 (ex. 1, edition)
1920 Keiser, BIN 2 no. 35 (ex. 3 [NBC 2507], copy)
1927 Luckenbill, ARAB 2 pp. 373–375 §§968–973 (ex. 1, translation)
1930 Schott, UVB 1 p. 60 and pl. 29 no. 25 (ex. 3 [W 4444], copy, edition)
1931 Lutz, UCP 9/8 pp. 385–390 and pls. 7–8 (ex. 2, photo, copy, edition)
1932 Bauer, OLZ 35 cols. 254–255 (ex. 2, study)
1932–33 Meissner, AfO 8 p. 51 (exs. 1–2, study)
1933 Bauer, Asb. 2 p. 48 (exs. 1–2, study)
1957 Borger, Orientalia NS 26 p. 2 (ex. 3, study)
1969 Oppenheim, ANET[3] p. 297 (exs. 1–2, partial translation)
1970 Berger, ZA 60 pp. 128–129 (ex. 3, study)
1978 Foxvog, RA 72 p. 43 (ex. 2, study)
1982 Kessler, Bagh. Mitt. 13 pp. 14–15 no. 11 (ex. 4, copy, transliteration)
1995 Frame, RIMB 2 pp. 224–227 B.6.32.19 (exs. 1–4, edition)
1998 Borger, BiOr 55 col. 848 (study)

TEXT

1) ⸢*a*⸣-*na* ⸢^{d}INANNA⸣ UNUG.KI *e-tel-lat* AN-*e u* KI-*tim ga-šir-ti* DINGIR.MEŠ *ṣi-ir-ti*
2) ⸢*šá*⸣ *ina ṣi-tan u ši-la-an ur-tu ta-nam-di-nu ta-šak-kan ši*-⸢*ki-in-šá*⸣
3) *i-lat tam-ḫa-ri ez-ze-ti šá ina qé-reb te-še-e a-šam-šá-niš i-su-ur-ru*
4) *a-li-kát i-di* LUGAL *mi-gir-i-šá mu-ra-si*-⸢*bat*⸣ *ga-re-e-šú*
5) *be-let* KUR.KUR *ḫa-mi-mat par-ṣe muš-te-ši-rat gi-mir šu-luḫ-ḫu*
6) *a-ši-bat é-nir-gál-*^{d}*a-nim šá qé-reb é-an-na be-el-ti* GAL-*ti* GAŠAN-*šú*
7) ^{m}AN.ŠÁR-DÙ-A LUGAL GAL LUGAL *dan-nu* LUGAL ŠÚ LUGAL KUR *aš-šur* LUGAL *kib-rat* LÍMMU-*ti* LUGAL LUGAL.MEŠ NUN *la šá-na-an*
8) *šá ul-tu tam-tim e-liti a-di tam-tim šap-liti i-bé-lu-ma gi-mir ma-liki ú-šak-niš še-pu-uš-šú*
9) *šá e-li* URU.*ṣur-ru šá qa-bal tam-tim e-liti u* NI.TUK.KI *šá qa-bal tam-tim šap-liti*
10) *ni-ri be-lu-ti-šú ú-kin-nu-ú-ma i-šu-ṭu ab-šá-an-šú šá ep-še-tu-ú-šú e-li kal* DINGIR.MEŠ *ṭa-a-ba*
11) *e-li ṣal-mat* SAG.DU *du-uš-šu-pa-tu* SIPA-*ú-su šá ina* BALA-*šú* ^{d}IŠKUR ŠÈG.MEŠ-*šú* ^{d}*é-a nag-bi-šú*
12) *a-na ma-ti-šú uš-tab-ru-ú ina ṭuḫ-du u meš-re-e iš-te-né-ʾu-ú* UN.MEŠ-*šú*
13) *gi-mir um-ma-ni-šú ṭuḫ-ḫu-du i-ru-uš-šú da-ád-me-šú* DUMU ^{m}AN.ŠÁR-ŠEŠ-SUM.NA LUGAL GAL LUGAL *dan-nu*
14) LUGAL ŠÚ LUGAL KUR *aš-šur* GÌR.NÍTA TIN.TIR.KI LUGAL KUR EME.GI$_7$ *u* URI.KI *mu-še-šib* TIN.TIR.KI *e-piš é-sag-íl*
15) *mu-ud-diš eš-re-e-te kul-lat ma-ḫa-zi šá ina qer-bi-ši-na iš-tak-ka-nu si-ma-a-ti*
16) DUMU DUMU ^{md}30-ŠEŠ.MEŠ-SU LUGAL GAL LUGAL *dan-nu* LUGAL ŠÚ LUGAL KUR *aš-šur-ma ina* BALA-*e-a* EN GAL ^{d}AMAR.UTU
17) *ina ri-šá-a-ti a-na* TIN.TIR.KI ⸢*i-ru*⸣-[*um-ma*] *sat-tuk-ku é-sag-íl u* DINGIR.MEŠ TIN.TIR.KI *ú*-⸢*kin*⸣
18) *ki-din-nu-tu* TIN.TIR.KI *ak-ṣur áš-šú dan-nu a-na* SIG *la ḫa-ba-lu* ^{md}GIŠ.NU$_{11}$-MU-GI.NA
19) ŠEŠ *ta-li-mì a-na* LUGAL-*ú*-⸢*tu*⸣ KÁ.DINGIR.RA.KI *ap-qid u ši-pir é-sag-íl la qa-ta-*[*a*]
20) *ú-šak-lil ina* KÙ.BABBAR KÙ.GI *u ni-siq-ti* NA$_4$.MEŠ *é-sag-íl az-nun-ma ki-ma* ⸢*ši*⸣-[*ṭir bu-ru-mu*]

1–6) For the goddess Ištar of Uruk, sovereign of heaven and netherworld, most powerful of the gods, exalted one, who *executes* the command she gives in the east and in the west, the fierce goddess of battle who whirls around in the melee like a dust storm, who marches at the side of the king, her favorite, (and) slays his foes, (5) mistress of the lands, who has gathered to herself (all) divine offices (and) administers correctly all purification rites, who dwells in Enirgalanim — which is inside Eanna — great lady, his lady:

7–16a) Ashurbanipal, great king, strong king, king of the world, king of Assyria, king of the four quarters (of the world), king of kings, ruler who has no rival, who rules from the Upper Sea to the Lower Sea and who made all rulers bow down at his feet; who imposed the yoke of his rulership upon the city Tyre — which is in the midst of the Upper Sea — and Dilmun — which is in the midst of the Lower Sea — (10) so that they pulled his yoke; whose deeds are pleasing to all the gods (and) whose shepherdship is sweet to the black-headed people; during whose reign the god Adad made his rain (and) the god Ea his springs last a long time for his land, (who) continually seeks after his people with prosperity and wealth, whose people are all in a state of prosperity, and whose settlements rejoice; son of Esarhaddon, great king, strong king, king of the world, king of Assyria, governor of Babylon, king of the land of Sumer and Akkad, who (re)settled Babylon, (re)built Esagil, (15) renovated the sanctuaries of all the cult centers, and constantly established appropriate procedures in them; grandson of Sennacherib, great king, strong king, king of the world, (who was) also king of Assyria —

16b–22a) During my reign, the great lord, the god Marduk, [entered] Babylon amidst rejoicing. I (re)confirmed the regular offerings for Esagil and the gods of Babylon. I (re-)established the privileged status of Babylon (and) appointed Šamaš-šuma-ukīn, my favorite brother, to the kingship of Babylon in order that the strong might not harm the weak. I completed the work on Esagil which had not been finished. (20) I *decorated* Esagil with silver, gold, and precious stones and made Eumuša glisten like the [stars (lit. "writing") of the firmament]. I repaired the damaged parts of all their sanctuaries (and) extended (my) protection over all cult centers.

6 *é-nir-gál-*^{d}*a-nim* is presumably to be identified with *é-nir-gál-an-na*, "House, Prince of Heaven," which was restored by Esarhaddon (Leichty, RINAP 4 pp. 273–275 Esarhaddon 134).

13 *i-ru-uš-šú* "rejoice": One expects *iriššū* rather than *iruššū* since the verb is *riāšu*.

21) *ú-nam-mir é-umuš-a ù šá eš-re-e-te ka-li-ši-na ḫi-bil-ta-ši-na ú-šal-lim*

22) *e-li kul-lat* ⸢*ma-ḫa-zi*⸣ *ú-šat-ri-ṣi an-dul-lum ina* *u*$_4$*-me-šú-ma* É.GAR$_8$ *é-*⸢*an*$^?$*-na*$^?$⸣ *si-ḫir-ti* [...]

23) *šá la-ba-riš il-lik-u-ma i-qu-pu ik-kám-ru áš-ra-ti-šú-nu áš-te-ʾe-*[*ma eš-šiš ú-še-piš-ma*]

22b–24a) At that time, (with regard to) the (enclosure) wall of *Ea*[*nn*]*a*, the perimeter [...] which had become old, buckled, (and) a heap of ruin, I sought their (original) emplacement [and had (them) built anew. I] completed (them), raising their tops (as high) as a mountain.

24) [*ú*]-⸢*šak*⸣*-lil-ma ki-ma šá-di-i ul-la-a re-ši-šu-un a-na šat-ti* ⸢^{d}INANNA⸣ UNUG.KI GAŠAN GAL-[*ti*]

25) ⸢*ši*⸣*-pir šá-a-šú ḫa-diš lip-pa-lis-ma ia-a-ti* ^{m}AN.ŠÁR-DÙ-A LUGAL KUR *aš-šur* NUN *pa-liḫ-šú a-mat da-*⸢*mi*⸣-[*iq-ti-ia*]

26) *liš-šá-kin šap-tu-uš-šá* TI UD.MEŠ SÙ.MEŠ *še-bé-e lit-tu-tu ṭu-ub* UZU *ḫu-*⸢*ud*⸣ [*lìb-bi li-šim ši-ma-ti*]

27) *ù šá* ^{md}GIŠ.NU$_{11}$-MU-GI.NA LUGAL KÁ.DINGIR.RA.KI ŠEŠ *ta-lim-ia* UD.MEŠ-*šú li-ri-ku liš-*[*bi bu-ʾa-a-ri*]

24b–27) On account of this, may the goddess Ištar of Uruk, the great lady, look upon this work with pleasure and may a go[od] word for me — Ashurbanipal, king of Assyria (and) prince who reveres her— be set upon her lips! [May she determine as my fate] a long life, fullness of old age, good health, (and) happ[iness]! Moreover, with regard to Šamaš-šuma-ukīn, king of Babylon, my favorite brother, may his days be long (and) may he be fully [satisfied with (his) good fortune]!

28) ⸢*a*⸣*-a-um-ma* NUN EGIR-*ú šá ina u*$_4$*-me* BALA-*e-šú ši-pir šu-a-ti in-na-ḫu an-ḫu-us-*⸢*su*⸣ [*lu-diš*]

29) ⸢*šu-mì*⸣ *it-ti* MU-*šú liš-ṭur* MU.SAR-*u-a li-mur-ma* Ì.GIŠ *lip-šu-uš* ⸢UDU.SISKUR⸣ BAL-*qí*

28–30a) May any future ruler, during the days of whose reign this work falls into disrepair, [renovate its] dilapidated sections! May he write my name with his (own) name, find my inscribed object, anoint (it) with oil, offer a sacrifice, (and) place (my inscribed object) with his (own) inscribed object! The goddess Ištar of Uruk will (then) listen to his prayers.

30) ⸢*it*⸣*-ti* MU.SAR-*e-šú liš-kun ik-ri-bi-šú* ^{d}INANNA UNUG.KI *i-šem-me šá šu-mì it-ti* MU-*šú la i-šaṭ-ṭa-ru*

31) MU.SAR-*u-a i-a-ab-ba-tu lu-u a-šar-šú ú-nak-ka-ru-ma it-ti* MU.SAR-*e-šú la i-šak-ka-nu*

32) ^{d}INANNA UNUG.KI GAŠAN GAL-*ti ag-giš lik-kil-me-šú-ma* MU-*šú* NUMUN-*šú ina* KUR.KUR *li-ḫal-liq-ma a-a ir-ši-šú re-e-mu*

30b–32) (But) as for the one who does not write my name with his name, (or) destroys my inscribed object, or changes its position and does not place (it) with his (own) inscribed object, may the goddess Ištar of Uruk, great lady, glare at him angrily, make his name (and) his descendant(s) disappear from the lands, and have no pity on him!

264

A tablet fragment in the Iraq Museum has an Akkadian inscription which refers to the dedication of a ceremonial wagon (*attaru*). The inscription appears to belong to the reign of Ashurbanipal, who is mentioned on the obverse of the tablet. Furthermore, the 2fs pronominal suffixes in obv. 3′–4′ and the 2fs verbal forms in obv. 4′ and rev. 3–5 suggest that the dedication was possibly for a goddess whose name is no longer preserved.

---

263 line 22 *é-*⸢*an*$^?$*-na*$^?$⸣ ("*Ea*[*nn*]*a*") is only found on ex. 2 (collation D.A. Foxvog).

CATALOGUE

Museum Number	Excavation Number	Provenance	Dimensions (cm)	cpn
IM —	W 22669/3	Uruk	—	n

COMMENTARY

The script of the text is Babylonian. The original is probably in the Iraq Museum, but its museum number is not known. Given the tablet's provenance among the late Babylonian texts unearthed at Uruk, the inscription is likely a later copy. The edition is based on the published hand copy.

BIBLIOGRAPHY

1983 von Weiher, SpTU 2 pp. 2, 141, and 265 no. 31 (copy, transliteration, study)

1996 Borger, BIWA p. 383 (study)

2003 Beaulieu, Pantheon of Uruk p. 380 (rev. 6–7a, edition, study)

TEXT

Obv.
Lacuna
1′) [...] (traces) [x x] x x ⸢TAR ŠÚ BAD⸣
2′) [x x (x) ma-ka]-⸢le⸣-e KÙ.MEŠ mim?-ma? x-⸢sú?⸣ [x] DU? ma-ḫar?-ka kun?-nu?
3′) [x x (x) ia-a]-⸢ti⸣ ^{m}AN.ŠÁR-DÙ-A* MAN KUR aš-šur.⸢KI⸣ ARAD mi-gir lìb-bi-ki
4′) [...] x-tim re-ʾu-ú-⸢ti⸣ mi-šar šá taš-ru-ki* ina ⸢qí⸣-bi-ti-⸢ki⸣
Rev.
1) [...]-⸢le⸣ x ⸢TI.LA⸣ ZI-tim x x x x x [x]
2) [...] ⸢na⸣-mar ka-bat-ti x (x) x x TI x x x x
3) [x] x x x DU a-na ši-rik-ti šur-⸢ki⸣ ŠAR? RA? x (x) re-ṣu-ti
4) ⸢al⸣-ki-ma i-tap-pa-li i-da-a-a LÚ.KÚR-⸢ia⸣ né-e-ri SUḪUŠ GIŠ.GU.⸢ZA⸣ LUGAL-ti-ía
5) ⸢a⸣-na u_4-me SÙ.MEŠ ki-ma KUR-i šur-ši-di ⸢ma⸣-nam-ma ina LUGAL.MEŠ DUMU.MEŠ-e-[a]
6) ⸢e⸣-nu-ma GIŠ.at-ta-ri šu-a-ti in-na-⸢ḫu⸣-ma DU-ku la-ba-⸢riš⸣
7) [an]-⸢ḫu⸣-ut-su ⸢lu⸣-ud-diš ši-ṭir šu-mì-ia it-ti ši-ṭir MU-šú liš-⸢kun⸣
8) [...] x ik-ri-bi-(erasure)-šú i-šem-[mu-u]
9) [šá ... a]-⸢šar-šú⸣ ú-nak-ka-ru MU-šú i-šaṭ-⸢ṭa⸣-[ru]
10) [... a-na] ⸢ni⸣-ši ŠU.II*-šú a-a iz-⸢zi⸣-[zu-ma]
11) [... ag-gi]-⸢iš⸣ [x x]
Lacuna

Lacuna
1′) [...] ... [...] pure [food offer]ings, *anything ... set out before* you.

2′–Rev. 5a) [... m]e, Ashurbanipal, king of Assyria, the servant (who is) the favorite of your heart, [...] ... (and) the just shepherdship that you bestow at your command, [...] the preservation of (my) life ... [...] a [b]right spirit ... Grant ... as a gift, ... come to my aid and always *stand in for me*, kill m[y] enemy, (and) make the foundation of my royal throne as secure as a mountain for eternity.

Rev. 5b–8) When this ceremonial wagon becomes dilapidated and old, may one of the kings, [my] descendants, restore its [dilapid]ated section(s). May he place (on it) the writing of my name with the writing of his name. [The god(dess) ...] will (then) list[en to] his prayers.

Rev. 9–11) [(As for) the one who ...] changes its [pos]ition (or) writ[es] his (own) name, may [the god(dess) ...] not be pres[ent for] his prayers [and ... angri]ly [...]
Lacuna

4′ *taš-ru-ki** "that you bestow": The copy has *taš-ru*-KU.

rev. 10–11 and Lacuna For possible restorations to this damaged concluding section of the inscription, see Ssi 7 v 13′–16′ and Ssi 19 lines 46–47.

265

A fragment from a single-column clay cylinder now housed in the Yale Babylonian Collection (New Haven) preserves part of an Akkadian inscription of Ashurbanipal recording his restoration of Edimgalkalama ("House, Great Bond of the Land"), the temple of the god Anu rabû ("Great Anu" = Ištarān) at Dēr, in the east Tigris region. Although the name of neither the temple nor the city survives in this damaged text, it is fairly certain that the inscribed object was intended to be deposited in the mudbrick superstructure of Edimgalkalama since the god Anu rabû ("Great Anu") is invoked twice in the text's concluding formula. Ashurbanipal boasts that he raised the temple "as high as a mountain," a statement about the project that he does not record in his inscriptions from the Assyrian heartland.

CATALOGUE

Museum Number	Provenance	Dimensions (cm)	cpn
YBC 2368	Possibly Uruk	16×9	n

COMMENTARY

The inscription is written in contemporary Babylonian script and each line of text is separated by a horizontal ruling. The edition is based on E. Frahm's edition and copy.

Although the cylinder was meant to be deposited in the structure of Edimgalkalama at Dēr (modern Tell Aqar), it is highly plausible, as Frahm has already suggested (Studies Parpola pp. 63–64), that the object came from Uruk (modern Warka) (1) since that Babylonian city was the origin of thousands of cuneiform texts purchased by Yale University now housed in the Yale Babylonian Collection; and (2) since there appears to have been "a rather intensive cultural exchange between the ancient cities of Der and Uruk" (ibid p. 63), as demonstrated by the fact that at least two Late Babylonian scholarly tablets bearing colophons stating that they were written in Dēr were unearthed during the German excavations at Uruk, in the library of Iqīšāya, a well-known exorcist in the early Hellenistic Period. On these grounds, Frahm (ibid p. 64) postulated that YBC 2368 "had at first likewise been housed in Anu rabû's temple in Der, but was then brought to the south with the other [scholarly] tablets [including SpTU 4 nos. 125 and 185] that eventually found their way to Uruk. The scholars of Uruk might have been interested in the text because Assurbanipal's qualities as a learned king and patron of the scribes were still remembered in Late Babylonian times, and because the name of Der's principal god, Anû rabû and Ištaran, resembled those of their own main deities, Anu and Ištar." Nevertheless, it is not impossible that the cylinder originates from Dēr, although Tell Aqar has never been excavated and only a few texts have been reportedly discovered there. For further details, see Frahm, Studies Parpola pp. 63–64.

With regard to Edimgalkalama, see George, House Most High p. 76 no. 166; and Frahm, Studies Parpola pp. 55–63. The inscription might have been composed sometime between mid-648 (after Abu [V] 30th) and Abu (V) 645, since Ashurbanipal worked on Anu rabû's temple after the Šamaš-šuma-ukīn rebellion had come to an end and since Edimgalkalama's completion is first recorded (at least according to the extant textual record) in Novotny and Jeffers, RINAP 5/1 pp. 209–221 Asb. 10 (Prism T) iii 15–17, the earliest known copy of which was inscribed on 6-V-645 (eponymy of Nabû-šar-aḫḫēšu). Presumably, the inscription written on YBC 2368 (this text) was composed earlier than Prism T (Asb. 10).

BIBLIOGRAPHY

2009 Frahm, Studies Parpola pp. 59–64 (edition, copy, provenance)

TEXT

Lacuna

1′) [*é-dim-gal-kalam-ma* (*šá qé-reb* BÀD.AN.KI) É AN.GAL] EN ⸢GAL⸣ [EN-*ia šá la-ba-riš il-li-ku-ma*]

2′) [...] x x x x ⸢*áš-ra*⸣-*ti-šú* ⸢*áš-te-ʾe*⸣ *ina* ⸢*ši-pir*⸣ [^{d}*kulla eš-šiš*? *ú-še-piš-ma*?]

3′) [... *ú*]-⸢*zaq-qìr ḫur-sa-niš a-na*⸣ *šat-ti* AN.GAL EN *ṣi-i-ri ši*-⸢*pir*⸣ [*šá-a-šú*? *ḫa-diš lip-pa-lis-ma*]

4′) [*ia-a-ti*? ^{m}AN].⸢ŠÁR⸣-DÙ-IBILA LUGAL KUR *aš*-⸢*šur*⸣ NUN *pa-liḫ-ka* TI u_4-*me* SÙ.MEŠ *še*-⸢*bé*⸣-[*e lit-tu-tu*]

5′) [*ṭu-ub* UZU *ḫu*]-⸢*ud*⸣ *lìb-bi na*-⸢*ma-ri ka-bat-ti*⸣ *ši-i-mì ši-ma-ti ina* ⸢*li-i*⸣-[*ti u da-na-ni*?]

6′) [EDIN *na-ki*]-*ri-ia šu-zi-za*-⸢*an-ni*⸣-*ma ku*?-*šu-du a-a-bi-ia me-e*-x [...]

7′) [SUḪUŠ GIŠ.GU.ZA LUGAL]-⸢*ú*⸣-*ti-ia ú-ḫum*-⸢*meš šur-ši-di it*?⸣-*ti* ⸢AN⸣-*e* ⸢*ù* KI⸣-*tim ki*-⸢*i*?⸣-[*ni*? BALA-*ú-a*]

8′) [*a-a-um-ma* NUN] ⸢EGIR⸣ *šá ina* u_4-*me* BALA-*šú ši-pir šá*-⸢*a-šú*⸣ *in-na*-⸢*ḫu*⸣ *an-ḫu-us*-⸢*su*⸣ [*lu-ud-diš*]

9′) [*šu-mì it-ti* MU-*šú*] ⸢*liš*?-*ṭur*⸣ MU.SAR-⸢*ú*⸣-*a li-mur*-⸢*ma* Ì⸣.GIŠ *lip-šu-uš* ⸢UDU?.SISKUR? BAL?-*qí*? *it-ti*⸣ [MU.SAR-*e-šú*]

10′) [*liš-kun ik-ri-bi*]-⸢*i*⸣-*šú* AN.⸢GAL⸣ *i*-⸢*šem*⸣-*me šá šu-mì šaṭ-ru ina ši-pir ni-kil-ti i-pa*-⸢*aš*?⸣-[*ši-ṭu*]

11′) [MU.SAR-*ú-a i-ab-ba-tu*] ⸢*ù*?⸣ *lu-u a-šar-šú* ⸢*ú*⸣-*nak-ka-ru-ma it-ti* MU.SAR-*e-šú* ⸢*la*⸣ [*i-šak-kan*]

12′) [...] x ⸢*rik*⸣-*sa-ti-ia ú-paṭ-ṭa-ru* AN.GAL EN *ṣi*-⸢*i*?⸣-[*ru*? ...]

Lacuna

1′–3′a) [At that time], I sought the (original) emplacement [of Edimgalkalama, (which is inside (the city) Dēr), the temple of Great Anu], the gr[eat] lord, [my lord, which had become old, ...] ... [*I had* (*it*) *built anew*] with the craf[t of the god Kulla, ..., (and) ma]de (it) as high as a mountain.

3′b–7′) On account of this, [may] Great Anu, the exalted lord, [look upon *this*] wor[k with pleasure]. Determine [*for me* — Ash]urbanipal, king of Assyria, the ruler who reveres you — as my fate a long life, fulln[ess of old age, good health, ha]ppiness, and a bright spirit. Make me stand [ov]er my [enem]ies in mighty victor[ies]. *To drive off* my enemies ... [...]. Make [the foundation(s) of] my [royal throne] as secure as a mountain! *Make* [my reign] *as f*[*irm*] as heaven and netherworld!

8′–10′a) [May any futu]re [ruler], during the days of whose reign this work falls into disrepair, [renovate] its dilapidated sections! May he write [my name with his (own) name], find my inscribed object, anoint (it) with oil, offer a sacrifice, [(and) place (my inscribed object)] wit[h his (own) inscribed object]! Great Anu will (then) listen to his [prayer]s.

10′b–15′) (But) as for the one who eras[es] my inscribed name by some crafty device, [(or) destroys my inscribed object], (or) changes its position, or [does] n[ot place (it)] with his (own) inscribed object, [...] ... dismantles my construction, [may] Great Anu, the *exal*[*ted*] lord, [...] *di'u*-disease and anxiety, together with *his family*, [...] to destroy his people, to carry

---

Lacuna before 1′ The translation assumes that the end of the now-missing line before line 1′ ended with *ina* u_4-*me-šú-ma* "at that time."

1′ *é-dim-gal-kalam-ma* (*šá qé-reb* BÀD.AN.KI) "Edimgalkalama, (which is inside (the city) Dēr)": Compare Asb. 262 line 16, which has *é-babbar-ra šá qé-reb* ZIMBIR.KI "Ebabbar, which is inside Sippar."

2′ The signs before ⸢*áš-ra*⸣-*ti-šú* ⸢*áš-te-ʾe*⸣ ("I sought the (original) emplacement") are not sufficiently preserved to be able to read them with any degree of certainty. As E. Frahm (Studies Parpola p. 62) has already suggested, line 2′ might have begun with *i-qu-pu in-nab-tu* ("which had buckled and collapsed") or *i-qu-pu ik-kám-ru* ("which had become buckled (and) a heap of ruin"); see respectively Asb. 262 line 17 and Asb. 263 line 23. ^{d}*kulla eš-šiš*? *ú-še-piš-ma*? "[*I had* (*it*) *built anew*] with the craf[t of the god Kulla]": The restoration is based on Asb. 241 line 21, Asb. 253 line 21, Asb. 258 line 18, and Asb. 262 lines 17b–18a.

3′ [*ú*]-⸢*zaq-qìr ḫur-sa-niš*⸣ "[I ma]de (it) as high as a mountain": This orthography of *zaqāru* is attested also in an inscription of Ashurbanipal's older brother Šamaš-šuma-ukīn; see Frame, RIMB 2 p. 255 B.6.33.4 line 27. None of Ashurbanipal's other extant inscriptions recording work on Edimgalkalama record that he raised the superstructure of Great Anu's temple like a mountain; compare Novotny and Jeffers, RINAP 5/1 p. 217 Asb. 10 (Prism T) iii 15–17 and p. 304 Asb. 23 (IIT) lines 73–75. As one expects from Ashurbanipal's Babylonian inscriptions, this text does not record that Ashurbanipal had the temple's divine occupants (Anu rabû, Šarrat-Dēr, and Mār-bīti) placed once again on their daises; compare, for example, Asb. 244 lines 13–14a, Asb. 245 lines 13–14a, and Asb. 262 lines 16–18a.

12′ [...] x ⸢*rik*⸣-*sa-ti-ia ú-paṭ-ṭa-ru* "[...] ... dismantles my construction": Compare Grayson and Novotny, RINAP 3/2 p. 317 Sennacherib 223 (Bavian Inscription) lines 57b–58a: *šá e-piš-ti e-pu-šú ú-saḫ-ḫu-ú rik-sa-te ar-ku-sa i-paṭ-ṭa-ru* "who desecrates the work that I have done, dismantles the (canal) system that I have constructed."

13′) [...] ⸢*di*$^{?}$-*ʾi*$^{?}$ *ù di*⸣-*lip-ti šá-a-šú ga-du* ⸢*kim*$^{?}$⸣-*ti-i*$^{?}$-*šú*$^{?}$ *x* [...]
14′) [...] *x a-na* ⸢*ḫa*⸣-*pe*-⸢*e*⸣ UN.MEŠ-*šú a-na šá-la*-⸢*la*$^{?}$⸣ [...]
15′) [MU-*šú* NUMUN-*šú i-na* KUR.KUR$^{?}$] *li-ḫal-liq-ma a-a* ⸢*ir*⸣-[*ši-šú re-e-mu*]

off [..., ...]. May he make [his name (and) his descendant(s)] disappear [from the lands], and h[ave] no [pity on him]!

266

This five-line dedicatory inscription of Ashurbanipal to the goddess Sutītu is known from a black and grey scorched onyx eye-stone discovered at the Persian capital Persepolis; Asb. 267 might be an exact duplicate of this inscription. With regard to the goddess Sutītu ("the Sutian"), see Frame in Spar and Jursa, CTMMA 4 pp. 309–311.

CATALOGUE

Excavation Number	Provenance	Dimensions (cm)	cpn
PT4 455	Persepolis, Treasury, near the center of Room 33	Dia.: 3.8; thickness: 0.7	p

COMMENTARY

Because the current whereabouts of the bead are unknown, although it might be in Tehran (Iran) as R. Borger (BIWA p. 386) has suggested, the present edition of the inscription written on PT4 455 is based on the published photograph (Schmidt, Persepolis 2 pl. 25 no. 3). The script is Neo-Assyrian.

BIBLIOGRAPHY

1957 Schmidt, Persepolis 2 p. 58 and pl. 25 no. 3 (photo, edition)
1996 Borger, BIWA p. 386 (study)

TEXT

1) [*ana* ^{d}]*su-ti-ti*
2) ⸢GAŠAN⸣-*šú* ^{m}AN.ŠÁR-DÙ-A
3) MAN KUR *aš-šur*
4) *ana* ⸢TIN⸣-*šú*
5) BA-*ìš*

1–5) [For the goddess] Sutītu, his [la]dy: Ashurbanipal, king of Assyria, presented (this object) for the sake of his [lif]e.

267

This polished, cylinder-shaped bead from Persepolis has a four-line dedicatory inscription written on it. Assuming that the royal name in line 2 is correctly restored, then this inscription is an exact duplicate of Asb. 266. If not, then this bead would have likely borne an inscription of Ashurbanipal's father Esarhaddon. Based on the fact that the text written on this bead appears to have been an exact duplicate of the preceding inscription, this short dedication to the goddess Sutītu is edited in the present volume among the certain inscriptions of Ashurbanipal.

CATALOGUE

Excavation Number	Provenance	Dimensions (cm)	cpn
PT4 1180	Persepolis, Treasury, in debris in the area of Room 33	Length: 1.9; Dia.: 1.5	n

COMMENTARY

This polished banded white, grey, and pink chalcedony cylinder-shaped bead is perforated lengthwise. Because no photograph or copy of PT4 1180 has ever been published and because the original could not be examined since the bead's present location is not known, the edition in the present volume is based on E.F. Schmidt's published edition (Persepolis 2 p. 59). R. Borger (BIWA p. 386) has suggested that the original might be in Tehran (Iran). The script is presumed to have been Neo-Assyrian, just like Asb. 266 and 269. As mentioned in the introduction above, the inscription might be an exact duplicate of Asb. 266, which is inscribed on PT4 455.

BIBLIOGRAPHY

1957 Schmidt, Persepolis 2 p. 59 (edition)

1996 Borger, BIWA p. 386 (study)

TEXT

1) *ana* ᵈ*su*-[*ti-ti*]
2) GAŠAN-*šú* ᵐAN.[ŠÁR-DÙ-A]
3) MAN KUR *aš-šur*
4) *ana* TIN-*šú* ⸢BA⸣-[*iš*]

1–4) For the goddess Su[tītu], his lady: As[hurbanipal], king of Assyria, prese[nted] (this object) for the sake of his life.

268

An inscribed fragment of a grey and white chalcedony bead found at the Persian capital Persepolis bears a short, proprietary inscription of a late Neo-Assyrian king, possibly Ashurbanipal.

CATALOGUE

Excavation Number	Provenance	Dimensions (cm)	cpn
PT4 1173	Persepolis, Treasury, in debris in the area of Room 33	1.5×1.9	n

COMMENTARY

This inscribed, flat-ellipsoid-shaped bead is pierced through its short axis and it has an octagonal cross section. Since no copy or photograph of PT4 1173 has ever been published and since the original could not be examined, as its current whereabouts are unknown, the present edition is based on E.F. Schmidt's published transliteration (Persepolis 2 pp. 57–58). R. Borger (BIWA p. 386) has suggested that the object might be in Tehran (Iran). The script is presumed to have been Neo-Assyrian, just like Asb. 266 and 269. The proposed restorations are based on those two inscriptions.

BIBLIOGRAPHY

1957 Schmidt, Persepolis 2 pp. 57–58 (transliteration, study)
1996 Borger, BIWA p. 386 (study)

TEXT

1) [KUR ᵐAN.ŠÁR-DÙ]-A ⸢MAN⸣ [KUR *aš-šur*]

1) [Palace of Ashurbani]pal, kin[g of Assyria].

269

An impressive, sculptured bowl with four lion handles found at Persepolis has a one-line proprietary inscription of Ashurbanipal written on it.

CATALOGUE

Excavation Number	Provenance	cpn
PT4 368 + PT5 156 + PT5 244	Persepolis, Treasury, Hall 41 and Corridor 31	n

COMMENTARY

This shattered, decorated stone bowl is reported to have been made from granite, but since its current whereabouts are unknown, the authors were not able to confirm the material support; R. Borger (BIWA p. 386) has suggested that the object might be in Tehran (Iran). The bowl, as E.F. Schmidt (Persepolis 2 p. 84) has already proposed, might have originally been from Nineveh and was very likely removed by the Medes in 612, when the Assyrian capital was captured, looted, and destroyed; this is probably also the case for text Asb. 266–268. The inscription, which is engraved on the bowl's exterior, is written in Neo-Assyrian script. The edition presented here is based on the published hand-drawn facsimile since the original was not available for firsthand examination and since the inscription is not visible in the published photograph of PT4 368 + PT5 156 + PT5 244 (Schmidt, Persepolis 2 pl. 49 no. 1).

BIBLIOGRAPHY

1957 Schmidt, Persepolis 2 pp. 83–84 and pl. 49 no. 1 (photo, copy, edition)

1996 Borger, BIWA p. 386 (study)

TEXT

1) KUR AN.ŠÁR-DÙ-A MAN ⌜GAL⌝ [MAN *dan-nu*] ⌜MAN⌝ ŠÚ MAN KUR AN.ŠÁR.KI

1) Palace of Ashurbanipal, grea[t] king, [strong king, kin]g of the world, king of Assyria.

270

A silver vessel with gold leaf now housed in the Miho Museum (Japan) bears a one-line proprietary inscription of Ashurbanipal. The inscription is written on the outer rim of the vessel's lip in small cuneiform characters. The object, which has been part of the museum's collection since 1998, might have come from one of the cave treasures discovered in Iran during the early 1990s, but its ultimate provenance is unknown. Although the text appears to be a genuine Ashurbanipal inscription, the authenticity of the gold-leafed beaker cannot be verified given its uncertain provenance and the highly unusual medium upon which this short Akkadian inscription is written (compare, for example, a silver bucket of Esarhaddon [Leichty, RINAP 4 pp. 281–282 Esarhaddon 140; photo in Seipel, 7000 Jahre p. 205 no. 117]). Because the text could possibly be an actual seventh-century Assyrian inscription, based on its contents and orthography, this inscription is included — albeit tentatively — in the present volume.

CATALOGUE

Museum Number	Provenance	Dimensions (cm)	cpn
Miho Museum, SF 4.061	Purchased	Height: 24.5; Max. dia.: 21	n

BIBLIOGRAPHY

1999 Bleibtreu, Vergoldeter Silberbecher (copy, edition, study, provenance)

2000 Muscarella, Source 20/1 pp. 29–37 (photo, study)

2001 Albenda, JAOS 121 pp. 145–146 (study)

TEXT

1) KUR ^{m}AN.ŠÁR-DÙ-⸢A⸣ [MAN GAL MAN *dan*]-*nu* MAN ŠÚ MAN KUR AN.ŠÁR.⸢KI⸣ A ^{m}AN.ŠÁR-PAP-AŠ MAN KUR AN.ŠÁR.KI A ^{md}30-PAP.MEŠ-SU MAN KUR AN.ŠÁR.KI

1) Palace of Ashurbanipal, [great king, stro]ng [king], king of the world, king of Assyria, son of Esarhaddon, king of Assyria, son of Sennacherib, king of Assyria.

1001

Sm 1937 is a fragment from the upper left corner of a clay tablet that contains an inscription of a late Neo-Assyrian king. The text begins with the royal name, but unfortunately only the initial theophoric element AN.ŠÁR "Aššur" is preserved, indicating that the text belongs to either Esarhaddon or Ashurbanipal. The tablet was part of a series since the subscript (rev. 4′) identifies it as the *nis-ḫu 2-ú*, "second extract." The type of object upon which the inscription was originally written is unknown. However, two lines from the conclusion of the text (rev. 1′–2′) parallel rev. 4′–5′ of 82-3-23,12 (unpublished), another tablet of a Neo-Assyrian king whose subscript (rev. 6′) states that its text was written upon an *úsu-mit-te* "stele." This could suggest that the present inscription was also intended for such an object. Moreover, compare Leichty, RINAP 4 pp. 103–109 Esarhaddon 48 (Aššur-Babylon A), which is the first extract of an inscription that was copied from the left side of a stele (lines 109–110).

CATALOGUE

Museum Number	Provenance	Dimensions (cm)	cpn
Sm 1937	Nineveh, Kuyunjik	6.1×7.5	p

BIBLIOGRAPHY

1896 Bezold, Cat. 4 p. 1518 (study)

1996 Borger, BIWA p. 341; and LoBl pp. 83–84 (transliteration, study)

TEXT

Obv.
1) ^{m}AN.ŠÁR-[...]
2) ⸢DUMU ^{m}⸣[...]
3) *e*-[...]
4) KIN *x* [...]
5) *ša* [...]
6) *ša* [...]
7) *ša* [...]
8) DIŠ *x* [...]
9) ŠE$^{?}$/60$^{?}$ *x* [...]
10) ⸢*man*$^{?}$-*ma*$^{?}$⸣ [...]
11) *x* [...]
12) *x* [...]
Lacuna
Rev.
Lacuna
1′) ⸢TA ŠÀ *mal-qi*⸣-*te* ⸢*ša*⸣ [É *tuk-la-ti-šú*$^{?}$ ...]
2′) ⸢1/2⸣ NINDA 1/2 ⸢KAŠ TA⸣ ŠÀ *mal-qi*-⸢*te*⸣ [...]
3′) *x*.⸢MEŠ$^{?}$ ŠAḪ$^{?}$⸣ URU *x* [...]

4′) [(*x x*)] ⸢*nis-ḫu*⸣ 2-*ú* [...]

Obv. 1–2) Ashur/Esar/Aššur-[..., ...], son of [..., ...]

Obv. 3–12) (No translation possible)

Lacuna

Lacuna

Rev. 1′–3′) [f]rom the watering place fo[r *his stronghold* ...] 1/2 bread (and) 1/2 beer from the watering plac[e ...] ... *the city* [...].

Rev. 4′) [(...)] second extract [...].

1002

This fragment, K 9155, comes from the bottom half of a small clay tablet and contains an inscription of a late Neo-Assyrian king, possibly Esarhaddon or Ashurbanipal. The inscription mentions several deities — Ninurta, the Queen of Nineveh, the Lady of Arbela, Gula, and the Sebetti, with more likely named in the portion of the obverse that is now broken away — along with a short statement about what each of these deities did for the king. Nothing in the inscription allows for a specific identification of the ruler to whom it belongs, although the language of the text is generally reminiscent of those two Neo-Assyrian kings. Obv. 9′–12′ are written on the bottom edge of the tablet.

CATALOGUE

Museum Number	Provenance	Dimensions (cm)	cpn
K 9155	Nineveh, Kuyunjik	3.8×6.7	p

BIBLIOGRAPHY

1893 Bezold, Cat. 3 p. 989 (study)
1924–39 Geers, Heft A p. 44 (copy)
1996 Borger, BIWA p. 336; and LoBl p. 43 (transliteration, study)
1997 Weissert in Parpola and Whiting, Assyria 1995 p. 347 n. 21 (obv. 7′, study)

TEXT

Obv.
Lacuna
1′) [*x*] *x x* [...]
2′) ⸢*ú*⸣-[*x*]-*al*-[...]
3′) ⸢^{d}*nin*⸣-*urta* ⸢AB ŠÚ$^{?}$/ŠI$^{?}$⸣ [...]
4′) ⸢*ṣu*⸣-*um-me-rat* [*lìb-bi-ia*]
5′) ⸢*ú*⸣-*šak-ši*-⸢*da*⸣ [...]
6′) *ú-ter-ra* [...]
7′) ^{d}*šar-rat*-NINA.KI ⸢AMA⸣ *réme-ni*-⸢*tu*$^{?}$⸣
8′) Á.II-*a-a it-tas-ḫar-ma*
9′) *ṭa-biš tu-še-ši-ba-an-ni*
10′) *ina* GIŠ.GU.ZA AD *ba-ni*-⸢*ia*⸣
11′) ^{d}*be-let*-URU.LÍMMU-DINGIR
12′) *be-el-tu* GAL-⸢*tum*⸣
Rev.
1) *šá e-peš* LUGAL-*ti*-⸢*ia*⸣
2) *ú-sa-di-ra ši-pir* SIG$_5$.MEŠ
3) ^{d}*gu-la ak-ṣu*-⸢*ti*⸣-*ia*

Lacuna
Obv. 1′–2′) (No translation possible)

Obv. 3′–6′) The god Ninurta, ... [...], allowed [me] to achieve [my heart's] desire [...] (and) he returned [...].

Obv. 7′–10′) The goddess Queen of Nineveh, the merciful [mot]her, came to my side and gladly made me sit on the throne of the father who had engendered me.

Obv. 11′–Rev. 2) The goddess Lady of Arbela, the great lady, regularly sent me favorable message(s) concerning my exercising kingship.

Rev. 3–4) The goddess Gula *pacified* those who were

obv. 11′–rev. 2 The declaration that the goddess Lady of Arbela sent the Assyrian king favorable messages is reminiscent of Esarhaddon's oracle collections (see Parpola, SAA 9 pp. 4–27 nos. 1–3).

4) *tu-ni*$^{?}$*-iḫ-ma tu-šak-*⌈*niš*⌉ [*x*] *x x*
5) ^{d}IMIN.BI DINGIR.⌈MEŠ *qar-du*⌉*-*[*tum* ...]
6) *šu-me-*⌈*lu*$^{?}$⌉ *x* [...]
7) *il-x* [...]
8) ⌈*ta*$^{?}$⌉ *x* [...]
Lacuna

insolent to me and she made ... bow dow[n (to me)].
Rev. 5–7) The Sebetti, valiant gods, [...] *the left* [...] ... [...]

Rev. 8) (No translation possible)
Lacuna

1003

A fragment (K 6371) from the middle section of one face of a clay tablet preserves parts of seven lines of text from an inscription of a late Neo-Assyrian king, perhaps Esarhaddon or Ashurbanipal. With so little of the text preserved, the identification of the Assyrian ruler to whom it belongs is based on a reference to the DUMU LUGAL-*u-ti* "heir designate" (line 4′), the position to which Ashurbanipal was appointed during Esarhaddon's reign in order to ensure a smooth transition of power from one ruler to the next.

CATALOGUE

Museum Number	Provenance	Dimensions (cm)	cpn
K 6371	Nineveh, Kuyunjik	3.2×3.6	p

BIBLIOGRAPHY

1891 Bezold, Cat. 2 p. 783 (study)
1898 Winckler, OLZ 1 cols. 70–71 (lines 4′–6′, transliteration; study)
1916 Streck, Asb. pp. LXXXIV–LXXXV (study)
1996 Borger, BIWA p. 335; and 8°-Heft p. 167 (transliteration, study)

TEXT

Lacuna
1′) [...] *x x* [...]
2′) [...]-⌈*ni*$^{?}$⌉ DINGIR.MEŠ *du-*⌈*un*$^{?}$*-ni*$^{?}$⌉ [...]
3′) [...] *x-ti mé-lam-me nam-*⌈*ri*⌉*-*[*ri* ...]
4′) [...] *x-nu*$^{?}$ DUMU LUGAL-*u-ti* ⌈*iq*$^{?}$⌉-[...]
5′) [...] ⌈LUGAL⌉ GAL LUGAL KAL ⌈LUGAL⌉ [...]
6′) [...] *x x* ⌈AL$^{?}$⌉ [...]
7′) [...] *x* [...]
Lacuna

Lacuna
1′–4′) [...] ... [...] the gods [... *with*] *power*, [...] ..., awe-inspiring radiance, (and) bril[liance ...] ... heir designate [...].

5′–7′) [...], great [kin]g, strong king, kin[g of ..., ...] ... [...]

Lacuna

1002 rev. 4 *tu-ni*$^{?}$*-iḫ-ma* "*pacified* and": CAD N/1 (p. 149 sub *nâhu* A 5.a) read the signs as *tu-ni-iḫ-ma* "pacified and," but CAD S (p. 35 sub *saḫāpu* 4.a) instead construed them as *tu-sa-aḫ-ḫap* "lays flat (and)." The second sign appears to have three vertical strokes for SA, but the final stroke slants away from the first two and does not seem to have a clear head for the wedge (compare the SA sign of rev. 2, which also appears to have an additional, extraneous vertical stroke). Thus, the sign is interpreted here as NI rather than SA. This reading is buttressed by the fact that the final sign has three horizontal wedges, making a reading *ḫap* (the LAGAB sign) rather than *ma* difficult.
1002 rev. 6 There appears to be a scribal notation in the left margin next to this line of the tablet, but due to damage it is unclear what the sign is or what it is meant to indicate.

1004

A tablet fragment, 82-3-23,125, that only preserves a small portion of two faces near the top of a tablet contains part of an account of the conflict between an Assyrian king and Taharqa, the king of Egypt, thus indicating that the tablet belongs to either Esarhaddon or Ashurbanipal. The subscript (rev. 4′) records that the tablet's contents were inscribed inside the cella (*atmanu*) of a temple to one of the gods, but the name of the deity is not preserved due to damage. If the text belongs to the reign of Ashurbanipal, it is possible that the inscription is related to his building activity on the temple of the god Sîn in the city Ḫarrān since the "Large Egyptian Tablets" (Jeffers and Novotny, RINAP 5/2 pp. 277–286 Asb. 207 [LET]) record that king's Egyptian campaigns as a historical prelude to the building account for that temple, which specifically mentions the refurbishment of the god Sîn's cella. In his analysis, M. Streck (Asb. pp. LX–LXI) classified the tablet with those that he believed contain drafts or models for epigraphs to be carved on stone slabs. The inscription has not been collated and is based on Bauer's copy (Asb. pl. 59).

CATALOGUE

Registration Number	Provenance	Dimensions (cm)	cpn
82-3-23,125	Nineveh, Kuyunjik	5.1×6.4	n

BIBLIOGRAPHY

1896 Bezold, Cat. 4 p. 1823 (rev. 4′, copy; study)
1916 Streck, Asb. pp. LX–LXI and CCLXXV (study)
1933 Bauer, Asb. p. 54 and pl. 59 (copy, transliteration, study)
1996 Borger, BIWA pp. 175 and 349 (study)

TEXT

Obv.	
Lacuna	Lacuna
1′) [...] ⸢EN-*ia*⸣ AN.ŠÁR *šá* (traces) [...]	1′–4′) [...], my [lo]rd, (the god) Aššur, who ... [... for rul]ing over the lands and people [...] set out, Taharqa [...], governors, [...]
2′) [... *a-na be*]-⸢*lu*⸣-*ut* KUR.KUR *ù* UN.MEŠ [...]	
3′) [...] ⸢*it*⸣-*ba-a* ^{m}*tar-qu-u* [...]	
4′) [...] ⸢LÚ⸣.NAM.⸢MEŠ⸣ [...]	
Lacuna	Lacuna
Rev.	
Lacuna	Lacuna
1′) [...] KUR *x* [...]	Rev. 1′–3′) (No translation possible)
2′) [...] *x* IB *x* [...]	
3′) [...] NA *it-ti* [...]	
4′) *ša ina* UGU *at-man* É [...]	Rev. 4′) That which is (written) upon the inner sanctum of the temple of [...].

1005

A small fragment from the middle of one face of a clay tablet contains a text belonging to a late Neo-Assyrian king, possibly Ashurbanipal. Although there is nothing preserved in the inscription that allows for a definitive ascription to a specific Assyrian king, the language of the text might reflect an account of Ashurbanipal's conflict with either Taharqa, the king of Egypt, or Teumman, the king of Elam.

CATALOGUE

Museum Number	Provenance	Dimensions (cm)	cpn
K 14127	Nineveh, Kuyunjik	2.9×2.7	p

BIBLIOGRAPHY

1893 Bezold, Cat. 3 p. 1362 (study)
1924–39 Geers, Heft A p. 166 (copy)
1996 Borger, BIWA p. 338; and LoBl p. 51 (transliteration, study)

TEXT

Lacuna
1′) [...] *x* ⸢LU MA?⸣ [...]
2′) [...] *x*-⸢*ia*⸣ *e-mu*-⸢*qí*⸣-[*ia*? ...]
3′) [...] *lib-bu ig-pu*-[*uš* ...]
4′) [...] *in-ši-ma da-mì-iq*-[*ti* ...]
5′) [...] ⸢*ṭè*⸣-*me-šu-ma ba*-⸢*lu*⸣ [DINGIR.MEŠ? ...]
6′) [... *a-na e-muq ra-ma-ni-šú*] ⸢*it*⸣-*ta-kil-ma da-ṣa*-[*a-ti* ...]
7′) [... *la*?] *iṣ-ṣur-ma* ⸢*iḫ*?⸣-[...]
8′) [...] *x* ÁB DINGIR.MEŠ *la* [...]
9′) [...] *x x* (*x*) [...]
Lacuna

Lacuna
1′–9′) [...] ... [...] my [..., *my*] strength [...] (his) heart was prou[d ...] he forgot [...] and [*did not remember* my] favo[r(s) ... (5′) ...] his own judgment and without [*divine approval* ... He] trusted [in his own strength] and [*answered*] with disrespect. [...]. He did [*not*] honor [...] and he [... *He did*] *not* [...] ... the gods [...] ... [...]
Lacuna

1006

A fragment from the upper left corner of a clay tablet preserves part of a historical inscription of an Assyrian king, most likely Ashurbanipal. Little of the original inscription is preserved, but the last line of the text (rev. 9′) mentions the Elamites. Moreover, this tablet may have belonged to a series given that rev. 9′ is on the top edge of the tablet and thus likely served as the catchline for the next tablet of the series.

CATALOGUE

Registration Number	Provenance	Dimensions (cm)	cpn
81-2-4,286	Nineveh, Kuyunjik	3.1×7	p

BIBLIOGRAPHY

1896 Bezold, Cat. 4 p. 1779 (study)
1916 Streck, Asb. p. LXXXVII (study)
1933 Bauer, Asb. p. 67 and pl. 57 (copy, transliteration)
1996 Borger, BIWA p. 348 (collations)

TEXT

Obv.
1) (traces) [...]
Lacuna
Rev.
Lacuna
1′) *x* ⸢ME⸣ *x* [...]
2′) ⸢*ša*⸣ MURUB$_4$ ⸢URU⸣ [...]
3′) *ina su-up-pe-e* [...]
4′) *ina dun-ni zik-*[*ru-te* ...]
5′) *ina qí-bit* ^{d}*aš-šur* [...]
6′) *it-ti* KÙ.GI KÙ.⸢BABBAR⸣ [...]
7′) ANŠE.KUR.RA.MEŠ GAL.⸢MEŠ⸣ [...]
8′) *ina ul-ṣi ri-šá-a-*⸢*ti*⸣ [...]

1) (No translation possible)
Lacuna

Lacuna
Rev. 1′–8′) ... [...] of the citad[el of ...]. Through supplications [...] with power, viril[ity, ...] (rev. 5′) by the command of the god Aššur [...] with gold, silver, [...], large horses, [...], in (the midst of) joyous celebration [...].

9′) LÚ.*e-la-mu-u šá ana gi-piš x x* [*x*] *x-ma* [...]

Rev. 9′) The Elamites who *trusted* in the mass(ed might) of ... and [...].

1007

An inscription of a Neo-Assyrian king is found on a fragment from the right side of one face of a clay tablet. The fragment only preserves parts of ten lines of text, however, it mentions Egypt and Kush, as well as some form of direct speech about Babylonia. Thus, the fragment might belong to the reign of Ashurbanipal, although this is not certain since such locations are also mentioned in texts of Esarhaddon.

CATALOGUE

Museum Number	Provenance	Dimensions (cm)	cpn
K 4496	Nineveh, Kuyunjik	3.8×4.4	p

BIBLIOGRAPHY

1891 Bezold, Cat. 2 p. 637 (study)

1898 Winckler, OLZ 1 col. 69 (lines 3′–7′, 9′, transliteration; study)

1916 Streck, Asb. pp. LXXXIV–LXXXV and CCLXXXVIII (study)

1933 Bauer, Asb. pp. 69–70 and pl. 41 (copy, transliteration)

1996 Borger, BIWA p. 333 (study)

TEXT

Lacuna

1′) [...] ⸢E LI⸣ [...]

2′) [...] *ina* ⸢*da*⸣-*x* [...]

3′) [...] ⸢MAN⸣ KUR AN.ŠÁR.KI ERIM.ḪI.A-*šú iš-pu*-⸢*ru*⸣

4′) [... KUR.*mu*]-⸢*ṣur*⸣ *u* KUR.*ku-ú-si*

5′) [...] *x-u-ni* KUR EME.GI$_7$ *u* URI.KI

6′) [... KUR.*kár*-^{d}*dun*]-⸢*ía*⸣-*àš* DÙ-*šá nu-mal-la-a qa-tuk-ka*

7′) [...] *la ḫa-sis* MUN-*ti*

8′) [...].⸢MEŠ⸣ *ša* DINGIR.MEŠ *ú-maš-šir-ma*

9′) [...] *x x-ia* ⸢*im*⸣-*ši-ma*

10′) [...] *x* SI *x* [*x* (*x*)]

Lacuna

Lacuna

1′–10′) [...] ... [...] in ... [..., *who*] had sent his troops [*to fight with* (*the troops of*) ..., the k]ing of Assyria, [... Egy]pt and Kush [...] to me, the land of Sumer and Akkad, (5′) [*saying*: "... of Karduni]aš (Babylonia), all of it, we will deliver into your hand." [...] (who) did not remember my kindness, [...], abandoned [the ...]s of the gods, and [...]. He forgot my ... and (10′) [...] ... [...]

Lacuna

1008

A flake from a clay tablet (K 16776) contains an inscription of a late Neo-Assyrian king, possibly Ashurbanipal. This fragment preserves very little of the original text, but it mentions Babylon and what language of the inscription is preserved in line 2′ appears to mirror that found in texts of Ashurbanipal.

CATALOGUE

Museum Number	Provenance	Dimensions (cm)	cpn
K 16776	Nineveh, Kuyunjik	1.3×4.1	p

BIBLIOGRAPHY

1996 Borger, BIWA p. 339; and LoBl p. 61 (transliteration, study)

TEXT

Lacuna
1′) [...] *x x x x* (*x*) [...]
2′) [... SIG$_5$-*tu*$^?$ *e*]-⸢*pu*$^?$-*šú*⸣-*uš im-ši-ma iḫ-ṭa-a* [...]
3′) [...] ⸢KÁ⸣.DINGIR.RA.KI *x x* [...]
4′) [...] *x* ⸢*a-na*⸣ [...]
5′) [...] *x x* [...]
Lacuna

Lacuna
1′–5′) [...] ... [...]. He forgot [*the kindness* that I had do]ne for him and sinned against me. [... B]abylon ... [...] to/for [...] ... [...]
Lacuna

1009

Parts of only eleven lines of text are preserved on a tablet fragment containing an inscription of a late Neo-Assyrian king. The attribution is uncertain given that the tablet's contents do not preserve sufficient information to enable a definitive determination, but the language of the fragment (especially line 7′) is generally reminiscent of Ashurbanipal's inscriptions.

CATALOGUE

Museum Number	Provenance	cpn
K 19448	Nineveh, Kuyunjik	p

BIBLIOGRAPHY

1992 Lambert, Cat. p. 35 (study)
1996 Borger, BIWA p. 340; and LoBl p. 72 (transliteration, study)

TEXT

Lacuna
1′) [...] *x* [...]
2′) [...] TUR [...]
3′) [...] *x* ⸢*pa-ni*⸣ *ta-x* [...]
4′) [...] *pa-an* ERIM.ḪI.A-[*ia* ...]
5′) [...] ⸢*iš*⸣-*te-ʾu-u* ⸢*na*⸣-[...]
6′) [... *il-li*]-⸢*ku*⸣-*nim-ma ú*-⸢*na*⸣-[*áš-ši-qu* ...]
7′) [...] *x la ka*-⸢*ṣir*⸣ [*ik-ki*$^?$ ...]
8′) [...] *x*-⸢*nu*⸣-*ti* [...]
9′) [...] ⸢E$^?$ Á$^?$⸣ [...]
10′) [...] ⸢*ša*⸣ [...]
11′) [...] *x* [...]
Lacuna

Lacuna
1′–2′) (No translation possible)

3′–7′) [...] before ... [...] *for* [my] troops [...] were constantly searching for [...]. They [cam]e to me and k[issed *my feet*. ...], the magnani[mous (*and*) *forbearing* one, ...].

8′–11′) (No translation possible)
Lacuna

1009 line 4′ Possibly restore [*a-li-kut*] *pa-an* ERIM.ḪI.A-[*ia*] "[who march] ahead of [my] troops" (see, for example, Tadmor and Yamada, RINAP 1 p. 83 Tiglath-pileser III 35 [Iran Stele] i 12) or *pa-an* ERIM.ḪI.A-[*ia ul ad-gul*] "[I did not wait] for [my] troops" (see, for example, Leichty, RINAP 4 p. 13 Esarhaddon 1 [Nineveh A] i 63).
1009 line 7′ R. Borger (BIWA LoBl p. 72) questioned whether the traces before *la* could be read as [AN.ŠÁR$^?$-DÙ$^?$]-⸢A$^?$⸣, but they do not appear to conform to such an interpretation.

1010

K 6868 + K 9248 is a fragment that preserves parts of two faces from the center of a clay tablet and contains an inscription of a late Neo-Assyrian king, possibly Ashurbanipal. The inscription appears to have been drafted for the fashioning of several objects for the goddess Ištar — including a curtain (TÚG.*mar-du-tu*, rev. 3′) and a statue of the goddess (rev. 4′) — that were presumably to be set up in one of her temples, although no temple name is extant. What is preserved of the obverse describes the Assyrian king's devotion to Ištar and her care in protecting and guiding him in preparation for his tenure as king. Very little remains of the military report of the inscription (rev. 1′–3′a), but it makes mention of the king's capture of an enemy who had fled into the mountains.

CATALOGUE

Museum Number	Provenance	Dimensions (cm)	cpn
K 6868 + K 9248	Nineveh, Kuyunjik	4.5×11	p

BIBLIOGRAPHY

1891 Bezold, Cat. 2 p. 815 (K 6868, study)
1893 Bezold, Cat. 3 p. 996 (K 9248, study)
1996 Borger, BIWA p. 335; and LoBl p. 38 (transliteration, study)

TEXT

Obv.
Lacuna
1′) [...] x [...] x [...]
2′) [...] x AN.ŠÁR x [...] x NIŠ$^{?}$ x [...]
3′) [... ^{d}*iš*]-⸢*tar*$^{?}$⸣ GAŠAN *ta-ra-ma-an-ni x x* ⸢TA$^{?}$ LA$^{?}$⸣ [*x x* (*x*)] *x x x* KUR$^{?}$ *a-na x* [...]
4′) [... *ul-tu*] ⸢*ṣe*⸣-*ḫe-ri-ia a-di ra-bé-ia* TÚG.⸢SÍG$^{?}$⸣ [DINGIR$^{?}$]-⸢*ti*$^{?}$⸣-*šá*$^{?}$ ⸢*aṣ*$^{?}$-*bat at*$^{?}$⸣-*tal-lak x* [...]
5′) [...] *x* ⸢*ta-aṣ*⸣-*ṣur ina* GIŠ.MI-*šá ṭa-a-*[*bi x x*] *x* A *e-pu-uš x* [...]
6′) [...] ⸢*ta*⸣-*at-tar-ra-an-ni* ⸢*qa-as-sa*⸣ *šá ba-la-ṭi* ⸢TA$^{?}$⸣ [...]
7′) [... *ši-pir*] ⸢LÚ⸣.*maḫ-ḫe-ia ka-a-a-an ta-áš-ta-*⸢*nap-pa-ra*$^{?}$⸣ [...]
8′) [...] ⸢LÚ.KÚR.MEŠ⸣-*ia a-nir as-pu-na x x* [...]
9′) [...] x ŠA$^{?}$ TA ḪA x x x x [...]
10′) [...] x x x x [x] x x [...]
Lacuna
Rev.

Lacuna
Obv. 1′–10′) [...] (the god) Aššur [...] ... [... *the goddess Išta*]*r*, the lady who loves me, ... [...] ... to/for [... from] my childhood until I became an adult, I took hold of *the he*[*m of*] *her* [*divinit*]*y* (and) *I* constantly followed [... (5′) ...] she guarded (me) with her benevole[nt] protection [...] *I* made [..., h]er hand, which [*sustains*] my life, guided me [...] she constantly kept *sending* [*me* message(s) from] my ecstatics [...] I killed my enemies (and) flattened ... [...] ... [...] ... [...]
Lacuna

obv. 4′ TÚG.⸢SÍG$^{?}$⸣ [DINGIR$^{?}$]-⸢*ti*$^{?}$⸣-*šá*$^{?}$ ⸢*aṣ*$^{?}$-*bat*⸣ "I took hold of *the he*[*m of*] *her* [*divinit*]*y*": This reading, which was suggested by R. Borger (BIWA LoBl p. 38), is supported by Jeffers and Novotny, RINAP 5/2 p. 325 Asb. 220 (L^{4}) ii 27′.

Lacuna
1′) [...] x *al-lik* x x x (x) [...] x x [...]
2′) [...] ⸢*qé*$^{?}$⸣*-reb* KUR*-e a-šar maš-qí-ti-šú* ⸢KI⸣ [...] x *bal-ṭu-us-*⸢*su*⸣ x [...]
3′) [... *ina*$^{?}$] ⸢*u*$_{4}$$^{?}$⸣*-me-šú* DÙ*-uš* TÚG*.mar-du-tu šu-a-*⸢*tu*⸣ [...].⸢MEŠ$^{?}$⸣ *mu-še-ri-bu ḫi-ṣib* [...]
4′) [...] ⸢ALAM⸣ ^{d}15 GAŠAN*-ia* x x x [... *ep-še-e*]*-ti-ia* EDIN-⸢*uš*⸣-[*šú* ...]
5′) [... *ḫa*]*-diš nap-li-*⸢*si*⸣*-*[*ma* ...] x x *mut-tal-li-*[*ku*$^{?}$ ...]
6′) [...] x *ina ki-rim-*[*mì-ki* DÙG.GA ...] x DI *nap-šat-su* ŠUM$^{?}$ RU [...]
7′) [...] x ŠÚ$^{?}$ DIŠ$^{?}$ x x [...] x *in-*x x x [...]
8′) [...] x*-na* UD$^{?}$ [...] x [...]
Lacuna

Lacuna
Rev. 1′–3′a) [...] I went ... [...] ... [... *i*]*nside* the mountains, *his* watering place, [..., *I captured*] him alive. [...].

Rev. 3′b–4′) [*At*] that [*t*]*ime*, I made that curtain (and) [...]s that bring in the yield of [*mountain and sea* ... a st]atue of the goddess Ištar, my lady, ... [... (*and*) *I had*] my [dee]ds [*written*] upon [it].
Rev. 5′–6′) [*O Ištar*, ...], look with pleasure upo[n ... and ...] ... *the mobil*[*e* ...] in [your sweet] embra[ce ...] his life ... [...].

Rev. 7′–8′) (No translation possible)

Lacuna

1011

K 18219 is a tiny flake from a clay tablet that contains an inscription of a late Neo-Assyrian king, although the identification of the ruler is uncertain. The text mentions a king of the land Elam (rev. 3′), but the name is not preserved, so this text could belong to the reign of Sargon II, Sennacherib, Esarhaddon, or Ashurbanipal.

CATALOGUE

Museum Number	Provenance	cpn
K 18219	Nineveh, Kuyunjik	p

BIBLIOGRAPHY

1992 Lambert, Cat. p. 20 (study)
1996 Borger, BIWA p. 340; and LoBl p. 69 (transliteration, study)

TEXT

Lacuna
1′) [...] x ⸢A⸣ x [...]
2′) [...] x *ina* [...]
3′) [...] LUGAL KUR.⸢ELAM⸣.[(MA).KI ...]
4′) [...] *ú-še-*⸢*ṣa*⸣*-*[*am-ma* ...]
5′) [...] x (x) [...]
Lacuna

Lacuna
1′–5′) [...] ... [...] *in* [...], the king of the land Ela[m, ...] I brought [out and ...]

Lacuna

1010 rev. 4′–5′ The scribe appears to have inserted [... *ep*]-⸢*še-e-ti*⸣*-ia* ⸢TE$^{?}$⸣ [...], "[...] my [d]eeds [...]," in the space between rev. 4′ and 5′ in much smaller script, likely as part of some type of scribal addition or correction.

1012

K 19386 is a flake from the center of a clay tablet that contains a text dealing with the deportation of a royal family. The language of the text has strong affinities to that of Ashurbanipal's inscriptions (compare, for example, Novotny and Jeffers, RINAP 5/1 pp. 75–76 Asb. 3 [Prism B] vii 47, 53–54, 70, and 84), and thus most likely dates to his reign, but this is not certain.

CATALOGUE

Museum Number	Provenance	cpn
K 19386	Nineveh, Kuyunjik	p

BIBLIOGRAPHY

1992 Lambert, Cat. p. 35 (study)

1996 Borger, BIWA p. 340; and LoBl p. 70 (transliteration, study)

TEXT

Lacuna
1′) [...] *x x* [...]
2′) [...] ⸢*ú*⸣-*še-bil-šu-ma* [...]
3′) [...] ⸢*qin*⸣-*nu-šú* NUMUN É AD-⸢*šú*⸣ [...]
4′) [... LÚ.*šu-ut*] ⸢SAG⸣-*ia ša a-na šá-ʾa*-⸢*al*⸣ [*šul-mì-šú* ...]
5′) [...]-⸢*i*⸣-BI *ik-lu*-⸢*ú*⸣ [...]
6′) [... *mi-ra-nu-uš-šú-un*$^{?}$ *ina*$^{?}$ UGU$^{?}$] ⸢ŠÀ$^{?}$-*šú*⸣-*nu ip*-⸢*ši*⸣-[*lu-nim-ma*$^{?}$ ...]
Lacuna

Lacuna
1′–2′) [...] ... [...] I sent to him and [...].

3′–6′) [RN, (...,) *his brothers*], his [fa]mily, (and) the seed of hi[s] father's house [... the eun]uch of mine whom [*I had sent*] to inquire abo[ut his well-being ... (5′) ..., whom ...] ... had confined [*in prison, ... they*] *cra*[*wled naked upon*] their [*belli*]es [*and* ...].

Lacuna

1013

A tablet fragment (Rm 283) from the bottom of the obverse of a clay tablet contains an inscription of a late Neo-Assyrian king, probably Ashurbanipal. Although H. Winckler (AOF 2 pp. 20–21) originally thought that the inscription likely belongs to Esarhaddon, R. Borger (Asarh. p. 119 §99) stated that there is no reason for ascribing the text to him, and then later (BIWA p. 344) suggested "Assurbanipal Spätzeit?". If the inscription belongs to Ashurbanipal, then it must have been written at a later date in his reign given that obv. 12′ mentions the lands Parsumaš and Dilmun, locations that only appear in texts composed at that time. Parsumaš is mentioned in Novotny and

1012 line 5′ [...]-⸢*i*⸣-BI "[...] ...": If this text belongs to the reign of Ashurbanipal, R. Borger (BIWA LoBl p. 70) raised the possibility that these signs could be read as [^{m}*um-man*]-⸢*i*⸣-*gaš* "[Umman]igaš (Ḫumban-nikas II)," one of the kings of Elam in that period.

Jeffers, RINAP 5/1 p. 270 Asb. 12 (Prism H) vi 7′ and p. 307 Asb. 23 [IIT] line 114, and Dilmun is mentioned in ibid. p. 308 Asb. 23 [IIT] lines 131 and 137; the Prism H inscription dates to 639, while the Inscription from the Ištar Temple (IIT) dates to ca. 638.

CATALOGUE

Museum Number	Provenance	Dimensions (cm)	cpn
Rm 283	Nineveh, Kuyunjik	4.9×7.3	p

BIBLIOGRAPHY

1896 Bezold, Cat. 4 p. 1601 (study)
1898 Winckler, AOF 2 pp. 19–21 (edition, study)
1898 Winckler, OLZ 1 col. 75 (study)
1927 Luckenbill, ARAB 2 p. 223 §572 (translation)
1956 Borger, Asarh. p. 119 §99 (study)
1996 Borger, BIWA p. 344; and LoBl p. 93 (transliteration, study)

TEXT

Obv.
Lacuna
1′) [...] *x x x* (*x*) [...]
2′) [...] *x*.⸢MEŠ⸣ *u* GAL-*u ša* AD.MEŠ-*ia* ⸢*ú*⸣-*x* [...]
3′) [... *a-na*$^{?}$] ⸢*na*⸣-*še-e man-da-at-ti šá šat-ti-šam*-⸢*ma*⸣ [...]
4′) [...] *x tak-lum* GIM TI$_{8}$.MUŠEN *ina šá-ḫat* KUR-*e šit-ku-na*-⸢*at*⸣ [*šu-bat-su*]
5′) [...] ⸢*šit*$^{?}$⸣-*ku-nu da-ad-me-šú kàṣ-rat el-lat-su e-mu*-⸢*qi*⸣-[*šú x x* (*x*)]
6′) [...] *x* ^{d}MUATI ^{d}30 ^{d}15 ^{d}U.GUR *a-li-ku* Á.⸢II⸣-[*ia*]
7′) [...] *x-ti ti-bu-ut* ERIM-*ni di-ku-ut a-na*-⸢*an*⸣-[*ti*]
8′) [...]-⸢*ti*$^{?}$⸣-*ma ir-šú-u gi-lit-tú ina la ṣa-bat ṭè-e-me im-šú-u x* [*x x*]
9′) [...]-*li-ip* LUGAL-*ú-ti a-di gi-mir* ERIM.ḪI.A-*šú* ⸢DAGAL⸣.[MEŠ]
10′) [...] *e-piš* MÈ-*šú a-di* ANŠE.KUR.RA.MEŠ ANŠE.KUNGA.MEŠ *ṣi-mit-ti* ⸢GIŠ⸣.[ŠUDUN]
11′) [...] ⸢GÌR.II⸣ LUGAL-*ti-ia iṣ-ba-tu ú-ṣal-lu-u* EN-[*ti-ia*]
12′) [... KUR.*par*]-⸢*su*⸣-*ma-áš ù* KUR.NI.TUK.KI *šá a-šar-šú-un ru-qu ma-la* MA SU *x* [...]
Rev.
Reverse completely missing

Lacuna
Obv. 1′–5′) [...] ... [...]s and the noble(s), who(m) my ancestors ... [... *to* d]eliver payment, which [...] yearly [...] *trusted* [...], like an eagle [whose dwelling] is situated in a mountain cleft, [...] whose settlements *are* [s]*ituated* [...], whose forces are organized (and) [whose] troo[ps *are* ...].

Obv. 6′–11′) [The deities ...], Nabû, Sîn, Ištar, (and) Nergal, who march at [my] side, [...] ... the assault of troops (and) the setting of an atta[ck] in motion, [...] and they became terrified. They foolishly forgot [...] royal ..., including all of his extens[ive] troops, (10′) [...], (and) his fighter(s), together with horses, mules, (and) harness-b[roken (steeds), ...]. They grasped [the fe]et of my royal majesty (and) made appeals to [my] lordly majes[ty].

Obv. 12′) [... (of) the land Pars]umaš and the land Dilmun, whose location(s) are remote, *as many as* ... [...].
Reverse completely missing

obv. 1′–11′ Although the subject matter of these lines is uncertain, A. Fuchs (personal communication) raises the possibility that they represent another narrative about the end of Tabal (compare Novotny and Jeffers, RINAP 5/1 p. 309 Ashurbanipal no. 23 [IIT] lines 141–146a).
obv. 8′ The translation follows CAD's rendering of the phrase *ina la ṣa-bat ṭè-e-me* (lit. "by not grasping reason") as "foolhardily" (see CAD L p. 3 sub *la* c 3′).

1014

K 3150 is a fragment from the center of a clay tablet that preserves parts of two faces, although what little appears on Side B of the fragment is not decipherable. The text belongs to one of the late Neo-Assyrian kings, but the specific ascription is uncertain. The text mentions the city Ḫarrān, which otherwise only appears in inscriptions of Sargon II and Ashurbanipal. If the city protected in A 11′ is Ḫarrān from A 10′, this might find its closest parallel in Sargon II's texts (compare, for example, Frame, RINAP 2 p. 166 Sargon II 9 line 9), but this is only speculation since the present context is unclear.

CATALOGUE

Museum Number	Provenance	Dimensions (cm)	cpn
K 3150	Nineveh, Kuyunjik	5.8×5.4	p

BIBLIOGRAPHY

1891 Bezold, Cat. 2 p. 508 (study)

1996 Borger, BIWA p. 332; and LoBl p. 22 (transliteration, study)

TEXT

Side A

Lacuna
1′) [...] ⌜*aš*$^{?}$-*šur* IB/LU⌝ *x x* [...]
2′) [...] BA$^{?}$ *mu*$^{?}$-*kil*$^{?}$ DINGIR *u* LUGAL [...]
3′) [...] *x-nu-šu*$^{?}$ *i-na pu-ḫur x* [...]
4′) [... $^{d?}$]⌜UTU$^{?}$⌝ *u* ⌜^{d}IŠKUR *pi*$^{?}$⌝-*i-šú-nu i-x* [...]
5′) [...] ⌜*kib*⌝-*rat* LÍMMU-*ti ki-i iš*-⌜*tén*$^{?}$⌝ [...]
6′) [...] ⌜LUGAL⌝-*ú-tu* KUR *aš-šur*.KI *e-x* [...]
7′) [...]-*šú ez-zu-te i-na* KIN *ni*-⌜*kil*⌝-[*ti* ...]
8′) [...] ⌜*e*⌝-*ṭè-er na-piš-ti-šú a*-⌜*na*⌝ [...]
9′) [...] ⌜*ṭè*$^{?}$⌝-*em* DINGIR-*ti-šú* GAL-*ti x* [...]
10′) [...] ⌜*pa*$^{?}$⌝-*aṭ* URU.*ḫar-ra-na x x* [...]
11′) [... *ṣu-lu*]-⌜*ul*⌝-*šú ṭa-a-bu an-du-ul-la*-[*šú* ...]
12′) [...]-*šú bi-in ma-li-ki mim-ma* [...]
13′) [...] *x* Ú *x* [...]
14′) [...] *x x* [...]
Lacuna

Lacuna
A 1′–6′) [...] (*the god*) *Aššur* ... [...] *the one who holds* god and king [..., ...], *his* [..., ...] in *the assembly of* [..., ...] the *command(s)* of [*the god Š*]*amaš* and the god Adad ... [... (A 5′) ..., *who* ...] the four quarters (of the world) as *on*[*e*, ..., *the one who*] ... [the kin]gship of Assyria [...].

A 7′–12′) [...] his furious [...] in a cr[afty] maneuver [...] to save his (own) life, to [..., *he* ... *the w*]*ill of* his great divinity [... (A 10′) ... *the bo*]*rder of* the city Ḫarrān ... [...] his benevolent [protecti]on (and) [his *beneficent*] aegis [...] the son of the king, who(m)ever [...].

A 13′–14′) (No translation possible)

Lacuna

Side B

Lacuna
Traces of 1 or 2 signs in 9 lines
Lacuna

Lacuna
(Traces of 1 or 2 signs in 9 lines)
Lacuna

1015

A fragment (K 6370) from the middle of one face of a clay tablet preserves an inscription belonging to a late Neo-Assyrian king, perhaps Ashurbanipal. The fragment only contains parts of ten lines of text that provide little information for determining to which king this text belongs. It is possible that line 2′ mentions Indabibi, an Elamite king during the time of Ashurbanipal, but the line is too damaged to be certain of the reading (see the on-page note). Moreover, line 9′ could mention the Chaldeans — a term that otherwise only appears in texts of Sargon II and Sennacherib, even though the land Chaldea is mentioned by the other late Neo-Assyrian kings — but this is again uncertain (see the on-page note).

CATALOGUE

Museum Number	Provenance	Dimensions (cm)	cpn
K 6370	Nineveh, Kuyunjik	3.2×3.8	p

BIBLIOGRAPHY

1891	Bezold, Cat. 2 p. 782 (study)
1898	Winckler, OLZ 1 col. 70 (line 9′, transliteration, study)
1916	Streck, Asb. p. LXXXVII (study)
1996	Borger, BIWA p. 335; and 8°-Heft p. 167 (transliteration, study)

TEXT

Lacuna	Lacuna
1′) [...] *x x* [...]	1′–3′) (No translation possible)
2′) [...] ⸢*in*⸣-*da*-BI-[...]	
3′) [...] *x* KI KA LU [...]	
4′) [...] *x-ti-ia ú-še*-[...]	4′–10′) [...] *he* [...] my [*lord*]*ly*/[*roy*]*al* [...] ...s without [... he] was regularly receivin[g ... my] furious m[ood was *not* paci]fied [...]. I sent him a messag[e of ...] *Chaldeans* [...] ... [...]
5′) [...] *x* ŠE$^{?}$.MEŠ *ina la x* [...]	
6′) [...] ⸢*im*⸣-*da-na-ḫa*-⸢*ra*⸣ [...]	
7′) [... *ul*$^{?}$ *ip*]-⸢*šaḫ*⸣ *ez-ze-tú* ⸢*ka*⸣-[*bat-ti* ...]	
8′) [...] *x áš-pur-šú ši-pir*-⸢*ti*⸣ [...]	
9′) [...] ⸢LÚ$^{?}$.*kal*$^{?}$⸣-*da-a-a x* [...]	
10′) [...] *x* (*x*) [...]	
Lacuna	Lacuna

2′ These signs could be interpreted as [*ni*]-⸢*in*⸣-*da-bé*-[*e*] "[*ni*]*ndab*[*û*]-offerings," or as [^{m}]⸢*in*⸣-*da-bi*-[*bi*] "[I]ndabi[bi]," a servant of the Elamite king Tammarītu who deposed him and assumed the throne during Ashurbanipal's reign (see, for example, Novotny and Jeffers, RINAP 5/1 p. 75 Asb. 3 [Prism B] vii 41–42).

9′ H. Winckler (OLZ 1 [1898] col. 70) read this line as [LÚ].⸢*kal*⸣-*da-ai* for "[C]haldeans"; however, R. Borger (BIWA 8°-Heft p. 167) stated that the traces before *da* are not *kal*. Because of damage to the tablet, it is difficult to ascertain exactly what signs are before *da*, but the traces do not appear to exclude the present reading.

1016

An inscription of a late Neo-Assyrian king is found on K 16021, a fragment most likely from the bottom of a clay tablet. Very little in the inscription can be used for determining to which king this text belongs, but based on the general language, it could belong to the reign of Ashurbanipal.

CATALOGUE

Museum Number	Provenance	Dimensions (cm)	cpn
K 16021	Nineveh, Kuyunjik	4.4×3.2	p

BIBLIOGRAPHY

1996 Borger, BIWA p. 339; and LoBl p. 58 (transliteration, study)

TEXT

Obv.
Lacuna
1′) [...] *x* (*x*) [...]
2′) [...] *x* ⸢UD?⸣ [...]
3′) [...] ŠU *x* [...]
4′) [...] *ul* ⸢*iḫ*⸣-*x* [...]
5′) [...] *ba-lu* DINGIR.MEŠ [...]
6′) [...] ⸢*a*⸣-*na-ku ina qí-bit* ⸢AN?⸣.[ŠÁR? ...]
7′) [...] *x-su* GIŠ.TUKUL.⸢MEŠ⸣ [...]
8′) [...] *ik-ka-lu a*-⸢*kal*?⸣-[*šú*?-(*nu*?) ...]
9′) [...] *pa-an* ERIM.ḪI.A-⸢*ia*⸣ [...]
10′) [...] *x-lu* GIŠ *x* [...]
Rev.
Reverse completely missing

Lacuna
Obv. 1′–3′) (No translation possible)

Obv. 4′–6′a) [...] he did not [...] without divine approval [...].
Obv. 6′a–10′) I myself, by the command of (*the god*) A[*ššur*, ...] ... [*his/my*] weapons [...] who/they were eating [*his/their*] fo[*od* ...] *for* m[y] troops [...] ... [...].

Reverse completely missing

1017

K 17809 comes from the top left corner of a clay tablet and contains an inscription of a Neo-Assyrian king (identification uncertain). The small fragment only preserves a handful of lines, but obv. 1 mentions an "Elamite" (⸢LÚ⸣.ELAM.MA.KI-*a*-⸢*a*⸣), which could place the text in the reign of Ashurbanipal, even though a name for this Elamite is not preserved. Furthermore, rev. 1′ begins with the prepositional use of *šūt*, "Because of/On account of," a usage that is common in inscriptions of Ashurbanipal.

1016 obv. 6′ *ina qí-bit* ⸢AN?⸣.[ŠÁR?] "by the command of (*the god*) A[*ššur*]": Or possibly read *ina qí-bit* ⸢d?⸣[...] "by the command of *the go*[*d/dess* ...]."
1016 obv. 9′ For possible restorations, see the on-page note to Asb. 1009 line 4′.

CATALOGUE

Museum Number	Provenance	cpn
K 17809	Nineveh, Kuyunjik	p

BIBLIOGRAPHY

1992 Lambert, Cat. p. 14 (study)

1996 Borger, BIWA p. 340; and LoBl p. 67 (transliteration, study)

TEXT

Obv.
1) ⌈LÚ⌉.ELAM.MA.KI-*a*-⌈*a*⌉ *x* [...]
2) *x x x x* [...]
Lacuna
Rev.
Lacuna
1′) *šu*-⌈*ut ep-šet*⌉ ḪUL-⌈*tim*⌉ *x* [...]
2′) TA *qé*-⌈*reb* NUMUN?⌉-*šú* GIŠ.⌈GU?⌉.[ZA? ...]
3′) *ina ni-ṭi-il* IGI.II-*šú x* [...]

Obv. 1–2) The Elamite [...] ... [...]

Lacuna

Lacuna

Rev. 1′–3′) On account of the evil deed(s), [*may he/they* ...] from his *progeny*, [...] the *thr*[*one* (*of*) ... *May he/they* ...] through his gaze.

1018

K 17999 is a small flake from one face of a clay tablet that contains an inscription of a late Neo-Assyrian king. Little is preserved of the tablet's original contents, but the language is compatible with that of Ashurbanipal's inscriptions; especially compare line 3′ with Novotny and Jeffers, RINAP 5/1 p. 59 Asb. 3 (Prism B) i 73 and p. 233 Asb. 11 (Prism A) i 79b–80a.

CATALOGUE

Museum Number	Provenance	cpn
K 17999	Nineveh, Kuyunjik	p

BIBLIOGRAPHY

1992 Lambert, Cat. p. 17 (study)

1996 Borger, BIWA p. 340; and LoBl p. 68 (transliteration, study)

TEXT

Lacuna
1′) [...] *x x* [...]
2′) [...] *x-nu ú-*⸢*šam-kír*⸣ KAL$^{?}$⸣ *x* [...]
3′) [... *a-na e*]-⸢*peš*⸣ GIŠ.TUKUL MURUB$_4$ *u* ⸢MÈ⸣ [...]
4′) [... ^{d}]⸢AG$^{?}$⸣ DINGIR.MEŠ GAL.MEŠ *x* [...]
5′) [...] *iz-zi-*⸢*zu*⸣ [...]
6′) [... *la*$^{?}$] ⸢*am*$^{?}$⸣-*ši*$^{?}$-*ma x* [...]
7′) [...] *x* KI *x* [...]
8′) [...] *x* [...]
Lacuna

Lacuna
1′–8′) [...] ... [...] ... he incited to become hostile ... [... to wag]e armed battle and wa[r ..., the gods/deities ...], (and) *Nabû*, the great gods, [... (5′) ...] who/they stood [... *I did not fo*]*rget* and [...] ... [...]
Lacuna

1019

A small flake (K 22138) from the right edge of a clay tablet bears a text mentioning the god Enlil and a prize bull (GU$_4$.MAḪ-*ḫu*). It may also refer to Ashurbanipal (A 5′), although the name is only partially preserved. If the latter is a reference to Ashurbanipal, it is uncertain if the text belongs to his reign or to that of one of his successors.

CATALOGUE

Museum Number	Provenance	cpn
K 22138	Nineveh, Kuyunjik	p

BIBLIOGRAPHY

1992 Lambert, Cat. p. 71 (study)
1996 Borger, BIWA p. 340; and LoBl p. 79 (transliteration, study)

TEXT

Side A

Lacuna
1′) [... ^{d}]⸢EN.LÍL⸣
2′) [...] ⸢ŠÁ$^{?}$⸣ ME

3′) [...] *x* GU$_4$.MAḪ-⸢*ḫu*⸣
4′) [...] ⸢*in*⸣-*nab-tú-*⸢*ma*⸣
5′) [... ^{m}AN.ŠÁR]-DÙ-A
6′) [...]-⸢*ti*$^{?}$⸣-*šú*
Lacuna

Lacuna
A 1′–2′) [... the god E]nlil [...] ...

A 3′–6′) [...] prize bul[l(s) ... he] fled an[d ... Ashur]banipal [...] *him*.
Lacuna

Side B

Lacuna
1′) [...] AN
Lacuna

Lacuna
B 1′) (No translation possible)
Lacuna

1019 B line 1′ The AN sign is written on the right edge of Side A next to a horizontal ruling, and it appears to be the final sign of a line from Side B that has run over the edge of the tablet.

1020

A fragment from the center of one face of a clay tablet contains an inscription of a late Neo-Assyrian king. Despite the fact that the text only preserves parts of nine lines, it most likely belongs to the reign of Sargon II or Ashurbanipal given that the phrase *šá-ʾa-al šul-mì-ia*, "to inquire about my well-being" (line 3′) only appears in the inscriptions of those two kings.

CATALOGUE

Museum Number	Provenance	Dimensions (cm)	cpn
Rm 2,467	Nineveh, Kuyunjik	4.1×4.4	p

BIBLIOGRAPHY

1896 Bezold, Cat. 4 p. 1677 (study)
1933 Bauer, Asb. p. 107 and pl. 55 (copy, study)
1996 Borger, BIWA p. 346 (study)

TEXT

Lacuna
1′) [...] *x* ˹E? KAL?˺ *x* [...]
2′) [...] ˹*la*?˺ *aq-bi ina* KAR? *x* [...]
3′) [... *iš*]-˹*pu*˺-*ra a-na šá-ʾa-al* ˹*šul*˺-[*mì-ia* ...]
4′) [...] *x-ka šá* IB LA? *ip-ru-sa x* [...]
5′) [...] *x na ša*?/*da*?-*a-ti la ki-iṣ*?-*x* [...]
6′) [...] ˹*iš*?-*kun*˺-*šú*-˹*nu*?˺-*ti* DI [...]
7′) [...] *x ú-sa-di-ra x* [...]
8′) [...] *x* KI *sa-ra-a*-˹*ti*?˺ [...]
9′) [...] *x x* [...]
Lacuna

Lacuna
1′–9′) [...] ... [...] I did [*n*]*ot* say [...]. In/from ... [... he se]nt [*his mounted messenger*] to inquire about [my] wel[l-being ...] ... *which* ... he *blocked/decided* [... (5′) ...] ... not ... [... *he p*]*l*[*a*]*ced them* [...] arranged [...] ... *lie*[*s* ...] ... [...]
Lacuna

1021

An inscription of a late Neo-Assyrian king is found on a fragment (K 13749) from the right side of one face of a clay tablet, but the king to whom it belongs is uncertain. The fragment preserves the ends of eleven lines that only contain five signs at most. However, the limited language that is extant might suggest that this part of the inscription dealt with renovations to some type of structure, with line 9′ indicating that the Assyrian king had an object constructed for it, although the reference to the type of object made is now broken away.

1020 line 6′ As shown in T. Bauer's copy (Asb. pl. 55), the sign before *ti* appears to be a single horizontal wedge with slight damage to its latter half. It is unclear if there was originally an oblique wedge present for a NU sign that is now broken away, or if this sign is actually the AŠ sign.

CATALOGUE

Museum Number	Provenance	Dimensions (cm)	cpn
K 13749	Nineveh, Kuyunjik	3.6×3.1	p

BIBLIOGRAPHY

1893 Bezold, Cat. 3 p. 1336 (study)

1996 Borger, BIWA p. 337; and LoBl p. 50 (transliteration, study)

TEXT

Lacuna
1′) [...] *x*
2′) [...]-⸢*uš*⸣-*šú*
3′) [...] *x* NA KI
4′) [...] ⸢*u*$^{?}$⸣ KÙ.BABBAR
5′) [... *a-na*] ⸢*si*⸣-*ḫir-ti-šú*
6′) [...] ⸢KI$^{?}$⸣-*ta ú-še-šib*
7′) [...]-⸢*tu*⸣ GAL-*tú*
8′) [... *lu*$^{?}$]-⸢*le*⸣-*e ú-mal-li*
9′) [...] ⸢*ú*⸣-*še-piš-ma*
10′) [...]-*šú*
11′) [...] *x*
Lacuna

Lacuna
1′–6′) [... *upon*] *it*. [...] ... [... *an*]*d* silver [... (5′) ... in] its [e]ntirety. [...] ... I made [...] reside [...].

7′–11′) [...] great [..., ...] I filled (it) with [*splen*]*dor*. [...] I had [...] made and [... (10′) ...] its [...]
Lacuna

1022

81-7-27,280 is small fragment from the center of a clay tablet containing an inscription of an Assyrian king, most likely Ashurbanipal. Little of the text's contents remain, but lines 1′–6′a describe work on an unnamed building, while line 6′b mentions Eḫulḫul ("House which Gives Joy"), the temple of the god Sîn at Ḫarrān. Work on the Eḫulḫul temple is mentioned once in an inscription of Sargon II (Frame, RINAP 2 p. 374 Sargon II 84 line 6′), but often in inscriptions of Ashurbanipal (see, for example, Novotny and Jeffers, RINAP 5/1 p. 217 Asb. 10 [Prism T] ii 29–43 and iii 5–12). Assuming that the text belongs to the reign of Ashurbanipal, J. Novotny (Eḫulḫul p. 107) suggested that lines 1′–6′a pertain to that king's rebuilding of the House of Succession at Nineveh (compare Novotny and Jeffers, RINAP 5/1 p. 207 Asb. 9 [Prism F] vi 55–56a and p. 263 Asb. 11 [Prism A] x 101–102) and lines 6′b–7′ deal with his work on the Eḫulḫul temple at Ḫarrān (the subject of the building report of Jeffers and Novotny, RINAP 5/2 pp. 285–286 Asb. 207 [LET] rev. 43–67). If this is correct, the inscription is possibly part of a prologue composed after the completion of these structures, which would mean that it was composed late in Ashurbanipal's reign.

1021 line 3′ In his transliteration, R. Borger (BIWA LoBl p. 50) questioned whether the signs could be read as [^{d}*a*]-⸢*nun*⸣-*na-ki* for "[the *Anu*]*nnakū gods*," but the traces before NA do not appear to conform with NUN. Possibly read [...]-⸢*in*⸣-*na*.KI.

CATALOGUE

Registration Number	Provenance	Dimensions (cm)	cpn
81-7-27,280	Nineveh, Kuyunjik	2.4×2.9	p

BIBLIOGRAPHY

1896 Bezold, Cat. 4 p. 1813 (study)

1996 Borger, BIWA p. 349; and LoBl p. 105 (transliteration, study)

2003 Novotny, Eḫulḫul pp. 43, 45, 107–108, 114–116, 394 (copy, transliteration, study)

TEXT

Lacuna

1′) [...] *x x* [...]

2′) [...]-⸢*ti*⸣-*ia* ⸢*šá*⸣ *x* [...]

3′) [...] *x e-pu-šú* ⸢A$^{?}$⸣ [...]

4′) [...] *x tam-le-e* ⸢KI$^{?}$⸣ [...]

5′) [... URUDU] ⸢*nam*⸣-*ru ú-ḫal-*⸢*lip*⸣-[(*ma*) ...]

6′) [... *é*]-⸢*ḫúl*⸣-*ḫúl* ⸢É⸣ [^{d}30 ...]

7′) [...] ⸢DUMU⸣ ^{m}*x*-[...]

8′) [...] *x* [...]

Lacuna

Lacuna

1′–6′a) [... (of)] my [...], which [..., which] he (*Sennacherib*) had built [...] the terrace [... (5′) ...] I covere[d *tall columns* with shi]ny [copper (and) ...].

6′b–8′) [Eḫ]ulḫul, the templ[e of the god Sîn, *which* ..., the s]on of [..., *had built*, ...]

Lacuna

1023

This fragment, K 16899 + Sm 1048, comes from the center of one face of a clay tablet and bears an inscription of a late Neo-Assyrian king, possibly Esarhaddon or Ashurbanipal. The extant text concerns the presentation of different types of stones, aromatics, and sacrifices to the gods. Although additional deities were likely mentioned in the lacunae, references to the deities Šerūa (line 6′), Nabû (line 6′), and Aššur (line 9′) are preserved. In addition, line 9′ mentions Esagil ("House Whose Top Is High"), the temple of Marduk at Babylon. The join of K 16899 and Sm 1048 was made by Z. Földi, and the authors would like to thank him for bringing this to their attention.

1022 line 3′ If lines 1′–6′a pertain to Ashurbanipal's rebuilding of the House of Succession at Nineveh as suggested in the introduction, then Sennacherib would likely have been the previous builder mentioned in the inscription.

1022 lines 6′b–7′ J. Novotny (Eḫulḫul pp. 107–108 n. 327) tentatively suggested that these lines might be restored as [*é*]-⸢*ḫúl*⸣-*ḫúl* ⸢É⸣ [^{d}30 *ša qé-reb* URU.*ḫar-ra-na ša* ^{md}*šùl-ma-nu*-MAS DUMU ^{m}*aš-šur*-PAP-IBILA (DUMU)] ⸢DUMU⸣ ^{m}⸢GIŠ$^{?}$⸣.[TUKUL-*ti*-^{d}MAŠ LUGAL *pa-ni maḫ-ri-ia e-pu-šú*], "[Eḫ]ulḫul, the templ[e of the god Sîn, which is (situated) inside the city Ḫarrān, which Shalmaneser (III), son of Ashurnaṣirpal (II), grands]on of T[ukultī-Ninurta (II), a king who preceded me, had built]."

CATALOGUE

Museum Number	Provenance	Dimensions (cm)	cpn
K 16899 + Sm 1048	Nineveh, Kuyunjik	3.9×4.6	p

BIBLIOGRAPHY

1896 Bezold, Cat. 4 p. 1458 (Sm 1048, study)

1924–39 Geers, Heft B p. 137 (Sm 1048, copy)

1992 Lambert, Cat. p. 2 (K 16899, study)

1996 Borger, BIWA p. 341; and LoBl p. 82 (Sm 1048, transliteration, study)

TEXT

Lacuna

1′) [...] *x x* [...]

2′) [...] ⸢Á⸣ *x* [...]

3′) [...] *x* DA ME *x* [...]

4′) [... NA$_4$].⸢ZA⸣.GÌN NA$_4$.BABBAR.DILI NA$_4$ *a-⸢qar⸣-[tu* ...]

5′) [...] ⸢GIŠ.ŠUR.MÌN⸣ GI DÙG.GA *kal* ŠIM.ḪI.A ⸢*šá*⸣ *x* [...]

6′) [... ^{d}*še*]-⸢*ru-u*$_8$*-a*⸣ *šar-ra-ti u* ^{d}*na-bi-um* [...]

7′) [...] ⸢*ṣu*⸣*-up-ri šuk-lu-lu šu-ʾe-e ma-ru-ti* UDU$^{?}$.[...]

8′) [...]-⸢*ti*⸣ UDU.SISKUR.MEŠ *taš-⸢ri⸣-iḫ-ti aq-qí* ME BI$^{?}$ [...]

9′) [...] *x-ti* AN.⸢ŠÁR⸣ *x* [*x* (*x*)] ⸢*a*⸣*-na é-sag-íl šá x* [...]

10′) [...] ⸢*šá*$^{?}$⸣ BAL ⸢AD$^{?}$⸣ [*x x* (*x*)] *x ba-ni-⸢šú*$^{?}$ *pa*$^{?}$*-rak*$^{?}$⸣ [...]

11′) [...] ⸢*pa*$^{?}$⸣*-qid kiš-⸢šat*$^{?}$⸣ [...] *x* [...]

12′) [...] ⸢MA$^{?}$⸣ A [...]

13′) [...] *x* UD$^{?}$ [...]

Lacuna

Lacuna

1′–3′) (No translation possible)

4′–11′) [... l]apis lazuli, (and) *pappardilû*-stone, pre[cious] stone(s), [... (5′) ...] cypress, sweet reed(s), all of the aromatics, *which* [... the goddess Šer]ūa, the queen, and the god Nabû [..., ... *whose horns and* h]ooves are perfect, fattened sheep, [...]. I offered sumptuous offerings ... [...] ... *of* (the god) Aššur [...] to/for Esagil, *which* [... (10′) ...] ... [...], *his* creator, *the da*[*is of* ... *who is en*]*trusted with al*[*l of* ...].

12′–13′) (No translation possible)

Lacuna

1024

A dedicatory inscription of a late Neo-Assyrian king, probably Ashurbanipal, to the goddess Zarpanītu is found on Rm 337 + Rm 451. The fragment comes from the upper portion of a clay tablet and preserves parts of two faces. The obverse contains an opening dedication to the goddess that gives her epithets, while the reverse preserves part of the text's curse formula. The name of the object that had been fashioned for Zarpanītu is no longer preserved, and the scribe did not include a subscript on the tablet that would have contained such information. However, an epithet in obv. 8 describes Zarpanītu as "the goddess of pleasure" (*i-lat tak-né-e*), and it is known from inscriptions of Ashurbanipal that he had a "pleasure bed" (*mayyāl taknê*) made and placed in her bed chamber, Kaḫilisu, for her and her husband, Marduk, to use (see, for example, Novotny and Jeffers, RINAP 5/1 p. 216 Asb. 10 [Prism T] i 46–54). Thus, it is possible that the present inscription related to the fashioning of this object (see also Asb. 1025–1026). Moreover, the divine trio Anu, Enlil, and Ea (obv. 10) are also mentioned in some of Ashurbanipal's Ḫarrān inscriptions (see Jeffers and Novotny, RINAP 5/2 p. 288 Asb. 208 obv. 11 and p. 312 Asb. 216 obv. 13 [partially restored]), and the phrase "the holy shrine" (*ki-iṣ-ṣi el-li*) in obv. 9 is used for the Emeslam temple in a dedicatory text of Ashurbanipal to Nergal (ibid. pp. 345–346 Asb. 227 obv. 6), which suggest that Rm 337 + Rm 451 belongs to the reign of Ashurbanipal as well.

CATALOGUE

Museum Number	Provenance	Dimensions (cm)	cpn
Rm 337 + Rm 451	Nineveh, Kuyunjik	8.1×7	p

BIBLIOGRAPHY

1896 Bezold, Cat. 4 pp. 1605 and 1613 (study)

1924–39 Geers, Heft M p. 7 (Rm 337, copy)

1996 Borger, BIWA p. 345; and LoBl pp. 94-95 (transliteration, study)

TEXT

Obv.

1) *[a-na ^{d}zar-pa-ni-tum ...] x-ti i-lá-a-ti qá-rit-⸢ti⸣* [DINGIR.MEŠ$^{?}$ ...]
2) *[... ku-uz]-⸢ba⸣ za-a᾽-na-at na-šat ⸢me-lam⸣-[me* ...]
3) *[... mul]-li-la-at nap-ḫar* EN.[MEŠ$^{?}$ ...]
4) *[... a-šá]-re-da-at* KI-*⸢tim⸣ šá mì-⸢su⸣-šá ⸢šu-qu⸣-[ru-(u)-tu$^{?}$* ...]
5) *[... ta]-⸢na⸣-da-a-ti šá gi-⸢mir⸣* [...]
6) [...] x-ḪAR *ši-tul-ti u mil-ki* DUMU.[MUNUS ...]
7) [...] *šá na-ad-nu-šú kiš-šá-tu* x [...]

Obv. 1–7) [For the goddess Zarpanītu, ...] ... of the goddesses, the heroic o[ne of *the gods* ..., *the one who*] is endowed with [sexual cha]rm (and) who bears the awe-inspir[ing radiance, ..., who pu]rifies all *the lord*[*s* ..., for]emost of the earth, whose *pre*[*cious*] cultic rites [are ..., (5) ... the pr]aise of all [...] ... deliberation and counsel, the daug[hter of ...] that was given to her (lit: "him"), the totality (of) [...];

8) [...] *ṣir-tu i-lat tak-né-e šá a-na* x [...]
9) [...] x *ki-iṣ-ṣi el-li* x [...]
10) [...] ⸢EŠ⸣.BAR *^{d}a-nim* ^{d}⸢EN⸣.LÍL *u ^{d}é-a ⸢la⸣* [...]
11) [...] *⸢pa⸣-ra-aṣ ^{d}a-⸢nù⸣-ú-ti* x [...]

Obv. 8–11) [...] exalted [*lady*], goddess of pleasure who [...] to/for [...] — the holy shrine — [... (10) ... *who does*] not [... the de]cision of the gods Anu, Enlil, and Ea [... *who gathers to herself*] (all) divine offices of the highest rank [...];

12) [...] *⸢šá⸣ ina ṣi-it ^{d}šam-ši ina šu-pi-i-šá* [...]
13) [...] *⸢šá⸣ ina e-reb ^{d}šam-ši ina* IGI.DU$_{8}$.A-*šá* [...]
14) [...] x *šá ina* GIŠ.DÌḪ *uš-ta-pa-a ú-*[...]
15) [...] *šá ina šá-lam* ^{d}UTU-*ši ina* IGI.DU$_{8}$.A-*šá* [...]
16) [...] *x-e šá ina ge-⸢gu$^{?}$⸣-né-e ab-ra-[a-ti$^{?}$* ...]
17) [...] *ina ṣi-ta-áš u ši-⸢la⸣-an ⸢la⸣* [...]
18) [...] *⸢mu⸣-diš-šá-at ḫi-⸢iṣ⸣-bi ⸢mu⸣-*[...]
19) [...] x [x x] x *šá* x [...]

Obv. 12–19) [...], at [w]hose manifestation at sunrise [...], at whose appearance at sunset [...], who, from *baltu*-plant(s), makes [...] manifest, [... (15) ...], at whose appearance at sunset [...] ..., who [...] *human*[*ity*] in *a sacred building*, [..., *who does*] not [...] in the east and west, [..., the one w]ho restores abundance, the one w[ho ...], who [...]

Lacuna

Lacuna

Rev.

Lacuna
1′) [...] *x x* [...]
2′) [...] *x* MA LI *x* [...]
3′) [...] *x liq-bi-*⸢*kim-ma*⸣ [...]
4′) [...] *x un-ni-ni-ia* [...]
5′) [...] *x in-na-ḫu-ma* ⸢*il*⸣-[*la-ku la-ba-riš* ...]
6′) [... *a-a*] ⸢*ú*⸣-*šá-an-ni-ma* [...]
7′) [*šá* ... ^{d}*zar*]-⸢*pa*⸣-*ni-tum ú-šá-an-nu-ma a-x* [...]
8′) [... *ú-nak-ka*]-⸢*ru*⸣-*ú-ma ni-bit* MU-⸢*ia*⸣ [...]
9′) [... *ar-rat*] ⸢*la*⸣ *nap-šú-ri li-ru-ur-šú-ma* [...]
10′) [...] ⸢^{d}⸣AMAR.UTU *ḫa-ʾi-i-*<*ri*>*-šá ka-a-a-an* ⸢*li*⸣-[...]

Blank

Lacuna
Rev. 1′–4′) [...] ... [...] ... [...] let him speak [...] to you an[d ...] my prayers [...].

Rev. 5′–6′) [... *when this* ...] becomes dilapidated and o[ld, *may he* ..., may he not] change [...], and [...].
Rev. 7′–10′) [(As for) the one who ...] changes [the ... of the goddess Zarp]anītu and ... [... remov]es [the ...] and [...] the mention of m[y] name [...] may she curse him with [an i]rreversible [curse] and [...] may she constantly [*speak inauspicious words about him before* the g]od Marduk, her husba<nd>, (and) [...].

Blank

1025

K 4498 is a fragment from the reverse of a clay tablet that contains the concluding blessings of an inscription of an Assyrian king, probably Ashurbanipal. Although the subscript is not preserved after the horizontal ruling, rev. 3′ mentions a "pleasure bed" (*mayyāl taknê*). Ashurbanipal had such an object made and placed in Zarpanītu's bed chamber, Kaḫilisu (see the introduction to Asb. 1024; compare also Asb. 1026).

CATALOGUE

Museum Number	Provenance	Dimensions (cm)	cpn
K 4498	Nineveh, Kuyunjik	4.5×3.8	p

BIBLIOGRAPHY

1891 Bezold, Cat. 2 p. 637 (study)
1924–39 Geers, Heft B p. 17 (copy)
1996 Borger, BIWA p. 333; and LoBl p. 26 (transliteration, study)

TEXT

Obv.
Obverse completely missing
Rev.
Lacuna
1′) (erased line)
2′) [...] ⸢*zik*$^{?}$⸣*-ri šu-mì-šú kab-te li-*⸢*na*$^{?}$⸣-[...]
3′) [...] ⸢*ma*⸣*-a-al tak-né-e mu-ši šá x* [...]

Obverse completely missing

Lacuna
Rev. 1′–9′) [...] may *she* [... *the men*]*tion of* his venerated name [...] the pleasure bed at night *that* [... may] *she* grant me [*progeny*] and expa[nd *my offspring* ... (rev. 5′)

1024 rev. 5′–10′ For potential restorations to these lines, see Novotny and Jeffers, RINAP 5/1 p. 311 Asb. 23 (IIT) lines 177b–183, Jeffers and Novotny, RINAP 5/2 p. 289 Asb. 208 rev. 8–13, p. 292 Asb. 209 rev. 4–21, and p. 295 Asb. 210 rev. 2′–9′.

4′) [... *šu-mu*?] ⸢*li*⸣-*šar-šá-an-ni-ma li-rap*-⸢*pi*⸣-[*iš* NUMUN ...]
5′) [...]-*ia li-dan-nin-ma li-x* [...]
6′) [...] x.MEŠ *li-šá-áš-ṭi-ra* [...]
7′) [...] ⸢u_4⸣-*me-šam li-ḫa-as*-⸢*si*⸣-[*sa*? ...]
8′) [...]-*a-a lik-tar-ra*-⸢*bu*⸣ [...]
9′) [...] x SIG_5-*tim* x [...]

...] may *she* strengthen my [...] and may *she* [...] may *she* have [...]s written [...] daily may *she remi*[*nd* ...] ... may th[ey] constantly bless [...] good thing(s) [...].

Subscript completely missing

Subscript completely missing

1026

A fragment (K 8361) from the bottom of a clay tablet, which preserves parts of two faces, contains an inscription of a late Neo-Assyrian king, probably Ashurbanipal. The text appears to be a dedicatory inscription from the king to the divine couple Marduk? and Zarpanītu, and it mentions a pleasure bed (*mayyāl taknê*) in rev. 8. Ashurbanipal had a pleasure bed made and placed in Kaḫilisu, Zarpanītu's bed chamber, for this divine pair to use (see the introduction to Asb. 1024; compare also Asb. 1025). One should also note that in the corpus of royal inscriptions, the god Dunga (rev. 4) is mentioned in Sennacherib's inscriptions dealing with the *akītu*-house at Aššur (see, for example, Grayson and Novotny, RINAP 3/2 pp. 254–255 Sennacherib 173).

CATALOGUE

Museum Number	Provenance	Dimensions (cm)	cpn
K 8361	Nineveh, Kuyunjik	5.2×7	p

BIBLIOGRAPHY

1893 Bezold, Cat. 3 p. 919 (study)
1924–39 Geers, Heft A p. 9 (copy)
1996 Borger, BIWA p. 336; and LoBl p. 43 (transliteration, study)

TEXT

Obv.
Lacuna
1′) [...] ⸢*zi*⸣-*kir be*-⸢*lu-ti-šú*⸣ x x x [...]
2′) [...] (traces) [...]
Rev.
1) [... *i*?]-⸢*ter*⸣-*ri-šú-uš* TI.LA x x (x) [...]
2) [...] ⸢DINGIR⸣.MEŠ *qé-reb-šú ú-šá-áš-ṭir-ma* x x [...]
3) [...] ⸢UGU⸣-*ka* DINGIR-*ut-ka lim-ḫur*

Lacuna
Obv. 1′–Rev. 2) [... the me]ntion of his lordly majesty ... [...] ... [...] they (*the gods*) were constantly [im]ploring him for (my) life ... [...] I had [... *of* the go]ds written therein and [...].

Rev. 3–7) [... *o*]*n* you, may your divinity accept (and)

1025 rev. 4′ The restorations are based on Leichty, RINAP 4 p. 301 Esarhaddon 1015 vi 6.
1026 rev. 3 ⸢*ka*⸣-[*bat-ta-ka*? *li-iḫ-ši-iḫ*?] "[*may your*] *m*[*ind desire*]": This restoration is based on Jeffers and Novotny, RINAP 5/2 pp. 297–298 Asb. 211 rev. 5.

⸢*ka*⸣-[*bat-ta-ka*? *li-iḫ-ši-iḫ*? (...)]
4) [...] ⸢LÚ⸣.NAR *ina* GIŠ.ZÀ.MÍ *šu-bat* ^{d}*dúnga* ITI.ŠE *x* [...]
5) [...]-*ka li-ṣa-a ḫi-tas*-[*sas* ...]
6) [...]-*tim ki-in* SUḪUŠ GIŠ.GU.⸢ZA⸣ [...]
7) [...] *x-ka* KÙ-*tum li-x* [...]
8) [... GIŠ].⸢NÁ⸣ *tak-né-e li*-[...]
9) [...] ⸢AN?⸣ KI ŠU ⸢UB⸣ [...]
10) [...] *x* NE-*ma* GIŠ *x* [...]
11) [...] ⸢^{d}⸣*zar-pa-ni*-⸢*tum*⸣ [...]
12) [...] *x* E *x* [...]
13) [...] *x x* [...]
14) [...] *x* [...]
Lacuna

[*may your*] m[*ind desire* ...] a singer with a lyre, the abode of the god Dunga, (in) the month Addaru (XII), [... (rev. 5) ...] may [(*the command for*) ...] come forth [*from*] your [*lips*]. Always remem[ber ..., ...], make firm the foundation(s) of [*my royal*] throne. [...]. May your holy [...].
Rev. 8–14) [...] may [... a] pleasure bed [...] ... [... (rev. 10) ...] ... and ... [...] the goddess Zarpanīt[u ...] ... [...] ... [...]
Lacuna

1027

K 6681 comes from the left side of the obverse of a clay tablet and bears an inscription of a late Neo-Assyrian king, possibly Ashurbanipal or Sîn-šarra-iškun. The extant contents are the epithets of the Assyrian king that appear at the beginning of the inscription subsequent to the mention of the royal name. Unfortunately, the general language of the epithets does not allow for a certain ascription to which king this text belongs.

CATALOGUE

Museum Number	Provenance	Dimensions (cm)	cpn
K 6681	Nineveh, Kuyunjik	6.3×6.4	p

BIBLIOGRAPHY

1891 Bezold, Cat. 2 p. 802 (study)
1996 Borger, BIWA p. 335; and LoBl p. 36 (transliteration, study)

TEXT

Obv.
Lacuna
1′) [...] *x x x x x* [...]
2′) ⸢SANGA ÉNSI⸣ *ke-e-nu e-pir é*-⸢*zi*⸣-[*da* ...]
3′) *mal-ku le-ʾu-u a-ḫi-iz né-me-eq* ^{d}AG *x* [...]
4′) *ša* DINGIR.MEŠ GAL.MEŠ *a-na šu-te*-⸢*šur*⸣ [...]
5′) *ù a-na ud-du-uš ši-pir* É.KUR [...]
6′) GIŠ.GIDRU *i-šìr-tú* GIŠ.ŠIBIR *ke-e-nu x* [...]
7′) AN.ŠÁR ^{d}EN ^{d}MUATI *re-ṣu-us*-⸢*su*⸣ [...]
8′) *mu-šal-lim-mu* ⸢*na-aš*⸣-*par-ti* AN.ŠÁR *u* ^{d}AMAR.[UTU ...]

Lacuna
Obv. 1′–6′) [...] ... [...], the priest, the true vice-regent, who provides for Ez[ida, ...], the capable ruler who comprehends the wisdom of the god Nabû, [...]; (to) who(m) the great gods [...] to dire[ct ..., (...)], (5′) and to restore the work of temple[(s), ...], a just scepter (and) a true staff [*for* ...];
Obv. 7′–14′) (for whom) the gods Aššur, Bel (Marduk), and Nabû [...] h[is] aid; the one who carries out in full the instruction(s) of (the god) Aššur and the

9′) *ka-ṣir ki-din-nu-ti-ku-nu mu-bal-*[...]
10′) ⸢*šá*⸣ *ana* MU ^{d}MUATI DINGIR-*šú x* (*x*) IM-*ku-nu* ⸢*ù*$^{?}$⸣ [...]
11′) ⸢*šá*$^{?}$⸣ A$^{?}$ *x x pa-ni-ku-nu mu-šal-*[...]
12′) (erasures) *mu-ter* ⸢*gi*⸣-[*mil-li* ...]
13′) ⸢*ù*$^{?}$⸣ *a-na* LÚ.*bár-sipa*.MEŠ *x* [...]
14′) [...] ⸢BÁRA$^{?}$.MAḪ⸣ (erasure?) *šu-bat* [...]
Lacuna
Rev.
Reverse completely missing

god Mar[duk ...], the one who (re)-established your privileged status, the one who [...]; (10′) who, at the *name* of the god Nabû, his god, your ... *and* [...; *w*]*ho* ... your *faces*, the one who [...], the one who exacts r[evenge ...] *and* for the people of Borsippa, [..., ...] *the throne-dais*, the seat of [*his* (*Marduk's*) *exalted divinity*, ...]
Lacuna

Reverse completely missing

1028

This small fragment (K 6806) comes from the reverse of a clay tablet and bears an inscription of a Neo-Assyrian king, possibly Esarhaddon or Ashurbanipal. The fragment only contains parts of three lines of text: rev. 1′–2′ comprise the conclusion of the text, while rev. 3′ after the horizontal ruling is the tablet's subscript. Although hardly anything of the original inscription remains, the subscript establishes that it was written on the wild bulls (AM.MEŠ) of Borsippa. Inscriptions of Esarhaddon (Leichty, RINAP 4 p. 117 Esarhaddon 54 [Smlt.] rev. 10b–16a) and Ashurbanipal (Novotny and Jeffers, RINAP 5/1 p. 216 Asb. 10 [Prism T] ii 1–6) describe how these two kings had wild bulls fashioned for Ezida ("True House"), Nabû's temple at Borsippa.

CATALOGUE

Museum Number	Provenance	Dimensions (cm)	cpn
K 6806	Nineveh, Kuyunjik	3.6×4.2	p

BIBLIOGRAPHY

1891 Bezold, Cat. 2 p. 811 (study)
1996 Borger, BIWA p. 335; and LoBl p. 36 (transliteration, study)

TEXT

Obv.
Obverse completely missing
Rev.
Lacuna
1′) [...] TI *x x* (*x*) [...]
2′) [...] *x x li-ni-*DIR$^{?}$/ŠUL$^{?}$ BAD *x* [...]

3′) *ša* UGU AM.MEŠ *ša bár-sipa*.⸢KI⸣ [(...)]

Obverse completely missing

Lacuna
Rev. 1′–2′) [...] ... [...] may he ... [...].

Rev. 3′) That which (is written) upon the wild bulls of Borsippa [(...)].

1029

A fragment from the upper right corner of a clay tablet preserves part of a dedicatory inscription to the god Nergal. Although neither the name of the deity nor that of the Assyrian king who commissioned the inscription are preserved, the text almost certainly belongs to the reign of Ashurbanipal and most likely pertains to his construction work on Nergal's temple Emeslam ("House, Warrior of the Netherworld") at Cutha (see Jeffers and Novotny, RINAP 5/2 pp. 344–357 Asb. 227–230). This interpretation is based on the fact that obv. 1–11 appear to supply the ends of the lines to the opening dedication and mention of the royal name and titles of the so-called "Nergal-Laṣ Inscription" (ibid. pp. 345–346 Asb. 227 obv. 1–11); restorations to those lines are tentatively taken from the latter. However, after the introductory sections, the contents of the historical narrative of these two texts differ, and despite the fact that several phrases appear in both, the account originally contained on the present tablet was most likely its own inscription (compare obv. 12–24 with ibid. p. 346 Asb. 227 obv. 12–25 and p. 350 Asb. 228 obv. 1′–12′). The reverse of the tablet preserves the conclusion of the inscription, which is followed by a horizontal ruling and then blank clay to the top edge of the tablet, but since the fragment comes from the right side of the tablet, it is possible that the scribe had included a subscript that is now completely broken away. The connection between this text and Ashurbanipal's Nergal material was identified by T. Mitto, and the authors would like to thank him for bringing this to their attention.

CATALOGUE

Registration Number	Provenance	Dimensions (cm)	cpn
Bu 91-5-9,204	Nineveh, Kuyunjik	7.3×7.3	p

BIBLIOGRAPHY

1896 Bezold, Cat. 4 p. 1947 (study)

1996 Borger, BIWA p. 352; and LoBl pp. 114-115 (transliteration, study)

TEXT

Obv.

1) [*a-na* ^{d}U.GUR *qar-ra-du gít-ma-lum dan-dan-nu* DINGIR.MEŠ *ma-am-lu a-šá-re-du* EN *ga*$^{?}$*-áš-ru* (...)] *ṣi-*⸢*ra*$^{?}$⸣-[*x* (*x*)]

2) [LUGAL *tam-ḫa-ri be-el a-ba-ri ù dun-ni be-el a-bu-bi šá*]-⸢*kin*⸣ *na-as*$^{?}$-[*pan-ti*$^{?}$]

3) [DUMU ^{d}EN.LÍL *ṣi-i-ru ga-áš-ru* DINGIR.MEŠ ŠEŠ.MEŠ-*šú bu-kúr* ^{d}*ku-tu*]-⸢*šar*⸣ *šar-ra-tum* ⸢GAL$^{?}$⸣-[*tum*$^{?}$]

4) [*ša* Á.II LUGAL *mi*$^{?}$*-gir*$^{?}$*-i-šú il-lak-ú-ma*

Obv. 1–6) [For the god Nergal, perfect warrior, mightiest of the gods, foremost hero, *powerful* lord, (...)] ..., [king of battle, lord of strength and power, lord of the Deluge that brings abo]ut *devas*[*tation*, the exalted son of the god Enlil, powerful one among the gods, his brothers, child of the goddess Kutuša]r (Mullissu), the *gr*[*eat*] queen, [who marches at the side of the king, his *favorite*, and kills his foes, (who) cuts d]own the en[emy, (5) (who) *spares* the ruler who reveres him

i-na-ar-ru ga-re-e-šú ú-šam]-⸢qa⸣-tu$_4$ a-[a-bi]
5) [ina šib-ṭi i-ga$^?$-mì-lu NUN pa-lìḫ-šú i-šar-ra-ku]-⸢uš⸣ da-na-nu ⸢u li⸣-[i]-⸢tu⸣
6) [a-šib é-mes-lam ki-iṣ-ṣu el-lu ša qé-reb GÚ.DU$_8$.A].⸢KI⸣ EN GAL-[e] EN-⸢šu⸣

from plague, (who) grant]s him mighty vic[tor]ie[s], who resides in Emeslam, the holy shrine that is inside Cutha], the great lord, hi[s] lord —

7) [a-na-ku ^{m}aš-šur-DÙ-A$^?$ LUGAL GAL-ú LUGAL dan-nu LUGAL ŠÚ LUGAL KUR] ⸢AN⸣.ŠÁR.KI ⸢LUGAL⸣ [kib]-⸢rat⸣ LÍMMU-⸢tim⸣
8) [DUMU ^{m}AN.ŠÁR-PAP-AŠ$^?$ LUGAL ŠÚ LUGAL KUR AN.ŠÁR.KI DUMU DUMU ^{md}30-PAP.MEŠ-SU$^?$] LUGAL ŠÚ [LUGAL] ⸢KUR⸣ AN.ŠÁR.⸢KI⸣
9) [NUMUN da-ru-ú ša LUGAL-ti a-na ku-un-ni sat-tuk-ki za-na-an eš-re-e-ti] ⸢iḫ⸣-šu-ḫu-in-ni ⸢DINGIR.MEŠ⸣ GAL.⸢MEŠ⸣
10) [AN.ŠÁR ^{d}NIN.LÍL u ^{d}U.GUR DINGIR.MEŠ GAL.MEŠ ú-kin-nu SUḪUŠ GIŠ.GU.ZA LUGAL-ti-ia] ⸢ú⸣-šá-te-ru ⸢EN$^?$-ú$^?$-ti$^?$⸣
11) [a-na tu-ur gi-mil-li LUGAL.MEŠ AD.MEŠ-ia UGU kul-lat na-ki-ri-ia] ú-šar-bu-u GIŠ.[TUKUL].MEŠ-ia

Obv. 7–11) [I, *Ashurbanipal*, great king, strong king, king of the world, king of A]ssyria, kin[g of the four quarte]rs (of the world)]; [son of *Esarhaddon*, king of the world, king of Assyria; grandson of *Sennacherib*], king of the world, [king of] Assyria; [the eternal seed of kingship] — the great g[od]s desired me [to secure the regular offerings (and) to provide for the shrines. (10) The deities Aššur, Mullissu, and Nergal, the great gods, made the foundation(s) of my royal throne firm], (and) they made *my lordship* more surpassing (and) made my [weapon]s greater [than (those of) all my enemies in order to exact revenge for the kings, my fathers]:

12) [...] ⸢zi⸣-kir-šu-nu ⸢la šaḫ⸣-tu
13) [...] x ID x [(x)] x-ma$^?$
14) [...] x e-liš u šap-liš
15) [...] ⸢uk⸣-ki-pa a-⸢dan⸣-nu
16) [... šal-pú-tim LÚ.e-la-me]-⸢e⸣ iq-bu-ú pu-ḫur-šú-un
17) [...] in-nam-ba-a ši-ma-a-⸢ti⸣
18) [... GIŠ.TUKUL] ⸢la⸣ pa-du-ú ú-šat-me-ḫu rit-tu-u-[a]
19) [...] ⸢i⸣-da-at le-mut-ti-[šu]
20) [...] x AD dan-ni šul-pu-ut ⸢URU⸣.[...]
21) [...] x iš-te-niš [...]
22) [...] x qí-bit-sa [...]
23) [...] x KUR [...]
24) [...] x x [...]

Obv. 12–24) [...] they (the Elamites) did n[ot re]vere their (the gods') pronouncement(s), [...] ... *and* [...] above and below. (15) [...] the appropria[te] time [d]rew near, [... *For 1,635 years*, the Elamite destruction] (that) their assembly had declared [...] was decreed as [my] fate, [...] (and) they (the gods) had m[y] hand take up the merciless [weapon. ...] inauspicious omens [about him ... (20) ...] *strong* ... the destruction of the city [...] together [...] her command [...] *land* [...] ... [...]

Lacuna

Lacuna

Rev.

Lacuna

1′) [...] x [x]
2′) [ša ... MU-šu] ⸢i⸣-šaṭ-⸢ṭa⸣-[ru]
3′) [...] x [x x (x)] ú-ḫal-[la-qu]
4′) [... la na]-⸢par$^?$⸣-ka-a ⸢NAM⸣.ÚŠ.⸢MEŠ ina KUR⸣-šú liš-tab-ri liš-gi-⸢šú⸣ [x x]

Lacuna

Rev. 1′) (No translation possible)

Rev. 2′–4′) [(As for) the one who ... (and)] writ[es his name ...], (or) makes (it) disa[ppear ...], may he (the god Nergal) [*cons*]*tantly* establish enduring pestilence in his land (so that) it may slaughter [...].

Subscript completely missing?

Subscript completely missing?

1030

A poorly-preserved late Neo-Assyrian relief, with parts of its thirty-six-line Akkadian inscription still intact, is carved on a rock face at Shakaft-i Gulgul, located in the Zagros Mountains, on the southwestern slopes of the Kabir Kuh in Iran. Although the identity of the ruler who had this round-topped, stele-shaped monument cut into this mountainous ridge is uncertain, it is highly plausible that it was Ashurbanipal or his father Esarhaddon. The proposed attribution is based on the author of the text's claims that (1) the god Aššur had decreed that he would be king while he was still in his mother's womb, (2) the gods Nabû and Marduk had endowed him with intelligence and wisdom, and (3) the great gods had safely installed him on the throne of his father. These themes are well known from many inscriptions dating to the long reign of Ashurbanipal. The passage recording the principal reason(s) for which the monument had been carved is unfortunately almost completely destroyed; sadly, only a few signs are legible in 17b–21. As is usually typical for late Assyrian rock reliefs, the inscription concludes with a short building report recording the creation of the monument, advice to a future ruler to respect the carved image and accompanying inscription, and curses against anyone who alters or destroys the king's record of his deeds.

CATALOGUE

Source	Provenance	Dimensions (cm)	cpn
Grayson and Levine, IrAnt 11 pp. 29–38	Shakaft-i Gulgul	Height: 128 cm; base width: 82 cm	p

COMMENTARY

This rock relief was discovered in the summer of 1972 by L. Vanden Berghe. The monument, which was already in very poor condition at the time of its discovery, depicts a left-facing Assyrian king, whose height extends from the top to the bottom of the shallowly-carved niche, and divine symbols, which are depicted on both sides of the king's head (seven circles [Sebetti], a crescent moon [Sîn], an eight-pointed star [Ištar], a winged disk [Šamaš], and a horned crown [Aššur]). In 2009, a similar monument was found by two mountaineers about eleven kilometers away, approximately two kilometers north of Heydarabad-e Mishkhas, in the Ilam province of Iran, near the source of the Sarab-e Mishkhas River; for details, see Alibaigi, Shanbehzadeh, and Alibaigi, IrAnt 47 (2012) pp. 29–33. Unlike the Shakaft-i Gulgul rock relief, which has an accompanying thirty-six-line Akkadian inscription, the Heydarabad-e Mishkhas monument was uninscribed.

The Shakaft-i Gulgul inscription uses a mixture of Assyrian and Babylonian sign forms, which is typical of late Neo-Assyrian inscriptions written on stone; on this phenomenon, see, for example, Grayson, AfO 20 (1963) pp. 88–89 and nn. 18–19. The Babylonian sign forms are: BU in lines 24, 31, and 35; LI in lines 28, 32, 34, 35, and 36; LU in line 13; LUGAL in lines 2 and 35; RU in lines 14, 23, 27, and 30; ŠEŠ in line 34; TA in lines 22, 23, 24, 28, and 34; TU in lines 3, 14, and 30; Ù in line 1: and UZ in lines 14 and 32. Each line of text is separated by a horizontal ruling and the inscription is written over the image of the king. As A.K. Grayson and L.D. Levine (IrAnt 11 [1975] p. 32) have already noted, the inscription appears to have been carefully prepared and, as far as the text is preserved, only one error is known; in line 31, the conjunction *u* ("and") is erroneously added before the adjective *rabûtu* ("great"; written GAL.MEŠ).

As for the identity of the king who had this monument commissioned, this is not certain because the relevant part of the inscription (especially lines 4–5) is completely destroyed. Grayson and Levine (IrAnt 11 p. 33) have suggested that Sennacherib, Esarhaddon, and, particularly, Ashurbanipal might have been the late Neo-Assyrian ruler in whose name the Shakaft-i Gulgul inscription was written. J.E. Reade (IrAnt 12 [1977] p. 35) has argued that the rock relief could not have been earlier than 688 since the "gesture of holding an object to the nose, instead of extending one finger, is clearly Babylonian in origin ... [and] Sennacherib introduced many Babylonian customs into Assyria, and into the cult of the national god Ashur, especially after his final capture of Babylon in 689 : this gesture must be another of them, signifying perhaps the integration of

Babylonian and Assyrian kingship, or Ashur's appropriation of many of Marduk's attributes." Although he dated the monument to the reign of Ashurbanipal since "[t]he only recorded campaigns, in the appropriate area, are those conducted on Ashurbanipal's behalf during the Elamite wars of 653–646," Reade believed that the rock relief had been executed by an Assyrian field commander, rather than by Ashurbanipal himself, on the basis of the "remarkably plain appearance" of the monument (ibid. pp. 42–43 and 36–37 respectively). R.J. van der Spek (IrAnt 12 [1977] pp. 45–47), however, has put forward the idea that it was more likely Ashurbanipal's father Esarhaddon, rather than Ashurbanipal himself, who had had the Shakaft-i Gulgul monument commissioned, although conceding that "to choose between them is ... very difficult, if not impossible"; he correctly noted that Sargon II and Sennacherib can be excluded as the possible royal author since these two kings generally did not refer to their fathers in their inscriptions (see the comments in the on-page note to line 5). Van der Spek's preference for Esarhaddon was based on (1) the divine sequence of Nabû then Marduk being more commonly attested in the known inscriptions of Esarhaddon (for example, Leichty, RINAP 4 p. 12 Esarhaddon 1 [Nineveh A] i 17) than in those of his son Ashurbanipal, where Nabû is mentioned before Marduk only once in extant inscriptions of that ruler (Jeffers and Novotny, RINAP 5/2 p. 324 Asb. 220 [L^{4}] i 34′); (2) the mention of Esarhaddon undertaking a campaign in Ellipi in contemporary textual sources, especially referring to himself as the *nāsiḫ Ellipi* ("the one who depopulated the land Ellipi") in one of his inscriptions (Leichty, RINAP 4 p. 181 Esarhaddon 97 [Monument B / Tel Barsip Stele] line 20); (3) no positively-identified rock reliefs being known from Ashurbanipal's reign, whereas at least one such monument is attested for Esarhaddon (ibid. pp. 191–193 Esarhaddon 103 [Monument C / Nahr el-Kelb Inscription]); and (4) the god Enlil not being enumerated among the gods who favored the king in Ashurbanipal's inscriptions, while that deity is in Esarhaddon's texts (for example, ibid. p. 104 Esarhaddon 48 [Aššur-Babylon A] line 3). Although van der Spek's Points 1–3 are valid, Point 4, however, is not correct as Ashurbanipal does list Enlil among the gods who favored him in at least one inscription (Jeffers and Novotny, RINAP 5/2 p. 105 Asb. 113 obv. 3); the text written on Rm 2,243 + 81-2-4,251 is probably a draft or archival copy of a text that was engraved on a stele or a rock face. Apart from the fact that under Ashurbanipal there were many opportunities for the creation of the Shakaft-i Gulgul rock relief, especially between 653 and 645, as Grayson and Levine (Iranica Antiqua 11 p. 35), as well as Reade (IrAnt 12 pp. 42–43), have already concluded, there are some pieces of textual evidence in support of Ashurbanipal being the monument's royal creator. In lines 8b–10a — which are very similar to Jeffers and Novotny, RINAP 5/2 p. 323 Asb. 220 (L^{4}) i 5′ — the god Aššur is the deity who determines Ashurbanipal's royal destiny while he is still in the womb. In the extant Esarhaddon corpus, this role is assigned to the goddess Ištar; Leichty, RINAP 4 p. 97 Esarhaddon 43 obv. 12b–14 uses different language to describe the king's pre-birth favor; specifically that text states *išruka ana* [*širikti*], "she gave me (a royal destiny) as [a gift]," rather than *išīm šīmtī*, "he determined (a royal destiny) as my lot." The closest parallel for lines 12–13a — ^{d}30 ^{d}UTU *šá ku-un-ni* ⸢BALA⸣*-ia i-da-at* SIG$_5$ *e-tap-pa-lu a-ḫa-meš* "the gods Sîn and Šamaš discussed with each other favorable omens concerning the stability of my r[eign]" — is Jeffers and Novotny, RINAP 5/2 p. 228 Asb. 186 ("Large Hunting Inscription") line 6: ^{d}30 ^{d}UTU *ina an-ni-šú-nu ke-e-ni* ITI*-šam iš-*⸢*ta*⸣*-nap-pa-ru-u-ni i-da-at dum-qí* "the gods Sîn (and) Šamaš regularly sent me auspicious signs every month through their firm 'yes.'" In lines 13b–15a, the inscription's royal author states that "the gods Nabû (and) Marduk granted me a broad mind (and) extensive knowledge as a gift" (^{d}AG ^{d}AMAR.UTU *uz-nu ra-*[*pa-áš*]*-tu ḫa-si-*⸢*su*⸣ *pal-ku-u iš-ru-ku ši-rik-ti*). In at least two inscriptions of Ashurbanipal, Marduk is credited with bestowing these gifts on his earthly representative; see Novotny and Jeffers, RINAP 5/1 p. 281 Asb. 15 i 2′–3′ and Jeffers and Novotny, RINAP 5/2 p. 323 Asb.l 220 (L^{4}) i 10′. Although *uznu rapaštu hasīsu palkû*, "broad mind (and) extensive knowledge," is known from texts of Esarhaddon (Leichty, RINAP 4 p. 107 Esarhaddon 48 [Aššur-Babylon A] line 62b and p. 205 Esarhaddon 105 [Babylon C] iii 29–30), it is the god Ea, in his manifestation as Nudimmud, not Nabû and/or Marduk, who grants these gifts to Esarhaddon. At present, the content and language of lines 8b–17a have more in common with Ashurbanipal's inscriptions than they do with those of Esarhaddon. As van der Spek (IrAnt 12 p. 45) has already noted, given the complete absence of a royal name in the text itself, it is "very difficult, if not impossible," to know for certain if Ashurbanipal or Esarhaddon was the late Neo-Assyrian king who had had the Shakaft-i Gulgul monument commissioned.

BIBLIOGRAPHY

1973 Vanden Berghe, Iran 11 p. 209 and pls. 13–14a (photo, study)
1975 Grayson and Levine, IrAnt 11 pp. 29–38 (photo, edition, study)
1977 Reade, IrAnt 12 pp. 33–44 and pl. 1 (photo, study)
1977 van der Spek, IrAnt 12 pp. 45–47 (study)
1982 Börker-Klähn, Bildstelen p. 215 no. 223 (study)
2002 Kreppner, AoF 29 p. 370 (study)
2006 Mayaheri, Payam-e Bastan Shenas 3 pp. 63–74 (study)
2012 Alibaigi, Shanbehzadeh, and Alibaigi, IrAnt 47 pp. 29–32 (study)
2014 Grayson and Novotny, RINAP 3/2 p. 3 (study)
2017 Malekzadeh and Khosroshahi, Pazhohesh-ha-ye Bastanshenasi Iran 7 pp. 89, 94 and 96 (photo, study)

TEXT

1) ^{d}*aš-šur ù* DINGIR.[MEŠ] ⸢GAL⸣.MEŠ
2) ⸢*ša*⸣ *i-di* LUGAL *mi-[ig]-ri-šú-un [i]-*⸢*za*⸣*-zu-ma*
3) *[ú]-šam-*⸢*qa*$^{?}$⸣*-tu [(kul-lat*$^{?}$*) na]-ki-ri-*⸢*šú*⸣
4) [...] ⸢MAN$^{?}$⸣ ŠÚ$^{?}$ [...] *x x* [...] *x* [*x x*]
5) ⸢DUMU$^{?}$⸣ [...]
6) *x* [...]
7) [...]*-nu*
8) [...] *x* [...] ^{d}[*aš-šur*$^{?}$ AD$^{?}$] ⸢DINGIR$^{?}$⸣.MEŠ
9) *x x x* [*ina*$^{?}$] ⸢*lìb*$^{?}$*-bi*$^{?}$⸣ [AMA-*ia*$^{?}$ *ši-mat*$^{?}$ LUGAL$^{?}$]*-ti*
10) *i-šim šim-ti* [...] ^{d}EN.LÍL
11) *a-na* EN-*ut* KUR *u* UN.MEŠ [*iz-kur*$^{?}$] *ni-bit-ti*
12) ^{d}30 ^{d}UTU *šá ku-un-ni* ⸢BALA⸣*-ia i-da-at* SIG$_{5}$

1–3) The god Aššur and the [grea]t gods [w]ho [sta]nd at the side of the king, their fav[or]ite, and [who] *cut down* [(*all of*)] his [en]emies:

4–8a) [...], *king of the world*, [...], ... [...], (5) *son of* [..., ...]:

8b–17a) *The god* [*Aššur, the father of the go*]*ds*, ... determined [*a roya*]*l destiny* as my lot [(*while I was*) *in my mother's wo*]*m*[*b* (*and*) ...]; the god Enlil [*nominated*] me for ruling over the land and people; the gods Sîn and Šamaš discussed with each other favorable omens

1–3 ^{d}*aš-šur ù* DINGIR.[MEŠ] ⸢GAL⸣.MEŠ ⸢*ša*⸣ *i-di* LUGAL *mi-[ig]-ri-šú-un [i]-*⸢*za*⸣*-zu-ma [ú]-šam-*⸢*qa*$^{?}$⸣*-tu [(kul-lat*$^{?}$*) na]-ki-ri-*⸢*šú*⸣ "The god Aššur and the [grea]t gods [w]ho [sta]nd at the side of the king, their fav[or]ite, and [who] *cut down* [(*all of*)] his [en]emies": Compare Grayson and Novotny, RINAP 3/2 p. 308 Sennacherib 222 (Judi Dagh Inscription) lines 1–5: ^{d}*aš-šur* ^{d}30 ^{d}UTU ^{d}IŠKUR ^{d}MAŠ *ù* ^{d}INANNA DINGIR.MEŠ GAL.MEŠ *ša i-di* LUGAL *mì-ig-ri-šú-un i-za-zu-ma* UGU *kul-lat na-ki-ri ú-šam-ra-ru* GIŠ.TUKUL.MEŠ*-šú* "The deities Aššur, Sîn, Šamaš, Adad, Ninurta, and Ištar, the great gods who stand at the side of the king, their favorite, and make his weapons prevail over all enemies." [(*kul-lat*$^{?}$) *na*]*-ki-ri-*⸢*šú*⸣ "[(*all of*)] his [en]emies": Compare Grayson and Levine, IrAnt 11 (1975) p. 36–37, where this passage is read as [KUR *na*]*-ki-ri-*⸢*šú*⸣ "[*the land of*] his [en]emies." *māt nakirī* is not commonly attested in late Neo-Assyrian inscriptions, whereas *kullat nakirī* is. Moreover, one does not expect the verb *maqātu* ("to fall"; Š stem "to cut down") with the phrase *māt nakirīšu*.

4 Based on the position of the title ⸢MAN$^{?}$⸣ ŠÚ$^{?}$, "*king of the world*" within the frame of the stele-shaped monument, that title appears to have immediately followed the name of the king in whose name the text was written. This sequence is not presently attested in the known and published Neo-Assyrian rock relief inscriptions. Compare Frame, RINAP 2 p. 440 Sargon II 116 (Tang-i Var Inscription) line 11a: ^{m}MAN-GIN MAN GAL MAN *dan-nu* MAN ŠÚ "Sargon (II), great king, strong king, king of the world"; and Grayson and Novotny, RINAP 3/2 p. 308 Sennacherib 222 (Judi Dagh Inscription) lines 6–7a and p. 313 Sennacherib 223 (Bavian Inscription) line 3a ^{md}30-PAP.MEŠ-SU MAN / LUGAL GAL MAN / LUGAL *dan-nu* MAN / LUGAL ŠÚ "Sennacherib, great king, strong king, king of the world." Note that the title *šar kiššati* is not used in Tadmor and Yamada, RINAP 1 p. 91 Tiglath-pileser III 37 (Mila Mergi Inscription) line 12 and Leichty, RINAP 4 p. 192 Esarhaddon 103 (Monument C / Nahr el-Kalb Inscription) lines 4–6a.

5 ⸢DUMU$^{?}$⸣ "*son of*": If the reading of the sign is correct, and it is not RA$^{?}$ (as alternatively suggested by Grayson and Levine, IrAnt 11 [1975] p. 36 in addition to DUMU), then the most likely candidates for royal author of the Shakaft-i Gulgul rock relief inscription is Esarhaddon or Ashurbanipal since both of these kings generally refer to their fathers and grandfathers in their inscriptions. In the extant late Neo-Assyrian text corpus, Tiglath-pileser III, Sargon II, and Sennacherib very rarely mention their fathers. For the handful of instances where they do, see Tadmor and Yamada, RINAP 1 p. 148 Tiglath-pileser III 58 line 2; Frame, RINAP 2 p. 308 Sargon II 66 line 1; and Grayson and Novotny, RINAP 3/2 p. 170 Sennacherib 135 obv. 2 (name restored) and p. 232 Senacherib 163 obv. 5′.

8b–10a ^{d}[*aš-šur*$^{?}$ AD$^{?}$] ⸢DINGIR$^{?}$⸣.MEŠ *x x x* [*ina*$^{?}$] ⸢*lìb*$^{?}$*-bi*$^{?}$⸣ [AMA-*ia*$^{?}$ *ši-mat*$^{?}$ LUGAL$^{?}$]*-ti i-šim šim-ti* "*The god* [*Aššur, the father of the go*]*ds*, ... determined [*a roya*]*l* destiny as my lot [(*while I was*) *in my mother's wo*]*m*[*b*]": The proposed restorations are based on Jeffers and Novotny, RINAP 5/2 p. 323 Asb. 220 (L^{4}) i 5′ [AN.ŠÁR] AD DINGIR.MEŠ *ina lìb-bi* AMA-*ia ši-mat* LUGAL-⸢*u-ti*⸣ [*i-šim*$^{?}$ *šim-ti*$^{?}$] "[(The god) Aššur], the father of the gods, [*determined*] a roya[l] destiny [*as my lot*] (while I was) in my mother's womb." The motif of the gods determining the king's destiny or shaping him for kingship is known from the inscriptions of Sennacherib, Esarhaddon, and Ashurbanipal, but only one inscription of Ashurbanipal records that the god Aššur performed this task (see the commentary of this text); the goddess Bēlet-ilī is credited with creating Sennacherib's kingly features while in the womb, and the goddess Ištar is said to have determined Esarhaddon's royal lot before his birth. See Grayson and Novotny, RINAP 3/2 p. 57 Sennacherib 43 lines 3–4a; and Leichty, RINAP 4 p. 97 Esarhaddon 43 obv. 12b–14. Thus, if the restorations of these lines are correct, then Ashurbanipal might have been the king in whose name this inscription was written, especially since the language is a near parallel to Jeffers and Novotny, RINAP 5/2 p. 323 Asb. 220 (L^{4}) i 5′.

10b–11 ^{d}EN.LÍL *a-na* EN-*ut* KUR *u* UN.MEŠ [*iz-kur*$^{?}$] *ni-bit-ti* "the god Enlil [*nominated*] me for ruling over the land and people": Compare Jeffers and Novotny, RINAP 5/2 p. 323 Asb. 220 (L^{4}) i 6′ [^{d}]⸢NIN⸣.LÍL AMA GAL*-tu a-na be-lut* KALAM *u* UN.MEŠ *taz-*⸢*ku-ra*⸣ [*šu-mì*$^{?}$] "[the goddess Mul]lissu, the great mother, nominate[d *me*] for ruling over the land and people." Based on this parallel, the verb *zakāru* ("to name") is restored instead of *nabû* ("to name"; see Grayson and Levine, IrAnt 11 [1975] p. 36). Note that the orthography of *nibītu* ("name") as *ni-bit-ti* is at present not otherwise attested in extant late Neo-Assyrian inscriptions.

12–13a ^{d}30 ^{d}UTU *šá ku-un-ni* ⸢BALA⸣*-ia i-da-at* SIG$_{5}$ *e-tap-pa-lu a-ḫa-meš* "the gods Sîn and Šamaš discussed with each other favorable omens concerning the stability of my r[eign]": *idāt dumqi* "favorable omens" is presently attested only in the inscriptions of Esarhaddon and

13) *e-tap-pa-lu a-ḫa-meš* ^{d}AG ^{d}AMAR.UTU
14) *uz-nu ra-[pa-áš]-tu ḫa-si-*⸢*su*⸣ *pal-ku-u iš-ru-ku*
15) *ši-rik-ti* ⸢DINGIR⸣.MEŠ GAL.MEŠ *ina* UKKIN-*šú-nu*
16) *ṭa-biš ú-še-ši-[bu-in-ni ina* GIŠ].GU.ZA AD-*ia* EN-*ut* KUR

concerning the stability of my r[eign]; (and) the gods Nabû (and) Marduk granted me a broad mind (and) extensive knowledge as a gift. The great gods in their assembly gladly made [me] si[t on the] throne of my father (and) they entrust[ed m]e with dominion over the land [and] (its) people.

17) [*u*] ⸢UN⸣.MEŠ *ú-ma-al-[lu-u ana* ŠU.II-*u]-a* URU.*x*-[...]-*x*-⸢*da*$^{?}$⸣
18) [...] *x* GI/ZI-*šú x x* [...] *x* [...]
19) [...] *x* [...]
20) [...]
21) [...]-*ú-ṣu*

17b–21) (As for) the city [...]*da* [...] ... [...].

22) [...]-*x-ia* [*ab*$^{?}$]-*ta-ni*
23) ⸢*ṣe*$^{?}$⸣-*ru-uš-šú ta-*[*nit-ti*$^{?}$ (...)] *ep-še*$_{20}$-*tú*
24) *e-pu-šú* UGU-*šú* [*ú-šá-áš-ṭir-ma*] ⸢*a*⸣-*na ta-mar-ti*
25) LUGAL.MEŠ DUMU.MEŠ-[*ia* (...) *ana ár*]-*kàt* *u*$_4$-*me e-zib*

22–25) [(I ... and) I *f*]*ashioned* [...], my [..., up]on it. [I had] the *pr*[*aise of*] the deeds that I had performed [written] on it [and] I left (it) [for the fu]ture, for the admiration of the kings, [my] descendants.

26) NUN EGIR-*ú ina* [LUGAL.MEŠ DUMU.MEŠ]-*ia ša* ^{d}*aš-šur u* DINGIR.MEŠ
27) GAL.MEŠ *a-na* EN-[*ut* KUR *u*] UN.⸢MEŠ⸣ *i-zak-ka-ru* MU-*šú*
28) NA$_4$.NA.RÚ.A *ta-*[*nit*]-⸢*ti*⸣ DINGIR.⸢MEŠ⸣ GAL.MEŠ *li-mur-ma*
29) Ì.GIŠ *lip-šú-uš* [UDU].⸢SISKUR⸣ *liq-*⸢*qí*⸣ *šá* *ṣa-al-mu šú-a-tú*
30) *ul-tu áš-ri-*[*šú*] *ú-nak-ka-ru* ^{d}*aš-šur u* DINGIR.MEŠ
31) <<*u*>> GAL.MEŠ *ma-la* [*i-na*] NA$_4$.NA.RÚ.[A] *an-né-e šu-mu na-bu*
32) *ez-zi-iš li-*[*ik-kil*]-⸢*mu-šú*⸣-[(*ma*) *ina mit*]-*ḫu-uṣ* GIŠ.TUKUL.MEŠ
33) *qé-reb* MURUB$_4$ ⸢EDIN$^{?}$⸣ [*i-da-šú a*]-*a i-zi-zu-ma*

26–29a) May a future ruler, one of [the kings], my [descendants], whose name the god Aššur and the great gods call for rul[ing over the land and] peop[le], find (this) monument (and) the pr[aise] of the great gods; and (then) anoint (it) with oil (and) make an offering.

29b–36) (As for) the one who changes this image from its position, may the god Aššur and the great gods, as many as are named [on] this monume[nt], gl[ar]e at him angrily [(and) n]ot stand [by his side in a cl]ash of weapons in the midst of a *pitc*[*hed*] battle. May they lead him [*in bondag*]*e* under [*his*] *enemy*. (35) May they overthrow [his] roy[al] dynasty and [m]ake his name (and) seed [di]sappear from the land.

Ashurbanipal. The closest parallel, with both the moon-god Sîn and the sun-god Šamaš sending good omens, is Jeffers and Novotny, RINAP 5/2 p. 228 Asb. 186 ("Large Hunting Inscription") line 6: ^{d}30 ^{d}UTU *ina an-ni-šú-nu ke-e-ni* ITI-*šam iš-*⸢*ta*⸣*-nap-pa-ru-u-ni i-da-at dum-qí* "the gods Sîn (and) Šamaš regularly sent me auspicious signs every month through their firm 'yes.'"

13b–15a ^{d}AG ^{d}AMAR.UTU *uz-nu ra-[pa-áš]-tu ḫa-si-*⸢*su*⸣ *pal-ku-u iš-ru-ku ši-rik-ti* "the gods Nabû (and) Marduk granted me a broad mind (and) extensive knowledge as a gift": Compare Novotny and Jeffers, RINAP 5/1 p. 281 Asb. 15 i 2′–3′ and Jeffers and Novotny, RINAP 5/2 p. 323 Asb. 220 (L[4]) i 10′; ^{d}AMAR.UTU ABGAL DINGIR.MEŠ *uz-nu ra-pa-áš-tu ḫa-si-su pal-ku-u iš-ru-ka ši-rik-te* "the god Marduk, the sage of the gods, granted me a broad mind (and) extensive knowledge as a gift" (conflated transliteration and translation). The phrase *uznu rapaštu hasīsu palkû*, "broad mind (and) extensive knowledge," is also attested in inscriptions of Sargon II and Esarhaddon; see, for example, Frame, RINAP 2 p. 190 Sargon II 17 lines 6b–7a; and Leichty, RINAP 4 p. 107 Esarhaddon 48 (Aššur-Babylon A) lines 62b and p. 205 Esarhaddon 105 (Babylon C) iii 29b–30. Note that Ea, in his manifestations of Ninšiku and Nudimmud, grants wisdom and intelligence to Sargon II and Esarhaddon, while Marduk grants these gifts to Ashurbanipal.

15b–16a ⸢DINGIR⸣.MEŠ GAL.MEŠ *ina* UKKIN-*šú-nu ṭa-biš ú-še-ši-[bu-in-ni ina* GIŠ].GU.ZA AD-*ia* "The great gods in their assembly gladly made [me] si[t on the] throne of my father": The theme of the gods peacefully placing the king on the throne of his father is presently attested only for Esarhaddon, Ashurbanipal, and Sîn-šarra-iškun. See, for example, Leichty, RINAP 4 p. 15 Esarhaddon 1 (Nineveh A) ii 45b–47a; Novotny and Jeffers, RINAP 5/1 p. 232 Asb. 11 (Prism A) i 41–44; Jeffers and Novotny, RINAP 5/2 p. 325 Asb. 220 (L[4]) ii 10′–11′; and, in the present volume, Ssi 10 (Cylinder A) lines 16b–19.

22–23a [...]-*x-ia* [*ab*$^{?}$]-*ta-ni* ⸢*ṣe*$^{?}$⸣-*ru-uš-šú* "[(I ... and) I *f*]*ashioned* [...], my [..., up]on it": Compare Grayson and Novotny, RINAP 3/2 p. 317 Sennacherib 223 (Bavian Inscription) line 55a: 6 NA$_4$.NA.RÚ-[*e* DÙ$^{?}$]-⸢*uš*$^{?}$⸣ *ṣa-lam* DINGIR.MEŠ GAL.MEŠ EN.MEŠ-*ia ab-ta-ni qé-reb-šú-un* "[I ma]de six stele[s] (and) I *fashioned* image(s) of the great gods, my lords, upon them." Perhaps this passage in the Shakaft-i Gulgul inscription could be tentatively restored as follows: [NA$_4$.NA.RÚ.A$^{?}$ DÙ-*uš*$^{?}$ *ṣa-lam*$^{?}$ DINGIR.MEŠ$^{?}$ GAL.MEŠ$^{?}$ EN].⸢MEŠ⸣-*ia ab-ta-ni* ⸢*ṣe*$^{?}$⸣-*ru-uš-šú* "[*I made a stele (and) I f*]*ashioned image(s) of the great gods*, my [*lord*]s [up]on it." Alternatively, one could read [*ṣa-lam*$^{?}$ LUGAL$^{?}$]-⸢*ti*$^{?}$⸣-*ia*, "[*an image of*] my [*royal majest*]*y*." Compare, for example, Tadmor and Yamada, RINAP 1 p. 92 Tiglath-pileser III 37 (Mila Mergi Inscription) line 46a: *ṣa-*⸢*lam*⸣ MAN-*ti-ia ina qer-bi-šá ab-ni-ma* "I had an image of my royal majesty fashioned on it."

24b–25 ⸢*a*⸣-*na ta-mar-ti* LUGAL.MEŠ DUMU.MEŠ-[*ia* (...) *ana ár*]-*kàt u*$_4$-*me e-zib* "I left (it) [for the fu]ture, for the admiration of the kings, [my] descendants": Compare Grayson and Novotny, RINAP 3/2 p. 317 Sennacherib 223 (Bavian Inscription) line 57a: *a-na* LUGAL.MEŠ-*ni* DUMU.MEŠ-*ia e-zib ṣa-ti-iš ma-ti-ma* "I left (them) for ever after for the kings, my descendants."

34) *ina* KI.TA LÚ?.KÚR?-[*šú*? *ka-mì*]-⸢*iš*?⸣ *li-ir-du-šú*
35) *pa-le-e* LUGAL-[*ti-šú lis-ki*]-*pu-ma* MU-*šú*
36) NUMUN-*šú ina* KUR [*lu*]-*ḫal-li-qu*

34 *ina* KI.TA LÚ?.KÚR?-[*šú*? *ka-mì*]-⸢*iš*?⸣ *li-ir-du-šú* "may they lead him [*in bondag*]*e* under [*his*] *enemy*": For the reading tentatively proposed here, compare, for example, Frame, RINAP 2 p. 171 Sargon II 9 (Bull Colossi Inscription) line 106: *i-na* KI.TA LÚ.KÚR-*šú li-še-ši-bu-uš ka-meš* "may they make him live in bondage under his enemy"; Leichty, RINAP 4 p. 186 Esarhaddon 98 (Monument A / Zinçirli stele) rev. 5b6: *ina* KI.TA LÚ.KÚR-*šú lu-še-šib-šú ka-meš*; and, in this volume, Ssi 6 (Cylinder C) rev. 11′b *ina* KI.⸢TA⸣ LÚ.KÚR-*šú li-*⸢*še-ši*⸣-*bu-uš ka-mì-iš*.

2001–2002

Numerous inscriptions of members of Ashurbanipal's family are known, including two texts ascribed to his wife/wives. The first (Asb. 2001), which is written in the name of Libbāli-šarrat, is engraved on a round-topped stele that was discovered in the so-called "row of steles," in the religious capital Aššur. The second (Asb. 2002), which might also be attributed to Libbāli-šarrat, is known from an archival copy inscribed on a single-column clay tablet. The inscriptions of his sons and successors Aššur-etel-ilāni and Sîn-šarra-iškun are edited in the present volume (see pp. 156–166 and 168–208), while those of his older brother, Šamaš-šuma-ukīn, who was king of Babylon from 667–648, are not. For editions of Šamaš-šuma-ukīn's inscriptions, see Frame, RIMB 2 pp. 248–259 B.6.33.1–2001.

Figure 11. VA 8847 (Ass 15756 + Ass 15758; Asb. 2001), fragments of the upper portion of a stele of Ashurbanipal's wife Libbāli-šarrat that were discovered in the "row of steles" at Aššur. © Staatliche Museen zu Berlin – Vorderasiatisches Museum. Photo: Olaf M. Teßmer.

2001

The reverse of a fragmentarily-preserved, round-topped stele from Aššur is engraved with a five-line Akkadian inscription of Ashurbanipal's wife Libbāli-šarrat. The face of monument, which was found in the "row of steles" ("Stelenreihe"), depicts this Assyrian queen with a mural crown.

CATALOGUE

Museum Number	Excavation Number	Photograph Number	Provenance	Dimensions (cm)	cpn
VA 8847	Ass 15756 + Ass 15758	Ass ph 4569, 4951	Aššur, hC11I	56×55	c

COMMENTARY

The inscription, as one expects from a stone stele discovered at Aššur, is written in Neo-Assyrian script. Each line of text is separated by a horizontal ruling.

The inscription was collated by J. Novotny from the original in January 2019.

BIBLIOGRAPHY

1913 Andrae, Stelenreihen pp. 6–8 and pl. 10 no. 1 (photo, copy, study)
1915 Meissner, Grundzüge p. 140 fig. 233 (drawing [image of the queen])
1915 Meissner, OLZ 18 cols. 37–38 (study)
1916 Streck, Asb. pp. CCXVI–CCXXII and 390–391 no. 1 (edition)
1920 Meissner, BuA 1 p. 76 and p. 77 fig. 16 (drawing [image of the queen], study)
1929 Weissbach, RLA 1/3 p. 225 and pl. 36a (photo [image of the queen], study)
1938 Andrae, WEA p. 83 with fig. 59, and pp. 146 and 151 (drawing [image of the queen], study)
1941 Bittel et al., Yazılıkaya p. 117 with fig. 48 (drawing [image of the queen], study)
1982 Börker-Klähn, Bildstelen p. 217 no. 227 (drawing, study)
1987 Vorderasiatisches Museum p. 152 fig. 184 and p. 154 (photo [image of the queen], study)
1997 Pedersén, Katalog p. 58 (study)
2002 Ornan, CRRA 47 p. 461 and p. 462 fig. 2 (drawing, study)
2012 Macgregor, SAAS 21 pp. 88–89, 90–91, 94, and 125 (translation, drawing, study)
2012 Svärd, Power and Women pp. 68–69, 116, and 268 no. 123 (edition, study)
2015 Svärd, SAAS 23 pp. 49, 75–77 (with fig. 1), and 210 no. 126 (edition, photo, study)
2018 Brereton, I am Ashurbanipal pp. 16–17 and fig. 9* (photo [inscription not visible], study)

TEXT

1) ⸢*ṣa-lam*⸣
2) [^{f}]URU.⸢ŠÀ⸣.URU-⸢*šar*⸣-[*rat*]
3) ⸢MUNUS⸣.É.[GAL]
4) *šá* ^{m}AN.ŠÁR-DÙ-[A]
5) MAN ŠÚ ⸢MAN⸣ KUR *aš*-[*šur*]

1–5) [I]mage of Libbāli-šar[rat], que[en] of Ashurbani[pal], king of the world, ki[ng] of As[syria].

2002

The obverse of a horizontal clay tablet (an *u'iltu*-tablet) has a draft or archival copy of an inscription of Ashurbanipal's wife (possibly Libbāli-šarrat) written on it. This short, eight-line Akkadian text records that a woman close to Ashurbanipal, almost certainly his wife based on the occurrence of *narāmiša* ("her beloved") in line 4 and *hā'eriša* ("her husband") in line 7, dedicated a reddish-gold-plated object to a goddess (possibly Tašmētu, the consort of the god Nabû). Because Libbāli-šarrat is the only known-by-name wife of Ashurbanipal, this dedicatory inscription might have been written in her name, although this cannot be proven.

CATALOGUE

Registration Number	Provenance	Dimensions (cm)	cpn
83-1-18,332	Nineveh, Kuyunjik or Kalḫu	3.3×5.6	p

COMMENTARY

For details about *u'iltu*-tablets, horizontal tablets with a 1:2 ratio, see, for example, Radner, Nineveh 612 BC pp. 72–73 (with fig. 8); Grayson and Novotny, RINAP 3/2 pp. 5–6; and Weiershäuser and Novotny, RINBE 2 p. 81. The script is Neo-Assyrian. Based on the concluding formula of the text, especially line 7, K. Deller has suggested that the tablet originated from Kalḫu, rather than Nineveh. See Deller, OrAnt 22 (1983) pp. 23–24 for details.

With regard to the identity of the royal lady in whose name the inscription is written, M. Streck (Asb. pp. CCXXVI–CCXXIX) wrongly suggested that it was Ešarra-ḫammat, Esarhaddon's queen who is presumed to have been Ashurbanipal's birth-mother. Because the inscription refers explicitly to the royal lady's husband in line 7 (*hā'eriša*, "her husband"), Streck's proposal cannot be correct, as Deller (OrAnt 22 [1983] p. 23) and E. Weissert (PNA 1/1 p. 161 sub Aššur-bāni-apli I.1.-b.-2′.-b′) have already pointed out. Since the only known-by-name wife of Ashurbanipal is Libbāli-šarrat, Deller tentatively proposed restoring the beginning of line 2 as [^{f}URU.ŠÀ.URU-*šar-rat* MUNUS.KUR *ša* ^{m}*aš-šur*-D]Ù-A "[Libbāli-šarrat, queen of Ashurba]nipal." Although this restoration is very likely correct, it cannot be proven with absolute certainty. Therefore, it is best to leave the name of Ashurbanipal's queen at the beginning of line 2 unrestored, as it might have been a hitherto unknown wife of that king who commissioned this text and inscribed object.

BIBLIOGRAPHY

1896	Bezold, Cat. 4 p. 1881 (study)
1898	Johns, ADD 1 p. 498 no. 644 (copy)
1903	Meissner, MVAG 8/3 pp. 16–17 (transliteration)
1905–6	Fossey, ZA 19 pp. 181–183 and pl. III (copy, edition)
1913	Ungnad, ARU no. 17 (edition)
1916	Streck, Asb. pp. CCXXVI–CCXXIX and 392–395 no. 3 (edition, study)
1969	Postgate, Royal Grants p. 123 (lines 4–5, collations)
1983	Deller, OrAnt 22 p. 22–24 (edition)
1998	Weissert, PNA 1/1 p. 161 sub Aššur-bāni-apli I.1.b.2′.b′ (lines 2, 7, translation; study)
1999	Melville, SAAS 9 p. 72 (line 4–6, edition, study)
2012	Macgregor, SAAS 21 p. 88 (line 4–6, translation, study)
2012	Svärd, Power and Women pp. 69, 116, and 268–269 no. 124 (translation, study)
2015	Svärd, SAAS 23 pp. 55, 61, 81–82 and 210–211 no. 127 (translation, study)

TEXT

Obv.

1) [*a-na* ^{d}... (...) GAŠAN] ⸢GAL⸣-*tum* GAŠAN-*šá*
2) [^{f}... MUNUS.É.GAL *šá* ^{m}*aš-šur*]-⸢DÙ⸣-A MAN ŠÚ MAN KUR AŠ
3) [*tu-še-piš-ma x x*] *x* KÙ.GI *ruš-ši-i*
4) [*a-na* TI.LA *šá*] ^{m}*aš-šur*-DÙ-A *na*-⸢*ram*⸣-*i-šá*
5) [GÍD.DA UD.MEŠ-*šú la*]-*bar* GIŠ.GU.ZA-*šú u*

1) [For the goddess ..., (...) the grea]t [lady], her lady:
2–3) [..., the queen of Ashurba]nipal, king of the world, king of Assyria, [had a ... made of] reddish gold.

4–8) She set up and presented (this object) [for the life of] Ashurbanipal — her beloved — [to prolong his

1 On the reading of the line, see Deller, OrAnt 22 (1983) p. 23: "Die bisher allgemein angenommene Ergänzung [*a-na* d.*Taš-m*]*e-*tu_4 GAŠAN*-*šá* ist nach der Kollation I. L. Finkels in hohem Grade unwahrscheinlich, da vor dem vermeintlichen M]E-tu_4 Raum verfügbar ist für wenigstens sieben Zeichen durchschnittlicher Länge. Die obige Ergänzung folgt einem Vorschlag I. L. Finkels; es darf jedoch als so gut wie sicher angenommen werden, dass ^{f}GN = Tašmētu ist, wie unten zu Z. 7 nachzuweisen sein wird."
2 ^{f}...: K. Deller (OrAnt 22 [1983] p. 23) tentatively restored the royal name at the beginning of line 2 as ^{f}URU.ŠÀ.URU-*šar-rat* "Libbāli-šarrat." See the commentary for further information. MUNUS.É.GAL "queen": The restoration is based on Asb. 2001 line 3. As Deller has suggested (ibid.), one could restore MUNUS.KUR instead of the more commonly-attested MUNUS.É.GAL; compare Leichty, RINAP 4 p. 314 Esarhaddon 2001 line 2.
3 *tu-še-piš-ma* "she had ... made": The reconstruction of this verb is taken from similar dedicatory texts (see Leichty, RINAP 4 pp. 319-320 Esarhaddon 2005 obv. 4 and Esarhaddon 2006 rev. 4).

šá-a-⸢*šá*⸣

6) *a-na* TI.⸢LA⸣-*šá* GÍD.DA UD.⸢MEŠ⸣-*šá kun-nu* BALA-*e-šá*

7) UGU LUGAL *ḫa-ʾe-e-ri-šá at-mu-šá* ⸢*šu*⸣-*ṭu-bi-ma*

8) ⸢*it*⸣-*ti a-ḫa-meš lu-ub-bu-*⸢*ri* GÁ⸣-*ma* BA-*iš*

Rev.

Blank

days (and) to length]en (his time on) his throne, and, for her very own life, to lengthen her days, (and) to firmly establish her reign, (so that) you (the goddess to whom this object is dedicated) make her (the queen's) speech pleasing to the king, her husband, and allow (them both) grow old with each other.

Blank

2003–2018

For at least part of the reigns of Ashurbanipal in Assyria and Šamaš-šuma-ukīn in Babylonia, Sîn-balāssu-iqbi, son of Ningal-iddin, was governor of the southern Babylonian city of Ur. He has left several Sumerian and Akkadian inscriptions that record the restoration or construction of various structures there. While none of these mention the king of Babylon, Šamaš-šuma-ukīn, three specifically refer to Ashurbanipal, the king of Assyria (Asb. 2006 and 2008–2009). Thus, the inscriptions of this important governor have been edited with those of Ashurbanipal instead of Šamaš-šuma-ukīn (Frame, RIMB 2 pp. 248–259 B.6.33.1–2001). Sîn-balāssu-iqbi was preceded in office by his father Ningal-iddin, who held that position in the reign of Esarhaddon, Ashurbanipal's father, and, quite likely, already in the time of Sennacherib, his grandfather. Two Babylonian economic texts composed in 658 and 657 refer to Sîn-balāssu-iqbi as governor, but he may have already taken office in the reign of Esarhaddon (680–669). He was succeeded by two of his brothers, Sîn-šarra-uṣur (see Frame, RIMB 2 pp. 258–259 B.6.33.2001) and Sîn-tabni-uṣur, the latter of whom is known to have held the governorship of Ur in at least 650 and 649. For details, see Frame, Babylonia pp. 278–279; and Baker, PNA 3/2 pp, 1129–1130 sub Sīn-balāssu-iqbi no. 3. With regard to Sîn-balāssu-iqbi's building activities at Ur, see Hätinen, dubsar 20 pp. 337–359.

2003

This Sumerian inscription of Sîn-balāssu-iqbi, which is dedicated to the moon-god Nanna (Sîn), the tutelary deity of the city of Ur, is written on a stone door socket excavated at Ur. The text records that governor's renovation of Etemennigurru ("House, Foundation Clad in Awe-Inspiring Radiance"), in particular, the construction of a new door.

CATALOGUE

Museum Number	Excavation/ Registration No.	Provenance	Dimensions (cm)	cpn
BM 119065	1927-10-3,60; U 2674	Ur, Edublalmaḫ, in situ in a brick-lined cavity against the jamb of the southwestern doorway of the outer sanctuary chamber	Height: 8″; base dia.: 12″×10″	p

COMMENTARY

The door socket was found in 1924–25, during C.L. Woolley's excavations at Ur. The piece was assigned the excavation number U 2674 and it is shown on British Museum negative U 342. The door socket was made from (the upper) half of a kudurru. The inscription is written in archaizing Babylonian script. The text is inscribed in two columns: col i = lines 1–19 and col. ii = 20–38.

BIBLIOGRAPHY

1925 Woolley, AJ 5 pp. 384–385 and pl. XLI no. 1 (provenance, photo, translation)
1925 MJ 16 p. 294 (photo)
1928 Gadd, UET 1 no. 169 (photo, copy, edition)
1929 Langdon, JRAS p. 371 (study)
1962 Woolley, UE 9 p. 14 (provenance, partial translation)
1965 Woolley, UE 8 pp. 11, 15–16, 21, and 101 (provenance, partial translation, study)
1982 Woolley and Moorey, Ur p. 224 (partial translation)
1995 Frame, RIMB 2 pp. 230–232 B.6.32.2001 (edition)
2013 May, CRRA 56 pp. 206–207 (study)
2021 Hätinen, dubsar 20 pp. 358–359 (lines 10–31, edition)

TEXT

1) ^{d}suen an-na
2) pirig digir-re-e-ne
3) lugal ^{d}en-líl-e-ne
4) lugal-a-ni-ir

1–4) For the god Sîn of heaven, lion of the gods (and) king of the Enlil (circle of) gods, his lord:

5) ^{md}EN.ZU-TI.LA.BI-DU$_{11}$.GA
6) šagina úri.KI-ma
7) dumu $^{m\ulcorner d\urcorner}$nin-gal-SUM.MA
8) šagina úri.KI-ma
9) ú-a é-kíš-nu$_{6}$-gal

5–9) Sîn-balāssu-iqbi, governor of Ur, son of Ningal-iddin, (who was also) governor of Ur, who provides for Ekišnugal —

10) é-temen-ní-gùr-ru
11) níg u$_{4}$ ul-lí*-a-ta
12) é-gar$_{8}$ dirig-ga-bi
13) te-me-en-bi a-ri-a
14) uš$_{8}$-bi bí-in-šú-šú
15) ká-bi ḫa-lam-me-e-ne
16) ki-bi bí-in-kin-kin
17) šà dub te-me-en-bi
18) u-me-ni-dù
19) sag-bi ba-ni-in-íl
20) GIŠ.ig GIŠ.taškarin giš sag
21) kur-bi-ta sù-ud-da

10–31) (With regard to) Etemennigurru, whose (enclosure) wall had collapsed in the distant past, whose foundation terrace had lain waste, (and) whose foundations were covered over, I sought the location of (15) its forgotten gate(s). I put its foundation inscription inside a box and raised its (the temple's) top. I inlaid with silver (20) a door of boxwood, wood of finest quality from a distant mountain, fixed with a copper peg, whose band(s) were strong, (whose) *bottom* was of gold, (25) (whose) door bolt was of shining silver, (and whose) bar and pivot were of strong copper, in order that it might stand forever in the doorway of Esagdili

3 ^{d}en-líl-e-ne: The "Enlil (circle of) gods" was a group of deities, generally of minor importance, who were associated with the god Enlil, the patron of the city Nippur. Some of the deities in this group are mentioned in Asb. 2010–2015.
11 ul-lí*-a-ta "distant": The text has ul-DÙ-a-ta.
12 dirig-ga-bi "had collapsed": With regard to the translation of dirig-ga, see Frame, RIMB 2 p. 39 B.2.6.1 (on-page note to line 10).
15 ká-bi ḫa-lam-me-e-ne "its forgotten gate(s)": One could also translated this passage as "its ruined gate(s)."

22) gag urudu bí-in-dù-a
23) kéš-da-bi kala-ga
24) uš kù-sig$_{17}$-a-ke$_{4}$
25) si-gar kù-babbar zálag-zálag
26) aškud nu-kúš-ù
27) urudu kala-ga
28) kù-babbar u-me-ni-dab-dab
29) ká é sag-dili
30) é ḫal-la-ta dù-a
31) da-rí-šè gub-bu-dè

("House of Secrets"), the house built in secret.

32) lú mu-sar-ra-mu
33) šu bí-íb-ùr-e-a
34) ḫa-ba-ki-bi kúr-ru-da
35) ^{d}suen ^{d}nin-gal
36) digir bàd-gal-gu$_{10}$
37) mu-bi
38) ḫé-en-ḫa-lam-e-ne

32–38) May the god Sîn (and) the goddess Ningal, the god(s), my helpers, destroy the name of anyone who erases my inscription or changes its position!

2004

This Sumerian inscription of Sîn-balāssu-iqbi is written on a clay nail and records the restoration of Etemennigurru, the same structure mentioned in the previous text.

CATALOGUE

Museum Number	Excavation/ Registration No.	Provenance	Dimensions (cm)	cpn
BM 116987	1924-9-20,250; U 1262	Ur, main gateway, southwest of the Great Court	Height: 7.2; dia.: 5.9	c

COMMENTARY

The nail was found by the British expedition to Ur and was given the excavation number U 1262. The inscription — whose sign forms are Babylonian and display some archaizing features — is found running along the side of the object.

BIBLIOGRAPHY

1928 Gadd, UET 1 no. 183 (copy, edition)
1995 Frame, RIMB 2 pp. 232–233 B.6.32.2002 (edition)
2013 May, CRRA 56 pp. 206–207 (study)
2021 Hätinen, dubsar 20 pp. 346–347 (edition)

2003 lines 29–30 The translation follows George, House Most High pp. 138–139; and Hätinen, dubsar 20 p. 358 and n. 2019.

TEXT

1) ^{d}suen an-na
2) pirig digir-re-⌜e⌝-ne
3) lugal ^{d}en-líl-e-ne
4) lugal-a-ni-ir
5) ^{md}EN.ZU-TI.LA.BI-DU_{11}.GA
6) šagina
7) úri.KI-ma
8) dumu ^{md}nin-gal-SUM.MA
9) šagina
10) úri.KI-ma
11) é-temen-ní-gùr-ru
12) é ki ág-gá*-na
13) gibil-bi
14) in-na-dù

1–4) For the god Sîn of heaven, lion of the gods (and) king of the Enlil (circle of) gods, his lord:

5–14) Sîn-balāssu-iqbi, governor of Ur, son of Ningal-iddin, (10) (who was also) governor of Ur, built anew Etemennigurru, his beloved temple.

2005

This Sumerian inscription of Sîn-balāssu-iqbi, which is known from clay nails that were discovered at Ur, states that that pro-Assyrian governor rebuilt the Gipāru and constructed a statue of the goddess Ningal, the consort of the god Nanna (Sîn) and that building's principal divine occupant.

CATALOGUE

Ex.	Museum Number	Excavation/ Registration No.	Provenance	Dimensions (cm)	Lines Preserved	cpn
1	BM 119021	1927-10-3,16; U 3249c	Ur, beneath pavement of the sanctuary of the Ningal temple	Length: 12.4; Dia. 7	1–17	c
2	BM 119023	1927-10-3,18; U 3249m	As ex. 1	Length: 13; Dia. 6.8	1–17	c
3	BM 119024	1927-10-3,19; U 3249l	As ex. 1	Length: 13.6; Dia. 7.3	1–17	c
4	CBS 15905	U 3249i	As ex. 1	Length: 13.9; Dia. 7.3	1–17	c
5	CBS 15905	U 3249g$^{?}$	As ex. 1	Length: 13.8; Dia. 7.2	1–17	c

COMMENTARY

Sir L. Woolley found thirteen nails bearing this text "set upright, bedded in a little bitumen, in holes below the walls and pavement of the sanctuary" (AJ 5 [1925] p. 368). In addition to the three in the British Museum and the two in the Penn Museum listed above, six further exemplars are reported to be in the Iraq Museum (Baghdad) and to bear the museum number IM 1081 (see Edzard, Sumer 13 [1957] p. 178). The present locations of the remaining two exemplars are not known. Ex. 4 bears a faint museum number, CBS 1590x, where x stands for an illegible numeral, and ex. 5 has no museum number written on it; however, the Penn Museum registration book records that the number 15905 was given to "Clay cones of Sin-balatsu-iqbi" that bore the Ur number 3249. The identification of the letter

2004 line 12 ki ág-gá*-na "his beloved": The scribe of the text did not correctly write out the gá sign on the clay nail. For a copy of the sign, see the minor variants at the back of the book.

at the end of the excavation number marked on ex. 5 is not certain. The text is written in archaizing Babylonian script. Ex 1 is the master exemplar in the edition presented here. A score of the text is presented on Oracc.

The inscription literally states that Sîn-balāssu-iqbi rebuilt "the Gipāru, the house *of* the goddess Ninlil, beloved wife of the god Sîn" for the goddess Ningal. As J.A. Brinkman has argued (Orientalia NS 38 [1969] pp. 337–338 n. 2), it is likely that dnin-líl should be taken "as an epithet referring to Ningal and connoting 'supreme goddess' or something similar." His suggestion has been adopted here. It is likely that one should regard the inscription as indicating a syncretism between Ningal and Ninlil, just as previous texts appear to reflect a syncretism between Ningal's spouse Nanna (Sîn) and Ninlil's spouse Enlil (see introduction to Asb. 2010).

BIBLIOGRAPHY

1925 Woolley, AJ 5 p. 368 and pl. XXXV no. 1 (provenance, photo [inscription illegible])
1925 Woolley, MJ 16 p. 47 (provenance)
1928 Gadd, UET 1 no. 171 (exs. 1–3, copy, edition)
1931 Van Buren, Found. p. 60 (provenance)
1939 Woolley, UE 5 pp. 63–64 and pl. 27b (provenance, photo [inscription illegible])
1965 Brinkman, Orientalia NS 34 p. 250 (study)
1968 Ellis, Foundation Deposits p. 83 (provenance)
1969 Brinkman, Orientalia NS 38 pp. 337–338 n. 2 (study)
1982 Woolley and Moorey, Ur pp. 226–227 (translation)
1995 Frame, RIMB 2 pp. 243–244 B.6.32.2014 (exs. 1–5, edition)
2013 May, CRRA 56 pp. 206–207 (study)
2021 Hätinen, dubsar 20 pp. 350–351 (edition)

TEXT

1) dnin-gal UN-gal
2) é-giš-nu$_{11}$-gal
3) dnin-men-na ki ág-gá
4) úri.KI-ma nin-a-ni-ir
5) mdEN.ZU-TIN-*su-iq-bi*
6) šagina úri.KI-ma
7) gi$_{6}$-pàr é dnin-líl-le
8) nìta-dam ki ág-gá
9) dsuen
10) gibil-bi mu-na-dù
11) alam níg-dím-dím-ma
12) dnin-gal-ke$_{4}$ u-me-ni-dím
13) šà é digir ḪU-dù-šè
14) u-mu-un-ku$_{4}$-ku$_{4}$
15) é-nun-ta
16) ki-tuš nam-en-na-ni dù
17) bí-in-ri-a

1–4) For the goddess Ningal, queen of Ekišnugal, divine Ninmenna ("Lady-of-the-Crown"), beloved of Ur, his lady:

5–17) Sîn-balāssu-iqbi, governor of Ur, built anew the Gipāru, the house of the supreme goddess, beloved wife of the god Sîn. After he constructed a statue, a (re-)creation of the goddess Ningal, (and) brought it into the house of the wise god, she took up residence in Enun, (which was) built (to be) her lordly abode.

2006

An Akkadian text stating that Sîn-balāssu-iqbi, "governor of Ur, Eridu, and the Gurasimmu (tribe)," rebuilt a well named Puḫilituma ("Well That Brings Luxuriance") for the goddess Ningal, the consort of the moon-god Nanna (Sîn), is inscribed on eight clay disks discovered at Ur. His (good) deeds are recorded to have been "in order to ensure the good health of Ashurbanipal, king of Assyria."

2005 line 13 ḪU-dù-šè (pa$_{7}$-dù-šè or paq-dù-šè) "wise": ḪU-dù can stand for Akkadian *mūdû* (see AHw p. 666 and CAD M/2 p. 1 64).

CATALOGUE

Ex.	Museum Number	Excavation/ Registration No.	Provenance	Dimensions (cm)	Lines Preserved	cpn
1	BM 124351	1933-10-13,4; U 18529c	Ur, foundation deposit, bottom of Kurigalzu brickwork, in a well in the Ningal temple	Dia.: 8.3	1–16	c
2	BM 124350	1933-10-13,3; U 18529g$^{?}$	As ex. 1	Dia.: 7.5	1–16	c
3	IM 16429	U 18529h	As ex. 1	—	1–16	n
4	IM 48412	U 18529e	As ex. 1	—	1–16	n
5	IM 48413	U 18529f	As ex. 1	—	1–16	n
6	IM 48414	U 18529b	As ex. 1	—	1–16	n
7	UM 33-35-191a	U 18529a	As ex. 1	Dia.: 8	1–16	c
8	UM 33-35-191b	U 18529d (Ur photo 2178)	As ex. 1	Dia.: 8	1–16	c

COMMENTARY

Sir Leonard Woolley discovered the disks during the eleventh season of excavations at Ur. Ex. 2 has U 18529b written on it, but as noted by J.A. Brinkman, the "b" is probably an error for "g" (Orientalia NS 38 [1969] p. 340, n. 4 from p. 339). The disks are inscribed on both sides and the text is written in contemporary Babylonian script. The arrangement of lines varies in the exemplars; however, the master line follows ex. 1. Exs. 2 and 6 have the inscription on 18 lines. For exs. 4–6, the score on Oracc presents only the variants given by Brinkman (ibid. p. 340 n. 2) and nothing is given for ex. 3 since that exemplar was not available to him for examination and could not be collated by the authors. The minor (orthographic) variants are listed at the back of the book.

Because the reverse of ex. 7 has been cleaned since it was studied by Brinkman (ibid. p. 348), it is now clear that it is not the disk whose reverse is shown on the right side of UE 5 pl. 22b. The disk on the photograph must be identified with one of exs. 3–5.

BIBLIOGRAPHY

1933 Woolley, AJ 13 p. 370 and pl. LVI no. 1 (provenance, photo [inscription illegible])
1939 Woolley, UE 5 p. 33 (provenance), pl. 22a (photo [inscription illegible]) and pl. 22b right (ex. unknown, photo) and left (ex. 8, photo)
1965 Brinkman, Orientalia NS 34 pp. 249–250 n. 5 (study)
1965 Sollberger, UET 8 no. 102 (exs. 1–2, copy [ex. 2 as variants to ex. 1]; exs. 1–8, study)
1968 Ellis, Foundation Deposits pp. 96, 104, and 194 no. 83 (study)
1969 Brinkman, Orientalia NS 38 pp. 339–342 and 348 (exs. 1–2, 4–8, edition; exs. 1–8, study)
1995 Frame, RIMB 2 pp. 244–245 B.6.32.2015 (exs. 1–8, edition)
2021 Hätinen, dubsar 20 p. 234 (lines 1–3, edition)

TEXT

1) *a-na* ^{d}*nin-gal* GAŠAN *ṣir-ti*
2) *šar-rat i-la-a-ti qa-rit-ti*
3) DINGIR.MEŠ GAL.MEŠ
4) *ana* TIN ZI.MEŠ *šá* AN.ŠÁR-DÙ-IBILA
5) LUGAL KUR *aš-šur*.KI LUGAL *dan-nu* LUGAL *kiš-šat*
6) *be-lí-šú* ^{md}30-TIN-*su-iq-bi*
7) DUMU ^{md}*nin-gal*-MU
8) LÚ.GÌR.NÍTA ÚRI.KI
9) *eridu*.KI *u* LÚ.*gu-ra-sim-mu*

1–3) For the goddess Ningal, exalted lady, queen of the goddesses, (most) valiant of the great gods:

4–13) In order to ensure the good health of Ashurbanipal, king of Assyria, strong king, (and) king of the world, his lord, Sîn-balāssu-iqbi, son of Ningal-iddin, governor of Ur, Eridu and the Gurasimmu (tribe), (10) opened up (its) emplacement, built (the well named) Puḫilituma, and established (it) for all time. He made inexhaustible spring water appear in it.

---

2 Exs. 2 and 6 add AMA ("mother") after *qa-rit-ti*, that is, "the valiant, the mother of the great gods."

10) *áš-ri ip-te-e-ma pú-ḫi-li-tùm-ma*
11) *ib-ni-ma ú-kin aḫ-ra-taš*
12) A.MEŠ *nag-bi da-ru-ti*
13) *ú-šab-ra-a qé-reb-šú*
14) *šá* NUN *pe-tu-ú* PÚ *šu-a-ti*
15) *li-ri-ku u*$_4$*-mu-šú*
16) *liš-ta-an-dil* NUNUZ-*šú*

14–16) With regard to any (future) ruler who (re)opens this well, may his days be long (and) his offspring extensive!

2007

Sîn-balāssu-iqbi's workmen discovered a brick with a Sumerian inscription of the Ur III king Amar-Suen (2046–2038) while looking for the (original) ground plan of the Ekišnugal temple complex at Ur. Sîn-balāssu-iqbi had one of his scribes, Nabû-šuma-iddin (a lamentation priest), make a copy of that Sumerian text on a clay drum-shaped object which, in view of the poorly-preserved notation written on the top of the object, might have been a model for an altar or dais. Only the colophon, which is written in Akkadian, and the inscription on the top of the object are edited here; the inscription of Amar-Suen is edited in Frayne, RIME 3/2 (pp. 256–257 E3/2.1.3.11).

CATALOGUE

Museum Number	Excavation/ Registration No.	Provenance	Dimensions (cm)	cpn
BM 119014	1927-10-3,9; U 2757	Ur, Giparu, "museum" of En-nigaldi-nanna, ES 2 or "room 5" (= ES 5$^?$)	10.8; Dia: 6.8	c

COMMENTARY

This clay object was found in the Giparu, in the so-called "museum" of En-nigaldi-nanna, a daughter of the Neo-Babylonian king Nabonidus (555–539). Sir Leonard Woolley indicates that the piece was found in room ES 2 of the building in AJ 5 [1925] p. 383 and in "room 5" (= ES 5$^?$) in UE 9 p. 17; for a plan of the Giparu at Ur, see UE 9 pl. 65.

The colophon (col. iv) is written in contemporary Babylonian script, while the remainder of the text is written in an archaizing script. Since the passage on the top of the object is written in an archaizing script, it may well be a copy of an older inscription just like cols. i–iii. However, since it is not specifically a part of the Amar-Suen inscription, the Sîn-balāssu-iqbi colophon is edited here.

Amar-Suen's inscription seems to be based upon "Amar-Suen 3" (Steible, NSBW 2 pp. 221–225 = Frayne, RIME 3/2 pp. 255–256 E3/2.1.3.10). However, if so, the lamentation-priest Nabû-šuma-iddin, the person who copied the text on Sîn-balāssu-iqbi's behalf, either did a bad job of copying the original text or made the copy from a different or damaged version of that inscription. Nabû-šuma-iddin's copy includes several errors and differs significantly from the so-called "Amar-Suen 3" inscription, as already pointed out by D.R. Frayne.

2006 line 13 *ú-šab-ra-a* "He made ... appear": M. Worthington (personal communication) suggests that this may be a faulty form of the verb *šutebrû*, thus intended to mean here "he made permanent."

BIBLIOGRAPHY

1925 Woolley, AJ 5 pp. 383–384 and pl. XL no. 1 (provenance, photo, translation)
1925 Woolley, MJ 16 p. 34 (photo)
1928 Gadd, UET 1 no. 172 (photo, copy, edition)
1962 Woolley, UE 9 pp. 14, 17, and 111 and pl. 29 (provenance, photo, study)
1965 Brinkman, Orientalia NS 34 p. 250 (study)
1965 Woolley, UE 8 pp. 4 and 102 (study)
1968 Hunger, Kolophone no. 73 (edition)
1971 Sollberger and Kupper, IRSA IIIA3e n. 1 (translation)
1980 Edzard, RLA 6/1–2 pp. 64–65 (translation)
1982 Woolley and Moorey, Ur p. 231 (photo)
1991 Steible, NSBW 2 pp. 221–225 Amarsuen 3 Text B (edition)
1995 Frame, RIMB 2 pp. 246–247 B.6.32.2016 (edition)
1997 Frayne, RIME 3/2 pp. 256–257 E3/2.1.3.11 (edition)
2013 May, CRRA 56 p. 206 (study)

Figure 12. BM 119014 (Asb. 2007), a clay drum-shaped object with a Sumerian inscription of the Ur III king Amar-Suen and an Akkadian text of Sîn-balāssu-iqbi, a governor of Ur during the reign of Ashurbanipal.

TEXT

Lines 1-28 [= col. i–iii], which contain an inscription of Amar-Suen, are not edited here.

Col. iv

29) GABA.RI ⸢SIG$_4$⸣.AL.ÙR.RA

30) *nap-pal-ti* ÚRI.KI

31) *ep-šet amar-*^{d}EN.ZU LUGAL *ú-ri*

32) *ina ši-te-ʾe-ú ú-ṣu-ra-a-ti*

33) *é-giš-nu*$_{11}$*-gal* ^{md}EN.ZU-TIN-*su-*⸢*iq-bi*⸣

34) GÌR.NÍTA ⸢URI$_5$⸣.KI *iš-te-*⸢*ʾu-ú*⸣

35) ^{md}AG-MU-SUM.NA DUMU ^{m}MU-^{d}*pap-sukkal*

36) LÚ.GALA ^{d}EN.(erasure).ZU

37) *a-na ta-mar-*(erasure)*-ti*

(Lines 1-28 [= col. i–iii], which contain an inscription of Amar-Suen, are not edited here.)

Col. iv

29–38) Copy from a baked brick from the debris of Ur, the work of Amar-Suen, the king of Ur, (which) Sîn-balāssu-iqbi, the governor of Ur, had discovered while looking for the ground plan of Ekišnugal. Nabû-šuma-iddin, son of Iddin-Papsukkal, the lamentation-priest of the god Sîn, saw (it) and wrote (it) down for display.

38) *i-mur-ma iš-ṭur*

Top

39) [(*x*)] ^{d}BÁRA ^{d}EN.LÍL *x*

40) [...] ⸢AN⸣ ME

41) [...]-⸢*ú*$^{?}$⸣

42) [...] *x*

Top

39–42) (No translation possible)

2008

This Sumerian inscription of Sîn-balāssu-iqbi records that he renovated Elugalgalgasisa ("House, King of Righteous Counsel"). This text is found on several bricks from Ur and mentions Ashurbanipal. The same temple is also mentioned in the next text.

CATALOGUE

Ex.	Museum Number	Excavation/ Registration No.	Provenance	Dimensions (cm)	Lines Preserved	cpn
1	BM 114277	1919-10-11,4708	Ur	29×19.5×8	1–12	p
2	BM 114278	1919-10-11,4709	As ex. 1	13×7.5×3	7–12	n
3	BM 137345	1935-1-13,5; U 1664	Ur, top of main staircase of the ziggurat, in debris	14.5×13×6	1–5	p
4	BM 137349	1935-1-13,9; U 3161	As ex. 1	27×25.5×7.5	1–12	n
5	BM 137381	1979-12-18,16	As ex. 1	25.5×25.5×8	1–12	p
6	BM 137408	1979-12-18,43	As ex. 1	13×9×7	1–2	p
7	CBS 15337	U 152$^{?}$	As ex. 1	24×25×8	1–12	c
8	CBS 16491	—	As ex. 1	26×26×8	1–12	c
9	CBS 16555a	—	As ex. 1	26×26×8	1–12	c
10	CBS 16555b	—	As ex. 1	26×26×7.5	1–12	c
11	IM —	U 3161	As ex. 1	27×27×7.5	1–12	n

COMMENTARY

H.R. Hall's excavations produced exs. 1–2, while exs. 3–4 and 7–10 come from Sir Leonard Woolley's work at Ur, as probably do exs. 5–6. C.J. Gadd states that U 3161 was found "loose in Nin-gal temple" and is in the Iraq Museum (ex. 11; see UET 1 p. xviii); Woolley says that it was "from the temple of Nin-gal" and also indicates that it is in the Iraq Museum (UE 8 p. 103). According to C.B.F. Walker (CBI p. 68), BM 137349 (ex. 4) is U 3161. The Ur registry in the British Museum does not indicate that more than one brick was given this number and simply says it was found "loose on top." Ex. 7 has the Ur excavation number 152 crossed out on it; according to the Ur registry U 152 is a "string of beads." Ex. 7 also has the notation T.T.B. 17 written upon it.

U 3136 and 7824 (present locations not known) may also bear this inscription; see UE 6 pp. 50 and 99. The Ur registry states that U 3136 is a molded brick fragment from the front of the Dublal. U 7824 was found loose in room 6 of the Enunmaḫ; the Ur registry indicates that it has the same inscription as U 3161, except for za-nam-til-la-šu in line 2.

While exs. 1–2 and 4–10 are stamped, ex. 3 is inscribed. It is not clear if ex. 11 was stamped or inscribed. The area stamped on exs. 1–2 and 4–6 measures 16.2/16.8×9.5/10.0 cm. Information for exs. 1–6 comes from Walker. No score for this brick inscription is presented on Oracc.

2007 line 39 The sign at the end of the line cannot be *lá* (as tentatively proposed by H. Steible).

BIBLIOGRAPHY

1928 Gadd, UET 1 no. 170 (ex. 11, copy, edition; ex. 3, study)
1965 Woolley, UE 8 p. 103 (ex. 11, study)
1981 Walker, CBI pp. 68–69 no. 82 (exs. 1–6, transliteration)
1985 Behrens, JCS 37 p. 240 no. 56 (exs. 7–10, study)
1995 Frame, RIMB 2 pp. 233–234 B.6.32.2003 (exs. 1–11, edition)
2013 May, CRRA 56 pp. 206–207 (study)
2021 Hätinen, dubsar 20 pp. 344–345 (edition)

TEXT

1) ^{d}nanna lugal an ki-a
2) zi nam-ti-la-šè
3) AN.ŠÁR-DÙ-IBILA-ke$_4$
4) lugal lugal-e-ne lugal-a-ni
5) ^{d}30-TIN-*su-iq-bi*
6) šagina úri.KI-ma
7) eridu.KI-ga-ke$_4$
8) ú-a é-giš-nu$_{11}$-gal
9) èš abzu zálag-ga-ke$_4$
10) é-lugal-galga-si-sá
11) é ki ág-gá-a-ni
12) gibil-bi mu-un-na-dù

1–12) (For) the god Nanna, king of heaven (and) netherworld: in order to ensure the good health of Ashurbanipal, king of kings, his lord, (5) Sîn-balāssu-iqbi, governor of Ur (and) Eridu, who provides for Ekišnugal, the shining shrine of the Watery Abyss (*apsû*), built anew (10) Elugalgalgasisa, his beloved temple.

2009

This eight-line Sumerian inscription, which is stamped on the edge of a fragmentary brick found at Ur, states that Sîn-balāssu-iqbi had the shrine Elugalgalgasisa (the same structure mentioned in the previous text) rebuilt. Ashurbanipal, the king of Assyria, is mentioned by name in the inscription.

CATALOGUE

Museum Number	Excavation/ Registration No.	Provenance	Dimensions (cm)	cpn
BM 119278	1927-10-3,273; U 6341	Ur, loose, south of the Egipar	21×10.5×7.5	c

COMMENTARY

During Sir Leonard Woolley's excavations at Ur, the brick was discovered and assigned the excavation number U 6341. The text is inscribed in two columns: col i = lines 1–4 and col. ii = 5–8. Walker, CBI no. 81, provides collation notes for lines 2 (⸢A⸣, not IB[I]LA of UET 1 copy) and 5 (úri, not uri$_5$ of UET 1 copy). C.J. Gadd has suggested that a word for "god" or "protector" should be restored at the beginning of line 2 (that is, "[god of As]hurbanipal" or "[protector of As]hurbanipal").

2008 line 1 lugal "king": Ex. 3 has en gal "great lord."
2008 line 5 ^{d}30-TIN-*su-iq-bi* "Sîn-balāssu-iqbi": Exs. 3 and 7–10 have ^{md}30-TIN-*su-iq-bi*, that is, they insert a masculine determinative before the name.

BIBLIOGRAPHY

1928 Gadd, UET 1 no. 168 (copy, edition)
1965 Brinkman, Orientalia NS 34 p. 251 (study)
1981 Walker, CBI p. 68 no. 81 (transliteration)
1995 Frame, RIMB 2 p. 234 B.6.32.2004 (edition)
2013 May, CRRA 56 pp. 206–207 (study)

TEXT

1) [^{d}nanna] ⸢lugal⸣-a-ni
2) [(x) AN].ŠÁR-DÙ-⸢A⸣
3) [lugal] ki-šár-ra-ke$_{4}$
4) [^{md}]⸢30-TIN-*su-iq-bi*⸣
5) šagina ⸢úri.KI⸣-ma
6) eridu.⸢KI-ga zi⸣-ni-<<ki>>-šè
7) é-⸢lugal⸣-galga-si-sá
8) ⸢gibil⸣-bi mu-na-⸢an-dù⸣

1–8) [(For) the god Nanna], his [lo]rd, [... of As]hurbanipal, [king] of the world, [Sî]n-balāssu-iqbi, (5) governor of Ur (and) Eridu, for the sake of his life (re)built Elugalgalgasisa [an]ew.

2010

The construction of Eušumgalana ("House, Dragon of Heaven"), the dwelling of the deity Ninkasi, is recorded in this Sumerian text inscribed twice on a brick from Ur. The work is dedicated to the moon-god Nanna (Sîn). This inscription is the first of nine similar inscriptions from Ur that deal with shrines at that Babylonian city (Asb. 2010–2018). Two of these inscriptions mention only the god Nanna (Asb. 2016–2017) and one assigns a shrine to the god Enlil (Asb. 2018). The remaining six inscriptions, however, for the most part, ascribe shrines to relatively minor deities: Ninkasi, Šuzianna, Kusu, Nusku, Ninimma, and Ennugi (Asb. 2010–2015). Each of these six deities was one of the "sons of Enmešarra," a god who was connected with the netherworld and viewed as an ancestor of Enlil (see Gadd, UET 1 p. 56; and Hibbert, OrAnt 21 [1982] pp. 256–257). Each is also known to have had a shrine in Nippur, Enlil's principal cult center (see Bernhardt and Kramer, Orientalia NS 44 [1975] p. 98; and George, House Most High pp. 12–13). All except Ninkasi are known to have been specifically associated with Enlil in some way (see An = Anum i 184, 252, 306, 318, and 324). Thus, it appears that in carrying out his renovations at Ur, Sîn-balāssu-iqbi was modelling his work upon the cultic topography at Nippur. Since several of this governor's texts refer to Nanna/Sîn as "king of the Enlil (circle of) gods" (Asb. 2003–2004 and 2010–2018) and since one refers to Nanna's Enlilship (nam-^{d}en-líl-lá-a-ni; Asb. 2017 line 7), it seems that Sîn-balāssu-iqbi was attempting to promote a syncretism between the gods Nanna (Sîn) and Enlil.

CATALOGUE

Ex.	Museum Number	Excavation Number	Provenance	Dimensions (cm)	Lines Preserved	cpn
1	CBS 16483, face	U 3250	Ur, Ningal temple, wall, room left of the sanctuary	26×12.5×7.5	1–8	c
2	CBS 16483, edge	U 3250	As ex. 1	As ex. 1	1–6, 8	c

COMMENTARY

The brick was discovered in 1925–26, during the fourth season of Sir Leonard Woolley's excavations at Ur. The inscriptions on it are inscribed, not stamped. Contrary to a statement in the Ur registry in the British Museum that U 3301 has the same inscription as U 3250 and one in JCS 37 that CBS 16490 (U 3301) and CBS 16483 (U 3250) both have this text, CBS 16490 has Asb. 2014, as previously noted by C.J. Gadd (UET 1 p. xviii) and L. Woolley (UE 8 p. 103).

Ex. 2, the inscription on the edge of CBS 16483, omits line 7. Gadd (UET 1 p. 55 sub no. 174) states that eight further brick inscriptions (UET 1 nos. 175–182 = Asb. 2011–2018) show the same feature: the complete text on the brick's face and a shorter version, omitting line 7, on the brick's edge. None of the exemplars of Asb. 2011–2018 that were examined firsthand has a text on the edge that omits line 7. In every case in which the inscription was collated, however, the edge inscription of Asb. 2010–2018 had ^{d}50-e-ne in line 1, not ^{d}en-líl-e-ne, as found on the brick's face. Following RINAP editorial practice, no score for this brick inscription is presented on Oracc.

The deity Ninkasi, who is named in line 7, is sometimes described as the goddess of beer; see Civil, Studies Oppenheim pp. 67–89.

BIBLIOGRAPHY

1925 Woolley, AJ 5 p. 368 (provenance)
1928 Gadd, UET 1 nos. 173–174 (exs. 1–2, copy, edition)
1939 Woolley, UE 5 pp. 32–33 and 60 (provenance)
1965 Woolley, UE 8 pp. 70 and 103 (provenance, study)
1985 Behrens, JCS 37 p. 240 no. 57 (exs. 1–2, study)
1995 Frame, RIMB 2 pp. 235–236 B.6.32.2005 (exs. 1–2, edition)
2013 May, CRRA 56 pp. 206–207 (study)
2021 Hätinen, dubsar 20 p. 353 and n. 1989 (study)

TEXT

1) ^{d}nanna lugal ^{d}en-líl-e-ne
2) lugal-a-ni
3) ^{md}EN.ZU-TI.LA.BI-DU$_{11}$.GA
4) šagina úri.KI-ma
5) ú-a eridu.KI-ga
6) é-ušumgal-an-na
7) ⸢ki⸣-gub ^{d}nin-ka-si-ke$_{4}$
8) mu-na-dù

1–8) (For) the god Nanna, king of the Enlil (circle of) gods, his lord: Sîn-balāssu-iqbi, governor of Ur, (5) who provides for Eridu, built Eušumgalana, the station of the goddess Ninkasi.

---

1 ^{d}en-líl-e-ne "the Enlil (circle of) gods": Ex. 2 has ^{d}50-e-ne.
7 This line is omitted in ex. 2.

2011

A brick found at Ur has a Sumerian text of Sîn-balāssu-iqbi inscribed on its face and edge. The inscription records that this governor of Ur had built Eešbanda (House, Little Chamber"), the abode of the goddess Šuzianna, for the moon-god Nanna (Sîn). According to An = Anum i 184–84a, Šuzianna was a junior wife (dam bàn-da) of the god Enlil and the wet-nurse of Sîn. The text is similar to Asb. 2010 and 2012–2018. Following RINAP editorial practice, no score for this inscription is presented on Oracc.

CATALOGUE

Ex.	Museum Number	Excavation Number	Provenance	Dimensions (cm)	Lines Preserved	cpn
1	CBS 16484, face	U 3326	Ur, well of the Ningal temple	27×12×8	1–8	c
2	CBS 16484, edge	U 3326	As ex. 1	As ex. 1	1–8	c

BIBLIOGRAPHY

1925 Woolley, AJ 5 p. 368 (provenance)
1928 Gadd, UET 1 no. 175 and sub no. 174 (exs. 1–2, copy, edition [as variant to UET 1 no. 173])
1939 Woolley, UE 5 pp. 32–33 and 60 (provenance)
1965 Woolley, UE 8 pp. 70 and 103 (provenance, study)
1985 Behrens, JCS 37 p. 240 no. 58 (study)
1995 Frame, RIMB 2 p. 236 B.6.32.2006 (exs. 1–2, edition)
2013 May, CRRA 56 pp. 206–207 (study)
2021 Hätinen, dubsar 20 p. 354 and n. 1991 (study)

TEXT

1) dnanna lugal den-líl-e-ne
2) lugal-a-ni
3) mdEN.ZU-TI.LA.BI-DU$_{11}$.GA
4) šagina úri.KI-ma
5) ú-a eridu.KI-ga
6) é-èš-bàn-da
7) ki-tuš dšu-zi-an-na
8) mu-na-dù

1–8) (For) the god Nanna, king of the Enlil (circle) of gods, his lord: Sîn-balāssu-iqbi, the governor of Ur, (5) who provides for Eridu, built Eešbanda, the abode of the goddess Šuzianna.

2012

A Sumerian inscription stating that Sîn-balāssu-iqbi, the governor of Ur, constructed for the moon-god Nanna (Sîn) the shrine Eankikuga ("House of the Pure Heaven and Netherworld"), the station of the goddess Kusu, is found inscribed twice on a brick from Ur. Kusu was apparently a purification

2011 line 1 den-líl-e-ne "the Enlil (circle of) gods": Ex. 2 has ⸢d50⸣-e-⸢ne⸣.
2011 line 6 é-èš-bàn-da "Eešbanda": The reading of the temple name is clear on ex. 2. Ex. 1 has é-èš-(x)-bàn-da. With regard to the reading of the Sumerian temple name, see George, House Most High p. 83 no. 265.
2011 line 7 Contra C.J. Gadd (UET 1 p. 55 sub no. 174), ex. 2 does not omit line 7; see the commentary of Asb. 2010.

priest of the god Enlil and one of the children of the god Enmešarra. (For problems understanding the nature of this deity, see Michalowski, Studies Hallo pp. 158–159; and Simons, RA 112 [2018] pp. 123–148 and NABU 2020/1 pp. 58–59 no. 26.) The text is similar to Asb. 2010–2011 and 2013–2018. No score is provided for this brick inscription on Oracc.

CATALOGUE

Ex.	Museum Number	Excavation Number	Provenance	Dimensions (cm)	Lines Preserved	cpn
1	CBS 16485, face	U 3296	Ur, well of the Ningal temple	26×12×7	1–8	c
2	CBS 16485, edge	U 3296	As ex. 1	As ex. 1	1–8	c

BIBLIOGRAPHY

1925 Woolley, AJ 5 p. 368 (provenance)
1928 Gadd, UET 1 no. 176 and sub no. 174 (exs. 1–2, copy, edition [as variant to UET 1 no. 173])
1939 Woolley, UE 5 pp. 32–33 and 60 (provenance)
1965 Woolley, UE 8 pp. 70 and 103 (provenance, study)
1985 Behrens, JCS 37 p. 240 no. 59 (study)
1995 Frame, RIMB 2 p. 237 B.6.32.2007 (exs. 1–2, edition)
2013 May, CRRA 56 pp. 206–207 (study)
2021 Hätinen, dubsar 20 p. 354 and n. 1993 (study)

TEXT

1) ᵈnanna lugal ᵈen-líl-e-ne
2) lugal-a-ni
3) ᵐᵈEN.ZU-TI.LA.BI-DU_{11}.GA
4) šagina úri.KI-ma
5) ú-a eridu.KI-ga
6) é-an-ki-kù-ga
7) ki-gub ᵈkù-sù-ke_4
8) mu-na-dù

1–8) (For) the god Nanna, king of the Enlil (circle of) gods, his lord: Sîn-balāssu-iqbi, governor of Ur, (5) who provides for Eridu, built Eankikuga, the station of the god Kusu.

2013

Two copies of this Sumerian inscription of Sîn-balāssu-iqbi are found inscribed on a brick from Ur. The inscription states that he had built Eadgigi ("House, Counsellor"), the abode of the god Nusku, for the moon-god Nanna (Sîn). Nusku was a god of light and fire and the vizier of the god Enlil (see Tallqvist, Götterepitheta pp. 432–434). The inscription is similar to Asb. 2010–2012 and 2014–2018. Following RINAP editorial practice, no score is presented on Oracc.

2012 line 1 ᵈen-líl-e-ne "the Enlil (circle of) gods": Ex. 2 has ᵈ50-e-ne.
2012 line 7 Contra C.J. Gadd (UET 1 p. 55 sub no. 174), ex. 2 does not omit line 7; see the commentary of Asb. 2010.

CATALOGUE

Ex.	Museum Number	Excavation Number	Provenance	Dimensions (cm)	Lines Preserved	cpn
1	CBS 16489, face	U 3300	Ur, well of the Ningal temple	26×26×8	1–8	c
2	CBS 16489, edge	U 3300	As ex. 1	As ex. 1	1–8	c

BIBLIOGRAPHY

1925 Woolley, AJ 5 p. 368 (provenance)
1928 Gadd, UET 1 no. 180 and sub no. 174 (exs. 1–2, copy, edition [as variant to UET 1 no. 173])
1939 Woolley, UE 5 pp. 32–33 and 60 (provenance)
1965 Woolley, UE 8 pp. 70 and 103 (provenance, study)
1985 Behrens, JCS 37 p. 241 no. 63 (study)
1995 Frame, RIMB 2 pp. 237–238 B.6.32.2008 (exs. 1–2, edition)
2013 May, CRRA 56 pp. 206–207 (study)
2021 Hätinen, dubsar 20 p. 354 and n. 1995 (study)

TEXT

1) ^{d}nanna lugal ^{d}en-líl-e-ne
2) lugal-a-ni
3) ^{md}EN.ZU-TI.LA.BI-DU$_{11}$.GA
4) šagina úri.KI-ma
5) ú-a eridu.KI-ga
6) é-ad-gi$_4$-gi$_4$
7) ki-tuš ^{d}nusku
8) mu-na-dù

1–8) (For) the god Nanna, king of the Enlil (circle of) gods, his lord: Sîn-balāssu-iqbi, governor of Ur, (5) who provides for Eridu, built Eadgigi, the abode of the god Nusku.

2014

This Sumerian inscription records that Sîn-balāssu-iqbi had built Ekišibgalekura (exact reading and interpretation of the ceremonial name are not certain), the abode of the goddess Ninimma, a daughter of the god Enlil; the work was carried out on behalf of the god Nanna (Sîn). The text is inscribed twice upon a brick discovered at Ur and is similar to Asb. 2010–2013 and 2015–2018. No score for this text is provided on Oracc.

CATALOGUE

Ex.	Museum Number	Excavation Number	Provenance	Dimensions (cm)	Lines Preserved	cpn
1	CBS 16490, face	U 3301	Ur, well of the Ningal temple	25×27×7	1–8	c
2	CBS 16490, edge	U 3301	As ex. 1	As ex. 1	1–8	c

2013 line 1 ^{d}en-líl-e-ne "the Enlil (circle of) gods": Ex. 2 has ^{d}50-e-ne.
2013 line 7 Contra C.J. Gadd (UET 1 p. 55 sub no. 174), ex. 2 does not omit line 7; see the commentary of Asb. 2010.

COMMENTARY

H. Behrens (JCS 37 [1985] p. 240 sub no. 57) indicated that CBS 16490 (U 3301) has inscription Asb. 2010, but the brick actually has this text (Asb. 2014) inscribed on it. The Sumerian name of the temple might mean "House, Keeper of the Seal of the Ekur." A.R. George (House Most High p. 79 no. 202) has suggested that it might instead be é-dub-(sar)-gal-é-kur-ra ("House of the Great Scribe of the Ekur"). For the goddess Ninimma's position as a scribe and her connection with the god Enlil (whose temple was Ekur at Nippur), see George, BTT p. 469.

BIBLIOGRAPHY

1925 Woolley, AJ 5 p. 368 (provenance)
1928 Gadd, UET 1 no. 181 and sub no. 174 (exs. 1–2, copy, edition [as variant to UET 1 no. 173])
1939 Woolley, UE 5 pp. 32–33 and 60 (provenance)
1965 Woolley, UE 8 pp. 70 and 103 (provenance, study)
1995 Frame, RIMB 2 pp. 238–239 B.6.32.2009 (exs. 1–2, edition)
2013 May, CRRA 56 pp. 206–207 (study)
2021 Hätinen, dubsar 20 p. 354 and n. 1997 (study)

TEXT

1) ^{d}nanna lugal ^{d}en-líl-e-ne
2) lugal-a-ni
3) ^{md}EN.ZU-TI.LA.BI-DU$_{11}$.GA
4) šagina úri.KI-ma
5) ú-a eridu.KI-ga
6) é-kišib-gal-é-kur-ra
7) ki-tuš ^{d}nin-ìmma-ke$_{4}$
8) mu-na-dù

1–8) (For) the god Nanna, king of the Enlil (circle of) gods, his lord: Sîn-balāssu-iqbi, governor of Ur, (5) who provides for Eridu, built Ekišibgalekura, the abode of the god Ninimma.

2015

This poorly preserved Sumerian inscription discovered at Ur states that Sîn-balāssu-iqbi had built the abode or station of the god Ennugi, for the god Nanna (Sîn); the Sumerian name of the structure in question is not fully preserved. The text is similar to Asb. 2010–2014 and 2016–2018.

CATALOGUE

Museum Number	Excavation/ Registration No.	Provenance	Dimensions (cm)	cpn
BM 119277	1927-10-3,272; U 3148	Ur, northwest of the ziggurat or in the Great Court of Nanna	19×16×7.5	c

2014 line 1 ^{d}en-líl-e-ne "the Enlil (circle of) gods": Ex. 2 has ^{d}50-e-[ne].
2014 line 7 Contra C.J. Gadd (UET 1 p. 55 sub no. 174), ex. 2 does not omit line 7; see the commentary of Asb. 2010.

COMMENTARY

The brick fragment with this inscription is variously said to have been found northwest of the ziggurat (Gadd, UET 1 p. xix) and in the Great Court of Nanna (Woolley, UE 8 p. 103). The text is inscribed, not stamped, on the brick's face. The fragment is not sufficiently well preserved to determine if it also had an inscription on its edge or not. Sir Leonard Woolley says that CBS 16559 also has this excavation number and inscription. A brick from the fourth season of excavations at Ur (1925–26) that was accessioned in the Penn Museum on April 19, 1927 was given this museum number (16559); however, no brick with this number or this inscription can currently be found in the museum. Thus the edition presented here represents only BM 119277, which was kindly collated by C.B.F. Walker on behalf of the then-active RIM Project.

The god Ennugi was associated both with looking after dikes and canals and with the netherworld; he was also the "throne-bearer" of the god Enlil; see Tallqvist, Götterepitheta p. 305 for details. The reading of the name of the shrine in line 6 is not certain. Walker reads the sign before kù as ga, while A.R. George reads gú$^{?}$ (House Most High p. 161 no. 1255). A copy of the sign is found in the list of minor variants at the back of this book.

BIBLIOGRAPHY

1928 Gadd, UET 1 no. 182 (copy, edition [as variant to UET 1 no. 173])
1965 Woolley, UE 8 pp. 70 and 103 (provenance, study)
1981 Walker, CBI p. 70 no. 86 (transliteration)
1995 Frame, RIMB 2 pp. 239–240 B.6.32.2010 (edition)
2013 May, CRRA 56 pp. 206–207 (study)
2021 Hätinen, dubsar 20 p. 354 and n. 1999 (study)

TEXT

1) [^{d}nanna lugal ^{d}en-líl-e]-⸢ne⸣
2) [lugal-a]-ni
3) [^{md}EN.ZU-TI.LA.BI-DU$_{11}$].GA
4) [šagina úri].KI-ma
5) [ú-a] ⸢eridu⸣.KI-ga
6) [é-x]-x-ga$^{?}$-kù-ga
7) [ki-tuš/gub] ^{d}en-nu-gi-ke$_{4}$
8) [mu-na]-dù

1–8) [(For) the god Nanna, king of the Enlil (circle of) gods], his [lord: Sîn-balāssu-iq]bi, [governor of Ur, (5) who provides for Eri]du, built [E...]kuga, [the abode/station] of the god Ennugi.

2016

Six bricks found at Ur are inscribed with a Sumerian text that states that Sîn-balāssu-iqbi had built the shrine Eanšar ("House, All Heaven") for the moon-god Nanna (Sîn). The inscription is similar to Asb. 2010–2015 and 2017–2018.

CATALOGUE

Ex.	Museum Number	Excavation/ Registration No.	Provenance	Dimensions (cm)	Lines Preserved	cpn
1	BM 119279, face	1927-10-3,274; U 3297	Ur, well of the Ningal temple	25.5×25.5×7.5	1–8	c
2	BM 119279, edge	1927-10-3,274; U 3297	As ex. 1	As ex. 1	1–8	c
3	CBS 16486, face	U 3297a	As ex. 1	25.5×15.5×8	1–8	c
4	CBS 16486, edge	U 3297a	As ex. 1	As ex. 3	1–8	c
5	CBS 16556a, face	U 3297b	As ex. 1	26×26×8	1–8	c
6	CBS 16556a, edge	U 3297b	As ex. 1	As ex. 5	1–8	c
7	CBS 16556b, face	U 3297c	As ex. 1	25.5×25.5×6.5	1–8	c
8	CBS 16556b, edge	U 3297c	As ex. 1	As ex. 7	1–8	c
9	IM 1101	U 3297	As ex. 1	—	—	n
10	IM 1102	U 3297	As ex. 1	—	—	n

COMMENTARY

C.B.F. Walker kindly collated exs. 1–2. The designation a–c after the Ur excavation number for exs. 3–8 is one added by the Penn Museum and is not part of the original excavation number. As for IM 1101 and IM 1102 (exs. 9–10), which have not been examined firsthand, it is possible that each has the inscription twice, once on the brick's face and once on the brick's edge. Sir Leonard Woolley did not indicate whether they do or do not, but also does not do so for exs. 1–2, 3–4, 5–6, and 7–8 (see UE 8 p. 103). C.J. Gadd indicated that his copy and edition come from BM 119279 (exs. 1–2), but the measurements he gives (25.5×12.0×7.0 cm) fit CBS 16486 (exs. 3–4) better than BM 119279. All of the exemplars are inscribed, not stamped. Following RINAP editorial practice, no score of the text is provided on Oracc.

BIBLIOGRAPHY

1925 Woolley, AJ 5 p. 368 (provenance)

1928 Gadd, UET 1 no. 177 and sub no. 174 (copy, edition [as variant to UET 1 no. 173])

1939 Woolley, UE 5 pp. 32–33 and 60 (provenance)

1965 Woolley, UE 8 pp. 70 and 103 (exs. 1–l0, provenance, study)

1981 Walker, CBI p. 69 no. 83 (exs. 1–2, transliteration)

1985 Behrens, JCS 37 p. 240 no. 60 (exs. 3–8, study)

1995 Frame, RIMB 2 pp. 240–241 B.6.32.2011 (exs. 1–10, edition)

2013 May, CRRA 56 pp. 206–207 (study)

2021 Hätinen, dubsar 20 pp. 352–353 (edition)

TEXT

1) ᵈnanna lugal ᵈen-líl-e-ne
2) lugal-a-ni
3) ᵐᵈEN.ZU-TI.LA.BI-DU$_{11}$.GA
4) šagina úri.KI-ma
5) ú-a eridu.KI-ga
6) é-an-šár
7) ki-tuš nam-lugal-la-ni
8) mu-na-dù

1–8) (For) the god Nanna, king of the Enlil (circle of) gods, his lord: Sîn-balāssu-iqbi, governor of Ur, (5) who provides for Eridu, built Eanšar, his royal abode.

---

1 ᵈen-líl-e-ne "the Enlil (circle of) gods": Exs. 2, 4, 6, 8 have ᵈ50-e-ne.
7 Contra C.J. Gadd (UET 1 p. 55 sub no. 174), exs. 2, 4, 6, 8 do not omit line 7; see the commentary of Asb. 2010.

2017

This Sumerian brick inscription is known from four bricks discovered at Ur. The text records that the governor of that Babylonian city, Sîn-balāssu-iqbi, constructed the shrine Ešaduga ("House that Pleases the Heart"); the work was undertaken on behalf of the god Nanna (Sîn). The inscription is similar to Asb. 2010–2016 and 2018.

CATALOGUE

Ex.	Museum Number	Excavation/ Registration No.	Provenance	Dimensions (cm)	Lines Preserved	cpn
1	BM 119271, face	1927-10-3,266; U 3298	Ur, well of the Ningal temple	25.5×25×7	1–8	c
2	BM 119271, edge	1927-10-3,266; U 3298	As ex. 1	As ex. 1	1–8	c
3	CBS 16487, face	U 3298a	As ex. 1	26×12×8	1–8	c
4	CBS 16487, edge	U 3298a	As ex. 1	As ex. 3	1–8	c
5	CBS 16557, face	U 3298b	As ex. 1	26×26×8	1–8	c
6	CBS 16557, edge	U 3298b	As ex. 1	As ex. 5	1–5	c
7	IM 1103	U 3298	As ex. 1	—	—	n

COMMENTARY

Exs. 1–2 were kindly collated by C.B.F. Walker. The designations a and b after the Ur excavation numbers for exs. 3–6 were added by the Penn Museum, Philadelphia, and are not part of the original excavation numbers. In view of the measurements given for the brick in UET 1 (25.5×12.0×7.0), it seems likely that C.J. Gadd used CBS 16487, or possibly IM 1103, for his model. It is possible that ex. 7 has the inscription twice, once on the face and once on the edge; however, it has not been possible to examine the brick in the Iraq Museum in Baghdad. The text is inscribed, not stamped. No score for this brick inscription is presented on Oracc.

BIBLIOGRAPHY

1925 Woolley, AJ 5 p. 368 (provenance)
1928 Gadd, UET 1 no. 178 and sub no. 174 (copy, edition [as variant to UET 1 no. 173])
1939 Woolley, UE 5 pp. 32–33 and 60 (provenance)
1965 Woolley, UE 8 pp. 70 and 103 (exs. 1–7, provenance, study)
1981 Walker, CBI p. 69 no. 84 (exs. 1–2, transliteration)
1985 Behrens, JCS 37 p. 241 no. 61 (exs. 3–6, study)
1995 Frame, RIMB 2 pp. 241–242 B.6.32.2012 (exs. 1–7, edition)
2013 May, CRRA 56 pp. 206–207 (study)
2021 Hätinen, dubsar 20 p. 353 (edition)

TEXT

1) ^{d}nanna lugal ^{d}en-líl-e-ne
2) lugal-a-ni
3) ^{md}EN.ZU-TI.LA.BI-DU$_{11}$.GA
4) šagina úri.KI-ma
5) ú-a eridu.KI-ga
6) é-šà-du$_{10}$-ga
7) ki-tuš nam-^{d}en-líl-lá-a-ni
8) mu-na-dù

1–8) (For) the god Nanna, king of the Enlil (circle of) gods, his lord: Sîn-balāssu-iqbi, viceroy of Ur, (5) who provides for Eridu, built Ešaduga, the abode of his Enlilship.

1 ^{d}en-líl-e-ne "the Enlil (circle of) gods": Exs. 2, 4, 6 have respectively ^{d}50-e-ne, ⸢^{d}50-e-ne⸣, and ^{d}⸢50-e⸣-n[e].

7 Contra C.J. Gadd (UET 1 p. 55 sub no. 174), exs. 2, 4, 6 do not omit line 7; see the commentary of Asb. 2010. Unlike Asb. 2010–2015, we have an abstract noun (nam-^{d}en-líl-lá-a-ni, "his Enlilship" or "his position as chief deity") here rather than the name of a deity.

2018

This Sumerian inscription, which is written on three bricks found at Ur, states that Sîn-balāssu-iqbi had built for the god Nanna (Sîn) Eašanamar (exact reading and meaning uncertain), the abode of the god Enlil. The text is similar to Asb. 2010–2017.

CATALOGUE

Ex.	Museum Number	Excavation/ Registration No.	Provenance	Dimensions (cm)	Lines Preserved	cpn
1	BM 119274, face	1927-10-3,269; U 3299	Ur, well of the Ningal temple	26×26×7	1–8	n
2	BM 119274, edge	1927-10-3,269; U 3299	As ex. 1	As ex. 1	3–8	n
3	CBS 16488, face	U 3299	As ex. 1	26×26×8	1–8	c
4	CBS 16488, edge	U 3299	As ex. 1	As ex. 3	1–8	c
5	CBS 16558	U 3299	As ex. 1	—	—	n

COMMENTARY

According to C.J. Gadd (UET 1 p. 55 sub no. 174), the inscription on the edge of BM 119274 (ex. 2) omitted line 7; however, C.B.F. Walker does not indicate this in CBI. The brick could not be located in the British Museum for collation, but in view of the same erroneous statement by Gadd about Asb. 2011–2017, it seems likely that the line was not omitted. According to Woolley, UE 8 p. 103, CBS 16558 (ex. 5) has this inscription, but this brick cannot be located at present in the Penn Museum, although it was registered in the museum on April 19, 1927. All of the exemplars are inscribed, not stamped. Following RINAP editorial practice, no score of this text is presented on Oracc.

The exact reading of the temple's Sumerian name in line 6 is not certain. A.R. George tentatively suggested é-tilla$_{x}$-maḫ$^{!}$ ("House, Exalted Open Place"); see House Most High p. 69 no. 91 and p. 150 no. 1101, but, as noted by A. Hätinen (dubsar 20 pp. 354–355 n. 2001), AŠ.AN.AMAR.UTU is used "for the name Dilimbabbar/Namraṣīt [the moon god] in one of the manuscripts for the prayer 'Šamaš 1.'"

BIBLIOGRAPHY

1925 Woolley, AJ 5 p. 368 (provenance)
1928 Gadd, UET 1 no. 179 and sub no. 174 (exs. 1–2, copy, edition [as variant to UET 1 no. 173])
1939 Woolley, UE 5 pp. 32–33 and 60 (provenance)
1965 Woolley, UE 8 pp. 70 and 103 (exs. 1–5, provenance, study)
1981 Walker, CBI pp. 69–70 no. 85 (exs. 1–2, transliteration)
1985 Behrens, JCS 37 p. 241 no. 62 (ex. 3, study)
1995 Frame, RIMB 2 pp. 242–243 B.6.32.2013 (exs. 1–5, edition)
2013 May, CRRA 56 pp. 206–207 (study)
2021 Hätinen, dubsar 20 pp. 354–355 and n. 2001 (study)

TEXT

1) ^{d}nanna lugal ^{d}en-líl-e-ne
2) lugal-a-ni
3) ^{md}EN.ZU-TI.LA.BI-DU$_{11}$.GA
4) šagina úri.KI-ma
5) ú-a eridu.KI-ga

1–8) (For) the god Nanna, king of the Enlil (circle of) gods, his lord: Sîn-balāssu-iqbi, governor of Ur, (5) who provides for Eridu, built *Eašanamar*, the abode of the god Enlil.

1 ^{d}en-líl-e-ne "the Enlil (circle of) gods": Ex. 4 has ^{d}⸢50⸣-e-n[e]; ex. 2 might also have had the same variant but it cannot be located for collation.

6) é-AŠ-AN-AMAR
7) ki-tuš ^{d}en-líl-lá-ke$_4$
8) mu-na-dù

---

6 é-AŠ-AN-AMAR "*Eašanamar*": The final sign in ex. 3 looks more like ŠEŠ than AMAR; the sign is damaged on ex. 4.
7 Contra C.J. Gadd (UET 1 p. 55 sub no. 174), ex. 4 and likely ex. 2 (latter not collated) do not omit line 7; see the commentary of Asb. 2010. ^{d}en-líl-lá-ke$_4$ "of the god Enlil": Ex. 3–4 omit -ke$_4$.

Aššur-etel-ilāni

Only a handful of inscriptions are known for Ashurbanipal's son and immediate successor Aššur-etel-ilāni (631–627) and more texts of his are attested from Babylonia than from Assyria. This king's texts are presently found on numerous bricks, a clay cylinder, and a few single-column clay tablets. All but one inscription are written in the Standard Babylonian dialect of Akkadian; a brick inscription discovered at Nippur is composed in the Sumerian language. This group of texts provides some details about his building activities and support of temples, and one text records that he had the remains of an earlier Chaldean ruler returned from Assyria to its proper burial place in Bīt-Dakkūri. Aššur-etel-ilāni is known to have sponsored building on or donated inscribed objects to the temples Eešerke (Sippar-Aruru), E-ibbi-Anum (Dilbat), Ekur (Nippur), Esagil (Babylon), and Ezida (Kalḫu). For further information about Aššur-etel-ilāni's reign, see pp. 31–33 of the present volume (with references to earlier scholarly literature).

1

Numerous bricks are inscribed with a short Akkadian inscription stating that Aššur-etel-ilāni had bricks made for rebuilding Ezida ("True House"), the temple of the god Nabû at Kalḫu. As one generally expects from brick inscriptions, no details about the project are recorded in the text.

CATALOGUE

Ex.	Museum Number	Excavation/ Registration No.	Provenance	Dimensions (cm)	Lines Preserved	cpn
1	BM 90184	1979-12-20,100	Kalḫu, Ezida	15.5×33×9	1–7	p
2	BM 90185	1979-12-20,101	As ex. 1	15×33.5×9.5	1–7	p
3	BM 90186	1979-12-20,102	As ex. 1	32.5×32×9	1–7	p
4	BM 90187	1979-12-20,103	As ex. 1	15×33×9	1–7	p
5	BM 90188	1979-12-20,104	As ex. 1	32×33×9	1–7	p
6	BM 90189	1979-12-20,105	As ex. 1	30.5×32×9	1–7	p
7	BM 90190	1979-12-20,106	As ex. 1	31.5×32.5×8.5	1–7	p
8	BM 90191	1979-12-20,107	As ex. 1	32×31.5×9	1–7	p
9	BM 90192	1979-12-20,108	As ex. 1	33×32.5	1–7	p
10	BM 90193	1979-12-20,109	As ex. 1	31.5×26×8	1–7	p
11	BM 90194	1979-12-20,110	As ex. 1	31.5×31.5×9	1–7	p
12	BM 90195	1979-12-20,111	As ex. 1	15×32.5×9	1–7	p
13	BM 90196	1979-12-20,112	As ex. 1	15×33.5×8.5	1–7	p
14	BM 90197	1979-12-20,113	As ex. 1	15×33.5×9	1–7	p
15	BM 90198	1979-12-20,114	As ex. 1	15×27×9.5	1–7	p
16	BM 90199	1979-12-20,115	As ex. 1	15×33×9	1–7	p
17	BM 90706	1979-12-20,314	As ex. 1	—	4–7	n
18	BM 90725	1979-12-20,326	As ex. 1	—	1–7	n
19	BM 90741	1979-12-20,332	As ex. 1	17.5×15.5×9	1–7	p
20	IM 60624	—	As ex. 1	—	1–7	p
21	IM 56282	ND 1130	Kalḫu, Burnt Palace, Room 18	33×33×9	1–7	n

22	IM 59296	ND 4406A	Kalḫu, Ezida or Burnt Palace	—	—	n
23	IM 59296	ND 4406B	As ex. 22	—	—	n
24	IM —	ND 4407A	As ex. 22	—	—	n
25	IM —	ND 4407B	As ex. 22	—	—	n
26	IM 60634	ND 6215	As ex. 1	—	—	n

COMMENTARY

All of the bricks that contain this inscription of Aššur-etel-ilāni are inscribed by hand rather than stamped. The master text is based on ex. 7. The inscription is written over seven lines in the majority of exemplars (with the lineation the same in each), but exs. 15 and 16 only contain six lines and ex. 18 is written over nine lines. The shorter lineation of exs. 15–16 has separate causes, however, since the scribe of the former wrote lines 5–6 of the master text on a single line, while the scribe of the latter erroneously omitted line 5 entirely.

Exs. 20 and 26 also have an impression from a brick stamp. On ex. 20, the lineation of the text follows the majority of the exemplars as it is written in seven lines, but there is a large blank space of about four lines separating lines 4 and 5 of the inscription, in between which a stamped image appears. The impression is of a *mušḫuššu*-dragon carrying the spade of the god Marduk and the wedge/stylus of the god Nabû on its back, with the seven circles of the Sebetti behind those; the image is rotated about eighty degrees clockwise in relation to the inscription, thus primarily facing to the left. Ex. 26 also contains a stamp impression of a *mušḫuššu*-dragon carrying those divine emblems in the middle of the brick, but this brick was not available for study to provide more specific information about the inscription or image on it. Interestingly, BM 132263 (1958-2-8,6; ND 6216) is a brick discovered in Ezida that apparently has the same stamped image as these two exemplars, although it is uninscribed. Despite the fact that it lacks an inscription, the shared stamp impression suggests that this brick was created for Aššur-etel-ilāni's work on that temple as well. The information for exs. 21–26 (and BM 132263) beyond the little that has been published was provided by C.B.F. Walker, and the authors would like to thank him for this contribution.

No score for this brick inscription is presented on Oracc, following RINAP editorial practices. The minor (orthographic) variants, however, are listed at the back of the book. Given that exs. 17 and 18 were not available for study, the variants contained on these objects are taken from Walker, CBI pp. 127–128 no. 190.

BIBLIOGRAPHY

1861 1 R pl. 8 no. 3 (copy)
1916 Streck, Asb. pp. CXCIX and 380–381 (edition)
1922 BM Guide p. 75 nos. 314–329 (exs. 1–15, study)
1927 Luckenbill, ARAB 2 p. 408 §1130–1131 (translation)
1952 Wiseman, Iraq 14 p. 67 (ex. 21, study)
1957 Mallowan, Iraq 19 p. 11 (exs. 22–25, translation, provenance)
1957 D. Oates, Iraq 19 p. 33 (provenance)
1973 Postgate, Governor's Palace p. 264 (ex. 21, provenance)
1981 Walker, CBI pp. 127–128 no. 190 (exs. 1-19, transliteration, variants)
1991 J. Oates, CAH^2 3/2 p. 172 (study)
1998 Brinkman, PNA 1/1 p. 183 sub Aššūr-etel-ilāni 2.a.2′ (study)
2001 D. Oates and J. Oates, Nimrud pp. 115, 118 and 132 (exs. 21–26, study, provenance)
2009 Novotny and Van Buylaere, Studies Oded p. 234 (translation, study)

TEXT

1) *ana-ku* ^{m}AN.ŠÁR-*e-tel*-DINGIR.MEŠ MAN ŠÚ MAN KUR AŠ
2) A ^{m}AN.ŠÁR-DÙ-A MAN ŠÚ MAN KUR AŠ
3) A ^{m}AN.ŠÁR-PAP-AŠ MAN ŠÚ MAN KUR AŠ-*ma*
4) *ú-še-piš-ma* SIG$_4$.AL.ÙR.RA
5) *a-na e-peš é-zi-da*
6) *šá qé-reb* URU.*kal-ḫa*
7) *ana* TI.LA ZI.MEŠ-*ia* BA-*ìš*

1–7) I, Aššur-etel-ilāni, king of the world, king of Assyria; son of Ashurbanipal, king of the world, king of Assyria; son of Esarhaddon, king of the world, (who was) also king of Assyria; had baked brick(s) made for (re)building Ezida, which is inside Kalḫu. I dedicated (this brick) for the preservation of my life.

4 Ex. 18 omits *ú-še-piš-ma*.
5 Ex. 16 omits this line.

2

A copy of an Akkadian inscription of Aššur-etel-ilāni is written on a crudely-fashioned, single-column clay tablet. That text records that this successor of Ashurbanipal had an offering table made of *musukkannu*-wood and *ṣāriru*-gold for the god Marduk, Babylon's tutelary deity. A two-line note appears after the inscription and mentions food offerings, the name of an individual (a certain Nādin, son of Bēl-aḫḫē-iqīša), and a date (the eleventh day of Ulūlu [VI] of the king's third regnal year). M. Jursa has argued convincingly that the tablet probably comes from Uruk and was copied in the reign of Cambyses, and that the date on the tablet refers to Cambyses' reign (NABU 2013/1 pp. 19–21 no. 13 and Current Research in Cuneiform Palaeography pp. 187–198).

CATALOGUE

Museum Number	Provenance	Dimensions (cm)	cpn
PTS 2253	Possibly Uruk	11.8×8.7	c

COMMENTARY

In 1915, Princeton Theological Seminary purchased their collection of cuneiform tablets, including the present one, from Yale University. Because Yale had earlier acquired the items from various dealers, the original provenance of the inscription is not known. Since the god Marduk is described as "lord of Babylon, who dwells in Esagil" (lines 8–9), it is plausible that the *musukkannu*-wood table mentioned in the text was to be placed in the Esagil temple and, thus, this might indicate that the inscription originally comes from Babylon, Marduk's principal place of worship. The inscription is written in Babylonian script, although a few sign forms are Neo-Assyrian. E. Leichty suggested that lines 1–20 are the text for the inscription which was to be carved or painted on the offering table and that they were written by the individual who is mentioned by name in line 22 (Nādin, son of Bēl-aḫḫē-iqīša) to serve as a draft or model for the craftsmen. Leichty suggested also that the offerings mentioned in line 21 were perhaps to have been presented to Marduk in Nādin's name when the table was dedicated. M. Jursa, however, has argued that the tablet is likely a late copy of an original written in Assyrian script and that it likely comes from Uruk, since Nādin, son of Bēl-aḫḫē-iqīša (line 22), is probably to be identified with a scribe by that name who is known at Uruk from the reign of Neriglissar into the reign of Cambyses, who was the author of texts composed between the third year of Nabonidus and the fourth year of Cambyses, and who is known to have on occasion carried out his duties in Babylon, including probably in the sixth month of Cambyses' third year. Jursa's careful study of the paleography of the inscription has also made him suggest a later date for the tablet than the reign of Aššur-etel-ilāni, a date in the second half of the sixth century. For details, see Jursa, NABU 2013/1 pp. 19–21 no. 13 and Current Research in Cuneiform Palaeography pp. 187–198.

The tablet is roughly oval in shape, crudely formed, and has been flattened at the edges. Leichty had suggested that it appears that a previously inscribed tablet had been moistened and flattened for reuse.

Line 12 is unintelligible and appears to have been inserted in between lines 11 and 13; there is no contextual break between lines 11 and 12. In the left margin between lines 16 and 17 are traces of what may be two signs, possibly ŠÀ NU. Leichty suggested that "they, as well as the blank spaces on the tablet, have to do with the placing of the inscription on the table ... Perhaps these notes refer to decoration on the table in which case we should probably read NU as *ṣalam* 'relief, drawing.'"

BIBLIOGRAPHY

1983 Leichty, JAOS 103 pp. 217–220 (photo, edition)
1986 Brinkman and Kennedy, JCS 38 p. 103 no. Mn.2 (study)
1995 Frame, RIMB 2 pp. 262–263 B.6.35.1 (edition)
1997 Hurowitz, RA 91 p. 40 nn. 5–6 (study)
1998 Brinkman, PNA 1/1 p. 183 sub Aššūr-etel-ilāni 2.b.1′ (study)
2013 Jursa, NABU 2013/1 pp. 19–21 no. 13 (lines 21–22, edition; study)
2015 Jursa, Current Research in Cuneiform Palaeography pp. 187–198 (study)

Figure 13. PTS 2253 (Aei 2) is a crudely-fashioned, single-column clay tablet inscribed with a text recording the dedication of an offering table to the god Marduk. © Special Collections, Wright Library, Princeton Theological Seminary.

TEXT

Obv.
1) [*a-na* ^{d}AMAR].⸢UTU$^{?}$ *kab*⸣*-tu šit-ra-ḫu* ^{d}EN.LÍL DINGIR.MEŠ *šá-qu-ú*
2) [*e-li* DINGIR].⸢MEŠ⸣ *a-*⸢*šir*⸣ DINGIR.MEŠ *ka-la-me mu-kil mar-kas* ^{d}*í-gì-gì*
3) [*ù* ^{d}*a*]-⸢*nun*⸣*-na-ki mu-ma-ʾe-er an-durun-na* LUGAL ŠÚ AN-*e ù* KI-*tim*
4) ⸢*šá*$^{?}$ *a*$^{?}$*-na*$^{?}$ *zik*⸣*-ri-šú* DINGIR.MEŠ GAL.MEŠ ⸢*pal*⸣*-ḫiš ú-taq-qu-ú qí-bit-su*
(3 lines blank)

Obv. 1–4) [To the god] Marduk, venerable, splendid, the Enlil of the gods, most exalted of [the] gods, the one who directs all of the gods (and) holds the link between the Igīgū- [and] Anunnakū-gods, controller of the heavenly abode, king of the totality of heaven and netherworld, at whose mention the great gods fearfully attend his command,
3 blank lines

---

5) *šaḫ-tú la-a-nu ši-i-ḫu šá ina* ZU.AB *ir-bu-ú bal-ti šur-ru-ḫu*
6) *mì-na-a-ta šu-tu-ru ṣu-ub-bu-ú nab-ni-ti le-eʾ-um*
7) *le-eʾ-ú-tu mu-du-ú ka-la-me la-mid ṭè-em* ZU.AB
8) *a-ḫi-iz pi-riš-ti làl-gar* EN KÁ.DINGIR.RA.KI

Obv. 5–9a) respectful, large of stature, one who grew up in the Watery Abyss (*apsû*), (whose) dignity is splendid, (whose) body is superior, (and whose) features are perfect, most capable of all (of the gods), one who knows everything, understands the will of the Watery Abyss, (and) comprehends the secret(s) of the *lalgar*, lord of Babylon, who dwells in Esagil, great lord, his lord:

---

3 For *andurunna* "heavenly abode," see Borger, MZ p. 250.
7 *ṭè-em* "will": Perhaps translate instead "affair(s)."
8 CAD L p. 47 describes *lalgar* as "cosmic subterranean water."

9) *a-šib é-sag-íl* EN GAL-*ú* EN-*šú* ^{m}AN.ŠÁR-*e-tel-li*-DINGIR.MEŠ
10) LUGAL ŠÚ LUGAL KUR AN.ŠÁR.KI GIŠ.BANŠUR GIŠ.MES.MÁ.KAN.NA
11) *iṣ-ṣi da-ru-ú* ⸢*šá ṣa*⸣*-ri-ri* ḪUŠ.A *uḫ-ḫu-zu*
Rev.
12) ŠÁ NU KÁT MAŠ *x*
13) [*i*]-⸢*na*⸣ *ši-pir* ⸢DUMU⸣.ME ⸢*um-ma-nu nak*⸣*-liš šu-pu-šú a-na si-ma-a-ta*
14) ⸢*ma-ka-le*⸣*-e* KÙ.ME *šu-lu-ku a-na* TIN ZI.MEŠ-*šú še-me-e*
15) *su-pe-e-šú sa-kap* LÚ.KÚR.MEŠ-*šú* BA-*iš*
16) ^{d}AMAR.UTU EN GAL-*ú* (erasure) GIŠ.BANŠUR *šu-a-ti*
17) *ḫa-diš ina nap-lu-si-ka* ^{d}*šul-pa-è-a* EN GIŠ.BANŠUR
18) *ina ra-kas* GIŠ.BANŠUR *šá-rak sur-qin-nu ka-a-a-an la na-par-ka-a*
19) *a-mat* MUNUS.SIG$_{5}$ ^{m}AN.ŠÁR-*e-tel-li*-DINGIR.ME LUGAL KUR AN.ŠÁR.KI
20) NUN *mi-gir lìb-bi-ka lit-tas-qar ma-ḫar-ka*
Erased line
Blank line
21) 2 SÌLA 3 *šal-šú* NINDA SISKUR 1 (PI) 1 (BÁN) GIŠ.PÈŠ ḪÁD.A *ina maš-šar-ti šá* ITI.DU$_{6}$
22) ^{m}*na-din* A ^{md}EN-PAP.ME-BA-*šá* ITI.KIN UD.11.KAM MU.3.KAM

Obv. 9b–Rev. 15) Aššur-etel-ilāni, king of the world (and) king of Assyria, in order to ensure his good health, so that his prayers be heard, and to overthrow his enemies presented (this) table of *musukkannu*-wood, a durable wood, which is mounted with red *ṣāriru*-gold ... artistically made by the skill of craftsmen, (and) suitable for the fitting things of pure food offerings.

Rev. 16–20) O god Marduk, great lord, when you look upon this table with pleasure, (and) when (this) table is set (and) regular, ceaseless offerings are presented, may the god Šulpaea, the lord of the table, speak well of Aššur-etel-ilāni, king of Assyria (and) your favorite ruler, before you!

Erased line
Blank line
Rev. 21–22a) Two *qû* (and) the three and one-third *akalu* (as) offerings; one *pānu* (and) one *sūtu* of dried figs from the *maššartu*-deliveries of the month Tašrītu (VII). Nādin, son of Bēl-aḫḫē-iqīša.
Rev. 22b) Ulūlu (VI), eleventh day, third year.

3

This clay tablet, which was found at Babylon in 1911, is inscribed with an Akkadian text stating that Aššur-etel-ilāni, Ashurbanipal's son and immediate successor, had a gold scepter made for the god Marduk. The scepter was placed in Eešerke ("House, Shrine of Weeping"), that god's shrine at Sippar-Aruru.

CATALOGUE

Museum Number	Excavation Number	Photograph Number	Provenance	Dimensions (cm)	cpn
VAT 13142	BE 42262	Bab ph 2329	Babylon, Merkes, Temple	6.8×3.5×1.9	c

2 line 12 There is a blank space after line 12, the first line on the reverse.
2 line 21 Two *qû* and three and one-third *akalu* are equivalent to approximately two and one-third liters. One *pānu* and one *sūtu* are equivalent to approximately forty-two liters (assuming a *sūtu* of 6 *qû*, see Powell, RLA 7/7–8 p. 498 §IV.7).

COMMENTARY

This clay tablet was identified by W.G. Lambert as the object published in the Deimel Festschrift by E. Ebeling (who gave no museum or excavation number for the tablet and stated that it was among the Aššur texts of the Vorderasiatisches Museum). The inscription is written in Neo-Assyrian script and shows evidence of several erasures. The tablet was kindly collated by J. Marzahn on behalf of the RIM Project.

The Sumerian name of the temple *é-èš-ér-ke*$_4$ means "House, Shrine of Weeping" and that building is not otherwise attested. A.R. George tentatively suggested that the name might be a corrupted form of *é-še-ri-ga* ("House Which Gleans Barley"), the temple of the deity Šidada at Dūr-Šarrukku (=Sippar-Aruru), which might have contained a secondary cult of the god Marduk (George, House Most High p. 83 no. 269). W.G. Lambert suggested to G. Frame that "weeping" might refer to that of the deities Tiāmat and Kingu (or Qingu), together with their allies, whose defeat by Marduk is mentioned in lines 5–6.

BIBLIOGRAPHY

1935 Ebeling, Studies Deimel pp. 71–73 (edition)

1995 Frame, RIMB 2 pp. 263–264 B.6.35.2 (edition)

1996 Marzahn and Frame, JCS 48 pp. 95–96 (copy, study)

1998 Brinkman, PNA 1/1 p. 183 sub Aššūr-etel-ilāni 2.b.1′ (study)

1999–2000 Da Riva and Frahm, AfO 46–47 p. 166 (lines 16–18, study)

TEXT

1) ⸢*a*⸣-*na* ^{d}MES EN *šur-bé-e* UR.⸢SAG⸣ MAḪ
2) EN EN.EN *šá-qu-u šá gat-tú šur-ru-ḫu*
3) UGU *kal* DINGIR.MEŠ *ma-aʾ-diš šur-bu-ú*
4) *na-ši* ⸢*me-lam*⸣-*me ez-zu-ti la-biš na-mur-ra-te*
5) *ṭa*-⸢*rid* ^{d}⸣*kin-gu ka-šid tam-tim gal-la-ti*
6) *ka*-⸢*mu lem-nu*⸣-*ti a-šib é-èš-ér-ke*$_4$
7) *šá qé-reb* ZIMBIR.KI-^{d}*a-ru-ru* EN GAL-*e* EN-*šú*

8) ⸢^{m}AN⸣.[ŠÁR]-⸢*e*⸣-*tel-li*-DINGIR.MEŠ MAN ŠÚ MAN KUR *aš-šur*.KI
9) ⸢DUMU ^{m}AN.ŠÁR-DÙ-A⸣-A MAN ŠÚ MAN KUR *aš-šur*.KI
10) *ú-še-piš-ma* GIŠ.NÍG.GIDRU KÙ.GI ḪUŠ.A
11) *šá a-na ṣi-bít* ŠU.II-*šú* KÙ-*tum šar-ku*
12) *a-na* TI.LA ZI.MEŠ-*šú* GÍD.DA UD.MEŠ-*šú*
13) GIN BALA.MEŠ-*šú šá-lam* NUMUN-*šú šur-šú-du* GIŠ.GU.ZA MAN-*ti-šú*
14) *še-me-e su**-*up-pi-šú ma-ḫa-ri tés-lit-i-šú*
15) *ina qé-reb é-èš-ér-ke*$_4$ *ú-kin da-riš*
16) *ù šá* LÚ.KU$_4$.É LÚ.*ki-na-al-ti* UN.MEŠ *šú-a-te*
17) *mal ba-šú-u mu-šal-li-mu al-ka-ka-ti-šú*
18) *šu-bar-ra*-<*šú*>-*nu a-na u*$_4$-*me ṣa-a-ti iš-kun*

---

19) (erasure) *šá ina* UGU GIŠ.NÍG.GIDRU KÙ.GI *šá* ^{d}MES

1–7) For the god Marduk, supreme lord, exalted hero, lord of lords, exalted, wh(ose) figure is splendid (and who) is vastly superior to all of the (other) gods, bearer of the awe-inspiring, terrible radiance, clothed in splendor, (5) who drove [off] the god Kingu, defeated the *angry* sea, (and) overcame the evil ones, who dwells in Eešerke — which is inside Sippar-Aruru — great lord, his lord:

8–15) Aššur-etel-ilāni, king of the world (and) king of Assyria, son of Ashurbanipal, king of the world (and) king of Assyria, (10) had a scepter of red gold made which was (then) presented for his (Marduk's) pure hands to grasp. He (Aššur-etel-ilāni) set (it) up forever inside Eešerke in order to ensure his good health, to prolong his days, to confirm his reign, to ensure the well-being of his descendant(s), to make his royal throne secure, (and) to ensure that his prayers are heard (and) his supplication(s) granted.

16–18) Moreover, he established for (all) future days the freedom from taxation of those privileged to enter the temple, the collegium, *those* people, as many as there are, who look after his (Marduk's) ways.

---

19) That which is (written) upon the gold scepter of the god Marduk.

---

5 The "sea" *tam-tim*, is the goddess Tiāmat, who, like her son and supporter Kingu, was defeated by Marduk in the Babylonian creation epic *Enūma eliš*. *tam-tim gal-la-ti* "*angry* sea" could also be translated as "roiling sea."

16 Instead of the singular form *šuāte*, one would expect a plural form to modify UN.MEŠ, "people." Thus, possibly translate instead "that collegium of people."

4

This six-line Akkadian text is inscribed on a brick now housed in the Weld-Blundell Collection of the Ashmolean Museum (Oxford). The inscription records Aššur-etel-ilāni's restoration of E-ibbi-Anum ("House the God Anu Named"), the temple of the god Uraš and the goddess Ninegal at Dilbat. Moreover, the text states that this successor of Ashurbanipal had debris cleared from a well of that temple.

CATALOGUE

Museum Number	Provenance	Dimensions (cm)	cpn
Ash 1922.190	Possibly Dilbat	38×9.5×8	c

COMMENTARY

S. Langdon states that the brick originates from Dilbat (Langdon, OECT 1 p. 37), but it is unclear if this provenance was determined solely by means of the text's contents or by some knowledge about where the piece was actually found. The text is inscribed along the edge of the brick in Babylonian script.

With regard to E-ibbi-Anum, see Unger, RLA 2/3 (1935) pp. 222–223; George, House Most High p. 102 no. 493; and Almamori and Bartelmus, ZA 111 (2021) pp. 174–190. Unusually, the name of the temple includes an Akkadian word, *ibbi*, "(he) named."

BIBLIOGRAPHY

1923 Langdon, OECT 1 pp. 37–38 and pl. 29 (copy, edition)
1927 Luckenbill, ARAB 2 p. 409 §1135A (translation)
1957 Borger, Orientalia NS 26 p. 7 (study to line 3)
1981 Walker, CBI pp. 70–71 no. 87 (transliteration)
1995 Frame, RIMB 2 pp. 264–265 B.6.35.3 (edition)
1998 Brinkman, PNA 1/1 p. 183 sub Aššūr-etel-ilāni 2.b.1′ (study)

TEXT

1) *a-na* ^{d}*uraš* EN MAḪ SAG.KAL DINGIR.ME GAL.ME *é-i-bí-*^{d}*a-num* BÁRA *ra-aš-bu* EN GAL-*u* EN-*šú* ^{m}AN.ŠAR$_{4}$-NIR.GÁL-DINGIR.ME MAN KUR AN.ŠÁR.KI

2) *mu-ud-diš* BÁRA DINGIR.ME GAL.MEŠ <<GAL.ME>> DUMU ^{m}⸢AN⸣.ŠÁR-DÙ-A MAN KUR AN.ŠÁR.KI SIPA *ṣal-mat* SAG.DU *é-i-bí-*^{d}*a-num áš-ri el-lu*

3) *šá qé-reb dil-bat*.KI *šu-bat* ^{d}*uraš u* ^{d}*nin-é-*⸢*gal*⸣ *uš-šiš a-gur-ru pi-ti-iq* ^{d}*báḫar eš-šiš ib-ni-ma* SUḪUŠ PÚ KI-*šú*

4) *ki-i pi-i la-bi-ri-im-ma ú-kin* ⸢*a-na*⸣ *du-ur u*$_{4}$*-me*

1a) For the god Uraš, exalted lord, foremost of the great gods of E-ibbi-Anum — the shrine (which is) worthy of honor — great lord, his lord:

1b–4a) Aššur-etel-ilāni, king of Assyria, who renovated the shrine(s) of the great gods, son of Ashurbanipal, king of Assyria, shepherd of the black-headed, renovated E-ibbi-Anum, the holy place which is inside Dilbat, the abode of the god Uraš and the goddess Ninegal. He built (it) anew with baked bricks, the craft of the god Baḫar and, with regard to the foundation of the well, he (re-)established its position just as (it had been) in ancient times.

4b–6) He cleaned this entire well for all time (in order

3 Baḫar was the god of potters.

zu-mur PÚ MU.MEŠ GIM ÍD.IDIGNA *u* ÍD.<BURANUN> *ub-bi-ib-ma*
5) *ana nap-ta-nu* DINGIR.ME GAL.MEŠ *ú-kin* A.⸢MEŠ⸣ *šu-nu-te*$_9$*-e-ma a-na nap-ta-nu uš-taḫ-ma-ṭu u*$_4$*-mi-šam ana* ^{d}AG
6) ^{d}AMAR.UTU ^{d}*uraš u* ^{d}*nin-é-gal a-ši-bu* ⸢*qé-reb*⸣ É MU*.ME SIG$_5$-*tim* ^{m}AN.ŠÁR-NIR.GÁL-DINGIR.ME* MAN *mi-gir-šú-un li-iq-bu-u li-ri-ik* BALA-*šú*

to make its water as pure) as (that of) the Tigris and <Euphrates> Rivers, and (5) he established its water for the meals of the great gods. That water should be brought every day in good time for (their) meals. May they say good things about Aššur-etel-ilāni, the king, their favorite, to the deities Nabû, Marduk, Uraš, and Ninegal, who dwell in that temple (so that) his reign may be long!

5

This thirteen-line Sumerian inscription of Aššur-etel-ilāni recording that he had Ekur ("House, Mountain"), the temple of the god Enlil, rebuilt is known from a fragment of a brick discovered at Nippur that is now in the Hilprecht collection of the Friedrich-Schiller-Universität (Jena). The text is inscribed, not stamped.

CATALOGUE

Museum Number	Provenance	Dimensions (cm)	cpn
HS 1958 (former HS 42)	Probably Nippur	15.2×9.6×6.6	c

COMMENTARY

The brick probably originates from the University of Pennsylvania's excavations at Nippur, which were undertaken between 1888 and 1900. The text's contents also suggest such a provenance. Although the fragment presently measures 15.2×9.6×6.6 cm, the brick had been cut down to this size in modern times. The inscription is written in Babylonian script, with some of the sign forms having archaizing features. The inscription was collated by J. Oelsner on behalf of the RIM Project.

As already noted by D.O. Edzard, both this inscription and one of Ashurbanipal's (Asb. 259) appear to be based upon an inscription of the Kassite king Adad-šuma-uṣur (1216–1187) which has been found on several bricks from Nippur (Hilprecht, BE 1/1 no. 81 and duplicates).

BIBLIOGRAPHY

1959-60 Edzard, AfO 19 p. 143 (photo, edition)
1969 Oelsner, WZJ 18 p. 54 no. 33 (study)
1995 Frame, RIMB 2 pp. 265–266 B.6.35.4 (edition)
1998 Brinkman, PNA 1/1 p. 183 sub Aššūr-etel-ilāni 2.b.1′ (study)

4 line 5 The understanding of the passage follows a suggestion by J.N. Postgate.

TEXT

1) [^{d}en-líl]
2) [lugal kur]-⌜kur⌝-[ra]
3) [lugal-a]-ni-ir
4) [AN].⌜ŠÁR⌝-*e-tel-lu*$_4$-DINGIR.MEŠ
5) ⌜sipa⌝ še-ga-bi
6) ú-a nibru.KI*
7) sag-ús* é-kur-ra
8) lugal kalag-ga
9) lugal ub-da límmu-ba
10) é-kur-ra
11) é ki ág-gá-a-ni
12) sig$_4$ al-ùr-ra-ta
13) mu-un-na-dù

1–13) For [the god Enlil, lord of the la]nds, his [lord: Aššu]r-etel-ilāni, (5) his obedient [shephe]rd, who provides for Nippur, supporter of Ekur, mighty king, king of the four quarters (of the world), (re)built (10) Ekur, his beloved temple with baked bricks.

6

Copies of this Akkadian inscription of Aššur-etel-ilāni are known from a clay tablet and two small clay cylinders. This text records that Aššur-etel-ilāni had the remains of a seventh-century chieftain of Bīt-Dakkūri returned from Assyria to the latter's ancestral home, Dūru-ša-Ladīni ("Fortress of Ladīnu"). The tribal leader in question, Šamaš-ibni, was likely the Dakkurian leader whom Esarhaddon (680–669) had taken to Assyria and executed in 678. This good deed on the part of Aššur-etel-ilāni presumably reflects his attempt to win the support of that important Chaldean tribe in Babylonia.

CATALOGUE

Ex.	Museum Number	Provenance	Object	Dimensions (cm)	Lines Preserved	cpn
1	YBC 2151	Purchased	Cylinder	10.6×5.4	1–20	c
2	NBC 6069	As ex. 1	Tablet	9.7×2.7	1–2, 19–20	c
3	NBC 6070	As ex. 1	Cylinder	10.3×4.9; Dia. of end 3.3	1–2, 2–17	c

COMMENTARY

The dealer from whom ex. 1 was purchased stated that it had been found at "Tel Khaled a few miles to the southeast of Hilla, near the present course of the Euphrates" according to A.T. Clay (YOS 1 p. 60). Tel Khaled might be Tulūl al-Ḫālidija; see Zadok, WO 16 (1985) pp. 54–55 and n. 166. There is no information on the provenances of the other two exemplars, which had passed through the antiquities market (Clay, YOS 1 p. 60 n. 1). Ex. 1 was collated by G. Frame both before and after it was baked. Several tiny fragments — at least some of which do not belong to this cylinder — had been attached to the piece in modern times and these were removed at the time of baking. These fragments are currently stored with YBC 2151 and preserve all or parts of one or more signs. These fragments are not taken into consideration in the score edition present on Oracc. The three exemplars are inscribed in contemporary Babylonian script and the line arrangement is identical for all three (as far as they are preserved).

The master line follows ex. 1, with help from exs. 2–3 in line 2 and ex. 3 in lines 3 and 7–12. The minor (orthographic) variants are listed at the back of the book.

Two Babylonian chronicles record that the governor of Nippur (...-aḫḫē-šullim) and Šamaš-ibni, "the Dakkurian" (that is, leader of the Bīt-Dakkūri tribe), were taken to Assyria and executed in the third year of Esarhaddon (678); see Leichty, RINAP 4 pp. 7–8. While nothing more is known about that particular governor of Nippur, Esarhaddon's royal inscriptions tell us about Šamaš-ibni's crime. They state that he had forcibly taken possession of fields belonging to the inhabitants of Babylon and Borsippa; for example, see Leichty, RINAP 4 p. 18 Esarhaddon 1 (Nineveh A) iii 62–70. Undoubtedly, Šamaš-ibni had taken control of this land while Babylon lay abandoned after its destruction by Sennacherib in 689 and problems had probably arisen over ownership of the land when Esarhaddon began the restoration of Babylon. Esarhaddon sent Assyrian troops south, plundered Bīt-Dakkūri, returned the land to its original owners, and made Nabû-ušallim, son of Balāssu, head of the tribe instead of Šamaš-ibni. On this matter, see in particular Frame, Babylonia pp. 79–80; see also Baker and Gentili, PNA 3/2 pp. 1198–1999 sub Šamaš-ibni no. 4.

As for Dūru-ša-Ladīni, to which the tomb was transferred, it was a fortified settlement in the area of the Bīt-Dakkūri tribe. See Unger, RLA 2/4 (1936) p. 247 sub Dûr-Ladinna; and Bagg, RGTC 7/3-1 p. 192 sub Dūr-Ladīni.

BIBLIOGRAPHY

1915 Clay, YOS 1 no. 43 (ex. 1, copy, edition)
1918 Meissner, OLZ 21 col. 223 (ex. 1, partial translation)
1922 Ungnad, OLZ 25 col. 3 (ex. 1, study)
1927 Luckenbill, ARAB 2 pp. 408–409 §§1132–1135 (ex. 1, translation)
1937 Stephens, YOS 9 no. 81 (ex. 2, copy) and no. 82 (ex. 3, copy)
1982 Bottéro in Gnoli and Vernant, La mort pp. 383–386 no. 6 and p. 403 (exs. 1–3, edition)
1988 Hecker, TUAT 2/4 p. 478 (exs. 1–3, translation)
1995 Frame, RIMB 2 pp. 266–268 B.6.35.5 (exs. 1–3, edition)
1998 Brinkman, PNA 1/1 p. 183 sub Aššūr-etel-ilāni 2.b.2′ (study)

TEXT

1) KI.MAḪ *šá* ^{md}UTU-*ib-ni* DUMU ^{m}*da-ku-*⌜*ru šá*⌝ ^{m}AN.ŠÁR-NIR.GÁL-DINGIR.MEŠ LUGAL KUR *aš-šur*
2) *re-e-mu ir-šá-áš-šum-ma ul-tu qé-reb* KUR *aš-šur a-na* É-^{m}*da-kur* KUR-*šú*
3) *ú-bil-la-áš-šum-ma ina* KI.MAḪ *ina qé-reb* É-*šú šá* BÀD-*šá-la-di-ni ú-šá-aṣ-li-lu-šú*
4) *man-nu at-ta lu-ú* LÚ.*šak-nu* LÚ.*šá-pi-ru lu-ú da-a-a-nu*
5) *lu-ú* NUN *šá ina* KUR *iš-šak-ka-nu a-na* KI.MAḪ *u e-ṣe-et-ti*
6) *šu-a-ti la ta-ḫa-aṭ-ṭu a-šar-šú ú-ṣur*
7) *ṣi-il-li ṭa-a-bi e-li-šú tu-ru-uṣ*
8) *a-na šu-a-ti* ^{d}AMAR.UTU EN GAL-*ú pa-le-e-ka lu-ur-*⌜*rik*⌝
9) *ṣu-lul-šú ṭa-a-bu e-li-ka li-iš-*⌜*kun*⌝
10) ⌜MU⌝-*ka* NUMUN-⌜*ka ù ba-la-ṭu* u_4⌝-*me-*⌜*ka* GÍD.DA.MEŠ *a-na* u_4-*me ṣa-a-ta*⌝ *lik-*⌜*ru*?-*bu*?⌝
11) *šum-ma* NUN *šu-ú lu-ú* LÚ.*šak-nu lu-ú* LÚ.*šá-pi-ru lu-ú da-a-a-nu*
12) *lu-ú* GÌR.NÍTA *šá ina* KUR *ib-ba-áš-šu-ú*
13) *a-na* KI.MAḪ *u e-ṣe-et-ti šu-a-ti i-ḫa-aṭ-ṭu-ú*
14) *a-šar-šú ú-nak-ka-ri a-na a-šar šá-nam-ma i-leq-qu-ú*
15) *ù man-ma a-na le-mut-tum ú-šad-ba-bu-šú-ma*

1–3) The tomb of Šamaš-ibni, the Dakkurian, upon whom Aššur-etel-ilāni, king of Assyria, had pity, brought from Assyria to Bīt-Dakkūri, his (own) country, and laid to rest in a tomb inside his home of Dūru-ša-Ladīni ("Fortress of Ladīnu").

4–10) Whoever you are, whether governor or commander or judge or prince, who is appointed in the land, do not harm this tomb or (its) bone(s)! (But rather) look after its position (and) extend (your) good protection over it! For (doing) this, may the god Marduk, the great lord, lengthen your reign, establish his good protection over you, (and) *bless* your name, your descendant(s), and your long life for all time!

11–20) (But) if that prince or governor or commandant or judge or governor who appears in the land harms this tomb or (its) bone(s), (or) changes its position, taking (it) to another place, (15) or (if) another person incites him to plan wicked things (against this tomb) and he listens (to him), may the god Marduk, the great lord, make his name, his descendant(s), his

5 and 13 *e-ṣe-et-ti* "bone(s)": Note the Assyrian form of the word *eṣemtu*.

i-šem-mu-ú
16) ^{d}AMAR.UTU EN GAL-*ú* MU-*šú* NUMUN-*šú* NUNUZ-*šú ù na-an-nab-šú*
17) *i-na pi-i* UN.MEŠ *li-ḫal-liq*
18) ^{d}AG *sa-ni-iq mit-ḫur-ti mi-na-a-ta* u_4*-me-*⸢*šú* GÍD.DA⸣.MEŠ ⸢*li-kar-ri*⸣
19) ⸢^{d}U.GUR⸣ *ina di-iʾ šib-*⸢*ṭu*⸣ *u šag-*⸢*ga*⸣*-áš-ti*
20) *la i-gam-mi-il nap-šat-su*

offspring, and his seed disappear from (mention by) the mouth(s) of the people! May the god Nabû, who makes opposing forces agree, cut short the number of his days (lit. "the number of his long days")! May the god Nergal not spare his life from *malaria*, plague, or slaughter!

Sîn-šuma-līšir

No inscriptions of Sîn-šuma-līšir, a man who was Aššur-etel-ilani's chief eunuch and who was probably not a member of the Assyrian royal family, are attested from either Assyria or Babylonia. This is hardly surprising because he appears to have vied for power for the entire duration that he held authority (627). Given that nearly all of his time was spent fighting against Sîn-šarra-iškun, a son of Ashurbanipal, and perhaps a few other members of the royal family, it is unlikely that any inscriptions were composed in Sîn-šuma-līšir's name. If any had been written, these inscribed objects were probably (systematically) destroyed by Sîn-šarra-iškun when he gained the upper hand, brought back civil order to Assyria, and ascended the Assyrian throne. For further information about Sîn-šuma-līšir, see pp. 31–33 of the present volume.

Sîn-šarra-iškun

Relatively few inscriptions are known for Sîn-šarra-iškun (626–612), the last Assyrian king to have ruled from Nineveh. Scholars have identified twenty-one official texts of his, although several of these might in fact belong to his much more powerful father, Ashurbanipal. At present, Sîn-šarra-iškun's texts come from cities in the Assyrian heartland, Nineveh (Ssi 1–6 and possibly 21), Aššur (Ssi 7–18), and Kalḫu (Ssi 19–20). The extant inscriptions are all written in the Akkadian language and are inscribed on clay cones (Ssi 11), clay cylinders (Ssi 1–5, 10, and 19), clay prisms (Ssi 7–9), clay tablets (Ssi 6 and 15–18), a clay bulla (Ssi 20), mud bricks (Ssi 13–14), a stone block (Ssi 12), and a stone vessel (Ssi 21). It is clear from scribal notes written on drafts or archival copies of inscriptions that official texts were also engraved on the metal plating of ceremonial tables (Ssi 17–18) and on metal cultic vessels and utensils (Ssi 15–16). Note that YBC 2171 (Stephens, YOS 9 no. 80), an Assyrian inscription written on a clay cylinder that A.K. Grayson (Studies Winnet p. 168) attributed to Sîn-šarra-iškun, is not edited here since that text more likely dates to the time of the much earlier Assyrian king Ninurta-tukultī-Aššur.

These texts record some of his building activities. Sîn-šarra-iškun is known to have sponsored construction on Sennacherib's "Palace Without a Rival" (South-West Palace; Ssi 1); the city wall of Nineveh (Ssi 6); the temple of the god Nabû at Aššur, Egidrukalamasumu ("House Which Bestows the Scepter of the Land"; Ssi 7–14); and the Nabû temple at Kalḫu, Ezida ("True House"; Ssi 19). Presumably, he undertook other building projects, but inscriptions recording those activities are either not sufficiently preserved to allow their identification or no longer extant (Ssi 2–5). Moreover, he dedicated metal(-plated) objects to various deities at Aššur (Ssi 15–18).

Seven inscriptions of Sîn-šarra-iškun bear eponym dates. These are as follows: Nabû-tappûtī-alik, chief eunuch (Ssi 1); Sîn-šarru-uṣur, governor of Ḫindānu (Ssi 3); Bēl-aḫu-uṣur, palace overseer (Ssi 6 and 10); Aššur-mātu-taqqin, governor of (U)pummu (Ssi 9); Sa'īlu, chief cook (Ssi 11); and Dādî, (chief) treasurer (Ssi 19). For information about the chronological sequence of these six post-canonical eponym officials, see pp. 41–42 of the present volume.

1

Several clay cylinders discovered at Nineveh, including a few found by L.W. King, appear to bear the same inscription of Sîn-šarra-iškun. That text, at least according to one exemplar, records the renovation of the western entrance of the "Palace Without a Rival" (South-West Palace) at Nineveh. Sîn-šarra-iškun calls his great-grandfather's royal residence the "Alabaster House," which undoubtedly refers to its numerous sculpted and inscribed limestone slabs and colossal apotropaic figures. In addition to boasting that he rebuilt that part of the palace from its foundations to its crenellations, Sîn-šarra-iškun claims to have expanded the building's structure beyond what it had been in the reign of Sennacherib. One copy of this text was inscribed in the eponymy of Nabû-tappûtī-alik, the chief eunuch. The inscription is generally referred to in scholarly publications as "Cylinder C."

CATALOGUE

Ex.	Museum Number	Registration Number	Provenance	Dimensions (cm)	Lines Preserved	cpn
1	BM 99320	Ki 1904-10-9,352 + Ki 1904-10-9,353	Nineveh, probably Kuyunjik	—	1–6, 6′–21′	c
2	BM 99324	Ki 1904-10-9,357	As ex. 1	4.1×5.1	1′–5′	c
3	—	81-7-27,8 + 82-5-22,26	As ex. 1	6.3×15.4	1′–12′	c
4	DT 64 + 82-5-22,27	82-5-22,7	As ex. 1	—	1–15, 17′–21′	c
5	K 8541	—	As ex. 1	5.7×3.2	10–20	c

COMMENTARY

The five fragments that bear the present inscription originate from hollow clay cylinders; ex. 4 preserves part of the cylinder's right end, which has a round opening in its base. A horizontal ruling separates each line of text in all of the exemplars. The lineation of lines 1–19 comes from exs. 1 and 4–5 and is the same in these exemplars where they overlap, while the lineation of lines 1′–12′ comes from ex. 3 and that of lines 13′–20′ from ex. 1. The subscript of the text containing the date (line 21′) is only preserved on ex. 1. A full score of the inscription is presented on Oracc and the minor (orthographic) variants are listed at the back of the book in the critical apparatus.

Note that M. Streck's edition of this inscription (Asb. pp. 382–387), which utilizes only exs. 4 and 5, is conflated with Ssi 19 (Cylinder B) exs. 1 [only K 1662] and 4.

BIBLIOGRAPHY

1880 Schrader, Berichte der Sächsischen Gesellschaft der Wissenschaften, Philologisch-Historische Klasse 32 pp. 29–30, 35–37 and 41 (exs. 3 [DT 64], 4, copy [typeset], study; ex. 3 [DT 64] lines 1–7, transliteration)
1892 Winckler, RA 2 p. 67 (ex. 3 lines 2′–4′, edition)
1890 Winckler, KB 2 p. 271 n. 2 (ex. 4 [DT 64], study)
1893 Bezold, Cat. 3 p. 937 (ex. 5, study)
1896 Bezold, Cat. 4 pp. 1547 and 1795 (exs. 3–4, study)
1914 King, Cat. p. 45 nos. 367–368 and 372 (exs. 1–3, study; lines 1–4, 21′ [ex. 1], copy [typeset])
1914 King, CT 34 p. 5 and pls. 2–3 and 5–7 (exs. 1–5, copy, study)
1916 Streck, Asb. pp. CCVII–CCIX, CDXCIV–CDXCV, 382–385, and 838–840 (exs. 4–5, edition [conflated with Ssi 19]; ex. 1, partial edition [lines 1–4, 21′]; exs. 2–3, study)
1926 Luckenbill, ARAB 2 pp. 411–413 §§1142–1147 (with n. 1) and 1150 (exs. 1–4, translation)
1952–53 Falkner, AfO 16 pp. 306 (exs. 1–5, study)
1967 von Soden, ZA 58 p. 252 (line 5, study)
1972 Grayson, Studies Winnett pp. 157–168 (exs. 1, 3–5 [conflated with Ssi 6], edition, study)
1991 Na'aman, ZA 81 p. 255 (line 5, study)
1991 J. Oates, CAH^2 3/2 p. 176 n. 29 (line 5, study)
1994 Millard, SAAS 2 p. 109 (study)
2001 Mattila, PNA 2/2 p. 894 sub Nabû-tappūtī-alik a (line 21′, study)
2002 Novotny, PNA 3/1 p. 1143 sub Sīn-šarru-iškun b.1′ (study)
2009 Frahm, KAL 3 p. 91 (study)
2009 Meinhold, Ištar p. 445 no. 16 (study)
2009 Novotny and Van Buylaere, Studies Oded pp. 218–219 (exs. 1–5, study)
2014 Novotny, JCS 66 p. 111 (line 13′, study)
2018 Novotny in Yamada, SAAS 28 p. 261 (line 13′, study)

TEXT

1) *a-na-ku* ^{md}⌈EN⌉.ZU-LUGAL-GAR-*un* LUGAL GAL LUGAL *dan-*⌈*nu*⌉ [LUGAL ŠÚ LUGAL KUR] ⌈AN⌉.ŠÁR.KI
2) *ni-iš* IGI.II AN.ŠÁR ^{d}EN.LÍL ^{d}NIN.LÍL ⌈GÌR.NÍTA *mut*⌉-*nen-*⌈*nu*⌉-[*ú* LÚ.*x*] *x é-šár-ra*
3) *ma-al-ku šuk-nu-šu* ⌈*i*⌉-*tu-ut kun lìb-bi* ^{d}30 ^{d}⌈NIN⌉.[GAL ^{d}UTU *u* ^{d}*a-a na-ram* ^{d}AMAR.UTU ^{d}NUMUN]-⌈DÙ⌉-*tum* ^{d}AG ^{d}PAPNUN
4) ⌈*ni*$^{?}$-*šu*⌉-*ut* ^{d}*iš-tar a-ši-bat* ⌈URU.NINA⌉ ^{d}*iš-tar a-ši-bat* [LÍMMU-DINGIR.KI *mi-gir* ^{d}U.GUR] ⌈*ù*⌉ ^{d}*nusku*
5) [*šá* AN.ŠÁR ^{d}]⌈NIN.LÍL⌉ *ù* DINGIR.MEŠ ⌈GAL.MEŠ⌉ [EN.MEŠ-*ia i-na*] ⌈*bi*⌉-*rit maš-ši-*⌈*ia*⌉ [*ke-niš ip-pal-su-ni-ma is-su-qu*]-⌈*ni*⌉ *a-na* LUGAL-*u-ti*
6) [*za-ni-nu-ú-ti kiš-šat ma-ḫa-zi* É.BAR-*ú-ti gi-mir eš-re-e-ti re-ʾu-ú-ut nap-ḫar ṣal-mat* SAG.DU *e*]-⌈*pe*⌉-*šu iq-bu-ni*

1–6) I, Sîn-šarra-iškun, great king, stron[g] king, [king of the world, king of A]ssyria, favored by the deities Aššur, Enlil, (and) Mullissu; pio[us] governor, [...] of Ešarra, humble ruler; chosen by the steadfast hearts of the deities Sîn, Ni[ngal, Šamaš, and Aya; beloved of the deities Marduk, Zarpa]nītu, Nabû, (and) Tašmētu; *the one chosen by* the goddess Ištar who resides in Nineveh (and) the goddess Ištar who resides in [Arbela, favorite of the gods Nergal] and Nusku; (5) [the one whom (the god) Aššur, the goddess Mul]lissu, and the grea[t] gods, [my lords, steadfastly looked upon am]ong m[y] *brothers* and [selected] for kingship; they commanded me [to per]form [the roles of provisioner of all cult centers, priest of all sanctuaries, (and) shepherd of the totality of the black-headed (people)];

7) [*ki-ma* AD *u* AMA *it-ta-nar-ru-in-ni-ma i-na-ru a-a-bi-ia ú-šam-qí-tú*] ⌈*ga*$^{?}$⌉-*re-ia*
8) [*ṭa-biš ú-še-šib-u-in-ni ina* GIŠ.GU.ZA LUGAL-*u-ti* AD] DÙ-*ia*
9) [^{d}*é-a* ^{d}*be-let*-DINGIR.MEŠ *a-na e-nu-ti kiš-šá-ti ib-nu-in-ni ina nap-ḫar x x ú-šá*]-⌈*ti*$^{?}$⌉-*ru nab-ni-ti*
10) [^{d}30 LUGAL *a-ge-e a-na kun-ni* SUḪUŠ KUR *šu-te-šur ba-ʾu-la-a-ti a-ge-e* EN-*u-ti e-pir-an-ni* GIŠ.GIDRU LUGAL-*u*]-⌈*ti*⌉ *ú-šat-me-eḫ rit-tu-u-a*
11) [^{d}NIN.LÍL *a-ši-bat* NINA.KI *an-tum* ...] *x* SAG.MEŠ-*ia*
12) [*eṭ-lu šu-pu-ú a-a-ru šu-tu-ru a-ḫi-iz ṭè-e-me ù mil-ki mu-ta*]-⌈*mu*⌉-*ú dam-qa-a-ti*

7–16) [they guided me like a father and a mother, killed my foes, (and) cut down] my [*adv*]*ersaries*; [they gladly placed me on the royal throne of the father] who had engendered me; [the god Ea (and) the goddess Bēlet-ilī created me for dominion over the world] (and) [*they made*] my form [*surpas*]*sing* [among all ...; (10) the god Sîn, king of the crown, crowned me with the crown of lordship] (and) he made my hand grasp [the scepter of kingshi]p [to make the foundation of the land firm (and) to direct the people; the goddess Mullissu who resides in Nineveh, (the goddess) Antu, ... *raised up*] my head; [resplendent young man, superb man, who comprehends reason and counsel, who spea]ks eloquent (words), [magnanimous,

---

4 ⌈*ni*$^{?}$-*šu*⌉-*ut* "*the one chosen by*": As already noted by A.K. Grayson (Studies Winnett p. 167), the interpretation of the first word of this line, which he reads as *tab-šu-ut*, is problematic, although it is almost certainly an epithet of Sîn-šarra-iškun. If Grayson's interpretation of the first sign is correct, then *tabšûtu* might be a variant form of *tabšītu* ("*creation*); see AHw p. 1299 sub *tabšītu* and CDA p. 393 sub *tabšītu*. Given that *binût* (*qāti*) ("creation (of the hands) of") is commonly attested in inscriptions of Ashurbanipal, Sîn-šarra-iškun's father, the reading of the first word of line 4 of this text as *tab-šu-ut* seems highly unlikely. Recently, the CAD (T p. 33 sub *tabšītu*), has tentatively suggested reading this word as ⌈*ni*$^{?}$-*šu*⌉-*ut*; compare D.D. Luckenbill (ARAB 2 p. 411 §1143), who translated the beginning of line 4 as "companion(?)," presumably from *nišūtu*, which according to the CAD (N p. 297–299) means "family, relatives (by consanguinity or by marriage)," and "people." The known meanings of *nišūtu*, however, do not seem to fit the context of this passage. Assuming that the first three signs of line 4 are to be read as ⌈*ni*$^{?}$-*šu*⌉-*ut*, then *nišût* might be interpreted as a rare variant of *nišītu* ("one chosen by"); see CAD N p. 281 sub *nišītu* 2.b.2′. For example, compare Leichty, RINAP 4 p. 14 Esarhaddon 1 (Nineveh A) ii 17 *ni-šit* ^{d}AG ^{d}AMAR.UTU ("chosen by the gods Nabû (and) Marduk") and p. 185 Esarhaddon 98 (Monument A / Zinçirli stele) rev. 21: *ni-šit* AN.ŠÁR ^{d}AG *u* ^{d}AMAR.UTU ("chosen by the gods Aššur, Nabû, and Marduk"). Alternatively, *nišût* could be from the word *nišûtu* (CAD N p. 299 sub *nišûtu*), with the meaning in this passage as "*the one enthroned by*." Given that the word *nišītu* is more commonly used in Neo-Assyrian royal inscriptions (although normally as *nišītu īnī* "the desired object of"), and the word *nišûtu* is at present unattested in the currently-extant corpus, the authors have tentatively interpreted the first word as ⌈*ni*$^{?}$-*šu*⌉-*ut*, "*the one chosen by*."

5 *maš-ši-*⌈*ia*⌉ "m[y] *brothers*": This word has sometimes been interpreted in the inscriptions of Sîn-šarra-iškun as "twin" or "twin brother." For example, see AHw p. 631 sub *māšu*; CAD M p. 4 sub *māšu* 1.a; and Grayson, Studies Winnett pp. 164 and 167. J. Oates (CAH^{2} 3/2 p. 176 n. 29) — followed by U. Bock (Kinderheit p. 288 [with n. 170] — suggests simply translating *māšu/maššû* as "brothers," with the sense of "full brother," instead of "twin brother." Compare, for example, von Soden, ZA 58 (1967) p. 252 and Meinhold, Ištar p. 458, where this word is taken to mean "biological brother(s)" (leiblicher Bruder/leibliche Brüder). N. Na'aman (ZA 81 [1991] p. 255) tentatively suggests translating *maššû* as "equals," with the implication that it referred to Sîn-šarra-iškun's brothers, who were also contenders for the Assyrian throne. Although Sîn-šarra-iškun's inscriptions seem to imply that he was young when he came to the throne, he could not have been that young since Aššur-uballiṭ II, assuming that he was indeed a son of his, must have been old enough to take over the duties of king when Sîn-šarra-iškun died in 612 and, therefore, Aššur-uballiṭ must have been born prior to Sîn-šarra-iškun becoming king in late 627. Thus, it is not impossible that Sîn-šarra-iškun was an older brother of Aššur-etel-ilāni, rather than his twin brother.

7 *it-ta-nar-ru-in-ni-ma* "they guided": Or possibly "they picked up again and again," as suggested by U. Bock (Kinderheit p. 114 [with nn. 597–598] and pp. 288–289), who proposes that *ittanarrûinnima* is a Gtn form of the verb *tarû* (AHw p. 1336 sub *tarû* II).

13) [*lìb-bu rap-šú ka-raš ta-šim-ti šá at-mu-šú* UGU UN.MEŠ] *ar-ma-niš* DÙG.GA
14) [*šá*? *ú-sa-a-ti u ta-ḫa-na-ti* ...]*-ru du-un-qu-šu*
15) [...] *x* ⸢*zik*⸣*-ri-šú-un*
16) [...] SAG.MEŠ*-šú*

discerning, whose words] are as sweet [to the people] as the *armannu*-fruit; [*to whom* ... assistance and succor ... as] his good fortune; (15) [...] their words; [...] his head;

17) [DUMU ^{m}AN.ŠÁR-DÙ-IBILA LUGAL GAL LUGAL *dan-nu* LUGAL ŠÚ LUGAL KUR AN.ŠÁR.KI LUGAL KUR EME.GI$_7$ *u* URI.KI LUGAL *kib-rat*] ⸢LÍMMU⸣*-tim*
18) [DUMU ^{m}AN.ŠÁR-ŠEŠ-SUM.NA LUGAL GAL LUGAL *dan-nu* LUGAL ŠÚ LUGAL KUR AN.ŠÁR.KI GÌR.NÍTA KÁ.DINGIR.RA.KI LUGAL KUR EME.GI$_7$ *ù*] URI.KI
19) [DUMU ^{md}30-ŠEŠ.MEŠ-SU LUGAL GAL LUGAL *dan-nu* LUGAL ŠÚ LUGAL KUR AN.ŠÁR.KI NUN *la šá*]-⸢*na*⸣*-an*
20) [ŠÀ.BAL.BAL ^{m}LUGAL-GI.NA LUGAL GAL LUGAL *dan-nu* LUGAL ŠÚ LUGAL KUR AN.ŠÁR.KI GÌR.NÍTA KÁ.DINGIR.RA.KI LUGAL KUR EME.GI$_7$ *u*] ⸢URI.KI⸣

17–20) [son of Ashurbanipal, great king, strong king, king of the world, king of Assyria, king of the land of Sumer and Akkad, king of the f]our [quarters (of the world); son of Esarhaddon, great king, strong king, king of the world, king of Assyria, governor of Babylon, king of the land of Sumer and] Akkad; [son of Sennacherib, great king, strong king, king of the world, king of Assyria, ruler who has no riv]al; [descendant of Sargon (II), great king, strong king, king of the world, king of Assyria, governor of Babylon, king of the land of Sumer and Akka]d;

Lacuna

Lacuna

1′) [...] *x* DÙG.GA *iḫ-*⸢*ti*⸣*-x x* [*x*] *x* [*x x*] ⸢BAN? NI KI?⸣ [...]
2′) [*x x* (*x*)]-⸢*ú*⸣*-tu* DINGIR.MEŠ GAL.MEŠ *pit-lu-ḫa-ku* ⸢*áš-ra-te*⸣*-šú-nu áš-te-ʾu-ú ú-ṣal-lu-ú* EN-⸢*us*⸣-[*su-nu* ...]

1′–2′) [...] ... [...] ... I constantly revered the great gods, (and) I was assiduous towards their sanctuaries (and) beseeched [their] lordly maje[sties ...].

3′) [*i*]-⸢*da*?⸣*-a-a i-zi-zu-ma ú-sa-at dum-qí e-pu-šu-*⸢*ú-ni ke*⸣*-mu-ú-a i-tap-pa-lu i-na-ru a-a-bi-*⸢*ia*⸣ [...]
4′) [LÚ].⸢KÚR⸣.MEŠ*-ia ik-mu-ú a-a-*⸢*ab*⸣ KUR *aš-*⸢*šur*.KI *la ma-gi*⸣*-ru-ti* LUGAL*-ti-ia iṣ-bu-*⸢*tu*$_4$⸣ [...]
5′) [*x*] (*x*) *x* IM.MEŠ *ti-bu-ti-ia ú-šab-bi-ru kap-*[...]

3′–5′) They stood by my [*sid*]*e*, carried out correct procedures for me, constantly answered (enemies) in my stead, killed m[y] foes, [...], bound my [en]emies, capture[d] the enemies of Assyria who had not bowed down to my royal majesty, [... (5′) ...] they broke the ...s of the assault against me, [...];

6′) [*ina*] ⸢SAG LUGAL⸣*-ú-ti-ia i-*⸢*na*⸣ *maḫ-re-*⸢*e*⸣ BALA*-ia ša ina* GIŠ.GU.ZA LUGAL*-ú-ti* [*ra-biš ú-ši-bu*]
7′) [*za-na*]-⸢*an*⸣ *ma-ḫa-zi šuk-lul eš-ret* BÀD.MEŠ*-ni da-*⸢*ád*⸣*-me* KUR *aš-*⸢*šur*.KI⸣ [...]
8′) [*x x*] *x-e-ri ka-*⸢*a*⸣*-a-an uš-*⸢*ta*⸣*-da-*⸢*na*⸣ [*kar-šú-u-a*]
9′) [DINGIR.MEŠ] ⸢GAL⸣.MEŠ *ša ap-tal-la-ḫu-šú-nu-ti* DINGIR*-us-su-nu* [...]
10′) [*x x*] ⸢*en*⸣*-né-ti-ia de-e-ni e-pu-šu-ma* UGU EDIN *x* [...]
11′) [...] *x-*⸢*in*⸣*-ni* [...]

6′–11′) [At the beginnin]g of my [k]ingship, in my first regnal year when [I sat in greatness] on (my) royal throne, I constantly gave [thought to providi]ng for cult centers (and) completing the sanctuaries of fortresses (and) settlements of Assyria, [...] ... [The gre]at [gods], whose divinity I constantly revered, [... (10′) ...] rendered judgment on [*those who had* s]inned against me, and, in the open country, [...] me [...].

12′) [*ina*] ⸢*u*$_4$⸣*-me-šú* É NA$_4$.GIŠ.NU$_{11}$.GAL *né-reb* IM.MAR.TU *ša a-na* ⸢É⸣ [...]
13′) [*ša* ^{md}]⸢30⸣-PAP.MEŠ-SU LUGAL ⸢KUR⸣ [*aš*]-⸢*šur*⸣.KI ⸢AD⸣ AD DÙ-⸢*ia*⸣ [*e-pu-šu e-na-aḫ-ma la-ba-riš il-lik*]
14′) [*an-ḫu*]-⸢*us-su ad*⸣*-ke ul-*⸢*tu*⸣ [UŠ$_8$*-šú a-di gaba-dib-bi-šú ar-ṣip ú-šak-lil*]

12′–15′) [At] that [t]ime, the Alabaster House, the western entrance which [...] to the *palace* [..., that S]ennacherib, king of [Assyri]a, the (grand)father of the father who had engendered m[e, had built, had become dilapidated and old — I] removed it[s dilapidated sectio]n(s). [I built (and) completed (it)] fro[m its foundation(s) to its crenellations, (15′) *made*] its

3′–5′ and 10′–11′ For an interpretation of these lines, see the on-page note to Ssi 3 line 12.

5′ As tentatively suggested by J.N. Postgate (personal communication), based on the Amarna version of Adapa line 5, possibly read this line as [*x*] (*x*) *x* IM.MEŠ *ti-bu-ti-ia ú-šab-bi-ru kap-*[*pi*?*-šú*?*-nu*? ...], "with the winds of my assault, they (the gods) broke [*their*] *wi*[*ngs*]."

15′) [UGU *šá pa-ni*]-⸢*ti*⸣-*im-ma ši-kit-ta-šú ú*-[*rab-bi*? ...]
16′) [NUN] ⸢EGIR⸣-*ú i-na* LUGAL.MEŠ-*ni* DUMU.⸢MEŠ⸣-[*ia e-nu-ma* É *šu-a-tú in-na-ḫu-ma il-la-ku la-ba-riš*]
17′) [*an*]-*ḫu-us-su lu-ud-diš* [MU.SAR-*ú ši-ṭir* MU]-*ia*$_5$
18′) ⸢*ù* MU.SAR-*ú ši-ṭir*⸣ *šu-me ša* ^{md}30-[PAP.MEŠ-SU MAN KUR *aš-šur*].⸢KI? AD? AD?⸣ [DÙ-*ia li*]-⸢*mur*⸣-*ma*
19′) [Ì].⸢GIŠ *lip-šu*⸣-*uš* UDU.SISKUR BAL-*qí it-ti* MU.⸢SAR⸣-[*e ši-ṭir* MU-*šú liš*]-*kun*
20′) ⸢AN⸣.ŠÁR ^{d}NIN.LÍL *ik-ri-bi*-⸢*šu*⸣ [*i-šem-mu*]-*ú*

structure [*larger* than the one bef]ore, [...].

16′–20′) May [a futu]re [ruler], one of the kings, [my] descendants, renovate its [dila]pidated section(s) [when that house becomes dilapidated and old. May he fi]nd [an inscribed object bearing] my [name] and an inscribed object bearing the name of Sen[nacherib, king of Assyria], *the (grand)father of the father* [who had engendered me], and (then) anoint (them) with [o]il, make an offering, (and) [pl]ace (them) with an inscribed obje[ct bearing his name. (20′) (The god) A]ššur (and) the goddess Mullissu [will (then) hear] h[is] prayers.

Date ex. 1

21′) ITI.ŠU.GAR.NUMUN.NA *li-mu* ^{md}AG-*tap-pu-ti*-⸢*a*⸣-[*lik*]

Date ex. 1

21′) Du᾿ūzu (IV), eponymy of Nabû-tappûtī-a[lik].

2

A piece of a clay cylinder preserves part of the prologue of an inscription of Sîn-šarra-iškun. Although the royal name and the king's genealogy are completely broken away, the attribution to this son of Ashurbanipal is certain based on parallels with other texts of Sîn-šarra-iškun from Nineveh, Aššur, and Kalḫu; compare Ssi 1, 6–7, 10, and 19. Because the building account is missing, it is not known what construction project it recorded. Since the object bears a "Kuyunjik" registration number, it is generally assumed that the fragment was discovered at Nineveh. Scholars commonly refer to this text as "Cylinder D."

CATALOGUE

Museum Number	Provenance	Dimensions (cm)	cpn
K 2744	Probably Nineveh, Kuyunjik	7.9×12.7×1.9	c

BIBLIOGRAPHY

1891 Bezold, Cat. 2 p. 471 (study)
1975–76 Schramm, WO 8 pp. 45–48 (edition, copy)
2002 Novotny, PNA 3/1 p. 1143 sub Sīn-šarru-iškun b.1′ (study)
2009 Meinhold, Ištar p. 203 with n. 1217 and p. 445 (line 11′a, edition, study)
2009 Novotny and Van Buylaere, Studies Oded p. 219 (study)

TEXT

Lacuna

1′) [...] ⸢*ú-kin par*⸣-*ṣe ki-du-de*-⸢*e*⸣ *x* [...]

2′) [... *ir*]-⸢*te-ʾu-u*⸣ *ba-ʾu-la-ti* AGA EN-*u-ti x* ⸢*e-pi-ru*⸣-[*uš na-an-nàr* AN-*e* ^{d}30]

3′) [GIŠ.GIDRU *i-šar-tú*] ⸢*uš*⸣-*pa-ru ke-e-nu* ⸢*a*⸣-*na* SIPA-*u-ti* UN.MEŠ DAGAL.MEŠ ^{d}AMAR.⸢UTU⸣ [... *ú-šat-me-ḫu rit-tu-uš-šú*]

4′) [*lìb-bu*] ⸢*rap*⸣-*šú ka-raš ta*-⸢*šim*⸣-*ti ša a-na ṭu-ub* UZU UN.⸢MEŠ⸣ [...]

5′) [*a-ḫi*]-⸢*iz*⸣ *ṭè-e-me la-mid ši-tul-ti ša né-me-qí-šú ú-šá-ḫi-zu*-⸢*šú*⸣ [^{d}*é-a* ...]

6′) ⸢NUN⸣ *na-aʾ-du* GÌR.NÍTA *it-pe-šú* SIPA *ke-e-nu iš-šak-ku ṣi-i-ru* [...]

7′) ⸢*ša*⸣ *ina tukul-ti* AN.ŠÁR ^{d}NIN.LÍL ^{d}AMAR.UTU ^{d}*zar-pa-ni-tum* ^{d}AG ^{d}*taš-me-tum ul-tú ṣi-it* ^{d}UTU-⸢*ši*⸣ [*a-di e-reb* ^{d}UTU-*ši* ...]

8′) *ina qí-bit* DINGIR-*ti-šú-nu ṣir-ti a-a-bi-šú ik-mu-u ú-šam-qí-tu ga-re-šú gi-mir za-ma-ni-šú is-pu-nu* [...]

9′) *a-na zi-kir* MU-*šú kab-ti šá im-bu-šú* AN.ŠÁR ^{d}NIN.LÍL ^{d}AMAR.UTU ^{d}*zar-pa-ni-tum* ^{d}AG ^{d}*taš-me-tum mal-ki ša x* [...]

10′) *le-ʾu-ú mu-du-ú šá* KUR AN.ŠÁR.KI KI.TUŠ *ne-eḫ-tú a-na šu-šu*-⸢*bi*⸣ [...]

11′) *pa-liḫ* AN.ŠÁR ^{d}NIN.LÍL ^{d}30 ^{d}UTU ^{d}EN ^{d}GAŠAN-MU ^{d}AG ^{d}*taš-me-tum* ^{d}15 *šá* NINA.KI ^{d}15 *šá* LÍMMU-⸢DINGIR⸣.[KI DINGIR.MEŠ GAL.MEŠ (EN.MEŠ-*šú*)]

12′) *šá ul-tu ṣe-ḫe-ri-šú a-di* GAL-*šú* EGIR-*šú-nu* ⸢*it*⸣-*tal-lak-u-ma ú-ṣal-lu-u be-lut-sún ina su-up-pe*-⸢*e*⸣ [...]

13′) *na-ṣir kit-ti ra-ʾi-im mi-šá-ri e-piš ú-sa-a-ti a-lik tap*-⸢*pu*⸣-[*ut a-ki-i* ...]

14′) *mut-nen-nu-u mun-dal-ku ša ta-nit-ti* AN.ŠÁR ^{d}NIN.LÍL ^{d}30 ^{d}UTU ^{d}AMAR.UTU ^{d}*zar-pa-ni-tum* ^{d}⸢AG⸣ [^{d}*taš-me-tum* ...]

15′) ⸢*mu-kin*⸣ *iš-di* KUR-*šú mu-ṭib lìb-bi* ERIM.ḪI.A-*šú ša ina kit-te u me-šá-ri* GIM *x* [...]

16′) *ḫa*-⸢*tin*⸣ LÚ.ERIM.MEŠ *ki-din-ni ma-la ba-šú-u mu-ub-bi-ib* ⸢*sat*⸣-[*tuk-ki* ...]

17′) AN.ŠÁR ^{d}NIN.LÍL ^{d}EN ^{d}AG ⸢*ep-še-ti-ia*⸣ [SIG$_5$].⸢MEŠ *ḫa-diš ip*⸣-[*pal-su-ma* ...]

18′) UGU LUGAL.⸢MEŠ *a-šib* BÁRA⸣.[MEŠ ...]

Lacuna

Lacuna

1′–5′) [...] firmly established; [...] cultic rites (and) *kidudû*-rites [... cons]tantly shepherded the people; [whom the light of heaven, the god Sîn], crow[ned] with the crown of lordship; [whose hand] the god Mardu[k, ..., made grasp a just scepter] (and) a true [s]taff for shepherding a widespread population; [magnanim]ous, discerning, who [...] for the good health of the people; (5′) [who comprehen]ds reason, who learned deliberation; the one to whom [the god Ea, ...], taught his wisdom;

6′–9′) pious [r]uler, capable governor, true shepherd, exalted vice-regent, [...]; the one who, with the support of the deities Aššur, Mullissu, Marduk, Zarpanītu, Nabû, (and) Tašmētu [...] from sunrise [to sunset]; who, by the exalted command of their divinity, binds his foes, cuts down his adversaries, flattens all of his enemies, [...]; at the mention of whose venerated name, which the deities Aššur, Mullissu, Marduk, Zarpanītu, Nabû, (and) Tašmētu gave to him, the rulers *of/who* [...];

10′–13′) the capable one who knows how to make Assyria dwel[l] in a peaceful abode [...]; who reveres the deities, Aššur, Mullissu, Sîn, Šamaš, Bēl (Marduk), Bēltiya (Zarpanītu), Nabû, Tašmētu, Ištar of Nineveh, (and) Ištar of Arb[ela, the great gods, (his lords)]; who, from his childhood until he became an adult, constantly followed after them (the great gods), beseeched their lordly majesties, (and) with supplication[s ...]; who guards truth, who loves justice, who renders assistance, who goes to the ai[d of the weak, ...];

14′–16′) the pious (and) judicious one, who [*constantly speaks*] the praise of the deities Aššur, Mullissu, Sîn, Šamaš, Marduk, Zarpanītu, Na[bû, (and) Tašmētu]; (15′) who makes the foundation of his land firm, who pleases the hearts of his troops, who [...] in truth and justice like [...]; who protects the privileged people, as many as there are; who maintains the purity of regu[lar offerings; ...].

17′–18′) The deities Aššur, Mullissu, Bēl (Marduk), (and) Nabû lo[oked] with pleasure upon my [good] deeds [and ... They ...] than (those of all other) kings who sit on (royal) dais[es. ...]

Lacuna

3

A fragmentarily preserved clay cylinder of a seventh-century Assyrian king, presumably Sîn-šarra-iškun (or his father Ashurbanipal), bears an inscription that commemorates the king's construction work on a terrace. Only parts of the introduction, concluding formulae, and date line remain. The cylinder was inscribed during the eponymy of Sîn-šarru-uṣur, governor of Ḫindānu (date of tenure as eponym-official unknown).

CATALOGUE

Museum Number	Registration Number	Provenance	Dimensions (cm)	cpn
BM 122613	1930-5-8,2	Nineveh, Kuyunjik, Asn. Palace, Square H	11.5×18	p

COMMENTARY

The inscription is written in Neo-Assyrian script and horizontal rulings separate each line of text. A.R. Millard (Iraq 30 [1968] p. 111) proposed that BM 122613 might have belonged to the same cylinder as BM 122616 + BM 127966 (+)? BM 128073 (Novotny and Jeffers, RINAP 5/1 pp. 290–292 Asb. 21), which is inscribed with a text summarizing some of Ashurbanipal's building activities in Assyria and Babylonia and a few of his military conquests, most notable of which is the defeat of the Cimmerian ruler Tugdammî. This join is highly unlikely since BM 122613 probably bears an inscription of Sîn-šarra-iškun, as E. Weissert (*apud* Borger, BIWA p. 356) has already pointed out. Therefore, the inscription written on that fragment is edited in the present volume together with the certain inscriptions of Assyria's penultimate ruler.

For the possible contents of the introduction in lines 1–4, compare the introductions of Ssi 1, 6–7, 10, and 19.

BIBLIOGRAPHY

1968	Lambert and Millard, Cat. p. 13 (study)
1968	Millard, Iraq 30 p. 111 and pl. XXVII (copy, study)
1994	Millard, SAAS 2 p. 116 (study)
1996	Borger, BIWA p. 356 (study)
1998	Reade, Orientalia NS 67 p. 257 (study)
2000	Reade, RLA 9/5–6 p. 410 §13.5 (study)
2002	Novotny, PNA 3/1 p. 1143 sub Sīn-šarru-iškun b.1′ (study)
2005	Reade, Iraq 67/1 p. 381 (study)
2009	Novotny and Van Buylaere, Studies Oded p. 219 with n. 9 (study)

TEXT

1) [... LUGAL] ŠÚ LUGAL ⸢KUR⸣ AN.⸢ŠÁR.KI$^{?}$⸣ [...]
2) [... ^{d}AMAR.UTU ^{d}*zar*]-⸢*pa-ni*⸣-*tum na-ram* ^{d}AG ^{d}⸢*taš-me-tum*⸣ (traces) [...]
3) [... LUGAL KUR AN.ŠÁR].⸢KI$^{?}$⸣ LUGAL ⸢KUR EME.GI$_7$⸣ [*u*] ⸢URI.KI DUMU$^{?}$ ^{m}AN$^{?}$.ŠÁR$^{?}$⸣-(traces) [...]
4) [... GÌR.NÍTA] ⸢KÁ$^{?}$.DINGIR$^{?}$.RA$^{?}$.KI$^{?}$ LUGAL⸣ KUR ⸢EME.GI$_7$ *u*$^{?}$⸣ [URI.KI]
5) [...] ⸢*ša*⸣ *x* ŠÚ *x* ⸢*ú*⸣-*še-ṣu-u a-na re-še*-⸢*e*⸣-[*ti*]
6) [...] *x-niš* SAG.DU *ú-šá-qí-ru nab*-⸢*ni*⸣-[*ti*]

1–4) [*I, Sîn-šarra-iškun*, ... king of] the world, king of Assyria, [... of the god Marduk (and) the goddess Zarp]anītu, beloved of the god Nabû (and) the goddess Tašmētu, [...; son of Ashurbanipal, ..., king of Assyria], king of the land of Sumer [and] Akkad; *son of Esarhaddon*, ... [...; son of Sennacherib, ...; descendant of Sargon (II), ..., governor of B*]abylon*, king of the land of Sumer *and* [Akkad]:

5–7) [...] ... whom they (the gods) made pre-emine[nt, ...] ..., they held [my] for[m] in high esteem [...] ... for

7) [...] *x* (*x*) ŠÚ ⸢*a*⸣-*na* ⸢LUGAL⸣-[*u-ti*]
8) [...] (traces) [...]
9) [...] (traces) [...]
10) [...] *x-nu-šú* (traces) [...]
11) [...] ABGAL DINGIR.MEŠ [...]
12) [...] *x* ⸢*ina*$^{?}$ *lìb*$^{?}$-*bi*$^{?}$⸣ *e*-⸢*šá*⸣-[*a*$^{?}$-*ti*$^{?}$ ...]
13) [...] *x x x x* (*x*) [...]

Lacuna

1′) [...] (*x*) [...]
2′) [...] *x x x x* [...]
3′) [...] *x*.MEŠ (*x*) *x x x*.MEŠ *ḫu-ud lìb-bi x x x x x* (*x*) [...]
4′) [...] (*x*) *x x a-lik it-bal* Á.II-*a-a* LÚ.KÚR.MEŠ-⸢*ia*⸣ *x x x* [...]
5′) [...] *ḫu-ud* ⸢*lìb*⸣-*bi ina ṭu-ub* ⸢UZU.MEŠ$^{?}$⸣ [*na-mar*] ⸢*ka-bat-ti*⸣ [...]
6′) [NUN EGIR-*ú ina* LUGAL.MEŠ-*ni* DUMU].⸢MEŠ-*ia e-nu*⸣-*ma tam-lu-u* ⸢*šu*⸣-*a*-⸢*tú in*$^{?}$-*na*$^{?}$⸣-[*ḫu-ma il-la-ku*] ⸢*la*$^{?}$-*ba*$^{?}$-*riš*$^{?}$⸣ [*an-ḫu-us-su lu-ud-diš*]
7′) [MU.SAR-*u ši-ṭir* MU-*ia*] ⸢*li*⸣-*mur*-⸢*ma* Ì.GIŠ⸣ *lip-šu*-⸢*uš*⸣ [UDU.SISKUR BAL-*qí it*]-⸢*ti* MU.SAR-*e ši*⸣-[*ṭir* MU-*šú liš-kun*]
8′) [AN.ŠÁR ^{d}NIN.LÍL ^{d}AMAR.UTU ^{d}*zar-pa-ni*]-⸢*tum*$^{?}$ ^{d}AG⸣ ^{d}*taš-me*-⸢*tum*⸣ [*ik-ri-bi-šú i-šem-mu-ú*]
9′) [*šá* MU.SAR-*u ši-ṭir* MU]-⸢*ia ú-nak*⸣-*ka-ru ši-pir* ŠU.⸢II-*ia*⸣ [...] *x x* A$^{?}$ MU$^{?}$-*ia* [...]
10′) [...] (*x*) ⸢*a-na ni*⸣-*iš* ŠU.II-⸢*šú a*⸣-*a* ⸢*iz*⸣-*zi*-⸢*zu-ma a-a iš-mu-u su-up-pi-šú ag-giš*⸣ *li-ru-ru-šú-ma* [MU-*šú* NUMUN-*šú ina* KUR *li-ḫal-li-qu*]

king[ship ...].
8–13) [...] ... [...] ... [...] ... [...], the sage of the gods, [...] in *the midst of the ch*[*aos* ...] ... [...]

Lacuna

1′–5′) [...] ... [...] ... happiness ... [...] ... my side ... my enemies [...] happiness, good health, (and) a [bright] spiri[t ...].

6′–8′) [May a future ruler, one of the kings], my [descendant]s, [renovate its dilapidated section(s)] when tha[t] terrace *be*[*co*]*m*[*es dilapidated* and] *old*. [M]ay he find [an inscribed object bearing my name] and (then) anoin[t (it)] with o[i]l, [make an offering, (and) place (it) wi]th an inscribed object bea[ring his name. The deities Aššur, Mullissu, Marduk, *Zarpanīt*]*u*, Nabû, (and) Tašmētu [will (then) hear his prayers].
9′–10′) [(As for) the one who] removes [an inscribed object bearing m]y [name, ...] m[y] handiwork, [...] my ..., (10′) may [the deities ...] not be pres[ent] for his prayers and not heed his supplications. May they curse him an[g]rily and [make his name (and) seed disappear from the land].

Date

11′) [... *lim-mu* ^{m}]⸢^{d}⸣30-MAN-PAP ⸢LÚ.EN.NAM⸣ [URU$^{?}$].⸢*ḫi*⸣-[*in-da-na*]

11′) [..., ... day, eponymy of] Sîn-šarru-uṣur, governor of [*the city*] Ḫi[ndānu].

4

A tiny piece of a clay cylinder is inscribed with a text that records some building activity at Nineveh. Although the ruler's name is not preserved in the text, the attribution to Assyria's penultimate king is based on several criteria: (1) the assumed provenance (Nineveh); (2) the material support (clay cylinder, which is commonly attested for Sîn-šarra-iškun, whereas it is not for his father Ashurbanipal); and (3) the script density (which is similar to the objects bearing Ssi 1). Almost nothing of the inscription remains, so it is no longer possible to determine what accomplishment it described. Of note, the Tigris River is mentioned.

---

3 line 12 ⸢*ina*$^{?}$ *lìb*$^{?}$-*bi*$^{?}$⸣ *e*-⸢*šá*⸣-[*a*$^{?}$-*ti*$^{?}$] "*the midst of the ch*[*aos*]": The phrase *ina libbi ešâti*, which is tentatively suggested here, is not otherwise attested in extant Neo-Assyrian inscriptions. However, compare, for example, *ina e-šá-a-ti u saḫ-ma-šá-a-ti* ("because of chaos and disruption") in Grayson and Novotny, RINAP 3/2 p. 148 Sennacherib 168 line 26. If interpreted correctly, then this would be a direct reference to the chaos that ensued in 627 when Sîn-šarra-iškun came to the throne. Moreover, it not implausible that Ssi 1 (Cylinder C) lines 3′–5′ and 10′–11′ also refer to the violence that ensued in the Assyrian heartland at that time. With this in mind, the foes and adversaries that Sîn-šarra-iškun's inscriptions regularly state as being killed and cut down by the gods (for example, Ssi 10 [Cylinder A] line 16) might refer to his rivals for the Assyrian throne, the "*brothers*" (*maššû*) among whom his patron deities had singled him out to be the king of Assyria, and Sîn-šuma-līšir, the chief eunuch of Aššur-etel-ilāni.

CATALOGUE

Registration Number	Provenance	Dimensions (cm)	cpn
80-7-19,13	Probably Nineveh, Kuyunjik	4.7×3.5	n

BIBLIOGRAPHY

1896 Bezold, Cat. 4 pp. 1729 (exs. 3–4, study)

1914 King, CT 34 p. 5 and pl. 3 (copy, study)

1916 Streck, Asb. p. CCIX (study)

1926 Luckenbill, ARAB 2 p. 413 §1151 (translation)

1952–53 Falkner, AfO 16 p. 306 (study)

2009 Novotny and Van Buylaere, Studies Oded p. 219 (study)

TEXT

Lacuna
1′) [...] (blank) [...]
2′) [...]-*bi* [...]
3′) [...] ⸢ÍD.IDIGNA⸣ [...]
4′) [...] ⸢*šu*⸣-*bat*-⸢*su*?⸣ [...]
5′) [...] *e-pu-*[*šu* ...]
6′) [... *ar*]-⸢*ṣip*⸣ *ú*-⸢*šak*⸣-[*lil* ...]
7′) [... *ú*]-⸢*mal*⸣-*li* [...]
8′) [...] *x* [...]
Lacuna

Lacuna
1′–8′) [... the] Tigr[is Ri]ver [... *who*]*s*[*e* s]ite [... which ...] bui[lt ... I bui]lt (and) com[pleted (it) ... I] filled [...]
Lacuna

5

A small fragment of a clay cylinder, presumably from Nineveh, bears an inscription of a late Neo-Assyrian king, most likely Ashurbanipal's son Sîn-šarra-iškun. The proposed attribution to Sîn-šarra-iškun, which was first suggested by L.W. King, is based on the following three criteria: (1) the assumed provenance (Nineveh); (2) the material support (clay cylinder); and (3) the script density (which is similar to the objects bearing Ssi 1). The text is not sufficiently preserved to be able to determine which building activity it commemorated. Since the É sign appears in line 7′, the inscription probably recorded work on a palace, possibly the South-West Palace, or one of Nineveh's many temples.

CATALOGUE

Museum Number	Registration Number	Provenance	Dimensions (cm)	cpn
K 8540 + 82-5-22,28	82-5-22,28	Probably Nineveh, Kuyunjik	4.1×7.5	c

BIBLIOGRAPHY

1893 Bezold, Cat. 3 p. 937 (study [K 8540])
1896 Bezold, Cat. 4 p. ix (study)
1914 King, CT 34 p. 5 and pl. 4 (copy, study)
1916 Streck, Asb. p. CCIX (study)
1952–53 Falkner, AfO 16 p. 306 (study)
2009 Novotny and Van Buylaere, Studies Oded p. 219 (study)

TEXT

Lacuna
1′) [...] *x* A [(*x*)] AD [...]
2′) [... LUGAL KUR] ⸢AN⸣.ŠÁR.KI *x* [...]
3′) [... *e*]-⸢*pu*⸣-*šu e-na-aḫ-*[*ma*] *la-*⸢*ba*⸣-[*riš il-lik* ...]
4′) [... *ul-tu*] ⸢UŠ$_8$⸣-*šú a-di gaba-dib-*⸢*bi*⸣-[*šú*] *ar-ṣip* [*ú-šak-lil* ...]
5′) [...] *x ši-*⸢*kit-ta*⸣-*šu* [*ú-rab-bi*? ...]
6′) [...] *x* [*x x*] *x* [...]
7′) [... *e-nu-ma*?] ⸢É⸣ [*šu-a-tu*? ...]
Lacuna

Lacuna
1′–6′) [...] ... [... that ..., king of A]ssyria, [... had bu]ilt became dilapidated [and] o[ld ...] I built (and) [completed (it) from] its [fo]undation(s) to [its] crenellatio[ns. ... *I enlarged*] its struc[tu]re. [...] ... [...]
7′) [... *when that*] *house* [...]
Lacuna

6

A draft or archival copy of an inscription that is similar to Ssi 1 is written on a fragmentary clay tablet, possibly from Nineveh. Although the building report is completely missing, it is certain from the subscript (a scribal note) that the text commemorated Sîn-šarra-iškun's work on the wall of Nineveh, which had been built by his great grandfather Sennacherib. Presumably, copies of this Akkadian inscription were written on clay cylinders (just like Ssi 1–5, 10, and 19) and deposited in the mud-brick structure of Nineveh's city wall, which went by the Sumerian ceremonial name Badnigalbilukurašušu ("Wall Whose Brilliance Overwhelms Enemies") when it was first built. Like Ssi 1, this inscription is generally referred to as "Cylinder C" in scholarly publications. The edition is based on A.K. Grayson's published copy.

CATALOGUE

Museum Number	Provenance	Dimensions (cm)	cpn
IM 3209 + IM 3249	Probably Nineveh, Kuyunjik	—	n

BIBLIOGRAPHY

1972 Grayson, Studies Winnett pp. 157–168 (edition [conflated with Ssi exs. 1, 3–5], copy)
1994 Millard, SAAS 2 p. 87 (rev. 14′, transliteration)
1999 Frahm, PNA 1/2 p. 284 sub Bēl-aḫu-uṣur 8c (rev. 14′, study)
2002 Novotny, PNA 3/1 p. 1143 sub Sīn-šarru-iškun b.1′ (study)
2009 Frahm, KAL 3 p. 91 (study)
2009 Meinhold, Ištar p. 445 no. 16 (study)
2009 Novotny and Van Buylaere, Studies Oded pp. 218–219 (study)
2017 Baker, PNA 4/1 p. 168 sub ša-pān-ekalli Bēl-aḫu-uṣur 8 (rev. 14′, study)

TEXT

Obv.

1) [*a-na-ku* ^{md}EN.ZU]-⸢LUGAL⸣-GAR-*un* LUGAL GAL LUGAL *dan-nu* LUGAL ŠÚ ⸢LUGAL⸣ [KUR AN.ŠÁR.KI]

2) [*ni-iš* IGI.II AN.ŠÁR] ⸢^{d}⸣EN.LÍL ^{d}NIN.LÍL GÌR.NÍTA *mut-nen-nu-ú* ⸢LÚ⸣.[*x x é-šár-ra*]

3) [*ma-al-ku šuk-nu-šu i-tu*]-*ut kun lìb-bi* ^{d}30 ^{d}NIN.GAL ^{d}UTU *u* ^{d}*a-a na-ram* [^{d}AMAR.UTU ^{d}NUMUN-DÙ-*tum* ^{d}AG ^{d}PAPNUN]

4) [*ni*$^{?}$-*šu-ut* ^{d}*iš-tar a*]-⸢*ši*⸣-*bat* ⸢NINA⸣.KI ^{d}*iš-tar a-ši-bat* LÍMMU-DINGIR.KI *mi*-⸢*gir*⸣ [^{d}U.GUR *ù* ^{d}*nusku*]

5) [*šá* AN.ŠÁR ^{d}NIN].⸢LÍL *ù*⸣ DINGIR.MEŠ GAL.MEŠ ⸢EN⸣.MEŠ-*ia ina bi-rit maš-ši-ia* ⸢*ke-niš ip*⸣-[*pal-su-ni-ma is-su-qu-ni a-na* LUGAL-*u-ti*]

6) *za*-⸢*ni*⸣-[*nu*]-⸢*ú*⸣-*ti kiš-šat ma-ḫa-zi* ⸢É⸣.BAR-*ú*-⸢*ti*⸣ [*gi-mir eš*]-⸢*re-e-ti*⸣

7) *re*-⸢*ʾu-ú-ut*⸣ *nap*-⸢*ḫar*⸣ *ṣal-mat* ⸢SAG⸣.DU *e*-⸢*pe*⸣-[*šu iq*]-⸢*bu*⸣-*u-ni*

1–7) [I, Sîn-šar]ra-iškun, great king, strong king, king of the world, k[ing of Assyria, favored by the deities Aššur], Enlil, (and) Mullissu; pious governor, [... of Ešarra, humble ruler; chos]en by the steadfast hearts of the deities Sîn, Ningal, Šamaš, and Aya; beloved of [the deities Marduk, Zarpanītu, Nabû, (and) Tašmētu; *the one chosen by* the goddess Ištar who res]ides in Nineveh (and) the goddess Ištar who resides in Arbela, favorit[e of the gods Nergal and Nusku; (5) the one whom (the god) Aššur, the goddess Mulliss]u, and the great gods, my lords, steadfastly l[ooked upon] among my *brothers* [and selected for kingship]; they [command]ed me to perf[orm] the roles of pro[vision]er of all cult centers, priest [of all san]ctua[ri]es, (and) she[p]her[d of] the totalit[y of] the black-headed (people);

8) *ki*-⸢*ma* AD⸣ *u* [AMA] ⸢*it*⸣-*ta*-⸢*nar*⸣-*ru-in-ni-ma i-na*-⸢*ru*⸣ [*a-a-bi-ia ú-šam-qí-tú*] *ga-re-ia*

9) ⸢*ṭa-biš ú*⸣-*še-šib-u-in-ni ina* ⸢GIŠ⸣.[GU.ZA LUGAL-*u-ti* AD] ⸢DÙ⸣-*ia*

10) ⸢^{d}⸣*é-a* ^{d}⸢*be-let*⸣-DINGIR.MEŠ *a-na e-nu-ti kiš-šá-ti ib-nu*-⸢*in*⸣-[*ni ina nap-ḫar x x ú-šá-ti*$^{?}$]-⸢*ru*⸣ *nab-ni-ti*

11) ^{d}30 LUGAL *a-ge-e a-na kun-ni* SUḪUŠ KUR *šu*-[*te-šur ba-ʾu-la-a-ti a-ge-e* EN-*u*]-*ti e-pir-an*-[*ni*]

12) GIŠ.GIDRU LUGAL-*u-ti* [*ú-šat-me-eḫ*] *rit-tu*-⸢*ú*⸣-[*a*]

13) ^{d}NIN.LÍL *a-ši-bat* NINA.KI *an-tum x* [...] *x* ⸢SAG⸣.[MEŠ]-⸢*ia*$^{?}$⸣

14) ⸢*eṭ*⸣-*lu šu-pu-ú a-a-ru šu*-⸢*tu*⸣-[*ru a-ḫi-iz ṭè-e-me ù mil-ki mu-ta-mu*]-⸢*u*⸣ *dam*-[*qa*]-*a-ti*

15) [*lìb*]-⸢*bu*⸣ *rap-šú ka-raš ta-šim*-⸢*ti*⸣ [*šá at-mu-šú* UGU UN.MEŠ *ar*]-⸢*ma*⸣-*niš* DÙG.GA

16) [*šá*$^{?}$] ⸢*ú*⸣-*sa-a-ti u ta-ḫa*-⸢*na*⸣-[*ti ...-ru du*]-⸢*un*⸣-*qu-šú*

8–19) they guided me like a father and [a mother], th[ey] killed [my foes (and) cut down], my adversaries; they g[l]adl[y] placed me on the [royal throne of the father who had enge]ndered me; (10) the god Ea (and) the goddess Bēlet-ilī created m[e] for dominion over the world (and) *they* [*made*] my form [*surpassing* among all ...]; the god Sîn, king of the crown, crowned m[e] with [the crown of lordsh]ip (and) [he made] m[y] hand [grasp] the scepter of kingship to make the foundation of the land firm (and) to di[rect the people; the goddess Mullissu who resides in Nineveh, (the goddess) Antu, [... *raised up*] *my* hea[d]; resplendent [yo]ung man, sup[erb] man, [who comprehends reason and counsel, who speak]s elo[qu]ent (words), (15) [magn]animous, discerning, [whose words] are as sweet [to the people as the *arm*]*annu*-fruit; [*to whom* ...] assistance and succ[or ... as] his [good fo]rtune; [...] ... [...] their [wor]ds; [...] ... [...] ... [...] his [head];

---

4 [*ni*$^{?}$-*šu-ut*] "[*the one chosen by*]": See the on-page note to Ssi 1 (Cylinder C) line 4 for the interpretation of the first word of this line.
5 *maš-ši-ia* "my brothers": See the on-page note to Ssi 1 (Cylinder C) line 5 for the interpretation of *maššîya*.
8 ⸢*it*⸣-*ta*-⸢*nar*⸣-*ru-in-ni-ma* "they guided me": Or possibly "they picked me up again and again." See the on-page note to Ssi 1 (Cylinder C) line 7.

17) [...] x x [... *zik*]-*ri-šú-un*

18) [...] *x* [...] MA$^{?}$ ŠU$^{?}$ BI

19) [...] LU *x* [... SAG].⸢MEŠ⸣-*šú*

20) [DUMU ^{m}AN.ŠÁR-DÙ-IBILA LUGAL GAL MAN *dan-nu* LUGAL ŠÚ MAN KUR AN.ŠÁR.KI MAN] ⸢KUR⸣ EME.GI$_{7}$ *u* ⸢URI⸣.[KI MAN] ⸢*kib-rat*⸣ [LÍMMU]-⸢*tim*⸣

21) [DUMU ^{m}AN.ŠÁR-ŠEŠ-SUM.NA MAN GAL MAN *dan-nu* MAN ŠÚ MAN KUR AN.ŠÁR.KI GÌR.NÍTA KÁ.DINGIR.RA.KI MAN KUR EME.GI$_{7}$] ⸢*ù* URI.KI⸣

20–21) [son of Ashurbanipal, great king, strong king, king of the world, king of Assyria, king of the l]and of Sumer and A[kkad, king of] the [fou]r quarte[rs (of the world); son of Esarhaddon, great king, strong king, king of the world, king of Assyria, governor of Babylon, king of the land of Sumer] and Akkad;

Lacuna

Rev.

Lacuna

1′) [NUN EGIR-*ú i-na* LUGAL.MEŠ-*ni* DUMU.MEŠ-*ia e-nu-ma* BÀD *šu-a-tú in*]-⸢*na*$^{?}$-*ḫu*$^{?}$-*ma*$^{?}$⸣

2′) [*il-la-ku la-ba-riš an-ḫu-us-su lu-ud-diš* MU].⸢SAR-*ú*⸣ [*ši*]-*ṭir* MU-*ia*

3′) [*ù* MU.SAR-*ú ši-ṭir šu-me ša* ^{md}30-PAP.MEŠ-SU MAN KUR *aš-šur*.KI AD AD] ⸢DÙ⸣-*ia* ⸢*li*⸣-*mur-ma*

4′) ⸢Ì.GIŠ *lip-šu-uš*⸣ [UDU.SISKUR BAL-*qí it-ti* MU].⸢SAR⸣-*e ši*-⸢*ṭir*⸣ MU-*šú liš-kun*

5′) AN.ŠÁR ^{d}⸢NIN⸣.[LÍL *ik-ri*]-*bi-šú i-šem-mu-u*

Rev. 1′–5′) [May a future ruler, one of the kings, my descendants, renovate its dilapidated section(s) when that wall becomes *dilap*]*id*[*a*]*ted a*[*nd* old]. May he find [an inscribed obje]ct [bea]ring my name [and an inscribed object bearing the name of Sennacherib, king of Assyria, the (grand)father of the father who had enge]ndered me, and (then) anoint (them) with o[i]l, [make an offering], (and) place (them) [with an inscribed obje]ct bearing his name. (rev. 5′) (The god) Aššur (and) the goddess M[ullissu] will (then) hear his [pray]ers.

6′) *ša* MU.SAR-*u ši*-⸢*ṭir*⸣ [MU-*ia*] ⸢*ul*⸣-*tú áš-ri-šú ú-nak-ka-ru*

7′) *it-ti* ⸢MU.SAR⸣-*e* ⸢*ši*⸣-[*ṭir*] MU-*šú la i-šak-ka*-⸢*nu*⸣

8′) AN.ŠÁR ^{d}NIN.⸢LÍL⸣ ^{d}30 ^{d}UTU ^{d}[AMAR].⸢UTU⸣ ^{d}NUMUN-DÙ-*tum* ^{d}MUATI ^{d}⸢PAPNUN⸣ ^{d}15 *šá* NINA.KI

9′) ^{d}*šar-rat-kid-mu-ri* ^{d}15 *šá* ⸢LÍMMU-DINGIR⸣.KI DINGIR.MEŠ GAL.MEŠ *šá* AN-*e u* KI-*tim*

10′) GIŠ.GU.ZA-*šú li-šá-bal-ki-tú li-ru-ru* BALA-*šú*

11′) GIŠ.GIDRU-*šú li-ṭi-ru* Á.II-*šú lik-su-u ina* KI.⸢TA⸣ LÚ.KÚR-*šú li*-⸢*še-ši*⸣-*bu-uš ka-mì-iš*

12′) *ag-giš li-ru-ru-šú-ma* MU-*šú* NUMUN-*šú* BALA-*šú na*-⸢*an-nab*⸣-*šú ina nap*-⸢*ḫar*⸣ [KUR].KUR *li-ḫal-li*-⸢*qu*⸣

Rev. 6′–12′) (As for) the one who removes an inscribed object bear[ing my name f]rom its place (and) does not place (it) with an inscribed object be[aring] his name, may the deities Aššur, Mullissu, Sîn, Šamaš, [Mardu]k, Zarpanītu, Nabû, Tašmētu, Ištar of Nineveh, Šarrat-Kidmuri, (and) Ištar of A[rb]ela, the great gods of heaven and netherworld, (rev. 10′) overthrow his throne, curse his reign, take away his scepter, bind his arms, (and) make him [s]it bound at the feet of his enemy. May they curse him angrily and make his name, his offspring, his dynasty, (and) his progeny disappe[ar] from all[l of the la]nds.

13′) MU.SAR-*ú ša* BÀD NINA.⸢KI⸣

Rev. 13′) Inscription concerning the wall of Nineveh.

Date

14′) ⸢ITI⸣.KIN *lim-mu* ^{m}EN-PAP-PAP LÚ.⸢*šá*⸣ IGI ⸢KUR⸣

Rev. 14′) Ulūlu (VI), eponymy of Bēl-aḫu-uṣur, [pala]ce overseer.

7

Several fragmentarily-preserved clay prisms discovered at Aššur are inscribed with a text stating that Ashurbanipal's son and successor Sîn-šarra-iškun constructed a temple for the god Nabû in that city. The inscription records that the building had been so neglected in the past that Nabû and his consort Tašmētu were forced to live in the (neighboring) temple of the

Assyrian Ištar, where they scraped by on meager portions of leftover offerings. In typical Assyrian style, Sîn-šarra-iškun claims that he built the temple from top to bottom. Afterwards, the king reports that he had Nabû and Tašmētu ushered into their newly-constructed home and fêted with an overabundance of food offerings. The text, as far as it is preserved, is a (near or exact) duplicate of Ssi 10. Three exemplars bear dates, but those lines are not sufficiently preserved to identify in which eponym year(s) the prisms were inscribed. Scholars generally refer to this inscription as "Cylinder A."

Figure 14. The Nabû temple at Aššur showing the general find spots of inscribed objects of Sîn-šarra-iškun. Adapted from Bär, Ischtar-Tempel p. 391 fig. 5.

CATALOGUE

Ex.	Museum Number	Excavation Number	Photograph Number	Provenance	Lines Preserved	cpn
1	VA 7501	Ass 948	—	Aššur, iC5I, by the southeast corner of the Aššur temple	i 10′–22′, v 14–17, date	c
2	VA 8418	Ass 13374	Ass ph 3616	Aššur, eB7II, Nabû temple, south cella, in debris, under later stone foundations	ii 2–13, iii 3′–7′	c
3	VA 8419 + VA 5059	Ass 13266 + Ass 13594	Ass ph 3461, 3616, S 3618	Aššur, eC7II, Nabû temple, level of the brick pavement	i 1'–11′, iii 17′–23′, iv 9′–28′, v 9–17, date	c

4	A 3620	Ass 18738	—	Aššur, iD4V, in the forecourt of the Aššur temple, ca. 30 cm above the Sargon II pavement	iii 1′–7′	p
5	SE 155 (+) SE 156	—	—	Probably Aššur	ii 15–28, iii 5′–22′, iv 1′–27′, v 2–17, date	p

COMMENTARY

The master text is a conflation of the exemplars. In the places where the exemplars overlap but the lineation is different in those exemplars, the lineation of the master text is taken from the following: ex. 3 for i 10′; exs. 4 and 5 for iii 3′–6′; and ex. 5 for iv 9′–27′ and v 9–17. Ex. 1 preserves the lower portion of col. i and ex. 2 preserves the upper portion of col. ii. However, neither exemplar preserves a top or bottom edge for its respective prism, and so the division between cols. i and ii in the master text is somewhat arbitrary since there is only one line missing after the contents of ex. 1 and before the contents of ex. 2. Regarding cols. iii and iv, the master text for the end of those columns is taken from ex. 3, which does not preserve a bottom edge for its col. iii, while iv 28′ appears to be the final line of its col. iv. In contrast, the last line of col. iii in ex. 5 is iii 22′ and the final line of its subsequent column is iv 27′. A complete score is presented on Oracc. The orthographic variants that appear in this inscription are listed at the back of the book.

BIBLIOGRAPHY

1908 Jordan, MDOG 38 p. 28 (ex. 3, study)
1913 Scheil, RA 10 pp. 199–205 (ex. 5, copy, edition)
1914 Scheil, Prisme pp. 51–56 (ex. 5, copy, edition)
1916 Streck, Asb. p. CCXIV, CDXCIV, 838, and 840–843 (ex. 5, edition; ex. 3, study)
1922 Schroeder, KAH 2 pp. 86–88 nos. 131 and 135–137 (exs. 1–3, copy)
1926 Luckenbill, ARAB 2 pp. 414–416 §§1156–1164 (exs. 1–3, translation [conflated with Ssi 10 ex. 1])
1936 Böhl, MLVS 3 p. 33 (exs. 1–3, 5, study)
1939–41 Weidner, AfO 13 p. 312 (study)
1952–53 Falkner, AfO 16 p. 305 (exs. 1–3, ex. 5, study)
1984 Donbaz and Grayson, RICCA p. 61 and pl. 37 no. 265 (ex. 4, copy, study)
1986 Borger, ZA 76 p. 302 (ex. 4, study)
1986 Pedersén, Archives 2 p. 13 n. 9 (ex. 1, study)
1997 Pedersén, Katalog pp. 153, 157, and 159 (exs. 1–4, study)
2002 Novotny, PNA 3/1 p. 1144 sub Sīn-šarru-iškun b.3′ (study)
2009 Novotny and Van Buylaere, Studies Oded pp. 216–217 (iii 3′–18′, translation [conflated with Ssi 10]; exs. 1–5, study)
2009 Frahm, KAL 3 pp. 90–91 (iii 2′–7′, transliteration; exs. 1–5, study)
2009 Meinhold, Ištar pp. 445–466 no. 16 (exs. 1–5, edition [conflated with Ssi 9–10], study)
2010 Novotny, Studies Ellis p. 468 no. 5.28 (iii 3′–18′, translation [conflated with Ssi 10]; study)
2012 Schmitt, Ischtar-Tempel pp. 82 n. 254, 86, 89–90, and 145–146 and pls. 205–207 nos. 456 and 458–459 (exs. 2–3, photo, study)
2014 Novotny, Kaskal 11 pp. 162–168 (study; iii 1′–iv 1′, translation [conflated with Ssi 10]; exs. 1–5, provenance)

TEXT

Col. i
Lacuna of 3 or 4 lines
1′) ^{d}⸢AG ^{d}⸣[*taš-me-tum*]
2′) *ina ni-iš* IGI.II.⸢MEŠ⸣-[*šú-nu* SIG$_{5}$.MEŠ]
3′) *ke-niš ip-pal-*⸢*su*⸣-[*šú-ma*]
4′) *is-su-qu-šú a-na* [LUGAL-*u-ti*]
5′) *a-na kun-ni* (erasure) SUḪUŠ [KUR]
6′) *šu-te-šur ba-ʾu-la**(over erasure)-[*a-ti*]
7′) ⸢*dal*⸣-*ḫa-a-ti a-*<*na*> *tu-*⸢*qu*⸣-[*ni*]
8′) [*ab*]-⸢*ta*⸣-*a-ti a-na ke-še*$_{20}$*-ri a-*⸢*ge*⸣-[*e*]

Lacuna of 3 or 4 lines
i 1′–ii 4) [*I, Sîn-šarra-iškun, great king, strong king, king of the world, king of Assyria; the one whom the deities Aššur, Mullissu, Marduk, Zarpanītu*], Nabû, (and) [Tašmētu] steadfastly looked [upon] with [their benevolent] glance [and] selected for [kingship]; whom the light of he[aven, the god Sîn, cr]owned with the cro[wn of lordship] (i 5′) to make the foundation of [the land] firm, to direct the peop[le], t<o> put in o[rder]

Lacuna before i 1′ Based on Ssi 10 (Cylinder A) lines 1–2a, the translation assumes that the now-missing lines before i 1′ contained *a-na-ku* ^{md}30-LUGAL-*iš-kun* LUGAL GAL LUGAL *dan-nu* LUGAL ŠÚ LUGAL KUR AN.ŠÁR.KI *ša* AN.ŠÁR ^{d}NIN.LÍL ^{d}AMAR.UTU ^{d}*zar-pa-ni-tum* "I, Sîn-šarra-iškun, great king, strong king, king of the world, king of Assyria; the one whom the deities Aššur, Mullissu, Marduk, Zarpanītu."

Figure 15. VA 8419 + VA 5059 (Ass 13266 + Ass 13594; Ssi 7 ex. 3), a fragment of a clay prism with an inscription recording Sîn-šarra-iškun building the Nabû temple at Aššur. Image courtesy of Aaron Schmitt. © Staatliche Museen zu Berlin – Vorderasiatisches Museum. Photo: Olaf M. Teßmer.

9′) [*be-lu-ti i*]-⸢*pi-ru*⸣-*uš na-an-nàr* ⸢AN⸣-[*e* ^{d}30]
10′) [GIŠ.GIDRU *i-šar-tú*] *uš*-⸢*pa*⸣-*ru ke*-[*e-nu*]
11′) *a-na* ⸢*re*⸣-[*ʾu-u-ti* UN].⸢MEŠ DAGAL⸣.[MEŠ]
12′) ^{d}⸢AG⸣ [*pa-qid kiš-šá-ti*]
13′) *ú-šat-me*-[*ḫu rit-tu-uš-šú*]
14′) *lib-bu* ⸢*rap*⸣-[*šú ka-raš ta-šim-ti*]
15′) *a-ḫi-iz* ⸢*ṭè*⸣-[*e-me*]
16′) *ù* [*mil-ki*]
17′) *la-mid* ⸢*ši*⸣-[*tul-ti*]
18′) *da-a-a-nu* [*ke-e-nu*]
19′) *da-bi-ib kit*-⸢*ti*⸣ [*ù meš-šá-ri*]
20′) ⸢*ša*$^{?}$ *ik*⸣-*kib-šú* [*nu-ul-la-a-ti*]
21′) [*an-zil*]-⸢*la*⸣-*šú* ⸢*sur*⸣-[*ra-a-ti*]
22′) [NUN *na-aʾ-du*] ⸢GÌR⸣.[NÍTA *it-pe-šú*]

Col. ii
1) [LÚ.SIPA *ke-e-nu mut-tar-ru-ú*]
2) ⸢UN.MEŠ⸣ [DAGAL.MEŠ *ša* DINGIR.MEŠ GAL.MEŠ]
3) LUGAL-⸢*us*⸣-[*su ki-ma ú-lu* Ì.MEŠ *uš-ṭib-bu*]
4) UGU *gi*-[*mir ma-ti-tan*]

what is confused, (and) to repair [what is de]stroyed; [whose hand] the god N[abû, overseer of the world], made gra[sp (i 10′) a just scepter (and)] a tr[ue] st[a]ff for sh[epherding a] wi[despread populati]on; magnani[mous, discerning], (i 15′) who comprehends r[eason] and [counsel], who learned d[eliberation; reliable] judge, who speaks about trut[h and justice; (i 20′) to *wh*]om [treacherous talk] is anathema (and) l[ies an abominat]ion; [pious ruler, capable] gov[ernor, true shepherd, leader of a widespread popula]tion; [whose] kingship [the great gods made as pleasing] in al[l of the lands as the finest oil];

5) DUMU ^{m}AN.ŠÁR-DÙ-[IBILA LUGAL GAL LUGAL *dan-nu*]
6) LUGAL ŠÚ LUGAL KUR AN.ŠÁR.⸢KI⸣ [LUGAL KUR EME.GI$_{7}$]
7) *ù* URI.KI LUGAL ⸢*kib-rat* LÍMMU⸣-[*tim*]
8) DUMU ^{m}AN.ŠÁR-PAP-AŠ LUGAL GAL LUGAL *dan-nu*

ii 5–15) son of Ashurban[ipal, great king, strong king], king of the world, king of Assyria, [king of the land of Sumer] and Akkad, king of the [fo]u[r] quarters (of the world); son of Esarhaddon, great king, strong king, king of the world, king of Assyria, governor of Babylon, (ii 10) king of the land of Sumer and Akkad; son of Sennacherib, great king, strong king, king of

9) LUGAL ŠÚ LUGAL KUR AN.ŠÁR.KI GÌR.NÍTA KÁ.DINGIR.RA.KI
10) LUGAL KUR EME.GI$_{7}$ *ù* URI.KI
11) DUMU ^{md}30-PAP.MEŠ-SU LUGAL GAL LUGAL *dan-nu*
12) ⸢LUGAL ŠÚ LUGAL KUR⸣ [AN].⸢ŠÁR.KI⸣ NUN *la šá-na-an*
13) [ŠÀ.BAL.BAL ^{m}LUGAL]-⸢GI.NA LUGAL GAL⸣
14) [LUGAL *dan-nu* LUGAL ŠÚ LUGAL KUR AN.ŠÁR.KI GÌR.NÍTA]
15) [KÁ.DINGIR.RA.KI LUGAL KUR EME.GI$_{7}$ *ù*] ⸢URI.KI⸣

the world, king of [Assyri]a, ruler who has no rival; [descendant of Sarg]on (II), gr[eat] king, [strong king, king of the world, king of Assyria, governor of Babylon, king of the land of Sumer and] Akkad;

16) [*ina* SAG LUGAL-*u-ti-ia ul*]-*tú* AN.ŠÁR
17) [^{d}EN ^{d}AG ^{d}30] ^{d}UTU
18) [^{d}*nin-urta* ^{d}U.GUR *u*] ^{d}*nusku*
19) [*ina bi-rit maš-ši-ia ut*]-*tu-un-ni-ma*
20) [*iḫ-ši-ḫu*] ⸢LUGAL⸣-*u-ti*
21) [*ki-ma* AD *u*] ⸢AMA⸣ *it-ta-nar-ru-un-ni-ma*
22) [*i-na-ru*] ⸢*a*⸣-*a-bi-ia*
23) [*ú-šam-qí-tu*] ⸢*za*⸣-*ʾi-i-ri-ia*
24) [*ú-sa-at* SIG$_{5}$] ⸢*i*⸣-*pu-šú-u-ni*
25) [*ṭa-biš ú*]-⸢*še*⸣-*šib-u-in-ni*
26) [*i-na* GIŠ.GU.ZA LUGAL-*u*]-⸢*ti*⸣ AD DÙ-*ia*
27) [*ša za-na-an*] ⸢*ma*⸣-*ḫa-zi*
28) [...] *x* [(*x*)] *x x*

ii 16–28) [At the beginning of my kingship, af]ter the gods Aššur, [Bēl (Marduk), Nabû, Sîn], Šamaš, [Ninurta, Nergal, and] Nusku [ch]ose me [among my *brothers*] and (ii 20) [desired (me)] as king, guided me [like a father and a moth]er, and [killed] my [f]oes, [cut down] my [e]nemies, performed [good deeds] for me, (and) (ii 25) [gladly p]laced me [on the roya]l [throne] of the father who had engendered me; [*I constantly gave thought* to providing for cu]lt centers, [...] ...

Lacuna

Lacuna

Col. iii

Lacuna

Lacuna

1′) *x* (*x*) [...]
2′) ⸢*la*⸣-*ba*-⸢*riš*⸣ [*il-lik*]
3′) [TA$^{?}$ UD].⸢MEŠ⸣ *ma-aʾ-du-te ni*-⸢*du*⸣-[*tú il-lik-ma*]
4′) [*i-te*]-*me qaq*-⸢*qa*⸣-[*riš*]
5′) ^{d}⸢AG ^{d}⸣*taš-me**-*tum* EN.MEŠ-⸢*ia*⸣
6′) <*ina*> É ^{d}[*iš-tar*] *aš-šur-i*-⸢*ti*⸣ [*áš-bu-ma*]
7′) *i-maḫ*-⸢*ḫa-ru sur*⸣-[*qé-ni*]
8′) LUGAL.MEŠ-*ni* [AD.MEŠ-*ia*]
9′) *a-li-kut* ⸢*maḫ*⸣-[*ri-ia*]
10′) DÙ-*eš* É *šú-a-tú la* ⸢*iḫ*⸣-[*su-su-nim-ma*]
11′) *ul iš-ku-nu uz-nu*

iii 1′–11′) [... it became o]ld. [*For* a] long [tim]e, [it fell] into dis[repair and beca]me level [with] the groun[d]. (iii 5′) The god Na[bû] (and) the goddess Tašmētu, m[y] lords, [took up residence] <in> the temple of the Assyria[n Ištar and] (there) they receiv[ed] str[ewn offerings]. The kings, [my ancestors] who came be[fore me], (iii 10′) did not th[ink about] (re)building that temple [and] they did not pay (it any) attention.

12′) *a-na-ku* ^{md}30-LUGAL-GAR-⸢*un*⸣
13′) LUGAL *kiš-šá-ti* LUGAL KUR AN.ŠÁR.KI
14′) *pa-liḫ* DINGIR.MEŠ GAL.MEŠ
15′) *muš-te-eʾ-u áš-ri-šú-nu*
16′) *e-pe-eš* É *šu-a-tú*
17′) *ina lìb-bi-ia ib-ba-ši-ma*
18′) *ka-bat-ti ub-la*
19′) ⸢*ina*⸣ GIŠ.ḪUR-*šú la-bir-tú*
20′) [*ina* MAŠ].⸢KÁN-*šú*⸣ *maḫ-ri-ti*
21′) [*ina* ITI DÙG.GA] ⸢*u*$_{4}$-*me*⸣ *še-me-e*
22′) [*ina ši-pir ka-kù-gal-lu-ti ina*] ⸢NA$_{4}$$^{?}$.*pi*$^{?}$-*li*$^{?}$⸣
23′) [...] *x*

iii 12′–23′) I, Sîn-šarra-iškun, king of the world, king of Assyria, the one who reveres the great gods, (iii 15′) who is assiduous towards their places (of worship), conceived in my heart to (re)build that temple and wanted (to carry it out). According to its original plan, (iii 20′) [on] its former [sit]e, [in a favorable month], (on) an auspicious day, [according to the craft of the incantation priest, *I filled in (its) foundation with*] *limestone*

Lacuna of 1 or 2 lines

Lacuna of 1 or 2 lines

Col. iv

---

iii 5′ ⸢^{d}⸣*taš-me**-*tum* "the goddess Tašmētu": In the text, the ME sign appears to have an extra horizontal wedge.

iii 23′ Based on Ssi 10 (Cylinder A) line 30a, the translation tentatively assumes that iii 23′ contained *tem-me-en-ši uš-mal-li*$^{?}$-*ma* "*I filled in (its) foundation.*"

Lacuna of 1 or 2 lines
1′) [*ar-ṣip ú-šak*]-⸢*lil*⸣
2′) [...]-⸢*ia*⸣
3′) [...] *x-ma*
4′) [*ki-ma* UD.MEŠ *ú*]-⸢*nam*⸣-*mir*
5′) [^{d}AG ^{d}]⸢*taš*⸣-*me-tum*
6′) [DINGIR.MEŠ GAL].⸢MEŠ⸣ EN.MEŠ-*ia*
7′) [*ul-tu* É] ⸢^{d}⸣*iš-tar aš-šur-i-te*
8′) [*ú-še*]-⸢*ṣa*⸣-*am-ma*
9′) [*ina* ITI DÙG].⸢GA⸣ *u*$_{4}$*-me še-me-e*
10′) [*qé*]-*reb*-[*šú*] *ú-še-rib-ma*
11′) [*ú*]-*šar-me* BÁRA *da-ra-a-ti*

Lacuna of 1 or 2 lines
iv 1′–11′) [I built (and) complet]ed (it) [*from its foundations to its crenellations. ...* m]y [...] and [made (it) s]hine [like daylight. I brou]ght [the god Nabû (and) the goddess Ta]šmētu, [the great gods], my lords, out [of the temple of] the Assyrian Ištar and, [in a favorab]le [month], (on) an auspicious day, (iv 10′) I made (them) enter [in]side [it] and made (them) dwell on (their) eternal dais(es).

12′) ⸢GU$_{4}$⸣.MAḪ-*ḫi reš-tu-u-ti*
13′) ⸢GUKKAL⸣.MEŠ *ma-ru-ti*
14′) *zi-i-bi qa-áš-du-ti*
15′) *ina ma-ḫar* ^{d}AG ^{d}*taš-me-tum*
16′) EN.MEŠ-*ia aq-qí-ma*
17′) *uš-par-zi-ḫa qé-reb é-kur-ri*
18′) ^{d}AG ^{d}*taš-me-tum*
19′) *ep-še-ti-ia* SIG$_{5}$.MEŠ
20′) *ḫa-diš ip-pal-su-ma*
21′) *ik-tar-ra-bu* LUGAL-*u-ti*

iv 12′–21′) I offered prime quality [pr]ize bulls (and) fattened fat-tailed sheep as pure food offerings before the god Nabû (and) the goddess Tašmētu, my lords, and (thus) I lavishly provided (for them) inside (that) temple. The god Nabû (and) the goddess Tašmētu (iv 20′) looked with pleasure upon my good deeds and constantly blessed my kingship.

22′) NUN EGIR *ina* LUGAL.MEŠ
23′) DUMU.MEŠ-*ia* ⸢*e*⸣-*nu-ma* É *šu-a-tú*
24′) *in-na-ḫu-ma* [*il*]-⸢*la*⸣-*ku la-ba-riš*
25′) *an-ḫu-us-su* [*lu-ud*]-*diš*
26′) MU.SAR-*u* [*ši-ṭir*] ⸢MU⸣-*ia*
27′) *li-mur-ma* [Ì.GIŠ] *lip-šu-uš*
28′) [*ni-qa-a*] ⸢*li*?-*iq*?⸣-[*qí*]
Col. v
1) [*it-ti* MU.SAR-*e*]
2) *ši*-[*ṭir* MU-*šú liš-kun*]
3) AN.⸢ŠÁR⸣ [^{d}NIN.LÍL]
4) ^{d}AMAR.⸢UTU⸣ [^{d}*zar-pa-ni-tum*]
5) ^{d}AG ⸢^{d}⸣[*taš-me-tum*]
6) *ik-ri-bi-šú* ⸢*i*⸣-[*šem-mu-ú*]

iv 22′–v 6) [May] a future ruler, one of the kings, my descendants, [reno]vate its dilapidated section(s) [w]hen that temple becomes dilapidated and [o]ld. May he find an inscribed object [bearing] my [na]me, and (then) anoint (it) with [oil], *m*[*a*]*k*[*e* an offering (and) (v 1) place (it) with an inscribed object] be[aring his name]. The deities Ašš[ur, Mullissu], Mard[uk, Zarpanītu], Nabû, (and) [Tašmētu will (then) hear] his prayers.

7) *ša* MU.SAR-*ú ši*-[*ṭir* MU-*ia*]
8) *ú-nak-kar*-[*ú-ma*]
9) *it-ti* MU.SAR-*e ši*-⸢*ṭir* MU-*šu*?⸣
10) *la i-šak-ka-nu ù šu-mì it-ti* MU-*šú*
11) *la i-šaṭ-ṭa-ru*
12) AN.ŠÁR ^{d}NIN.LÍL ^{d}AMAR.UTU
13) ^{d}*zar-pa-ni-tum* ^{d}AG ^{d}*taš-me-tum*
14) *a-na ni-iš* ŠU.II-*šú a*-⸢*a*⸣ *iz-zi-zu-ma*
15) *a-a iš-mu-ú su-up-pi-šú*
16) *ag-giš li*-⸢*ru*⸣-*ru-šú-ma*
17) MU-*šú* NUMUN-*šú* NUNUZ-*šú* [*ina* KUR *li*]-⸢*ḫal*⸣-*li-qu*

v 7–17) (As for) the one who removes an inscribed object be[aring my name and] does not place (it) with an inscribed object bearing *his* name and does not write my name with his name, may the deities Aššur, Mullissu, Marduk, Zarpanītu, Nabû, (and) Tašmētu not be present for his prayers and (v 15) not heed his supplications. May they curse him angrily and [make] his name, his seed, (and) his offspring [dis]appear [from the land].

Date ex. 1

18A) [...] *x*.KAM
19A) [...]

Date ex. 1

v 18A–19A) [...], ...th [day, eponymy of ...].

Lacuna before iv 1′ The translation assumes that the now-missing line(s) before iv 1′ contained *ul-tu* UŠ$_{8}$-*šú a-di gaba-dib-bi-šú* "*from its foundations to its crenellations*"; compare Ssi 10 (Cylinder A) line 30b.

Date ex. 3

18B) ⸢ITI⸣.[...]
19B) *lim-⸢mu⸣* [...]

Date ex. 3

v 18B–19B) [..., ...th day], epony[my of ...].

Date ex. 5

18C) ITI.DU$_6$ [...]
19C) ⸢*lim-mu* ^{m}⸣[...]

Date ex. 5

v 18C–19C) Tašrītu (VII), [...th day], eponymy of [...].

8

A small portion of a clay prism, now comprising two fragments, is inscribed with a text reporting on Sîn-šarra-iškun's construction of the temple of Nabû at Aššur. Its preserved contents are similar to Ssi 7 and 10.

CATALOGUE

Museum Number	Excavation Number	Photograph Number	Provenance	cpn
VAT 9524 (+) A 494	Ass 13183a (+) Ass 13183b	Ass ph 3430	Aššur, eB7II, Nabû temple, north cella, on the brick pavement, east of the dais	c

BIBLIOGRAPHY

1997 Pedersén, Katalog p. 157 (study)
2009 Frahm, KAL 3 pp. 89–91 and 230 (edition, copy)
2012 Schmitt, Ischtar-Tempel pp. 82 n. 254, 88, and 145 and pl. 203 nos. 453–454 (photo, study)
2014 Novotny, Kaskal 11 p. 166 (provenance)

TEXT

Col. i′
Lacuna
1′) [*ba*$^{?}$-*ne*$^{?}$]-*e*
2′) [É] ⸢*šu*⸣-*a-tú*
3′) [*ina lìb-bi*]-*ia*
4′) [*ib-ba*]-⸢*ši*⸣-*ma*
5′) [*ka-bat-ti*] ⸢*ub*⸣-*la*
6′) [*ina* GIŠ].⸢ḪUR⸣-*šú*
7′) [*la-bir-tú ina* MAŠ].⸢KÁN⸣-*šú*
8′) [*maḫ-ri*]-*ti*
9′) [*ina* ITI DÙG.GA *u*$_4$-*me*] ⸢*še*⸣-*me-e*
10′) [*ina ši-pir ka-kù-gal-lu*]-*te*$^{*?}$ (over erasure)
11′) [...] KA
12′) [*ina* NA$_4$.*pi-i*]-*li*
13′) [*tem-me*]-⸢*en*⸣-*ši*
14′) [*uš-mal*]-⸢*li*$^{?}$⸣-*ma*
15′) [*ú-zaq-qir ḫur*]-⸢*šá*⸣-*niš*
16′) [*ul-tu* UŠ$_8$]-*šú*
17′) [*a-di gaba-dib-bi*]-*šú*

Lacuna
i′ 1′–20′) [conceiv]ed [in] my [heart to *(re)buil*]*d* [t]hat [temple] and [want]ed (to carry it out). [According to] its [original pla]n, [on] its [form]er [sit]e, [in a favorable month, (on) an au]spicious [day, according to the craft of the incantation pri]est, [... *I fille*]*d in* its [foundat]ion [with limesto]ne and [made (it) as high] as [a mount]ain. [I built (and) complet]ed (it) [from] its [foundation(s) to] its [crenellations. ...]

18′) [*ar-ṣip ú-šak*]-⸢*lil*⸣
19′) [...] *x*
20′) [...] *x*
Lacuna
Col. ii′
Lacuna
1′) ⸢GUKKAL?⸣.[MEŠ]
2′) ⸢*ma*⸣-*ru*-⸢*ti*?⸣
3′) *zi-i*-[*bi*]
4′) *qa-áš*-⸢*du*⸣-[*ti*]
5′) *ina ma*-⸢*ḫar*⸣
6′) ^{d}AG ^{d}[*taš-me-tum*]
7′) EN.MEŠ-[*ia*]
8′) ⸢*aq*⸣-*qí-ma uš*-⸢*par*⸣-[*zi-ḫa*]
9′) [*qé*]-⸢*reb*⸣ *é-kur*-[*ri*]
10′) [^{d}]⸢AG⸣ ^{d}*taš*-[*me-tum*]
11′) [*ep-še*]-⸢*ti*⸣-[*ia*]
12′) [SIG$_{5}$.MEŠ *ḫa-diš*]
13′) [*ip-pal*]-⸢*su*⸣-[*ma*]
Lacuna

Lacuna

Lacuna
ii′ 1′–13′) [I] offered [*prime quality prize bulls* (*and*) f]atten[ed *fat-t*]*ai*[*led sheep*] as pu[re] food offe[rings] befo[re] the god Nabû (and) the goddess [Tašmētu, my] lords, and (thus) I lavis[hly provided (for them) [insi]de (that) temp[le. The god Na]bû (and) the goddess Taš[mētu loo]ke[d with pleasure upon my good deed]s [and]
Lacuna

9

Two small fragments of a clay prism discovered at Aššur bear an Akkadian text of Sîn-šarra-iškun. Although little of the inscription is extant, it is presumed that it recorded this king's construction of the Nabû temple at Aššur; for example, compare Ssi 7–8 and 10–12. This inscription is likely a shorter version of Ssi. 7 and 10 (Frahm, KAL 3 pp. 90–91); it is also earlier than those two inscriptions. The object was inscribed during the eponymy of Aššur-mātu-taqqin, governor of the city (U)pummu.

CATALOGUE

Museum Number	Excavation Number	Provenance	cpn
VA 7506 (+) VA 7518	Ass 3518 (+) Ass 3830	Aššur, gC4III, north of the ziggurat, in debris, at the west end of the wall of Aššur-rêm-nišēšu	c

8 Lacuna before ii′ 1′ The translation tentatively assumes that the now-missing line(s) before ii′ 1′ contained GU$_{4}$.MAḪ-*ḫi reš-tu-u-ti* "*prime quality prize bulls*"; *compare Ssi 10 (Cylinder A) line 33b.*

BIBLIOGRAPHY

1922 Schroeder, KAH 2 p. 86 nos. 130 and 132 (copy)
1936 Böhl, MLVS 3 p. 33 (study)
1939–41 Weidner, AfO 13 p. 312 (study)
1952–53 Falkner, AfO 16 p. 305 (study)
1994 Millard, SAAS 2 p. 85 (vi 3′–6′, study)
1997 Pedersén, Katalog p. 154 (study)
1998 Radner, PNA 1/1 p. 196 sub Aššūr-mātu-taqqin 14 (vi 3′–6′, study)
2009 Frahm, KAL 3 p. 91 (study)
2009 Meinhold, Ištar pp. 448, 450, 452, 457–459, 460–461, and 465–466 (edition [conflated with Ssi 7 and 10])
2009 Novotny and Van Buylaere, Studies Oded p. 216 n. 3 (study)
2014 Novotny, Kaskal 11 p. 168 (provenance)
2017 Baker, PNA 4/1 p. 81 sub pāḫutu Aššūr-mātu-taqqin 14 (vi 3′–6′, study)

TEXT

Col. i
Lacuna
1′) ⸢KUR AN⸣.[ŠÁR.KI]
2′) *ša* [AN.ŠÁR]
3′) LUGAL [DINGIR.MEŠ]
4′) *ina ni-*[*iš* IGI.II-*šú*]
5′) *dam-qa-*⸢*a*⸣-[*ti*]
6′) *ḫa-*[*diš*]
7′) *ip-pal-*⸢*su*⸣-[*šú-ma*]
8′) *is-su-*⸢*qu*⸣-[*šú*]
9′) ⸢*a-na* LUGAL⸣-[*u-ti*]
10′) [*a-na*] ⸢*kun*⸣-[*ni*]
Lacuna

Lacuna
i 1′–10′) As[syria]; the one who[m (the god) Aššur], the king [of the gods], with [his] benevol[ent] g[lance], looked [with] ple[asure upon and] selecte[d] for king[ship; to] ma[ke firm]
Lacuna

Col. ii
1) [...]-*ú*
2) [...]-*u-a*
3) [*a-na*] ⸢*kun*$^{?}$⸣-*ni*
4) [SUḪUŠ] KUR
5) [*šu-te*]-*šur*
6) [*ba-ʾu-la*]-⸢*a*⸣-*ti*
7) [KUR AN].⸢ŠÁR⸣.KI
8) [...] *x* PA
Lacuna

ii 1–8) [...] ... [to *make* the foundation of] the land [*f*]*irm*, [to dir]ect [the peo]ple of [As]syria, [...] ...
Lacuna

Col. iii
1) *šak-ka-nak-ku*
2) KÁ.DINGIR.RA.⸢KI⸣
3) LUGAL KUR EME.⸢GI$_7$⸣
4) *ù* ⸢URI⸣.KI
5) DUMU ^{md}30-PAP.⸢MEŠ⸣-[SU]
6) LUGAL ⸢GAL⸣-[*ú*]
7) LUGAL ⸢*dan*⸣-[*nu*]
8) LUGAL [ŠÚ]
Lacuna

iii 1–8) governor of Babylon, king of the land of Sum[er] and Akk[ad]; (5) son of Sennac[herib], grea[t] king, stro[ng] king, king of [the world],
Lacuna

Col. iv
1) *it-*⸢*ta*⸣-[*nar-ru-un-ni-ma*$^{?}$]
2) *x x* [...]
Lacuna

iv 1–2) *they* (*the gods*) [*guided me and*] ... [...]
Lacuna

Col. v
Lacuna

Lacuna

Col. vi
Lacuna
1′) [MU-*šú* NUMUN-*šú*] ⸢NUNUZ$^{?}$-*šú*⸣
2′) [*ina* KUR *lu-ḫal*]-*liq-qu*

Lacuna
vi 1′–2′) [May they (the gods) make his name, his seed], (and) his *offspring* [disa]ppear [from the land].

Date		**Date**
3′)	[...] *lim-mu*	vi 3′–6′) [..., ... day], eponymy of [Aššur-mātu]-taqqin, [gover]nor of [the city (Up)pummu].
4′)	[^{m}*aš-šur*-KUR]-LAL-*in*	
5′)	[LÚ.EN].⌜NAM⌝	
6′)	[URU.*pu-um-mu*]	

10

A (near or exact) duplicate of Ssi 7 is inscribed on three clay cylinders discovered at Aššur. This inscription fills in several gaps in the prism version of the text, including some details about the alleged building history of Nabû's temple. According to this text, which is also commonly referred to as "Cylinder A" in scholarly publications, Sîn-šarra-iškun had Nabû's temple rebuilt from top to bottom on the foundations of an earlier building, one that had been worked on by the Middle Assyrian kings Shalmaneser I and Aššur-rēša-iši I and the Neo-Assyrian ruler Adad-nārārī III. This statement, however, is contradicted in Ssi 12, which states that the Nabû temple was constructed anew on a vacant plot of land. Since the archaeological record supports what is stated in Ssi 12, one should disregard the building history included in "Cylinder A." It appears that when the building report of this text was drafted, its composer(s) might have believed that there had been an earlier Nabû temple built at Aššur (on that exact spot) and (partly) conflated its building history with that of the Ištar temple; early twentieth-century German excavations have revealed that the foundations of the western part of the Nabû temple were laid above the remains of several earlier temples. Later, when the scribes realized their mistake, references to the temple's history were no longer included in reports of this accomplishment of Sîn-šarra-iškun; compare Ssi 11–12. For further details, see Novotny, Kaskal 11 (2014) pp. 162–165. Ex. 1 was inscribed in the eponymy of Bēl-aḫu-uṣur, the palace overseer.

CATALOGUE

Ex.	Museum Number	Excavation Number	Photograph Number	Provenance	Lines Preserved	cpn
1	VA 5060 (+) LB 1323	Ass 13595	Ass ph S 3615	Aššur, eB7II, Nabû temple, south cella, on the pavement of the door, in debris	1–44, date	c
2	VA Ass 2316	Ass 13158 (+) Ass 13158a	Ass ph 3361	Aššur, eB7II, Nabû temple, north cella, east of the dais	1–21, 39–44, date	c
3	A 3634	Ass 19423	—	Aššur, city area	7–8	n

COMMENTARY

The master text is based on ex. 1 with help from ex. 2 where the former is damaged; the lineation of the inscription differs in several places among the exemplars. Ex. 1 has a horizontal ruling between every two lines of text and then two horizontal rulings before the date; this pattern of horizontal rulings may have also been followed in ex. 3, which contains one horizontal ruling among the three lines of text that it preserves. In contrast, ex. 2 contains no horizontal rulings except for one before the first line and after the final line of text that precedes the date. A full score of the inscription is presented on Oracc. All of the minor (orthographic) variants are listed in the critical apparatus, at the back of the book.

BIBLIOGRAPHY

1908 Andrae, MDOG 38 p. 23 (ex. 2, study)
1908 Jordan, MDOG 38 p. 28 (ex. 2, study)
1916 Streck, Asb. p. CCXIV (ex. 2, study)
1922 Schroeder, KAH 2 p. 84 no. 128 (ex. 1 [VA 5060], copy)
1926 Luckenbill, ARAB 2 pp. 414–415 §§1156–1158 (ex. 1 [VA 5060], translation [conflated with Ssi 7 ex. 1])
1936 Böhl, MLVS 3 pp. 31–42 (exs. 1–2, conflated edition, study)
1939–41 Weidner, AfO 13 p. 312 (study)
1947 Böhl, Chrestomathy 1 pp. 34–36 no. 25 (ex. 1, copy)
1952–53 Falkner, AfO 16 p. 305 (exs. 1–2, study)
1967 von Soden, ZA 58 p. 252 (line 17, study)
1973 Kampman, Studies Böhl pp. 230–231 (ex. 1, study)
1977 Andrae, WEA pp. 232 and 313 n. 212 (exs. 1–2, study)
1984 Donbaz and Grayson, RICCA p. 63 and pl. 41 no. 306 (ex. 3, copy)
1986 Borger, ZA 76 p. 302 (ex. 3, study)
1988 Deller, JAOS 108 p. 517 (lines 7–9a, transliteration; ex. 3, study)
1991 Na'aman, ZA 81 p. 255 (line 17, study)
1991 J. Oates, CAH^2 3/2 p. 176 n. 29 (line 17, study)
1994 Millard, SAAS 2 p. 87 (line 45A, transliteration)
1997 Pedersén, Katalog pp. 159 and 207 (exs. 1–3, study)
1999 Frahm, PNA 1/2 p. 284 sub Bēl-aḫu-uṣur 8c (line 45A, study)
2002 Novotny, PNA 3/1 p. 1144 sub Sīn-šarru-iškun b.3′ (study)
2009 Frahm, KAL 3 p. 90 (exs. 1–3, study)
2009 Meinhold, Ištar pp. 445–466 no. 16 (exs. 1–3, edition [conflated with Ssi 7 and 9], study)
2009 Novotny and Van Buylaere, Studies Oded pp. 216–217 (lines 24b–28, translation [conflated with Ssi 7]; exs. 1–3, study)
2010 Novotny, Studies Ellis p. 468 no. 5.28 (lines 24b–28, translation [conflated with Ssi 7]; study)
2012 Bock, Kinderheit pp. 289–290 (lines 16b–22a, edition [conflated with Ssi 7])
2012 Schmitt, Ischtar-Tempel pp. 82 n. 254, 88–89, and 146 and pls. 208–209 nos. 461–462 (exs. 1–2, photo, study)
2014 Novotny, JCS 66 p. 111 (lines 22b–24a, study)
2014 Novotny, Kaskal 11 pp. 162–168 (lines 22b–30, translation [conflated with Ssi 7], study; exs. 1–3, provenance)
2017 Baker, PNA 4/1 p. 168 sub ša-pān-ekalli Bēl-aḫu-uṣur 8 (line 45A, study)
2018 Novotny in Yamada, SAAS 28 pp. 262–263 with nn. 40–42 (lines 22b–24a, translation, study)

TEXT

1) *a-na-ku* $^{m⸢d⸣}$[30-LUGAL]-⸢*iš*⸣-*kun* ⸢LUGAL⸣ GAL LUGAL *dan-nu* LUGAL ŠÚ LUGAL KUR AN.ŠÁR.KI

2) *ša* AN.ŠÁR $^{⸢d⸣}$[NIN.LÍL ^{d}]⸢AMAR⸣.UTU ^{d}*zar-pa-ni-tum* ^{d}AG ^{d}*taš-me-tum ina ni-iš* IGI.II-*šú-nu* SIG$_5$.MEŠ

3) *ke-niš ip-pal-*⸢*su*⸣*-šú-ma is-su-qu-šú a-na* LUGAL-*u-ti a-na kun-ni* SUḪUŠ KUR

4) *šu-te-šur* ⸢*ba-ʾu-la-a-ti*⸣ *dal-ḫa-a-ti a-na tu-qu-ni ab-ta*-a-ti*

5) *a-na ke-še*$_{20}$*-ri a-ge-e be-lu-ti i-pi-ru-*⸢*uš na*⸣*-an-nàr* AN-*e* ^{d}30

6) GIŠ.GIDRU *i-šar-tú uš-pa-ru ke-e-nu a-na re-*⸢*ʾu*⸣*-u-ti* UN.MEŠ DAGAL.MEŠ

7) ^{d}AG *pa-qid kiš-šá-ti ú-šat-me-ḫu rit-tu-uš-šú lìb-bu rap-šú ka-raš ta-šim-ti*

1–11) I, [Sîn-šarra-i]škun, great king, strong king, king of the world, king of Assyria; the one whom the deities Aššur, [Mullissu, M]arduk, Zarpanītu, Nabû, (and) Tašmētu steadfastly looked upon with their benevolent glance and selected for kingship; whom the light of heaven, the god Sîn, crowned with the crown of lordship to make the foundation of the land firm, to direct the people, to put in order what is confused, (5) (and) to repair what is destroyed; whose hand the god Nabû, overseer of the world, made grasp a just scepter (and) a true staff for shepherding a widespread population; magnanimous, discerning, who comprehends reason and counsel, who learned deliberation; reliable judge, who speaks about truth and justice; to whom treacherous talk

4 *ab-ta*-a-ti* "what is destroyed": The text of ex. 1 has *ab-*RA*-a-ti*.

Figure 16. VA Ass 2316 (Ass 13158 [+] Ass 13158a; Ssi 10 ex. 2), a fragmentarily-preserved clay cylinder inscribed with a text recording the construction of the temple of the god Nabû at Aššur. Image courtesy of Aaron Schmitt. © Staatliche Museen zu Berlin – Vorderasiatisches Museum. Photo: Olaf M. Teßmer.

8) *a-ḫi-iz ṭè-e-me ù mil-ki la-mid ši-tul-ti da-a-a-nu ke-e-nu da-bi-ib kit-ti*

9) *ù meš-šá-ri šá ik-kib-šú nu-ul-la-a-ti an-zil-la-šú sur-ra-a-ti*

10) NUN *na-a*ʾ*-du* GÌR.NÍTA *it-pe-šú* LÚ.SIPA *ke-e-nu mut-tar-ru-ú* UN.MEŠ DAGAL.MEŠ

11) *ša* DINGIR.MEŠ GAL.MEŠ LUGAL-*us-su ki-ma ú-lu* Ì.MEŠ *uš-ṭib-bu* UGU *gi-mir ma-ti-tan*

12) DUMU ^{m}AN.ŠÁR-DÙ-IBILA LUGAL GAL LUGAL *dan-nu* LUGAL ŠÚ LUGAL KUR AN.ŠÁR.[KI] LUGAL KUR EME.GI$_7$ *u* URI.KI

13) LUGAL *kib-rat* LÍMMU-*tim* DUMU ^{md*}*aš*-šur**(over erasure)-ŠEŠ-SUM.NA LUGAL GAL LUGAL *dan-nu* LUGAL ŠÚ LUGAL KUR AN.ŠÁR.KI

14) GÌR.NÍTA KÁ.DINGIR.RA.KI LUGAL KUR EME.GI$_7$ *u* URI.KI DUMU ^{md}30-ŠEŠ.MEŠ-⸢SU LUGAL⸣ GAL LUGAL *dan-nu* LUGAL ŠÚ

15) LUGAL KUR AN.ŠÁR.KI NUN *la šá-na-an* ŠÀ.BAL.BAL ^{m}LUGAL-GI.NA LUGAL GAL ⸢LUGAL *dan*⸣*-nu* LUGAL ŠÚ LUGAL KUR AN.ŠÁR.KI

16) GÌR.NÍTA KÁ.DINGIR.RA.KI LUGAL KUR EME.GI$_7$ *u* URI.KI *ina* SAG LUGAL-*u-ti-ia* ⸢*ul*⸣*-tu* AN.ŠÁR ^{d}EN ^{d}AG

17) ^{d}30 ^{d}UTU ^{d}*nin-urta* ^{d}U.GUR *ù* ^{d}*nusku ina bi-rit maš-ši-ia ut-*⸢*tu*⸣*-un-ni-ma iḫ-ši-ḫu* LUGAL-*u-ti*

is anathema (and) lies an abomination; (10) pious ruler, capable governor, true shepherd, leader of a widespread population; whose kingship the great gods made as pleasing in all of the lands as the finest oil;

12–16a) son of Ashurbanipal, great king, strong king, king of the world, king of Assyria, king of the land of Sumer and Akkad, king of the four quarters (of the world); son of Esarhaddon, great king, strong king, king of the world, king of Assyria, governor of Babylon, king of the land of Sumer and Akkad; son of Sennacheri[b], great [k]ing, strong king, king of the world, (15) king of Assyria, ruler who has no rival; descendant of Sargon (II), great king, [s]trong ki[ng], king of the world, king of Assyria, governor of Babylon, king of the land of Sumer and Akkad;

16b–22a) At the beginning of my kingship, a[f]ter the gods Aššur, Bēl (Marduk), Nabû, Sîn, Šamaš, Ninurta, Nergal, and Nusku chose me among my *brothers* and desired (me) as king, guided me like a father and a mother, killed my foes, c[u]t down my enemies,

9 *meš-šá-ri* "justice": This is an unusual writing for *mīšari/mēšari*.

17 *maš-ši-ia* "my *brothers*": See the on-page note to Ssi 1 (Cylinder C) line 5 for the interpretation of *maššîya*. *ut-*⸢*tu*⸣*-un-ni-ma* "they chose me": This is a contracted form for *uttûninni*.

18) *ki-ma* AD *u* AMA *it-ta-nar-ru-un-ni-ma i-na-ru a-a-bi-ia* ⸢*ú-šam*⸣*-qí-tú za-ʾi-i-ri-ia*

19) *ú-sa-at* SIG$_5$ *i-pu-šú-u-ni ṭa-biš ú-še-šib-u-in-ni* ⸢*ina*⸣ [GIŠ.GU].⸢ZA⸣ LUGAL-*u-ti* AD DÙ-*ia*

20) *ša za-na-an ma-ḫa-zi šuk-lul eš-re-e-ti šu-te-šur* ⸢*pe-lu*⸣*-de-e ka-a-a-an uš-ta-da-na kar-šú-u-a*

21) *áš-rat* DINGIR.MEŠ GAL.MEŠ EN.MEŠ-*ia áš-te-ʾe-e-ma mim-*⸢*ma ša*⸣ [UGU DINGIR]-⸢*ti*⸣*-šú-nu* GAL-*ti* DÙG.GA *a-na e-pe-še*

22) *lìb-bi ub-la ina u*$_4$*-mi-šú-ma* É ^{d}AG *šá qé-*⸢*reb bal*⸣-[*til*.KI *šá* ^{md}]⸢*sál*⸣*-ma-nu*-MAŠ DÙ É AN.ŠÁR *e-pu-uš*

23) *e-na-aḫ-ma* ^{md}⸢*aš-šur*-SAG$^?$-*i*$^?$-*ši*$^?$ A$^?$ $^{m?}$*mu*$^?$⸣-[*tak-kil-*^{d}*nusku*$^?$ *e-pu-uš*] ⸢*e*⸣*-na-aḫ-ma* ^{md}IŠKUR-ERIM.TÁḪ DUMU ^{m}*šam-ši-*^{d}IŠKUR

24) *e-pu-uš-*⸢*ma e-na*⸣-[*aḫ-ma la-ba-riš il-lik ul-tu* UD.MEŠ *ma-aʾ*]*-du-ti ni-du-tú il-lik-ma i-te-me qaq-qa-riš*

25) [^{d}AG ^{d}*taš-me-tum ina* É ^{d}*iš-tar aš-šur-i-ti*] *áš-bu-ma i-maḫ-ḫa-ru sur-qé-ni*

26) [LUGAL.MEŠ AD.MEŠ-*ia a-li-kut maḫ-ri-ia* DÙ-*eš*] ⸢É⸣ *šú-a-tú la iḫ-su-su-nim-ma*

27) [*ul iš-ku-nu uz-nu a-na-ku* ^{md}30-LUGAL-GAR-*un* LUGAL] ŠÚ LUGAL KUR AN.ŠÁR.KI *pa-liḫ* DINGIR.MEŠ GAL.MEŠ

28) [*muš-te-eʾ-u áš-ri-šú-nu e-pe-eš* É *šú-a-tú ina lìb*]-⸢*bi*⸣*-ia ib-ba-ši-ma ka-bat-ti ub-la*

29) [*ina* GIŠ.ḪUR-*šú la-bir-tú ina* MAŠ.KÁN-*šú maḫ-ri-ti ina* ITI DÙG].⸢GA⸣ *u*$_4$*-me še-me-e ina ši-pir ka-kù-gal-lu-ti ina* NA$_4$.*pi-i-li*

30) [*tem-me-en-ši uš-mal-li*$^?$*-ma ú-zaq-qir ḫur-šá*]-⸢*niš*⸣ *ul-tu* UŠ$_8$-*šú a-di gaba-dib-bi-šú ar-ṣip ú-šak-lil*

31) [...-*ia* ...]-⸢*ma*⸣ *ki-ma u*$_4$*-me ú-nam-mir* ^{d}AG ^{d}PAPNUN DINGIR.MEŠ GAL.MEŠ EN.<MEŠ>-*ia*

32) [*ul-tu* É ^{d}*iš-tar aš-šur-i-ti ú-še-ṣa*]*-am-ma ina* ITI DÙG.GA *u*$_4$*-me še-me-e qé-reb-šú ú-še-rib-ma*

33) [*ú-šar-me* BÁRA *da-ra-a-ti* GU$_4$.MAḪ-*ḫi*] ⸢*reš*⸣*-tu-u-ti* GUKKAL.MEŠ *ma-ru-u-ti zi-i-bi qa-áš-du-ti*

34) [*ina ma-ḫar* ^{d}AG ^{d}PAPNUN EN.MEŠ-*ia aq*]-⸢*qí*⸣*-ma uš-par-zi-ḫa qé-reb é-kur-ri* ^{d}AG ^{d}PAPNUN

35) [*ep-še-ti-ia* SIG$_5$.MEŠ *ḫa-diš ip-pal*]-⸢*su*⸣*-ma ik-tar-ra-bu* LUGAL-*u-ti*

36) [NUN EGIR-*u ina* LUGAL.MEŠ DUMU.MEŠ]-⸢*ia*⸣ *e-nu-ma* É *šú-a-tú in-na-*⸢*ḫu*⸣*-ma*

37) [*il-la-ku la-ba-riš an-ḫu-us*]-⸢*su*⸣ *lu-ud-diš* MU.SAR-*ú ši-ṭir* MU-*ia*

38) [*li-mur-ma* Ì.GIŠ *lip-šu-uš ni-qa-a*] ⸢*li*⸣*-iq-qí it-ti* MU.SAR-*e ši-ṭir* MU-*šú liš-kun*

performed good deeds for me, (and) gladly placed me o[n the] royal [thro]ne of the father who had engendered me; (20) I constantly gave thought to providing for cult centers, completing sanctuaries, (and) putting in order *p*[*ell*]*udû*-rites; I was assiduous towards the sanctuaries of the great gods, my lords, and wanted to do whatev[er] was suitable [for] their great [divinit]y.

22b–27a) At that time, the temple of the god Nabû that is inside B[altil (Aššur), which Sha]lmaneser (I) — the builder of the temple of (the god) Aššur — had built, became dilapidated and *Aššur-rēša-iši* (*I*), *son of Mu*[*takkil-Nusku* (re)built (it) (and)] it became dilapidated (again); and Adad-nārārī (III), son of Šamšī-Adad (V) (re)built (it) and it became dilap[idated and old. For a lo]ng [time], it fell into disrepair and became level with the ground. (25) [The god Nabû (and) the goddess Tašmētu] took up residence [in the temple of the Assyrian Ištar] and (there) they received strewn offerings. [The kings, my ancestors who came before me], did not think about [(re)building] that temple and [they did not pay (it any) attention].

27b–33a) [I, Sîn-šarra-iškun, king of] the world, king of Assyria, the one who reveres the great gods, [who is assiduous towards their places (of worship)], conceived [in] my [hear]t [to (re)build that temple] and wanted (to carry it out). [According to its original plan, on its former site, in a favorab]le [month], (on) an auspicious day, according to the craft of the incantation priest, (30) [*I filled in* its foundation] with limestone [and made (it) as high] as [a mounta]in. I built (and) completed (it) from its foundations to its crenellations. [... my ... a]nd made (it) shine like daylight. [I brought] the god Nabû (and) the goddess Tašmētu, the great gods, my lord<s>, out [of the temple of the Assyrian Ištar] and, in a favorable month, (on) an auspicious day, I made (them) enter inside it and [made them dwell on (their) eternal dais(es)].

33b–35) [I offe]red prime quality [prize bulls] (and) fattened fat-tailed sheep as pure food offerings [before the god Nabû (and) the goddess Tašmētu, my lords], and (thus) I lavishly provided (for them) inside (that) temple. The god Nabû (and) the goddess Tašmētu (35) [looke]d [with pleasure upon my good deeds] and constantly blessed my kingship.

36–39) May [a future ruler, one of the kings, m]y [descendants], renovate [it]s [dilapidated section(s)] when that temple becomes dilapidated and [old. May he find] an inscribed object bearing my name, [and (then) anoint (it) with oil], make [an offering], (and) place (it) with an inscribed object bearing his name. [The

22b–24a For a discussion of the building history, see Novotny, Kaskal 11 (2014) pp. 162–165; and Novotny in Yamada, SAAS 28 pp. 262–263 with nn. 40–42.

39) [AN.ŠÁR ^{d}NIN.LÍL ^{d}AMAR.UTU ^{d}]⸢*zar*⸣-*pa*-⸢*ni*⸣-[*tum* ^{d}]⸢AG⸣ ^{d}*taš-me-tum ik-ri-bi-šú i-šem-mu-u*

40) [*šá* MU.SAR-*u ši*]-⸢*ṭir*⸣ MU-⸢*ia*⸣ *ú-nak-kar-ú-ma*

41) [*it-ti* MU.SAR-*e ši*]-⸢*ṭir*⸣ MU-*šú la i-šak-ka-nu ù šu-mi it-ti* MU-*šú*

42) [*la i-šaṭ-ṭa-ru* AN.ŠÁR ^{d}NIN].⸢LÍL⸣ ^{d}AMAR.UTU ^{d}*zar-pa-ni-tum* ^{d}AG ^{d}*taš-me-tum*

43) [*a-na ni-iš*] ⸢ŠU.II-*šú*⸣ *a-a iz-zi-zu-ma a-a iš-mu-ú su-up-pi-šu*

44) [*ag-giš*] ⸢*li*⸣-*ru-ru-šú-ma* MU-*šú* NUMUN-*šú* NUNUZ-*šú ina* KUR *lu-ḫal-li-qu*

deities Aššur, Mullissu, Marduk, Za]rpanī[tu, Na]bû, (and) Tašmētu will (then) hear his prayers.

40–44) [(As for) the one who] removes [an inscribed object bear]ing my name and does not place (it) [with an inscribed object bearin]g his name and [does not write] my name with his name, may [the deities Aššur, Mullis]su, Marduk, Zarpanītu, Nabû, (and) Tašmētu not be present [for h]is [pra]yers and not heed his supplications. [M]ay they curse him [angrily] and make his name, his seed, (and) his offspring disappear from the land.

Date ex. 1

45A) [... *lim*]-⸢*mu*⸣ ^{m}EN-ŠEŠ-ŠEŠ LÚ.*šá* IGI KUR

45A) [..., epon]ymy of Bēl-aḫu-uṣur, palace overseer.

Date ex. 2

45B) ITI.DU$_{6}$.KÙ UD.4$^{?}$.KAM *lim*-⸢*mu* ^{m}EN⸣-ŠEŠ-*ú*-⸢*ṣur* LÚ⸣.*šá* IGI É.GAL

45B) Tašrītu (VII), the *fourth* day, eponymy of Bēl-aḫu-uṣur, palace overseer.

11

A short inscription stating that this son and successor of Ashurbanipal built a temple for the god Nabû at Aššur is inscribed on numerous clay cones. The text claims that Sîn-šarra-iškun had the foundations laid during a favorable month, on an auspicious day, and that the workers performed their work happily. Several of the exemplars were inscribed during the month Tašrītu (VII), in the eponymy of Sa'īlu, the chief cook.

CATALOGUE

Ex.	Museum Number	Excavation Number	Photograph Number	Provenance	Lines Preserved	cpn
1	VA 8416	Ass 12727	Ass ph 3093, 3095	Aššur, eE7I, under the Parthian foundation, near the entrance to the Nabû temple	1–5	c
2	VA Ass 2128	Ass 10625	—	Aššur, city area	1–3	c
3	A 3448	Ass 6626	—	Aššur, eB5V	1–4	p
4	A 3547	Ass 12548	Ass ph 3129	Aššur, eE7I, dump, "west"	1–5	p
5	A 3549	Ass 12726	Ass ph 3093–3094, 3359–3360	As ex. 1	1–5	p
6	A 3550	Ass 12729	Ass ph 3093	As ex. 1	1–4	p
7	A 3554	Ass 12946	Ass ph 3253	Aššur, eE7I, south of the test trench	1–4	p
8	A 3555	Ass 12951	Ass ph 3253	Aššur, eE7I, north of the test trench	1–3	p
9	A 3557	Ass 13014	Ass ph 3334	Aššur, eE6V, north of the "Hallan" foundation	1–5	p
10	A 3558	Ass 13105	—	Aššur, eE7I, level of second Assyrian stratum	2–5	p
11	A 3560	Ass 13165	Ass ph 3334	Aššur, eD7I, Nabû temple, north courtyard	1–4	p
12	A 3561	Ass 13223	Ass ph 3536	Aššur, eC7I, Nabû temple, Room 4, on the floor	2–4	p

13	A 3563	Ass 13331	Ass ph 3536	Aššur, eC7III, Nabû temple, south courtyard, west corner, in debris ca. 40 cm above the brick pavement	1–2	p
14	A 3565	Ass 13458	Ass ph 3584	Aššur, eC7III, Nabû temple, south courtyard, south corner, on the floor	1–2	p
15	A 3567	Ass 13591	Ass ph 4203	Aššur, e7, dump	3–5	p

COMMENTARY

On the majority of exemplars (exs. 1–11), the inscription is written in five (although ex. 8 seems to have a few more) progressively shorter lines that form concentric circles around the opening on the top of the cone. The way in which the contents of the inscription are divided into those five lines varies among the exemplars (compare the division of lines in exs. 1, 5, and 6). The lineation (and text) of the master text follows ex. 5. The remaining exemplars have the inscription written in blocks of lines that appear in various locations on the head of the cones. Ex. 13 has the first half of the inscription written as a square block of text above a round opening that is in the center of the cone's head, while ex. 12 has the second half of the inscription written as a square block of text below the opening in the head of its cone. The other half of the inscription on these exemplars would have appeared on the opposite side of the openings in the cones, but those portions of the exemplars are not preserved. Exs. 14 and 15 seem to have the inscription written as a single block of text that covers the entire top of the cone, although not enough of these two exemplars is preserved to be certain.

The lineation of the conflated transcription provided in the initial publication of these objects by V. Donbaz and A.K. Grayson (RICCA p. 56) is unfortunately the result of a misunderstanding of Donbaz' copy of A 3549 (ex. 5 here). Like ex. 1, A 3549 is a fairly complete exemplar of the inscription, and so it was published as their "source a" and used as the basis for their transcription. In line with the majority of exemplars, the inscription on this object is written in five lines that form concentric circles around the opening on the top of the cone (see the photo in Nunn, Knaufplatten pl. 32 no. 1519). Given the fact that the intact lines of that exemplar are relatively long, Donbaz copied them (see RICCA pl. 32 no. 236) as consecutive lines of text in which long lines were continued on subsequent lines in the copy rather than how they appeared on the object itself, as was done for his copies of the other exemplars of this inscription. In this way, lines 1, 2, and 3 of A 3549 are each presented as three consecutive lines in the copy, line 4 is presented as two consecutive lines, and then line 5 appears as its own line. Since Donbaz did not provide line numbers in his copy, it gives the impression that the inscription on A 3549 was written as twelve consecutive lines, and this was taken as the lineation for their conflated transcription though no exemplar bearing this text preserves such a lineation. A score of the text is presented on Oracc and the minor (orthographic) variants are listed at the back of the book.

BIBLIOGRAPHY

1908 Andrae, MDOG 36 p. 35–36 (exs. 1, 5–6, study, provenance)
1908 Andrae, MDOG 38 p. 23 (exs. 1, 5–6, study)
1916 Streck, Asb. pp. CCXIII–CCXIV (exs. 1, 5–6, study)
1922 Schroeder, KAH 2 pp. 85–86 nos. 129 and 133 (exs. 1, 13, copy; ex. 12, variants)
1926 Luckenbill, ARAB 2 pp. 413–414 §§1152–1155 (ex. 1, translation, study)
1952–53 Falkner, AfO 16 p. 305 (exs. 1, 7, 11, 13, 15, study)
1982 Jakob-Rost, FuB 22 pp. 146 and 175 no. 111 (ex. 2, copy, study)
1984 Donbaz and Grayson, RICCA pp. 55–60 and pls. 32–34 J nos. 236–248 (exs. 3–12, 14–15, copy; exs. 1–15, transliteration, study)
1986 Deller, Bagh. Mitt. 16 p. 376 (line 5, transliteration, study)
1988 Deller, JAOS 108 p. 517 (line 5, study)
1994 Millard, SAAS 2 p. 113 (line 5, transliteration)
1997 Pedersén, Katalog pp. 136, 143, and 145–146 (exs. 1–15, study)
2006 Nunn, Knaufplatten pp. 63, 73–75 and 164–165 nos. 1516–1530 and pl. 32 no. 1519 (ex. 5, photo; exs. 1–15, study)
2017 Baker, PNA 3/1 p. 1046 sub Sa'īlu 19.a (line 5, study)
2002 Novotny, PNA 3/1 p. 1143 sub Sīn-šarru-iškun b.3′ (study)
2009 Frahm, KAL 3 p. 91 (study)
2009 Meinhold, Ištar p. 445 no. 16 (study)
2009 Novotny and Van Buylaere, Studies Oded p. 216 (exs. 1–15, study)
2010 Novotny, Studies Ellis pp. 120 and 124 (lines 3b–4, study)
2012 Schmitt, Ischtar-Tempel pp. 86, 88, and 168–169 and pls. 230–231 nos. 745–748, 751–752, 754–755, 757, 759, 761, and 763 (exs. 1, 4, 6–9, 11–14, photo; exs. 1, 4–9, 11–15, study)

2014 Novotny, Kaskal 11 pp. 164 n. 11 and 166–168 (exs. 1–15, provenance; line 5, study)

2017 Baker, PNA 4/1 p. 111 sub rab nuḫatimmi Saʾīlu 19 (line 5, study)

Figure 17. VA 8416 (Ass 12727; Ssi 11 ex. 1), a clay cone discovered at Aššur recording Sîn-šarra-iškun's construction of Nabû's temple. Image courtesy of Aaron Schmitt. © Staatliche Museen zu Berlin – Vorderasiatisches Museum and Deutsche Orient-Gesellschaft. Ass ph 3093, photographer unknown, 11.18.1907.

TEXT

1) *a-na-ku* ^{md}30-⸢LUGAL⸣-GAR-*un* MAN GAL MAN *dan-nu* MAN ŠÚ LUGAL KUR *aš-šur*.KI A ^{m}*aš-šur*-DÙ-A MAN GAL MAN *dan-nu* MAN ŠÚ MAN KUR *aš-šur*.⸢KI⸣ MAN KUR EME.GI$_7$ *u* URI.KI A ^{m}*aš-šur*-PAP-AŠ MAN GAL MAN *dan-nu* MAN ŠÚ MAN KUR *aš-šur*.KI GÌR.NÍTA KÁ.DINGIR.KI MAN KUR EME.GI$_7$ *u* URI.KI A ^{md}30-PAP.MEŠ-SU

1–2a) I, Sîn-šarra-iškun, great king, strong king, king of the world, king of Assyria; son of Ashurbanipal, great king, strong king, king of the world, king of Assyria, king of the land of Sumer and Akkad; son of Esarhaddon, great king, strong king, king of the world, king of Assyria, governor of Babylon, king of the land of Sumer and Akkad; son of Sennacherib, great king, strong king, king of the world, king of Assyria, ruler who has no rival; descendant of Sargon (II), great king, strong king, king of the world, king of Assyria, governor of Babylon, king of the land of Sumer and Akkad:

2) MAN GAL MAN *dan-nu* MAN ŠÚ MAN KUR *aš-šur*.KI NUN *la šá-na-an* ŠÀ.BAL.BAL ^{m}LUGAL-GI.NA MAN GAL MAN *dan-nu* MAN ŠÚ MAN KUR *aš-šur*.⸢KI⸣ GÌR.NÍTA KÁ.DINGIR.KI MAN KUR EME.GI$_7$ *u* URI.KI *ina* SAG LUGAL-*ti-ia ki-i ṭè-me* DINGIR-*ma*

3) *a-na* DÙ-*eš* É ^{d}⸢AG⸣ *šá qé-reb bal-til*.KI *lìb-bi*

2b–4) At the beginning of my kingship (and) in accordance with the will of the god(s), I wanted to (re)build the temple of the god Nabû that is inside Baltil (Aššur). In a favorable month, (on) an auspicious day, I laid its foundation(s) and I mixed its *kalakku*-mortar with beer (and) wine. Its brick maker(s and) hod carrier(s) spent their days in rejoicing

1 Ex. 11 omits MAN GAL "great king" and MAN ŠÚ "king of the world" after ^{m}*aš-šur*-PAP-AŠ "Esarhaddon."
2 Ex. 11 omits MAN GAL "great king" after ^{m}LUGAL-GI.NA "Sargon (II)."
3 Ex. 12 has [(*x*) *x*]-⸢*šur*?⸣ after *bal-til*.KI, "Baltil (Aššur)." Could this possibly be [(URU).*aš*]-⸢*šur*?⸣ as a gloss for Baltil?

ub-la ina ITI DÙG.GA *u_4-mu še-me-e te-me-en-šú ad-di-ma ina* KAŠ.SAG GEŠTIN *ka-lak-ka-šu ab-lul la-bin* SIG_4.MEŠ-*šú*
4) *za-bíl ku-dúr-ri-šú ina e-le-li nin-gu-tu ub-ba-la* UD-*šu-un* TA $UŠ_8$-*šú a-di gaba-dib-bi-šu ar-ṣip ú-šak-lil*

(and) singing. I built (and) completed (it) from its foundation(s) to its crenellations.

Date

5) ITI.DU_6.KÙ *lim-mu* ^{m}*sa-ʾi-lu* LÚ.GAL MUḪALDIM

5) Tašrītu (VII), eponymy of Saʾīlu, the chief cook.

12

This stone block is inscribed with a sixteen-line Akkadian text recording the construction of Nabû's temple at Aššur. Unlike other texts of Sîn-šarra-iškun recording this accomplishment, this inscription indicates that the new structure was constructed on an empty plot of land, and not rebuilt on the foundations of an earlier temple, as Ssi 7 and 10 record. This recently-published inscription confirms what has been long known from the archaeological record: Sîn-šarra-iškun did not simply rebuild an existing temple of the god Nabû at Aššur, but rather constructed an entirely new place of worship for him.

CATALOGUE

Source	Provenance	cpn
ISIMU 14-15 pp. 39-43	Aššur	p

BIBLIOGRAPHY

2011–12 Kessler, ISIMU 14–15 pp. 39–43 (photo, copy, edition)
2014 Novotny, Kaskal 11 pp. 159–165 and 168 (edition, study)

TEXT

1) *a-na-ku* ^{md}30-LUGAL-*iš-kun*
2) MAN GAL MAN KAL MAN ŠÚ MAN KUR *aš-šur*.KI
3) A ^{m}*aš-šur*-DÙ-A MAN ŠÚ MAN KUR *aš-*⸢*šur*⸣.[KI]
4) A ^{m}*aš-šur*-PAP-AŠ MAN ŠÚ MAN KUR *aš-*⸢*šur*⸣.KI
5) A ^{m}30-PAP.MEŠ-SU MAN ŠÚ MAN KUR AŠ
6) ⸢ŠÀ⸣.[BAL].BAL ^{m}LUGAL-GI.NA MAN ŠÚ MAN KUR AŠ
7) [GÌR.NÍTA] ⸢KÁ⸣.DINGIR.KI MAN KUR EME.GI_7 *u* ⸢URI.KI⸣

1–7) I, Sîn-šarra-iškun, great king, strong king, king of the world, king of Assyria; son of Ashurbanipal, king of the world, king of Assyri[a]; son of Esarhaddon, king of the world, king of Ass[yria]; (5) son of Sennacherib, king of the world, king of Assyria; [de]s[cenda]nt of Sargon (II), king of the world, king of Assyria, [governor of B]abylon, king of the land of Sumer and Akkad:

8) *ina* [SAG] ⸢LUGAL⸣-*ti-ia šá* AN.ŠÁR ⸢^{d}EN$^{?}$ ^{d}⸣MUATI
9) ^{d}[*iš-tar*$^{?}$] ⸢*ṭa*⸣-*biš ú-*⸢*še-šib-u-in*⸣-*ni*

8–14a) At [the beginning of] my [king]ship, when the deities Aššur, *Bēl* (*Marduk*), Nabû, (and) [*Ištar*] gladly

11 line 4 As noted by V. Donbaz and A.K. Grayson (RICCA p. 60), this line in ex. 11 is garbled. It contains about six or seven inconstruable signs (see the photo in Schmitt, Ischtar-Tempel pl. 231 no. 755).

10) *ina* GIŠ.⸢GU⸣.[ZA] ⸢AD⸣ DÙ-*ia* É ⸢^{d}AG⸣ [*šá*]
11) ⸢*qé-reb*⸣ *bal-til šá ul-*⸢*tú*⸣ UD.MEŠ SÙ.MEŠ
12) *la*$^{?}$ *ma*$^{?}$*-al*$^{?}$*-du ke*$^{?}$*-e-mu-u* ⸢*ni-du-tú*⸣
13) *ul-tú* UŠ$_{8}$*-šú a-di gaba-dib-bi-šú ar-ṣip*

placed me (10) on the th[rone of the fa]ther who had engendered me, *in place of* an empty lot I built (and) completed the temple of the god Nabû [that is] i[nsi]de Baltil (Aššur), which *had not been created* (lit: "born") from distant days, from its foundations to its crenellations.

14) *ú-šak-lil* ^{d}AG ^{d}PAPNUN *qé-reb-*⸢*šú*$^{?}$⸣
15) *ú-še-rib-ma ú-*⸢*šar*$^{?}$*-ma*$^{?}$⸣*-a*
16) *pa-*⸢*rak*$^{?}$⸣ *da-ra-a-ti*

14b–16) I made the god Nabû (and) the goddess Tašmētu enter inside *it* and *made (them) dwell on* (their) eternal *da*[*i*]*s*(*es*).

13

Numerous inscribed bricks record that Sîn-šarra-iškun had one of the enclosed courtyards of the Nabû temple at Aššur paved with baked bricks; the work was carried out according to the craft of the deity Nunurra.

CATALOGUE

Ex.	Museum Number	Excavation/ Registration No.	Photograph Number	Provenance	Lines Preserved	cpn
1	VA Ass 3284a	Ass 6655	Ass ph 994	Aššur, city area	4–8	p
2	VA Ass 3284b	Ass 13189	Ass ph 3330	Aššur, eB7II, Nabû temple, north cella, floor near the dais	1–13	p
3	VA Ass 3284c	Ass 13352	Ass ph 3460	Aššur, eC7III, Nabû temple, south ante-cella, floor	1–12	p
4	VA Ass 3284d	Ass 13463	—	Aššur, eC7II, Nabû temple, north ante-cella, floor	1–13	p
5	VA Ass 3284e	Ass 13464	—	As ex. 4	1–13	p
6	VA Ass 3284f	Ass 13607	—	Aššur, eC7III, Nabû temple, south ante-cella, floor	1–13	p
7	VA Ass 3284g	Ass 13799	—	Aššur, eB7I, Nabû temple, north ante-cella, floor	1–13	p
8	VA Ass 3284h	Ass 13946a (+) Ass 13946b	Ass ph 4178	Aššur, hE8I, west	1–12	(p)
9	VA Ass 3284i	—	—	Aššur	1–13	p
10	—	Ass 13123	Ass ph 4178	Aššur, eE7I, in test trench, ca. 2 m deep	1–6	p
11	—	Ass 13188	Ass ph 3329	Aššur, eB7II, Nabû temple, from the stack of bricks	1–13	p
12	—	Ass 13444	—	Aššur, eB7II, Nabû temple, north cella, floor	—	n
13	—	Ass 13445	Ass ph 3516	As ex. 12	1–13	n
14	—	Ass 13446	—	Aššur, eC7II, Nabû temple, north cella, floor	—	n
15	—	Ass 13447	—	Aššur, eC7II, Nabû temple, north cella, floor of the entrance	—	n
16	—	Ass 13448	—	As ex. 15	—	n
17	—	Ass 13449	Ass ph 4480–4481	Aššur, eC7II, Nabû temple, south ante-cella, floor	1–13	p
18	—	Ass 13450	—	As ex. 17	—	n
19	—	Ass 13462	Ass ph 4482–4483	As ex. 4	1–13	p
20	—	Ass 13465	—	As ex. 4	—	n
21	—	Ass 13466	Ass ph 4484–4485	As ex. 4	1–13	p
22	—	Ass 13606	—	As ex. 6	—	n

23	BM 115697	1922-8-12,72; Ass 13467	—	Probably Aššur, Nabû temple	1–13	p
24	BM 108856	1914-4-7,22	—	Ex. ex. 23	1–13	n

COMMENTARY

Although several of the bricks were not available for study (exs. 12–16, 18, 20, and 22), the text on the remaining exemplars is inscribed by hand and not stamped. The lineation of the inscription varies drastically among the exemplars; it is written over eight lines (ex. 6), twelve lines (ex. 8), thirteen lines (exs. 2–3, 7, 13, 17, 19, and 24), fourteen lines (exs. 5, 9, and 23), fifteen lines (exs. 4 and 21), and sixteen lines (ex. 11). Even when exemplars share the same number of lines, the division of those lines is inconsistent. The majority of the bricks contain no additional markings other than the inscription; however, exs. 2, 4, 13, 17, 19, and 21 have a vertical ruling to the left of the text that serves as a left margin and the inscription on ex. 23 is surrounded by a square box. The most unique brick is ex. 6. Its text is written in a rectangular box, with horizontal rulings between each line of text. Given that the text was written over only eight lines, it appears that the scribe had to draw an additional right vertical ruling for the right margin after several of the lines went past the initial vertical ruling set for the margin (see the copy in Jakob-Rost and Marzahn, VAS 23 pl. XLIV no. 148). The master text is taken from ex. 17.

No score for this brick inscription is presented on Oracc, following RINAP editorial practices. The minor (orthographic) variants, however, are listed at the back of the book.

Figure 18. BM 115697 (Ass 13467; Ssi 13 ex. 23), a brick with an Akkadian inscription recording the construction of the temple of the god Nabû. © Trustees of the British Museum.

BIBLIOGRAPHY

1908 Andrae, MDOG 38 pp. 24–25 (study)
1908 Jordan, MDOG 38 p. 28 (study)
1916 Streck, Asb. pp. CCXIII (study)
1922 BM Guide p. 75 nos. 330–331 (exs. 23–24, study)
1922 Schroeder, KAH 2 p. 87 no. 134 (ex. 17, copy; exs. 2, 8, 10–11, 19, 21, variants)
1926 Luckenbill, ARAB 2 p. 416 §1165 (ex. 17, translation; ex. 23, study)
1935 Andrae, JIT p. 122 and pl. 54a (ex. 13, photo; study)
1952–53 Falkner, AfO 16 p. 305 (ex. 17, study)
1977 Andrae, WEA pp. 232 and 313 n. 212 (study)
1981 Walker, CBI pp. 126–127 no. 189 (ex. 24, transliteration; ex. 23, variants; exs. 23–24, study)
1984 Marzahn and Jakob-Rost, Ziegeln 1 pp. 145–148 nos. 389, 391–392, and 394–395 (exs. 1, 3–4, 6–7, study)
1985 Jakob-Rost and Marzahn, VAS 23 p. 9 and pls. XLII–XLV nos. 143–145, 148, and 151 (exs. 1, 3–4, 6–7, copy, study)
1986 Galter, ZA 76 p. 304 (study)
1997 Pedersén, Katalog pp. 182 and 190–192 (exs. 1–23, study)
2002 Novotny, PNA 3/1 pp. 1143–1144 sub Sīn-šarru-iškun b.3′ (study)
2009 Meinhold, Ištar p. 445 no. 16 (study)
2009 Novotny and Van Buylaere, Studies Oded p. 217 (exs. 1–4, 6–23, study)
2012 Schmitt, Ischtar-Tempel pp. 82 n. 254, pp. 87–89 with n. 307, and pp. 147–148 and pls. 131a and 210–211 nos. 472–488, 490–491, and 495–496 (exs. 10, 13, 17, 19, 21, photo; exs. 2–8, 10–23, study)
2014 Novotny, Kaskal 11 pp. 166–168 (exs. 1–4, 6–23, provenance)

TEXT

1) *a-na-ku* ^{md}30-LUGAL-GAR-*un* MAN GAL-*u* MAN *dan-nu* MAN ŠÚ
2) MAN KUR *aš-šur*.KI DUMU ^{m}*aš-šur*-DÙ-A MAN GAL-*u* MAN *dan-nu* MAN ŠÚ
3) MAN KUR *aš-šur*.KI MAN KUR EME.GI$_7$ *u* URI.KI MAN *kib-rat* LÍMMU-*ti*
4) DUMU ^{m}*aš-šur*-PAP-AŠ MAN GAL-*u* MAN *dan-nu* MAN ŠÚ MAN KUR *aš-šur*.KI
5) GÌR.NÍTA KÁ.DINGIR.KI MAN KUR EME.GI$_7$ *u* URI.KI
6) DUMU ^{md}30-PAP.MEŠ-SU MAN GAL-*u* MAN *dan-nu* MAN ŠÚ MAN KUR *aš-šur*.KI
7) NUN *la šá-na-an*
8) ŠÀ.BAL.BAL ^{m}LUGAL-GI.NA MAN GAL-*u* MAN *dan-nu* MAN ŠÚ
9) MAN KUR *aš-šur*.KI GÌR.NÍTA KÁ.DINGIR.KI MAN KUR EME.GI$_7$ *u* URI.KI
10) *mu-ud-diš é-kur-ri* É ^{d}AG EN-*ia*
11) *šá qé-reb bal-til*.KI TÙR *šú-a-tú*
12) *ina a-gúr-ri pi-ti-iq* ^{d}*nun-ùr-ra*
13) *ak-šir*

1–13) I, Sîn-šarra-iškun, great king, strong king, king of the world, king of Assyria; son of Ashurbanipal, great king, strong king, king of the world, king of Assyria, king of the land of Sumer and Akkad, king of the four quarters (of the world); son of Esarhaddon, great king, strong king, king of the world, king of Assyria, (5) governor of Babylon, king of the land of Sumer and Akkad; son of Sennacherib, great king, strong king, king of the world, king of Assyria, ruler who has no rival; descendant of Sargon (II), great king, strong king, king of the world, king of Assyria, governor of Babylon, king of the land of Sumer and Akkad; (10) the one who renovates the chapels of the temple of the god Nabû, my lord, that is inside Baltil (Aššur): I repaired its (lit. "that") enclosed courtyard with baked bricks, the craft of the god Nunurra.

3, 5, and 9 KUR EME.GI$_7$, "the land of Sumer": Exs. 3–4 and 21 appear to have KUR EME.KI (with the third attestation in ex. 21 only written KUR EME without a following GI$_7$ or KI sign), while exs. 19 and 24 have KUR EME-*ri*. Based on these spellings, it is possible that the scribes were reading the logogram EME as *šumeri* with KI as a determinative in the former case and *ri* as a phonetic complement in the latter.
5 Ex. 3 omits GÌR.NÍTA KÁ.DINGIR.KI "governor of Babylon."
6 Ex. 3 adds MAN KUR EME.⸢KI *u* URI⸣.KI "king of the land of Sumer and Akkad" after MAN KUR *aš-šur*.KI "king of Assyria."
11 Ex. 4 leaves the space after an incomplete *qé-reb* (the text has *qé*-GIŠ) uninscribed, thus omitting *bal-til*.KI.

14

A fragment of a brick discovered at Aššur preserves part of the beginning of an Akkadian inscription of Sîn-šarra-iškun. Although it is not sufficiently preserved to be able to determine which project of this Assyrian king it records, it might have stated that Sîn-šarra-iškun constructed the Nabû temple in that city since all of the extant texts of his from Aššur record that accomplishment.

CATALOGUE

Museum Number	Excavation Number	Photograph Number	Provenance	cpn
VA Ass 3285	Ass 2043	Ass ph 408	Aššur, hB4II, Peripteros, northwest corner, in debris	p

BIBLIOGRAPHY

1911 Messerschmidt, KAH 1 p. 53* no. 56 (copy)
1916 Streck, Asb. pp. CCXIII and 388–389 (edition, study [wrongly cited as Ass 2041])
1926 Luckenbill, ARAB 2 p. 416 n. 1 (study)
1935 Andrae, JIT p. 122 with fig. 86 (copy, study)
1952–53 Falkner, AfO 16 p. 305 (study)
1997 Pedersén, Katalog p. 167 (study)
2002 Novotny, PNA 3/1 p. 1144 sub Sīn-šarru-iškun b.3′ (study)
2009 Meinhold, Ištar p. 445 no. 16 (study)
2009 Novotny and Van Buylaere, Studies Oded p. 217 (study)
2014 Novotny, Kaskal 11 p. 168 (provenance)

TEXT

1) [É].⸢GAL⸣ ^{md}30-LUGAL-GAR-*un* MAN GAL MAN [*dan-nu* MAN ŠÚ MAN KUR *aš-šur*.KI]
2) [A ^{m}*aš*]-*šur*-DÙ-A MAN GAL MAN *dan-nu* MAN ŠÚ MAN [KUR *aš-šur*.KI]
3) [A ^{m}*aš*]-*šur*-PAP-AŠ MAN GAL MAN *dan-nu* ⸢MAN⸣ [ŠÚ MAN KUR *aš-šur*.KI]
4) [A ^{md}30]-PAP.MEŠ-SU MAN GAL MAN ⸢*dan*⸣-[*nu* MAN ŠÚ MAN KUR *aš-šur*.KI]
5) [ŠÀ.BAL].⸢BAL? ^{m}⸣LUGAL-GI.NA ⸢MAN⸣ [GAL MAN *dan-nu* MAN ŠÚ MAN KUR *aš-šur*.KI]
6) [...] *x* (*x*) [...]

Lacuna

1–6) [Palac]e of Sîn-šarra-iškun, great king, [strong] king, [king of the world, king of Assyria; son of As]hurbanipal, great king, strong king, king of the world, king of [Assyria; son of Es]arhaddon, great king, strong king, k[ing of the world, king of Assyria; son of Senn]acherib, great king, s[trong] king, [king of the world, king of Assyria; (5) *descendan*]*t* of Sargon (II), [great] k[ing, strong king, king of the world, king of Assyria, ...]

Lacuna

15

A clay tablet discovered in the "N 2" Archive at Aššur (Pedersén, Archives 2 pp. 29–34) bears archival copies or drafts of two dedicatory inscriptions, both written in the name of Ashurbanipal's son Sîn-šarra-iškun. The text on the obverse (this inscription) records the fashioning of a *kallu*-bowl (and) a *šulpu*-bowl for the god Nabû in his temple at Aššur; for the inscription on the reverse, see the following text. The scribal note (subscript) indicates that the inscription was engraved on the reddish gold vessels.

CATALOGUE

Museum Number	Excavation Number	Provenance	cpn
VAT 9948	Ass 1328	Aššur, hB4V, trench 17, next to the edge of the terrace, N 2 Archive	n

BIBLIOGRAPHY

1952–53 Falkner, AfO 16 pp. 305–307 and pl. XV (edition, copy)
1986 Pedersén, Archives 2 pp. 29 and 33 Group E no. 18 (study)
2002 Novotny, PNA 3/1 p. 1144 sub Sīn-šarru-iškun b.3′ (study)
2009 Meinhold, Ištar p. 445 no. 16 (study)
2009 Novotny and Van Buylaere, Studies Oded pp. 217–218 (study)
2014 Novotny, Kaskal 11 p. 168 (provenance)

TEXT

1) [*a-na* ^{d}MUATI EN *nik-la-a*]-⸢*ti*⸣ *šit-ra-ḫi* ⸢DUMU NUN⸣ *mut-*[*tal-li*]
2) [*sa-ni*]-⸢*iq* ^{d}*í-gì-gì*⸣ ^{d}GÉŠ.U *a-ši-ir* DÙ *mim-ma šum-šu mu-du-ú* [NAM KUR]
3) [*réme*]-⸢*nu*⸣-*ú ta-a-a-ru a-šib qé-reb bal-til* EN GAL-*e* [EN-*šú*]

4) [^{m}]⸢^{d}⸣30-LUGAL-GAR-*un* LUGAL GAL-*ú* LUGAL *dan*-⸢*nu*⸣ LUGAL ŠÚ LUGAL KUR [*aš-šur*]
5) ⸢A⸣ ^{m}AN.ŠÁR-DÙ-A LUGAL GAL-*ú* LUGAL ⸢*dan-nu*⸣ LUGAL ŠÚ LUGAL KUR [*aš-šur*]
6) A ^{m}AN.ŠÁR-PAP-AŠ LUGAL GAL-*ú* LUGAL ⸢*dan*⸣-*nu* LUGAL ŠÚ LUGAL KUR ⸢*aš-šur*⸣
7) *ú-še-piš-ma* GIŠ.*kal-li šul-*⸢*pi* KÙ⸣.GI ḪUŠ.A *a-na me-si* ŠU.II-*šú* KÙ.MEŠ
8) *a-na* TI.LA ZI.MEŠ-*šú* GÍD.DA UD.⸢MEŠ-*šú šá*⸣-*lam* NUMUN-*šú šur-šú-du* GIŠ.GU.ZA LUGAL-*ti*-⸢*šú*⸣
9) *sa-kap* LÚ.KÚR.MEŠ-*šú ka-šad i-zi-im-ti-šú ú-kin ma-ḫar-*[*šú*]

1–3) [For the god Nabû, lord of ingenio]us things, the splendid one, s[on of] the ruler (Marduk), the nob[le one, the one who contr]ols the Igīgū (and) Anunnakū gods, the one who directs everything there is, the one who knows [the fate of the land, the merc]iful (and) compassionate one, the one who resides in Baltil (Aššur), the great lord, [his lord]:

4–9) Sîn-šarra-iškun, great king, strong king, king of the world, king of [Assyria]; (5) son of Ashurbanipal, great king, strong king, king of the world, king of [Assyria]; son of Esarhaddon, great king, strong king, king of the world, king of Assyria, had a *kallu*-bowl (and) *šulpu*-bowl of reddish gold made for washing his pure hands and had (them) firmly placed before [him (Nabû)] in order to preserve his life, lengthen his days, establish the well-being of his offspring, make the throne of his royal majesty secure, overthrow his enemies, (and) achieve his desires.

---

10) *šá ina* ⸢UGU⸣ *kal-li šul-pi šá* ^{d}MUATI [*šá* URU.ŠÀ.URU]

10) That which is upon a *kallu*-bowl (and) *šulpu*-bowl of the god Nabû [of the Inner City (Aššur)].

16

The text written on the reverse of the same tablet that is inscribed with Ssi 15 records that Sîn-šarra-iškun had a silver spoon made for Nabû's consort Tašmētu. Based on the subscript, it is assumed that the ceremonial spoon bore a copy of this inscription.

---

15 line 10 For the restoration at the end of the line, see the following text line 13.

CATALOGUE

Museum Number	Excavation Number	Provenance	cpn
VAT 9948	Ass 1328	Aššur, hB4V, trench 17, next to the edge of the terrace, N 2 Archive	n

BIBLIOGRAPHY

1952–53 Falkner, AfO 16 pp. 305–307 and pl. XV (edition, copy)

1986 Pedersén, Archives 2 pp. 29 and 33 Group E no. 18 (study)

2002 Novotny, PNA 3/1 p. 1144 sub Sīn-šarru-iškun b.3′ (study)

2009 Meinhold, Ištar p. 445 no. 16 (study)

2009 Novotny and Van Buylaere, Studies Oded pp. 217–218 (study)

2014 Novotny, Kaskal 11 p. 168 (provenance)

TEXT

1) *a-na* ^{d}PAPNUN *i-lat taš-me-e u sa-li-me* ⸢*qa-rit-ti*
DINGIR.MEŠ *šá-qu-ut* ^{d}⸣[INANNA.MEŠ]

2) *ḫi-rat* ^{d}MUATI IBILA *reš-tu-ú šá ku-uz-bu*
za-a'-nat ma-lat ⸢*nam*⸣-[*ri-ir-ri*]

3) *sa-ni-*⸢*qat*⸣ ^{d}*í-gì-gì* ^{d}GÉŠ.U *a-ši-ir* DÙ *mim-ma*
⸢*šum-šú le*⸣-*qàt* ⸢*un*⸣-[*ni-ni*]

4) [*šá*] *ina qé-*⸢*reb šá-áš-me u* MURUB$_{4}$ *ú-še*⸣-*zi-bu*
NUN *pa-liḫ* [DINGIR-*ti-šá*]

5) ⸢*il*⸣-*tum šur-bu-tú a-ši-bat qé-reb bal-til*.KI
GAŠAN GAL-*tú* ⸢GAŠAN⸣-[*šú*]

6) ⸢^{m}⸣^{d}30-LUGAL-GAR-*un* LUGAL GAL-*ú* LUGAL
dan-nu LUGAL ŠÚ LUGAL KUR *aš-*⸢*šur*⸣

7) A ^{m}AN.ŠÁR-DÙ*-A* LUGAL GAL-*ú* LUGAL *dan-nu*
LUGAL ŠÚ LUGAL KUR *aš-*⸢*šur*⸣

8) A ^{m}AN.ŠÁR-PAP-AŠ LUGAL GAL-*ú* LUGAL *dan-nu*
LUGAL ŠÚ LUGAL KUR *aš-*⸢*šur*⸣

9) *ú-še-piš-ma* GIŠ.DÍLIM KÙ.BABBAR *eb-bi a-na*
qur-ru-ub-e nap-tan še-rim

10) (erasures) *ù li-la-a-ti ma-ḫar* ⸢DINGIR⸣-*ti-šá*

11) *a-na* TI.LA ZI.MEŠ-*šú* GÍD.DA UD.MEŠ-*šú šá-lam*
NUMUN-*šú šur-šu-*⸢*du* GIŠ⸣.GU.ZA LUGAL-*ti-šú*

12) *sa-kap* LÚ.KÚR.MEŠ-*šú* ⸢*ka-šad i*⸣-*zi-im-ti-šú*
ú-kin ma-⸢*ḫar*⸣-*šá*

1–5) For the goddess Tašmētu, the goddess of acceptance and reconciliation, heroic one of the gods, sublime one of [goddesses], wife of the god Nabû — the firstborn son — who is endowed with sexual charm (and) filled with awe-insp[iring brilliance], the one who controls the Igīgū (and) Anunnakū gods, the one who directs everything there is, the one who accepts sup[plications, the one who] saves the ruler who reveres [her divinity] from the midst of combat and battle, (5) supreme [go]ddess, the one who resides in Baltil (Aššur), the great lady, [his] lady:

6–12) Sîn-šarra-iškun, great king, strong king, king of the world, king of Ass[yria]; son of Ashurbanipal, great king, strong king, king of the world, king of Ass[yria]; son of Esarhaddon, great king, strong king, king of the world, king of Assyria; had a spoon of shining silver made for serving the morning (10) and evening meals before her divinity and had (it) firmly placed before her (Tašmētu) in order to preserve his life, lengthen his days, establish the well-being of his offspring, make the throne of his royal majesty secure, overthrow his enemies, (and) achieve his desires.

---

13) *ša ina* UGU DÍLIM KÙ.BABBAR *šá* ^{d}PAPNUN *šá*
URU.⸢ŠÀ.URU⸣

13) That which is upon a silver spoon of the goddess Tašmētu of the Inner City (Aššur).

---

7 ^{m}AN.ŠÁR-DÙ*-A* "Ashurbanipal": The scribe has erroneously written ^{m}AN.ŠÁR-PAP-AŠ "Esarhaddon."

17

Another clay tablet discovered in the "N 2" Archive at Aššur (Pedersén, Archives 2 pp. 29–34) is also inscribed with two short texts of Sîn-šarra-iškun. The first inscription (this text) states that this Assyrian king dedicated an *ešmarû*-plated banquet table to the goddess Antu at Aššur (for the second inscription, see the following text); the table was constructed from *musukkannu*-wood, a hard wood often used in the manufacture of divine and royal furniture. This draft or archival copy of the inscription was presumably written on the table's metal plating.

CATALOGUE

Museum Number	Excavation Number	Provenance	cpn
VAT 9975	Ass 1702	Aššur, hB4V, trench 17, next to the edge of the terrace, N 2 Archive	p

BIBLIOGRAPHY

1920 Schroeder, KAV pp. X and 97 no. 171 (copy, study)
1952–53 Falkner, AfO 16 p. 305 (study)
1956 Borger, Asarh. p. 84 n. 1 (study)
1986 Pedersén, Archives 2 pp. 29 and 33 Group I no. 21 (study)
2002 Novotny, PNA 3/1 p. 1144 sub Sīn-šarru-iškun b.3′ (study)
2009 Novotny and Van Buylaere, Studies Oded p. 218 (study)
2014 Novotny, Kaskal 11 p. 168 (provenance)

TEXT

1) *a-na an-tum* GAŠAN ⸢DINGIR⸣.[MEŠ ...]
2) *ba-na-at* DÙ *mim-ma* ⸢MU-*šú*⸣ [...]
3) *a-ši-bat* URU.*aš-šur* GAŠAN GAL-⸢*tú*⸣ [GAŠAN-*šú* ^{md}]⸢30⸣-[MAN-GAR MAN KUR AŠ]
4) DUMU ^{m}*aš-šur*-DÙ-A MAN KUR AŠ A ^{m}*aš*-⸢*šur*⸣-[PAP-AŠ MAN] ⸢KUR⸣ AŠ A [^{md}30-PAP.MEŠ-SU MAN KUR AŠ]
5) ŠÀ*.BAL*.BAL* (*x**) (erased) (blank) [(...)]
6) *ú-še-piš-ma* GIŠ.BANŠUR GIŠ.MES.MÁ.⸢KAN GIŠ⸣ *da-re-e eš*-[*ma-ra-a*]
7) *eb-bu ú-šal-biš-ma a-na ra-kas nap-tan eb-bi si*-⸢*mat* DINGIR⸣-[*ti-šá*]
8) *ša ka-a-a-an la na-par-ka-a i-maḫ-ḫa-ru* GAL-*tum* DINGIR-[*ut-sa*]
9) *a-na* u_4*-me ṣa-a-ti ú-kin ma-ḫar-šá*
10) *a-na šat-ti an-tum* GAŠAN GAL-*tú* GIŠ.BANŠUR *šú-a-tu ḫa-diš ina nap-lu-si*-⸢*ki*⸣

1–3a) For (the goddess) Antu, lady of the go[ds, ...], the one who created everything there i[s, ...], who resides in the city Aššur, the grea[t] lady, [his lady]:

3b–9) [S]în-[šarra-iškun, king of Assyria]; son of Ashurbanipal, king of Assyria; son of Esar[haddon, king of] Assyria; son of [Sennacherib, king of Assyria]; had a table made of *musukkannu*-wood, a durable wood, and clad (it) with shining *eš*[*marû*-metal], and (then) had (it) firmly placed before her (Antu) to set out pure meal(s) befitting [her] di[vinity] so that [her] great divin[ity] may constantly (and) unceasingly receive (meals) forever.

10–16) On account of this, O Antu, great lady, when you look with pleasure upon this table, with your

---

5 In approximately half of the inscriptions of Sîn-šarra-iškun, the scribes have enumerated the king's genealogy down to Sargon II. Oddly, the scribe of VAT 9975 began to write the expected ŠÀ.BAL.BAL ^{m}LUGAL-GI.NA MAN KUR AŠ in this line, but then erased the first word of the entry and left the rest of the line blank. Later, in line 8 of the second inscription that is recorded on this tablet (Ssi 18), the same scribe simply omits the entry for Sargon II in Sîn-šarra-iškun's genealogy altogether.

11) *ia-a-ti* ^{md}30-MAN-GAR GÌR.NÍTA* *mi*-gir** ŠÀ*-*ki** NUN* *pa*-liḫ*-ki* ina* bu*-un-ni-ki nam-ru-ti ḫa-diš nap-lis-in-ni* x.A.AN ⸢SIG$_5$⸣ *lib-šá-a kar-ši*$^?$
12) *ur-ri-ki* UD.MEŠ-*ia šum-dili* MU.AN.NA.MEŠ-*ia* MU *na-an-na-bi ki-in-ni ana ṣa-a-*⸢*ti*⸣
13) LÚ.KÚR.MEŠ-*ia né-e-ri ki-šad la ma-gi-re-ia šuk-ni-*⸢*še*⸣ *ana* GÌR.II-⸢*ia*⸣
14) ⸢*na*$^?$⸣-*piš-ti šá ta-qí-še* GIM *ú-lu-ú* Ì.GIŠ *ṭib-bi* UGU UN.MEŠ DAGAL.[MEŠ]
15) [*ina*$^?$ *ma*$^?$]-⸢*ḫar*$^?$⸣ DINGIR.MEŠ *u ina ma-ḫar* DINGIR-*ti-ki* GAL*-*ti** *šul-biri tal-lak-ti ana u*$_4$*-me da-ru-te*
16) [...] ⸢AD⸣ DINGIR.MEŠ *ḫa*-'i-i-ri na-ra-mi-ki ab-bu-ti ṣab-ti qí-bi-i* <*dum*>-*qí*

bright countenance (also) look with pleasure upon me, Sîn-šarra-iškun — the governor who is the favorite of your heart, the ruler who reveres you — *so that good ... is on* (*my*) *mind*, prolong my days, increase my years, make my name (and) progeny firm for eternity, kill my enemies, (and) make the neck of those insubmissive to me bow down at my feet. Make *my life*, which you have granted (me), as pleasing to a widespread population as the finest oil. Make my walking about [*befor*]*e* the gods and before your great divinity endure for eternity. Intercede on my behalf (and) speak <favor>ably about me [*to the god Anu*], the father of the gods, your beloved husband.

18

The same tablet that is inscribed with Ssi 17 bears a draft or archival copy of a second dedicatory inscription. This text immediately follows the previous one on the tablet's obverse and continues onto the reverse, with lines 3–4 written on the bottom edge. It records that Sîn-šarra-iškun had a *musukkannu*-wood and *ešmarû*-metal table made and dedicated to the goddess Šala (the wife of the storm-god Adad), presumably for her cult at Aššur. The inscription was probably incised on the table's metal plating.

CATALOGUE

Museum Number	Excavation Number	Provenance	cpn
VAT 9975	Ass 1702	Aššur, hB4V, trench 17, next to the edge of the terrace, N 2 Archive	p

BIBLIOGRAPHY

1920 Schroeder, KAV pp. X and 97 no. 171 (copy, study)
1952–53 Falkner, AfO 16 p. 305 (study)
1956 Borger, Asarh. p. 84 n. 1 (study)
1986 Pedersén, Archives 2 pp. 29 and 33 Group I no. 21 (study)
2002 Novotny, PNA 3/1 p. 1144 sub Sīn-šarru-iškun b.3′ (study)
2009 Novotny and Van Buylaere, Studies Oded p. 218 (study)
2014 Novotny, Kaskal 11 p. 168 (provenance)

17 line 11 The scribe wrote *mi-gir* ŠÀ-*ki* and NUN *pa-liḫ-ki* with smaller signs and wrote *mi-gir* ŠÀ-*ki* in the upper half of the line with NUN *pa-liḫ-ki* underneath it in the lower half of the line. All of these signs, including NÍTA of GÌR.NÍTA and *ina bu-* of *ina bu-un-ni-ki*, are written over erasures in the middle of the line.
17 line 15 GAL-*ti* is written with smaller signs underneath the -*ti-ki* of DINGIR-*ti-ki*.
17 line 16 *ḫa*-'i-i-ri* "your husband": The text has visially similiar ZA-*'i-i-ri*.

TEXT

1) [*a-na* ^{d}*ša-la*] ⸢GAŠAN⸣ *šur-bu-tú ḫi-rat* ^{d}IŠKUR *šá-ga-pí-ri šá* KAŠ$_{4}$ *mur-ta-aṣ-nu*
2) [...] (*x*) *x* DINGIR.MEŠ GAL.MEŠ *mu-šim*-mu** (over erasures) <*ši-ma*>-*a-ti* ILLU DÙ-*at* DÙ.A.BI
3) [*x x* (*x*)]-⸢*at*⸣ *aš-na-an u ṭuḫ-di mu-kil-lat* ZI-*tì* UN.MEŠ ⸢*mu*⸣-*bal-liṭ-ṭa-at*
4) [(...)] (blank) *ka-la mim-ma-ma*
5) [...] *kul-lat rag-gi na-si-iḫ na-gab za-ma-ni a*-⸢*li*⸣-*kàt* Á.II LUGAL *mi-gir*-⸢*i-šá*⸣
6) [...] *x da-na*-⸢*ni u*⸣ *li-i-ti ṣa-bi*-⸢*ta*⸣-[*at*] ⸢*ab*⸣-*bu-ti qa-bat* MUNUS.SIG$_{5}$
7) [*a-ši-bat qé*]-*reb* ⸢*bal-til*⸣.KI GAŠAN (erasure?) GAL-*tú* [GAŠAN-*šú* ^{md}]⸢30⸣-MAN-GAR MAN KUR AŠ
8) [A ^{m}*aš-šur*-DÙ]-⸢A⸣ A ^{m}*aš-šur*-PAP-AŠ [A ^{md}]30-PAP.MEŠ-SU
9) [*ú-še-piš*]-⸢*ma*⸣ GIŠ.BANŠUR GIŠ.MES.MÁ.KAN.NA ⸢GIŠ⸣ [*da*]-⸢*re*⸣-*e eš-ma-ra-a eb-bu ú*-⸢*šal*⸣-[*biš-ma*]
10) [*a-na ra-kas*] ⸢*nap*⸣-*tan eb-bi si-mat* DINGIR-*ti-šá* ⸢*ša*⸣ *ka-a-a-an la na-par-ka-a i-maḫ-ḫa-ru* ⸢GAL⸣-[*tum* DINGIR-*ut-sa*]
11) [*a-na u*$_{4}$]-⸢*me*⸣ *ṣa-a-ti ú-kin ma-ḫar-šá*
12) [*a-na*] ⸢*šat-ti*⸣ ^{d}*ša-la* GAŠAN GAL GIŠ.⸢BANŠUR⸣ *šú-a-tú ḫa-diš ina nap-lu-si*-⸢*ki*⸣
13) ⸢*ia*⸣-*a-ti* ^{m}<^{d}>30-⸢MAN-GAR⸣ <MAN KUR> AŠ (blank)
14) ⸢SI⸣.SÁ BURU$_{14}$ ⸢*na-pa*⸣-*áš**(text: PA) ^{d}*nisaba šat-ti-šam* ⸢*la*⸣ *na-par-ka-a šu-tab-ri-i ina re-ši-ia*
15) *ina qí-bit-ki ṣir*-⸢*ti*⸣ *ina* ḪÉ.NUN *ṭuḫ-di šal-meš la-ar-te-ʾa-a ba-ʾu-lat aš-šur*
16) *ina é*-⸢*šár*⸣-*ra* É.⸢GAL DINGIR⸣.MEŠ (blank)

1–7a) [For the goddess Šala], supreme [lad]y, wife of the god Adad — the majestic, the runner, the roaring one — [...] the great gods who determine the <fat>es of flood water, the one who creates everything, [who ...] grain and abundance, who supports life for the people, who keeps everything alive, [*who exterminates*] all of the wicked, who rips out all enemies, who marches at the side of the king — [he]r favorite — [...] might[y] victories, who inte[rce]des on (his) behalf, who speaks favorable thing(s) (about him), [who resides i]n Baltil (Aššur), the great lady, [his lady]:

7b–11) [S]în-šarra-iškun, king of Assyria, [son of Ashurbani]pal, son of Esarhaddon, [son of] Sennacherib, [had] a table [made] of *musukkannu*, a [dura]ble wood, [an]d c[lad (it)] with shining *ešmarû*-metal, [and] (then) had (it) firmly placed before her (Šala) [to prepare] pure [m]eal(s) befitting her divinity so that [her] grea[t divinity] may constantly (and) unceasingly receive (meals) [for]ever.

12–16) [On ac]count [of] this, O Šala, great lady, when you look with pleasure upon this table, make successful harvest(s) (and) the pr[osperi]ty of grain, occur for me — Sîn-šarra-iškun, the <king of> Assyria — yearly, without ceasing. By your exalted command, in Ešarra, the palace of the gods, let me always safely shepherd the subjects of (the god) Aššur with abundance (and) plenty.

19

Numerous clay cylinders discovered in the debris of Ezida ("True House") at Kalḫu are inscribed with a text stating that Sîn-šarra-iškun had (part) of the god Nabû's temple rebuilt; Adad-nārārī III (810–783) is cited as a previous builder. Because the inscription's building report is poorly preserved, the full extent of the renovation project is not entirely certain. The king claims that the work was carried out according to the craft of the incantation priest, that (some of) the foundations were relaid, that he built (part of) the

18 line 5 Possibly restore at the beginning of the line *mu-bal-lat* "*who exterminates*." Compare Jeffers and Novotny, RINAP 5/2 p. 337 Asb. 224 line 6 (*mu-bal-lu-u nap-ḫar rag-gi*).

18 line 8 For the missing reference to Sargon II, who appears in the genealogies of every other inscription of Sîn-šarra-iškun, see the on-page note to Ssi 17 line 5.

18 line 13 There is a blank space of about one line separating lines 13 and 14.

18 line 14 ⸢*na-pa*⸣-*áš** "the pr[osperi]ty of": The text has ⸢*na-pa*⸣-PA.

superstructure (presumably from the foundations to the crenellations), did something with its "grand designs," and returned the temple's divine owners Nabû and Tašmētu to their daises. If the inscription is to be believed, the work started in his accession year (627); however, it is very likely that this is just royal rhetoric. The dated cylinders were inscribed in the eponymy of Dādî, the treasurer. In scholarly literature, this text is generally referred to as "Cylinder B."

CATALOGUE

Ex.	Museum Number	Excavation/ Registration No.	Provenance	Dimensions (cm)	Lines Preserved	cpn
1	K 1662 (+) IM — (Sumer 44 no. 5)	—	IM —: Kalḫu, Nabû temple, NT 12 or NT 13, in back fill	12.7×13.3 (K 1662); 5.7×6.7 (IM —)	1–10, 35–48	(c)
2	IM —	ND 4315	Kalḫu, Nabû temple, entrance of Tašmētu's cella, on the pavement	—	1–8, 23–47	n
3	BM —	ND 1123	Kalḫu, fill outside the southwest corner of the South-East Palace	—	1–7	c
4	K 1663	—	Probably Kalḫu, Nabû temple	7.6×8.3	7–17	c
5	K 1664	—	As ex. 4	4×2×1.2	7–11	c
6	BM 123414	1932-12-10,357	Nineveh, Kuyunjik	10×6.3	7–40	c
7	BM —	ND 6209	Kalḫu, South-East Palace, in fill	9×7.2	19–29	c
8	IM —	ND 4314	Kalḫu, Nabû temple, SEB XIII, floor	7×10	20–32	n
9	IM —	ND 4313	Kalḫu, Nabû temple, SEB XI, north-west corner, at a depth of 2.4 m	5×7	24–31	n
10	BM —	ND 4312	As ex. 9	5×7	38–46	c
11	BM —	ND 4323	Kalḫu, Nabû temple, SEB XIII, on the floor	—	46–48	c
12	—	Bu 89-4-26,154	Possibly Kalḫu, Nabû temple	6.3×7	18–25	c
13	BM —	ND 6222	Kalḫu, Nabû temple, courtyard, south of the doorway of the tablet room, in debris at floor level	4.5×5.8	10–16	c
14	IM —	ND 6221	As ex. 13	—	—	n

COMMENTARY

The fourteen fragments that bear this text all come from hollow clay cylinders. Ex. 3 preserves most of the right end of its cylinder, which has a round opening in its base; ex. 2, which preserves the left end of its cylinder, might also have a round opening in its base, but the exemplar was not available for study. A horizontal ruling separates each line of text in all exemplars. Note, however, that D.J. Wiseman's copy of ex. 2 (Iraq 26 [1964] pl. XXVII) does not have any horizontal rulings. The authors were unable to confirm the accuracy of Wiseman's copy since ND 4315 was not examined against the original in the Iraq Museum (Baghdad).

Despite statements in earlier literature, ex. 1 originates from Kalḫu, not Nineveh. See Weissert, NABU 1990/4 pp. 103–105 no. 126 for details. The same is probably true of exs. 4 and 5. Note that M. Streck's edition of this text (Asb. pp. 382–387), which utilizes only exs. 1 (just K 1662) and 4, is conflated with Ssi 1 (Cylinder C) exs. 4–5.

Since many of the exemplars are fragmentary, the master text is a conflation of the exemplars. However, the lineation of lines 1–8 and 23–47 is established by ex. 2 and that of lines 9–11 is set by ex. 5 since both of these exemplars preserve parts of the left side of their respective cylinders. A score of the text is presented on Oracc and the minor (orthographic) variants are listed at the back of the book. G. Van Buylaere kindly collated exs. 1 (K 1662 only), 3–7, and 10–13 from the originals in the British Museum (London). The authors were unable to collate exs. 2, 8–9, and 14 as they are in the Iraq Museum (Baghdad) and were not accessible during the preparation of the present volume.

BIBLIOGRAPHY

1861 1 R pl. VIII no. 6 (ex. 1 [K 1662], copy)
1875 G. Smith, Assyrian Discoveries pp. 382–384 (ex. 1 [K 1662], translation, study)
1880 Schrader, Berichte der Sächsischen Gesellschaft der Wissenschaften, Philologisch-Historische Klasse 32 pp. 29–30, 33–40 (exs. 1 [K 1662], 4, copy [typeset], study; ex. 1 [K 1662] lines 1–7, transliteration)
1889 Bezold, Cat. 1 p. 327 (exs. 1 [K 1662], 4–5, study)
1890 Winckler, KB 2 pp. 270–273 (ex. 1 [K 1662], edition)
1892 Winckler, RA 2 p. 66 (ex. 1 [K 1662] line 1, study)
1892 Oppert, ZA 7 pp. 337–338 (ex. 1 [K 1662], translation, study)
1896 Bezold, Cat. 4 p. 1929 (ex. 12, study)
1914 King, CT 34 p. 5 and pls. 4–6 (exs. 1 [K 1662], 4–5, copy, study)
1916 Streck, Asb. pp. CCVII–CCXVIII, 382–387, and 838–839 (exs. 1 [K 1662], 4, edition [conflated with Ssi 1]; ex. 5, study)
1926 Luckenbill, ARAB 2 pp. 409–410 §§1137–1141 and 412 §§1148–1149 (exs. 1 [K 1662], 4, translation)
1952 Wiseman, Iraq 14 pp. 66 and 68 (pl. XXII) (ex. 3, copy, study)
1952–53 Falkner, AfO 16 pp. 305–306 (exs. 1 [K 1662], 4–5, study)
1964 Wiseman, Iraq 26 pp. 122–124 and pl. XXVII (exs. 2, 8–10, copy; exs. 8, 11, transliteration; exs. 2, 8–11, study)
1965 Borger, JCS 19 pp. 68 and 76–78 (exs. 1–5, 8–11, transliteration, study)
1967 von Soden, ZA 58 p. 252 (line 5, study)
1968 Lambert and Millard, Cat. p. 24 (ex. 6, study)
1968 Millard, Iraq 30 p. 111 and pl. XXVI (ex. 6, copy, study)
1972 Grayson, Studies Winnett pp. 157–160 and 167–168 (study)
1973 Postgate, Governor's Palace p. 263 (ex. 3, provenance)
1985–86 Mahmud and Black, Sumer 44 pp. 137 and 152 no. 5 (ex. 1 [IM —], copy, study)
1990 Weissert, NABU 1990/4 pp. 103–105 no. 126 (lines 39–40, edition; ex. 1, study)
1991 Na'aman, ZA 81 p. 255 (line 5, study)
1991 J. Oates, CAH^{2} 3/2 p. 176 n. 29 (line 5, study)
1994 Millard, SAAS 2 p. 93 (line 48, transliteration)
1996 Borger, BIWA pp. 351, 357 and LoBl 113 (ex. 12, transliteration; exs. 6, 12, study)
1999 Mattila, PNA 1/2 p. 361 Dādî 21.a (line 48, study)
2002 Novotny, PNA 3/1 p. 1143 sub Sîn-šarru-iškun b.1′ (study)
2009 Meinhold, Ištar p. 445 no. 16 (study)
2009 Novotny and Van Buylaere, Studies Oded pp. 218–241 (edition, study; exs. 7, 11–13, copy)
2012 Bock, Kinderheit pp. 288–289 (lines 1–8, 26–29, edition)
2014 Novotny, JCS 66 p. 111 (line 31, study)
2017 Baker, PNA 4/1 p. 57 sub masennu Dādî 21 (line 48, study)
2018 Novotny in Yamada, SAAS 28 pp. 262–263, esp. n. 43 (line 31, study)

TEXT

1) ⸢*a**⸣-[*na-ku* ^{md}30]-⸢LUGAL⸣-GAR-*un* LUGAL GAL LUGAL *dan-nu* LUGAL ŠÚ [LUGAL KUR] ⸢AN⸣.ŠÁR.⸢KI⸣
2) *ni-*⸢*iš*⸣ [IGI.II] ⸢AN⸣.ŠÁR ^{d}NIN.LÍL *na-ram* ^{d}AMAR.UTU ^{d}*zar-pa-ni-tum bi-bil* ⸢*lìb*⸣-[*bi* ^{d}30] ⸢^{d}NIN.GAL⸣
3) *i-tu-*⸢*ut*⸣ *ku-un lìb-bi* ^{d}AG *u* ^{d}AMAR.UTU *mi-*⸢*gir*⸣ [DINGIR.MEŠ] ⸢*šu*⸣-*ut* AN KI
4) *šá* AN.ŠÁR ^{d}NIN.LÍL ^{d}EN ^{d}AG ^{d}30 ^{d}NIN.GAL ^{d}15 *šá* NINA.KI ^{d}15 ⸢*šá*⸣ [LÍMMU-DINGIR.KI] ⸢^{d}⸣U.GUR *u* ^{d}*nusku*
5) *i-na* ⸢*bi-rit*⸣ *maš-ši-šú ke-niš ip-pal-su-šú-ma* ⸢*is*⸣-[*su-qu-šú a*]-⸢*na*⸣ LUGAL-*u-ti*
6) *za-nin-*[*ut*] ⸢*nap*⸣-*ḫar ma-ḫa-zi šá-an-gu-tu gi-mir eš-ret* SIPA-*u-*⸢*ut*⸣ [*nap-ḫar ṣal-mat* SAG.DU *e-pe-šú*] ⸢*iq*⸣-*bu-u-šú*
7) *ki-ma* [AD *u* AMA *it*]-⸢*ta*⸣-*nar-ru-šú-ma i-na-ru a-a-bi-šú ú-šam-qí-*⸢*tú*⸣ [*ga*]-⸢*re-šú*⸣
8) *šá* ^{d}⸢*é-a*$^{?}$⸣ *a-na e-nu-te kiš-šá-ti ib-nu-šú-ma ina*

1–6) I, [Sîn-šarr]a-iškun, great king, strong king, king of the world, [king of A]ssyria, favor[ed by (the god) A]ššur (and) the goddess Mullissu, beloved of the god Marduk (and) the goddess Zarpanītu, the desire of the h[earts of the god Sîn] (and) the goddess Ningal, chosen by the steadfast hearts of the gods Nabû and Marduk, the favori[te of the gods o]f heaven (and) netherworld; the one whom the deities Aššur, Mullissu, Bēl (Marduk), Nabû, Sîn, Ningal, Ištar of Nineveh, Ištar o[f Arbela], Nergal, and Nusku (5) steadfastly looked upon a[mo]ng his *brothers* and se[lected fo]r kingship; whom they commanded [to perform] the roles of provisio[ner of a]ll cult centers, priest of all sanctuaries, (and) shepher[d of the totality of the black-headed (people)];

7–16) whom they [gu]ided like [a father and a mother], whose foes they killed, (and) whose [adve]rsaries they cut down; the one whom the god *Ea* cre-

1 ⸢*a**⸣-[*na-ku*] "I": D.J. Wiseman's copy of ND 4315 (ex. 2) appears to have the masculine determinative (a single vertical wedge). However, since Sîn-šarra-iškun's other inscriptions written on clay cylinders, prisms, and cones all begin with *anāku* ("I"), rather than with the king's name, this inscription probably also began with *anāku*. Compare, for example, Ssi 10 (Cylinder A) line 1. Because ND 4315 was unavailable for examination, the authors were unable to confirm the accuracy of Wiseman's copy.

5 *maš-ši-šú* "his *brothers*": See the on-page note to Ssi 1 (Cylinder C) line 5 for the interpretation of *maššīšu*.

7 [*it*]-⸢*ta*⸣-*nar-ru-šú-ma* "whom they [gu]ided": Or possibly "who they picked up again and again." See the on-page note to Ssi 1 (Cylinder C) line 7.

nap-ḫar x [...]
9) *a-na* ⸢*kun*⸣-[*ni* SUḪUŠ KUR *šu-te-šur*] ⸢*ba*⸣-*ʾu-ú-la-a-ti a-ge-e* EN-*u-ti e-pi-ru-uš* [*na-an-nàr* AN-*e* ^{d}30]
10) GIŠ.GIDRU ⸢*i*⸣-[*šar-tú uš-pa-ru ke-e-nu a*]-⸢*na*⸣ SIPA-*u-ti* UN.MEŠ DAGAL.MEŠ ^{d}AG *pa-qid* ⸢*kiš*⸣-[*šá-ti ú-šat-me-ḫu rit-tu-uš-šú*]
11) ⸢*dal*⸣-[*ḫa-a-ti a-na tu*]-⸢*qu*⸣-*ni ab-ta-a-ti* [*a-na ke-še*$_{20}$-*ri* ...]
12) [... *a*]-*na šu-šu-bi* ^{d}EN *u* ^{d}AG *ul-lu-*[*u* SAG.MEŠ-*šú*]
13) [...]-*mu a-ḫi-iz ṭè-e-me u mil-ki mu-ta-*⸢*mu*⸣-[*ú dam-qa-a-ti*]
14) [...] x *da-in de-en mi-šá-ri šá at-mu-šú* UGU UN.MEŠ ⸢*ar*⸣-[*ma-niš* DÙG.GA]
15) [*šá ik-kib-šú nu-ul-la-a-ti an-zil-la-šú sur-ra*]-⸢*a*⸣-*te la ka-ṣir ik-ki pa-ši-šú* [...]
16) [...] ⸢*ik*⸣-*ki-bi-šú-nu na-ṣi-ru* [...]

ated for dominion over the world and [...] among all [...; whom the light of heaven, the god Sîn], crowned with the crown of lordship to make [the foundation of the land] fi[rm (and) to direct the p]eople; (10) [whose hand] the god Nabû, overseer of the w[orld, made grasp] a j[ust] scepter (and) [a true staff fo]r shepherding a widespread population; [... to put in o]rder what is c[onfused (and) to repair] what is destroyed; [whose head ...] raise[d up t]o make the gods Bēl (Marduk) and Nabû dwell [...; ...], who comprehends reason and counsel, who spea[ks eloquent (words), ...], who administers just verdicts, whose words [are as sweet] to the people [as] the *a*[*rmannu*-fruit; (15) to whom treacherous talk is anathema (and) li]es [an abomination]; the forbearing one, the *pašīšu*-priest [...; who ...] their taboo; who protects [...];

17) [DUMU ^{m}AN.ŠÁR-DÙ-IBILA LUGAL GAL LUGAL] ⸢*dan*⸣-*nu* LUGAL ŠÚ LUGAL KUR ⸢AN.ŠÁR⸣.[KI] ⸢LUGAL KUR⸣ [EME.GI$_{7}$ *u* URI.KI LUGAL *kib-rat* LÍMMU-*tim*]
18) [DUMU ^{m}AN.ŠÁR-ŠEŠ-SUM.NA LUGAL GAL LUGAL *dan-nu* LUGAL *kiš*]-⸢*šá*⸣-*ti* ⸢LUGAL⸣ [KUR AN.ŠÁR.KI GÌR.NÍTA KÁ.DINGIR.RA.KI LUGAL KUR EME.GI$_{7}$ *u* URI.KI]
19) [DUMU ^{md}30-ŠEŠ.MEŠ-SU LUGAL GAL LUGAL *dan-nu* LUGAL] ⸢*kiš*⸣-*šá-ti* LUGAL KUR *aš-*⸢*šur*⸣.[KI NUN *la šá-na-an*]
20) [ŠÀ.BAL.BAL ^{m}LUGAL-GI.NA LUGAL GAL] ⸢LUGAL *dan*⸣-*nu* LUGAL ŠÚ LUGAL KUR *aš-šur*.KI GÌR.NÍTA KÁ.DINGIR.RA.[KI LUGAL KUR EME.GI$_{7}$ *u* URI.KI]
21) [... NUN *na-aʾ*]-*du* GÌR.NÍTA *it-pe-e-šú na-*⸢*ram*⸣ ^{d}AG *u* ^{d}*taš-me-*⸢*tum*⸣ x [...]

17–21) [son of Ashurbanipal, great king, st]rong [king], king of the world, king of Assyria, [ki]ng of the land of [Sumer and Akkad, king of the four quarters (of the world); son of Esarhaddon, great king, strong king, king of the wo]rld, k[ing of Assyria, governor of Babylon, king of the land of Sumer and Akkad; son of Sennacherib, great king, strong king, king of the w]orld, king of Assyria, [ruler who has no rival; (20) descendant of Sargon (II), great king], strong [kin]g, king of the world, king of Assyria, governor of Babylon, [king of the land of Sumer and Akkad; ..., pio]us [ruler], capable governor, beloved of the god Nabû and the goddess Tašmētu [...];

22) [*ul-tu* AN.ŠÁR ^{d}EN ^{d}]AG ^{d}30 ^{d}UTU *be-lut* KUR *u* UN.MEŠ *ú-*[*šad-gi-la*$^{?}$ *pa-nu-u-a*$^{?}$ ...]
23) ŠU.⸢II$^{?}$⸣-[*u-a ú-mal-lu-u*$^{?}$ *ú-sa*]-⸢*at*⸣ *dum-qí e-pu-šú-u-in-ni za-ʾi-i-ri-ia ik-mu-u* x [...]
24) *ṭu-da-*⸢*at*⸣ [...]-⸢*ni*⸣-*ma ṭa-biš ú-še-šib-ú-in-ni ina* GIŠ.GU.ZA ⸢LUGAL⸣-[*u-ti* AD DÙ-*ia*]
25) *i-na* GIŠ.MI-*šú-nu* DÙG.⸢GA⸣ [*ṣu-lu-li-šú*]-*nu rap-ši ke-niš ar-te-ʾa-a ba-ʾu-ú-*[*lat* ^{d}EN.LÍL]
26) *ul-tu ṣe-ḫe-ri-ia a-*⸢*di*⸣ [*ra-bé*]-*ia ar-ki* DINGIR.MEŠ GAL.MEŠ EN.MEŠ-*ia lu at-tal-lak-ma lu ab-ri* x [x x]
27) *áš-ra-te-šú-nu áš-te-ʾe-*⸢*e-ma*⸣ *mim-ma šá* UGU DINGIR-*ú-ti-šú-nu* GAL-*ti* DÙG.GA *a-na e-pe-še* ⸢*lìb*⸣-[*bi ub-la*]
28) *šá za-na-an ma-ḫa-zi šuk-*⸢*lul*⸣ [*eš-re-e*]-⸢*ti*$^{?}$⸣ *šu-te-šur par-ṣe* ⸢*ki-du-de*$^{?}$*-e*$^{?}$⸣ *ma-*⸢*šu-ú*⸣-*ti*
29) *ka-a-a-an uš-ta-ad-*⸢*da*⸣-*nu* [*kar-šú-u-a*]

22–29) [After the gods Aššur, Bēl (Marduk)], Nabû, Sîn, (and) Šamaš [*nominated me*] for ruling over the land and people, [*they placed ... into my*] hands, performed good [dee]ds for me, bound my enemies, [...] the path [of ...] and gladly placed me on the r[oyal] throne [of the father who had engendered me], (25) under their benevolent protection (and) [th]eir extensive [aegis], I constantly shepherded the subje[cts of the god Enlil] in a just manner. From my childhood unt[il] I [became an adult], I constantly followed after the great gods, my lords, and I beheld [...]. I was assiduous towards their sanctuaries [a]nd wa[nted] to do whatever was suitable for their great divinity. [I] constantly gave [thought] to providing for cult centers, completing [*sanctuarie*]s, (and) putting in order forgotten cultic rites (and) *kidudû-rites.*

30) *i-na* SAG LUGAL-*ti-*⸢*ia*⸣ [*i-na maḫ*]-*re-e* BALA-*ia* [*šá ina* GIŠ.GU.ZA] ⸢LUGAL⸣-*u-ti ra-*⸢*biš*⸣ [*ú-ši-bu*]

30–37) At the beginning of m[y] kingship, [in] my [fi]rst regnal year [when I sat] in greatness [on (my)]

31) ⸢É⸣ [^{d}AG šá qé-reb URU.kal-ḫa] ⸢šá ^{m}⸣^{d}IŠKUR-ERIM.⸢TÁḪ⸣ [x x (x)] x LUGAL pa-⸢a⸣-<ni> maḫ-ri-ia [e-pu-šú e-na-aḫ-ma]
32) i-na [...] x KI i-na ši-⸢pir⸣ [ka-kù-gal-lu-ti ...]
33) i-na x [...]
34) te-me-en-⸢šú ad⸣-di-⸢ma É⸣ x x x [...]
35) É šu-a-⸢tú⸣ [...] x ⸢ar-ṣip⸣ [ú-šak-lil ...]
36) GIŠ.ḪUR.MEŠ-šú GAL.⸢MEŠ⸣ [...] x x [...]
37) ^{d}AG u ^{d}taš-me-⸢tum⸣ [...] šub-tu [...]

royal [throne], the temple of [the god Nabû that is inside Kalḫu, whic]h Adad-nārār[ī (III) ...], a king of the pa<st> (who had come) before me, [had built, became dilapidated and] in [...] ..., according to the cra[ft of the incantation priest, ...] through [... I] laid its foundation(s) and the temple ... [...] (35) I built (and) [completed] that temple [...] its grand designs [...] ... [...] the god Nabû and the goddess Tašmētu [...] seat(s).

38) ^{d}AG IBILA gaš-[ru ...] ⸢ḫa⸣-diš ⸢nap⸣-[lis]-⸢ma⸣ lim-ma-ḫir pa-[nu-uk-ka ...]
39) ur-rik u_{4}-me-⸢ia⸣ [MU.AN.NA].⸢MEŠ⸣-ia ⸢šu⸣-[um]-⸢dil⸣ na-an-na-bi ⸢ki⸣-[in? ana ṣa-a-ti?]
40) kur-bu LUGAL-u-⸢ti⸣ [ḫu-ud lìb-bi ṭu-ub UZU].⸢MEŠ⸣ na-mar ka-bat-ti a-na da-riš ki-i-[na]
41) LÚ.KÚR.MEŠ-⸢ia⸣ [né-er ki-šad la ma]-⸢gi⸣-re-ia šuk-niš še-pu-ú-a

38–41) O Nabû, power[ful] heir, l[ook] with [pl]easure [upon ... a]nd may it be acceptable to y[ou ...]. Prolong m[y] days, in[creas]e my [year]s, (and) *ma*[*ke*] my progeny [*firm for eternity*]. (40) Bless [my] kingship (and) make fi[rm for me happiness, good health], (and) a bright spirit forever. [Kill] my enemies (and) make [the neck of those insubm]issive to me bow down at my feet.

42) NUN EGIR-⸢ú⸣ [ina LUGAL.MEŠ DUMU.MEŠ-ia] e-nu-ma É šu-a-tú in-na-ḫu-ma il-la-ku ⸢la⸣-ba-riš
43) an-ḫu-us-[su lu-ud-diš MU.SAR-u ši]-⸢ṭir⸣ MU-ia li-mur-ma Ì.GIŠ lip-šu-⸢uš⸣ UDU.SISKUR BAL-qí
44) ⸢it⸣-ti MU.[SAR-e ši-ṭir MU-šú liš]-⸢kun⸣ ^{d}AG u ^{d}taš-me-tum ik-ri-⸢bi⸣-šú i-šem-mu-ú

42–44) [May] a future ruler, [one of the kings, my descendants, renovate its] dilapidated sections(s) when that temple becomes dilapidated and old. May he find [an inscribed object beari]ng my name, and (then) anoin[t] (it) with oil, make an offering, (and) [pla]ce (it) with an inscr[ibed object bearing his name]. The god Nabû and the goddess Tašmētu will (then) hear his pray[e]rs.

45) šá ⸢MU⸣.SAR-⸢ú⸣ [ši-ṭir MU-ia ú-nak-ka-ru-ma it]-⸢ti⸣ ši-ṭir MU-šú la i-šak-ka-nu
46) AN.ŠÁR ^{d}EN ⸢^{d}⸣[AG a-na ni-iš ŠU.II-šú] ⸢a⸣-a iz-zi-zu-ma a-a iš-mu-u su-up-pe-e-šú
47) LUGAL-us-⸢su⸣ [lis-ki-pu?] ⸢ag⸣-giš li-ru-ru-šú-ma ⸢MU⸣-[šú] ⸢NUMUN-šú⸣ ina KUR li-ḫal-liq-qu

45–47) (As for) the one who [removes] an inscribed object [bearing my name and] does not place (it) [wit]h (an inscribed object) bearing his name, may the gods Aššur, Bēl (Marduk), (and) [Nabû] not be present [for his prayers] and not heed his supplications. [*May they overthrow*] hi[s] kingship, curse him [a]ngrily, and make [his] na[me] (and) his [se]ed disappear from the land.

Date exs. 1 and 11

48) [ITI.x x (x)] ⸢UD⸣.3.KAM lim-mu ^{m}da-ad-di-i LÚ.⸢AGRIG⸣

48) [...], the third day, eponymy of Dādî, the treasurer.

20

A proprietary label on a clay sealing discovered in the Review Palace at Kalḫu records that the object to which the bulla was attached was the property of Sîn-šarra-iškun.

19 line 31 ⸢^{m}⸣^{d}IŠKUR-ERIM.⸢TÁḪ⸣ [x x (x)] x "Adad-nārār[ī (III) ...]": Based on Ssi 10 line 23, possibly read ⸢^{m}⸣^{d}IŠKUR-ERIM.⸢TÁḪ⸣ [DUMU ^{m}šam-ši-^{d}]⸢IŠKUR?⸣, "Adad-nārār[ī (III), son of *Šamšī-Ada*]*d* (V)." Although this may appear to result in an overly long line, the signs of the line are written more closely together than those of other lines.

19 line 45 [it]-⸢ti⸣ ši-ṭir MU-šú "[wit]h (an inscribed object) bearing his name": The master text comes from ex. 10. In this common concluding forumla, one expects it-ti MU.SAR-e ši-ṭir MU-šú "with an inscribed object bearing his name." However, the damaged sign before ši-ṭir MU-šú in the exemplar cannot be read as ⸢e⸣ and thus interpreted as [MU.SAR]-⸢e⸣. It instead appears to be the right half of a winkelhaken, suggesting the reading [it]-⸢ti⸣ ši-ṭir MU-šú in which the scribe has omitted MU.SAR-e.

CATALOGUE

Museum Number	Excavation Number	Provenance	cpn
IM 60592	ND 6228	Kalḫu, Fort Shalmaneser, Room NW 15	n

BIBLIOGRAPHY

1984 Dalley and Postgate, Fort Shalmaneser p. 139 and pl. 45 no. 83 (copy, edition, study)

2002 Novotny, PNA 3/1 p. 1143 sub Sîn-šarru-iškun b.2′ (study)

2009 Novotny and Van Buylaere, Studies Oded p. 218 n. 7 (study)

TEXT

1) ⸢KUR$^{?}$⸣ ^{m}30-MAN-GAR

1) *Palace of* Sîn-šarra-iškun.

21

A stone vessel, possibly from Nineveh, is inscribed with a one-line proprietary label of Sîn-šarra-iškun.

CATALOGUE

Registration Number	Provenance	Dimensions (cm)	cpn
81-2-4,25A	Possibly Nineveh, Kuyunjik	Height: 3.7; Dia.: 14.6	n

COMMENTARY

In addition to 81-2-4,35A, there may be a few other stone vessel fragments that bear proprietary inscription(s) of Sîn-šarra-iškun. As stated in Novotny and Jeffers, RINAP 5/1 p. 364 Asb. 68 and p. 365 Asb. 69, these are 82-5-22,603A, BM 118779 (K 8551, 82-5-22,607A), Ki 1902-5-10,25, Sm 2243, Sm 2220, and 55-12-5,11. See Searight, Assyrian Stone Vessels p. 23 nos. 62 and 64, p. 25 no. 82, p. 26 no. 89, and p. 56 nos. 389 and 391. As far as 82-5-22,603A, BM 118779, and Ki 1902-5-10,25 are preserved, the texts on these three vessel fragments read: [...] MAN ŠÚ MAN KUR AŠ.KI A [...] "[...], king of the world, king of Assyria, son of [..., ...]" (82-5-22,603A); [...] ⸢A⸣ ^{md}AN.ŠÁR-PAP-AŠ MAN KUR AŠ.KI A [^{m}]⸢^{d}⸣30-PAP-MEŠ-SU [...] "[...], son of Esarhaddon, king of Assyria, son of Sennacherib, [...]" (BM 118779); and [... A ^{md}AN.ŠÁR-PAP-A]Š MAN KUR [AŠ.KI$^{?}$ ...] "[..., son of Esarhaddo]n, king of [Assyria, ...]" (Ki 1902-5-10,25). There are several pieces of evidence that might indicate that the inscription(s) written on those three stone vessels were written in the name of Sîn-šarra-iškun (or his brother and predecessor Aššur-etel-ilāni), rather than in that of Ashurbanipal. These are: (1) the name of Assyria (*māt aššur*) is written as KUR AŠ.KI, instead of KUR AN.ŠÁR.KI or KUR AŠ, in 82-5-22,603A and BM 118779; and (2) and Esarhaddon is only given the title *šar māt aššur* ("king of Assyria"), and not the titles *šar kiššati šar māt aššur* ("king of the world, king of Assyria"). Note that on 81-2-4,35A, the only certainly attested vessel inscription of Sîn-šarra-iškun, *māt aššur* is written KUR AŠ, not KUR AŠ.KI. Assuming that proprietary inscriptions of Assyria's penultimate king also included four generations in his genealogy, one could tentatively suggest that the complete text might have been KUR md30-LUGAL-GAR-*un* MAN GAL MAN *dan-nu* MAN ŠÚ MAN KUR AŠ A mAN.ŠÁR-DÙ-A MAN KUR AŠ A mAN.ŠÁR-PAP-AŠ MAN KUR AŠ A md30-PAP.MEŠ-SU MAN KUR AŠ A mMAN-GIN MAN KUR AŠ-*ma* "Palace of Sîn-šarra-iškun, great king, strong king, king of the world, king of Assyria, son of Ashurbanipal, king of Assyria, son of Esarhaddon, king of Assyria, son of Sennacherib, king of Assyria, son of Sargon (II), (who was) also king of Assyria."

BIBLIOGRAPHY

2008 Searight, Assyrian Stone Vessels pp. 58–59 and fig. 30 no. 418 (copy, edition, study)

TEXT

1) KUR md30-LUGAL-GAR-*un* MAN [GAL ...] MAN KUR AŠ-*ma*

1) Palace of Sîn-šarra-iškun, [great] king, [...], (who was) also king of Assyria.

2001

A stone vessel, possibly from Nineveh, is inscribed with a one-line proprietary label of an Assyrian royal lady by the name of Ana-Tašmētu-taklāk, who might have been the queen of Sîn-šarra-iškun (see the commentary for further details).

CATALOGUE

Registration Number	Provenance	Dimensions (cm)	cpn
55-12-5,252	Registered as coming from Sherif Khan, but possibly from Nineveh, Kuyunjik	Height: 3.6; Dia.: 9.5	n

COMMENTARY

As for the identity of Ana-Tašmētu-taklāk, I.L. Finkel (NABU 2000/1 p. 12 no. 8) has suggested that she "seems likely to have been most probably the second wife of Esarhaddon ... or perhaps the wife/widow of Sargon II, the second wife of Assurbanipal, or the wife of one of Assurbanipal's sons" (Aššur-etel-ilāni or Sîn-šarra-iškun). Compare also Searight, Assyrian Stone Vessels p. 74, where Finkel states that she was "Sargon's widow or a wife of a seventh-century king." More recently, S. Svärd (Power and Women pp. 100–101, 117, and 278) has argued that Ana-Tašmētu-taklāk was the queen of Aššur-etel-ilāni or Sîn-šarra-iškun. Since this inscription was not included in Frame, RINAP 2 or Leichty, RINAP 4, since it is uncertain if this queen was the (second or first) wife of Ashurbanipal, Aššur-etel-ilāni, or Sîn-šarra-iškun, and since there are more attested Assyrian inscriptions for Sîn-šarra-iškun than there are for Aššur-etel-ilāni, this one-line proprietary inscription is tentatively included with the texts of Assyria's penultimate king, although there is no firm evidence to suggest that Ana-Tašmētu-taklāk was the queen of Sîn-šarra-iškun rather than some other late-eighth or seventh century Assyrian ruler.

BIBLIOGRAPHY

2000 Finkel, NABU 2000/1 p. 12 no. 8 (edition, study)

2008 Searight, Assyrian Stone Vessels pp. 74 and 108 and fig. 49 no. 511 (copy, edition, study)

2012 Macgregor, SAAS 21 p. 71 n. 99 (study)

2012 Svärd, Power and Women pp. 100–102, 117 and 278 no. 156 (transliteration, translation, study)

2015 Svärd, SAAS 23 pp. 47–49, 61, 218 no. 150, and 223 (transliteration, translation, study)

TEXT

1) [*šá* ^{f}*ana*-^{d}*taš*]-*me-tum*-⸢*tak*⸣-*lak* MUNUS.⸢É⸣.GAL [... MAN KUR AŠ]

1) [Belonging to Ana-Taš]mētu-taklāk, queen of [..., (...,) king of Assyria].

Aššur-uballiṭ II

There are no known inscriptions of Aššur-uballiṭ II (611–609), a man — likely the son and designated heir of Sîn-šarra-iškun — who declared himself king of Assyria in Ḫarrān. This is hardly a surprise given the short duration of his reign, the limited extent of his sphere of direct influence (the northwestern part of the once-great Assyrian Empire, in particular, the area around the cult center of the moon-god Sîn), and the fact that he had to spend most of his time preparing for battle and fighting against Nabopolassar of Babylon and his Median ally Cyaxares for Assyria's survival as a political entity. Should he have had time to have carried out building activities that were not devoted to strengthening the defenses of his makeshift capital, which seems highly implausible according to the information provided in the Fall of Nineveh Chronicle (see pp. 43–46 of the present volume for a translation), then one would expect that any inscriptions written in his name would have been composed for and deposited/displayed in cities located outside of the Assyrian heartland (the "Aššur-Nineveh-Arbela" triangle), for example, Dūr-Katlimmu, Guzana, and Ḫarrān. Because Aššur-uballiṭ's reign was not only short, but very turbulent, it is highly unlikely that any inscription of his will ever be discovered. For further information about the final days of the Assyrian Empire, see p. 37.

Minor Variants and Comments

Ashurbanipal 241

1.2 MAN for LUGAL. **2**.1 *a-ši-ib**: form anomalous or over erasure. **2**.2, 15 TIN.TIR.KI for KÁ.DINGIR.RA.KI. **2**.6, 16 *ra-bi-[i]* and *ra-bi-*⸢*i*⸣ respectively for GAL-*i*. **2**.8 EN-*ia* for *be-li-ia*. **3**.10, 14, 17 ^{m}AN.ŠÁR-*ba-ni*-A for ^{m}AN.ŠÁR-DÙ-A; exs 5, 10, 14, 17 have ^{m}AN.ŠÁR-DÙ-IBILA for ^{m}AN.ŠÁR-DÙ-A. **3**.2, 4–6, 8–11, 14–17, 19 MAN for LUGAL in all occurrences preserved; only exs. 1 and 7 have LUGAL. **3**.2, 5–6, 8–11, 14–15, 17, 19 ŠÚ for ŠÁR; only ex. 1 has ŠÁR. **3**.8, 19 have *kib-ra-ti* for LÍMMU-*ti*; exs. 9, 17 have *kib-ra-a-ti*; and ex. 11 has *kib-*⸢*ra*⸣-[*a-ti*]. **4**.2, 4–6, 8–11, 14–15, 17, 19 MAN for LUGAL on all occurrences preserved; only exs. 1 and 7 have LUGAL. **4**.2, 4–6, 8–11, 14–15, 17, 19 ŠÚ for ŠÁR; only ex. 1 has ŠÁR. **4**.4–5 KÁ.DINGIR.RA.KI for TIN.TIR.KI. **5**.2, 4–5, 9–11, 17, 19 MAN for LUGAL; only 1, 7–8 have LUGAL. **5**.2, 8–11, 15 KUR *šu-me-ri* for KUR EME.GI. **5**.20 ⸢*ù*⸣ for *u*. **5**.2, 8–10, 15, 17 TIN.TIR.KI for KÁ.DINGIR.RA.KI; ex. 4 has [TIN.T]IR.KI.. **5**.10 *é-sag-íl**: The text has a form which appears to be a mixture of IL and ÍL. **6**.2 *eš-re-e-te* for *eš-re-e-ti*. **6**.5–11, 17 *ša* for *šá*. **6**.2, 5–6, 17 *ina* for *i-na*. **7**.2, 4–8, 11, 14, 20 *si-ma-a-te* for *si-ma-a-ti*. **7**.2 *u* for *ù*. **7**.2 *baṭ-lu-te* has for *baṭ-lu-tu*; exs 7.8–11, 17, 19 have *baṭ-lu-tú* for *baṭ-lu-tu*. **7**.2 *ú-kin-[nu]* for *ú-ki-nu*. **7**.15 Possibly insufficient room to restore all of line 7. **8**.4 *ki-du-de*-DU for *ki-du-de-e*. **8**.2, 4–6, 8–9, 11, 14 *la-bi-rim-ma* for *la-bi-ri-im-ma*. **8**.2, 10 *áš-ru-šú-[un]* and *áš-ru-šú-un* for *áš-ru-šu-un* respectively. **9**.4 ^{md}30-ŠEŠ.MEŠ-SU-*ba* for ^{md}30-ŠEŠ.MEŠ-SU. **9**.17 ^{md}30-ŠEŠ.MEŠ-SU*: The copy has ŠA (Assyrian form) for SU (not visible on photograph). **9**.2, 4–5, 8–11, 14–15, 17, 20 MAN for LUGAL on all occurrences preserved; only exs. 1 and 6–7 have LUGAL. **9**.2, 4–5, 8–11, 17, 20 ŠÚ for ŠÁR; only ex. 1 and 6–7 have ŠÁR.

10.2, 4–5, 8, 11, 20 *ri-šá-a-te* for *ri-šá-a-ti*. **10**.6 [K]Á.DINGIR.RA.KI for TIN.TIR.KI. **11**.10, 17 *ša* for *šá*. **11**.2, 5, 8–9, 11 *da-ra-a-te* for *da-ra-a-ti*; ex. 4 has [*da-r*]*a-a-te*. **11**.2 *sat-tuk-ku* for *sat-tuk-ki*. **12**.7, 10, 17 KÁ.DINGIR.RA.KI for TIN.TIR.KI in both occurrences; KÁ.DINGIR.RA.KI for TIN.TIR.KI in first occurrence only. **12**.2, 5–8, 10–11 have *ú-kin* for *ú-ki-in*, while exs. 4 and 9 have *ú-*⸢*kin*⸣ and *ú-k[in]* resectively; only exs. 1 and 17 have *ú-ki-in*. **12**.2 *ki-din-ú-te* for *ki-din-ú-tu*. **12**.6 K[Á].DINGIR.RA.KI for TIN.TIR.KI in second occurrence (first occurrence not preserved). **13**.2 omits masculine determinative (^{m}) in ^{md}GIŠ.NU$_{11}$-MU-GI.NA. **14**.2 LUGAL-*ú-te* for LUGAL-*ú-tu*. **14** Instead of KÁ.DINGIR.RA.KI exs. 2 and 9 have TIN.TIR.KI, ex. 8 has [TI]N.⸢TIR⸣.KI, and ex. 11 has TIN.[T]IR.KI. **14**.1 *ap-qí-di* for *ap-qid*. **14**.2 *u* for *ù*. **14**.2, 5–11, 17 *ina* for *i-na*; only ex. 1 has *i-na*. **15**.2 *ni-siq-tú* for *ni-siq-ti*. **15**.2, 9, 11 *az-nun-ma* for *az-nu-un-ma*; ex. 8 has *az-n*]*un-ma*. **16**.11 omits *ú* in *ú-nam-mir*. **17**.2, 8–11, 17 TIN.TIR.KI for KÁ.DINGIR.RA.KI. **17**.5, 8–9 *šal-ḫu-u-šú* for *šal-ḫu-ú-šú*. **18**.5, 7 *šá* for *ša*. **18**.2, 7, 11 *il-lik-u-ma* for *il-lik-ú-ma*. **18**.9 [*in-n*]*ab-*⸢*tu*⸣ for *in-na-ab-tu*. **19**.2, 5–8, 10, 17 EN.NUN for *ma-aṣ-ṣar-ti*; only exs. 1 and 9 have *ma-aṣ-ṣar-ti*. **19**.2 *u* for *ú*. **19**.2, 8, 11 *eš-re-e-te* for *eš-re-e-ti*. **19**.7–8, 10–11 TIN.TIR.KI for KÁ.DINGIR.RA.KI.

20.3, 9 ⸢*dun*⸣*-nu-nu* and *dun-nu-n[u]* respectively for *du-un-nu-nu*. **20**.9 *i-na* for *ina*. **20**.2–3, 9, 17 *e-mu-qu* for *e-muq*. **20**.2, 8, 9 omit *-a-* in *un-ma-na-a-ti-ia*; ex. 11 has *-iá* for *-ia* in *un-ma-na-a-ti-ia*. **21**.3, 9 *šal-ḫu-u-šú* for *šal-ḫu-ú-šú*. **21**.9 *i-na* for *ina*. **21**.5, 10, 17 *ú-rak-ki-si* for *ú-rak-kis*. **22**.8–9, 11 *i-na* for *ina*. **23** For *ar-ku-ú* exs. 2, 5, 9–10, 17 have EGIR-*ú*, and ex. 7 has [EGI]R-⸢*ú*⸣; only exs. 1 and 8 have *ar-ku-ú*. **23**.7–9, 11 *ša* for *šá*. **23**.8–9, 11 *i-na* for *ina*. **23**.5, 7–8, 11 omit *-e-* in BALA-*e-šú*. **23**.3, 10 *šu-a-tú* and *šú-a-ti* respectively for *šu-a-ti*. **23** For *um-ma-ni*, exs. 5–7, 10, 17 have LÚ.*um-ma-a-ni* and ex. 3 has ⸢*um-ma*⸣*-a-ni*. **23**.8–9 have respectively *en-qu-tú* and *en-qu-t[ú]* for *en-qu-tu* respectively; ex. 1 has *en-qu-t[u]/t[ú]/t[e]* (reading of the last sign is uncertain). **24**.3, 8–9, 11, 17 *šal-ḫu-u* for *šal-ḫu-ú*; ex. 10 has *šal-ḫu-*⸢*šú*⸣ for *šal-ḫu-ú*. **25**.10 *si-ma-ti-šu-nu* for *si-ma-ti-šu-nu*. **25**.17 MU.SAR-*ú-a* for MU.SAR-*u-a*. **27**.5, 7–11, 16–17 *ù* for *u*; only ex. 1 has *u*. **27**.10, 17, 19 *ta-li-mi-ia* for *ta-lim-ia*. **28**.6 *i-ab-ba-tu* for *i-ab-bat*. **28**.17 MU.SAR-*ú-a* for MU.SAR-*u-a*. **29**.2, 3, 5–6, 8–10, 15, 17 *gim-ri* for *gi-im-ri*; only exs. 1 and 11 have *gi-im-ri*. **29**.11 *ag-gi-iš* for *ag-giš*.

30.5, 8–10, 17, 19 *ina* for *i-na*. **30**.11 *ma-ta-a-ti* for KUR.KUR. **30**.1 *li-ḫal-li-qi* for *li-ḫal-liq*.

Ashurbanipal 244

10.2 *ki-din-nu-tú* for *ki-din-nu-tu*. **11**.1 omits -MU- in ^{md}GIŠ.NU$_{11}$-MU-GI.NA ; the other exemplars are not preserved at this point. **15**.2 IGI.[BAR-*ma*] for *lip-pal-lis-ma*. **19**.1 omits -MU- in [^{md}]⸢GIŠ.NU$_{11}$⸣-MU-GI.NA; the other exemplars are not preserved at this point. **22**.1* *i-ab-bat lu* for *i-ab-ba-tu lu-u*.

Ashurbanipal 245

1.2 ^{m}AN.ŠÁR-DÙ-IBILA for ^{m}AN.ŠÁR-DÙ-A. **10**.2 *ú-ki-in ki-di[n-ú-tu]* for *ú-kin ki-di-nu-tu*. **20**.2 *ta-lim-ia* for *ta-lim-iá*.

Ashurbanipal 246

18.2 [*an*]-⸢*dul*⸣*-lum* for *an-dul-lu*. 19.2 [U]GU for *e-li*.

Ashurbanipal 253

8.3 [K]UR *šu-me-ri* for KUR EME.GI$_{7}$; the end of line 8 on ex. 3 is on a separate, indented line, which has [MAN K]UR *šu-me-ri u* ⸢URI.KI⸣. **19**.2 *il-lik-u-m[a]* for *il-lik-ú-ma*. **20**.2 [*eš-re-e*]*-ti* for *eš-re-e-te*. **24**.2 [*la-bi-r*]*a-ti* for *la-bi-ra-a-te*.

Ashurbanipal 257

1.1–2 *dan-dan-nu**: Both texts have *dan-dan*-PAP. **1**.2 *šur-*⸢*bu*⸣*-ú* ⸢*kaš*⸣-[*kaš* (DINGIR.MEŠ)] for *kaš-kaš* DINGIR.MEŠ *šur-bu-ú gít-ma-la*. **2**.2 Omits *mut-tal-la e-tel-lu* ŠEŠ-*šú*. **3**.2 ^{m}AN.ŠÁR-DÙ-A for ^{m}AN.ŠÁR-DÙ-IBILA. **2**.1–2 *é-šà-ḫúl**-*a*: The copies have a sign that looks more like Ù than ḪÚL (see Frame RIMB 2 p. 336). **3**.1–2 *dan-nu**: The texts have *dan*-PAP. **4**.1–2 -*dan-nu**: The texts have *dan*-PAP. **6**.1–2 *dan-nu**: The texts have *dan*-PAP. **8**.2 *ina* for *i-na*. **8**.1–2 KÙ*: The copies of the sign are anomalous (see Frame RIMB 2 p. 336). **9** *é-šà-ḫúl**-*a*: As in line 2 (see above and Frame RIMB 2 p. 336). **10**.2 *ki-ma* <<*ki-ma*>>.

Ashurbanipal 258

10.1 KUR EME.<<UR>>.GI$_7$; ex. 2 not preserved at this point. 10.2 ù for u (second occasion; first occasion not preserved). 12.2 UD.ME for u$_4$-me-šú.

Ashurbanipal 261

10 Ex. 1 has: A-  Ex. 2 appears to have A-NE.UD.

Ashurbanipal 262

1.7 ^{m}AN.ŠÁR-DÙ-IBILA for ^{m}AN.ŠÁR-DÙ-A. 4.5 ⸢MAN⸣ ŠÚ MAN KUR aš-šur GÌR.NÍTA KÁ.DINGIR.RA.KI for LUGAL ŠÁR LUGAL KUR aš-šur GÌR.NÍTA TIN.TIR.KI. 5.5 MAN [...] for LUGAL KUR EME.GI$_7$ u URI.KI. 6.5 si-ma-a-ti for si-ma-ti. 8.5 [MA]N dan-nu MAN ŠÚ MAN KUR aš-šur for LUGAL dan-nu LUGAL ŠÁR LUGAL KUR aš-šur. 9.5 [KÁ.DINGI]R.RA.KI for TIN.⸢TIR⸣.KI. 10.5 KÁ.DINGIR.RA.K[I] for TIN.TIR.KI. 12.2 LUGAL-ú-tu for LUGAL-ú-ut. 14.2, 4 u for ù. 14.4 eš-re-e-te for eš-re-e-ti. 15.4 UGU for e-li. 18.4 DÙ-ma for ú-še-piš-ma. 19.4 [dam-qa]-⸢a⸣-te for dam-qa-a-ti. 19.4 IGI.BAR-ma for lip-p[a-lis]-ma. 25.3 ⸢lip-šú-uš⸣ for lip-šu-uš. 26.3 ta-li-<mi>-ia for ta-lim-ia. 27.7 MU.SAR-u-a for MU.SAR-ú-a. 28.7 e-la-a-ti for e-la-ti. 29.7 i-n[a] for ina.

Ashurbanipal 263

1.2 Although none of the writings of the divine name in this exemplar (lines 2, 24, 30, and 32) is entirely clear, the sign ^{d}INANNA appears to be written with the ligature: AŠ+MUŠ rather than AN+MUŠ (information courtesy of D.A. Foxvog). 4.2 mu-ra-si-bat*: The text has mu-ra-si-MU. 7.2 ^{m}AN.ŠÁR-DÙ-IBILA for ^{m}AN.ŠÁR-DÙ-A. 9.2 e-li-ti for e-liti. 10.1 ṭa-a-ba*: The text has ṭa-a-ŠU. 12.2 The form of MEŠ in UN.MEŠ*-šú is anomalous. 14.2 KÁ.DI[NGIR.RA.KI] for TIN.TIR.KI (second occurrence only). 15.2 eš-re-e-ti for eš-re-e-te. 17.2 ú-⸢kin$_7$⸣ for ú-⸢kin⸣. 23.2 il-lik-ú-ma for il-lik-u-ma. 25.3 lip-pa-l[i?-is-ma] for lip-pa-lis-ma. 26.2 liš-šá-kin$_7$ for liš-šá-kin. 27.2–3 TIN.TIR.KI and TIN.TIR.<KI> respectively for KÁ.DINGIR.RA.KI. 29.2–3 MU.SAR-ú-a for MU.SAR-u-a. 31.3 lu-ú for lu-u.

Ashurbanipal 2004

12 The text has  for gá in ki ág-gá*-na.

Ashurbanipal 2006

1 In lieu of ṣir-ti, ex. 4 has ṣir-ta, and exs. 5 and 8 have ṣir-tú. 3.4–5, 7–8 DINGIR.ME for DINGIR.MEŠ. 3 Instead of GAL.MEŠ, exs.5 and 7–8 have GAL.ME, and ex. 2 has GAL.MEŠ-te. 4.2, 6 a-na for ana. 5.4 kiš-šá-ti for kiš-šat. 7.2, 8 ^{md}nin-gal-SUM.NA for ^{md}nin-gal-MU. 9.5–8 LÚ.gu-ra-sim-ma for LÚ.gu-ra-sim-mu. 12.2 nag-bu for nag-bi. 12.2, 6–7 da-ru-tu for da-ru-ti. 15 In place of u$_4$-mi-šú ex. 2 has UD.MEŠ-šú and ex. 6 has u$_4$-mi-šú. 16.2, 6 liš-ta-an-di-il for liš-ta-an-dil.

Ashurbanipal 2015

6 The published copy has  for ga? in [é-x]-x-ga?-kù-ga.

Aššur-etel-ilāni 1

1 ^{m}AN.ŠÁR-e-tel-DINGIR.MEŠ: exs. 1, 8–9, 20 have ^{m}AŠ-e-tel-DINGIR.MEŠ; ex. 3 has ⸢^{m}aš⸣-šur-e-tel-DINGIR.MEŠ; exs. 4–5 have ^{m}aš-šur-e-tel-DINGIR.MEŠ; ex. 10 has ^{m}⸢aš-šur⸣-e-tel-DINGIR.MEŠ; ex. 12 has ^{m}AN.ŠÁR-NIR.GÁL-DINGIR.MEŠ; and ex. 16 has ^{m}aš-šur-⸢e-tel-DINGIR.MEŠ⸣. 1 AŠ: ex. 6 has ⸢AŠ.KI⸣; and exs. 11–13, 16 have AŠ.KI. 2 ^{m}AN.ŠÁR-DÙ-A: exs. 1, 4, 8–9, 12, 14, 20 have ^{m}AŠ-DÙ-A; exs. 3, 5, 10 have ^{m}aš-šur-DÙ-A; and ex. 16 has ^{m}⸢aš-šur-DÙ-A⸣. 2.6, 11–13, 16 AŠ.KI for AŠ. 3 ^{m}AN.ŠÁR-PAP-AŠ: exs. 1, 4–5, 8–9, 12, 14, 20 have ^{m}AŠ-PAP-AŠ; ex. 3 has ⸢^{m}aš⸣-šur-PAP-AŠ; ex. 10 has ^{m}⸢aš-šur-PAP-AŠ⸣; and ex. 16 has ^{m}aš-šur-PAP-AŠ. 3 AŠ-ma: ex. 6 has ⸢AŠ.KI?-ma?⸣; and exs. 11–13, 16 have AŠ.KI-ma. 4.9 omits ma in ú-še-piš-ma. 4 SIG$_4$.AL.ÙR.RA: ex. 2 omits ÙR and ex. 18 omits RA. 5.1, 3–5, 9, 12, 14, 20 ana for a-na. 5.2 e-zi-da for é-zi-da. 6.12 ša for šá. 6.18 omits URU in URU.kal-ḫa. 7.3–5, 8, 13–14, 16, 18 omit LA in TI.LA. 7.4, 18 ZI.MEŠ-ía for ZI.MEŠ-ia.

Aššur-etel-ilāni 3

6 The -ti in ⸢lem-nu⸣-ti is written over an erasure. 10 The KÙ in KÙ.GI is written over an erasure. 14 su*-up-pi-šú: The text has ŠU-up-pi-šú. 15 ina, the -reb in qé-reb, and the é in é-èš-ér-ke$_4$ are all written over erasures. 16 šá, the KU$_4$ in LÚ.KU$_4$.É, the MEŠ in UN.MEŠ, and šú-a-te are written over erasures.

Aššur-etel-ilāni 4

6 MU*.ME: The form of the MU sign is different from that of the MU in line 2 and it might be an attempt to present an archaic form of the sign. 6 ME* in ^{m}AN.ŠÁR-NIR.GÁL-DINGIR.ME: The copy has DIŠ. On the brick, one can see a trace of a horizontal line passing through the middle of the sign, but this appears to be a continuation of the final wedge of the preceding sign rather than a new horizontal wedge.

Aššur-etel-ilāni 5

6 nibru.KI*: The KI sign has no horizontal wedges and is somewhat similar to the A sign in lines 6 and 11. 7 sag-ús*: The text has sag-DÙ.

Aššur-etel-ilāni 6

1.2 A ^{m}da-ku-<ru šá> for DUMU ^{m}da-ku-⸢ru šá⸣. 2.3 ⸢É-^{m}da-ku-ri⸣ for É-^{m}da-kur. 3 Ex. 1 has qé-reb É* (text: RIB)-<šú> šá and not qé-reb <É-šú> šá as copied in YOS 1. 10 For the end of the line, ex. 1 has ⸢lik⸣-r[u?-bu?] and ex. 3 has lik-⸢ru?-bu?⸣ (see the collations in Frame, RIMB 2 p. 336); this passage is not preserved in ex. 2. 14.3 ú-nak-ka-ru-ma for ú-nak-ka-ri.

Sîn-šarra-iškun 1

6′.3 ina for i-⸢na⸣. 7′ Ex. 3 has eš-⸢re⸣-e-ti for eš-ret and omits ni in BÀD.MEŠ-ni. 9′.3 šá for ša. 10′.3 i-pu-šu-⸢ma⸣ for e-pu-šu-ma.

Sîn-šarra-iškun 7

iv 14′.5 qa-áš-du-u-ti for qa-áš-du-ti. 22′.5 EGIR-⸢ú⸣ for EGIR.
v 16.1 [li-ru]-ru-šu-ma for li-⸢ru⸣-ru-šú-ma. 17.1 [NUMUN]-šu for NUMUN-šú and NUNUZ-šu for NUNUZ-šú.

Sîn-šarra-iškun 10

1.2 KAL for dan-nu and aš-šur.KI for AN.ŠÁR.KI. 4.2 tuq-qu-ni for tu-qu-ni. 5.2 [i]-⸢pi⸣-ru-šú for i-pi-ru-⸢uš⸣ and ^{d}ŠEŠ.KI for ⸢na⸣-an-nàr. 6.2 ⸢SIPA⸣-ti for re-⸢ʾu⸣-u-ti. 7.1 omits tu in rit-tu-uš-šú. 8.2 u for ù and ši-tul$_5$-ti for ši-tul-ti. 10.2 omits LÚ in LÚ.SIPA. 11.2 [ú-lu]-⸢ú⸣ for ú-lu and omits MEŠ in Ì.MEŠ. 12.2 ^{m}aš-šur-DÙ-IBILA for ^{m}AN.ŠÁR-DÙ-IBILA and aš-šur.KI for AN.ŠÁR.[KI]. 13.2 [^{m}aš-

šur-ŠEŠ.(MEŠ)]-⸢AŠ⸣ for ^{md*}*aš**-*šur**(over erasure)-ŠEŠ-SUM.NA and *aš-šur*.KI for AN.ŠÁR.KI. **14**.2 *šu-me-ri* for EME.GI$_{7}$, *ak-ka-de-e* for URI.KI, and ^{md}EN.ZU-ŠEŠ.MEŠ-⸢SU⸣ for ^{md}30-ŠEŠ.MEŠ-⸢SU⸣. **15**.2 *aš-šur*.KI for AN.ŠÁR.KI. **16**.2 MAN for LUGAL and omits *u* in LUGAL-*u-ti-ia*. **19**.2 ⸢*dum*⸣-[*qi*] for SIG$_{5}$.

Sîn-šarra-iškun 11

1.13 *ana-ku* for *a-na-ku*. **1**.13 ^{m}30-MAN-GAR for ^{md}30-⸢LUGAL⸣-GAR-*un*. **1**.1, 6 MAN for LUGAL. **1** A: ex. 6 has DUMU before ^{m}*aš-šur*-DÙ-A; and ex. 14 has DUMU for all three occurences of A. **1**.4 omits KI in *aš-šur*.⸢KI⸣ before MAN KUR EME.GI$_{7}$. **2**.13 ⸢KAL⸣ for first *dan-nu*. **2**.13 ^{m}MAN-GIN for ^{m}LUGAL-GI.NA. **2**.9. KAL for probably the second *dan-nu*. **2**.8 LUGAL-*te-ia* for LUGAL-*ti-ia*. **3** ^{d}⸢AG⸣: exs. 1, 12 have ^{d}MUATI; and ex. 6 has ^{d}⸢MUATI⸣. **3**.12 *šà* for *šá*. **3**.10 omits KI in *bal-til*.KI. **3** *u*$_{4}$-*mu*: exs. 3, 9 have *u*$_{4}$-*me*; and ex. 15 has [*u*$_{4}$]-⸢*me*?⸣. **3**.1 *te-me-en-šu* for *te-me-en-šú*. **3**.12 ŠUB-*ma* for *ad-di-ma*. **3**.6, 15 *ka-lak-ka-šú* and [*ka-lak*]-⸢*ka*⸣-*šú* respectively for *ka-lak-ka-šu*. **3**.1 SIG$_{4}$.MEŠ-⸢*šu*⸣ for SIG$_{4}$.MEŠ-*šú*. **4** *nin-gu-tu*: ex. 4 has ⸢*nin*⸣-*gu-tú*; ex. 5 has *nin*-<<*nin*>>-*gu-tu*; and ex. 9 has [*nin*]-⸢*gu*⸣-*tú*. **4**.1 *ub-bal* for *ub-ba-la*. **4**.6–7 *u*$_{4}$-*mu-šu-un* and *u*$_{4}$-*mu-šú*-⸢*un*?⸣ respectively for UD-*šu-un*. **4**.1 UŠ$_{8}$-*šu* for UŠ$_{8}$-*šú*. **4**.15 *gaba-dib-bi*-⸢*šú*⸣ for *gaba-dib-bi-šu*. **5**.1, 9 ^{m}⸢*sa*⸣-*i-lu* and ^{m}*sa*-⸢*i*⸣-[*lu*] respectively for ^{m}*sa-ʾi-lu*.

Sîn-šarra-iškun 13

1 Ex. 8 has ... [3]0-MAN-GAR for ^{md}30-LUGAL-GAR-*un*, while ex. 11 omits ^{d}. **1**.2–5, 8, 11, 19, 21, 23–24 omit *u* in GAL-*u*. **2**.2–6, 8, 10, 19, 21, 23–24 omit *u* in GAL-*u*. 3.23 omits MAN KUR *aš-šur*.KI. **4**.2–5, 8, 10–11, 19, 21, 23–24 omit *u* in GAL-*u*. **4**.3 omits KI in *aš-šur*.KI. **5**.19 omits KI in KÁ.DINGIR.KI. **6**.3–4, 21 A for DUMU. **6**.2, 19, 23–24 omit ^{d} in ^{md}30-PAP.MEŠ-SU. **6**.2–5, 8, 11, 19, 21, 23–24 omit *u* in GAL-*u*. **6**.3 omits KI in *aš-šur*.KI. **8**.2–5, 8, 11, 19, 21, 23–24 omit *u* in GAL-*u*. **9**.4 omits KI in *aš-šur*.KI. **9**.19 omits KI in KÁ.DINGIR.KI. **10**.2, 19 ^{d}MUATI for ^{d}AG. **10**.2, 19 EN-*ía* for EN-*ia*. **11**.2, 19, 24 omit KI in *bal-til*.KI. **12**.6, 19 appear to have KUR for *gúr* in *a-gúr-ri*.

Sîn-šarra-iškun 19

20.12 [*kiš*]-⸢*šá-ti*⸣ for ŠÚ. **21**.8 omits *e* in *it-pe-e-šú*. **23**.12 omits *u* in *e-pu-šú-u-in-ni*. **24**.6, 8 [*ú*]-*še-šib-u-in-ni* and *ú-še-šib-u-in-ni* respectively for *ú-še-šib-ú-in-ni*. **27**.9 ⸢*áš*⸣-*ra-ti-šú-nu* for *áš-ra-te-šú-nu* and *áš**(copy: PA)-*te*-ʾ*e*-⸢*e*⸣-[*ma*] for *áš-te-ʾe*-⸢*e-ma*⸣.

Index of Museum Numbers

Babylon, Nebuchadnezzar Museum

No.	RINAP 5
A Babylon 9	Asb. 241.18
A Babylon 55	Asb. 241.17

Baghdad, Iraq Museum

No.	RINAP 5
IM 1101	Asb. 2016.9
IM 1102	Asb. 2016.10
IM 1103	Asb. 2017.7
IM 3209+	Ssi 6.1
IM 3249+	Ssi 6.1
IM 16429	Asb. 2006.3
IM 48412	Asb. 2006.4
IM 48413	Asb. 2006.5
IM 48414	Asb. 2006.6
IM 56282	Aei 1.21
IM 59296	Aei 1.22–23
IM 60592	Ssi 20
IM 60629?	Aei 1.20
IM 60634	Aei 1.26
IM 124171	Asb. 241.19
IM —	Asb. 264
IM —	Asb. 2008.11
IM —	Aei 1.24
IM —	Aei 1.25
IM —	Ssi 19.1
IM —	Ssi 19.2
IM —	Ssi 19.8
IM —	Ssi 19.9
IM —	Ssi 19.14

Berkeley, Hearst Museum of Anthropology, University of California at Berkeley

No.	RINAP 5
HMA 9-1793	Asb. 263.2

Berlin, Vorderasiatisches Museum

No.	RINAP 5
VA 3587	Asb. 253.1
VA 4054a	Asb. 251.4
VA 4054b	Asb. 251.5
VA 4054c	Asb. 251.3
VA 4902	Asb. 241.5
VA 5059+	Ssi 7.3
VA 5060+	Ssi 10.1
VA 7501	Ssi 7.1
VA 7506+	Ssi 9
VA 7518+	Ssi 9
VA 8409	Asb. 245.1
VA 8416	Ssi 11.1
VA 8418	Ssi 7.2
VA 8419+	Ssi 7.3
VA 8847	Asb. 2001
VA —	Asb. 250
VA —	Asb. 251.6
VA —	Asb. 251.7
VA —	Asb. 251.8
VA Ass 2128	Ssi 11.2
VA Ass 2316	Ssi 10.2
VA Ass 3284a	Ssi 13.1
VA Ass 3284b	Ssi 13.2
VA Ass 3284c	Ssi 13.3
VA Ass 3284d	Ssi 13.4
VA Ass 3284e	Ssi 13.5
VA Ass 3284f	Ssi 13.6
VA Ass 3284g	Ssi 13.7
VA Ass 3284h	Ssi 13.8
VA Ass 3284i	Ssi 13.9
VA Ass 3285	Ssi 14.1
VA Bab 601	Asb. 241.10
VA Bab 602	Asb. 241.7

No.	RINAP 5
VA Bab 603	Asb. 241.9
VA Bab 604	Asb. 241.8
VA Bab 614	Asb. 244.1*
VA Bab 632	Asb. 241.11
VA Bab 634	Asb. 241.6
VA Bab 4052	Asb. 247.1, 25
VA Bab 4052h	Asb. 249
VA Bab 4052i	Asb. 247.2
VA Bab 4052k	Asb. 247.3
VA Bab 4073	Asb. 247.24
VA Bab 4073a	Asb. 247.4
VA Bab 4073b	Asb. 248.2
VA Bab 4073c	Asb. 248.4
VA Bab 4073d	Asb. 248.5
VA Bab —	Asb. 247.5
VA Bab —	Asb. 247.6
VA Bab —	Asb. 247.7
VA Bab —	Asb. 247.8
VA Bab —	Asb. 247.9
VA Bab —	Asb. 247.10
VA Bab —	Asb. 247.11
VA Bab —	Asb. 247.12
VA Bab —	Asb. 247.13
VA Bab —	Asb. 247.14
VA Bab —	Asb. 247.15
VA Bab —	Asb. 247.16
VA Bab —	Asb. 247.17
VA Bab —	Asb. 247.18
VA Bab —	Asb. 247.19
VA Bab —	Asb. 247.20
VA Bab —	Asb. 247.21
VA Bab —	Asb. 247.22
VA Bab —	Asb. 247.23
VA Bab —	Asb. 247.26
VAT 9524+	Ssi 8
VAT 9948	Ssi 15–16
VAT 9975	Ssi 17–18
VAT 13142	Aei 3

Bristol, Museum and Art Gallery

No.	RINAP 5
H-5097	Asb. 259.5

Heidelberg, Seminar für Assyriologie, Universität Heidelberg

No.	RINAP 5
—	Asb. 263.4

Istanbul, Archeological Museum

No.	RINAP 5
A 494+	Ssi 8
A 3448	Ssi 11.3
A 3547	Ssi 11.4
A 3549	Ssi 11.5
A 3550	Ssi 11.6
A 3554	Ssi 11.7
A 3555	Ssi 11.8
A 3557	Ssi 11.9
A 3558	Ssi 11.10
A 3560	Ssi 11.11
A 3561	Ssi 11.12
A 3563	Ssi 11.13
A 3565	Ssi 11.14
A 3567	Ssi 11.15
A 3620	Ssi 7.4
A 3634	Ssi 10.3
B 9	Asb. 241.3
B 15	Asb. 241.4
B 42	Asb. 241.20
B 46	Asb. 241 comm.
B 65	Asb. 244.2*
D 240	Asb. 241.3
D 251	Asb. 241.4
D 277	Asb. 241.20
D 281	Asb. 241 comm.
D 300	Asb. 244.2*
EŞ 7893	Asb. 243
EŞ 9027	Asb. 248.3
EŞ 9028	Asb. 251.2
EŞ —	Asb. 247.27
EŞ —	Asb. 259.15
EŞ —	Asb. 259.16
EŞ —	Asb. 259.17
EŞ —	Asb. 259.18
EŞ —	Asb. 259.19
EŞ —	Asb. 259.20

Jena, Fr. Schiller University

No.	RINAP 5
HS 1958	Aei 5
HS 2981	Asb. 259.24

Jerusalem, Couvent Saint-Étienne

No.	RINAP 5
SE 155+	Ssi 7.5
SE 156+	Ssi 7.5

Koka, Miho Museum

No.	RINAP 5
SF 4.061	Asb. 270

Leiden, Liagre Bohl Collection

No.	RINAP 5
LB 1323+	Ssi 10.1

Leiden, Rijksmuseum van Oudheden

No.	RINAP 5
1968/12.1	Asb. 259.26

Liverpool, World Museum Liverpool

No.	RINAP 5
WML unnumbered 1	Asb. 259.28

London, British Museum

No.	RINAP 5
BM 12064	Asb. 244.1
BM 12110+	Asb. 246.1
BM 22533	Asb. 246.2
BM 28384+	Asb. 262.7
BM 33338	Asb. 245.2
BM 40074	Asb. 244.2
BM 47655	Asb. 241.12
BM 47656	Asb. 241.13
BM 50662	Asb. 241.14
BM 50843+	Asb. 262.7
BM 56634	Asb. 262.4
BM 56639	Asb. 262.2
BM 68613	Asb. 241.15
BM 77223	Asb. 241.16
BM 78264	Asb. 262.5
BM 83000+	Asb. 253.2
BM 83001+	Asb. 253.2
BM 86918	Asb. 241.1
BM 90184	Aei 1.1
BM 90185	Aei 1.2
BM 90186	Aei 1.3
BM 90187	Aei 1.4
BM 90188	Aei 1.5
BM 90189	Aei 1.6
BM 90190	Aei 1.7
BM 90191	Aei 1.8
BM 90192	Aei 1.9
BM 90193	Aei 1.10
BM 90194	Aei 1.11
BM 90195	Aei 1.12
BM 90196	Aei 1.13
BM 90197	Aei 1.14
BM 90198	Aei 1.15
BM 90199	Aei 1.16
BM 90285	Asb. 248.1
BM 90706	Aei 1.17
BM 90187	Aei 1.4
BM 90188	Aei 1.5
BM 90189	Aei 1.6
BM 90190	Aei 1.7
BM 90191	Aei 1.8
BM 90192	Aei 1.9
BM 90193	Aei 1.10
BM 90194	Aei 1.11
BM 90195	Aei 1.12
BM 90196	Aei 1.13
BM 90197	Aei 1.14
BM 90198	Aei 1.15

No.	RINAP 5
BM 90199	Aei 1.16
BM 90285	Asb. 248.1
BM 90706	Aei 1.17
BM 90725	Aei 1.18
BM 90741	Aei 1.19
BM 90807	Asb. 259.1
BM 90864+	Asb. 246.1
BM 90865	Asb. 254
BM 90935	Asb. 244.1
BM 91115	Asb. 262.1
BM 99320	Ssi 1.1
BM 99324	Ssi 1.2
BM 108856	Ssi 13.24
BM 114277	Asb. 2008.1
BM 114278	Asb. 2008.2
BM 114299	Asb. 259.2
BM 115697	Ssi 13.23
BM 116987	Asb. 2004
BM 118779	Ssi 21 comm.
BM 119014	Asb. 2007
BM 119021	Asb. 2005.1
BM 119023	Asb. 2005.2
BM 119024	Asb. 2005.3
BM 119065	Asb. 2003
BM 119271	Asb. 2017.1–2
BM 119274	Asb. 2018.1–2
BM 119277	Asb. 2015
BM 119278	Asb. 2009
BM 119279	Asb. 2016.1–2
BM 122613	Ssi 3
BM 123414	Ssi 19.6
BM 124350	Asb. 2006.2
BM 124351	Asb. 2006.1
BM 130712	Asb. 251.1
BM 132263	Aei 1 comm.
BM 137345	Asb. 2008.3
BM 137349	Asb. 2008.4
BM 137381	Asb. 2008.5
BM 137408	Asb. 2008.6
BM —	Ssi 19.3
BM —	Ssi 19.7
BM —	Ssi 19.10
BM —	Ssi 19.11
BM —	Ssi 19.13
51-10-9,78R	Asb. 259.1
55-12-5,252	Ssi 2001
80-6-17,2	Asb. 254
80-7-19,13	Ssi 4
81-2-1,38	Asb. 244.2
81-2-1,103	Asb. 244.1
81-2-4,174	Asb. 252
81-2-4,286	Asb. 1006
81-3-24,367	Asb. 246.1
81-7-27,8+	Ssi 1.3
81-7-27,280	Asb. 1022
81-11-3,360	Asb. 241.12
81-11-3,361	Asb. 241.13
82-3-3,125	Asb. 1004

No.	RINAP 5
82-3-23,1653	Asb. 241.14
82-3-23,1837+	Asb. 262.7
82-5-22,7+	Ssi 1.4
82-5-22,26+	Ssi 1.3
82-5-22,28+	Ssi 5
82-5-22,603A	Ssi 21 comm.
82-5-22,607A	Ssi 21 comm.
AH 82-7-14,1032	Asb. 262.4
AH 82-7-14,1043	Asb. 262.1
AH 82-7-14,1044	Asb. 262.2
82-9-18,8612	Asb. 241.15
83-1-18,332	Asb. 2002
83-1-21,163+	Asb. 253.2
83-1-21,164+	Asb. 253.2
83-6-30,3	Asb. 241.16
Bu 88-5-12,120	Asb. 262.5
Bu 89-4-26,154	Ssi 19.12
Bu 91-5-9,204	Asb. 1029
94-1-15,335	Asb. 246.2
98-10-11,20+	Asb. 262.7
1900-3-10,2	Asb. 241.1
Ki 1902-5-10,25	Ssi 21 comm.
Ki 1904-10-9,352+	Ssi 1.1
Ki 1904-10-9,353+	Ssi 1.1
Ki 1904-10-9,357	Ssi 1.2
1914-4-7,22	Ssi 13.24
1919-10-11,4708	Asb. 2008.1
1919-10-11,4709	Asb. 2008.2
1919-10-11,4743	Asb. 259.2
1922-8-12,72	Ssi 13.23
1924-9-20,250	Asb. 2004
1927-10-3,9	Asb. 2007
1927-10-3,16	Asb. 2005.1
1927-10-3,18	Asb. 2005.2
1927-10-3,60	Asb. 2003
1927-10-3,266	Asb. 2017.1–2
1927-10-3,269	Asb. 2018.1–2
1927-10-3,272	Asb. 2015
1927-10-3,273	Asb. 2009
1927-10-3,274	Asb. 2016.1–2
1930-5-8,2	Ssi 3
1932-12-10,357	Ssi 19.6
1933-10-13,3	Asb. 2006.2
1935-1-13,5	Asb. 2008.3
1935-1-13,9	Asb. 2008.4
1942-1-28,1	Asb. 251.1
1958-2-8,6	Aei 1 comm.
1979-12-18,16	Asb. 2008.5
1979-12-18,43	Asb. 2008.6
1979-12-20,100	Aei 1.1
1979-12-20,101	Aei 1.2
1979-12-20,102	Aei 1.3
1979-12-20,103	Aei 1.4

No.	RINAP 5
1979-12-20,104	Aei 1.5
1979-12-20,105	Aei 1.6
1979-12-20,106	Aei 1.7
1979-12-20,107	Aei 1.8
1979-12-20,108	Aei 1.9
1979-12-20,109	Aei 1.10
1979-12-20,110	Aei 1.11
1979-12-20,111	Aei 1.12
1979-12-20,112	Aei 1.13
1979-12-20,113	Aei 1.14
1979-12-20,114	Aei 1.15
1979-12-20,115	Aei 1.16
1979-12-20,314	Aei 1.17
1979-12-20,326	Aei 1.18
1979-12-20,332	Aei 1.19
DT 64+	Ssi 1.4
DT 272	Asb. 262.3
DT 381	Asb. 248.1
K 1662+	Ssi 19.1
K 1663	Ssi 19.4
K 1664	Ssi 19.5
K 2744	Ssi 2
K 3150	Asb. 1014
K 4496	Asb. 1007
K 4498	Asb. 1025
K 6370	Asb. 1015
K 6371	Asb. 1003
K 6681	Asb. 1027
K 6806	Asb. 1028
K 6868+	Asb. 1010
K 8361	Asb. 1026
K 8540+	Ssi 5
K 8541	Ssi 1.5
K 8551	Ssi 21 comm.
K 9155	Asb. 1002
K 9248+	Asb. 1010
K 13749	Asb. 1021
K 14127	Asb. 1005
K 16021	Asb. 1016
K 16776	Asb. 1008
K 16899+	Asb. 1023
K 17809	Asb. 1017
K 17999	Asb. 1018
K 18219	Asb. 1011
K 19386	Asb. 1012
K 19448	Asb. 1009
K 22138	Asb. 1019
Rm 283	Asb. 1013
Rm 337+	Asb. 1024
Rm 451+	Asb. 1024
Rm 2,467	Asb. 1020
Rm 3,11	Asb. 245.2
Sm 1048+	Asb. 1023
Sm 1937	Asb. 1001

Montreal, McLennan Library, McGill University

No.	RINAP 5
ML 1.18	Asb. 259.25

New Haven, Yale Babylonian Collection

No.	RINAP 5	No.	RINAP 5	No.	RINAP 5
NBC 2507+	Asb. 263.3	YBC 2151	Aei 5.1	YBC 2372	Asb. 259.21
NBC 6069	Aei 5.2	YBC 2180	Asb. 263.1		
NBC 6070	Aei 5.3	YBC 2368	Asb. 265		

New York, Metropolitan Museum of Art

No.	RINAP 5	No.	RINAP 5	No.	RINAP 5
MMA —	Asb. 262.6	MMA 59.41.85	Asb. 259.27	MMA 86.11.51	Asb. 253.4

Oxford, Ashmolean Museum

No.	RINAP 5	No.	RINAP 5	No.	RINAP 5
Ash 1922.181	Asb. 259.3	Ash 1924.627	Asb. 259.4	W-B 190	Aei 4
Ash 1922.190	Aei 4	W-B 181	Asb. 259.3		

Paris, Bibliothèque Nationale

No.	RINAP 5
Inv. 65 no. 5929	Asb. 241.2

Paris, Louvre

No.	RINAP 5
AO 7752	Asb. 253.3

Philadelphia, Philadelphia Museum of Art
(pieces on loan to the University of Pennsylvania Museum of Archaeology and Anthropology, Philadelphia)

No.	RINAP 5	No.	RINAP 5	No.	RINAP 5
PMA F29-6-387a+	Asb. 258.1	PMA F29-6-387b+	Asb. 258.1	PMA F29-6-387e+	Asb. 258.1

Philadelphia, University of Pennsylvania Museum of Archaeology and Anthropology (Penn Museum)

No.	RINAP 5	No.	RINAP 5	No.	RINAP 5
CBS 733+	Asb. 255	CBS 16487	Asb. 2017.3–4	UM 33-35-191a	Asb. 2006.7
CBS 1632a	Asb. 259.6	CBS 16488	Asb. 2018.3–4	UM 33-35-191b	Asb. 2006.8
CBS 1757+	Asb. 255	CBS 16489	Asb. 2013.1–2	UM 55-21-384	Asb. 258.2
CBS 8632	Asb. 259.7	CBS 16490	Asb. 2014.1–2	UM 84-26-8	Asb. 259.10
CBS 8633	Asb. 259.8	CBS 16491	Asb. 2008.8	UM 84-26-9	Asb. 259.11
CBS 8644	Asb. 260	CBS 16555a	Asb. 2008.9	UM 84-26-10	Asb. 259.12
CBS 8654	Asb. 259.9	CBS 16555b	Asb. 2008.10	UM 84-26-11	Asb. 259.13–14
CBS 15337	Asb. 2008.7	CBS 16556a	Asb. 2016.5–6	UM 84-26-12	Asb. 261.1
CBS 15905	Asb. 2005.4–5	CBS 16556b	Asb. 2016.7–8		
CBS 16483	Asb. 2010.1–2	CBS 16557	Asb. 2017.5–6	UM L-29-632+	Asb. 258.1
CBS 16484	Asb. 2011.1–2	CBS 16558	Asb. 2018.5	UM L-29-636+	Asb. 258.1
CBS 16485	Asb. 2012.1–2	CBS 16559	Asb. 2010 comm.	UM L-29-633+	Asb. 258.1
CBS 16486	Asb. 2016.3–4				

Princeton, Princeton Theological Seminary

No.	RINAP 5
PTS 2253	Aei 2

PRIVATE COLLECTIONS

de Clercq

Asb. 242

Harper, R.F.

Asb. 259.22

Index of Excavation Numbers

Aššur

No.	RINAP 5
Ass 948	Ssi 7.1
Ass 1328	Ssi 15-16
Ass 1702	Ssi 17-18
Ass 2043	Ssi 14
Ass 3518+	Ssi 9
Ass 3830+	Ssi 9
Ass 6626	Ssi 11.3
Ass 6655	Ssi 13.1
Ass 10625	Ssi 11.2
Ass 12548	Ssi 11.4
Ass 12726	Ssi 11.5
Ass 12727	Ssi 11.1
Ass 12729	Ssi 11.6
Ass 12946	Ssi 11.7
Ass 12951	Ssi 11.8
Ass 13014	Ssi 11.9
Ass 13105	Ssi 11.10
Ass 13123	Ssi 13.10
Ass 13158+	Ssi 10.2
Ass 13158a+	Ssi 10.2
Ass 13165	Ssi 11.11
Ass 13183a+	Ssi 8
Ass 13183b+	Ssi 8
Ass 13188	Ssi 13.11
Ass 13189	Ssi 13.2
Ass 13223	Ssi 11.12
Ass 13266+	Ssi 7.3
Ass 13331	Ssi 11.13
Ass 13352	Ssi 13.3
Ass 13374	Ssi 7.2
Ass 13444	Ssi 13.12
Ass 13445	Ssi 13.13
Ass 13446	Ssi 13.14
Ass 13447	Ssi 13.15
Ass 13448	Ssi 13.16
Ass 13449	Ssi 13.17
Ass 13450	Ssi 13.18
Ass 13458	Ssi 11.14
Ass 13462	Ssi 13.19
Ass 13463	Ssi 13.4
Ass 13464	Ssi 13.5
Ass 13465	Ssi 13.20
Ass 13466	Ssi 13.21
Ass 13467	Ssi 13.23
Ass 13591	Ssi 11.15
Ass 13594+	Ssi 7.3
Ass 13595	Ssi 10.1
Ass 13606	Ssi 13.22
Ass 13607	Ssi 13.6
Ass 13799	Ssi 13.7
Ass 13946a+	Ssi 13.8
Ass 13946b+	Ssi 13.8
Ass 15756+	Asb. 2001
Ass 15758+	Asb. 2001
Ass 18738	Ssi 7.4
Ass 19423	Ssi 10.3

Babylon

No.	RINAP 5
81-B-3	Asb. 241.19
BE 5457	Asb. 245.1
BE 8010	Asb. 247.6
BE 8044	Asb. 247.7
BE 8045	Asb. 247.8
BE 8046	Asb. 247.9
BE 8047	Asb. 247.10
BE 8048	Asb. 247.11
BE 8049	Asb. 247.12
BE 8051	Asb. 247.13
BE 8052	Asb. 247.14
BE 8053	Asb. 247.15
BE 8054	Asb. 247.16
BE 8072	Asb. 247.5
BE 8073	Asb. 247.17
BE 8074	Asb. 247.18
BE 8075	Asb. 247.19
BE 8076	Asb. 247.20
BE 8077	Asb. 247.21
BE 8078	Asb. 247.22
BE 8079	Asb. 247.23
BE 8080	Asb. 247.24
BE 8081	Asb. 247.25
BE 8082	Asb. 247.26
BE 8083	Asb. 247.2
BE 8086	Asb. 247.1
BE 8763	Asb. 241.3
BE 12131	Asb. 241.4
BE 28510	Asb. 243
BE 29275	Asb. 241.5
BE 29362	Asb. 241.6
BE 29482	Asb. 244.1*
BE 30112	Asb. 241.7
BE 30130	Asb. 241.8
BE 30160	Asb. 241.9
BE 30161	Asb. 241.10
BE 30164	Asb. 241.11
BE 33896	Asb. 241.20
BE 36072	Asb. 251.4
BE 38119	Asb. 244.2*
BE 39436	Asb. 251.5
BE 39807	Asb. 251.6
BE 39849	Asb. 251.2
BE 40145	Asb. 248.2
BE 40855	Asb. 248.3
BE 41032	Asb. 248.4
BE 41143	Asb. 249
BE 41171	Asb. 251.7
BE 41186	Asb. 250
BE 41232	Asb. 248.5
BE 41252	Asb. 251.3
BE 46433	Asb. 251.8

Nimrud

No.	RINAP 5	No.	RINAP 5	No.	RINAP 5
ND 1123	Ssi 19.3	ND 4323	Ssi 19.11	ND 6215	Aei 1.26
ND 1130	Aei 1.21	ND 4406A	Aei 1.22	ND 6216	Aei 1 comm.
ND 4312	Ssi 19.10	ND 4406B	Aei 1.23	ND 6221	Ssi 19.14
ND 4313	Ssi 19.9	ND 4407A	Aei 1.24	ND 6222	Ssi 19.13
ND 4314	Ssi 19.8	ND 4407B	Aei 1.25	ND 6228	Ssi 20
ND 4315	Ssi 19.2	ND 6209	Ssi 19.7		

Nippur

No.	RINAP 5	No.	RINAP 5	No.	RINAP 5
3 NT 840	Asb. 258.2	5 NT 703	Asb. 259.23	18 N —	Asb. 261.2

Persepolis

No.	RINAP 5	No.	RINAP 5	No.	RINAP 5
PT4 368+	Asb. 269	PT4 1173	Asb. 268	PT5 156+	Asb. 269
PT4 455	Asb. 266	PT4 1180	Asb. 267	PT5 244	Asb. 269

Ur

No.	RINAP 5	No.	RINAP 5	No.	RINAP 5
U 152	Asb. 2008.7	U 3297	Asb. 2016. 1–2, 9–10	U 18529a	Asb. 2006.7
U 1262	Asb. 2004			U 18529b	Asb. 2006.6
U 1664	Asb. 2008.3	U 3297a	Asb. 2016.3–4	U 18529c	Asb. 2006.1
U 2674	Asb. 2003	U 3297b	Asb. 2016.5–6	U 18529d	Asb. 2006.8
U 2757	Asb. 2007	U 3297c	Asb. 2016.7–8	U 18529e	Asb. 2006.4
U 3148	Asb. 2015	U 3298	Asb. 2017.1–2, 7	U 18529f	Asb. 2006.5
U 3161	Asb. 2008.4, 11	U 3298a	Asb. 2017.3–4	U 18529g	Asb. 2006.2
U 3249c	Asb. 2005.1	U 3298b	Asb. 2017.5–6	U 18529h	Asb. 2006.3
U 3249g$^{?}$	Asb. 2005.5	U 3299	Asb. 2018.1–5		
U 3249i	Asb. 2005.4	U 3300	Asb. 2013.1–2	U —	Asb. 2008.5
U 3249l	Asb. 2005.3	U 3301	Asb. 2014.1–2	U —	Asb. 2008.6
U 3249m	Asb. 2005.2	U 3326	Asb. 2011.1–2	U —	Asb. 2008.8
U 3250	Asb. 2010.1–2	U 6341	Asb. 2009	U —	Asb. 2008.9
U 3296	Asb. 2012.1–2	U 16558	Asb. 2013.5	U —	Asb. 2008.10

Uruk/Warka

No.	RINAP 5	No.	RINAP 5	No.	RINAP 5
W 4444	Asb. 263.3	W 20942	Asb. 263.4	W 22669/3	Asb. 264

Index of Names

Personal Names

Adad-nārārī III: Ssi 10 23; Ssi 19 31.
Amar-Suen: Asb. 2007 iv 31.
Ana-Tašmētu-taklāk: Ssi 2001 1.
Ashurbanipal (Aššur-bāni-apli): Asb. 241 3; Asb. 242 1; Asb. 243 1; Asb. 244 1; Asb. 245 1; Asb. 246 2, 68; Asb. 247 2; Asb. 248 2; Asb. 249 1; Asb. 250 1; Asb. 251 1; Asb. 253 7; Asb. 254 1, 39; Asb. 255 4; Asb. 256 2; Asb. 257 3; Asb. 258 6, 22; Asb. 259 4; Asb. 260 6; Asb. 261 6; Asb. 262 1, 20; Asb. 263 7, 25; Asb. 264 obv. 3′; Asb. 265 4′; Asb. 266 2; Asb. 267 2; Asb. 268 1; Asb. 269 1; Asb. 270 1; Asb. 1007 3′; Asb. 1019 5′; Asb. 1029 obv. *7*; Asb. 2001 4; Asb. 2002 obv. 2, obv. 4; Asb. 2006 4; Asb. 2008 3; Asb. 2009 2; Aei 1 2; Aei 3 9; Aei 4 2; Ssi 1 17; Ssi 3 3; Ssi 6 obv. 20; Ssi 7 ii 5; Ssi 10 12; Ssi 11 1; Ssi 12 3; Ssi 13 2; Ssi 14 2; Ssi 15 5; Ssi 16 7; Ssi 17 4; Ssi 18 8; Ssi 19 17; Ssi 21 *1*.
Aššur-aḫu-iddina: See Esarhaddon.
Aššur-bāni-apli: See Ashurbanipal.
Aššur-etel-ilāni: Aei 1 1; Aei 2 obv. 9, rev. 19; Aei 3 8; Aei 4 1, 6; Aei 5 4; Aei 6 1.
Aššur-mātu-taqqin: Ssi 9 vi 4′.
Aššur-rēša-iši I: Ssi 10 23.
Aššur-[...] (Ashurbanipal, Esarhaddon, or Aššur-etel-ilāni): Asb. 1001 obv. 1.
Bēl-aḫḫe-iqīša: Aei 2 rev. 22.
Bēl-aḫu-uṣur: Ssi 6 rev. 14′; Ssi 10 45A, 45B.
Dādî: Ssi 19 48.
Dakkūru: Aei 6 1.
Esarhaddon (Aššur-aḫu-iddina): Asb. 241 4; Asb. 242 3; Asb. 243 5; Asb. 244 5; Asb. 245 5; Asb. 246 21; Asb. 248 4; Asb. 250 2; Asb. 251 2; Asb. 253 8; Asb. 254 14; Asb. 257 4; Asb. 258 8; Asb. 262 4; Asb. 263 13; Asb. 270 1; Asb. 1029 obv. *8*; Aei 1 3; Ssi 1 18; Ssi 3 3; Ssi 6 obv. 21; Ssi 7 ii 8; Ssi 10 13; Ssi 11 1; Ssi 12 4; Ssi 13 4; Ssi 14 3; Ssi 15 6; Ssi 16 8; Ssi 17 4; Ssi 18 8; Ssi 19 18; Ssi 21 *1*.
Iddin-Papsukkal: Asb. 2007 iv 35.
Libbāli-šarrat: Asb. 2001 2.
Mutakkil-Nusku: Ssi 10 23.
Nabû-šuma-iddin: Asb. 2007 iv 35.
Nabû-tappûtī-alik: Ssi 1 21′.
Nādin: Aei 2 rev. 22.
Ningal-iddin: Asb. 2003 7; Asb. 2004 8; Asb. 2006 7.
Saʾīlu: Ssi 11 5.
Salmānu-ašarēd: See Shalmaneser I.
Sargon II (Šarru-(u)kīn): Ssi 1 20; Ssi 3 4; Ssi 7 ii 13; Ssi 10 15; Ssi 11 2; Ssi 12 6; Ssi 13 8; Ssi 14 5; Ssi 19 20.
Sennacherib (Sîn-aḫḫē-erība): Asb. 241 9; Asb. 242 6; Asb. 243 6; Asb. 244 7; Asb. 245 7; Asb. 246 33; Asb. 253 12; Asb. 254 22; Asb. 257 6; Asb. 258 9; Asb. 262 7; Asb. 263 16; Asb. 270 1; Asb. 1029 obv. *8*; Ssi 1 19, 13′, 18′; Ssi 3 4; Ssi 6 rev. 3′; Ssi 7 ii 11; Ssi 9 iii 5; Ssi 10 14; Ssi 11 1; Ssi 12 5; Ssi 13 6; Ssi 14 4; Ssi 17 4; Ssi 18 8; Ssi 19 19; Ssi 21 *1*.
Shalmaneser I (Salmānu-ašarēd): Ssi 10 22.
Sîn-aḫḫē-erība: See Sennacherib.
Sîn-balāssu-iqbi: Asb. 2003 5; Asb. 2004 5; Asb. 2005 5; Asb. 2006 6; Asb. 2007 iv 33; Asb. 2008 5; Asb. 2009 4; Asb. 2010 3; Asb. 2011 3; Asb. 2012 3; Asb. 2013 3; Asb. 2014 3; Asb. 2015 3; Asb. 2016 3; Asb. 2017 3; Asb. 2018 3.
Sîn-šarra-iškun: Ssi 1 1; Ssi 6 obv. 1; Ssi 7 iii 12′; Ssi 10 1, 27; Ssi 11 1; Ssi 12 1; Ssi 13 1; Ssi 14 1; Ssi 15 4; Ssi 16 6; Ssi 17 3, 11; Ssi 18 7, 13; Ssi 19 1; Ssi 20 1; Ssi 21 1.
Sîn-šarru-uṣur: Ssi 3 11′.
Šamaš-ibni: Aei 6 1.
Šamaš-šuma-ukīn: Asb. 241 13; Asb. 242 14, 24; Asb. 243 11; Asb. 244 11, 19; Asb. 245 11, 19; Asb. 246 52, 74; Asb. 253 16; Asb. 254 31, 46; Asb. 262 11, 21; Asb. 263 18, 27.
Šamšī-Adad V: Ssi 10 23.
Šarru-(u)kīn: See Sargon II.
Taharqa (Tarqû): Asb. 1004 obv. 3′.
[...]: Asb. 1001 obv. 2; Asb. 1003 5′; Asb. 1007 3′; Asb. 1009 7′; Asb. 1022 6′, 7′; Asb. 1030 4, 5; Asb. 2002 2; Ssi 5 2′; Ssi 7 v 19A, 19B, 19C; Ssi 2001 1.

Geographic, Ethnic, and Tribal Names

Agade: See Akkad.
Akkad (Agade): Asb. 252 3′, 8′. See also Ištar of Akkad.
Akkad (Māt-Akkadî): Asb. 241 5; Asb. 242 5; Asb. 243 6; Asb. 244 6; Asb. 245 6; Asb. 246 23; Asb. 253 8; Asb. 254 16; Asb. 257 5; Asb. 258 10; Asb. 262 5; Asb. 263 14; Asb. 1007 5′; Ssi 1 17, 18, 20; Ssi 3 3, 4; Ssi 6 obv. 20, 21; Ssi 7 ii 7, 10, 15; Ssi 9 iii 4; Ssi 10 12, 14, 16; Ssi 11 1, 2; Ssi 12 7; Ssi 13 3, 5, 9; Ssi 19 17, 18, 20.
Amanus (Mount; Ḫamānu): Asb. 246 60.
Arbela: Ssi 1 4; Ssi 2 11′; Ssi 6 obv. 4, rev. 9′; Ssi 19 4. See also Ištar of Arbela.
Assyria (Māt-Aššur): Asb. 241 3, 4, 9; Asb. 242 2, 4, 7;

Asb. 243 2, 5, 7; Asb. 244 1, 5, 7; Asb. 245 1, 5, 7; Asb. 246 4, 22, 35, 69; Asb. 247 3; Asb. 248 3, 5; Asb. 249 2; Asb. 250 2; Asb. 251 2, 3; Asb. 253 7, 8, 12; Asb. 254 2, 15, 23; Asb. 256 2; Asb. 257 3, 4, 7; Asb. 258 6, 8, 9, 22; Asb. 262 1, 4, 8, 20; Asb. 263 7, 14, 16, 25; Asb. 264 obv. 3′; Asb. 265 4′; Asb. 266 3; Asb. 267 3; Asb. 268 1; Asb. 269 1; Asb. 270 1; Asb. 1003 5′; Asb. 1007 3′; Asb. 1014 Side A 6′; Asb. 1029 obv. 7, 8; Asb. 2001 5; Asb. 2002 obv. 2; Asb. 2006 5; Aei 1 1, 2, 3; Aei 2 obv. 10, rev. 19; Aei 3 8, 9; Aei 4 1, 2; Aei 6 1, 2; Ssi 1 1, 17, 18, 19, 20, 4′, 7′, 13′, 18′; Ssi 2 10′; Ssi 3 1, 3; Ssi 5 2′; Ssi 6 obv. 1, 20, 21, rev. 3′; Ssi 7 ii 6, 9, 12, 14, iii 13′; Ssi 9 i 1′, ii 7; Ssi 10 1, 12, 13, 15, 27; Ssi 11 1, 2; Ssi 12 2, 3, 4, 5, 6; Ssi 13 2, 3, 4, 6, 9; Ssi 14 1, 2, 3, 4, 5; Ssi 15 4, 5, 6; Ssi 16 6, 7, 8; Ssi 17 3, 4; Ssi 18 7, 13; Ssi 19 1, 17, 18, 19, 20; Ssi 21 1; Ssi 2001 1.

Assyrian(s): See Assyrian Ištar.

Aššur (Baltil): **Asb. 242** 9; **Asb. 246** 41; **Asb. 254** 26; **Ssi 10** 22; **Ssi 11** 3; **Ssi 12** 11; **Ssi 13** 11; **Ssi 15** 3; **Ssi 16** 5; **Ssi 17** 3; **Ssi 18** 7. See also Libbi-āli (Aššur).

Bābili: See Babylon.

Babylon (Bābili): **Asb. 241** 2, 4, 5, 10, 12, 14, 17, 19; **Asb. 242** 5, 10, 11, 12, 15, 24; **Asb. 243** 9, 10; **Asb. 244** 6, 9, 10, 12, 13, 14, 19, 23; **Asb. 245** 6, 9, 10, 12, 13, 19; **Asb. 246** 22, 23, 43, 47, 49, 55, 75; **Asb. 248** 6; **Asb. 251** 3; **Asb. 253** 8, 9, 13, 15, 17; **Asb. 254** 15, 16, 27, 28, 29, 32, 47; **Asb. 257** 5; **Asb. 262** 4, 5, 9, 10, 12, 22; **Asb. 263** 14, 17, 18, 19, 27; **Asb. 1008** 3′; **Aei 2** obv. 8; **Ssi 1** 18, 20; **Ssi 3** 4; **Ssi 6** obv. 21; **Ssi 7** ii 9, 15; **Ssi 9** iii 2; **Ssi 10** 14, 16; **Ssi 11** 1, 2; **Ssi 12** 7; **Ssi 13** 5, 9; **Ssi 19** 18, 20. See also Ištar of Babylon.

Babylonia: See Karduniaš.

Baltil: See Aššur.

Barsipa: See Borsippa.

Bīt-Dakkūri: **Aei 6** 2.

Borsippa (Barsipa): **Asb. 253** 6, 19, 20, 21, 24; **Asb. 1028** 3′.

Borsippa, gen.: **Asb. 1027** 13′.

Calah: See Kalḫu.

Chaldeans (Kaldāyu): **Asb. 1015** 9′.

Cutha (Kutû): **Asb. 1029** obv. 6.

Dēr: **Asb. 265** 1′.

Diglat: See Tigris.

Dilbat: **Aei 4** 3.

Dilmun: **Asb. 263** 9; **Asb. 1013** 12′.

Dūru-ša-Ladīni: **Aei 6** 3.

Elam (Elamtu): **Asb. 1011** 3′.

Elam, gen: **Asb. 1006** rev. 9′; **Asb. 1017** obv. 1; **Asb. 1029** obv. 16.

Eridu: **Asb. 2006** 9; **Asb. 2008** 7; **Asb. 2009** 6; **Asb. 2010** 5; **Asb. 2011** 5; **Asb. 2012** 5; **Asb. 2013** 5; **Asb. 2014** 5; **Asb. 2015** 5; **Asb. 2016** 5; **Asb. 2017** 5; **Asb. 2018** 5.

Euphrates (Purattu): **Aei 4** 4.

Egypt (Muṣur): **Asb. 1007** 4′.

Gurasimmu: **Asb. 2006** 9.

Ḫamānu: See Amanus (Mount).

Ḫarrān: **Asb. 1014** Side A 10′.

Ḫindānu: **Ssi 3** 11′.

Inner City: See Libbi-āli.

Kaldāyu: See Chaldeans.

Kalḫu (Calah): **Aei 1** 6; **Ssi 19** 31.

Karduniaš (Babylonia): **Asb. 1007** 6′.

Kush (Kūsu): **Asb. 1007** 4′.

Labnāna: See Lebanon (Mount).

Lebanon (Mount; Labnāna): **Asb. 246** 60.

Libbi-āli (Aššur): **Ssi 15** 10; **Ssi 16** 13. See also Aššur (Baltil).

Lower Sea (Tâmtu šaplītu; also Tâmtu elītu u šaplītu): **Asb. 243** 3; **Asb. 244** 3; **Asb. 245** 3; **Asb. 246** 10–11; **Asb. 254** 6; **Asb. 262** 3; **Asb. 263** 8, 9.

Māt-Akkadî: See Akkad.

Māt-Aššur: See Assyria.

Muṣur: See Egypt.

Nineveh (Ninua): **Ssi 1** 4, 11; **Ssi 2** 11′; **Ssi 6** obv. 4, 13, rev. 8′, 13′; **Ssi 19** 4. See also Ištar of Nineveh and Queen of Nineveh.

Nippur: **Asb. 258** 5, 15; **Aei 5** 6.

Parsumaš (Persia): **Asb. 1013** 12′.

Purattu: See Euphrates.

Sippar: **Asb. 262** 16.

Sippar-Aruru: **Aei 3** 7.

Sirara (in Mê-Turān): **Asb. 257** 2.

Sumer (Māt-Šumerî): **Asb. 241** 5; **Asb. 242** 5; **Asb. 243** 6; **Asb. 244** 6; **Asb. 245** 6; **Asb. 246** 23; **Asb. 253** 8; **Asb. 254** 16; **Asb. 257** 5; **Asb. 258** 10; **Asb. 262** 5; **Asb. 263** 14; **Asb. 1007** 5′; **Ssi 1** 17, 18, 20; **Ssi 3** 3, 4; **Ssi 6** obv. 20, 21; **Ssi 7** ii 6, 10, 15; **Ssi 9** iii 3; **Ssi 10** 12, 14, 16; **Ssi 11** 1, 2; **Ssi 12** 7; **Ssi 13** 3, 5, 9; **Ssi 19** 17, 18, 20.

Ṣurru: See Tyre.

Tâmtu elītu: See Upper Sea.

Tâmtu šaplītu: See Lower Sea.

Tigris (Diglat): **Aei 4** 4; **Ssi 4** 3′.

Tilmun: See Dilmun.

Tyre (Ṣurru): **Asb. 263** 9.

Upper Sea (Tâmtu elītu; also Tâmtu elītu u šaplītu): **Asb. 243** 3; **Asb. 244** 3; **Asb. 245** 3; **Asb. 246** 9–10; **Asb. 254** 5; **Asb. 262** 2; **Asb. 263** 8, 9.

Uppumu: **Ssi 9** vi 6′.

Ur: **Asb. 2003** 6, 8; **Asb. 2004** 7, 10; **Asb. 2005** 4, 6; **Asb. 2006** 8; **Asb. 2007** iv 30, 31, 34; **Asb. 2008** 6; **Asb. 2009** 5; **Asb. 2010** 4; **Asb. 2011** 4; **Asb. 2012** 4; **Asb. 2013** 4; **Asb. 2014** 4; **Asb. 2015** 4; **Asb. 2016** 4; **Asb. 2017** 4; **Asb. 2018** 4.

Uruk: **Asb. 263** 1, 24, 30, 32. See also Ištar of Uruk.

[...]: **Asb. 1006** rev. 2′; **Asb. 1029** *obv. 20*; **Ssi 7** *v 19A, 19B, 19C*.

[...]...da: **Asb. 1030** 17.

Divine, Planet, and Star Names

Adad: **Asb. 263** 11; **Asb. 1014** Side A 4′; **Ssi 18** 1.

Antu: **Ssi 1** 11; **Ssi 6** obv. 13; **Ssi 17** 1, 10.

Anu: **Asb. 1024** obv. 10; **Ssi 17** *16*.

Anu rabû: See Great Anu.

Anunnakū: **Asb. 241** 1; **Asb. 253** 3; **Asb. 258** 3; **Aei 2** obv. 3; **Ssi 15** 2; **Ssi 16** 3.

Asari: **Asb. 251** 1; **Asb. 253** 5. See also Bēl and Marduk.
Assyrian Ištar (Ištar Aššurītu): **Ssi 7** iii 6′, iv 7′; **Ssi 10** 25, 32.
Aššur: **Asb. 246** 7; **Asb. 254** 4; **Asb. 258** 10; **Asb. 1004** obv. 1′; **Asb. 1006** rev. 5′; **Asb. 1010** obv. 2′; **Asb. 1014** Side A *1*′; **Asb. 1016** obv. 6′; **Asb. 1023** 9′; **Asb. 1027** 7′, 8′; **Asb. 1029** obv. 10; **Asb. 1030** 1, *8*, 26, 30; **Ssi 1** 2, 5, 20′; **Ssi 2** 7′, 9′, 11′, 14′, 17′; **Ssi 3** 8′; **Ssi 6** obv. 2, 5, rev. 5′, 8′; **Ssi 7** ii 16, v 3, 12; **Ssi 9** i 2′; **Ssi 10** 2, 16, 22, 39, 42; **Ssi 12** 8; **Ssi 18** 15; **Ssi 19** 2, 4, 22, 46.
Aya: **Ssi 1** 3; **Ssi 6** obv. 3.
Bahar: **Aei 4** 3.
Bēl (Marduk): **Asb. 243** 2′; **Asb. 244** 16, 23; **Asb. 245** 16, 23; **Asb. 1027** 7′; **Ssi 2** 11′, 17′; **Ssi 7** ii 17; **Ssi 10** 16; **Ssi 12** 8; **Ssi 19** 4, 12, 22, 46. See also Asari and Marduk.
Bēlet-Arba'il: See Lady of Arbela.
Bēlet-ilī: **Ssi 1** 9; **Ssi 6** obv. 10.
Bēltīya: **Asb. 243** 2′; **Asb. 244** 16, 23; **Asb. 245** 16, 23; **Ssi 2** 11′. See also Zarpanītu.
Dunga: **Asb. 1026** rev. 4.
Ea: **Asb. 243** 2′; **Asb. 246** 66, 67, 82, 89; **Asb. 263** 11; **Asb. 1024** obv. 10; **Ssi 1** 9; **Ssi 2** 5′; **Ssi 6** obv. 10; **Ssi 19** 8.
Enlil: **Asb. 256** 1; **Asb. 258** 1, 10, 20; **Asb. 259** 1; **Asb. 260** 1; **Asb. 261** 1; **Asb. 1019** 1′; **Asb. 1024** obv. 10; **Asb. 1029** obv. 3; **Asb. 1030** 10; **Asb. 2003** 3; **Asb. 2004** 3; **Asb. 2007** iv 39; **Asb. 2010** 1; **Asb. 2011** 1; **Asb. 2012** 1; **Asb. 2013** 1; **Asb. 2014** 1; **Asb. 2015** 1; **Asb. 2016** 1; **Asb. 2017** 1; **Asb. 2018** 1, 7; **Aei 2** obv. 1; **Aei 5** 1; **Ssi 1** 2; **Ssi 6** obv. 2; **Ssi 19** 25.
Ennugi: **Asb. 2015** 7.
Erua: **Asb. 253** 5. See also Zarpanītu.
Great Anu (Anu rabû): **Asb. 265** 1′, 3′, 10′, 12′.
Gula: **Asb. 1002** rev. 3.
Igīgū: **Asb. 241** 1; **Asb. 253** 3; **Asb. 258** 3; **Aei 2** obv. 2; **Ssi 15** 2; **Ssi 16** 3.
Ištar: **Asb. 1010** *obv. 3*′, rev. 4′; **Asb. 1013** 6′; **Ssi 12** 9.
Ištar Aššurītu: See Assyrian Ištar.
Ištar of Akkad: **Asb. 252** 3′, 3′, 8′.
Ištar of Arbela: **Ssi 1** 4; **Ssi 2** 11′; **Ssi 6** obv. 4, rev. 9′; **Ssi 19** 4.
Ištar of Babylon: **Asb. 244** 13, 14, 23.
Ištar of Nineveh: **Ssi 1** 4; **Ssi 2** 11′; **Ssi 6** obv. 4, rev. 8′; **Ssi 19** 4.
Ištar of Uruk: **Asb. 263** 1, 24, 30, 32.
Kingu: **Aei 3** 5.
Kulla: **Asb. 241** 21; **Asb. 253** 21; **Asb. 258** 18; **Asb. 262** 17; **Asb. 265** 2′.
Kusu: **Asb. 2012** 7.
Kutušar: **Asb. 1029** obv. 3. See also Mullissu.
Lady of Arbela (Bēlet-Arba'il): **Asb. 1002** obv. 11′.
Marduk: **Asb. 241** 1, 10, 27, 29; **Asb. 242** 7, 20, 30, 32; **Asb. 246** 8, 37; **Asb. 247** 1; **Asb. 248** 1; **Asb. 249** 1; **Asb. 250** 1; **Asb. 253** 13; **Asb. 254** 5, 23; **Asb. 262** 8; **Asb. 263** 16; **Asb. 1024** rev. 10′; **Asb. 1027** 8′; **Asb. 1030** 13; **Aei 2** obv. 1, rev. 16; **Aei 3** 1, 19; **Aei 4** 6; **Aei 6** 8, 16; **Ssi 1** 3; **Ssi 2** 3′, 7′, 9′, 14′; **Ssi 3** 2, 8′; **Ssi 6** obv. 3, rev. 8′; **Ssi 7** v 4, 12; **Ssi 10** 2, 39, 42; **Ssi 19** 2, 3. See also Asari and Bēl.
Mullissu: **Asb. 1029** obv. 10; **Ssi 1** 2, 5, 11, 20′; **Ssi 2** 7′, 9′, 11′, 14′, 17′; **Ssi 3** 8′; **Ssi 6** obv. 2, 5, 13, rev. 5′, 8′; **Ssi 7** v 3, 12; **Ssi 10** 2, 39, 42; **Ssi 19** 2, 4. See also Ninlil.
Nabû: **Asb. 253** 1, 26, 28; **Asb. 254** 37, 62, 71; **Asb. 1013** 6′; **Asb. 1018** 4′; **Asb. 1023** 6′; **Asb. 1027** 3′, 7′, 10′; **Asb. 1030** 13; **Aei 4** 5; **Aei 6** 18; **Ssi 1** 3; **Ssi 2** 7′, 9′, 11′, 14′, 17′; **Ssi 3** 2, 8′; **Ssi 6** obv. 3, rev. 8′; **Ssi 7** i 1′, 12′, ii 17, iii 5′, iv 5′, 15′, 18′, v 5, 13; **Ssi 8** ii′ 6′, 10′; **Ssi 10** 2, 7, 16, 22, 25, 31, 34, 39, 42; **Ssi 11** 3; **Ssi 12** 8, 10, 14; **Ssi 13** 10; **Ssi 15** 1, 10; **Ssi 16** 2; **Ssi 19** 3, 4, 10, 12, 21, 22, 31, 37, 38, 44, 46.
Nanna: **Asb. 2008** 1; **Asb. 2009** 1; **Asb. 2010** 1; **Asb. 2011** 1; **Asb. 2012** 1; **Asb. 2013** 1; **Asb. 2014** 1; **Asb. 2015** 1; **Asb. 2016** 1; **Asb. 2017** 1; **Asb. 2018** 1. See also Sîn.
Nergal: **Asb. 257** 1; **Asb. 1013** 6′; **Asb. 1029** obv. 1, 10; **Aei 6** 19; **Ssi 1** 4; **Ssi 6** obv. 4; **Ssi 7** ii 18; **Ssi 10** 17; **Ssi 19** 4.
Ninegal: **Aei 4** 3, 6.
Ningal: **Asb. 2003** 35; **Asb. 2005** 1, 12; **Asb. 2006** 1; **Ssi 1** 3; **Ssi 6** obv. 3; **Ssi 19** 2, 4.
Ninimma: **Asb. 2014** 7.
Ninkasi: **Asb. 2010** 7.
Ninlil: **Asb. 2005** 7. See also Mullissu.
Ninmah: **Asb. 245** 13, 14, 23.
Ninmena: **Asb. 2005** 3.
Ninurta: **Asb. 258** 10; **Asb. 1002** obv. 3′; **Ssi 7** ii 18; **Ssi 10** 17.
Nisaba: **Ssi 18** 14.
Nunurra: **Ssi 13** 12.
Nusku: **Asb. 2013** 7; **Ssi 1** 4; **Ssi 6** obv. 4; **Ssi 7** ii 18; **Ssi 10** 17; **Ssi 19** 4.
Queen of Nineveh (Šarrat-Ninūa): **Asb. 1002** obv. 7′.
Sebetti: **Asb. 1002** rev. 5.
Sîn (Suen): **Asb. 1013** 6′; **Asb. 1022** 6′; **Asb. 1030** 12; **Asb. 2003** 1, 35; **Asb. 2004** 1; **Asb. 2005** 9; **Asb. 2007** iv 36; **Ssi 1** 3, 10; **Ssi 2** 2′, 11′, 14′; **Ssi 6** obv. 3, 11, rev. 8′; **Ssi 7** i 9′, ii 17; **Ssi 10** 5, 17; **Ssi 19** 2, 4, 9, 22. See also Nanna.
Suen: See Sîn.
Sutītu: **Asb. 266** 1; **Asb. 267** 1.
Šala: **Ssi 18** 1, 12.
Šamaš: **Asb. 246** 7; **Asb. 254** 4; **Asb. 262** 16, 18, 26, 28; **Asb. 1014** Side A 4′; **Asb. 1030** 12; **Ssi 1** 3; **Ssi 2** 11′, 14′; **Ssi 6** obv. 3, rev. 8′; **Ssi 7** ii 17; **Ssi 10** 17; **Ssi 19** 22.
Šarrat-Kidmuri: **Ssi 6** rev. 9′.
Šarrat-Ninūa: See Queen of Nineveh.
Šerūa: **Asb. 1023** 6′.
Šulpaea: **Aei 2** rev. 17.
Šuziana: **Asb. 2011** 7.
Tašmētu: **Ssi 1** 3; **Ssi 2** 7′, 9′, 11′, 14′; **Ssi 3** 2, 8′; **Ssi 6** obv. 3, rev. 8′; **Ssi 7** i 1′, iii 5′, iv 5′, 15′, 18′, v 5, 13; **Ssi 8** ii′ 6′, 10′; **Ssi 10** 2, 25, 31, 34, 39, 42; **Ssi 12** 14; **Ssi 16** 1, 13; **Ssi 19** 21, 37, 44.
Uraš: **Aei 4** 1, 3, 6.
Zarpanītu: **Asb. 1024** obv. 1, rev. 7′; **Asb. 1026** obv. 11; **Ssi 1** 3; **Ssi 2** 7′, 9′, 14′; **Ssi 3** 2, 8′; **Ssi 6** obv. 3, rev. 8′; **Ssi 7** v 4, 13; **Ssi 10** 2, 39, 42; **Ssi 19** 2. See also Bēltīya and Erua.
[...]: **Asb. 265** rev. 8, 10; **Asb. 1004** rev. 4′; **Asb. 1013** 6′.

Gate, Palace, Temple, and Wall Names

Object Names

Concordances of Selected Publications

Bauer, Asb.

P.	RINAP 5	P.	RINAP 5	P.	RINAP 5
48	Asb. 263.1–2	54	Asb. 1004	69–70	Asb. 1007
50	Asb. 241.1–11	67	Asb. 1006	107	Asb. 1020

Pl.	RINAP 5	Pl.	RINAP 5
41	Asb. 1007	57	Asb. 1006
55	Asb. 1020	59	Asb. 1004

Behrens, JCS 37 (1985) pp. 229–248

No.	RINAP 5	No.	RINAP 5	No.	RINAP 5	No.	RINAP 5
53	Asb. 259.6–14	56	Asb. 2008.7–10	59	Asb. 2012	62	Asb. 2018.3
54	Asb. 260	57	Asb. 2010.1–2	60	Asb. 2016.3–8	63	Asb. 2013
55	Asb. 261.1	58	Asb. 2011	61	Asb. 2017.3–6		

Borger, BIWA (8°-Heft and LoBl)

8°-Heft P.	RINAP 5
167	Asb. 1003; 1015

LoBl P.	RINAP 5	LoBl P.	RINAP 5	LoBl P.	RINAP 5
22	Asb. 1014	67	Asb. 1017		Asb. 1022
26	Asb. 1025	68	Asb. 1018	107	Asb. 241.14
36	Asb. 1027;	69	Asb. 1011	108	Asb. 262.7
	Asb. 1028	70	Asb. 1012	110	Asb. 241.15
38	Asb. 1010	72	Asb. 1009	112	Asb. 241.16;
43	Asb. 1002;	79	Asb. 1019		Asb. 262.5
	Asb. 1026	82	Asb. 1023	113	Ssi 19.12
50	Asb. 1021	83–84	Asb. 1001	114–115	Asb. 1029
51	Asb. 1005	93	Asb. 1013	123	Asb. 245.2
58	Asb. 1016	94–95	Asb. 1024	134	Asb. 242
61	Asb. 1008	105	Asb. 241.12–13;		

Frame, RIMB 2

P.	No.	RINAP	P.	No.	RINAP
196–198	B.6.32.1	Asb. 241.1–19	230	B.6.32.23	Asb. 255
199–202	B.6.32.2	Asb. 246	230–232	B.6.32.2001	Asb. 2003
202–203	B.6.32.3	Asb. 243	232–233	B.6.32.2002	Asb. 2004
203–204	B.6.32.4	Asb. 244	233–234	B.6.32.2003	Asb. 2008
205–206	B.6.32.5	Asb. 245	234	B.6.32.2004	Asb. 2009
206–208	B.6.32.6	Asb. 242	235–236	B.6.32.2005	Asb. 2010
208–209	B.6.32.7	Asb. 247	236	B.6.32.2006	Asb. 2011
209–210	B.6.32.8	Asb. 248	237	B.6.32.2007	Asb. 2012
210–211	B.6.32.9	Asb. 251	237–238	B.6.32.2008	Asb. 2013
211–212	B.6.32.10	Asb. 250	238–239	B.6.32.2009	Asb. 2014
212	B.6.32.11	Asb. 249	239–240	B.6.32.2010	Asb. 2015
212–214	B.6.32.12	Asb. 262	240–241	B.6.32.2011	Asb. 2016
215–216	B.6.32.13	Asb. 253.1–2	241–242	B.6.32.2012	Asb. 2017
217–219	B.6.32.14	Asb. 254	242–243	B.6.32.2013	Asb. 2018
219–221	B.6.32.15	Asb. 258	243–244	B.6.32.2014	Asb. 2005
221–222	B.6.32.16	Asb. 259.1–25	244–245	B.6.32.2015	Asb. 2006
223	B.6.32.17	Asb. 260	246–247	B.6.32.2016	Asb. 2007
223–224	B.6.32.18	Asb. 261	262–263	B.6.35.1	Aei. 2
224–227	B.6.32.19	Asb. 263	263–264	B.6.35.2	Aei. 3
227–228	B.6.32.20	Asb. 252	264–265	B.6.35.3	Aei. 4
228	B.6.32.21	Asb. 256	265–266	B.6.35.4	Aei. 5
229	B.6.32.22	Asb. 257	266–268	B.6.35.5	Aei. 6

Gadd, UET 1

No.	RINAP 5	No.	RINAP 5	No.	RINAP 5	No.	RINAP 5
168	Asb. 2009	172	Asb. 2007	176	Asb. 2012	180	Asb. 2013
169	Asb. 2003	173	Asb. 2010.1	177	Asb. 2016	181	Asb. 2014
170	Asb. 2008.3, 11	174	Asb. 2010.2	178	Asb. 2017	182	Asb. 2015
171	Asb. 2005.1–3	175	Asb. 2011	179	Asb. 2018.1–2	183	Asb. 2004

Lehmann-Haupt, Šamaššumukîn pls. I–XLVII

Pl.	RINAP 5	Pl.	RINAP 5	Pl.	RINAP 5
XIII–XVI no. 6 (S^2)	Asb. 254	XXV–XXVI no. 9[a] (L^2)	Asb. 262.1	XXVIII–XXIX no. 10 (P^1)	Asb. 242
XVII–XXII no. 7 (S^3)	Asb. 246.1	XXVI no. 9b	Asb. 262.2	XXX–XXXI no. 11 (P^2)	Asb. 241.2
XXIII–XXIV no. 8[a] (L^1)	Asb. 244.1	XXVI no. 9c	Asb. 262.3		
XXIV no. 8[b]	Asb. 244.2	XXVII no. 9d	Asb. 262.4		

Luckenbill, ARAB 2

P.	RINAP	P.	RINAP	P.	RINAP
223 §572	Asb. 1013	390 §1019	Asb. 258.1	411–412 §§1142–1147	Ssi 1.1–3
369–370 §§953–955	Asb. 244.1–2	405 §1118	Asb. 248.1	412 §§1148–1149	Ssi 19.4
370–372 §§956–959	Asb. 262.1	405 §§1119–1120	Asb. 247.5	412–413 §1150	Ssi 1.4
372 §§960–962	Asb. 242	405 §1121	Asb. 259.7, 22	413 §1151	Ssi 4
372–373 §§963–964	Asb. 241.1–2			413–414 §§1152–1155	Ssi 11.1
373 §§965–967	Asb. 245.1	408 §§1130–1131	Aei 1	414–415 §§1156–1158	Ssi 10.1
373–375 §§968–973	Asb. 263.1	408–409 §§1132–1135	Aei 6.1	414–416 §§1156–1164	Ssi 7.1–3
375–376 §§974–977	Asb. 254	409 §1135A	Aei 4	416 §1165	Ssi 13.17
376 §§978–980	Asb. 246.1	409–410 §§1137–1141	Ssi 19.1	416 n. 1	Ssi 14

Marzahn, FuB 27 (1989) pp. 53–64

No.	RINAP 5	No.	RINAP 5	No.	RINAP 5	No.	RINAP 5
VI	Asb. 249	10	Asb. 249	14	Asb. 247.2	18	Asb. 248.4
VII	Asb. 251	11	Asb. 251.4	15	Asb. 247.3	19	Asb. 248.5
VIII	Asb. 247	12	Asb. 251.5	16	Asb. 247.4		
IX	Asb. 248	13	Asb. 251.3	17	Asb. 248.2		

Oppenheim, ANET[3]

No.	RINAP 5
297	Asb. 263.1–2

Streck, Asb. pp. 1–397

P.	RINAP 5	P.	RINAP 5	P.	RINAP 5
226–229 no. 1 (L^1)	Asb. 244.1–2	244–249 no. 7 (S^3)	Asb. 246.1	382–385	Ssi 1.1, 4–5
228–233 no. 2 (L^2)	Asb. 262.1–6	350–351 no. 3.a.α	Asb. 248.1	382–389	Ssi 19.1, 4–5
232–235 no. 3 (P^1)	Asb. 242	350–351 no. 3.a.β	Asb. 247.5	388–389	Ssi 14
234–239 no. 4 (L^6 [P^2])	Asb. 241.1–2	352–353 no. 3.b	Asb. 259.7, 22	390–391 no. 1	Asb. 2001
238–241 no. 5 (E-maḫ)	Asb. 245.1	352–353 no. 4	Asb. 258.1	392–395 no. 3	Asb. 2002
240–245 no. 6 (S^2)	Asb. 254	380–381	Aei 1		

Walker, CBI

P.	No.	RINAP 5	P.	No.	RINAP 5
66–67	78	Asb. 248.1	69	84	Asb. 2017.1–2
67	79	Asb. 251.1	69–70	85	Asb. 2018.1–2
67–68	80	Asb. 259.1–5	70	86	Asb. 2015
68	81	Asb. 2009	70–71	87	Aei 4
68–69	82	Asb. 2008.1–6	126–127	189	Ssi 13.23
69	83	Asb. 2016.1–2	127–128	190	Aei 1.1–19

Wetzel and Weissbach, Hauptheiligtum pp. 38–56

No.	RINAP 5	No.	RINAP 5	No.	RINAP 5
A.II.a	Asb. 247.1–2, 5–26	A.II.c	Asb. 249	A.II.e	Asb. 251.2–8
A.II.b	Asb. 250	A.II.d	Asb. 248.2–5		